MURDER AND THE DEATH PENALTY IN MASSACHUSETTS

MURDER
AND THE
DEATH PENALTY
IN
MASSACHUSETTS

ALAN ROGERS

UNIVERSITY OF MASSACHUSETTS PRESS

Amherst & Boston

Copyright © 2008 by University of Massachusetts Press

All rights reserved

Printed in the United States of America

LC 2007022051

ISBN 978-1-55849-633-0 (paper); 632-3 (library cloth)

Designed by Richard Hendel

Set in Monotype Bulmer and The Serif Bold by dix!

Printed and bound by The Maple-Vail Book

Manufacturing Group

Library of Congress Cataloging-in-Publication Data

Rogers, Alan, 1936–

Murder and the death penalty in Massachusetts / Alan Rogers.

p. cm.

Includes bibliographical references and index.

ISBN 978-1-55849-633-0 (pbk. : alk. paper)—ISBN 978-1-55849-632-3

(library cloth : alk. paper)

1. Capital punishment—Massachusetts—History. 2. Murder—
Massachusetts—History. I. Title.

KFM2965.C2R64 2008

345.744'0773—dc22

2007022051

British Library Cataloguing in Publication data are available.

To Lisa and Nora, with love

CONTENTS

William Hardy, an African American living in Boston just twenty-five years after the 1780 adoption of the Massachusetts Declaration of Rights, was indicted for the murder of an infant. Witnesses said they saw Hardy standing in the Charles River submerging an object he held by a chain. At trial, a jury found him guilty of murder. Before sentence could be pronounced, Hardy's court-appointed attorney raised a technical objection. Hardy had been arraigned incorrectly. Chief Justice Theophilus Parsons granted the exception and ordered a new trial. "A man may quibble for his life," Parsons declared. On re-trial a jury acquitted Hardy.[1]

This book is about murder, due process, and the abolition of the death penalty in Massachusetts. For most of Massachusetts history, murder was punishable by death. Seventeenth- and eighteenth-century English migrants to Massachusetts were no strangers to capital punishment. On the eve of the Puritans' Great Migration, English law listed dozens of capital crimes, a number that swelled to more than two hundred in the decades before the American Revolution. By contrast, English settlers in Massachusetts imposed the death penalty for only a handful of crimes, and by the Reconstruction era only rape and first-degree murder carried the ultimate penalty. The average number of people executed for murder annually remained small well into the twentieth century. Occasionally, a murder captured headlines and abolitionists stirred public and political debate about the necessity, or the justness, of the death penalty, and in the 1970s and 1980s the Massachusetts Supreme Judicial Court became the center of that divisive debate.[2]

I argue that for more than 350 years the state's belief that it had a right to take the life of a person convicted of murder existed in tension with the court's commitment to protecting the rights of a capital defendant and with the public's ambivalence about the death penalty. From 1630 to 1947, when the last persons were put to death, the state executed 237 convicted murderers—men and women, Native Americans, African Americans, Chinese, and whites from various ethnic groups. While the machinery of death clunked along, mercy tempered justice, due process was transformed, abolitionists came within a handful of votes of outlawing the death penalty by legislative enactment, jurors sentenced a majority of defendants convicted of first-degree murder after 1951 to life imprisonment rather than death, and a string of governors refused to sign death warrants for those men who were sentenced to death. In 1984 the Massachusetts Supreme Judicial Court abolished capital punishment.[3]

The origins of the court's decision lay in the state's founding documents. *The Laws and Liberties* (1648) and the Massachusetts Declaration of Rights (1780) share a belief that individual rights and liberty are linked and that neither can exist without due process of law—fair and reasonable rules consistently applied. The United States Bill of Rights—available to state criminal defendants beginning in the 1960s—also outlines a code of criminal procedure based on the assumption that due process safeguards individual liberty from arbitrary governmental power. Supreme Court justice Felix Frankfurter recognized the importance of due process to liberty: "The history of American freedom," he wrote in 1945, "is, in no small measure, the history of procedure."[4]

Despite the government's constitutional commitment to procedural fairness, a criminal defendant on trial is no match for the enormous power of the state. To improve the balance of power between the accused and the state, a defendant's rights are held to be inviolable and any abridgement is grounds for an appeal and possibly an acquittal. For this reason, if convicted, capital defendants in Massachusetts routinely appealed to the Supreme Judicial Court, urging the court to exercise its role as the guardian of individual rights.

Changes in criminal due process also occurred because trials are adversarial. A murder defendant is presumed to be innocent, a claim the prosecution must overcome by presenting evidence of guilt a jury will find convincing beyond a reasonable doubt. In rebutting the state's evidence a defendant may challenge its admissibility and call upon the trial judge to resolve the dispute by making a ruling. The judge's ruling may benefit the defendant and also provide a useful precedent for other criminal defendants to challenge the rules. In this way, the rules of the game may be permanently changed. The Supreme Judicial Court also is empowered to articulate new rules.

Criminal due process alone, however, cannot guarantee a fair trial or a just outcome. A community's social and political imperatives and its values and biases affect the way in which justice is defined and administered. At times, racism, ethnic hatred, or sexism has tainted the outcome of a murder trial. In 1927, for example, Harvard law professor Felix Frankfurter charged that Nicola Sacco and Bartolomeo Vanzetti had been sentenced to death at a trial dominated by anti-immigrant, antiradical fear and hatred. Conversely, during the civil rights movement, the Supreme Judicial Court declared that the guarantees contained in the Massachusetts Declaration of Rights are not static and that their meaning is subject to change. The constitutional prohibition against "cruel or unusual punishment" must be interpreted "in light of contemporary circumstances." On that basis the court found the death penalty unconstitutional.[5]

The chapters that follow tell the story of how and why the Supreme Judicial Court came to abolish the death penalty in Massachusetts. The outcome certainly was not inevitable, but rather, abolition was the result of the convergence of historical changes, the story, as United States Supreme Court Chief Justice Earl Warren put it, of the "evolving standards of decency that mark the progress of a maturing society."[6]

In the first six chapters the narrative moves chronologically from the seventeenth-century origins of "due proceeding" in Puritan Massachusetts to the trial of Sacco and Vanzetti in the 1920s. In addition to highlighting particularly significant murder trials and the legal issues to which they gave rise, these chapters examine several attempts to abolish the death penalty. Chapters 7, 8, 9, and 10 are thematic, each one focusing on a particular aspect of due process. The final two chapters return to center stage the effort to abolish the death penalty. In 1951 Sara Ehrmann and the Massachusetts Council Against the Death Penalty successfully pushed through the legislature a law allowing capital juries to decide whether a person convicted of first-degree murder should be executed or sentenced to life imprisonment. It was a turning point. The "mercy law," together with the wholesale changes made to due process by the Supreme Judicial Court, eventually led the court to abolish the death penalty.

Chapter 1 focuses on murder and the changes to "due proceeding" made by the Puritans and their eighteenth-century heirs. Puritans hoped to establish a godly, peaceful community, but animosity between master and servant, Native American and English settler, coastal pirates and hard-working mariners, and British soldiers and colonists occasionally led to murder. Free to make laws and rules to fit the local situation, Massachusetts magistrates ensured that a defendant's confession was voluntary, and, contrary to English practice, that capital defendants had the opportunity to be represented by an attorney.

Chapters 2 and 3 highlight the sweeping changes brought about by the American Revolution and by early nineteenth-century reformers. The decades following the Revolution were especially tumultuous: more felons were executed than at any other time in Massachusetts history, but, in that period, the courts took an active role in protecting and extending liberty. Spurred by democratic reformers and by the execution of two young friends, Robert Rantoul launched the first movement to abolish capital punishment in Massachusetts. His effort fell just short of its goal, but the movement did succeed in drastically reducing the number of executions until racism undercut goodwill.

Chapter 4 focuses on three major murder trials and a handful of significant procedural changes. Between John Webster's conviction for the murder of George Parkman and James Trefethen's trial for the murder of his alleged lover, the Massachusetts legislature enacted laws creating degrees of murder, replacing the common-law form of criminal indictment with a short, generic form, allowing the defendant to testify in his or her own behalf and giving the prosecutor peremptory challenges. These new rules were in place for the 1905 trial of Charles Tucker, but widespread doubt about his guilt fueled a "monster petition" signed by more than a hundred thousand people begging the state to spare his life.

The trial of nine Chinese men who allegedly had been part of a bloody "tong war" is the subject of Chapter 5. The trial revealed deep social, political, and religious fissures within Massachusetts society that stymied Florence Spooner's campaign to stop the execution of three of the convicted men and to abolish the death penalty. Twenty years later Sacco and Vanzetti's trial, examined in Chapter 6, also divided the American people and may have fatally tainted the outcome but certainly gave momentum to the campaign to abolish the death penalty in Massachusetts.

Chapters 7, 8, 9, and 10 highlight changes in due process and argue that procedural reform drove the court to embrace abolition. In an effort to integrate the law and science, the Supreme Judicial Court defined insanity in 1844 and then, as Chapter 7 makes clear, struggled to keep pace with modern psychiatry while assuring the public that insanity is not merely an excuse to escape punishment. As I show in Chapter 8, the *Laws and*

Liberties granted capital defendants the right to an attorney, but a jurisdictional change and the legal profession's emergence raised questions about an attorney's effectiveness that were not resolved until 1974; this chapter also uncovers the history of discovery, the reciprocal exchange of information between the prosecution and the defense. The rules defining an admissible confession and the means by which an impartial jury is sought are explored in Chapters 9 and 10.

Chapter 11 features Sara Ehrmann, the Brookline reformer whom many credited with single-handedly pushing the mercy law though the legislature and with keeping alive the Massachusetts campaign to abolish the death penalty. Chapter 12 follows the road taken by the U.S. Supreme Court leading to the abolition of the death penalty and the Supreme Judicial Court's use of state constitutionalism to achieve that goal for Massachusetts when the Supreme Court decided in 1976 that the death penalty is constitutional. The Epilogue outlines the most recent attempt to reinstate the death penalty in Massachusetts.

My goal in writing this book is to make explicit "the evolving standards of decency" that ultimately led Massachusetts to conclude that the death penalty is "cruel or unusual punishment," contrary to the fundamental values expressed in the Declaration of Rights.

to emulate God, applying wisdom and mercy to achieve justice. Permitting judges to "proportion their severall sentences, accordinge to the severall natures and degrees of their [defendants] offenses" made for a more just and humane system, he argued in the fall of 1644. He suggested, for example, that magistrates routinely distinguished between first and repeat offenders in sentencing and penalized gentlemen more severely than defendants from lower social classes. "Prescript penaltyes," Winthrop claimed, would take away a judge's flexibility to craft a punishment that fit the specific circumstances of the crime. The same held true for murder, Winthrop insisted, taking on the lawmakers' most powerful argument. The Bible was filled with examples in which murderers were not punished by death. God "variethe the punishment according to the measure and nature of the offense." Finally, Winthrop reminded the deputies of their place in the political structure and concluded, "It is yourselves who have called us to this office, and being called by you, we hath our authority from God." [19]

Winthrop's arguments were not unreasonable, but they were completely unsatisfactory to the deputies. If judges were allowed to make law by precedent not subject to public deliberation, the deputies asked, might not the people find themselves bound in the chains of slavery? There must be a law code to protect the people's liberties. Therefore, in 1645–46, the legislature appointed "severall persons out of each county . . . to drawe up a body of lawes, so we may have recourse to any of them upon all occasions, whereby we may manifest our utter disaffection to arbitrary government." While no record exists of the law's formal adoption by the legislature, the General Court ordered the code printed in March 1648 and distributed it throughout the colony. [20]

The legislature's hard line on capital punishment ended whatever possibility may have existed to reform the death penalty. To some degree, the deputies' political identity was now tied to their support for the death penalty. Their triumph over Winthrop and the court had solidified their argument that the Bible allows no flexibility when it comes to punishment for murder. For lawmakers, discretionary justice was simply another word for arbitrary government and they rejected it. Therefore, the Laws and Liberties of Massachusetts stipulated that "if any person shall commit any wilfull MURTHER, which is Man slaughter, committed upon premeditate malice, hatred, or cruelties not in a mans necessary and just defense, nor by meer casualty against his will, he shall be put to death." [21]

Although the law and penalty for murder was fixed in 1648, murder trials continued to stir up controversy over who would control the courtroom. Judges and juries struggled to differentiate their roles in the legal process. Juries wanted to be free to say what the law meant or to mingle law with fact in arriving at their decision. Judges insisted it was their function to say what the law was and that jurors should be limited to determining the facts. A murder trial heard by the Court of Assistants in the spring of 1653, for example, led to an open clash between judges and jurors and to the first appeal of a murder conviction in the colony's history.[22]

John Betts, a Cambridge farmer, was indicted for the "horrible and wicked" murder of his servant Robert Knight, who died August 28, 1652, allegedly from blows delivered by Betts and from neglect during his subsequent "sickness." Several witnesses told Judge Increase Nowell, one of the founders of the Bay colony and an elder of the First Church of Boston, who gathered testimony in the case, that Betts abused Knight. Thomas Pierce, a man about sixty years of age, testified that he saw Betts hit Knight, knocking him to the ground. A twenty-seven-year-old carter, Richard French, told Judge Nowell that on another occasion he saw Betts strike Knight with a stick he "held in both hands and with all his force as hard as he could . . . he gave him at least six blowes so that Robert began to cry out." Richard's father, William, verified his son's testimony, adding that Betts had said that he beat Knight because he was lazy. And Renew Andrews stated that Betts, whom she described as a "furious man," had punished Knight by tying him to a board in an upright position, where he left him for several hours after Knight complained that his back hurt. While Knight was "trussed up," Betts pushed excrement into the servant's mouth and punched him in the face. In his deposition, Dr. George Alcock said that at Goodwife Betts's request, he examined Knight and found that he had a dislocated vertebra. Alcock advised Knight not to do any heavy work. On a follow-up visit, Alcock found Knight lying without food or drink in a small, unheated room. He was partially paralyzed.

Captain Daniel Gookin, a Cambridge magistrate, and Justice Robert Bridge visited Knight before his death. They warned him that the Lord would punish him if he were faking. Weak and grimacing with pain, the young man talked freely and convincingly, giving details about how and when Betts had beaten him. Knight died two days later and Betts was charged with murder.

At trial, other witnesses told a different story. Thomas Abbott, another of Betts's young workmen, told Judge Nowell that Knight was lazy, that he had no interest in farming, and that he often feigned illness. Abbott also insisted that the blows Betts gave Knight were harmless. Likewise, testimony from two other workers, Goulding Moore and William Manning, cast doubt on the prosecution's case.

The jury found Betts not guilty, apparently because they did not think an explicit link between the blows Betts gave Knight and the servant's death had been established. Because the jury's verdict was contrary to the judge's instructions on the law, the court refused the verdict and appealed the case to the General Court. It seems unlikely that Betts's guilt or innocence alone motivated the court to take this unusual step. At issue was the popular belief that a criminal jury had the right to decide matters of law and fact. This perception clashed with the court's argument that a judge had the sole right to decide the law and a jury the right to determine the facts and to receive the law from the court. There were two arguments implicit in the court's position. First, if a jury ignored the judge's instructions about the law, a defendant's right to due process was violated. Allowing juries to determine the law meant its meaning would fluctuate from case to case and a defendant would have no solid basis on which to make an appeal. Second, the court insisted only judges had the skill and the experience to clarify questions of law.[23]

The context within which the General Court heard the Court of Assistants' appeal in Betts was the struggle over discretionary justice that had divided the court and lawmakers in 1648, five years earlier. Not surprisingly, therefore, the legislature sided with the jury, finding Betts not guilty of murder. At the same time, the General Court did conclude that there was a "strong presumption and great probabilities of his guilt of so bloody a fact." Therefore, the lawmakers sentenced Betts to stand for one hour on the gallows wearing a rope around his neck, to be whipped, to pay court costs, and to be on probation for one year.[24]

In the two decades following the controversial Betts decision, the court heard seven murder cases, all of which brought to trial young, rootless workingmen, several of whom seemed to be angry about their low social status. Gregory Cassell, a sailor, felt bullied by the master of a fishing boat on which he worked. While ashore in the fall of 1657, Cassell hit the captain in the head with a hammer, killing him. No one saw the fatal fight, but Cassell's shipmates placed him at the scene of the crime and a grand jury indicted him. At his trial, Cassell argued what seems to have been his wish—that he and Captain Matthew Kinnage were "loving friends," not merely master and servant. Therefore, it seems the young sailor was especially aggrieved by Kinnage's alleged rough treatment of him.[25]

Robert Driver and William Favor also stood trial for murdering their master, Robert Williams, a fisherman, whose position of power they resented. Both pleaded not guilty and neither exercised his right to object to any of the jurors who were summoned to hear the case. Despite their protestations of innocence, juries found both men guilty in 1674 and the court sentenced each to be hanged. According to custom, a condemned culprit was brought to the meetinghouse to be made the subject of a clerical discourse. Following his sermon, Rev. Cotton Mather walked with the men to the gallows. Along the way, each man confessed to committing murder. Favor told Mather that he knew now that pride was the cause of his downfall. While he worked for Williams, Favor told Mather, he vainly had thought to himself: *"I am Flesh and Blood as well as my Master, and therefore, I know no Reason why my Master should not obey me, as well as I obey him."* Driver added that his first step toward the gallows was not industriously following his calling as a servant, a confession Mather and the magistrates welcomed as affirming the necessity of a hierarchical social structure.[26]

The blood and thunder of King Philip's War and the Glorious Revolution made murder a political as well as a social problem and in the process contributed to a significant increase in the number of murders committed in 1675 and 1676 and in 1688 and 1689. Although the court was under enormous pressure during these times to abandon procedures guaranteeing individual rights, the justices held firm to due process guarantees protecting the accused. During King Philip's War, a large aggressive faction hostile to all Indians pushed the court to do its hateful bidding. In August 1675, for example, Captain Samuel Mosely, a popular and successful army officer, dragged before the court thirteen Indians who he charged had murdered William Flagg, a soldier in Marlborough. John Indian, Joseph Spoonhaut, Little John Indian, and ten others were indicted and tried for murder. At trial, however, Judge Daniel Gookin, who also served as superintendent of the Praying Indians, and Justice Thomas Danforth spoke critically of Mosely's evidence against the Indians. His testimony and that of some Marlborough residents, the court observed, was filled with a general hatred for Indians but contained few facts linking the Indians arrested to Flagg's murder. A jury found all but Little John Indian not guilty. Aware of the hostility with which their verdict would be greeted, the court moved cautiously. Those Indians found not guilty were released under cover of darkness, just hours before a mob intending to lynch the Indians arrived at the courthouse. Disappointed at not finding their prey, at least some in the crowd threatened to hunt down the justices of the court.[27]

In the summer of 1676 the court and Captain Mosely clashed again. Sometime the previous fall the government had placed a group of Indians under the personal supervision of John Hoar, a lawyer who came to Concord in 1660. He built a house for the Indians in which they worked during the day and were locked up at night. Some local people who resented this arrangement asked Mosely to come to Concord. He and his soldiers arrived on a Sunday and went to the meetinghouse, where Mosely harangued the congregation, urging them to follow him to the Indian workhouse. He had no warrant or commission to justify his actions, but at the workhouse Mosely took charge, bullying Hoar and denying his authority to protect the Indians. In the morning, Mosely seized the Indians and marched them to Boston, from where they were sent to Deer Island, an open-air prison that turned into a death pen the following winter. Mosely had seized the Indians living peacefully in Concord without warrant and they were imprisoned without criminal cause or a trial. Yet, no advocate stepped forward to protect the Indians and the court watched silently.[28]

Although this incident makes clear the limitations of the court's power in the face of popular hostility, hatred did not completely undermine the colony's legal system. A few months after Mosely's highhanded action, Stephen and Daniel Gobble, who lived south of Walden woods, Nathaniel Wilde, and Daniel Hoar, John's son, were arrested for the murder of three Indian women and three children who were camped at Whortleberry Hill in nearby Lincoln. The men were indicted by a grand jury, tried before the court, found guilty by a jury, and sentenced to death in September 1676. Only the Gobble brothers were executed. Stephen walked to the gallows on a raw, cold day in late September. Five days later, Daniel was "drawn in a cart upon bed-clothes to [his] execution."[29]

On the same day Daniel Gobble was executed, four Indians were hanged on the Boston Common, bringing to fifteen the total number that were put to death during the bloody summer of 1676. Two other Indians were executed October 12. Those Indians who survived the war lost their independence and autonomy. By law, all Indians who were not family servants were required to live in one of four towns, where they would be under constant observation. White guardians replaced Indian magistrates as chief judicial officers in the villages. In the decades after King Philip's War, when wartime passions had cooled, Indians who came before the court were treated fairly.[30]

Thirteen years after King Philip's War the people of Boston ousted the colony's royal governor during the Glorious Revolution. Eager to restore law and order, the magistrates took aim at the gangs of pirates operating against local shipping. Among other outlaws, Captain Thomas Pound, a crew of thirteen men, and the ship's sailing master, Thomas Hawkins, were after quick, if prosaic, profits. On August 8, 1689, Pound's pirate band forcibly boarded the ketch *Mary* at anchor in Boston harbor and seized its cargo of fish valued at £60. About a week later, they assaulted the *Merrimack* while she lay at Homes Hole, Martha's Vineyard, and seized the sloop *Good Speed*. Satisfied with his plunder, Hawkins went ashore at Cape Cod while his mates sailed for the Elizabeth Islands and the possibility of more plunder. On September 30, the governor and council commissioned Captain Samuel Pease to put to sea at once in an armed sloop with a crew of twenty to capture the pirates. Four days later, Captain Pease discovered the pirates in Vineyard Sound. During the fight that followed, Captain Pease was shot and killed. Eventually, however, the superior firepower of the colony's warship caused the pirates to surrender. Hawkins and thirteen crewmen, including Thomas Johnston, a seaman identified as Pease's assailant, were brought to Boston and indicted for murder and piracy, both capital offenses.[31]

Johnston was tried separately from his shipmates, who were arraigned and tried in two groups. A jury, basing its decision on sworn testimony from Johnston's captors and his shipmates, found Johnston guilty of murder. Of the first five men tried for Pease's murder, four were found guilty and one, Edward Browne, was set free. At an arraignment for Pound, Hawkins and the remaining seven crewmen, all but William Coward pleaded not guilty to the charge of murder. Coward refused to take the oath required of witnesses or to plead to the indictment. He was sent back to prison and warned that he would be held in contempt if he did not comply with the court's order. When Coward refused a second time to cooperate, the court entered a guilty plea for him and ordered the trial to proceed. A jury found all seven men guilty as charged and they were sentenced to death, bringing the total number to be hanged on Boston Common to fourteen.[32]

In fact, only Johnston was hanged. The other convicted men successfully petitioned Governor Sir William Phips for clemency, a decision that caused Justice Samuel Sewall considerable anxiety. Sewall had visited the men in jail, "prayed with them," and signed a petition arguing a point of law for at least one of the convicted pirate-murderers. Still, he confided to his diary he felt pushed into the decision by one of his colleagues on the bench, Justice Wait Winthrop. "Some" on the court, Sewall wrote in January 1690, "thought Hawkins, because he got out of the Combination before Pease was kill'd, might live as well as Coward; so I rashly signed." The governor's reprieve was delivered to Hawkins just before he was "to be turn'd off . . . , which gave great disgust to the People," Sewall added.[33]

It would appear that Governor Phips distinguished piracy (at least when carried out by local men) from murder and determined to punish only the latter crime, for which Johnston was found solely responsible. Phips also may have been swayed by the court's postconviction argument for reversing the murder convictions of Hawkins and Coward. Although a bit murky, this process sheds light on several aspects of colonial criminal procedure and on how the court arrived at its decisions. First, in a search for the truth the criminal justice system relied heavily on oaths. It was assumed that God-fearing witnesses under oath told the truth and, likewise, that it made no sense for criminal defendants to be sworn because they would lie if guilty. Aided by the fact there was no rule to encourage jurors to weigh the credibility of witnesses, the pirate-witnesses who testified against Johnston may well have been motivated primarily by self-interest. It was to their benefit to name Johnston as the sole gunman responsible for murdering Pease. At the same time, the pirate-witnesses gained nothing by naming Coward. It seems reasonable to assume these same witnesses did not implicate Coward either in the murder or in the piracy and, therefore, the court overturned his conviction. Since the court might have ordered Coward to be pressed for refusing to plea, his standing mute was a risky—though ultimately successful—strategy. Second, it seems clear that at least Hawkins received invaluable and sophisticated legal advice. Hawkins's alibi that he was ashore on Cape Cod—that he had "withdrawn from the

Combination"—before Captain Pease was murdered certainly saved his life. Third, to arrive at its decision the justices engaged in a spirited internal postconviction debate about the law. There is no reason to think other controversial or complex cases did not provoke similar discussion within the court. Fourth, the fact that Justice Sewall grumbled, but joined in the decision, suggests that the court believed in consensus as a means of enhancing its power. Finally, it is plain the court treated the death penalty with great care, tempering the severity of the law with mercy whenever uncertainty crept into the procedure.[34]

Trial juries provided another source of flexibility in the criminal justice system. Grand juries normally brought an indictment for homicide whenever they considered a nonaccidental death, leaving it to the trial jury to determine whether the crime was homicide, manslaughter, or "misadventure." For this reason, all of the prosecutions for homicide that came before the court from 1630 to 1692 were by grand jury indictment. In addition to the fourteen Indians who were illegally dragged before the court by Captain Mosely, and the fourteen pirates, thirty-two other men and three women were indicted for murder during this period, bringing the total to sixty-three. Seven men and women who were charged with murder eventually were convicted of a lesser offense, usually manslaughter, thirteen were convicted, and sixteen were acquitted, not including the fourteen Indians. Of the thirteen persons found guilty of homicide, all were men and all but one—Lodwick Fowler, whose 1673 murder conviction was overturned by the General Court—were hanged. Nearly three times as many men (twenty-three) as women (eight) were homicide victims.[35]

One-third of the English men and women indicted for murder worked with the person they were accused of killing. Masters who were accused of murdering their servants were without exception acquitted, but servants indicted for murdering their masters were hanged for the crime. Sailors seemed especially prone to violence, lending support to the popular belief that young, rootless men were likely to be undisciplined. In peacetime, cross-cultural conflict was not an important cause of violence in seventeenth-century Massachusetts. With the exception of the three Indian women and their children who were massacred by young white men during King Philip's War, there was only one case in which a white man was tried for the murder of an Indian. He was found not guilty. On two occasions, Indian men were tried for murdering other Indians and they too were found not guilty. The charge of murder brought against Robin, an African American slave accused of killing a white man in 1689, was reduced to manslaughter.[36]

These data sustain two conclusions about homicide trials in seventeenth-century Massachusetts. First, juries were not quick to convict homicide defendants. Men and women, Indians and African Americans all seem to have received fair trials according to contemporary due process. Due process included a grand jury indictment that was made available to the defendant, legal representation, a jury trial, the right to challenge potential jurors, the right to confront witnesses, the right to have evidence presented, and the right of appeal. Second, from 1677 to 1692 juries tended increasingly to return a verdict of manslaughter rather than murder. Only four men were convicted of homicide and hanged during the last fifteen years of the Court of Assistants' existence.[37]

The Salem witch trials, of course, spilled plenty of blood. Before the colony's new charter authorized the creation of the Superior Court of Judicature (SCJ), a special Court of Oyer and Terminer had sent twenty-two people convicted of witchcraft to the gallows. While there is no question that the justices appointed to the SCJ believed in witchcraft, they eventually stopped the craze and worked to restore credibility to the colony's legal system. In particular, Justice Thomas Danforth, who joined Justices John Richards, Wait Winthrop, Samuel Sewall, and Chief Justice William Stoughton on the new court, was known to "utterly condemn" the witchcraft court proceedings. By the spring of 1693, Justice Danforth's condemnation and Justice Sewall's doubts ended prosecution for witchcraft. During the Superior Court of Judicature's initial session in Suffolk County, for example, Captain John Alden, who had been in hiding, was discharged from "suspition of Witchcraft," and a month later in Ipswich, five women indicted for witchcraft were tried and found not guilty.[38]

The justices of the new SCJ were old friends who usually rode together on circuit. Each term they held court in Boston, York, Portsmouth, Cambridge, Worcester, Plymouth, and Barnstable. Judges and lawyers often lodged at the same inn or at the home of friends. At the end of a long ride or a day in court, they ate, drank, and talked with comfortable familiarity. In December 1693, for example, Justice Sewall rode from his home in Boston with Justice Danforth and Chief Justice Stoughton to attend court in Salem. Arriving around eight o'clock in the evening, the three ate supper at the Blue Bell Tavern before retiring. The court cleared its docket the following day, but a "great Storm of Rain" kept the justices in Salem another day. That night, Judge Sewall and his colleagues, together with the attorney general, the sheriff of Essex County, and attorney Thomas Newton, among others, had dinner at Stephen Sewall's home.[39]

With but small variations, the court's life while on circuit remained the same until the American Revolution. Each term a small ceremony honoring the court was repeated as it moved throughout the province. As the justices approached a town in which they were to hold court, the sheriff and other local magistrates rode out to escort the justices to the courthouse. On Sunday, the justices would attend church, adding a bit of pomp to a town's life, and sometimes winning praise from a country clergyman. In York, Rev. Samuel Moody said that of the "present four justices of our Court, that we had not in America a Court more accomplished." When the court completed a circuit and returned to Boston, Chief Justice Benjamin Lynde added the custom of "treating" the other justices. On January 26, 1732, for example, the court gathered at the Orange Tree Tavern in Boston to enjoy "ale, cakes, cheese and brandy punch."[40]

Above all, however, a commitment to the "right discharge of duty in Court where the lives, libertys and estates of [the people] are ultimately determined" bound together the justices, the law, and the people. A capital trial revealed how important that relationship was. There was no greater responsibility than to "Judge in the solemn and awful tryal of a capital crime," Chief Justice Lynde instructed a jury. He urged the jurors to "discover by sufficient evidence the horrid fact and circumstances as to satisfy your consciences of the truth of the indictment." If the jurors' verdict was guilty, their private deliberation was played out in a grim public drama.[41]

Executions in Massachusetts followed a strict pattern, with the convicted, the clergy, and the crowd each playing an important part. After the court passed a sentence of death, ministers would visit the condemned prisoners and encourage them to see the error of their ways, to seek God's forgiveness, and to make a public confession. On the Sunday prior to the execution, a sermon was preached in the meetinghouse closest to the jail, the condemned sitting in the front row for all to see and to judge. Some prisoners rode from the jail to the gallows in a cart, others chose to walk. A clergyman accompanied the condemned, initiating a dialogue about the possibility of salvation. Ideally, the condemned read their confessions from

that the convicted person had received his one-time privilege. At least five more persons successfully pleaded benefit of clergy during the next six years.[50]

The first successful use of the motion in arrest of judgment in a capital case came in 1745 in a case involving two Englishmen, John Fowles and John Warren, who were part of a press gang. Under the authority of a warrant issued by the Suffolk County sheriff, they hoped to impress fifteen men. Roaming the streets of Boston, the press gang tangled with a group of local sailors. During the struggle, two Boston sailors were killed. A grand jury indicted Fowles and Warren and they were brought to trial on February 18, 1745. After a jury trial lasting more than ten hours, the two men were found guilty of murder and sentenced to death. Their attorney moved in arrest of judgment, arguing that the indictment did not specify the day on which the murder occurred or specifically charge Fowles or Warren with the blows that killed the sailors. The court heard arguments for and against granting the motion for two full days before deciding to arrest judgment.[51]

While Lynde served as chief justice, he also heard three homicide cases that exposed the ugliness of New England slavery. In October 1736, Captain Jonathan Barnes was tried before a special admiralty court, of which Lynde was a member. The story presented to the court by William Shirley, advocate general of the Admiralty Court, was simple and brutal. En route from Guinea to Boston with a ship packed with slaves, Captain Barnes determined that water had to be rationed. One black slave repeatedly called out "watro," and after other methods to silence the man failed, Barnes murdered him. John Bowles, the captain's lawyer, argued that Barnes's brutality was not motivated by malice but by his concern for the well-being of his entire ship. The "negro boy Bawman's" cries for water might well cause unrest and anger among the other slaves. If Bowles's first argument was covered with a thin hypocritical veil of humanity, his second was stripped of pretense. He contended that a slave was mere cargo, and as master of the cargo, Captain Barnes "might do what he would with him, even to taking away his life." The court rejected both arguments and found Captain Barnes guilty of homicide.[52]

Two additional cases of racial violence came before the SCJ in 1737 and 1741. Captain Samuel Rhodes was ordered by the court to answer questions about the death of a "Negro man named Aava," whom the captain had ordered tied "to a Gun and whipt by four other Negroes." Within an hour after he was cut loose, Aava died. Although Captain Rhodes defended his actions as nothing more than normal discipline, the court ordered him to post a bond and to appear before the Massachusetts Vice-Admiralty Court. Four Boston men—Benjamin Eaton, a hatter; Samuel and Benjamin Sumner, laborers; and Ambrose Searle, a saddler—were indicted in 1741 for the murder of London, a slave belonging to Rev. John Walley. The circumstances and cause of London's death were argued "all day till sundown." The following day, the jury found the men guilty of homicide "by misadventure." The court's sentence was lenient. Each man was required to post a bond for future good behavior.[53]

Despite these and other episodes of racial violence, the people of Boston were shocked and fearful in 1755 when two black slaves were charged with petit treason for the murder of their master, the Charlestown merchant John Codman. It was believed that Mark and Phillis, the accused slaves, were neither overworked nor ill-treated. Like many other New England slaves, both had been educated and had considerable freedom of movement, Mark frequenting the taverns of Charlestown and Phillis crossing the Charles River to visit friends in Boston. Yet, early public information about the crime suggested that Mark and numerous other slaves hated all whites, giving rise to the fear that Codman's murder was one episode in a widespread conspiracy to murder whites generally. Hoping to head off lawless popular revenge against black slaves generally as had occurred in New York City a decade earlier, Attorney General Edmund Trowbridge conducted a careful investigation.[54]

Codman owned several slaves, employing them as laborers, artisans, and house servants. Mark chafed under Codman's discipline and planned to murder him, thinking that a new master would allow him more freedom. Mark searched the Bible for a method of murdering his master without inducing guilt. He concluded that no sin would be committed if the murder were carried out without bloodshed. This erroneous interpretation Mark folded in with a bit of misinformation—that sometime earlier a Boston slave had used poison to murder his master and had escaped detection— and concocted a scheme to poison Codman. To carry out his plan, Mark sought the help of several other slaves.

For the poison he wanted, Mark eventually went to Robin, the slave of William Clarke, an apothecary, to obtain arsenic, and to Essex, a black servant who had access to "black lead," or graphite, used by Charlestown potters, which Mark believed would, like the arsenic, be fatal if ingested. To administer the poison, Mark recruited Phillis. She made a solution using arsenic and black lead and mixed it into Codman's food and drink. Codman died on July 1, 1755. A coroner's jury found that Codman had died from arsenic poisoning and an official investigation was launched immediately.

Mark was questioned but released. It seems clear, however, that the attorney general suspected Mark and set about to build a case against him. On July 12, a slave named Quaco, "the nominal husband" of Phoebe, a friend of Phillis's, was interrogated. Quaco told Justice of the Peace William Stoddard that when he learned Mark wanted Phoebe to join in the murderous plot, he told his wife not to take part. While Quaco was being questioned, Robin was arrested and jailed. He apparently also provided specific information implicating Mark and Phillis. Ten days later, the two slaves were questioned, first Phillis and then Mark.

Phillis freely spelled out to Trowbridge and Thaddeus Mason, Esq., the details of the plot to murder Codman. She said it was Mark who got the potter's lead from Essex and Mark to whom Robin brought the poison and Mark who gave Phoebe a vial of arsenic that she delivered to Phillis. She and Phoebe mixed the deadly potion, hiding the vial in the kitchen until Codman called for drink. Although she said she felt "ugly" doing it, Phillis took responsibility for mixing poison into Codman's oatmeal and chocolate drink. Phillis added that after Codman's death, Robin came to Charlestown to talk with Mark.

Armed with this information, Trowbridge questioned Mark again. Mark denied he had masterminded the plot to murder Codman, claiming he had learned of the murder only after Codman was dead. Mark admitted he had carried poison from Robin to Phoebe, but he insisted he had not known that she and Phillis intended to use it to murder Codman. Yes, he told Trowbridge, he had asked Essex for some potter's lead, but his purpose was wholly innocent. He merely wanted to learn if it would melt in a fire. Finally, Mark gave the attorney general a piece of information clearly meant to deflect suspicion from him. The day before Codman died, he told Trowbridge, Phillis "got to dancing and mocking master and shaking herself and acting as master did in the Bed."

Trowbridge was not fooled, and on the first Tuesday in August 1755, a grand jury indicted Mark and Phillis for petit treason, defined as a breach of private or domestic faith or allegiance between a wife and husband or a servant and master. A man convicted of petit treason was to be hanged in chains and his body displayed on a specially built iron gibbet; a woman was to be burned at the stake. Chief Justice Stephen Sewall presided at the trial at which Quaco and Phoebe testified for the prosecution. On advice of counsel, Mark and Phillis pleaded not guilty, but the evidence presented by Attorney General Trowbridge was overwhelming and a jury found the two slaves guilty. Sewall sentenced Mark and Phillis to death.

The *Boston Evening Post* printed an account of their executions:

Thursday last, in the Afternoon, Mark, a Negro Man, and Phillis, a Negro Woman, both servants of the late Capt. John Codman, of Charlestown, were executed at Cambridge, for poisoning their said Master. The Fellow was hanged, and the Woman burned at the Stake about Ten Yards distant from the Gallows. They both confessed themselves guilty of the Crime for which they suffered, acknowledged the Justice of their Sentences, and died very penitent. After execution the Body of Mark was brought down to Charlestown Common, and hanged in chains, on a Gibbet erected there for that Purpose.[55]

The gruesome public punishment meted out to Mark and Phillis neither prevented similar crimes nor undermined New England slaveholders' naive belief that they were able to understand and control the black people they enslaved. Just eight years after Mark's and Phillis's executions, a sixteen-year-old black slave named Bristol murdered Elizabeth McKinstry, a Connecticut clergyman's daughter living with her brother and sister-in-law in Taunton. Early on the morning of June 4, 1763, the McKinstry's daughter discovered Elizabeth lying in a pool of blood. Her head was split open and one side of her face was horribly burned. She was still alive but unconscious. She "languished till the Evening of the next Day without the least Appearance of Reason and then died," the *Boston Evening Post* reported. By chance, Robert Treat Paine, a lawyer and family friend, arrived in Taunton just as news of the crime became public. He went immediately to the McKinstry home, which he found "full of curious Spectators, Confusion, Anxiety and distress."[56]

After assaulting McKinstry, Bristol fled to Newport, Rhode Island, "riding off on his master's horse on a full Gallop." Late that afternoon he was captured and brought back to Taunton. At the coroner's request, Paine took charge of the inquest. Paine knew Bristol, describing him in a newspaper story as "an exceeding good Servant, remarkable for his obsequious Behavior." During questioning at the inquest, Bristol, "appear'd sullen and denied the fact," but "strong evidence" led a grand jury to indict him for McKinstry's murder. About twelve hours later he confessed privately to Paine, saying an older slave had threatened to kill him unless he murdered McKinstry.[57]

Paine represented Bristol at trial held October 13. The McKinstry's young daughter testified that she, Elizabeth, and Bristol were the only persons awake in the house when she put some flat irons in the fire. While the irons heated she went upstairs to gather the clothing she intended to press. Returning to the kitchen she noticed one of the irons missing and the other lying on its side. At the same moment she heard a "bitter Groan," walked toward the parlor, and found a trail of blood that led to Elizabeth's body at the bottom of the basement stairs. Other witnesses testified they saw Bristol racing away from the McKinstry house shortly before the alarm was sounded. A jury found Bristol guilty of murder and Chief Justice Thomas Hutchinson pronounced a sentence of death. Bristol was "to hang by ye neck till you be dead." Paine asked for, and won a brief postponement of the execution date, although he was unhappy that Bristol showed no emotion when he was sentenced to death. Standing on the gallows, however, Bristol apologized to the McKinstry family, acknowledged his guilt, and admonished "those of his own Colour" to obey their masters. He recited the Lord's Prayer and was "turn'd off."[58]

Following Bristol's execution Paine wrote an introduction to a sermon preached on the occasion by his friend, Rev. Sylanus Conant. Paine's analysis of the murder was free of racism, but he did sound a warning about the treatment of slaves. He began by describing the context within which murder occurred, highlighting the "alarming frailities of human Nature," and expressing how much "Horror, Pity and Indignation" this "tragic scene aroused." Bristol was brought to New England from Africa when he was about eight years old and, according to Paine, he "was treated with all the Tenderness and Instruction that could be desired, and he always appeared happy in his Situation." For this reason, Bristol's murder of Elizabeth "fills us with Astonishment." It is a "striking Instance of the Weakness of human Nature." Although Paine did not distinguish Bristol from other sinful men, he argued that slaves needed to be treated differently. "Those who have the Care of Negroes," he said, "[must] be very vigilant in removing the Prejudices of their barbarous Disposition by Instruction." And we must prevent "their companying together," because slave groups are the "grand Source of all the Evils that have arisen so frequently from this Nation."[59]

Just one year after Bristol's execution Paine represented another murder defendant and in doing so effected a change in the rules of criminal procedure. Bail normally was prohibited in a capital case, but in 1764 Paine petitioned Chief Justice Thomas Hutchinson to allow an indicted murderer, Jonathan Shepardson, to remain free until his trial. Paine argued the murder indictment against Shepardson would not be sustained at trial and, therefore, to hold him until the court's next circuit would violate the defendant's right to due process. Shepardson was an Attleboro resident whose rumored sexual misconduct came under attack by his neighbors. Late in October, a group of men in blackface and disguise surrounded Shepardson as he worked in his field. The men intended to force Shepardson to "ride Skimmington," a wooden horse on which they planned to parade him through town. Shepardson had been warned, however, and he was armed with a knife. During the scuffle that followed, Shepardson killed Benjamin Ide, one of his taunters. Under the circumstances, Paine asked that his client be granted bail and the chief justice agreed, allowing Shepardson to remain free until his trial in October 1765. At trial, Paine argued that Shepardson acted in self-defense and he was acquitted. The *Boston Gazette* concluded: "These Schimeton Frolicks have been too frequent in many Parts of the Country; but it is hoped that this unhappy man's Fate of whom it may be said, that *as a Fool dieth, so died he*, it will be a Caution to others, not to take it upon them in this lawless Manner to punish their Neighbours for any supposed or real Misbehaviour, but have them to the due Course of Law."[60]

Within days following Shepardson's acquittal, Paine and Hutchinson, who had cooperated to create new criminal procedure, were on opposite sides of a political controversy that would eventually lead to Hutchinson's exile and Paine's selection as attorney general of the newly independent Commonwealth of Massachusetts. Paine's diary entry for November 1, 1765 reads: "The Dawn was overcast with Dark destructive Fogs and nature seem'd to Mourn the Arrival of this ill boded dreaded never to be forgotten first of Nov. NB Stamp Act takes place this day." The stamp tax, designed by Parliament to raise a revenue in the colonies to help support imperial administration, stimulated riots, demonstrations, and resolutions against the law beginning in July and August. Among other militant acts meant to defeat the Stamp Act, Hutchinson's Boston home was destroyed by a mob from which he barely escaped. The following May, Paine was at Plymouth for a session of the SCJ when news arrived that the Stamp Act had been repealed. "The day was spent in rejoicing for the repeal," he wrote.[61]

Other colonial taxes followed, however, and to enforce their acceptance, British troops arrived in Boston in 1768. For nearly a year and a half after the troops' landing Massachusetts was relatively peaceful, but on the night of March 5, 1770, groups of soldiers nursing a grudge from an earlier scuffle with townsmen left their barracks looking to settle the old score. Soon knots of Bostonians gathered in the streets around the Custom House, where a single sentry stood guard. When a handful of soldiers commanded by Captain Thomas Preston were sent to support the sentry the crowd pelted them with chunks of ice, shouted taunts, and menacingly swung clubs. Fearful, angry, and acting without Preston's command, the soldiers—first one, then another—fired into the crowd, killing five civilians. Preston ran along the line of soldiers pushing the musket barrels with his arm. "Stop firing!" he shouted. He then marched his men to military headquarters. When word of the shooting reached Chief Justice Hutchinson, he rushed from his home to the state house and, stepping onto the balcony, shouted to the crowd below, "Murder will not go unpunished. The law shall have its course!"[62]

Solicitor General Jonathan Sewall drew up the indictments against Captain Preston and the eight British soldiers. Each man's indictment used the law's ancient formulaic language: "Not having the Fear of God before their eyes, but being moved and seduced by the Instigation of the devil and their own wicked hearts . . . did with force and arms feloniously, willfully and of their malice aforethought assault one Crispus Attucks." A grand jury took testimony from dozens of witnesses and on March 26 declared there was sufficient evidence to bring Preston and the eight soldiers to trial for murder. At the last moment the trials of Preston and the soldiers were separated.[63]

John Adams and Robert Auchmuty represented Preston and at a separate trial Adams and Josiah Quincy Jr. were counsel for Private William

Weems and the other seven soldiers. The court appointed Samuel Quincy special prosecutor and Robert Treat Paine was chosen by the Boston selectmen to assist him at the soldiers' trial. After months of delay, Preston stood in the prisoner's dock. With an eye toward eliminating from the jury Bostonians who he believed were likely to be antagonistic to a British military officer, Preston challenged fifteen of the twenty-two men in the initial jury pool. The remaining five seats were filled with men thought to be sympathetic to the Crown. Because the prosecution was not permitted to challenge jurors, the result was a jury packed in the officer's favor. The trial lasted six days, the first colonial homicide trial to take more than one day; and, therefore, the first time a Massachusetts jury was sequestered.[64]

After nearly ninety witnesses had paraded before the jury, the two defense lawyers gave their closing arguments, first Adams and then senior counsel Auchmuty. Adams constructed a brilliant legal argument that would lead the jury to only one conclusion—not guilty. First, Adams reminded the jurors they held a man's life in their hands. Therefore, if there were doubts, they must acquit. He quoted the English jurist Sir Matthew Hale to reinforce his point: "It is better five guilty persons should escape unpunished than one innocent person should die." Second, Adams extolled the law. "No passion can disturb" the law, he told the jury. The law was "deaf, inexorable, inflexible" and certain in its application to the facts. Irrefutable evidence had shown that an angry, club-wielding mob, shouting threats, charged toward Preston and his men. Therefore, Preston lawfully acted in self-defense. Auchmuty added little to Adams's spirited closing and, speaking for the Crown, Paine plodded through the conflicting evidence with little enthusiasm.[65]

Following the usual practice, each of the court's judges instructed the jury in reverse order of seniority. The most junior member of the Superior Court of Judicature, Judge Edmund Trowbridge, spoke first. The only trained lawyer on the bench, Trowbridge began his charge to the jury with an appeal to common sense. Neither the crowd nor the soldiers had a "concerted plan," he said, but against the background of animosity and insults, "any little spark would inkindle a great fire—and five lives were sacrificed to a squabble." He urged the jurors to decide whether Preston had ordered the soldiers to load and fire. "If it remains only doubtful in your minds, you can't charge him with doing it." If Preston did order his

Paine, who had signed the Declaration of Independence six years after act-ing as prosecutor at the Boston Massacre trials, now held the post of attor-ney general of Massachusetts. Paine quickly shaped a trial strategy using Bathsheba's servants who were privy to her murderous plan as the state's key witnesses. Following its standard procedure, the court appointed two Worcester County attorneys to defend the prisoners, senior counsel John Sprague and young Levi Lincoln. A graduate of Harvard College in 1765, Sprague was one of only two lawyers in Worcester County following the Loyalists' flight from Massachusetts in 1775. For this reason, Lincoln, fol-lowing his graduation from Harvard in 1772, headed west to read the law with Joseph Hawley, John Adams's Northampton mentor. Admitted to the bar shortly after the clash between British troops and American mi-litia in Concord, Lincoln had not previously tried a capital case, but his notes indicate he prepared carefully and conducted a vigorous defense. The accused were arraigned and pleaded not guilty. Three days later a jury of twelve local residents was impaneled. When Chief Justice William Cushing called the court to order at eight o'clock in the morning on April 24, Worcester's Old South meetinghouse was packed with spectators.[71]

Whether people were drawn to the trial by the prospect of political re-venge or simply for titillation is not known. On the surface it would seem a trial held during the Revolution involving two British soldiers and the daughter of a local Loyalist who seduced a youthful American soldier while she was planning to have her husband murdered would have been conducted in a politically charged atmosphere. That a young American soldier was inseparably linked to the murder made it impossible, however, for partisan observers to wish the whole lot guilty. Furthermore, Worcester County was not a hotbed of revolutionary zeal and there is no evidence to suggest the men in the jury pool were chosen with regard to their politics. Also, not a single prosecution witness manifested political animus toward the defendants, nor did newspaper accounts published after the trial re-port any bias during the trial, or revel in the fate of the convicted murder-ers. Deep into the *Massachusetts Spy*'s story about the trial, for example, Brooks and Buchanan were identified as British soldiers, but the lengthy account of the trial made no mention of Bathsheba's Loyalist father.[72]

Curiosity rather than politics probably attracted a throng to the court-room. It had been nearly thirty years since the last person was executed for murder in Worcester and more than a century since a Massachusetts woman had been sentenced to death for murdering her husband. Women rarely murdered another adult and no Massachusetts woman ever had hired a killer to murder her husband. It also was extremely rare for a person of high social status to be facing the death penalty. Finally, Bathsheba's public and private conduct had mocked the existing consensual moral code. In short, the residents of Worcester County had plenty to be curious about on that spring day in 1778 when Bathsheba Spooner's trial began.[73]

Defense attorney Lincoln appealed to the jurors' pride. Addressing them as an "American jury," he called attention to the fact that this was the "first case of bloodshed, the first capital trial since the establishment of [an independent Massachusetts] government." He reminded the jurors they were "to consider it as the trial of A&B, banishing all prejudices, contracted by reports—all indignation [about] the enormity of the offense—all opinions from hearsay—from their country—profession, connexions [sic], political sentiments." Clearly, Lincoln's statement was at once a bit of due process boilerplate and an attempt to undercut whatever political prejudice may have existed among the jurors.[74]

Potential bias was only one of the formidable hurdles confronting Lincoln. First, under existing rules parts of the voluntary confessions made by Buchanan, Brooks, and Ross were used against them in court. The same rule permitting the prosecution to use the defendants' confessions, however, also forced the state to prove its case with evidence other than the confessions and allowed Lincoln to raise doubts in the juror's minds about the confessions' worth. Lincoln argued, for example, that an accused person often was motivated to confess because of fear or "the misdirected hopes of mercy." Second, the limitations of eighteenth-century due process forced Lincoln to defend all four prisoners simultaneously even though Buchanan, Brooks, and Ross were charged as "principals," or perpetrators of the crime and Bathsheba as an "accessory before the fact" to murder. Lincoln foresaw this problem and played a wild card. He filed a pretrial motion attempting to sever the trial of Buchanan and Brooks from that of Ross and Bathsheba. Following the four defendants' arraignment, Lincoln argued that the British soldiers should be tried by a so-called jury of aliens, or Englishmen. The court rejected Lincoln's motion, and, therefore, at trial his only option was to convince the jury it should judge Buchanan and Brooks differently than Bathsheba and Ross. He instructed the jury that it "will be necessary that you keep in your minds the evidence dure in which the accused had every opportunity to establish innocence. Most citizens cheered the new standards, although a handful argued that regardless of the court's legal safeguards, executions—especially public executions—were contrary to republican ideals.[3]

The Massachusetts Declaration of Rights was the starting point for the articulation of a republican due process and for the idea that the punishment of death was different. Article 12 spells out a defendant's right to a full explanation of the charges, a prohibition against self-incrimination, a right to confront the state's witnesses, a right to legal counsel, and the right to trial by jury. Article 26 forbids a magistrate or court of law from inflicting "cruel or unusual punishment," and Article 29 holds out to every citizen the right "to be tried by judges as free, impartial and independent as the lot of humanity will admit." Elaborating on these constitutional mandates, the SJC took the lead in protecting and expanding a capital defendant's rights. Over the next several decades, therefore, due process became instrumentalist—the authority of customary rules was subordinated in favor of rules that reflected republican principles—and the rash of court-ordered executions during the commonwealth's first two decades was followed by a remarkable change in the criminal law's purpose and practice. By the early nineteenth century the notion that the law's chief function was to be the guardian of liberty was firmly in place. Lawyers routinely placed a specific plea for their client within an argument about the importance of liberty. Judges responded in kind. James Neale, for example, urged Attorney General Robert Treat Paine to determine "points of liberty and justice" with an eye to the rights of all men, and in 1805 the SJC vowed to act "with that anxious regard for personal liberty and to prevent vexatious oppression." A capital trial heightened the law's concern for liberty, a commitment most clearly manifested by the precedent setting capital trials involving African American defendants. Specifically, capital procedure was based on the presumption that death was different, that extraordinary safeguards must be in place when a human life was at stake. A handful of critics went further. They argued that capital punishment was contrary to American republicanism, that it was British, brutish, and beyond the powers delegated to the state by the Massachusetts Constitution.[4]

Contemporaries and historians searching for the causes of an increase in the rate of crime and murder in postwar Massachusetts identified the decline of civic virtue and the emergence of liberal capitalism. Rev. Aaron

Bancroft, for example, told a crowd gathered to witness the hanging of the convicted murderer Samuel Frost in 1793 that the morals of youth were linked to the promise of the new nation. "Moral virtues are of the highest importance to the interests of civil society. We are told," Bancroft stated, "that they are more especially necessary to the support of a government like ours." Bancroft attributed Massachusetts's rising crime rate to a decline in social morality rather than to man's inherent wickedness. He believed education was the key to ending "impious, cruel and barbarous" behavior. George Minot, writing in 1788, highlighted new attitudes about wealth as the root cause of instability. "An emulation prevailed among men of fortune to exceed each other in the full display of their riches," he said. "This was imitated among the less opulent classes of citizens and drew them off from those principles of diligence and economy, which constitute the best support of all government." In a 1786 address to the people of the commonwealth, the Massachusetts legislature also emphasized the dark side of Boston's new prosperity: "Habits of luxury have exceedingly increased and we have indulged ourselves in fantastical and expensive fashions [and] the virtue which is necessary to support a Republic has declined." Justice Nathaniel Sargeant's assessment was more pointed. He charged that "vicious persons" were "roving about the countryside disturbing peoples rest and preying upon their property." [5]

Economic prosperity also contributed to Boston's escalating violent crime rate. With the coming of peace thousands of war-weary newcomers poured into Boston, pushing up the town's population from a low of ten thousand in 1780 to nearly twenty-five thousand people by 1800. Boston's black population also declined during the Revolution, but by 1800 rose to about eight hundred people. This remarkable growth spurt brought a building boom and employment opportunities and upward mobility for some. At the same time, prosperity coupled with the demise of a commitment to the common good caused some citizens to worry. Robert Treat Paine, the commonwealth's first attorney general, observed that "the course of the war has thrown property into channels, where before it never was, and has increased little streams to overflowing rivers." The *Massachusetts Centinel* complained about the results of this change. "We daily see men speculating with impunity on the most essential articles of life, and grinding the faces of the poor and laborious as if there were no God." [6]

Capital crimes and executions had pockmarked the prewar history of ware hoping to turn a quick profit by reselling it. He eventually offered his purchase to a Providence, Rhode Island, silversmith. The silversmith became suspicious, however, when he noticed the marks identifying the silverware maker had been damaged deliberately and sent his apprentice for the sheriff, who arrested Sheehan for burglary. Sheehan denied the charge, insisting that he bought the silverware from two strangers. But at trial, the prosecution showed that Sheehan was in Boston the day the silverware was stolen from one of the town's well-to-do residents. Sheehan was convicted and sentenced to death. Because the damning evidence against him was flimsy, an army officer under whom Sheehan had served made an attempt to win a pardon for the young Irishman. The effort failed, and Sheehan's "last words and dying speech" were published on a broadside meant "to satisfy the curious Publick" that was widely distributed on November 22, 1787, when he was hanged on Boston Common. The *Massachusetts Centinel* hinted that Sheehan may well have been innocent of the burglary and that the jury and the court should have given him the benefit of the doubt.[22]

Where there may have been doubt about Sheehan's guilt, there was no expressed sympathy for a gang of highwaymen operating on the roads linking Boston to the nearby towns. The gang pounced on Nathaniel Cunningham as he walked from Boston to Cambridge on the evening of November 6. Armed with pistols and knives, four assailants threatened to murder Cunningham if he did not given them his money and valuables. As the muggers fled on foot, Cunningham's shouts for help roused the night watchmen and he gave chase. The watchman grabbed two suspects and before long they stood before the bar of justice charged with the capital crime of highway robbery. The trial occurred only a few days after delegates— including several members of the SJC—had ratified the U.S. Constitution. The defendants, two brothers, Archibald and Joseph Taylor—the former from Philadelphia and the latter from Ireland—were found guilty. Under a tough new law the two men were sentenced to death and on May 8, 1788, hanged near the spot where they assaulted and robbed Cunningham. Interestingly, there were no printed last words from either of these unrepentant professionals, nor a sermon justifying the state's action.[23]

The silence that greeted the Taylors' execution may have been a reflection of some public doubt about the efficacy and severity of the law. Despite harsh punishment and a string of executions, both criminal cases and capital crimes soared far above pre-commonwealth levels. During the SJC's two Suffolk County sessions in 1789, for example, fifty-three criminal indictments were brought before the court, four times more than in 1781. Likewise, during the commonwealth's first decade twenty-five persons were executed, twenty for robbery and burglary, five times more than in the previous seven decades. Still, the republic seemed unable to turn back the crime wave.[24]

In 1789 three more persons were executed for highway robbery, including Rachel Wall. Like the Taylors before them, William Smith and William Denoffee, alias "Donogan," received little public notice for their brazen armed assaults on Boston citizens. During a single summer evening Smith and Denoffee attacked and robbed three men as they walked Boston's streets, taking from their victims a jacket, a silk handkerchief, and silver shoe buckles, among other items. The two were quickly captured, convicted of highway robbery, and sentenced to death by the SJC. Smith and Denoffee waited more than a month in jail before they joined on the gallows Rachel Wall, a twenty-nine-year-old woman also sentenced to death for highway robbery.[25]

Wall's route to the gallows was circuitous but not unusual. Born in rural Carlisle, Pennsylvania, in 1760 to a hardworking farmer and his pious wife, Wall was pulled to Boston by her husband, whom she married at a young age against her parents' advice. The couple lived together only a short time before he "went off." Left without resources, Rachel lived productively and happily until her husband unexpectedly and briefly returned to her. According to Rachel, before he disappeared again he entwined her in the sticky web of crime. Beginning in 1785, she claimed a string of successful robberies and but two unsuccessful criminal forays. Wall and another woman pleaded guilty in the summer of 1785 to stealing goods from the home of Perez Morton Esq., one of Boston's most prominent lawyers. The SJC sentenced Wall to pay triple damages of £18, to have fifteen lashes laid on her bare back, and to pay court costs. Because she was unable to make payment, the court stipulated that her labor might be purchased for three years. Three years later to the day, Wall was back before the SJC. Together with two accomplices Wall had been arrested for housebreaking and theft. She pleaded guilty and the court sentenced her to pay Lemuel Ludden £24 for the goods stolen, to sit on the gallows for one hour with a noose

eficial for the victim's family and friends were also false, according to
"Marcus." First, no one who commits a crime intends to be caught. To the
contrary, a "momentary" calculation leads the offender to believe he will
get away with the crime. Therefore, it makes no difference what the punishment might be. Second, if the death penalty were a deterrent crime rates
would be lower in states where it is imposed than in states that do not use
the death penalty. But there are a greater number of convictions for theft
per capita in New York than in Massachusetts, he pointed out, although
theft is a capital offense in New York and punishable by imprisonment in
Massachusetts. Third, in Great Britain, "from whom we learned the idea
of Capital Punishments," criminals risk the death penalty by picking the
pockets of people even as someone is executed for pick-pocketing. Fourth,
placing a murderer in an "iron cage" would be a far more effective deterrent than execution. Exposing the convict to public scrutiny would make
people aware of the "monumental pain, shame and disgrace" an offender
must suffer for a very long time. Finally, "Marcus" reminded his readers
that no one who participates in the process of "launching a soul into the
presence of its Maker and Judge" should believe "that what they are doing
is RIGHT." [35]

Despite the growing clamor against capital punishment, Irish-born
John Stewart was convicted of burglary and hanged on Boston Common
in 1797. Banished to America by his family, Stewart landed in Wilmington,
Delaware, a sixteen-year-old boy without family or friends. Rootless and
desperately poor, he bounced from menial job to menial job until he found
work with a Boston carpenter in the 1790s. Stewart fell in with a wild bunch
of boys and allegedly turned to crime to pay for his drinking and gambling
habits. A short jail term for theft did nothing to change Stewart. As soon
as he was released, he and two pals broke into the North End home of
Captain Enoch Rust. The armed trio terrorized Rust's family until one of
the captain's sons wrestled Stewart to the floor and took his gun. At this,
Stewart's accomplices fled from the house and Stewart was dragged off to
jail. He came to trial five days later for capital burglary and a jury found
him guilty. On April 7, 1797, less than a month after his crime, nineteen-
year-old John Stewart was "turned off." The Boston *Gazette* seemed troubled by Stewart's execution, noting that he had "not been guilty of many
crimes" before his foolish foray into Captain Rust's house.[36]

Stephen Smith was the last person hanged on Boston Common for

burglary and, two years later, Samuel Smith achieved the dubious distinction of being the last person hanged for burglary in Massachusetts. For
twenty-eight years Stephen Smith had struggled to be free. Born a slave
in Virginia, he rebelled by stealing from his master and other white plant-
ers. When caught by his master, Smith was shipped to the West Indies to
be worked to death on a sugar plantation, but somehow he managed to
escape and return to Virginia. He hid in the woods near Norfolk, stealing
food and clothing to survive. Caught again, Smith was sent back to the
West Indies but once again escaped. This time, he made his way to Nova
Scotia and then to Boston, a free man. By this time, however, his criminal
ways were deeply ingrained and after just seven months in the "cradle of
liberty" Smith stood before the bar of justice. Convicted of two counts of
housebreaking and two counts of arson, Smith was sentenced to death.[37]

At 1:45 P.M. on October 12, 1797, Smith walked from the Boston jail to
the Common, where a large crowd already had assembled to witness the
execution. With staff in hand, the sheriff paraded in front of Smith, and two
sheriff's deputies on horseback rode alongside him. Rev. Peter Thatcher
also accompanied Smith to the gallows, praying softly. At the bottom of the
Common the procession stopped and the sheriff read the execution order.
Thatcher briefly prayed aloud and then read a statement said to have been
written by Smith. "After a lengthy pause," Smith spoke to the crowd. In
what quickly had become a fixed part of the republican ritual of hanging,
he assured the crowd that he had received a fair trial and he confessed to
the crimes for which he was convicted, as well as several others. A noose
was put around Smith's neck and a white hood pulled over his head before he was led to the scaffold and "launched into ETERNITY." After about a
half an hour his body was cut down and put into a coffin.[38]

Samuel Smith, according to his gallows speech, turned to crime in
1787 after he abandoned his wife and five children for the vagabond's life.
Caught and jailed in Concord, Massachusetts, for stealing sheep, Smith
escaped. While he was free he learned how to counterfeit coin, a criminal
enterprise that led to some quick and easy profits but also jail, the loss
of his right ear, and a fifteen-year prison sentence in 1794. However, on
December 20, 1796, Smith joined a band of prisoners who escaped from
Castle Island by scaling a wall and running across the frozen channel separating the prison from Boston. Smith did not stop running until he reached
Pennsylvania, where he lay low for two years. In the summer of 1799 he

returned to Massachusetts to look for his family. Finding that his wife and children had moved, Smith turned to crime again. He burglarized homes in Sherborn and Natick before he was caught with a bag of stolen goods in Sudbury. Brought before the SJC sitting in Cambridge, Smith was found guilty and sentenced to death. On December 26, 1799, a crowd numbering in the thousands stood shivering in the cold on Concord Common to watch Smith's execution.[39]

A Boston publisher specializing in popular broadsides and pamphlets issued an account of Smith's execution. Although the author did not specifically articulate a position for or against public executions, his graphic description of Smith's hanging clearly was intended to undermine support for public hangings. There was nothing romantic or enlightened about the "heterogeneous, motley assemblage," who paraded to the gallows or the people who came to watch the gruesome spectacle, the author asserted. When the sheriff gave the signal, the condemned person was "suspended by the aid of Hemp from the Gallows, dancing a Spanish Fandango in the air—and screwing up the muscles of his phiz into the most ghastly distortions." After a few minutes the dying man lost control of his bodily functions, and women viewing this sight fainted away, exposing their bodies to the lewd gaze of men when they fell to the ground. In just these few sentences the author made clear the link between brutality and vulgarity and implicitly questioned the impact of public executions on American republican society.[40]

Two years later, following the trial and conviction of Jason Fairbanks for the murder of Elizabeth Fales, a Dedham clergyman also criticized the "dreadful apparatus of a public execution." Although the circumstantial evidence was weighted heavily against the defendant, the trial caused a huge stir throughout New England and some people clung to the belief Fairbanks was innocent. The trial also raised broad cultural issues, including the impact of romantic fiction on youngsters, parents' responsibility for their children's behavior, and competing political visions. All of this was capped by a jailbreak, a chase to Canada's border, and Fairbanks's eventual execution.[41]

The immediate events leading to Fales's death began on a warm, late spring day in 1801. Fairbanks and Fales arranged to meet near a brook in Mason's pasture, not far from Fales's Dedham home. According to Attorney General Sullivan, the twenty-one-year-old Fairbanks had "lived an indulged and idle life" since a childhood smallpox inoculation gone awry robbed him of the strength in his right arm. When it became apparent that the boy's physical condition made him unfit for farm work, his anxious parents sent him to Wrentham Academy, hoping that a liberal education might lead to a professional career. But academic work also proved too difficult for Fairbanks. Headaches, a fever, and hemorrhages–the signs of tuberculosis—ravaged his body. After a short stay at school, he returned home to Dedham, to a life as a sickly, small-town dilettante of literature and music. He also cultivated a romantic relationship with his eighteen-year-old neighbor, Betsy Fales.[42]

Jason's brother Ebenezer described Betsy Fales as "not strikingly beautiful," but "engaging," "enthusiastic," "healthy," and "self-taught." Jason, nearly six feet tall, slender, with a light complexion and dark hair, also had "downcast eyes" and was "weakly, sedentary, conciliating, and pacific." Yet, "in the deepest sentiment of their hearts," Ebenezer claimed, "they were equally united and invariable." He believed Betsy and Jason were in love, opposites passionately attracted to each other. Marriage was out of the question, however. Jason's poor health at once sapped his strength and his financial prospects. His clouded future also may have fostered an impertinent attitude Betsy's family found unacceptable. Jason was not welcome at the Fales home. For this reason, Betsy and Jason had been meeting secretly for more than a year. Just eleven days before Betsy's death, according to Jason's niece "Sukey," the two young people met at her parents' home. At trial, "Sukey" testified that Betsy and Jason were alone together from about 9:00 P.M. until near sunrise.[43]

Those hours of intimacy may have prodded Jason to act, to attempt to bring his relationship with Betsy to fruition. On May 17, the day before Betsy and Jason's final, tragic meeting, Jason asked "Sukey" to create a marriage certificate and to fill in his and Betsy's names in the appropriate blanks. The next day Jason told his friend Reuben Farrington he planned to meet Betsy "in order to have the matter settled." He "either intended to violate her chastity or carry her to Wrentham to be married," he boasted. A few hours later when the two boys met again, Reuben asked what Jason would do after he and Betsy were married. Jason replied, "Sometimes I will go and lay with her; and sometimes she shall come and lay with me." He promised to share with his friend the outcome of his meeting with

Betsy. But Jason knew it was not likely Betsy would agree to his marriage proposal, because of his fragile health and his inability to provide for her. To get over this hurdle, he apparently planned to suggest to Betsy an arrangement that stopped short of marriage but permitted a sexual relationship. The fake marriage certificate Jason carried to his secret meeting with Betsy was the key to this plan. He also carried a penknife he had borrowed from one of his father's farm workers.[44]

Betsy spent the morning helping with household chores. At noon she walked to a neighbor's house, where she spent some time reading *Julia Mandeville*, a popular English novel in which two star-crossed lovers die, Henry in a duel undertaken because he mistakenly believed Julia had been unfaithful to him and Julia of a broken heart. Sometime after one o'clock Betsy left her friend's home for Mason's pasture to join Jason. At about three o'clock, two friends heard her call out "O Dear! O Dear," but the girls were unable to decide whether Betsy was laughing or crying out for help. Within a few minutes they learned she was dead.[45]

Jason brought the grim news to the Faleses. He staggered down the road toward their home, bleeding profusely from more than fourteen wounds, including a long gash across his neck. "Betsy," he gasped, "has killed herself." Still holding the bloody knife, Jason added, "And I have killed myself too." Betsy's father and uncle ran to Mason's pasture, where they found Betsy lying on the ground. Her throat was cut. There were stab wounds in her breast and arms, and one in her back. She was conscious but unable to speak and within a few moments she died in her father's arms. Near his daughter's body her father found the forged marriage certificate torn to pieces and Jason's overcoat and purse.[46]

A coroner's jury convened in the Faleses' home the day following Betsy's death. Jason lay near death in another room in the same house. Two days later, the "greatest funeral procession" longtime Dedham residents recalled ever witnessing slowly followed Betsy's body to the burial ground. On May 21 Jason was charged with Betsy's murder and carried in a litter from the Fales home to jail. A grand jury heard the case about two weeks later and returned a murder indictment against Fairbanks that was written in the same legal language used 165 years earlier when Dedham was founded. "Not having the fear of God before his eyes, but being moved and seduced by the instigations of the devil with a certain knife of the value of ten cents, the said Jason Fairbanks did feloniously, wilfully and of his malice aforethought did strike, stab, thrust" and murder Elizabeth Fales.[47]

Trial began Thursday, August 6, 1801, at eight o'clock in the morning before the SJC sitting in Dedham. Chief Justice Francis Dana presided, flanked by Justices Robert Treat Paine, Thomas Dawes, and Simeon Strong. A 1762 graduate of Harvard College, Dana read the law with Edmund Trowbridge and was admitted to the Suffolk County bar five years later. Dana served in the Massachusetts Provincial Congress, the Continental Congress, and the U.S. Congress, before Governor John Hancock appointed him to the SJC in 1785. He succeeded Cushing as chief justice in 1791. Attorney General James Sullivan represented the commonwealth at the Fairbanks trial. A Revolutionary War veteran, an outspoken republican, and a prolific writer who earlier may have expressed opposition to capital punishment, Sullivan had served as the state's chief law enforcement officer for more than a decade. The court appointed two prominent attorneys to represent Fairbanks. Harrison Gray Otis and John Lowell were Boston Federalists with more than three decades of trial experience between them when they stood alongside the shackled defendant.[48]

In a pretrial motion, Otis and Lowell asked the court to admit into evidence an alleged confession made by Fairbanks. In his statement—later published under the title *Solemn Declaration*—Fairbanks denied he murdered Betsy or that they had made a murder-suicide pact before they met at Mason's pasture. According to Fairbanks, Betsy impulsively took her own life because of a rash but honest remark he made to her. They were talking about their love for one another and their desire to marry, when Fairbanks showed the forged marriage certificate to Betsy, saying he "believed this brought us as near the marriage state as would ever be our lot together." Then, according to Jason's statement, he tore up the fake certificate and Betsy blurted out that Jason did not love her. Of course he loved her, Fairbanks shot back. Hadn't he "already possessed her person and received the pledge of her most tender attachment!" Betsy then demanded, "if [he] had ever told any one of our connection?" Jason answered he had shared their secret with his friends Reuben and Isaac. "Oh, you are a monster," she exclaimed, grabbing the knife from Fairbanks's hand and plunging it repeatedly into her breast while he looked on frozen by surprise. When he

saw she had cut her throat, he finally took the knife from her and turned
it on himself "only leaving off when I had finished cutting my own throat,
and when I believed all was over with me!"[49]

Sullivan opposed the admission of Fairbanks's alleged confession,
arguing, "as he had not used the Prisoner's confession against him," the
defense "had no right to use it for him." The court agreed with Sullivan.
"The story of a prisoner is never given in evidence in his own favor, unless
some part of the same story is given in evidence by the government against
him," Chief Justice Dana ruled. If the defendant's own story were admitted, Dana added, "men might commit the most atrocious crimes, and by a
well formed tale escape with impunity." Once the court ruled Fairbanks's
confession inadmissible, the process of selecting a jury got under way. Exercising his right to challenge peremptorily jurors he suspected of bias,
Fairbanks struck several potential jurors before agreeing to a panel of Norfolk County farmers and tradesmen. The *Columbian Centinel* reported
the first day of the trial "was attended at the opening by so numerous a
concourse of people of both sexes that the Court found it necessary to
adjourn from the Court to the Meeting House."[50]

Sullivan opened the second day of the trial by sketching out the known
facts and the prosecution's case against Fairbanks. The state's case,
Sullivan acknowledged, rested largely on circumstantial evidence, but he
assured the jury that "a fair and natural deduction from facts proved to
exist [would] leave the mind without a reasonable doubt." Sullivan concluded by asserting "the Prisoner and the deceased were together when
she was murdered and that her death was caused by knife wounds made
by the Prisoner." Defense counsel argued that Betsy's heightened sense of
romantic passion together with her melancholy despair created a potent
psychological combination that caused her to take her own life.[51]

The prosecution called more than thirty witnesses, beginning with
Dr. Nathaniel Ames, who had examined Betsy's body and attended to
Fairbanks while he lay near death from his self-inflicted wounds. The attorney general's direct questions and defense counsel's cross-examination
of Ames sought to resolve the key issue of whether Betsy's wounds were
the result of a murderous assault or self-inflicted. To that end, Sullivan focused on a wound in Betsy's back, just below the shoulder blade, arguing
that only a slashing attack by Fairbanks could account for such a wound.

But, when defense counsel asked Ames whether that wound might have been self-inflicted, the doctor answered yes. Other witnesses offered contradictory evidence about the nature of the relationship between Betsy and Jason and about several threats allegedly made by Fairbanks against Betsy and her parents. The defense put in very little evidence, relying instead on undermining the state's case by cross-examining its witnesses and by suggesting that Jason's general frailty and his crippled arm in particular made it impossible for him to overpower Betsy had he wanted to do so.[52]

After all the witnesses had been heard, the lawyers delivered their closing arguments. Otis and Lowell talked for six hours and Attorney General Sullivan completed his two-hour argument at nine o'clock Friday night. Because the defense had neither the law nor the facts on its side, Otis and Lowell spun out a romantic tale of star-crossed lovers who agreed to kill themselves out of despair that their love could not be consummated. The *Boston Gazette* described the defense lawyers' plea as a "torrent of eloquence with all that ingenuity, sagacity and learning which the genius and wisdom of man could invent." Sullivan's nineteenth-century biographer characterized his closing argument as one of "unrivalled eloquence."[53]

This case, Otis began, was "without exaggeration, without the aid of fancy, one of the most awful catastrophes ever exhibited in real life, in any age, country, or sketched by the most eccentric imagination, or the most melancholly poet." Since Fairbanks's arrest he had been the target of prejudice, rumor, exaggeration, and "self-created courts, have, without trial, and without a knowledge of the facts, pronounced him guilty." But, Otis added quickly, he trusted this American jury to "discard all previous impressions and to repress the effects which external prejudices may have excited" and to spare the life of a defendant "while any one man of his twelve judges entertains a reasonable doubt of his guilt." Otis urged the jurors to be especially careful, because their decision would turn on problematic circumstantial evidence.[54]

Boilerplate in place, Otis concentrated on creating a picture of a young woman and a sickly, weak "young man of irreproachable character at the unripe age of twenty years," who were in love. Betsy's head and heart were "filled with melancholly and romantic tales, which adverse circumstances forbade the gratification of, [who] had in a moment of phrenzy, put a period to her own existence." The alternate scenario—that Fairbanks murdered the woman he loved—was impossible to believe, according to Otis.

To believe Fairbanks murdered Betsy, the jury would have to conclude he acted "without provocation, without passion, without motive, without even those ordinary inducements which prompt hardened villains, practiced in iniquity, to commit the smallest offenses." "This is a simple tale," Otis argued. "Is it impossible? Has disappointed love never produced despair? Has despair never induced suicide? Has the softer sex been peculiarly exempt from these feelings and these results? No—Every novel writer will establish the assertion, that no passion has so often terminated fatally as love."[55]

Otis concluded his argument with an appeal to the jurors' provincialism, their patriotism and their compassion. Jurors should consider the "exemplary virtues," of Jason's parents, the "virtuous preceptors" of Dedham village, and the character of the American nation. A boy raised in France may be "taught butchery," or an English adolescent become "inured to carnage and plunder under the tutors of the Old Bailey," but American values would not permit such a "sanguinary taste." Finally, Otis begged the jury to consider the consequences of their decision and not to be afraid to act on their doubts about Fairbanks's guilt. "If you condemn him, you sentence a whole family to inevitable distress, perhaps to ruin, and a miserable being, perhaps INNOCENT, to certain death."[56]

The attorney general's closing statement explored some of the same themes Otis had touched on, but Sullivan also pounded the facts. Following the briefest introduction, Sullivan asserted that "the evidence is conclusive," that Betsy was murdered "with a knife which is proved to have been in the possession of the prisoner. He, and he alone, was with her when the deed was consummated. The deduction is consequently irresistible that she either destroyed herself or that he was guilty of her murder." Sullivan left no doubt about his choice of these alternate scenarios. First, the attorney general flatly rejected the defense argument that Betsy's romantic passion drove her to suicide. "To say that she could be provoked to commit suicide because the object of her affection was not a better man, or in better circumstances, is a supposition too unnatural to be allowed any serious consideration." *If* she did love him, she had options other than death. Second, Betsy's wounds were not self-inflicted. "It is altogether impossible that that [wound] in her back, directly in, should have been made by her own arm." If she had wished to die, she would not have slashed her arms and hands and plunged the knife painfully, but ineffectively into her breast. In fact, Betsy was fighting for her life, he said, fighting to save her honor. When she ripped up the forged marriage certificate and rebuffed his scheme to win sexual license, Jason became infuriated and attacked her with the knife he had brought along. He jabbed the knife toward her throat. She turned away to avoid the cut and he plunged the knife into her back. He tried again to slash her throat. She warded off his attacks with her hands and arms. Her flesh was torn open. Finally, she weakened, and he "gave the fatal wound in the throat."[57]

To prove the validity of the circumstantial scenario he had sketched for the jury, Sullivan now linked it tightly to the facts. The cadence of his speech was measured by the phrase "there is evidence." "There is evidence" Fairbanks sought revenge against Betsy's parents. "There is evidence" he planned "*their* ruin by ruining her." "There is evidence" he intended to engage Betsy "in an unlawful marriage." "There is evidence" he intended "to violate her chastity by force." And a thunderous beat: "There can be no doubt he intended to effect her dishonor by violence, unless she would consent to her own ruin by a clandestine marriage, or by a conduct far more disgraceful."

Sullivan might have stopped at this point but, sounding more like a preacher than a lawyer, he spoke to larger themes aimed at an audience outside the courtroom. He chastised parents who failed to instruct their children properly. "False fondness and misapplied tenderness" too often characterize the relationship between parents and children. Parents must be firm and watchful to prevent a child from becoming wayward. They must also encourage their children to cultivate steady work habits; work is an indication of self-discipline and of commitment to the community. "Idleness is a rebellion against the mode of our existence," he said, and inevitably leads a child to "cultivate unlawful desires."

Sullivan's rhetoric and his known accomplishments lent power and legitimacy to his argument. But Sullivan's presence provided the most compelling proof of his familiar argument that discipline, hard work, and the assumption of social responsibility are the necessary prerequisites for one's success as a person and for a stable, virtuous republic. As Sullivan stood before the jurors, perhaps limping slowly from where they were seated to the defense table, his twisted, shriveled leg—the result of a childhood accident—was painfully evident to jurors and spectators, reminding them that he had overcome a handicap and gone on to play a significant part in the Revolutionary War effort and rise to the post of attorney general in the postwar republic. Sullivan himself provided the perfect counterexample to the picture he drew of Fairbanks and the choices he had made that led him to murder.

When Sullivan had completed his argument, each of the four justices instructed the jury about the law. In summarizing the evidence the judges highlighted Fairbanks's "expressed intentions toward the deceased on the day she was murdered and the improbability of her giving the wounds in her breast, side, and arms, even if she had intended to destroy her own life." One of the judges adopted the attorney general's aggressive argument: if Fairbanks "induced [Betsy] to commit murder on her own person, he was a principal in the felony" and still culpable under the indictment, "as if he gave the wounds with his own hand."[58]

About ten o'clock Friday night the jury began its deliberations, but after an hour the foreman informed the court it was unable to agree. The court adjourned until eight o'clock Saturday morning. At that time, the jurors filed into court. When asked by the clerk, the jury foreman stated they had found the prisoner guilty of murder. The jurors were polled and each one affirmed the guilty verdict. Fairbanks faced Chief Justice Dana, who described in "strong and glowing colors" the "very barbarous manner" in which Fairbanks had murdered Betsy Fales. Fairbanks, the *Boston Gazette* noted, seemed to be "the only person in the whole assembly who was not affected at the ceremony of the scene." Dana stated his belief that Fairbanks had received a fair trial and "during his few short remaining hours" the chief justice urged the condemned man to reflect on his "future state." But Fairbanks was not ready for thoughtful reflection; he tried to say something about the testimony of several witnesses, but Dana cut him off and pronounced the death sentence. Jason Fairbanks, you are to "be carried from hence to the gaol from whence you came, and from thence to the place of execution, and there to be hanged by the neck until you are DEAD, and may God Almighty have mercy on your soul."[59]

Ten days later, a daring late-night assault on the jail freed Fairbanks and two other prisoners. The Dedham resident and former congressman Fisher Ames was outraged. He and other Federalists blamed Republican party activists for assisting with the jailbreak. To clear themselves of blame and to publicly display their patriotism, Dedham Federalists volunteered to allow their homes to be searched and to account for their whereabouts during the jailbreak. Republicans denied the Federalists' charge, touting the results of an independent investigation that concluded "not more than two or three were actors in this horrid labor of setting a murderer free." In a rush to distance their party from Fairbanks' escape, both Republicans and Federalists publicly contributed to a $1,000 reward for the fugitive's capture. In the meantime, equipped with money and horses, Fairbanks and his accomplice fled across Massachusetts, rode over Hoosac Mountain, and spurred their horses north toward Bennington, Vermont. The two fugitives intended to cross into Canada, but they were captured at the head of Lake Champlain, just short of their goal.[60]

Brought back to Boston, Fairbanks was held under guard until September 10, when he was taken from jail by a writ of habeas corpus and delivered to the Norfolk County sheriff. A troop of cavalry bolstered by a guard of 250 Dedham volunteers escorted Fairbanks to the Dedham jail and to a gallows erected on the Common. Rev. Thomas Thacher, a Dedham clergyman who frequently had visited Fairbanks in the Boston jail, walked along side the condemned man. A crowd estimated at ten thousand persons—more than five times the population of Dedham—lined the short route from the jail and circled the gallows. Fairbanks refused an opportunity to speak. He stood silent and apparently emotionless. He was blindfolded and the rope was put around his neck. The sheriff gave him a handkerchief to hold in his hand, telling him to drop it as a signal when he was ready to be executed. Fairbanks dropped it almost immediately.[61]

Following Fairbanks's execution several accounts of the case were published, including a satirical broadside issued by the "Pandamonium Press," Fairbanks's alleged confession, titled *Solemn Declaration*, and Thacher's postexecution sermon. The broadside lampooned the supposed relationship between God's plan and man's execution of a sinner-murderer. At the hour the hanging was scheduled to take place, the day's bright sun disappeared on cue, giving way to "watery clouds," "forked lightening," and "thunder with tremendous claps." At that moment, God's wrath and earthly punishment came together and the condemned man was "launched into eternity." But, the broadside made clear, if the gruesome spectacle was meant to warn spectators to avoid the temptations of sin, the lesson was lost on the crowd attending the execution. The men, women, and children packed around the gallows were laughing and playing, leading a hypothetical foreign visitor to think he was observing a celebratory national festival. The "surmise would have been just," the broadside concluded.[62]

Although Ames had played an ambivalent role at Fairbanks's trial, he was outraged by the publication of *Solemn Declaration*. "It is a great perversion of the truth," Ames wrote in his diary. The alleged confession, he said, glossed over the question of how Betsy wounded herself, exaggerated Jason's positive traits, and unfairly criticized the court and jury. Although Ames acknowledged the Fairbanks family would profit from the sales of pamphlet, he claimed it "disgusts almost everybody!" Thomas B. Adams, for example, bought and read a copy, but he remained convinced Fairbanks "suffered a righteous punishment."[63]

On the Sunday following Fairbanks's execution, Thacher delivered a dispassionate and reflective sermon that booksellers—perhaps hoping for a prolonged and profitable debate about Fairbanks's guilt or innocence—offered free to purchasers of the *Solemn Declaration*.[64] Thacher began by offering the usual moral advice, urging his listeners to see the "tragical event" as a warning signal from God, encouraging sinners to reform. Punishing the "wicked in the present world is one of the loudest admonitions which can be given to sinners," Thacher said. He also believed that the Fales and Fairbanks families deserved "sympathy and condolences."[65]

Thacher told his congregation he had visited Fairbanks in the Dedham and Boston jails. At Dedham they merely chatted, avoiding talk about the murder, because Fairbanks—probably on advice of counsel—was concerned any conversation "might affect him at his trial." Thacher urged Fairbanks to repent, but Jason was too angry. He talked only about those witnesses whom he accused of testifying falsely. After the escape and recapture, Thacher visited Fairbanks in the Boston jail. He no longer complained about the fairness of his trial, but Thacher noted that a "want of candor and a reserve" still prevented Fairbanks from acknowledging his sinful status or confessing to Betsy's murder. Thacher made no judgment based on his conversations with Fairbanks. He equivocated on the question of Fairbanks's guilt and pointed out that not everyone in Fairbanks's situation reacted the same way.

On the day of Fairbanks' scheduled execution, Thacher—who previously had not witnessed an execution—accompanied Fairbanks from Boston to Dedham and walked alongside him to the gallows on Dedham

Common. After Fairbanks gave the signal he was ready to be hanged, something went wrong and the "dreadful apparatus of a public execution assumed added horrors." But, the incident—perhaps the rope was too long or not strong enough or not tight enough to effectively suffocate the condemned man—was only one reason Thacher criticized public executions. In fact, he told his congregation, he had concluded public executions were "pernicious in their influence on the minds and manners of the community." Although many men and women had brought along their children, thinking "their minds may be impressed with a horror of vice by witnessing its terrible effects," Thacher said, he was convinced the grim spectacle had the opposite effect on everyone in attendance. Watching a person be put to death "naturally hardens the heart and renders it callous to those mild and delicate situations which are our guards of virtue." For this reason, public executions undermine public virtue and do nothing to deter would-be criminals.

Thacher also argued that public executions were unnecessarily brutal for the condemned person. To "expose their last agonies before thousands of spectators" was "Gothic savageness" or worse, "cannibalism." Admitting for argument's sake that fear was a necessary means of social control, would it not make sense if the condemned were executed behind prison walls? Would not such a process, Thacher asked his listeners, "impress more fear and terror on the multitude than if they every day beheld wretches expiring under the protracted torments of a despot?"

Thacher's conclusion was unmistakable: no religious or moral good came from public executions and they should be abolished.

To be sure, there were romantic and sentimental themes running through the Fairbanks trial, but the case also highlighted Massachusetts's capital procedure and stimulated criticism of public executions. Whatever cultural spin lawyers put on their closing arguments in subsequent trials, the rules of capital procedure remained the bedrock on which justice for capital defendants was built. Capital procedure was neutral and transparent and characterized by the attitude that death was different. For these reasons, a capital trial was governed by clearly articulated rules of evidence manipulated by skilled lawyers and interpreted by respected jurists, and the verdict was placed in the hands of a jury of disinterested citizens who weighed the evidence to determine a defendant's guilt or innocence. These basic safeguards ensured a fair trial for capital defendants. At the

same time, critics outside the courtroom kept up a drumbeat against public executions, an argument that eroded support for executions generally.
Thacher's criticism of the circuslike atmosphere attending the Fairbanks
execution, for example, signaled the beginning of the end of religious support for public executions and may have prompted the legislature to take
steps to bring the punishment of criminals into closer conformity with republican ideals.

Just a short time after Fairbanks's execution a Massachusetts Senate committee reported that the capital law against burglary "is so severe
that many offenders escape punishment," because juries will not convict.
Governor Caleb Strong, a Federalist, responded positively to the legislature, stating he would pardon unarmed burglars sentenced to death. The
governor's motive was not strictly humanitarian. Rather, he feared putting
to death unarmed burglars "would only excite compassion for the delinquent" and undermine support for capital punishment. The year following the governor's 1802 speech, Massachusetts lawmakers took burglary
off the capital list and invested in an alternative means of punishment,
Charlestown prison. At the same time the legislature reduced the list of
crimes punishable by death and eliminated the stocks, the pillory, whip-
ping, and mutilation.[66]

The legislature also opened the judicial system by requiring the governor to appoint a reporter to record and publish the SJC's decisions.
Published court reports would serve many purposes. They would help to
create a permanent system of common law, satisfy the demand of a growing number of lawyers for legal guidelines, and highlight publicly that
Massachusetts was a government of laws. Dudley Tyng, reporter for vol-
umes two through seventeen of SJC *Reports*, added that publishing the
court's decisions would buttress republicanism by allowing the people of
Massachusetts to pay close attention to the "import and extent" of their
constitutional rights.[67]

In the first published volume of *Massachusetts Reports* the court used
a potentially explosive capital case involving rape and murder to elaborate on a rule that prohibited the admissibility of a confession obtained by
"promises, persuasions, or hopes of pardon." John Battis, a nineteen-year-
old African American, was charged with the rape and murder of a white
teenager, Salome Talbot, to whom he had spoken on two or three prior
occasions. According to evidence introduced at trial, on a hot summer

day, she walked along a path near where he was working hilling corn on the south side of Blue Hill. "An unpremeditated thought, an uncherished impulse," caused him to follow her into a "gloomy thicket." There, "deaf to her struggles," he raped her. While she lay motionless on the ground, Battis grabbed a heavy rock and repeatedly crashed it against her head. He then dragged Salome to a nearby pond and held her bloody, lifeless body below water.[68]

Battis fled south toward Providence, but he was captured in Attleborough, ten miles short of his goal. Questioned by a justice of the peace, he "readily confessed" to the rape and murder of Talbot. He was arraigned and jailed in Dedham, awaiting trial. During the next several weeks a number of "respectable gentlemen from Boston and other neighboring towns" visited him. He also shared his life story with a Dedham newspaper editor, telling him he had been born in Boston to an interracial couple and that shortly after his fifth birthday his father abandoned the family, leaving his mother to care for him alone. She taught him to read and write and apprenticed him to a good master. But "youthful foibles" led young Battis to crime and ultimately to murder.[69]

Four months after his capture, he stood before the SJC and pleaded guilty to "that most atrocious crime." But the court insisted he take a "reasonable time to consider" his plea, reminding him that "he was under no legal or moral obligation to plead guilty, that he had a right to deny the several charges and put the government to the proof of them." The court had reason to believe someone had encouraged him to confess and the justices questioned everyone who had visited Battis while he awaited trial. Following its inquiry, the court concluded his confession was voluntary, and, therefore, his guilty plea was admissible. Attorney General Sullivan formally moved for a sentence of death that Chief Justice Dana "delivered in a solemn, affecting and impressive address to the prisoner." Battis was hanged on November 8, 1804.[70]

The court introduced three other important changes in capital procedure shortly after *Battis*. In *Commonwealth v. Hardy* (1807) the SJC officially acknowledged two long-time practices and articulated a new rule permitting testimony about a capital defendant's character. Because the "life of a fellow being" was at stake, the SJC noted it had a responsibility to appoint counsel and to allow its procedural errors to be appealed. In fact, William Hardy's court-appointed counsel successfully persuaded the court to reverse his client's death sentence, a historic first.[71]

On December 2, 1806, Hardy, an African American laborer, was indicted for the murder of an infant, an illegitimate child born to Elizabeth Whelfry. The indictment charged Hardy had wrapped a small chain around the baby girl's neck and held her under water until she drowned. As he was being led from jail to the courthouse for trial, the *Boston Courier* reported, a skeptical black woman bystander said to Hardy and the prison guard accompanying him, " 'Har you Hardy—you no lawyer—you fool! Why you no take 'em down [S]tate street and shoot 'em, den you be clear.' "[72]

At trial, Hardy was found guilty. Before the court sentenced him to death, however, his court-appointed counsel filed a motion in arrest of judgment, claiming the court had erred because a single justice had arraigned Hardy rather than the three or more justices called for in an 1805 statute. The court stayed his sentence of death and scheduled argument on the motion during its 1807 term. Senior defense attorney George Thatcher argued the trial had been illegal and the court "cannot proceed to pass sentence of death on William Hardy," because Hardy was arraigned only before Justice Theodore Sedgwick. Parsing each word in the governing statute and citing a handful of English cases, Thatcher concluded Hardy's 1806 trial was "invalid and erroneous, because in all cases a prisoner ought to be arraigned at the same bar where he is to be tried." He had no desire to "frustrate public justice," Thatcher added, but "in establishing a precedent for trials of capital offenses, the greater caution should be used that it may not be quoted by evil men in future disastrous periods of the commonwealth to abridge the citizens of their rights." Co-counsel George Blake, a thirty-eight-year-old trial lawyer and U.S. attorney for Massachusetts, buttressed Thatcher's death-is-different approach. The "habits and prejudices of the country," he said, linking contemporary social and legal practices, argue for "strict construction" of capital punishment statutes. Attorney General Sullivan rebutted Hardy's argument, but he conceded, "if there is a doubt, the life of the prisoner ought not to be taken."[73]

Chief Justice Theophilus Parsons, who brought to the court a reputation as the "greatest living lawyer" in Massachusetts when he was appointed to the bench in 1806, ruled for the defense. Although Hardy had not objected to the court's procedural error in a timely fashion and his trial went ahead, "an objection founded in want of jurisdiction, however small, is not in capital cases, taken away by any implied consent. If ever quibbling is at any time justifiable," Parsons wrote, "certainly a man may quibble for his life." Hardy's guilty verdict was set aside. Over the solicitor general's objection, Parsons also ruled that Hardy and capital defendants generally might introduce evidence at trial about their good character. "Whenever the defendant chooses to call witnesses to prove his general character to be good," Parsons added, "the prosecutor may offer witnesses to disprove their testimony. But it is not competent for the prosecutor to go into this inquiry until the defendant has voluntarily put his character in issue." Parsons believed this rule should be extended to all criminal defendants, but Justices Samuel Sewall and Isaac Parker argued the new rule should be limited to capital cases, "in favor of life."[74]

Immediately following the court's ruling reversing Hardy's conviction, Attorney General Sullivan moved for a new trial on the same indictment. The court scheduled a motion hearing. Although Blake and Thatcher did not raise an objection to a new trial, it marked the first time in the court's recorded history that counsel represented a capital defendant other than at trial. In short, by inviting defense counsel to participate in motion hearings the court significantly expanded the protection afforded a capital defendant. Hardy was acquitted at his second trial and immediately freed.[75]

In the decade after Hardy won his freedom on a procedural technicality, several additional changes were made in capital procedure and practices that emphasized the court's perception that death was different. Those changes were manifest in the 1817 murder trial of twenty-five-year-old Henry Phillips, a Welsh sailor whose effort to help a friend culminated in the murder of an Italian man, Gaspar Denegri. Alcohol and bravado prompted the incident leading to Phillips's indictment. According to trial testimony, Phillips stayed at the Roe Buck tavern in the North End whenever one of his trans-Atlantic voyages brought him to Boston. On the evening of December 1, 1816, Denegri, a Boston confectioner's apprentice, was drinking at the Roe Buck with some friends. The young Italian began to tease Nathan Foster, a son of the tavern's owner who was seated in a dark corner reading the Bible quietly by candlelight. Denegri had had a good deal to drink and began showing off for his friends by repeatedly blowing out Foster's candle. As Phillips watched from across the room, his anger boiled over. He stepped between Denegri and young Foster and warned Denegri to stop. Laughing, Denegri blew out the candle again and the two young men scuffled. Charlotte Foster ordered Denegri and his friends out. About an hour after Foster had closed the tavern for the night, Denegri returned, pounding on the door and loudly demanding to be admitted. Phillips grabbed an iron bar and pulled open the front door, but Denegri had run around to the back door. Phillips and a friend followed him and Phillips knocked him over the head with the bar. Denegri died six days later.[76]

At trial, the SJC appointed George Sullivan and Lemuel Shaw to represent Phillips. A son of former Attorney General James Sullivan, George Sullivan read the law with his father and was admitted to the Suffolk bar in 1804 at age twenty-one. Shaw graduated from Harvard College in 1800, read the law with David Everett, and at age twenty-three was admitted as an attorney by the Court of Common Pleas in Boston. Both men were experienced criminal defense lawyers. The solicitor general, Daniel Davis, had held his office since 1800. Chief Justice Isaac Parker and Justices Charles Jackson and Samuel Putnam sat on the bench. Parker was a Maine native who graduated from Harvard College in 1786, read the law with Boston attorney William Tudor, and three years later started a practice in Castine, Maine. He was appointed to the SJC in 1806 and moved to the center seat in 1814. During his tenure on the court Parker also served as Royall Professor of Law at Harvard Law School.[77]

Following the defense team's successful pretrial motion separating the trials of Phillips and his accomplice and its challenge of a dozen potential jurors, Davis opened for the commonwealth on January 9, 1817. Phillips was a "stranger in this part of the country," Davis began, but he would receive "every protection and assistance" guaranteeing a "perfectly impartial trial." To that end, Davis told the jurors, two distinguished lawyers had been appointed to defend Phillips. Indeed, he said, the "law is so careful of the rights of the accused party in a capital offense that the Court are always to be counsel for the Prisoner." Davis acknowledged that "public sentiment is against the infliction of capital punishment," but he hoped the jury would do its duty if the facts he presented sustained the murder indictment against Phillips.

Beginning with Dr. George Shattuck, Davis called a number of witnesses to prove the facts of the case against Phillips. The doctor testified that Denegri died from several blows to his head delivered with great force. Sullivan carefully cross-examined Shattuck, suggesting the blows were only a contributing factor to Denegri's death and that greater medical skill might have saved his life. Shattuck cautiously countered that argument. At this point, Sullivan approached the bench and asked that all witnesses be removed from the courtroom so that each one might "testify out of the presence and hearing of the others." The court granted the motion, a ruling revealing the transformation that had occurred in the court's presumption about the veracity of witnesses since the postrevolutionary decline of religion. Colonial courts had assumed witnesses under oath necessarily told the truth, but the SJC realized the search for truth was a more complicated process. Specifically, because the case against Phillips turned on eyewitness accounts certain to vary, Sullivan wanted to insulate the testimony of each eyewitness to prevent the emergence of a detrimental homogenized account and to allow him to exploit differences in their testimony. Later, Sullivan would ask jurors to interpret each witness's testimony and to draw their own conclusion.[78]

The solicitor general's star witness was Mary Davis, a barmaid at the Roe Buck tavern. She testified she was standing near the tavern's locked rear door and saw Phillips hit Denegri from behind as the young man approached the door. The jury foreman asked whether Phillips was intoxicated. "I don't know," she replied. "He appeared as usual." On cross-examination, Sullivan asked Davis whether she knew if Denegri was armed with a knife. Someone inside the tavern had said he was armed, the barmaid answered. Sullivan did not pursue this line of questioning, but in closing he raised the issue again to lend support to his argument that Phillips's act was legally justifiable.

When Davis left the witness chair, it was two o'clock in the afternoon and Chief Justice Parker called a one-hour recess. The common law rule stipulated that jurors were to be deprived of food, drink, light, and fire until they reached a verdict, but a recent change in practice, Parker told the jury, made it possible for the sheriff to provide capital jurors with "moderate refreshment." He cautioned the twelve men they were not allowed "to drink spiritous liquor of any kind" or discuss the case among themselves.[79]

When the jurors returned, Davis concluded his presentation by quoting from legal authorities, including the text most relied upon by American lawyers—Sir William Blackstone's *Commentaries on the Laws of*

England. Davis wanted to counter the implied argument about justifiable homicide made by Sullivan just before recess. Malice aforethought distinguishes murder from other homicides. Malevolence, Davis told the jury, is "the dictate of a wicked, depraved, and malignant heart" and, according to Blackstone, may be either expressed or implied. If a person manifests an "evil design" and strikes a blow that causes another person's death, but "did not intend his death, yet he is guilty of murder by express malice." Even without a specific sign of evil intent, when a person deliberately kills another person, the law implies malice. Only a person with an "abandoned heart" would be guilty of killing another person. And, Davis emphasized, "no affront by words, or gestures only is sufficient provocation" for killing another person.[80]

Sullivan opened his defense of Phillips by calling to the stand two clusters of witnesses. Using the *Hardy* rule, the first group of witnesses testified to Phillips's good character. The second group of witnesses offered evidence that Denegri was carrying a knife. Nathan and Charlotte Foster both stated they had known Phillips for several years and that he was a good, hard-working, peaceable man. Phillips's commanding officer testified similarly. More important, Mary Davis and Joseph M'Cann told the court they and others inside the tavern that fatal night suspected Denegri had a knife when he pounded on the door shouting threats and insults.

Sullivan gave the first closing statement for the defense. His elaborate three-hour argument focused on whether Phillips had manifested malice aforethought, the prerequisite for a murder conviction. Phillips's acts that night at the Roe Buck tavern did not fit the criteria for either express or implied malice, Sullivan told the jury. The young sailor had "reasonable ground" to believe Denegri was armed with a knife. Therefore, if he were guilty of anything, it was the lesser charge of manslaughter. It was eight o'clock at night when Sullivan finished his closing argument. Chief Justice Parker ordered the court adjourned for the day. He instructed the court's officers to keep the jury together and sober until court resumed Saturday morning at nine o'clock.

When court reconvened, defense co-counsel Lemuel Shaw, Solicitor General Davis, and Chief Justice Parsons each addressed the jury. Shaw began by confessing how anxious he was about making an argument to save a man's life. He argued Phillips had a legal basis for striking Denegri. The defendant "honestly believed" Denegri was armed and that he intended to break into the tavern to carry out his threat against Phillips. Shaw concluded his argument by reminding the jury that "any reasonable doubt" must lead them to acquit the defendant. "This is not a mere rhetorical flourish," Shaw told the jury, "but a well established rule." Davis used only about half of the time Shaw had used. Davis repeated the key facts of the case. According to Mary Davis's testimony, he pointed out, no one inside the tavern was in danger, because the doors were locked. Yet, Phillips repeatedly struck Denegri, causing his death. He was guilty of murder. If there was any doubt in the jurors' minds when Davis sat down, Chief Justice Parker's instructions removed it. There was no hint of ambivalence in Parker's interpretation of the evidence. He stated matter-of-factly that Denegri did not have any criminal intent when he returned to the tavern and the entire episode would have ended without harm, except for the "unfortunate suggestion" that he had a knife. The willingness to believe Denegri was armed probably was prompted by the "dread our people have of an Italian," Parker stated. But without proof to sustain that cultural bias, he urged the jury to discount that testimony. On the key question of whether Phillips's behavior manifested malice aforethought, the prerequisite for a murder conviction, Parker was equally blunt. "When a homicide is committed the law implies malice," he said. Specifically, the blow Phillips dealt Denegri was a "sudden transaction" that fulfilled the definition of malice aforethought.

The jury retired at two o'clock in the afternoon to deliberate Phillips's fate and returned in less than an hour with a guilty verdict. On the following day, Solicitor General Davis moved for a sentence of death. Chief Justice Parsons asked Phillips whether he had anything to say before sentence was pronounced. "I was led into it," Phillips blurted out and then stood weeping. Parsons praised the Massachusetts criminal justice system for the protection it provided the defendant during his trial. Without irony, the chief justice told Phillips—whose troubles began when he came to the rescue of a Bible-reading friend—if he had been born and educated in the United States, "where the poorest people have access to the source of light and truth in the Scriptures," he would not now stand convicted of murder. Parsons then pronounced sentence. Phillips was to be hanged by the neck until dead. Sentence was carried out March 13, 1817, before a crowd of twenty thousand people.[81]

Phillips's fate makes it clear that murder defendants had only a slim

chance of winning an acquittal, despite changes made in capital procedure following the enactment of the Massachusetts Constitution. The
facts presented by the prosecution and the court's presumption of implied
malice were formidable hurdles blocking capital defendants' path to freedom. Still, the four decades following the ratification of the Massachusetts
Constitution were a formative period for the extension of rights to capital
defendants. Using its constitutional power, the SJC laid down new rules of
law that insisted official conduct in capital cases measure up to a republican standard of fairness, impartiality, and equality. Some people believed
the new commonwealth could not endure without the deterrent to crime
supposedly provided by capital punishment, and in the 1780s there was
an orgy of state-sanctioned executions. Within a short time, however, lawyers routinely insisted that arbitrarily imposed capital punishment and a
republican form of government were incompatible. Without taking a political position on that question, the court nevertheless transformed capital
procedure by putting in place extraordinary safeguards when the life of a
fellow being was at stake.

The SJC was especially careful to protect the rights of African American
defendants, men and women freed by the ratification of the Massachusetts
Constitution. "When the liberty of one man was attacked [it was] tanta-
mount to an attack on the liberties of all," counsel for a slave who brought
suit for his freedom in 1781 argued. Two years later at a criminal trial, Chief
Justice Cushing emphasized the same ideal. "The people of this Commonwealth have solemnly bound themselves to each other—to declare—that
all men are born free and equal; and that *every subject is entitled to liberty*
and to have it guarded by the laws as well as his life and property." [82] *Battis*
and *Hardy* elaborated on this commitment.

In addition to the procedural rights outlined in the Massachusetts Declaration of Rights, the court extended to capital defendants a cluster of
rights articulated by rule. Capital defendants had the right to an attorney—
one senior and one junior counsel routinely were assigned—and, as in
Hardy's trial, appointed counsel also argued motions and represented
the defendant before the SJC when it sat as an appeals court. A capital
defendant also had the right to a randomly chosen impartial jury. To ensure that the jury was impartial, the defendant (but not the prosecution)
had the right to an unlimited number of challenges aimed at potential jurors. The court also ruled that capital jurors must be fed and sequestered

during jury deliberations, ending the traditional practice of allowing jurors in search of food and drink to mingle with spectators. Capital defendants were encouraged by the court to force the state to prove its case. If the prosecution sought to use a defendant's own words as evidence of guilt, the court insisted the confession must have been obtained without force or favor. By rule a capital defendant also had the right to introduce evidence of good character. Most important, a capital defendant had the right to "quibble," to raise questions about procedure on appeal in the hope of winning a reversal and a new trial. Although these rule changes extended greater protection to capital defendants, procedural changes alone could not eliminate anxiety about executing an innocent person, nor silence critics of public executions.

The rule of law generally and capital procedure specifically also was influenced by the development of a postrevolutionary civic religion. Capital trials were framed by religion, but a new understanding of the nature of truth shaped the trial. Well into the nineteenth century, a murder trial began with an indictment charging a defendant with "not having the fear of God before his eyes," and "may God have mercy on your soul" were the last words pronounced by the court to a guilty capital defendant. However, the trial itself reflected a profound shift in the way people perceived the truth. The law's new republican formulation replaced the moral certainty that had characterized colonial-era trials. Gone was the presumption that jurors should accept without question the testimony of sworn witnesses. Rather, jurors were told by the court to weigh each person's testimony and to reach a conclusion whose validity was beyond a reasonable doubt. For these reasons, a jury's verdict was said to reflect "the mythical will of the whole people." The author of a pamphlet written in the wake of Jason Fairbanks's execution put it this way: "In a free State, where the laws are mild, [they are] in a great degree dependent for their salutary energy on the cooperation of public opinion."[83]

While this republican formulation was celebrated for protecting a capital defendant's rights and for enhancing the power of ordinary citizens, the fact that it rested on a cluster of rules subject to reinterpretation encouraged a debate about the death penalty. Defense lawyers urged the court to adopt tighter procedural rules and reformers focused on the moral and political objections to the death penalty. In the 1830s lawyers and reformers launched an all-out assault against the death penalty.

THREE
"UNDER SENTENCE OF DEATH"
THE FIRST EFFORT TO ABOLISH THE DEATH PENALTY

The decades from 1830 to the eve of the Civil War were a time of intense activity for opponents of the death penalty. The efforts of a cluster of determined reformers to abolish the death penalty stimulated public debate, legislative action, and a long string of jury nullifications. At the same time, three spotlighted capital trials, two of which led to executions, captured the public's attention and brought about important legal changes. The chief justice of the Supreme Judicial Court, Lemuel Shaw, furthered the transformation of capital procedure begun by the court in the aftermath of the American Revolution. Shaw's brilliant charge to an 1850 capital jury unified a constellation of concepts expressing the protection afforded by the common law against conviction of an innocent person. The effort to abolish the death penalty in Massachusetts once again ended in failure, however. This time, the effort was sapped by the coming of the Civil War.

On the morning of October 27, 1845, a fireman rushing into a smoke-filled room in a house of prostitution near Boston's fashionable Beacon Hill neighborhood stumbled over a woman's body. The charred corpse later was identified as Maria Bickford, a young married woman from Maine. She apparently had been murdered, "her throat cut nearly from ear to ear." Two days later, a coroner's jury determined that her lover, Albert Terrill, a twenty-two-year-old married man from a respectable middle-class family in Weymouth, had murdered Bickford. Terrill eventually was arrested near New Orleans, Louisiana, and brought back to Boston. Rufus Choate, a brilliant and flamboyant criminal lawyer, agreed to defend him; a veteran prosecutor, Samuel D. Parker, represented the commonwealth.

Trial was set for March 26, 1846, in the Supreme Judicial Court. After four days of conflicting testimony and the prosecution's presentation of a considerable amount of circumstantial evidence, the jury found Terrill not guilty of murder.[1]

On each of those four days hundreds of people shoved their way into the courtroom or gathered outside hoping to catch a glimpse of Terrill. The city's newspapers provided extensive coverage of the affair, and a novel published anonymously that year used the courtroom drama to explore the meaning of the "fallen woman's" death. Reformers opposed to the death penalty—who during the 1830s and 1840s had pushed for legislation, petitioned the governor, established a newspaper, published books and articles, and founded the Massachusetts Society for the Abolition of Capital Punishment—took the opportunity to press their views.[2]

The driving force behind the movement to abolish capital punishment in Massachusetts was Robert Rantoul Jr. Born in Beverly, the son of one of the town's political leaders, Rantoul graduated from Harvard College in 1826 and read the law with John Pickering in Salem before he was admitted to the Essex County bar in 1829. The following year, Rantoul helped to defend his close friends Joseph and Francis Knapp, who had been accused of murdering Joseph White, a wealthy Salem businessman. Before trial, Joseph Knapp confessed but denied that his brother had played any part in the crime. Nonetheless, eighteen-year-old Francis, known as Frank, also was tried for murder, and although the evidence against him was circumstantial, he was convicted and hanged. Rantoul bitterly vowed to end the unjust and barbaric rite of execution, a stand that alienated him from many of the people of Salem. Without hope of establishing a law practice in the port city, Rantoul moved first to South Reading and then, in 1833, to Gloucester.[3]

Rantoul quickly established himself in his new home. Running as a Democrat, he was elected to the Massachusetts House of Representatives in 1834 by the people of Gloucester. Although there were only a handful of Democrats in the legislature, Rantoul emerged as a leader by creating a coalition with the "country Whigs." He attacked corporations, worked to revise and codify the state's statute laws, opened up admission to the bar, and during the first two weeks of his term, introduced a measure to abolish capital punishment. The legislature voted to publish and distribute Rantoul's report against the death penalty, but after a weeklong debate, the bill was defeated in March 1835.[4]

When the House reconvened in January 1836, however, Governor Edward Everett, a moderate Whig, recommended that the legislature reconsider its decision. "An increasing tenderness for human life," the governor stated, "is one of the most decided characteristics of the civilization of the day." Within a month, Rantoul submitted a lengthy report and a bill proposing that arson, armed burglary, armed robbery, and treason be punished with life imprisonment rather than death. Individuals convicted of rape or murder would receive, in addition to their life sentences, a penalty Rantoul called "civil death," whereby the criminal's marriage would be dissolved and his property distributed according to his will.[5]

Rantoul's argument against capital punishment pursued four lines. First, he asserted, the government has no right to take a person's life, because *the whole object of government is negative.* That is, government is established for the protection of life, liberty, and property, and "not for the destruction of any of those rights." The chief purpose of government, he said, is to ensure that no one appropriate the property of another or restrain the liberty of another or "injure the person, or shorten the life of another." We surrender to government only as much liberty as is necessary to preserve our natural rights, Rantoul argued. Any act extending beyond that limit—even "by the division of a hair"—is thus "tyrannical." It would be an "obvious absurdity" to claim that if and when men enter into a social compact they give "unlimited powers for all purposes to its government." Individuals do not agree "to hold their lives as conditional grant from the State." No one specifically surrenders the right to life, nor can one. Using governmental power to take a life therefore violates the basic principle of limited government, well defined in both the U.S. Constitution and the fundamental law of Massachusetts.[6]

The second line of argument proceeded from the Enlightenment belief that man can change the society in which he lives, that the "power of improvement" can affect the "general progress of society." According to Rantoul's historical analysis, the era "when darkness covered the earth" and ordinary people were powerless was now distant; civilization had been bathed by the revolutionary light of the eighteenth century. Citizens were now free to use "knowledge, reason and reflection" to change any law, including that "remnant of feudal barbarity," the death penalty. Within an enlightened society every individual can and should be reformed. "Felons," Rantoul concluded, "still are men, and have the better title to commiseration the more deeply they are sunk in guilt."

Rantoul's third line of reasoning was practical rather than theoretical or moral. He hoped to convince the legislature that the death penalty does not work. Crimes against property that are punishable by death—arson, armed burglary, and highway robbery—are more likely to involve murder, Rantoul claimed. On one hand, since the law already subjects him to the death penalty, the criminal is tempted to kill the witness to conceal his crime. On the other hand, if no murder has been committed in those crimes against property, a jury is unlikely to convict the accused because the penalty is so absolute. In other words, "the severity of the law totally defeats its object." Moreover, no evidence has been amassed to show that the death penalty reduces the number of crimes against property. In fact, Rantoul pointed out, when highway robbery was removed from Massachusetts's list of capital offenses during the years 1805 to 1819 there was no increase in the number of armed robberies.

Capital punishment neither deterred murderers nor offered the best protection for society. It was an "awful perversion of all moral reasoning" to argue that killing a person would reform others. In fact, the death penalty had the opposite effect, Rantoul insisted. It diminished the "natural sensibility of man for the sufferings of his fellow man" and generally promoted "cruelty and a disregard of life." Even explicit knowledge of the death penalty was unlikely to prevent a murder. A recent survey, Rantoul noted, found that of 167 convicts under sentence of death, 164 had attended a public execution before they had committed their own crimes.

Finally, Rantoul addressed the religious arguments for and against capital punishment. He acknowledged that the Old Testament justified the death penalty. But, he asked, should the brutal practices of "a peculiar people, under the most peculiar circumstances" govern "a polished and humane people . . . under circumstances essentially opposite theirs?" Rather than basing the state's legal code on the ancient laws of revenge, the commonwealth should embrace the command that lies at the heart of the universal spirit of Christianity—"Thou shalt not kill."

Opponents of Rantoul's bill scoffed at his "visionary ideals of theoretical good" and declared that if fear of the death penalty prevented just one murder, the law should remain. Rantoul replied with statistics show-ing that wherever a crime was removed from the capital punishment list, fewer such crimes were committed. After three days of debate, the House amended Rantoul's bill, eliminating the provision for "civil death" in case of rape and retaining the death penalty for arson and murder. This bill passed 237 to 171, but the Senate rejected it. Three years later, however, both the House and Senate overwhelmingly approved a bill that elimi-nated the death penalty for armed burglary and armed robbery.[7]

In 1840, Governor Marcus Morton, a Democrat elected by a narrow margin after a bitter campaign, recommended eliminating the death pen-alty in most cases in a speech that essentially summarized Rantoul's argu-ments. But Rantoul was no longer a member of the House, and for the next several years the legislature was too divided to act on the issue. To organize public support for their initiative and to bring pressure to bear on elected officials, Rantoul and Charles Spear, together with a handful of other Boston reformers, founded the Massachusetts Society for the Aboli-tion of Capital Punishment in 1845.[8]

Spear, a Boston Universalist minister, who earlier in the year had pub-lished *Essays on the Punishment of Death*, had decided in 1841 to "labour for humanity." He traveled widely, delivered scores of lectures, sold copies of his books, and organized petition campaigns to save the lives of con-victed murderers. Spear believed in the benevolence of God, freedom of the will, and the salvation of all men. He rejected the Calvinist idea of eternal punishment, arguing a just and loving God would save mankind. These principles, Spear insisted, would overcome every existing evil. All criminals, including murderers, could, and should, be reformed.[9]

On January 1, 1845, Spear began publishing a weekly newspaper de-voted to the abolition of the death penalty. "Our principle aim," he wrote in the *Hangman*, "will be to show the entire inutility of the gallows." The paper was filled with essays against the death penalty, announcements of society meetings, news about the plight of convicted murderers, and calls to action. "Let all those who do not desire" to have a man hung "make great exertions to save his life by circulating petitions immediately ask-ing for a commutation of punishment," Spear pleaded. In May 1845, he boasted that the paper had over two thousand subscribers and that his *Es-says* on capital punishment had sold five thousand copies.[10]

The *Hangman* thoroughly covered the story of Bickford's murder. In addition to its own accounts of the crime, the paper reprinted a long profile of the "misguided" Mrs. Bickford that originally had appeared in the *Boston Herald*. When Terrill was arrested and jailed in New Orleans in December 1845, the paper reported that it "was feared that he would commit suicide and therefore was watched constantly." But the following issue carried a letter from Terrill, who scoffed at the report. "I am not gloomy, nor contemplating suicide," he wrote, adding that he felt certain of "an acquittal by a jury of my countrymen." [11]

A month before Terrill was returned to Massachusetts, Governor George Briggs, a devout Baptist and a Whig, called on the legislature to reform capital punishment. Briggs privately supported the death penalty but wanted to appear sympathetic to public opinion. He had two concerns about the public's current attitude toward the death penalty: first, convictions were nearly impossible to obtain; and second, if someone were convicted of a capital offense, the governor was subjected to intense pressure to pardon the criminal or to commute his sentence to life imprisonment. Briggs suggested that the law against murder should recognize degrees of guilt. "The penalty of death shall remain against the willful and deliberate murderer," but, he added, "murder in the second degree, committed under circumstances of mitigation should be punished by confinement in the State Prison during life." [12]

Rantoul seized the opportunity to push for abolition of the death penalty. Early in February 1846, he wrote a series of letters that were published in the *Boston Times* and the *Prisoner's Friend*. The heart of Rantoul's argument was that the death penalty does not prevent crime; indeed, data proved the opposite. In his fourth letter, for example, Rantoul noted that between 1780 and 1845 there had been twenty-three executions for murder in Massachusetts, yet there had been no decrease in the rate of murder. By comparison, in England abolishing the death penalty for certain crimes had sharply reduced the frequency with which those particular crimes were committed. The results were decisive, he wrote; no one in England wanted "to restore the bloody rubric from which the present generation has escaped." Rantoul concluded his series by noting that in 1835 he had made a principled argument against capital punishment, but "experience now confirms what then was called theory." [13]

Terrill was secretly arraigned before the chief justice of the Supreme Judicial Court, Lemuel Shaw, on February 25, 1846. The accused murderer was described as "a handsome young man, full six feet in height" with hazel eyes and fair skin. In the brief time he spent before Judge Shaw, Terrill conducted himself "with dignity and utmost coolness," the *Prisoner's Friend* reported. "We hope the people of this Commonwealth will not hang this man, Spear wrote. "We hope they will never hang another man." [14]

In the interval between Terrill's arraignment and his trial in March, the *North American Review* published a long review essay on the death penalty. In addition to Spear's *Essays on the Punishment of Death*, the unnamed reviewer considered John L. O'Sullivan's *Report in Favor of the Abolition of the Punishment of Death by Law* and Rev. George Cheever's argument for the death penalty. The reviewer's sympathies were readily apparent. He brushed aside Cheever's argument that Christianity justifies the death penalty, pointing out that the argument denied the "precepts of Christ and the spirit of Christianity" and was merely an opinion unsubstantiated by "any experience of its usefulness or proof of its necessity." The reviewer then hammered home the point that the death penalty "has never been sure or equal." However conscientious the jury, the law simply cannot be applied fairly. Given the probability of circumstantial evidence forming the basis of conviction, the fallibility of human judgment, and the "sway of prejudice, ignorance and excitement," the accused person is "doomed." Therefore, by attempting to punish the murderer, the legal system "has been the slayer of the innocent." The likelihood of committing judicial murder, the reviewer concluded, is an inherent, and unacceptable, liability of the system. [15]

When Terrill's trial finally began on March 26, 1846, it had the "appearance of a Camp Meeting." Prosecutor Samuel Parker opened the proceedings by outlining the long, adulterous relationship between Bickford and Terrill, which Parker argued culminated in a murder of passion and jealousy. Terrill met Bickford in the summer of 1844 at a tavern in New Bedford where she worked as a prostitute, having fled from her husband in Bangor, Maine. Terrill and Bickford traveled to New York, Baltimore, and Philadelphia as man and wife, and in 1845 they lived together under assumed names in various Boston locations. Early in October, Terrill was arrested and indicted for adultery, but his wife, mother, and friends secured his release on a promise of good behavior. [16]

Immediately upon gaining his freedom, however, Terrill went straight to Bickford, who was living in a house of prostitution near Charles Street.

The two were together on the night of October 26, according to the manager of the house, Joel Lawrence. He testified that early in the morning he had awakened to a loud noise coming from Bickford's room; he then heard a person walking down the stairs and unlocking the front door. Shortly after, two other residents of the house smelled smoke and saw fire coming from Bickford's room. A fireman who lived nearby found Bickford's body when he entered the room to put out the fire. At about the same time, a man walked into Fulham's stable, mumbled that he had had a quarrel with his girlfriend, and asked to be driven to Weymouth. During the trial, William Fulham identified that man as Albert Terrill. Fulham also testified that Terrill had said something about a house fire.[17]

In his summation, Parker, who had been Suffolk County district attorney since 1830, admitted that Bickford was "an unblushing harlot and an undisguised adulteress," but he reminded the jury that the law protected the "life of everyone, high and low, rich and poor, virtuous and depraved." The jurors were also asked to remember that Terrill was an immoral man who had disgraced his family and broken his pledge to the court. Parker contended that because Terrill was obsessed with this young, beautiful woman, his judgment had been overwhelmed by his passion. These facts, Parker argued, spun into a web of circumstantial evidence that tied Terrill to the scene of the crime, left no doubt that he had murdered Bickford.

Finally, Parker appealed to the jurors "to stand firmly on the principle" that the law must protect the "safety of human life." To achieve that goal, the commonwealth demanded the death penalty in the case of premeditated, cold-blooded murder. Speaking directly to the campaign against capital punishment that had engulfed Massachusetts for more than a decade, Parker urged the jurors "not to be terrified by the talk about judicial murder," a term thrown about by reformers opposed to the death penalty. The commonwealth had presented convincing evidence to show that a murder had taken place and that Terrill had committed it. If the jury believed that the commonwealth had proved its case beyond a reasonable doubt, Terrill should be convicted and executed.[18]

Rufus Choate, Terrill's defense attorney, was the most prominent criminal lawyer in Boston. Born in Ipswich, Massachusetts, in 1799, Choate graduated from Dartmouth College in 1819, briefly attended Harvard Law School, and read the law with U.S. Attorney General William Wirt in

Washington, D.C., before being admitted to the Essex County bar in 1823. While practicing in Salem, Choate had been elected to the Massachusetts House of Representatives and the state Senate. After serving one term in the U.S. Congress as a representative of Essex County, Choate moved to Boston in 1834, to build his law practice. But in 1840, Choate gave in to pressure from his old friend Daniel Webster and consented to stand for election to the U.S. Senate.[19]

Choate served five years in the Senate, departing with the vow, "to my profession, *totis virbus*, I am now dedicated." Within a few years he was handling nearly seventy cases a year, an unusually large number of which were criminal. He tried cases of murder, fraud, arson, abortion, embezzlement, insurance claims, assault, and slander. Some critics charged that the methods he used to defend clients accused of criminal acts "struck down the fair fabric of public virtue and public integrity." Even Choate's friends conceded that he would "stretch the law to the utmost limit" and that "from his lips fatal sweetness flowed," but they also argued that his "erudition was wide-ranging and his commitment to the majesty of the law unflagging.[20]

Choate's co-counsel in the Terrill case, Annis Merrill, who had been admitted to the practice just two years earlier, made the opening statement and presented most of the witnesses for the defense. Choate elaborated on the defense's argument during an eight-hour summation speech. Merrill began by cautioning the jury not to judge Terrill by the "shocking and exaggerated accounts" the city's newspapers had "poured over the country" or by the "polluted sources" the prosecution had called as its chief witnesses. Merrill contended Parker had failed to provide a convincing motive for the murder of which Terrill was accused. The duty of a jury, Merrill urged, was to provide "the best earthly hope" in a process that would determine the "eternal destiny of a man like ourselves." "Until the Deity shall proclaim himself implacable and unforgiving," he continued, "let no man assume to smother the feelings of compassion in his bosom." Even if the government presented a "perfect case" and there was "no valid defense," it would be the responsibility of each juror, Merrill insisted, "to look tenderly upon the defendant and not to render a verdict in the spirit of retaliation and revenge.[21]

When weighing the importance of compassion in a capital case, jurors should remember that the legal system neither has been, nor can be, perfect. There are, Merrill argued, "numerous accounts of cases in which people have been convicted upon circumstantial evidence and put to death, who afterwards have been proved innocent." To buttress his argument, Merrill began to read from Spear's *Essays on the Punishment of Death*. Parker objected. Choate argued that the cases in which innocent persons had been put to death might be "read as an illustration without insisting that these accounts are actually true." But the court upheld the objection, ruling that only "books of authority" might be read in court.[22]

By raising the issue of capital punishment at the outset to frame their strategy within the courtroom, Merrill and Choate also played to the controversy swirling around the issue outside the courtroom. Choate's intent was revealed when he called the former dean of the Harvard Medical School, Dr. Walter Channing, to testify. Channing was a popular spokesman and secretary of the Society for the Abolition of Capital Punishment. He told the jury that Bickford could have slit her own throat and still had enough "muscular energy" to throw herself from the bed where the fatal blow had been inflicted to a spot on the floor several feet away. He also commented on anecdotal evidence presented by Terrill's relatives that the accused was known to sleepwalk. A somnambulist, Channing confirmed, could rise from his bed, get dressed, commit murder, set a fire, and run into the street with no memory of having done so. The doctor's testimony may have lent some legitimacy to the defense's alternative hypotheses about the events of the previous October, but his most important role was to remind jurors of the campaign to abolish the death penalty.[23]

Choate's long closing statement to the jury also was framed by opposition to the death penalty. He began by reminding the jury that the life of a fellow human being was at stake. They must abandon the "delusive dream" that the governor would commute a death sentence; it was for them to decide whether the life of a man should be "violently cut off." Choate's final sentence transformed his argument against capital punishment from an issue advocated by reformers to one that was at the heart of civic patriotism and republicanism. "Under the iron law of old Rome," Choate told the jury, "it was the custom to bestow a civic wreath on him who should save the life of a citizen. Do your duty this day, gentlemen, and you too, will deserve the civic crown."[24]

Surprise and disagreement greeted the verdict when Terrill was acquitted, but conservatives and reformers alike agreed that the jury's aversion to the death penalty had played a significant role in their decision. A letter to the *Prisoner's Friend*, probably written by Harvard College president Edward Everett, contended that when the jurors were confronted with the issue of capital punishment, they said simply, "Away with the punishment of death." Everett added that the money spent by the commonwealth to stage the trial should have been used "to educate some wretched children, to give a little bread or shelter to persons driven to crime by want." An earlier editorial in the *Boston Courier* expressed the same sentiments. "From the result of this trial," the editorial ran, "we infer that no person will hereafter be convicted of murder in the courts of Massachusetts. There is prevalent in society such a feeling of horror" about executions, particularly "the possibility that the sufferer may be innocent that jurors will not hesitate to acquit." [25]

The reformer Lydia Maria Child maintained that the jurors had found Choate's controversial hypothesis about somnambulism a convenient hook on which to hang their opposition to the death penalty. "This is another indication," she wrote, "of the extreme unwillingness to convict in capital cases." Although the *Boston Evening Transcript* viewed the verdict from a perspective favoring the death penalty, the paper shared Child's conclusion, calling somnambulism "shallow humbug." Somehow Boston must find enough jurors who will impose the "highest penalty," the paper grumbled, or the "stigma now resting upon her character" will remain. [26]

Although Choate would continue to be criticized for his tactics, hostility did not deter him from again making use of the somnambulism defense, this time in January 1847 when Terrill was tried for arson, also a capital offense. Like his trial for murder, Terrill's arson trial received extensive newspaper coverage. The *Prisoner's Friend* reported that the courtroom was "densely crowded during the whole of the eight days" of the proceedings. Once again, Choate and Merrill used a two-pronged defense: they argued that if Terrill set fire to the house of prostitution where he and Bickford were living, he did so while somnambulate, and they attacked capital punishment. [27]

When Terrill was found not guilty of arson, there were groans from those who favored capital punishment. In response to the verdict, Governor Briggs compromised his opposition to the abolition of the death penalty. He feared that sentimental jurors would dissolve the connection between penalties and crimes, that the link between law and order would be broken. In a thinly veiled allusion to Terrill, Briggs acknowledged that a "strong current of public sentiment" against capital punishment had produced "a good deal of embarrassment in the criminal proceedings in our courts of justice, manifesting itself in the acquittal of persons charged with capital offense, when they would probably have been convicted, if the penalty, following conviction, had been less severe." Briggs therefore proposed doing away with the death penalty for all capital crimes except murder. He calculated that by reducing the number of crimes punishable by death, he would undermine the popular movement against the death penalty.[28]

In fact, the movement was in disarray. Wendell Phillips, Boston's foremost agitator for reform and an officer in the Society to Abolish Capital Punishment, blasted Choate's tactics, especially the somnambulism defense, arguing that the lawyer had made it "safe to murder." Other members of the society were more circumspect but no less eager to be counted among the advocates of law and order. While implicitly acknowledging widespread dissatisfaction with the verdict, Charles Spear was cheered by one development. "We find that many persons who have formerly been in favor of Capital Punishment, are now convinced," Spear wrote a few days after Terrill's acquittal for arson, "that it is better to substitute some other punishment which will be more certain than the death penalty."[29]

Just eighteen months after Terrill was acquitted for arson, Washington Goode, a twenty-nine-year-old black mariner, was accused of murdering Thomas Harding, also a black mariner. The two men were rivals for the affections of Mary Ann Williams. On January 1, 1849, Goode was put on trial for his life. Although there were clear differences between the two cases—race and class most obviously—the public's anger about the verdicts rendered in Terrill's cases undoubtedly helped undermine Goode's chances for escaping the gallows.

The evidence used by District Attorney Parker to build his case against Goode was largely circumstantial. No one could positively identify the man who had plunged a knife between Harding's ribs. But Parker contended that Goode had a motive. Goode, said the prosecutor, flew into a drunken, jealous rage when he learned that Harding had given Mary Ann Williams a gift. Witnesses testified that Goode had boasted that he would get even with Harding. Other witnesses for the prosecution told the court that the man who murdered Harding had a voice and clothing and a gait similar to Goode's. Parker told the jurors they had a responsibility to stem the rising tide of "crimes of violence." Echoing Briggs, he insisted that unless punishment was certain, law and order would collapse.[30]

Two young, distinguished attorneys, William Aspinwall and Edgar Hodges, defended Goode. Aspinwall was born in London, where his father was U.S. Consul, in 1819. He graduated from Harvard College in 1838, attended Harvard Law School, and read the law with George W. Phillips (Wendell's brother). He was admitted to the Suffolk County bar in 1841. Although Hodges was older than his co-counsel, he had practiced in Boston only since 1846.[31]

Aspinwall and Hodges argued that Goode was innocent. They impugned the testimony of the commonwealth's witnesses, and they punched holes in the wall of circumstantial evidence built by Parker. In closing, Aspinwall reminded the jurors of their fearful responsibility. They held in their hands "the life of human being." There were cases, he told the jurors in words reminiscent of Merrill's argument to the Terrill jury, where the accused had been found guilty, hanged, and "afterwards found to have been entirely innocent of the crime for which his life had paid the forfeit." Parker quickly objected and Chief Justice Shaw upheld the prosecutor.[32]

Undeterred, Hodges pressed the point. He reminded the jurors that murder was not always and everywhere punished by death, not the first "murder by the son of our first parents," nor many committed since, even in so-called savage societies. Hodges was about to "discuss the impropriety of capital punishment" in Massachusetts when Parker again objected. Shaw told Hodges that he "was out of order to discuss the expedience or justice of the death penalty." The jury deliberated just thirty-five minutes before finding Goode guilty. On January 15, after lecturing Goode about his abuse of alcohol and his association with "an abandoned married woman," Chief Justice Shaw sentenced him to death. Goode was to be hanged on May 25.[33]

The opponents of the death penalty hoped to save Goode from the gallows, as they had with a number of men during the past fourteen years. The community's opposition to capital punishment was solid and widespread, according to the *Boston Herald*. If anyone doubts this proposition, the paper challenged, let him go to the courthouse when the Supreme Judicial Court is impaneling a capital jury. There he "will find that a great number of summoned jurors are rejected by the Commonwealth because they are opposed to taking a life for murder." On April 6, Wendell Phillips, among others, spoke to a large audience gathered on behalf of Goode at Tremont Temple. Phillips did not address the general issue of capital punishment; rather, he focused on Goode's case and on the fact that Goode was a black man. If he had committed murder—and there were serious doubts about that—the act was driven by passion and alcohol. Goode was not a hardened criminal but "the victim of the worst social influences." As a black man "the doors were shut against him—he has a separate school, a separate church; other people were ashamed to be associated with him and by law he was ostracized." Goode deserved sympathy and help, not death. Finally, Phillips posed an invidious question: why had Goode been "selected" to be hanged when Terrill who had murdered a woman in "cold blood," was set free?[34]

Phillips's question was addressed in an editorial by the *Herald* and in an article in the *Prisoner's Friend*. The answer was simple: unlike Terrill, Goode was black and poor. "Shall Washington Goode be hanged?" the editorial asked. "Yes, hang him; he is poor and has no friends. Twist, turn, look at the proposition in any manner you please, if a criminal or his friends have plenty of money, there is no law in New England which can reach him."[35]

The *Friend* struck a similar dissonant chord that played on the anger aroused by Terrill:

> Yes, Washington, thou must die! Thou art too vulgar to excite compassion. Hadst thou found thyself at midnight where a wife could not follow, and in thy haste to depart had slain thee partner and set fire to her chamber, mental infirmity might have a kind word to utter and call thee a sleepwalker—or if done into Latin, and given thee out as "somnambulist" there would be little danger for thy neck.[36]

Following the Boston meeting, the Society for the Abolition of Capital Punishment sponsored meetings in a half a dozen other Massachusetts cities and towns. At each meeting petitions were circulated and Spear boasted that more than twenty-three thousand signatures were obtained. One petition, signed by more than one hundred "colored citizens of Boston," urged the governor to consider race as a mitigating factor. Goode, according to an account in the *Prisoner's Friend*, "belongs to a race against whom a cruel prejudice paralyzes his effort for self-improvement, shuts the halls of the Lyceums against him, and banishes him to separate schools and churches." It seemed especially harsh, the petitioners argued, that a man burdened throughout his life with racial prejudice should be hanged.[37]

Although only a handful of people publicly supported Goode's hanging, there were plenty of supporters of capital punishment. Members of Boston's orthodox clergy argued at a debate held at the Boston Latin School that "the right to inflict Capital Punishment can be proved to spring from a divine source." One Calvinist minister, for example, defended the death penalty as "one of the chief safeguards of society." Evangelical clergymen also denounced opponents of capital punishment for caring nothing for the victims of murder and for wanting to coddle murderers.[38]

Despite the powerful and numerous appeals made to spare Goode's life, Governor Briggs and his Council adamantly refused to commute the black man's death sentence. "A pardon here," Briggs insisted, "would tend toward the utter subversion of the law."[39]

In the evening before his scheduled execution Goode attempted to commit suicide. He swallowed large chunks of tobacco and wads of paper and stuffed a blanket in his mouth so that he might suffocate or drown in his own vomit. Goode also slashed his arm at the elbow with a piece of glass. By the time the prison guards entered his cell, he had lost a considerable amount of blood. The prison doctor stopped the flow of blood, saving Goode's life so that he could undergo "a more terrible death in the morning."[40]

Unlike the executions that took place in Suffolk County before 1849, Goode's hanging occurred within the walls of the Leverett Street jail. The public execution ritual at the center of capital punishment for more than two hundred years was dropped quietly in 1835. There was evidence that postrevolutionary crowds were more boisterous and less attentive to the all-important religious message than their Puritan ancestors had been. As early as 1801 Rev. Thomas Thacher had blasted public executions for undermining the virtue of on-lookers and hardening their hearts. After he gave his sermon following the execution of Jason Fairbanks, fewer and fewer execution sermons were given and the practice disappeared by about 1825. A decade later, Robert Rantoul's widely circulated pamphlet contained data demonstrating that public executions did not deter murderers. More generally, mobs and riots occurred throughout northeastern cities in the 1830s. Boston was "shaken to its foundations" in the summer of 1834 when a mob of Protestant laborers burned the Ursuline Convent in Charlestown. The next year the legislature strengthened the riot act and moved executions inside prison walls, joining Pennsylvania, New Jersey, and New York in ending public executions.[41]

Because Goode was weak from loss of blood, prison guards strapped him into a chair and carried him to the gallows built in a corner of the prison yard. Despite a heavy rain, a large crowd stood outside the walls, straining to catch a glimpse of the gruesome event. The *Herald* angrily suggested that "Briggs and his Council, or the deluded priests who are clamoring for the wretch's blood, be compelled to perform the duties of gallows builders and hangmen." At 9:45 A.M. Goode was placed on the platform, and at a signal the trap door on which he stood sprang open and Goode's body, still bound to the chair, plunged several feet. Twenty-five minutes later doctors pronounced Goode dead. The *Prisoner's Friend* claimed that more than one thousand people paraded through a North End tenement where Goode's body was sent after the execution, a testament to their continued support for the abolition of capital punishment in Massachusetts. The movement's opponents also made a statement: "Goode is hung," one Boston newspaper wrote. "We hope Spear and his gang will howl no longer."[42]

Although twenty-one men were tried for murder between 1835 and 1849, by the time of Goode's execution only two had been hanged. Eight murder defendants were acquitted and eight found guilty of the lesser crime of manslaughter. Five men were convicted and sentenced to death, but three had their sentences commuted to life in prison. The two men put to death were unsympathetic characters. Benjamin Cummings, a public drunk who beat his wife on numerous occasions and had served time in the state prison, stabbed to death the New Bedford constable's son when he caught Cummings vandalizing his father's home. Thomas Barrett, a poor Irish immigrant, was convicted of two capital crimes, the rape and murder of a seventy-year-old woman. When the opponents of capital punishment petitioned Governor Briggs to commute Barrett's death sentence, they were told that his "extraordinary turpitude and abandoned depravity" put him beyond redemption or mercy. Barrett was sent to the gallows on January 5, 1845.[43]

Terrill's trials and Goode's execution marked a turning point in the early nineteenth-century campaign to abolish the death penalty in Massachusetts. Goode seems to have been the victim of racism and a social back-lash. Fearful that the reckless defense tactics used by Choate and Merrill threatened order and that widespread opposition to the death penalty undermined the law, the advocates of capital punishment insisted that neither sentimentality nor circumstances peculiar to any individual should disturb the rigid equation between the death penalty and murder. Opponents of the death penalty were at once embarrassed and angry, and their cause was weakened by the cynical means used to win Terrill's freedom and by the state's refusal to heed the voice of the people and spare the life of poor, black, friendless Washington Goode.

Just seven months after Goode's execution another murder captured Boston's imagination, blurring the distinction between opponents and advocates of capital punishment, splitting the legal community, and turning Boston society upside down. The murder occurred at the Boston Medical School and involved Boston Brahmin families and members of the Harvard elite. Shortly before noon on November 23, 1849, Dr. George Parkman, a wealthy real estate speculator and philanthropist, left his Beacon Hill home for a prearranged meeting with John White Webster, a Harvard chemistry professor. Parkman had come to collect money Webster owed him. According to Webster's subsequent confession, when he told Parkman he did not have the money, Parkman insulted him and shouted that he would have him fired from his professorship. Unable to endure Parkman's "threats and invectives," Webster grabbed a heavy piece of wood and killed Parkman with a single powerful blow. "I stooped down over him," Webster later recalled, "and he seemed to be lifeless." After bolting the laboratory's doors, he tried to revive Parkman. When that effort failed, Webster instantly made a fatal decision. "I saw nothing," he wrote, "but the alternative of a successful removal and concealment of the body, on the one hand, and of infamy and destruction on the other." He dragged Parkman's body from the lecture hall into an adjoining room equipped with a sink and butchered it. The head and viscera he burned in a furnace, the thorax and a part of a thigh he hid in a trunk, and the pelvis and some of the other limbs he threw down a laboratory privy. At six o'clock he left the college for his Cambridge home. Later that evening Webster played cards with a friend.[44]

When Parkman's family publicized his disappearance, the college janitor, Ephraim Littlefield, who lived in a basement apartment next to

Webster's laboratory, became suspicious and began an investigation that ended in his discovery of fresh human remains. On November 30, Webster was arrested. Trial before the Supreme Judicial Court was set for March 19, 1850.[45]

Webster, aware of Rufus Choate's successful defense of Albert Terrill, hoped to employ him for his defense. But Choate refused. Two other skilled criminal defense lawyers were approached, but they also refused, claiming that as members of the Harvard Corporation they had a conflict of interest. According to long practice and an 1820 statute, therefore, the court appointed two attorneys to defend Webster: Pliny Merrick, a fifty-six-year-old former prosecutor with more than three decades of trial experience, and Edward D. Sohier, a Harvard-educated commercial lawyer described as "full of resources, forceful in argument, and sharp in repartee." Attorney General John H. Clifford, who had been appointed the commonwealth's top legal officer in 1849 following nearly two decades of private practice, and George Bemis, a forty-one-year-old attorney who struggled to balance his religious convictions with his distaste for capital punishment, represented the commonwealth. "In searching my own heart," Bemis wrote in his diary, "perhaps I feel too ready to see justice—stern justice, if it be so called—enforced against an offender and take pride, shall I say, in shutting my eyes to the dreadful character of the consequences to him."[46]

"Notwithstanding the severe storm of rain and snow," hundreds of people lined up to gain entrance to Webster's trial. Tickets were issued and the courtroom audience was changed every ten minutes, allowing sixty thousand people to glimpse some part of the eleven days of legal proceedings. Promptly at 8:45 A.M. Chief Justice Shaw and Associate Justices Charles Dewey, Theron Metcalf, and Samuel Wilde took their seats at the bench and the process of impaneling a jury began. Shaw put the "usual interrogatories" to each potential juror, including a question to ascertain whether a would-be juror had "conscientious scruples, or such opinions on the subject of capital punishment, as to preclude [him] from finding a defendant guilty." One potential juror, Benjamin Greene, said that "he was opposed to capital punishment; but that he did not think that his opinions would interfere with his doing his duty as a juror." Greene was sworn. The court subsequently challenged for cause three other would-be jurors, because they were unequivocally opposed to participating in a process that might lead to the imposition of the death penalty. After the entire panel had been completed, Greene asked to be excluded. Shaw refused, saying Greene's scruples "did not come within the statute." [47]

The challenge to the state was to prove that a murder had occurred without showing the *corpus delicti*, or proof of the murder. To overcome this missing evidence, Clifford paraded a string of medical experts before the jury who testified that the remains discovered in Webster's laboratory were those of Parkman. Dr. Nathan C. Keep, Parkman's dentist, gave the most compelling and convincing testimony. He recognized the human teeth found in Webster's laboratory as the ones he had made for Parkman years before and repaired the day before his disappearance. Littlefield, the suspicious janitor, established the connection between the experts' identification of Parkman's remains and their presence in Webster's lab. He testified that on November 23, he saw Parkman enter Webster's lab but never saw him leave. Later that afternoon, he found Webster's laboratory door bolted from the inside, heard water running, and felt the heat of the furnace. After consulting with college authorities, Littlefield broke through the wall into the privy beneath Webster's laboratory and discovered the butchered remains of a man's pelvis and a leg. "I knew that it was no place for these things," he said. Clifford had made his case and he called no additional witnesses. [48]

Defense attorney Sohier did the best with what little he had. First, he stressed the difference between direct and circumstantial evidence and suggested the latter created plenty of reasonable doubt. Given human fallibility, mistakes occurred in the "inferences and conclusions" drawn from circumstances, with the result that innocent people were convicted erroneously, he warned. Second, Sohier stretched the definition of alibi. He introduced witnesses who claimed to have spotted Parkman alive in the days following his disappearance. Third, Jared Sparks, the president of Harvard, and a host of other prominent Bostonians testified that Webster was a peaceful man without malice who was incapable of committing murder. [49]

Following closing statements by Merrick and Clifford, Chief Justice Shaw instructed the jury. During his three-hour charge Shaw focused briefly on whether a juror who manifested scruples in regard to capital punishment should be kept off a murder jury and spoke at length about circumstantial evidence and reasonable doubt. The jury deliberated just over two and a half hours and returned a verdict of guilty. According to the

Boston Evening Transcript, Webster "sank gradually into his chair," and his "whole frame shook" for a full minute "during which there was dead silence in the court and every eye was turned upon him."[50]

While Webster awaited execution, a fierce debate raged within the legal community over jury selection and Shaw's charge to the jury on the issue of malice. The contentious points focused on the constitutionality of the death penalty and the maxim that a murder defendant is innocent until proved guilty. Following Webster's conviction, Lysander Spooner, a lawyer and social reformer from central Massachusetts, published a widely circulated pamphlet arguing that the Massachusetts statute requiring the elimination of would-be jurors who opposed capital punishment was an unconstitutional exercise of governmental power. The jury that convicted Webster was "*packed* by the court, either with a view to a more easy conviction than could otherwise be obtained, or with a view to a conviction which otherwise could not be obtained at all." Excluding people opposed to the death penalty was contrary to the Sixth Amendment of the U.S. Constitution and Article 12 of the Massachusetts Declaration of Rights, because such a procedure "*destroyed the trial by jury itself.*" Only a jury made up of a true cross-section of the community—a sample that included both jurors who opposed and jurors who favored capital punishment—could be defined as impartial and, therefore, properly fulfill the requirement that a death sentence could be imposed only with a unanimous verdict. By excluding those would-be jurors who manifest a greater sensibility about the death penalty, the government established a "standard of sensibility" that biased the outcome and deprived the defendant of a trial by a jury representing "all the degrees of sensibility which prevail among the people at large." Spooner's plan, together with the fact that at the time Massachusetts prosecutors did not have peremptory strikes—the ability to remove potential jurors without stating a reason—might well have ended the use of capital punishment had he prevailed. But his argument explicitly linking jury selection to the abolition of capital punishment did not gain legitimacy for more than a hundred years.[51]

Shaw's post-*Webster* critics also focused on his interpretation of the law of homicide, proof of malice. His charge to the jury, according to an unnamed lawyer, made a "farce and a mockery" of trial by jury and provided the basis for "judicial murder." Boston's *Monthly Law Reporter* declared that the "whole community shudders at the law of malicious homicide as expounded by the learned Chief Justice." Harvard law professor Joel Parker's damning conclusion to an article on the trial was that Shaw's jury instructions had violated a "cherished tradition of Anglo-American criminal justice: every man is presumed to be innocent until he is proved guilty."[52]

The chief accusation Shaw's critics made was that he implied the existence of malice as a matter of law and, therefore, shifted the burden of proof from the prosecution to the accused. Actually he did no such thing. He began, in *Webster*, by distinguishing manslaughter and murder, identifying manslaughter as the "unlawful killing of another without malice" and murder as "the killing of any person with malice aforethought, either expressed or implied." In law, he said, malice means a guilty mind, knowledge by the person that an act is wrong. Because the existence of malice distinguishes murder from manslaughter, it is necessary, Shaw wrote, "to ascertain with some precision the nature of legal malice, and what evidence is requisite to establish its existence." If facts presented by the defendant show "justification, excuse, or palliation" the crime may be defined as manslaughter. But, if the fact of the killing is established by solid evidence and there are no such circumstances, "there is nothing to rebut the natural presumption of malice." This rule, Shaw explained, is founded on the principle that a person "must be presumed to intend to do that which he voluntarily and willfully does in fact do, and that he must intend all the natural, probable, and usual consequences of his own acts."[53]

Specifically, in Webster's case there was evidence showing Parkman was murdered in Webster's laboratory. Webster pleaded innocent, claiming that Parkman had left the college alive. But the evidence was overwhelming that an intentional homicide had occurred for which Webster's innocent plea obviously provided no excuses or mitigation. Therefore, according to Shaw, "there is nothing to rebut the natural presumption of malice."[54]

Shaw's charge to the Webster jury divided the responsibility for determining a verdict into two interdependent parts: the court had the right to decide the law and the jury the power to weigh the facts and reach a verdict. Specifically, the jury was to determine whether Parkman's death was caused "by an act of violence and human agency" and "whether the act was committed" by Webster, as the prosecution charged. Shaw acknowledged that the proof offered by Attorney General Clifford that Webster murdered Parkman with malice aforethought was entirely circumstantial, but he assured the jurors that, used properly, circumstantial evidence was "safe and reliable." Shaw articulated three rules the jury should apply to test the worth of circumstantial evidence: the basic facts of the crime must be carefully tested; they all must be consistent with each other; and all of the circumstances must lead to a "connection between the known and proved facts and the fact sought to be proved," specifically whether the accused committed the murder as charged. It is not adequate that a chain of circumstantial evidence supports a strong probability that the defendant is guilty. The circumstantial evidence must produce a "morality certainty, that the accused, and no one else" committed the murder, and that conclusion must be proved beyond a reasonable doubt. "What is reasonable doubt?" Shaw asked.[55]

> It is a term often used, probably pretty well understood, but not easily defined. It is not mere possible doubt; because everything relating to human affairs, and depending on moral evidence, is open to some possible or imaginary doubt. It is that state of the case, which, after the entire comparison and consideration of all the evidence, leaves the minds of the jurors in that condition that they cannot say they feel an abiding conviction, to a moral certainty, of the truth of the charge. The burden of proof is upon the prosecutor. All the presumptions of law independent of evidence are in favor of innocence; and every person is presumed to be innocent until he is proved guilty. If upon such proof there is reasonable doubt remaining, the accused is entitled to the benefit of it by an acquittal. For it is not sufficient to establish a probability, though a strong one arising from the doctrine of chances, that the fact charged is more likely to be true than the contrary; but the evidence must establish the truth of the fact to a reasonable and moral certainty; a certainty that convinces and directs the understanding, and satisfies the reason and judgment, of those who are bound to act conscientiously upon it. This we take to be proof beyond a reasonable doubt; because if the law which mostly depends upon considerations of a moral nature, should go further than this, and require absolute certainty, it would exclude circumstantial evidence altogether.[56]

Shaw's *Webster* charge did not originate the principles of "reasonable doubt," the "presumption of innocence," the prosecutor's "burden of proof," and "moral certainty," but it did pull together those principles

accomplishments but resisted any substantial changes in capital procedure. And finally, although capital defendants benefited from the Supreme
Judicial Court's commitment to the moral certainty standard, the risks of
an erroneous conviction and execution in a system predicated on the possibility of error were obvious.

FOUR

"THE MONSTER PETITION"

In the years between the Civil War and World War I, Massachusetts was transformed by successive waves of new immigrants and by the development of an industrial society. Yankee farmers and small-town lawyers were pushed to the wings and replaced at center stage by aggressive businessmen and law school–trained attorneys who worked to modernize private law (contract, property, and torts) to keep pace with economic change. During the same period, the Massachusetts legislature enacted a string of progressive reforms, including a ten-hour workday, a minimum-wage law, workmen's compensation, and protective legislation for working women. The Massachusetts Supreme Judicial Court (SJC) turned back all efforts to find these new laws unconstitutional.

The basic shape of the criminal trial hardly changed during this period, but important changes were made in criminal procedure. Among other safeguards, a defendant had the right to remain silent after arrest and the right to bar self-incriminating evidence. The accused also had the right to testify in his or her own behalf in court. If a defendant chose not to testify, a Massachusetts prosecutor could not mention that fact and the trial judge was required to instruct the jury not to regard the defendant's silence as prejudicial. A Massachusetts criminal defendant could also contest the prosecution's introduction of a confession won by favor or force. Both the defendant and the state could challenge potential jurors, a process critics thought eliminated the best-prepared potential jurors and lengthened a trial. Finally, a capital defendant had a right to a postconviction appeals process during which lawyers could argue that procedural errors had deprived the defendant of a fair trial.[1]

Although murder rates were low, judges and lawyers in Massachusetts and throughout the United States routinely decried the criminal law's slow pace and its uneven results, problems many professionals believed were caused in large part by the procedural safeguards extended to criminal defendants. In a speech to the American Institute of Criminal Law in 1913, Moorfield Storey, Boston's most prominent attorney and longtime advocate for civil rights and racial justice, argued that the state provided criminal defendants "needless protection and paralyzed its own arm." Contemporary criminal procedure, he said, not only encouraged long delays, increased crime and violence, and endangered law-abiding citizens, it also threatened "ordered liberty" for all Americans.[2]

The American Institute of Criminal Law and Criminology, founded in 1910, was the most outspoken group advocating reform of criminal procedure. Editorials and articles in the institute's journal consistently argued that existing rules of criminal procedure needed to be modernized, that ancient Anglo-Saxon safeguards as well as procedures added in the wake of the Civil War needed to be stripped away in the name of efficiency and public safety. A Massachusetts branch of the institute was organized in 1912 and included among its members SJC justices Henry N. Sheldon and Charles A. DeCourcey. While the Massachusetts group was more moderate than many contributors to the national organization, its argument for streamlining criminal procedure had a significant impact on criminal justice in Massachusetts. The SJC, for example, consistently rejected appeals based on procedural error (the court was not permitted to examine the facts of a capital trial until 1939) initiated by convicted capital defendants.[3]

Those who clung to the traditional belief that a criminal trial—especially when a defendant's life hung in the balance—that pitted the government against the accused was inherently unequal supported the procedural reforms condemned by progressives. Defense attorneys and a dose of lethargy sustained Massachusetts's longtime policy of appointing counsel for indigent capital defendants and in 1859 led legislators to create degrees of murder so that only the most heinous crime was punishable by death. Defense lawyers also fought the elimination of the long, detailed common law indictment in favor of a simple short form. A liberal impulse also motivated Massachusetts legislators to repeatedly debate the need for capital punishment and for citizen groups to campaign to end the death penalty.[4]

The shrill tone of the debate over due process belied the reality. The number of reported murders declined sharply in late nineteenth- and early twentieth-century Massachusetts and the SJC rarely upheld a capital defendant's claim that he or she had been denied a procedural right and a fair trial. On the contrary, the state insisted the procedures it grudgingly accepted guaranteed the defendant a fair trial although historically the contested right had been narrowly defined by the SJC. In the decade before World War I several murder trials feuled the battle over procedure. In the spring of 1904, a high-profile murder trial highlighted the tension between critics and supporters of a more expansive criminal procedure. The sensational trial of Charles L. Tucker for the murder of Mabel Page touched off a debate about capital procedure and the death penalty, as well as the need to protect "defenseless women" from murderous sexual predators. Chester Jordan's murder trial in 1908 raised similar issues about procedure, delay, and the slaying of women by brutal men.[5]

The new urban society that emerged in Massachusetts after the Civil War changed the lives of all its citizens. The state's population increased from 1.2 million people in 1860 to 3.8 million people in 1920, a third of whom were foreign-born and more than three-quarters of whom lived in cities. Italians, French Canadians, Russian Jews, and even a small number of Chinese surged into the Bay State's cities and towns, nearly eradicating its predominant Yankee features. Boston, the "Athens of America," whose citizens gave birth to the state's first anti–capital punishment movement in the 1830s, had become the nation's fourth largest manufacturing city by 1870. Captains of industry, workers, and a mix of ethnic groups in dozens of other manufacturing towns throughout the state competed for a share of the new wealth generated by the growth of industry. The scramble for wealth sometimes led to violent clashes, but the great irony of the era was that murder rates in Massachusetts fell below their antebellum peak. By the turn of the century full employment, aggressive policing, and a sharp drop in liquor consumption combined to push down the rate of violent crime and murder.[6]

The number of indictments for murder in Massachusetts relative to the state's population rose sharply from 1865 to 1875 but fell steadily each decade thereafter until 1920. The average annual number of murder indictments from 1876 to 1886 was twenty-one. From 1887 to 1897 the average yearly number of murder indictments fell to sixteen, and from 1900 to 1910 a mere eleven murder indictments were recorded each year. The Massachusetts Attorney General's office recorded fourteen murder indictments in 1892 (including Lizzie Borden), but only nine homicide indictments in

1895, and eight in 1896. The number of indictments increased to fourteen in 1900 and jumped to thirty-three in 1920, signaling a new trend. Measured by recorded indictments, the state's murder rate stood at a miniscule 0.5 per 100,000 people in 1900 and 1.2 per 100,000 people in 1920. From 1860 to 1920 just forty-seven men were executed for murder. Opponents of capital punishment argued that given the low number of murders and the small number of convicted murderers executed, the death penalty could be abolished without threatening social stability. Proponents of the death penalty pointed out, however, that a disproportionate number of the men executed for murder after the turn of the century were recent immigrants. For advocates of capital punishment that data raised the specter of an increase in lawless violence and argued for the death penalty.[7]

Massachusetts murder rates before 1920 were remarkably low, but outside the South they were not strikingly unusual. Murder rates fell sharply in many northeastern cities and states and the number of legal executions in the United States relative to population also declined during 1885 to 1904. Philadelphia's murder rate dropped from 3.2 per 100,000 population between 1860 and 1880 to 2.5 per 100,000 population between 1881 and 1901. In New York State, the number of murder convictions relative to population declined steadily from the Civil War to the turn of the century. Still, despite solid evidence of a decline in homicides, many Americans believed the number of murders was increasing. This belief led reformers such as New York's Charles Loring Brace and Boston's Moorfield Storey to urge state legislators to use their power to streamline criminal trials, to lengthen prison sentences, and to speed up the execution process to control urban violence. Storey spoke of a "well-defined class of people who live by plundering their fellow men," and "sections of the country where murder is committed with almost no risk of punishment." Neither Brace nor Storey named particular ethnic groups as being part of the "dangerous classes" they blamed for increasing crime and violence, but since they placed these men and women in urban environments, the implication that immigrant groups were to blame was clear.[8]

In fact, throughout the late nineteenth and early twentieth centuries the roster of convicted murderers was more diverse than in the earlier part of the nineteenth century, but the motivation for homicide in Massachusetts remained much the same. Generally, men and women were killed for money, or love, or lust. The majority of convicted murderers executed by the state were young unskilled men who robbed their employers or friends or neighbors of a few dollars and murdered them to cover up the crime. (The state's first armed robbery–murder by a criminal gang occurred in 1910.) A nearly equal number of men murdered women or young girls. From 1866 to 1923 a dozen men were convicted and executed for murdering their wives and four men were put to death for raping and murdering young girls. By a slight margin more victims were murdered with guns than with axes, but strangulation, fists, and clubs topped the list of lethal means chosen by murderers who were ultimately executed for their crime. After the turn of the century, Italians, Poles, and Chinese living in urban areas were likely to use guns to settle their disputes. A sizable number of homicides occurred in rural areas, but a majority of Massachusetts murder victims were killed in a manufacturing town or in the city of Boston.[9]

From 1836 to 1898 Massachusetts, like almost all other states that imposed the death penalty, executed convicted murderers by hanging them in a hidden corner of the county jail yard. In the latter year, Massachusetts followed New York's lead and adopted the electric chair, an allegedly instantaneous and more humane method of execution, and mandated that all executions take place at the Massachusetts State Prison in Charlestown, rather than in the county of conviction. The Supreme Court of the United States had held *In re Kemmler* (1890) that "the infliction of death by electricity" did not violate the Eighth Amendment's prohibition against cruel and unusual punishment. Still, when Luigi Storti was sentenced to death by electrocution for the murder of his North End roommate, he argued that the electric chair constituted "cruel or unusual" punishment and, therefore, violated Article 26 of the Massachusetts Declaration of Rights. With characteristic brusqueness, Chief Justice Oliver Wendell Holmes Jr. dismissed the argument. "The suggestion that the punishment of death, in order not to be unusual," Holmes wrote in 1901 just prior to his appointment to the Supreme Court of the United States, "must be accomplished by molar rather than by molecular motion seems to us a fancy unwarranted by the constitution." Holmes also brushed aside Storti's "hint at argument based on mental suffering." Storti's "suffering is due not to its being more horrible to be struck by lightening than to be hanged with the chance of slowly strangling, but to the general fear of death. The suffering due to that fear the law does not seek to spare. It means that it shall be felt."[10]

In the years before the SJC accepted as constitutional death by high voltage, the Massachusetts legislature made other changes in capital procedure. Prompted by John Webster's controversial trial, lawmakers changed arrest procedure. It had been widely reported at the time of Webster's arrest that the police had tricked him. When he was taken into custody on the evening of November 30, 1849, following the discovery of body parts in his Harvard Medical School laboratory, a police officer went to Webster's Cambridge home to arrest him for the murder of George Parkman. The officer deliberately did not tell Webster he was under arrest. Rather, the officer asked Webster for his help in making another search of the medical school where Parkman was last seen alive. "Under this pretense," the *Boston Daily Bee* reported, the police "took [Webster] to Boston in a carriage." En route, the officer and Webster chatted casually about Parkman's disappearance. Webster later stated that he "was in doubt whether [he] was under arrest." But his doubt vanished when the carriage stopped at the Leverett Street jail. When Webster stepped inside the jail, officials abruptly arrested him for the murder of Parkman. "What me," he blurted out and appeared "completely bewildered," a state of mind the police hoped to exploit by hurrying him from the jail to his Harvard laboratory, where he was asked to identify the recently discovered body parts. The technique was designed to shock Webster and cause him to say something incriminating.[11]

Webster said nothing that helped the jury convict him, although the *New York Tribune* thought Webster's silence damaged his assertion of innocence and should have convinced the public of his guilt. The *Tribune* condemned those people in Massachusetts who believed Webster was guilty of murder but should not be hanged. "If men have no doubt of his guilt, believe in hanging, and such is the law," the paper asked, "why not carry it out in this case?" Just as poor men convicted of murder are sent to the gallows, Webster must be hanged. "If it is wrong and too severe, it is because the Law is wrong."[12]

Eight years after Webster's controversial execution the Massachusetts legislature changed the law governing arrest and punishment for murder. It enacted a law restricting the use of duplicitous arrest techniques and another dividing murder into degrees. Although the 1858 law failed to close completely the loophole that allowed the police to dupe suspects in the hope of obtaining incriminating statements, it did prohibit an arresting officer from lying to the accused about the reason he or she was being detained or arrested. The accused was to be informed of "the true ground on which the arrest is made." A police officer who gave a suspect misinformation or refused to answer an accused person's questions was subject to a heavy fine or up to one year's imprisonment. Under this new law, however, police officers were still free to mislead a suspect until he or she formally had been detained or arrested.[13]

The second reform in criminal procedure enacted in the aftermath of Parkman's murder was far more sweeping. In 1858 the legislature adopted a statute establishing degrees of murder, a reform that aligned Massachusetts with a dozen other states. As defined at common law, murder was the killing of a human being with malice aforethought. The existence of malice distinguished murder from manslaughter. The difference had been at the heart of Webster's postconviction defense. In his confession, as reported in the *Boston Courier* July 20, 1850, Webster claimed that Parkman had shouted insults at him and threatened to have him fired from his Harvard position if he did not immediately repay the money he owed. "Excited to the highest degree of passion," Webster said, he grabbed a thick wooden stick lying on the counter and struck Parkman. He stated that the single blow was delivered "with all the force that passion could give, and that he did not think, nor know, nor care, where he should hit him, nor how hard, nor what the effect would be." By contending there was no premeditation or malice Webster sought to convince the Committee on Pardons that he was guilty of nothing more than manslaughter and, therefore, his death sentence for murder should be commuted to life imprisonment. But, as Leonard Levy points out, Webster's ploy, if believed, "would have rebutted the inference of premeditation, but not of malice, because he had killed on the provocation of mere words." At trial, Chief Justice Lemuel Shaw had explained the rule of law governing such a situation. "No provocation by words only, however opprobrious," Shaw told the jury, "will mitigate an intentional homicide, so as to reduce it to manslaughter."[14]

Shaw's explanation may have helped convince the jury Webster was guilty of murder, but the chief justice's argument did not undercut the widespread sympathy for Webster or convince the public that Webster's actions—as he later confessed to them—met the definition of murder. Not surprisingly, therefore, at the tail end of a legislative session that stretched into the early morning hours of March 26, 1858, the legislature changed the law of murder. The new law abandoned the common law of murder and divided the crime into two degrees. First-degree murder was defined as an offense committed with "deliberately premeditated malice aforethought, or in the commission of, or attempt to commit, any crime punishable with death or imprisonment for life; or committed with extreme atrocity or cruelty." A murder that did not fit this definition was murder in the second degree. Under the new law the jury determined the degree of murder. The punishment for a defendant found guilty of first-degree murder was death, while the punishment for a defendant found guilty of second-degree murder was imprisonment for life.[15]

Boston's *Monthly Law Reporter*, the nation's leading legal journal, praised the new law for eliminating implied malice—the doctrine that had lead to Webster's murder conviction—as "a doctrine too vague to form a part of a law on which depends the life of a human being." And with acceptance of the broad definition of second-degree murder as "murder not appearing to be in the first degree," the *Law Reporter* declared, "certainty and humanity" had been built into the criminal code and the accused granted the "benefit of the doubt."[16]

Just one year after the new law's passage, Alexander Desmarteau, a twenty-two-year-old French Canadian itinerant peddler, was tried for the rape and murder of seven-year-old Augustine Lucas, a girl being cared for by foster parents in Chicopee. Evidence showed that Desmarteau had lured the child from her home and taken her to an isolated spot near the Connecticut River, where he raped her, bludgeoned her to death, and hurled her body into the river. A jury convicted Desmarteau of first-degree murder committed with extreme atrocity and cruelty. He appealed the verdict to the full court.[17]

Before the SJC, George M. Stearns, a young, court-appointed attorney, asserted that the indictment charging Desmarteau with murder was "inconsistent, unintelligible, contradictory and insufficient." He also challenged the constitutionality of dividing murder into degrees while retaining use of the ancient common law indictment. In his opening statement, Stearns engaged the court's justices in an unprecedented dialogue. "Suppose the defendant had pleaded guilty," he asked, "for what should he have been sentenced?" Justice Pliny Merrick—who before his appointment to the bench in 1853 had served as co–defense counsel for Webster—answered: "Does not a plea of guilty admit the offence to the whole extent charged?" Of course, replied Stearns, "but that leaves open, what is the offense charged." The indictment did not charge Desmarteau with murder in the first degree, but with murder according to the common law definition, which the new statute labeled murder in the second degree. This confusion was compounded and made unconstitutional by permitting a jury to determine the degree of murder. Such a procedure violated Article 12 of the Massachusetts Declaration of Rights, which states that "no subject shall be held to answer for any crimes or offense until the same is fully and plainly, substantially and formally, described to him." Finally, Stearns argued that Desmarteau could not be found guilty of first-degree murder committed with extreme atrocity or cruelty because the indictment stated the child died instantly from blows to her head.[18]

Justice Charles A. Dewey, whose tenure on the court began in 1837, spoke for a unanimous court in rejecting Desmarteau's appeal. Dewey brushed aside the misspellings and inconsistencies in the indictment to which Stearn had called the court's attention and insisted that these mistakes did not add up to a "fatal variance." The court also dismissed Stearn's argument that the jury was obligated to give a separate verdict on each of the counts contained in the indictment. Rendering a general verdict of guilty without distinguishing between the particular counts was an ancient practice supported by Massachusetts and English authorities. Most important, Judge Dewey rejected the defense argument that to find Desmarteau guilty of murder in the first degree committed with atrocity and cruelty a jury must find that the atrocity and cruelty were premeditated. According to the court's reading of the statute, if the jury found the murder was committed with extreme atrocity or cruelty the defendant was guilty of first-degree murder. The prosecution did not need to show the cruelty was premeditated. "The mere recital of the facts that make up the history of this homicide," Dewey stated, "should silence every doubt of its being a case of most aggravated atrocity and cruelty." The trial judge's instruction to the jury on this point was correct: it was within the jury's discretion to find the defendant guilty of first-degree murder if it found the facts of the brutal rape and violent murder of the girl constituted extreme atrocity and cruelty.[19]

Although the SJC upheld the 1859 statute dividing murder into degrees and confirmed Desmarteau's death sentence, its failure to address the problems raised by the common law murder indictment's lack of specific-ity caused at least two attorneys general to fault the law. Attorney General Charles Allen believed the indictment's silence about the degree of murder with which the defendant was charged was responsible for increasing the number of murders. According to Allen's analysis, persons were more likely to commit murder because they believed they could avoid the death penalty by winning a second-degree verdict. To discourage murderers from taking advantage of the law's ambiguity, he urged the legislature to empower the grand jury to specify the degree of murder. Allen's successor, Attorney General Charles Train, interpreted the law's shortcomings differently. Train argued that since 1859, "experience has demonstrated that juries will return a verdict of guilty of murder in the second degree when there is the slightest ground for it, and sometimes when there is not." Jurors were quick to find a defendant guilty of murder in the second degree, because it did not "involve the possibility of taking the life of the prisoner." The danger that an innocent person may be executed "presses upon the jurymen with fearful power." For this reason, Train urged the legislature to amend the law dividing murder into degrees by abolishing the death penalty for first-degree murder in favor of life imprisonment without parole.[20]

The Massachusetts legislature finally adopted a short form of criminal indictment in 1899. Under the new statute, the ancient, lengthy common law form alleging the manner or means of death was scrapped in favor of a terse statement. To protect a defendant's constitutional right under Article 12 of the Massachusetts Declaration of Rights ("No subject shall be held to answer for any crimes or offense until the same is fully and plainly, substantially and formally described to him"), the law acknowledged a defendant's right to information gathered by the prosecution. The statute permitted the defendant to petition the court for an order requiring the state "to give the defendant reasonable knowledge of the nature and the ground of the crime charged."[21]

Desmarteau did not benefit from the legislature's step toward a criminal discovery rule. He was hanged in the Hampden County jail on April 26, 1861, two weeks after the Confederate attack on Fort Sumter. Eleven Massachusetts men were indicted for murder and two were executed while their neighbors fought and died to save the Union. Twenty-nine-year-old George Hersey was hanged for poisoning his pregnant lover, and the court sentenced to death James Callender, a twenty-year-old African American, for the murder of a young housewife and her two children.[22]

In the wake of the Civil War the U.S. Congress took steps to secure full civil rights for former black slaves. As one part of the government's effort, U.S. Senator Charles Sumner of Massachusetts sponsored legislation permitting criminal defendants to testify on their own behalf in federal court and extending to federal prosecutors the use of peremptory challenges. Sumner's motivation for urging passage of these changes in criminal procedure sprang from his desire to allow newly freed blacks to testify as competent witnesses and to arm federal prosecutors with the power to eliminate racially biased jurors. Congress later moved to extend these changes in federal procedure to state courts in the South. The *New York Times* endorsed the move to permit black defendants to testify, arguing in October 1865, that the "denial of the suffrage will not, of itself, be a fatal objection" to the readmission of Southern states, "but the denial to the freedman of the power to testify in court against the white man, would be a fatal objection. It strikes not at a mere civil franchise, but at a natural right—the right of protecting life and property." A few days later, the *Boston Daily Evening Transcript* stated the issue more boldly and broadly. Massachusetts not only should be willing to live by the same rules it sought to impose on the South, but it should also extend the right to testify to all criminal defendants. "Any one who loves justice," the front-page article stated, "will agree with the right of colored men to testify in the Courts of law." But, "when we insist, as in truth and justice we ought, that black men shall be admitted as witnesses in courts of law, let us insist that white men shall be admitted too." In fact, under the direction of John Quincy Adams II, the Massachusetts legislature passed a bill allowing state criminal defendants to testify in their own behalf. At the request of the accused, the 1866 law allowed a defendant to testify as a competent witness. The defendant's failure to testify, the law stated, shall not "create any presumption against the defendant."[23]

Without commenting on the law's origins, the *American Law Review* said the law should not have been passed and explained why. It undermined the presumption of innocence and weakened the defendant's protection against self-incrimination. The common law practice "was a better way of protecting the accused because there was a clear presumption of innocence and the accused could not be compelled to furnish evidence against himself." Under the new law a defendant will have no option but to testify, because "there is but one construction to be put on a refusal; and no statute can be devised that will prevent that construction from having its full force." And what if the accused is innocent, but is no angel? If he takes the stand, he will be torn to pieces by cross-examination. "He breaks down and the jury disbelieve him when he is really telling the truth, and find him guilty of the one crime of which he really is innocent." The *Review* condemned the law as potentially destructive of a defendant's rights and "demoralizing from its encouragement of perjury."[24]

Massachusetts attorney general Charles Train also condemned the change. He believed that a law allowing defendants to testify coupled with the ancient practice of allowing an unsworn prisoner to address the jury at the conclusion of a trial gave the defendant an advantage over the state. By testifying after the state had outlined its case, a prisoner would be able to tailor his or her story to counter the state's evidence. And, permitting the defendant to address the jury after closing arguments allowed the accused to appeal directly to the jury's sympathy, "which goes forth freely toward him" anyway, Train claimed.[25]

The anxiety expressed by the attorney general and by the *Review* proved to be exaggerated. Wary of facing a prosecutor's tough questions, capital defendants rarely took the stand in their own behalf. The experience of James Nicholson illustrates the pitfalls. At an 1885 trial for murdering his wife, Nicholson testified that alcohol had so befuddled his mind that he had no memory of shooting his wife or of fleeing to Canada or of using a false name while living as a fugitive in Montreal. In his closing argument to the jury, Attorney General Edgar Sherman ridiculed Nicholson's memory lapses. The jury must realize the "great inducement and the strong motive [Nicholson] has to swear falsely," Sherman began. "Although upon trial for his life, he defied the authority of the court and the power of the law, and stubbornly refused to answer" the prosecutor's questions. "Does that not show," Sherman asked the jury, "the character of the man, who, when he had determined to murder his wife, would carry it out; and does not this exhibition on the witness stand confirm all the evidence of the murder?" The jury found Nicholson guilty of murder in the first degree and he was sentenced to death.[26]

Three years after Massachusetts adopted the law permitting a defendant to testify in his or her own behalf, the legislature again followed Congress's lead by allowing state prosecutors in capital trials to use a discretionary, or peremptory, challenge to eliminate a potential juror without stating a reason. The common law and Massachusetts practice had restricted the use of peremptory challenges to the defendant, as did most states before 1860. Beginning as early as 1836, however, Massachusetts prosecutors had urged the legislature to permit the state as well as the defendant to use peremptory challenges, but the legislature held firm to its belief that only a defendant should be permitted that right. The number of peremptory strikes a capital defendant was permitted to use fluctuated—from an unlimited number in 1780 to twenty on the eve of the Civil War—but Massachusetts prosecutors were permitted to challenge potential capital jurors only for cause. If a juror stated that his opposition to the death penalty was such that he would not find the defendant guilty regardless of the evidence, he was struck for cause. The 1869 law changed that fundamental principle of due process by empowering prosecutors to strike a potential capital juror suspected of harboring a bias that would cause the juror to acquit the defendant. Some critics charged that arming prosecutors with peremptory strikes in addition to allowing the state to strike for cause jurors who were conscientiously opposed to capital punishment created a jury biased in favor of the death penalty. Nearly a century passed before the courts tackled that procedural controversy.[27]

While important aspects of capital procedure were changed in the 1860s, the general routine followed by the SJC during the decades following the Civil War was not very different from the court's colonial practices. The nineteenth-century court traveled around the state holding trial court sessions in county seats and hearing appeals in Boston. For a part of the year, two of the court's seven judges traveled, sitting as trial court judges, while the other five remained in Boston to make up an appeals court. In addition to capital cases, the court had original jurisdiction of equity and divorce cases. In 1883, Judge Oliver Wendell Holmes Jr. commented at the end of his first full year on the SJC, "We are very hard worked and some of the older judges affirm that no one can do all the work without breaking down." The court produced more than four hundred opinions each year. Holmes listed "about a thousand cases" in his personal docket book in which he kept a record of the court's decisions that fell to him to write during his twenty years on the bench. The SJC's workload was reduced in 1887 when the legislature ended the court's jurisdiction over divorce, annulment, and child custody cases and four years later when it shifted responsibility for capital trials from the SJC to the lower Superior Courts.

This change in capital procedure had profound repercussions, the most important of which was the appointment of counsel by the court.[28]

The practice of appointing counsel in capital cases had roots in Massachusetts's colonial origins and was buttressed by the postrevolutionary court's commitment to republicanism. As noted earlier, the 1806 trial of William Hardy, an African American laborer, was the first reported instance in which the court appointed counsel to represent a capital defendant. At trial, Hardy was found guilty of murder, but after the verdict was announced, attorneys George Thatcher and George Blake filed a motion for arrest of judgment, based on a procedural technicality. Contrary to law, Hardy had been arraigned by a single justice. Therefore, "all proceedings had on the said indictment were illegal, being *coram non judice*, and . . . this Court cannot proceed to pass sentence of death on the said William Hardy." [29]

Speaking for a unanimous court, Chief Justice Theophilus Parsons agreed. Although Hardy had allowed the trial to proceed and had not raised an objection to the pretrial irregularity until after the jury returned a verdict of guilty, his "implied assent" to the proceeding was not enough to legitimize it. "If ever quibbling is at any time justifiable," Parsons concluded, "a man may quibble for his life." The verdict was set aside. At a new trial Hardy was found not guilty.[30]

In 1820 the court's practice of appointing counsel in capital cases was enacted into law. During the next seventy-one years the SJC appointed two lawyers—usually one senior and one junior counsel—for every murder defendant facing the death penalty who could not afford to employ counsel. More than one hundred Massachusetts attorneys "ably and faithfully defended" accused murderers, giving them their "best service gratuitously." The senior lawyers appointed by the SJC were drawn from the elite of the Massachusetts bar. From 1873 to 1883, for example, there were twenty-two capital trials in Suffolk County to which the court appointed senior counsel. A collective portrait shows that they were middle-aged college graduates with nearly twenty years of legal experience at the time they took up their assignment to defend an indicted murderer. Only seven of this group of court-appointed counsel had criminal trial experience, but all were appellate lawyers who often had appeared before the SJC on other matters. George Searle, who at one time had been partners with Franklin Pierce and Benjamin F. Butler and had written treatises on the criminal law, was the only lawyer in this group appointed to more than one capital trial during this decade. The junior counsel assigned by the court to capital cases from 1873 to 1883 were young and relatively inexperienced, but they were more likely to have graduated from college and law school than their senior partners and they already had appeared before the SJC. Four of the junior counsel who had not attended law school had read the law with a founder of the Boston Bar Association. The court's appointment of these young men marked them as a part of an emerging elite, lawyers who were on course to rise to the top of their profession.[31]

Before 1891 the demands placed on court-appointed attorneys or on the court by a murder trial were not great. Only a handful of murder cases came to trial each year. An attorney's responsibility did not begin until a few days before the defendant appeared in court, and the trial rarely lasted more than a few days. But the SJC was eager for relief from its staggering caseload. The amount of civil litigation handled by the attorney general more than doubled during the 1870s and 1880s and, despite a national trend to create intermediate appeals courts to ease the appellate burden on state supreme courts, the Massachusetts legislature chose not to follow that reform path. For that reason, Governor Alexander Rice appointed a special commission in 1876 and charged it with making recommendations for reducing the SJC's workload. Headed by Augustus L. Soule, a forty-nine-year-old Springfield lawyer elevated to the SJC by Governor Rice in 1877, the commission urged the legislature to transfer jurisdiction for capital cases from the SJC to the Superior Court. Soule's argument for this change was tactless, politically naïve, and, perhaps, offensive to the SJC. He bluntly concluded that Superior Court judges knew more criminal law than did the justices sitting on the SJC and that the current appeals process was unfair because the SJC sat both as a court of original jurisdiction and an appeals court in murder cases.[32]

Attorney General Charles Train blasted the commission's report. He opposed transferring jurisdiction for capital trials from the SJC to the Superior Court. First, he rejected the commission's claim that Superior Court judges were more familiar with criminal law. In fact, a majority of the SJC's justices had been promoted to the high court from the Superior Court. Second, he said, trying murder cases in the Superior Court would "increase the delay in capital trials," because the appeals process would be longer and more cumbersome. "As it stood, exceptions raised during a capital trial were certified immediately for review by the full court and disposed of without delay," Third, Train appealed to tradition. For more than two hundred years Massachusetts had required that the "highest crime known to the law be tried in the highest tribunal of the Commonwealth and with the solemnity due to the magnitude of the crime." Finally, Train told the legislature, "unless the time has arrived for the abolition of the death penalty, I am opposed to the change suggested."[33]

Ten years later, Attorney General Andrew J. Waterman, a lawyer with more than thirty years of experience, including eight as a prosecutor in western Massachusetts, revived the idea of eliminating the SJC's original jurisdiction for murder trials. He cautioned that the SJC's crowded docket would prevent the court from fulfilling its constitutional obligation to provide a speedy trial for an indicted murderer. Since the number of judges on the Superior Court had been increased to fourteen, trials in that court "would be much more readily obtained," and the prisoner's rights protected. As a sop to legislators who worried about the ability of Superior Court judges, Waterman proposed that three judges sit as a court for a murder trial, a "sufficient guarantee," as he put it, "of an intelligent and sound administration of the law in such cases."[34]

Governor John Q. A. Brackett endorsed Waterman's proposal in his 1890 inaugural address. Before the legislature acted on the governor's recommendation, three sitting SJC justices died, a fact that may have prompted the Joint Committee on the Judiciary to embrace the change in capital procedure. The legislature easily passed the bill and Governor William E. Russell, one of only three Democrats to hold the governor's office since the Civil War, signed it into law, June 6, 1891.[35]

The year following passage of the law, Assistant Attorney General Hosea Knowlton praised the results in the attorney general's annual report. The change, "which was regarded by many as a doubtful, if not dangerous experiment, now has been tested and approved." Not only did the Superior Court handle effectively thirteen capital cases, but also, according to Knowlton, the change from the SJC to the Superior Court had stripped murder trials of their glamour. The "superstitious deference we have paid to murder, investing the accused with a dignity and importance above the level of common criminals is wholly unnecessary to the protection of the innocent and adds to the difficulty of convicting the guilty," Knowlton claimed.[36]

While there was truth to Knowlton's assessment, he failed to address the potential long-term changes initiated by homicide's new venue. As former attorney general Train had predicted, murder convictions in the lower courts brought both a greater number of appeals and appeals of greater complexity to the SJC. In fact, in the decade after the Superior Court began to try murder cases, there were four times as many appeals of murder convictions made to the SJC than in the decade prior to 1891. At the same time, the number of exceptions made by defense attorneys at trial, and subsequently argued before the SJC, skyrocketed. Although they may have been less well trained in criminal law, the pool of attorneys from which the Superior Court appointed counsel to represent accused murderers was a much more aggressive group than the elite lawyers appointed by the SJC.[37]

Former governor John D. Long, a lawyer with more than thirty years of experience, was one of only two elite attorneys appointed by the Superior Court to defend an accused murderer. In 1892, Long and junior counsel Marcellus Coggan were asked by the trial court to defend James Trefethen, a young Boston dry-goods wholesaler indicted for the murder of Deltena Davis, a twenty-six-year-old Charlestown shopkeeper. At trial, the commonwealth built a circumstantial case against Trefethen. The district attorney argued that Trefethen had seduced Davis—"a pure New England girl, wholly unsophisticated in the ways of the world"—but refused to marry her despite her heartfelt, desperate pleas. According to Davis's mother, Deltena and Trefethen met on the evening of December 23, 1891, to decide what to do. Witnesses saw them standing together in Everett Square. When Davis failed to return home, her mother alerted the police. Three days later Davis's body was found in the Mystic River. An autopsy revealed drowning caused her death and that she was five months pregnant. Two police officers testified that on the evening Davis disappeared they saw a buggy similar to Trefethen's heading from Everett Square toward the Mystic River.[38]

Long attacked the basic presumptions of the commonwealth's case. The relationship between Trefethen and Davis had not been romantic; it was strictly business. There was no evidence to substantiate the accusation Trefethen had seduced Davis, nor that he had murdered her. In fact, no evidence supported the commonwealth's claim that Davis had been murdered. Long suggested the young woman had committed suicide.

He wanted to call to the stand Sara Hubert, a "clairvoyant medium," who would testify Davis came to her the day prior to her death and allegedly said she would commit suicide if the man whose child she was carrying did not agree to marriage. The prosecution objected to Hubert and the trial court agreed, barring her testimony as hearsay. Long reserved an exception to the court's ruling, laying the basis for an appeal. The jury found Trefethen guilty of murder in the first degree.[39]

Before the SJC Long brilliantly distinguished the SJC's ten-year-old rule on the inadmissibility of hearsay evidence on which the trial court had relied from Davis's alleged statement to Hubert. He contended that Davis's statement was made close enough to the time of her death to show her state of mind—that an unmarried pregnant woman might commit suicide. Although the court acknowledged that "this was not the law" and that there was no case "exactly like the present," Chief Justice Walbridge Field embraced Long's argument. The jury should have had the opportunity to consider whether Davis may have committed suicide. "We are of the opinion that the presiding judge erred in refusing to receive this evidence," Field concluded, "and for that reason, the verdict against Trefethen must be set aside."[40]

In September 1893, Trefethen was tried a second time for Davis's murder. Long asserted that a "simple, natural case of suicide has been bloated into a charge of murder," despite the fact that the government had not produced "one scintilla of evidence to show homicide." Although the prosecution built a circumstantial case against Trefethen and introduced witnesses who cast doubt on Hubert's claim about Davis's visit prior to her death, a jury found Trefethen not guilty.[41]

Long's success in winning a new trial for Trefethen was unmatched for more than three decades. Until 1926 no other attorney—either court appointed or privately employed by a defendant—convinced the SJC to reverse a client's death sentence. Aside from the different factual situations, there were two general reasons accounting for this long stretch without reversible error. Before 1939 the SJC lacked the power to review the facts of a capital case; it could decide only questions of law and, on such matters, the court typically deferred to a trial judge's discretionary power to make rulings about the specific application of a general legal distinction. Also, argument about the constitutional protection extended to a capital defendant was rare before the late twentieth century. Therefore, the two most common issues of law raised before the SJC involved rulings by the trial court about the admissibility of evidence or the voluntariness of defendant's confession. In both matters the SJC consistently deferred to the trial judge's rulings.[42]

A survey of the twenty-one appeals of first-degree murder convictions made to the SJC from 1892 to 1920 reveals that fourteen involved reviews of rulings made at the trial-court level on evidence and four on confessions, and one raised a constitutional issue. Every exception to a trial judge's ruling by the defendant was denied by the SJC. The SJC upheld the admissibility of evidence about long-term marital discord, of photographs of the murder scene, of ballistic tests, and of the validity of circumstantial evidence. "It is difficult in dealing with this description of evidence," Justice John Wilkes Hammond wrote about John Howard's hostility toward his wife, Ida, in *Commonwealth v. Howard* (1910), "to define, as a matter of law, the precise limits which must practically control its admission; much must be left to the discretion of the trial court." Likewise, in *Commonwealth v. Williams* (1898), Justice Holmes praised Judge Henry K. Braley's ruling admitting circumstantial evidence that money held by the victim six months earlier was probably still in his possession when he was murdered and that it was the same money held by the defendant Alfred Williams after the murder of John Gallo. "The case at the bar," Holmes wrote, "is a striking example and proof of the general rule [that] the facts in a circle support one another, when if any one were withdrawn they would all fall to the ground."[43]

Holmes also ruled, in *Commonwealth v. Chance* (1899), that incriminating statements made by John Chance to police officers following his arrest on April 20, 1898, for the murder of Charles Russell and during an examination the following morning were correctly admitted by the trial judge. Chance initially told the police he spent several hours at his girlfriend's home on the night of the murder, but he admitted that a coat found near the murder scene belonged to him. On the morning following his arrest Chance told the police he went to sleep early on the night of the murder, but that statement contradicted his girlfriend's statement that he was away from the house for some time after 8:00 P.M. On the afternoon before he was arraigned and in the evening after his arraignment police questioned Chance again. During the evening examination one of the police officers suggested to Chance that he would benefit if he "came clean." At trial, Judge Robert Bishop ruled the officer's inducement made the entire third day's examination inadmissible. Hoping to have all of Chance's statements declared inadmissible, defense attorney H. P. Harriman asked Bishop to rule that the two previous examinations were connected to the third one, and therefore, they also should be excluded. Judge Bishop refused and the defendant excepted. On appeal, Holmes held Judge Bishop's ruling "went to the extreme in its anxiety to protect the defendant's rights. If it had gone further," Holmes concluded, "it clearly would have been wrong."[44]

Four years after Holmes left the SJC for the Supreme Court of the United States the Massachusetts court heard Charles L. Tucker's appeal of his conviction for the murder of Mabel Page, a forty-one-year-old unmarried woman from Weston. Tucker asked the SJC to review eighteen defense motions denied by trial judges Edgar J. Sherman and Henry N. Sheldon. Important as the legal issues argued before the court were to the defense claim that Tucker deserved a new trial because of errors in due process, the unspoken question before the court and the dominant issue in the public mind was Tucker's guilt.

Edward Page discovered his daughter Mabel's body in her bedroom when he returned home on the afternoon of March 31, 1904. Wounds on Mabel Page's hands suggested she had tried to ward off her assailant before she succumbed to stab wounds inflicted in her stomach, chest, throat, and back. There was no sign of a sexual assault, nor did robbery initially appear to be a motive since Page's jewelry lay undisturbed on a dresser. Page's handwritten note left on a hallway table for her father suggested to police that the assailant had gained entrance to the house sometime between 11:30 A.M. and 2:00 P.M. by telling Page her brother had been injured and was in a Boston hospital. Police also found a slip of paper on the floor near Page's body on which had been written, "J. L. Morton, Charlestown, Mass."[45]

Three days after the murder, a *Boston Globe* reporter sought out Charles Tucker, an unemployed twenty-three-year-old who lived with his parents in Auburndale, a short distance from Weston. The reporter knew Tucker "spent a great deal of time down by the Charles River boathouse near the Weston Bridge" and that a year earlier Tucker's wife had drowned in the Charles River as a result of a suspicious canoeing accident. Although the water was calm and shallow, Tucker swam to shore, leaving his wife to drown in mid-stream. No charges were brought against Tucker, but in retrospect, many people suspected foul play.[46]

In an April 4 *Globe* interview, Tucker acknowledged being at the Weston Bridge about noon on March 31, roughly the time police calculated Page had been murdered. Prompted by the interview, the Massachusetts State Police questioned Tucker for several hours and four days later placed him under arrest. When police searched Tucker they found in his pocket a Canadian shield pin believed to be Page's and three broken knife pieces that when put together fit a sheath discovered under the seat of a wagon in which Tucker had ridden the day of Page's murder. Under questioning, Tucker acknowledged the sheath to be similar to one he claimed to have lost. He also admitted purposely breaking the blade, because he feared being connected with Page's murder. On June 16, flanked by attorneys Thomas and James Vahey, Tucker entered a plea of not guilty to the murder of Mabel Page. Pending trial, the court ordered Tucker held without bail in the Cambridge jail.[47]

The court also scheduled a pretrial motion hearing for December. While legal proceedings slowly got under way, the *Globe* ran several stories about the case, leading up to two articles published in September about the "Morton" slip of paper found at the murder scene. Under the headline "Battle of the Experts Bids Fair to Be One of the Most Notable in the History of Murder Cases," the Sunday *Globe* printed photos of a sample of Tucker's handwriting and the Morton slip. The article accompanying the photos included analyses of the two handwriting samples, as well as interviews with the four handwriting experts who had been employed by the commonwealth. Each expert used a different method of analysis, but they all agreed Tucker had written the Morton note. Still, a skeptical tone permeated the article and it ended by encouraging readers to form "their own impressions as to [the note's] likeness to the hand of the prisoner." A follow-up article noted that there "were countless opinions on both sides of this question," a fact, the newspaper said "excited and interested" defense attorney James Vahey.[48]

Shortly after the articles appeared a Suffolk County Superior Court found the *Globe* guilty of contempt of court. The newspaper appealed the lower court's finding after the Tucker murder trial had concluded. Before the SJC, the *Globe* contended that because the articles were published several months before Tucker's trial began no harm had been done and that the articles were true and impartial and not intended "to interfere with the due administration of justice." The court brushed aside the newspaper's defense and characterized the articles as "sensational," "highly improper," and a "gross interference with the administration of justice in an important criminal case." Moreover, it was not an acceptable defense that statements made in the articles were true or that the *Globe* had not "intended to injure either of the parties to the case or to reflect upon the dignity of the court." Readers of the articles, the court stated in June 1905, might be disqualified from sitting as jurors, making it far more difficult for the court to impanel an impartial jury. On appeal, the SJC upheld the contempt ruling and the newspaper paid a heavy fine.[49]

In fact, jury selection for Tucker's January 1905 trial had encountered no such problem. The trial court excused for cause more than a dozen potential jurors, because they "were opposed to capital punishment" and defense attorney Vahey and Attorney General Herbert Parker each used seven peremptory challenges, but no one was excused because they had formed an opinion based on the *Globe* articles. The twelve men selected ranged in age from twenty-four to sixty years and included three farmers, a shoe worker, a stonemason, a plumber, a wheelwright, a molder, a laborer, a tax collector, a police officer, and a retired clergyman. Rev. William W. Nason was impaneled even though he told the court he was "strongly opposed to capital punishment." When asked if his views would preclude his finding the defendant guilty if the evidence warranted it, Nason answered, "No, but I should require very positive proof."[50] When the twelfth juror had been accepted, Judge Sherman spoke to the jury:

> To this indictment, gentlemen, the defendant, the prisoner at the bar, has pleaded that he is not guilty, and for the trial thereof puts himself upon the country, which country you are. You are sworn to try this issue; if he is guilty, you will say so; or if he is not guilty, you will say so, and no more. Good men and true, stand fast together and hearken to your evidence.[51]

District Attorney George A. Sanderson, a heavy-set, round-faced man with a walrus mustache, opened the commonwealth's case by sketching a vivid picture of an "inoffensive and unprotected woman in her home," her horrified discovery of Tucker's cruel deceit, and his sudden murderous attack. Sanderson and Parker produced witnesses who supported the prosecution's argument that robbery was Tucker's motive for murdering Page. The district attorney contended the unemployed Tucker wanted money to finance a trip to the St. Louis World's Fair. Amy Roberts, the Page's maid, testified that ten dollars and a stickpin with a Canadian design were missing from Page's purse. Roberts identified the stickpin found in Tucker's possession at the time of his arrest as Page's. A waiter at a Lynn restaurant added that a few days after the murder Tucker had a roll of money, including a ten-dollar bill. The prosecution also introduced Tucker's admission that he had been within sight of the Page home on the day of the murder and that he had broken his knife because he feared becoming a suspect. Finally, the state's expert witnesses testified that it was Tucker's handwriting on the slip of paper found at the Page home. In his closing, Attorney General Parker admitted the absence of a clear motive, but he reminded jurors of several past horrible, inexplicable murders in which jurors had rightly found the defendants guilty. He concluded simply. Tucker's conduct "was not that of man who is innocent."

Defense attorney James Vahey attacked the prosecution's case at every point. In his opening statement he turned Tucker's admission to the police about breaking his knife from a "confession" into the understandable reaction of a young man harassed by the media and the police. Vahey, a thin, clean-shaven man with a mass of dark curly hair, produced experts and eyewitnesses to buttress his argument that "this boy cannot be guilty; it is impossible for him to have had the opportunity." Medical experts testified Tucker's knife could not have caused Page's wounds and three handwriting analysts testified it was not Tucker's handwriting on the paper slip, but Page's. Friends of Page's maid added that she had said nothing had been taken from the home and Tucker's parents told the court their son's late wife had given him a Canadian design stickpin two years earlier. Finally, Vahey, paraded before the jury witnesses who placed Tucker on the Weston Bridge at 12:15 P.M. and near his home by 12:50 that afternoon, a time frame that if accepted made it impossible for Tucker to walk to and from the Page home.

After some public ambivalence, Tucker chose not to testify in his own behalf, but he did take advantage of the customary opportunity to make an unsworn statement to the jury following closing arguments. Standing in the prisoner's cage, his dark hair parted in the middle and slicked back,

in what may have been a fatal mistake, he blamed the press for his pre-
dicament, rather than professing his innocence. "On the 31st day of March
I was just as happy as any boy could be," he began, but reporters came
to me "so much and put things in the paper about me that I actually got
frightened and done things which I did do." Trial judges Sherman and
Sheldon instructed the jury on the law following Tucker's brief statement
and just after 11:00 A.M. on January 24, 1905, the jury began its deliberations. Eight hours later it returned a verdict of guilty of murder in the first
degree. Tucker slumped forward, his body nearly doubled in half and buried his head into his folded arms resting on the front railing of the witness
cage. Vahey "staggered to the cage to try to comfort" him. For several minutes the lawyer held Tucker's head in his arms. As the jurors filed out they
kept their eyes averted from the pathetic scene.

In its follow-up, the *Globe* focused on the guilty verdict's popular reception. Only a handful of people randomly interviewed privately came to
the same opinion as the jury, the paper reported, and even they "did not
believe the evidence strong enough to warrant a conviction." Most people
were "dazed and stupefied" by the guilty verdict. An anonymous veteran
defense attorney was quoted as saying, "It is the most awful verdict I ever
heard of." But two jurors, Nason and Thomas H. Murphy, a Chelmsford
plumber, stated that not a single juror had argued for acquittal. Standing in
front of his Watertown home the day following the verdict, Vahey vowed
to appeal.

In April, judges Sherman and Sheldon denied a defense motion for a
new trial. Before the SJC five months later, Vahey argued eighteen exceptions to the trial court's rulings, four of which raised substantive questions
of law. First, Vahey argued the trial court had erred in permitting the prosecution to introduce evidence about Tucker's financial difficulties, "because the poverty of a defendant is not admissible to show a motive in him
to commit the crime with which he is charged." Second, he claimed that
the broken knife pieces found in Tucker's pocket by the police should not
have been admitted, because the search was conducted without a valid warrant. Third, he argued that Tucker's incriminating statements to the police
about breaking the knife should have been excluded; and, fourth, that the
court erred in its charge to the jury explaining the link between deliberate
premeditated malice aforethought and murder in the first degree.[52]

Writing for a unanimous SJC, sixty-nine-year-old Justice John Wilkes

Hammond overruled every defense exception. He agreed with Vahey's general point that "before the law rich and poor stand alike." But, Hammond added, specific evidence about Tucker's financial situation was properly admitted "to show that at the time of the murder there was in the [Page] house a certain amount of money and that shortly after the murder this money was in the possession of the defendant." Hammond rejected the defense claim that Tucker's constitutional rights had been infringed by the search in which the knife pieces were found. Although the search warrant the police brought to Tucker's home made no mention of a knife, Tucker's mother voluntarily invited the officers to enter and search the home. They acted on her consent and, therefore, made no use of the warrant. Even if the police were liable for a trespass against the defendant that would not be sufficient to exclude the evidence. Furthermore, Tucker's incriminating statements to the police were properly admitted. The trial court had applied the "humane practice" rule in regard to the confession's admissibility. After hearing argument from both the prosecution and the defense as to the confession's voluntariness, the trial court ruled it was admissible but left the final decision up to the jury. "It's difficult to see," Hammond wrote, "how the defendant could be harmed by having another chance given to him by the submission of the question to the jury." Finally, Hammond upheld the trial court's definition and explanation of murder in the first degree. For more than a generation, he said, Massachusetts trial courts have adhered to the meaning of the phrase "deliberately premeditated malice aforethought" initially articulated by Chief Justice Shaw in *Webster*. The charge given to the Tucker jury conformed to that model and "the defendant has no ground for a valid exception."[53]

Following the SJC's denial of Tucker's appeal, the trial court set Tucker's execution for the week of June 10, 1906. A series of desperate moves to save Tucker's life ensued. In late January, Vahey filed another motion with the trial court asking for a new trial based on recently discovered evidence showing Tucker, not Page, owned the Canadian stickpin. Judge Sherman denied the motion. Two months later, Tucker filed an application for a writ of error in the U.S. Supreme Court, arguing that his Fourth Amendment right to be secure against an unreasonable search was violated. Without comment, but in keeping with the Court's position that the Bill of Rights did not extend to state criminal proceedings, Justice John Marshall Harlan denied Tucker's plea. Two weeks later, the law firm of

Vahey, Innes, and Mansfield called on the people of Massachusetts to sign a petition urging Republican governor Curtis Guild to commute Tucker's death sentence to life imprisonment.[54]

The "monster petition," as it came to be called, made a case for the people's direct participation in the state's decision to take a human life. The petition carved out a role in death penalty proceedings for the people. A petition campaign urging commutation, the preamble stated, should not be viewed as

> a reflection upon judicial proceedings, nor as an expression by the executive branch of the government that the orderly processes of the law should not be treated with the utmost consideration. [But,] the taking of a human life is the extreme penalty of the law, and in the performance of such a solemn duty certain rights have been reserved to the people. The declaration of the right we have to life and liberty, and to the freedom of thought and speech, states only in another way the sacred duty imposed upon us all to protect the lives and liberty of others accused and in distress. In such an exigency the voice of the people can, and should, manifest itself.[55]

As expected, the effort to gather petition signatures stirred a public debate. On successive Sundays in April and May, Massachusetts clergymen used their pulpits to debate Tucker's fate as well as the need for a death penalty. Rev. Alexander Blackburn of the First Baptist Church, Salem, urged his parishioners not to sign the Tucker petition. Every signature, Blackburn claimed, will be "an invitation to crime and an invitation to anarchy." Another Baptist minister, Rev. Frederick Heath of Boston, stressed the death penalty's social purpose. "People claim that from a humane standpoint [capital punishment] should be abolished, but they do not stop to consider there is a humane side for society. The safety of our mothers, wives and children, defenseless people on the streets attacked by murderers, demands that we have capital punishment." Heath added: "The law of capital punishment is not the law of man, but of God." On the contrary, Rev. F. A. Wiggin, a Boston Unitarian, and Rev. N. L. Bailey, a Peabody Baptist, believed the police and justice system had rushed to judgment. Even if Tucker were guilty, they said, a modern civilized society has "no right to take life."[56]

The Massachusetts House also took up the death penalty issue.

Although similar bills had been routinely defeated, Salem representative Thomas L. Davis sought to use the controversy over Tucker's conviction to win passage of a bill calling for a constitutional amendment abolishing capital punishment. Among other arguments, Davis and his supporters contended that a diseased brain might have driven Tucker to murder. By this reasoning, he was not capable of exercising free will, and therefore, there was no justification for state retribution. Opponents of the bill rejected this scientific explanation in favor of a moral argument. Several legislators labeled Tucker a "degenerate." In addition to talk about the suspicious circumstances in which Tucker's first wife died, there also were rumors that his teeth marks had been found on the body of his wife and the body of Mabel Page. For the most part, however, the bill's opponents stuck to familiar reasons for retaining the death penalty, including a need to deter violent crime and a state's right to take the life of a murderer. Tucker's murder of a "defenseless woman"—if no other crime—demanded the death penalty. The House easily defeated Davis's bill.[57]

On May 22, the petition asking Governor Guild to commute Tucker's death sentence to life imprisonment was delivered to the Massachusetts State House rolled up in a large, specially-made wooden box. Said to measure more than a mile in length and signed by 116,555 Massachusetts men and women (80,860 men and 35,695 women), plus an additional 10,000 people from outside the state, the petition was unceremoniously left at the governor's office. The usual procedure for a commutation hearing—and certainly that is what Vahey had in mind when he launched the petition campaign and enlisted prominent spokespeople—was for an unrestricted discussion before the governor and the Council, a ten-member elected body with statutory and advisory powers. But, with the approval of the SJC, Governor Guild, a forty-six-year-old former newspaper publisher, sidestepped the Council in favor of a hearing restricted to the presentation of new evidence before he and the two original trial judges. Because judges Sherman and Sheldon previously had ruled three times on the evidence, this novel arrangement offered Tucker little hope for success.[58]

For twelve hours on Tuesday, June 5, defense attorney Vahey and former Attorney General Parker squared off once again, this time at the State House. "The time has come," Parker began, "indeed, the time has passed when ... the presumption of innocence that surround and protect everyone accused has been torn from [Tucker] by the weight of truth." Anticipating that Vahey's plea for commutation of Tucker's death sentence would focus on the revised testimony of the medical examiner, Dr. F. A. Harris, Parker worked to minimize its impact. Was the testimony Harris gave at trial incorrect, or is the testimony he now gives incorrect? Aside from Harris's peace of mind, does it matter? Harris was but one of five experts who testified at trial that a single-bladed knife like the broken one found in Tucker's pocket caused Miss Page's fatal wounds. If all the evidence but Harris's revised opinion is set aside, Parker asked, "who shall sleep within the borders of this commonwealth serene tomorrow night? Where shall the rights of life and the safety of life be preserved?" Finally, Parker dismissed the monster petition and the democratic argument it represented. To decide Tucker's fate on the basis of a "popular, irresponsible outcry and not by steadfast adherence to the law" would be a grave mistake that would seriously undermine law and order.[59]

"After a long and weary trial of this case a verdict was obtained," Vahey began, "but the verdict has never satisfied the people of this commonwealth." An "overwhelming multitude of the people in this commonwealth believe Tucker to be innocent." The people believe the Tucker jury was wrong and that it is the governor's responsibility to right that wrong by commuting his death sentence to life imprisonment, he said. Such an act of mercy would not weaken the rule of law, but strengthen it. But there also was a substantial reason for the governor to act, according to Vahey. At trial, Harris had testified that a single-edged knife had caused Page's fatal wound and the other medical experts deferred to his opinion. At the commutation hearing, however, Harris offered proof that only a double-edged knife could have caused Page's death. To Vahey, the conclusion to be drawn from this new evidence seemed obvious: Harris's initial mistake had denied Tucker a fair trial and Guild should spare the prisoner's life.[60]

Just before midnight, two days after the hearing, Governor Guild announced he was not going to commute Tucker's death sentence. The governor's report to the people of Massachusetts was full and uncompromising. Before making his fateful decision Guild conducted his own investigation, studied the official record, and probed Tucker's character. Guild walked from Weston Bridge to the Page home and slipped Tucker's reconstructed knife through the slit in Mabel Page's bloodstained corset. Both exercises helped convince the governor of Tucker's guilt. Guild also satisfied himself that Tucker's right to due process—a fair trial and appellant review of legal questions—had been upheld. Skilled and dedicated legal counsel had represented Tucker at trial and the postconviction appeals process had included review by the trial court, the SJC, and the Supreme Court of the United States. Tucker also had another opportunity to introduce reasonable doubt at his commutation hearing. No authority wavered. "Every decision handed down by every judicial authority to whom disputed questions of law have been referred," Guild wrote, "has affirmed the correctness of the rulings in this case."[61]

If justice was served, what about mercy? The usual reasons argued for mercy, according to the governor, were youth, extreme provocation, or a previous blameless life. "No such plea can be entered" for Tucker. He is not a boy, but a young man at an age at which others have distinguished themselves either in public or private employment. There was no provocation for his murderous assault. Neither Mabel Page nor any of her family had ever harmed Tucker or any member of his family. Tucker's "miserable habit of life"—a series of immoral offenses allegedly including a sexual relationship with a woman on the day of Page's murder—also barred him from mercy. The governor also implicitly gave credence to the rumors about Tucker's aberrant sexual behavior. Tucker could not contain his passions "within the bounds established by nature."

Finally, Guild made three general points about capital punishment. The death penalty, he said, ensures the safety of every citizen, but it is particularly necessary for the protection of "women's chastity." Also, the people had no direct role in determining who could be executed. Referring to the monster petition, the governor insisted that "irresponsible agitation cannot be substituted for law and order in this commonwealth." Finally, sounding like a seventeenth-century Puritan, Guild told the people that Tucker's fate following his slide into immorality would "serve to warn the youth of our Commonwealth tempted by the allurements of vice to ignoble life, that the wages of sin is death."

Three days after Guild's stern report, at twelve minutes past midnight June 11, 1906, Tucker walked quickly and indifferently to the electric chair. Before he turned to sit he quietly read a brief statement asking for forgiveness. He tightly shut his eyes and sat down. Working quickly six men strapped him into the "grim engine of destruction." Death was instantaneous.

The incremental changes made in criminal procedure during the last half of the nineteenth century created a more elaborate and sophisticated due process structure and extended greater protection to capital defendants. The legislature and the SJC added to a convicted murderer's ancient right to an attorney and to the use of peremptory challenges, the right of a defendant to testify in his or her own behalf, and greater safeguards against the prosecution's use of a defendant's improperly obtained confession. At the same time, the legislature armed the state with peremptory challenges, allowing the prosecution to create a "death qualified" jury, and shifted murder jurisdiction to the lower Superior Courts. The latter change seems to have benefited the state. With a single exception, well into the twentieth century the SJC refused to overturn a trial court verdict on a question of law. In part for this reason, defendants rarely raised constitutional questions and had no success when they did, as Tucker's effort to use the Fourth Amendment made clear.

The fear stimulated by the Tucker case helped sweep away the rational arguments made for his innocence, for the abolition of the death penalty, or for a sentence of life imprisonment rather than death. Governor Guild cast the death penalty as part of a chivalric code buttressed by due process. The protection afforded Tucker by due process allowed Guild and others to argue that he had received a fair trial and, therefore, could be fairly executed.

While the protection of women ranked high as a justification for the death penalty, many Massachusetts residents believed immigrants posed the most serious threat to law and social order. When, about a year after Tucker's execution, a Chinese gang was tried for gunning down several of its rivals on the streets of Boston, immigration and the death penalty were linked in the public mind.

For centuries Anglo-American law had prided itself on balancing the contest between the government and the accused by restraining official power. The procedural reforms adopted by states after the Civil War sought to curb state power in the name of equality. Progressives argued that procedures to protect the individual are necessary to restrain governments who held absolute power, but they are unnecessary in a modern society where constitutional constraints are the rule. In short, critics of criminal procedure did not perceive due process—fair and reasonable rules of law consistently applied—as the means by which governmental power was restrained and a defendant's liberty safeguarded. From their perspective due process tilted the balance in favor of the criminal defendant and threatened social and political stability. The sharp increase in the number of reported murders after 1920 and the courts' narrow interpretation of due process ended the progressive debate about criminal procedure. More than four decades passed before the Supreme Court of the United States initiated a new effort to align criminal procedure and individual liberty by expanding due process.

───── FIVE ─────

A "TONG WAR" AND THE SECOND EFFORT TO ABOLISH THE DEATH PENALTY

Capital punishment for murder was under attack at the turn of the twentieth century in Massachusetts. Although some feared that non-English-speaking immigrants pouring into the state were especially prone to violence, a campaign to abolish the death penalty led by the Anti-Death Penalty League had at various times won support from Attorney General Hosea Knowlton, Governor Eugene Foss, dozens of legislators, and a galaxy of religious and social leaders. Together with the controversial execution of Charles Tucker in January 1906, a rash of murders in 1903 and 1907 in Boston's Chinatown splintered this fragile coalition. Fueled in part by anti-Chinese sentiment, proponents of capital punishment reasserted the state's right to execute convicted murderers.

Everything about the capital trials of the Chinese defendants was unique. The five victims and twelve defendants all were Chinese, and all were members of two warring tongs, or secret societies. Wong Chung and Charlie Chin were charged with homicide in 1903, found guilty and sentenced to life in prison. Just eight years later both men were pardoned. Then, in what the *Boston Globe* termed "the most remarkable and peculiar trial for murder ever known in Massachusetts," the state tried ten Chinese men for murder, more defendants than had been tried at once before or since 1908. With few exceptions, the defendants and nearly all the witnesses spoke and understood only Chinese. At the conclusion of weeks of contradictory testimony, interrupted by the illness of a juror and the death of one of the defendants, the *Globe* concluded that neither the prosecution nor the defense had told the truth. Nevertheless, the jury quickly found the defendants guilty as charged. On March 8, 1908, the court sentenced all nine men to death. Remarkably, the trial court overturned the verdict for four men, and following a string of appeals, two other defendants had their sentences commuted to life in prison. The state executed Min Sing, Leong Gong, and Hom Woon, the first time in the commonwealth's history that a Chinese person was put to death in the electric chair and the first time that more than one person was executed on the same day. Hundreds of protesters joined Senator James Vahey in condemning "this awful legal tragedy," while others cheered the "power of American law and the swift certainty of punishment" that it was said would "suppress defiant alien lawlessness."[1]

In addition to highlighting the debate over capital punishment, the Chinese murder trials focused public attention on the entire legal process leading to an execution. The trials plumbed the depths of anti-Chinese feeling and raised anew questions about the relationship between the exclusion of Chinese immigrants and the development of commercial relations between the United States and China. A history of violence between rival tongs, charges of police brutality and corruption, and the dread of miscegenation also helped to form a dense web connecting violence and legitimacy. In addition to anti-Chinese prejudice, the rise of Boston ethnic politics and a separatist Roman Catholic subculture converged after 1909, causing the Anti-Death Penalty League to collapse.[2]

Chinese laborers had been brought to Massachusetts beginning in 1870. Calvin T. Sampson, a North Adams manufacturer, was determined to break the shoemakers' union, the Secret Order of St. Crispin. For this reason, he contracted with a San Francisco agent to bring seventy-five Chinese workers to North Adams to replace the striking Crispins. Workingmen throughout the state were aroused. A "large and enthusiastic meeting" was held in Boston's Tremont Temple in the summer of 1870. At the end of a long day of speeches, the workingmen resolved to launch their own political movement, to avoid being "reduced to the Chinese standard of rice and rats." However, an economic depression, not organized labor's militancy, ended Sampson's use of Chinese workers. The number of unemployed American laborers willing to work for less than the wages demanded by the Crispins jumped dramatically. By 1875 only a handful of Chinese workers remained in North Adams; most returned to China or to San Francisco when their original three-year contract expired.[3]

However limited, Sampson's success encouraged other employers in New England to use Chinese laborers. A few dozen Chinese were brought to Boston to help meet the demand for laborers to rebuild the city after the devastating fire of 1872. Initially, the Chinese workers squatted in tents near the corner of Harrison Avenue and Beach Street, a previously undeveloped wasteland. During the next several decades the number of Chinese people living in the area grew slowly, despite Congress's enactment of a series of restrictive immigration laws. By 1902, when the final Chinese Exclusion Act was passed, there were about six hundred people living in Chinatown, 0.01 percent of the population of Boston. The men worked in restaurants and laundries scattered throughout greater Boston, as well as in Chinatown.[4]

Aside from the rudimentary relationship established between middle-class customers and Chinese businessmen, all but a few Chinese were isolated from English-speaking Boston. Only one Chinese man was qualified to vote; only a tiny number were able to speak English; and a mere handful adopted American dress. Likewise, most Bostonians had only occasional, and primarily negative, glimpses of Chinese culture. Besides Chinese New Year celebrations, opium dens, sexually aggressive Chinese males coveting white women, an absence of family values, gambling, gang violence, and a "peculiar legal cunning" were the subjects most often covered by the press. Chinatown was referred to factitiously as the "unknown" or "Celestial kingdom," or simply, "the colony," by Boston newspapers and public officials. When Judge William Emmons became Boston police commissioner in 1903, the *Boston Globe* described his tour of Chinatown as though he were visiting a foreign country, a place at once exotic, repugnant, and dangerous. Escorted by two veteran officers, Emmons ventured into a restaurant, where—the reporter sarcastically noted—he "withstood the temptation of the delicious food," stepped into a gambling room, and spied a dark, half-hidden building in a narrow alley-way where "Chinamen gather to smoke the forbidden opium." At the conclusion of his tour, the commissioner stated that he would not tolerate illegal activities by anyone, anywhere in the city.[5]

In fact, Emmons apparently made a corrupt bargain with the Hip Sing tong. In exchange for information about illegal activities conducted by the On Leong tong, the Boston police left Hip Sing alone. Throughout the summer and fall of 1903, for example, the police arrested scores of On Leong tong members for gambling but not a single member of Hip Sing. The tactic led directly to violence. While thousands of people lined

Federal Street to watch Boston's Ancient and Honorable Artillery Company parade with the London Honourables, On Leong retaliated against Hip Sing by murdering Wong Yak Chung in Chinatown. On Leong's so-called hatchet man, Wong Chung, was arrested running from the scene of the crime. The police then swept though Chinatown, rounding up other suspects. When the men were being led into the Pemberton Square police station, someone shouted, "Get the Chink murderers!" One of the suspects, Charlie Chin, was charged with murder. He emerged from police custody a few hours later. His face was covered with bruises and his nose was broken. The police claimed that members of Hip Sing had beaten Chin before the police arrested him. Chin said the police beat him.[6]

This bit of reportorial candor was unusual. For the most part, Boston newspapers used the supposed cultural and racial shortcomings of Chinese to frame their stories. Chinese were assumed to be dishonest, crafty, money grubbing, profoundly ignorant, and naturally violent, a stereotype white Bostonians routinely used to rationalize their own actions toward Chinese or to explain why Chinese acted as they did. For example, although the police acknowledged their part in intensifying the rivalry between the tongs by taking sides in their struggle and admitted they had been warned that a "tong war" was about to begin, Captain Lawrence Cain, a police spokesman, shrugged off responsibility for the murder by using a racial stereotype. "Those Chinamen are such liars," he declared, "We couldn't believe half they told us." That the Chinese in police custody were able to employ lawyers also was fit into a negative racial stereotype. The "array of legal talent that rushed" to the courthouse to represent Chinese suspects was paid for either by an individual's slavish devotion to work or by friends pooling their resources. Neither strategy was perceived as American: the first was presented as antifamily and the second as the ill-gotten fruit of racial solidarity. Finally, the story of the day's violent events was concluded with an anecdote meant to convey how ludicrous Chinese were. When Wong Chung was being interrogated he allegedly refused to sit down in a chair. "He thought he was being put into the electric chair," the *Globe* snickered, "and supposed he was going to be executed forthwith for the murder."[7]

About a week after the murder of Wong Chung, U.S. Immigration authorities, U.S. marshals, and more than fifty Boston police officers swooped down on Chinatown. Hundreds of Chinese who were unable to produce on-the-spot a certificate of identification as required by the Chinese Exclusion Act of 1882 were arrested. The police went door-to-door, dragging undocumented Chinese from their homes, herding them into wagons, and speeding them to the courthouse. Huddled together in the courtroom, some of the frightened men had to be propped up while they stood before the magistrate.[8]

White superiority or Chinese inferiority was an implicit theme in the coverage of the roundup. Three brief anecdotes illustrate this tendency. One suspect, whose "bright face had unmistakable evidence of Caucasian blood and good breeding," according to the *Globe*, told the police in "impeccable English" that he lived in New York City. Because of his appearance and style, he was believed and released. In contrast, those Chinese who were unable to speak English were so confused "they forgot their names." Another suspect's wife, who was white, angrily shouted at him and at the police. Her husband, Yee Koon, cowered in his chair, but the police merely laughed at the woman's ranting. The *Globe* also hinted there was an illicit connection between the jailed Chinese and the white people who owned property near Chinatown and who provided bail. The underlying assumption was that a white person would not post bail for a Chinese unless there were a hidden motive.[9]

The Chinese had some public support within the white community. Colonel Stephen Nickerson, Boston vice counsel for China, called the arrests and the manner in which they were made "an outrage." Nickerson condemned police "brutality," called for reparations for Chinese injured during the raid, and pointed out that the law required that persons have a "reasonable opportunity" to produce their certificates of identification. While Nickerson and his allies were genuinely concerned about protecting the legal rights of Chinese, they also were motivated by the hope for greater access to the China market and the fear that riding roughshod over Chinese in the United States would jeopardize the dream of huge profits. U.S. Senator George Frisbie Hoar, of Massachusetts, had opposed the Chinese Exclusion Acts for this very reason. Predicting that trade with China would bring "hundreds of millions a year" into the Northeast, Hoar warned against offending China. But, however popular Hoar's argument may have been with northeastern manufacturers, anti-Chinese sentiment remained strong. To guard against the possible adverse effects of racial bias, Nickerson was in the courtroom on November 30, 1903, when Wong Chung and Charlie Chin were put on trial for murder.[10]

Opening arguments by the defense and the prosecution were sharply contradictory. Defense counsel M. J. Creed insisted his clients were innocent and that an agent of the Hip Sing tong murdered Wong Yak Chung. Creed argued that Chung shot only in self-defense and that the Hip Sing framed Chin, a plot in which the police were complicit. Assistant District Attorney John McLaughlin told the jury that credible witnesses saw the two defendants at the scene of the crime and that when police officers arrested the two men they were armed, Chung with a pistol from which several shots had been fired and Chin with a hatchet. McLaughlin's argument was substantiated by three young white men and by two police officers: Augustine Gale, Russell Anthony, and James Clark identified Chung as the person they saw firing a revolver as he walked across Harrison Avenue toward Wong Yak Chung; officer Farrell told the jury that Chung was carrying a gun and was wearing an armored vest when he ran from the scene of the murder; officer Brooks added that he saw Chin toss aside a hatchet as he ran away. Finally, McLaughlin contended that both Chung and Chin had confessed while they were under police custody.

Chung and Chin took the stand in their own defense. Chung maintained he was walking casually across Harrison Avenue when someone began shooting. To protect himself, he returned fire. When asked why he was wearing an armored vest when he was arrested, Chung answered that he feared for his life because Hip Sing had threatened to kill him. Chin claimed he was in a restaurant eating supper when he heard shots. When he ran into the street, someone shouted to him to pick up a hatchet that was lying on the sidewalk. Just as he did so, officer Brooks ran toward him. Chin added that he heard a wounded man say Tow Kang shot him. Two defense witnesses corroborated Chin's story about Tow Kang, whom attorney Creed identified as "a recognized and dreaded agent of the infamous Hip Sing society."

In his closing statement, McLaughlin insisted that the government's case "was not affected by any question of race prejudice." The bullets fired from Chung's revolver were consistent with those that killed Wong Yak Chung. Chin was clutching a hatchet, proof that he was part of a murder plot. Finally, the district attorney charged that On Leong had not only paid for the defense attorneys but provided witnesses "who had been paid to go to court to testify falsely."

Charles W. Bartlett, a veteran criminal lawyer, made the closing statement for the defendants. He blasted the way in which the Boston police had handled the investigation, beginning with their withholding evidence. All of the weapons and spent cartridges from the crime scene had not been produced. Everyone agreed dozens of shots were fired. Yet, only those shells matching Chung's gun were introduced into evidence. Furthermore, the police were too slow in gathering evidence. Wong Yak Chung's body lay on the sidewalk for fifteen or twenty minutes before the police began to search for evidence. That the victim did not have a revolver when his body was carted away to the morgue cannot be taken to mean he did not have a gun when the shooting began. Bartlett also denounced Chin's treatment by the police, while he was "supposed to be under the protection of the law." Finally, Bartlett asked, why didn't the police make any attempt to arrest Tow Kang, whom several eyewitnesses identified as the gunman? The implication of Bartlett's argument was unmistakable: the Boston police were complicit in a murderous plot hatched by Hip Sing.

The jury apparently was untroubled by the possibility that either police corruption or racial prejudice played a part in the proceedings and had no difficulty sorting out the conflicting testimony or the tangled tong rivalry. After eating dinner, the jury deliberated just forty-five minutes to find both defendants guilty of murder in the second degree. Chin, who understood English, seemed shocked by the verdict, but Chung showed no emotion when told of his fate by a translator. Judge Lloyd E. White brought his first murder trial to a close by sentencing Chung and Chin to life imprisonment and by agreeing to hear defense motions on January 16, 1904.

Bartlett began his argument for a new trial by expressing his "surprise and dismay" that the court had departed from its "old custom" and allowed the jury to "go wandering about during a trial." Specifically, Bartlett contended that while the trial was in progress one juror said publicly that he was ready to convict Chung and Chin "on their looks." This same juror was an army deserter and a convicted felon and should have been disqualified from serving on the jury, Bartlett argued. Judge White rejected the motion, adding "counsel could try the case every two weeks in the year and not find a jury that would not convict Wong Chung." Bartlett promptly filed an appeal with the Supreme Judicial Court.

Chief Justice Marcus P. Knowlton, who was promoted to the center seat in 1902, delivered the court's unanimous opinion upholding Judge White's ruling denying Chung and Chin a new trial. The only issue addressed by the court was that of the juror's previous criminal record. Neither the juror's alleged desertion nor his felony conviction necessarily barred him from jury service. The juror may have been listed as a deserter, Knowlton reasoned, but he had not been found guilty of desertion by an official tribunal, as the law required. Therefore, he had not lost his rights as a citizen. Even the juror's admission of desertion before Judge White at the motion hearing would not automatically disqualify him, Knowlton wrote. It was within the trial judge's discretion to ask about the circumstances of the desertion and then to make a judgment about the juror's fitness to serve. Likewise, the juror's felony conviction would not necessarily strip him of his civil rights. After completing his punishment, the board of election commissioners may lawfully choose to place a former criminal on the jury list. Defense counsel is correct that this procedure is contrary to the common law, Knowlton acknowledged. "But," he noted, "in this Commonwealth it is not the law that persons convicted of a crime shall be permanently deprived of their civil rights. Our legislation, more humane and charitable than the law of early times, recognizes the possibility of repentance and reformation." Finally, Knowlton argued, the juror should have been challenged before the trial began. The defense has a responsibility "for the proper protection of their own rights. . . . Our system provides challenges of jurors by the parties . . . which may be peremptory as well as for cause." If an unqualified juror manages to slip through this system, the defendant may ask for a new trial, but as with other such motions, it is within the trial judge's discretion to grant it or not. "It would be most unfortunate," Knowlton concluded, echoing Judge White's candid remark about the presumed guilt of the defendants, "if for an accidental error or omission hardly more than technical, it should be necessary to set aside a correct verdict."[11]

Two Chinese high commissioners and their delegation visited Boston eighteen months after Wong Chung and Charlie Chin's appeal was denied. For three days in February 1906, the business elite's desire to gain greater access to the China market overwhelmed the usual expressions of anti-Chinese sentiment. The visiting Chinese were lavishly entertained

and shamelessly courted. Governor Curtis Guild welcomed the high commissioners and escorted them and their large entourage to the Somerset
Hotel, where Mayor John F. Fitzgerald waited. A quiet lunch with Harvard
president Charles Eliot was meant to prepare the Chinese for the next
day's hectic pace.

A special train carrying the Chinese delegation left Boston for Lawrence and Lowell on the morning of February 12. On board were politicians, some Chinese students studying at Harvard, and, most important,
officers of the area's largest textile mills. In Lawrence, the Chinese were
given a tour of Hamilton Mills, where they were shown cotton cloth manufactured for export to China. A group of female workers presented the
Chinese with an imperial red flag on which a golden fire-breathing dragon
had been stitched. A sumptuous lunch and more factory tours filled out
the day's schedule.

The following day, the Chinese toured Harvard, Wellesley College, and
Boston's historic sites. The main event of the day was an evening banquet
filled with speeches. Governor Guild opened the oratory by stressing the
importance of "trade relations between the United States and China," a
theme to which each successive speaker returned with some variation.
President Eliot placed the China trade in a broad historical perspective.
Mayor Fitzgerald was more specific: "We in Boston have not forgotten the
benefits of our early Chinese trade," and we "have high hopes for future
profits," he added. It was left to Amory Lawrence, president of the mer-
chants' association, to link economics and politics. Looking at the high
commissioners, he boasted of the "substantial sale in China of cotton
goods manufactured in the mills you have visited" and expressed the hope
that "every case of misunderstanding and ill feeling may be adjusted" so
that more business might be accomplished.

The plans for reinvigorating the China trade and for ending ill feeling
came to nothing. National and global economic forces steadily undermined the textile industry in the Northeast and harsh U.S. immigration
laws damaged political relations between China and the United States.
Likewise, within Massachusetts the relationship between Chinese and
whites was pockmarked by fear of miscegenation, hostility, and violence.
Over the next several months following the high commissioners' visit,
for example, there were critical stories about marriages between Chinese

men and white women, a lurid account of a New York brothel into which young, white women supposedly were enticed by Chinese men, a matter-of-fact statement by Boston police that Chinese men attended Christian Sunday schools only so that they might "become acquainted with the white women who conduct the classes," and alarming reports about illegal Chinese immigrants. In contrast, a brutal assault by six young men on a Chinese man working in his shop was described as "boys play." Then, on August 2, 1907, Boston was rocked by another deadly shootout between Chinatown's warring tongs.[12]

Just before 8:00 P.M., as men lounged in the doorways of shops or stood talking in small groups on Oxford Place, a narrow T-shaped alleyway in the center of Chinatown, a group of men quickly and quietly took up positions along the length of the alley. One man lit a string of firecrackers from a cigar he clenched in his mouth and tossed them onto the street. Instantly, the sound of gunfire filled the air and shooters poured a murderous rain of bullets into the narrow alleyway. Men scrambled for cover, fled into nearby stores, or raced the length of Oxford Place, hoping to reach safety on Harrison Avenue. Three men were shot dead and seven fell wounded. The assailants then sprinted out of the alley and scattered as quickly as they had come.[13]

Within minutes after the shooting, every available police officer and detective was dispatched to the bloody scene. An ambulance and an undertaker's wagon saw to the wounded and dead, while police "raiding parties" scoured the area for suspects. A door-to-door search was begun, policemen often forcing their way into "dirty and dingy" rooms where a gunman might be hiding. Because the police immediately formed the opinion that the shooting was the work of Hip Sing, officers smashed down the door of the tong's headquarters and searched the building for evidence that "would connect any member of the local society with the shooting." Nothing specific was found there, but dozens of suspects and witnesses were rounded up and taken to police headquarters, where a crowd of nearly two thousand people surged around the station.

By early morning the police had arrested five men and charged them with murder. All were thought to be members of Hip Sing. The first officer to arrive at the crime scene caught Min Sing. He was taken immediately to Captain Cain's private office, "where he was stood up for the identification of witnesses," who said he was one of the shooters. Hom Woon was arrested at South Station just as he was boarding a train for New York City. Dressed in "American clothes" and wearing a white straw hat, Woon "looked the part" of a gunman: "his deep-sunken eyes and heavy chin and sullen manner were extremely forbidding." A third suspect was arrested about 2:00 A.M.. Joe Guey was in a laundry on Dartmouth Street when the police burst into the shop. Two others charged with being gunmen were arrested in Worcester. Yee Wat waved a revolver at a crowd of people who had surrounded him in the train station and Leong Gong bolted into the women's waiting room before surrendering to police officers. The following day, the police arrested five more suspects, including Warry Charles, a well-known Boston businessman.

Charles was charged with being an accessory before the fact to murder, a crime that carried the death penalty. The police suspected that as a leader of the Hip Sing tong, he had ordered and planned the attack on On Leong, perhaps in retaliation for their murder of Wong Yak Chung in 1903. Two specific bits of information led detectives to connect Charles to the murders: three of the men arrested were carrying his business card, and several of the shooters were from New York City, where Charles had lived before coming to Boston. Charles denied all charges and appeared calm and comfortable before being released from police custody.

Although the *Herald* and the *Globe* wrote sympathetically about the "eternal fear" that gripped many Chinese caught in the midst of an unwanted tong war, and the "terror" felt by "top side Chinamen"—defined by one newspaper as those who were "superior in the way of education and ability to the average run of Chinaman"—both papers peppered their stories with negative racial stereotypes. Innocent bystanders were labeled "shivering, chattering Chinamen," or "panic-stricken celestials"; Chinese referred to the gunmen as " 'Velly bad men,' of whom they were 'velly 'fraid.'" Suspects were rounded up "over their laundry boards, tables of chop suey or pipes of opium." With a knowing snicker, it was reported that when Hom Woon was brought in by police, his "face bore signs of having met with some obstacle which had badly bruised the lips." [14]

The *Evening Transcript* used similar language in its news stories about the shootout but easily exceeded its rivals in the extent to which racism was generalized and politicized. The "massacre" in Boston's Chinatown, the newspaper stated, manifested "the spirit and tactics of the Mafia exemplified by yellow men, instead of swarthy men, and it is another sinister proof of the implacable savagery of these Old World feuds with which we are fated to wrestle in America." Taking for granted that the men charged were guilty, the paper focused on the larger political purpose that would be served by imposing the death penalty. "The important thing," the editor, Robert Lincoln O'Brien, contended, "is to suppress this defiant alien lawlessness with an iron hand and to teach these bloodthirsty conspirators that though this is a land of freedom, it is not a land of license." Finally, O'Brien warned would-be jurors that the "Oriental is an even more subtle and secretive individual than the Latin or Armenian," and that in the courtroom one-time Chinese opponents would "combine in a determination to deceive and baffle the American officers of law." [15]

Keenly aware of the pervasiveness of anti-Chinese feeling, counsel for the ten defendants asked the court to question prospective jurors about their attitudes toward Chinese. Not a single venireman (a person summoned to act as a juror) admitted to being prejudiced against the defendants because of their race, but of the 165 men called 73 were excused because they claimed to be opposed to capital punishment. Judge Francis Gaskill's patience wore thin as the number of men increased who said they would not convict a defendant if that meant sending him to his death. Albert Somer, for example, was asked whether he would violate his juror's oath to put aside his own interests and preconceptions and to decide the case solely on the evidence presented in open court if the defendant warranted conviction. When he answered, "I would your honor," Judge Gaskill snapped back, "Then we don't want you, a man who would violate his oath." Of the men who said they harbored no anti-Chinese bias and who were willing to convict a defendant on the evidence even if it meant the person would be executed, the defense challenged forty and the prosecution nine. Finally, twelve white, middle-class men were selected: a retiree, a druggist, a manufacturer, a clerk, a bookkeeper, a real estate broker, a shipper, and five skilled workers. [16]

The jury sworn to determine the guilt or innocence of the ten Chinese defendants met contemporary legal standards: it had been purged of opponents of capital punishment and it was presumed to be impartial. The process of eliminating anyone who opposed or had any scruples against the death penalty was enacted into law in 1836, during the first Massachusetts campaign to abolish the death penalty. Although the law was intended to recognize the validity of opposition to capital punishment, it had the effect of creating a jury that leaned toward the prosecution, a tendency that was masked by the common law ideal of impartiality. Specifically, the views of those jurors who survived elimination because they believed in the death penalty were given added weight because they were said to be impartial. Common law defined an impartial juror as genuinely capable of separating his own interests and preconceptions and of deciding the case solely on the evidence presented in court. In the words of the great common law jurist Lord Coke, "He that is of a jury, must be *liber homo*, that is, not only a freeman and not bond, but also one that hath such freedom of mind as he stands indifferent as he stands unsworne." As used in Massachusetts, this standard of impartiality paradoxically required a juror to be independent not only from the influence of others but also from his own opinions and biases, with the exception of his support for the death penalty.[17]

The jurors' commitment to be impartial was tested before either the prosecutor or defense counsel had said a word. Massachusetts criminal procedure required a defendant to be seated in a prisoner's dock, usually a square wooden structure, open at the top, located just in front of the bar separating the audience from the officers of the court. To accommodate the Chinese defendants, the state constructed a special steel cage, in which "the ten men had scarcely room to sit upright." An armed deputy sheriff led each man to and from the cage. These unusual arrangements seem likely to have reinforced in the juror's mind the stereotype of Chinese as dangerous and violent and may have eroded the presumption of innocence that is the hallmark of a fair trial.

There was no hint of prejudice in Assistant District Attorney Michael Dwyer's opening statement to the jury on January 21. He simply listed the charges and outlined the government's case against the ten defendants. Nine of the Chinese were charged with murder in the first degree, and the tenth, Warry Charles, was charged with being an accessory before the fact. Charles, explained Dwyer, "incited, procured, counseled and aided within the meaning of the law, the other defendants to commit the murders before their actual commission." If convicted, the defendants would be sentenced to death.

Each man played a specific role. Dwyer placed Hom Woon, Min Sing, and Leong Gong on the sidewalk opposite Moy Wing's store on the corner of Harrison Avenue and Oxford Place. Wong Duck and Wong How, Dwyer said, took up a position near number 7 Oxford Place. Three men—

Joe Guey, Dong Bok Ling, and Yee Wat—stood at a spot farther along the alleyway. Yee Jung went to the southern end of Oxford Place, near the small passage that connects to Oxford Street. At a signal, all nine men opened fire with their revolvers, shooting directly at the clusters of men who stood or sat along the alleyway. Within minutes three men lay dead and seven others were wounded badly. The defendants ran through the alley, some fleeing into Oxford Street, others into nearby Beach Street.

During the next few days, the police arrested nine alleged gunmen, along with Warry Charles, who, witnesses stated, had planned the murders at a meeting of the Hip Sing tong. Min Sing was running away from Oxford Place when he was grabbed by a police officer. Hom Woon was arrested at South Station; officers said he was trying to rub gunpowder from his hand. Joe Guey's "odd" behavior aroused the suspicion of an officer who arrested him five hours after the shooting. Yee Wat and Leong Gong were apprehended the next day in Worcester. Wong How was arrested and charged with murder because he gave "contradictory statements as to his whereabouts on the night of the shooting." The police found Wong Duck in a Quincy laundry and Yee Jung in Portsmouth, New Hampshire. Neither man was able to account satisfactorily for his whereabouts on the night of August 2. Warry Charles was arrested in his Myrtle Street laundry after eyewitnesses told the police they saw Charles hand a revolver to Hom Woon on the morning of the shooting.

Dwyer concluded his opening statement by stressing the importance of "preserving law and order in our community" and by reminding the jury that "no matter how humble or of whatever nationality . . . the exact truth must be declared by your verdict as to each of these defendants." He told the jurors that he intended to present ninety witnesses, nearly all of whom would testify through an interpreter. He asked for their patience and full attention.

The jurors struggled to pay attention, but without much success. Men squirmed in their seats or stared into the distance while the process of translating witnesses' testimony and attorneys' questions dragged slowly along. An article published in the *Globe* on January 22 described the process:

All the witnesses who have been called thus far have testified through an interpreter, and the interlude between question and answer as given to the jury in English is far from musical. The suggestive query of Asst. Dist. Atty. Dwyer or the incisive inquiry of Gen. Charles W. Bartlett or Harvey H. Pratt in cross-examination is worked over by the interpreter with many grimaces and gestures into some dialect of southern China, and then the witness responds with plentiful specimens of guttural punctuation while he is endeavoring to fathom the question and frame his answer. By the time this is put into English it is sometimes discovered that somewhere in the shuffle the exact meaning of the attorney has failed to penetrate the mind of one or the other celestials and the ground has to be traversed anew.

The slow parade of government witnesses came to an abrupt stop on January 23, when one of the jurors became too ill to continue. Following testimony from a doctor and consultation with the attorneys, Judge Gaskill discharged the jury and adjourned the court. He ordered a new trial to begin February 3, eleven days later. During the interlude between trials, Boston police announced a ban on outdoor public activities in Chinatown, prohibited the use of firecrackers, and kept a close watch on the clubhouses of the rival tongs. Still, according to a description published in the *Boston Herald* January 23, the celebration of Chinese New Year went on: "Indoors, behind drawn curtains the Chinamen are celebrating with as much weird ritual and hospitality as ever." There was no mention of the victims' families.

The process of impaneling a new jury to hear evidence against the ten Chinese defendants accused of murder began when Judges Edward Pierce and John Freeman Brown questioned prospective jurors. Nearly two hundred potential jurors were packed into a room adjoining the criminal court. The clerk called one man at a time into the courtroom for questioning. The judges used this method hoping to reduce the number of prospective jurors who said they were opposed to capital punishment. Pierce and Brown, who were hearing their first murder case, believed that expressions of opposition to the death penalty were contagious. Therefore, by isolating the would-be jurors the court would cure the disease. The strategy had only limited success.

The *Globe* reported the answers of twenty-six prospective jurors. Of that number, nine (35 percent) said they were opposed to capital punishment and were excused. If that percentage held for the entire number of

men questioned, it was just 10 percent less than those who expressed opposition to the death penalty at the first trial when veniremen answered
so that everyone could listen. In short, the judges seem to have undervalued the strength and depth of the sentiment against capital punishment.
While the jurors chosen for the second trial necessarily shared the same
opinion about capital punishment as the first jury, the second group ranked
lower on a socioeconomic scale. There were four small businessmen and
five skilled workers included on the first jury. By comparison, the second
jury included only one small businessman and no skilled workers. In addition to a salesman, a manager, and a business agent, the second jury also
included four clerks, a decorator's assistant, and a "colored caterer." The
court seemed eager to encourage the jurors, praising their "intelligence
and their determination to master all of the details of the case." [18]

Assistant District Attorney Dwyer's opening statement laid out the government's case. He named the nine gunmen, placed each of them at the
scene of the crime, and promised that a host of eyewitnesses would prove
the state's case against the accused gunmen. He contended that Warry
Charles, president of the Hip Sing tong, had masterminded the murderous attack to bolster the society's declining membership and influence
among local Chinese. Charles's scheme, Dwyer argued, was to terrorize
Chinatown residents into joining Hip Sing or to extort money from them
in exchange for protection.

The witnesses Dwyer called fell into three general categories. Law enforcement officers, medical examiners, a representative from the building
inspector's office, who provided a lesson on the layout of Chinatown, and
a psychiatrist made up the first group of witnesses. Dr. George Jelly, a frequent expert witness in Massachusetts capital trials, had been appointed
by the court to examine Hom Woon and determine whether he was competent to stand trial. After five observations of Woon, Jelly told the court
Woon was "fully capable of comprehending the court proceedings."

Most of the more than forty prosecution witnesses who testified at the
trial from February 4 through February 17 were eyewitnesses to the shooting. These witnesses either worked in or owned Chinatown businesses or
lived in the area. Their accounts of how a group of men dressed in American clothes walked into Oxford Place and began a ten-minute shooting
spree on the unarmed men sitting and talking in the alleyway varied little.
Still, in an unprecedented ruling, the court agreed to the jury's request that

it be permitted to "review the testimony from day to day in order to fix it in their minds, but to avoid all discussion of its value."[19]

The third group of witnesses presented by the prosecution was to connect Warry Charles to the murders. The state's star witness was a Hip Sing insider. Wabber Shoi Poy, a member of Hip Sing's ten-member council, testified on February 17 that he was in the secret meeting room of the tong's headquarters in July 1907 when Charles proposed making an attack in Chinatown. "I want to make every business man join the order," Charles said, according to Wabber Shoi Poy. To carry out the scheme, Charles suggested hiring additional gunmen from other cities. He offered every man taking part in the attack $20 and expenses. If any of the hired gunmen was caught, Charles promised the society would cover their legal expenses. A majority of the council enthusiastically agreed to the idea, Wabber Shoi Poy claimed. Then, standing in the witness box, Wabber Shoi Poy pointed out six men in the cage who were local members of Hip Sing. He called the others New York "hatchet men."[20]

Charles W. Bartlett and Harvey H. Pratt poked and punched at the stories told by the state's witnesses. The sixty-three-year-old Bartlett, who was defense counsel for Wong Chung and Charlie Chin in 1903, had made a run for governor in 1905 and was the first Massachusetts lawyer to argue before the U.S. Supreme Court that the Fourteenth Amendment's "due process" clause should be applied to state murder trials. Pratt was sixteen years younger than Bartlett and had served for six years as assistant district attorney in Plymouth County before launching his own practice in 1893. Both men were experienced criminal attorneys who had defended a long list of accused murderers.[21]

Their strategy was simple: discredit the accounts of eyewitnesses by calling attention, if possible, to their criminal record, pointing out inconsistencies and inaccuracies in their description of the shooting, or suggesting that they were motivated to testify against the defendants because of tong rivalry. Bartlett asked Moy Wing, for example, whether he had been arrested six times for gambling during the past year. Moy Wing said he used to gamble but had not done so for years. The courtroom burst into laughter when the attorney theatrically waved a copy of Moy Wing's arrest record. Bartlett then asked whether the police had dropped several of Moy Wing's gambling charges in exchange for his testimony against the defendants. Moy Wing said no. How did Moy Wing reconcile his initial statement made to the district attorney at police headquarters that there was too much smoke to see anyone clearly, with his unequivocal courtroom identification of Leong Gong as one of the gunmen? The witness blamed a poor translation for the confusion. Pratt employed the same tactic as his senior colleague, implying that Wabber Shoi Poy's testimony was part of a deal with the police. First he asked why Wabber Shoi Poy had not gone to the police with information about the shooting before it happened since he was at the meeting where plans were made. The witness was vague. Pratt's next question suggested a specific answer. "Did [police] officer Linton ask you to be a witness?"

The defense opened its case by putting Warry Charles on the stand. Perhaps hoping to portray himself as a successful American immigrant, Charles told his dramatic life story in clear, colloquial English. Born in China in 1857, Charles fled from a life of poverty to San Francisco at the age of eleven. During the next three years he worked for relatives in San Francisco and New Orleans before moving to Omaha, where he started his own business with money he had saved. In 1880 he married Mary Whitting, a woman he met at Sunday School. They had a son. Some time later, Charles moved to New York City. He opened a laundry, attended a commercial school, worked as a courtroom interpreter, and took an active part in a government probe into Chinese gambling, for which he earned the enmity of some Chinese. For that reason, Charles moved to Boston in 1896. He reestablished himself as a businessman, won work in the courts as an interpreter, and founded the Hip Sing tong.

Charles denied any part in the shooting that took place in Chinatown on August 3, 1907. On that day, Charles told the court, he was busy working until he left for Cambridge about 3:00 P.M., where he stayed until 8:30 P.M. He did not meet Hom Woon or hand him a revolver as had been testified, nor had he ever asked the members of Hip Sing to contribute to a fund for hiring gunmen, as Wabber Shoi Poy claimed. Charles's landlady and Sunday School teacher told the court that Charles was either at home or at church on each of the days the prosecution claimed he was planning the shooting.

Assistant District Attorney Felix McGettrick subjected Charles to a "severe cross examination." Again and again, McGettrick asked about Charles's participation in Hip Sing and about his whereabouts on the fatal day. The district attorney also wanted to know why Charles had not lived with his wife since he left New York eleven years ago. Charles insisted that he had had nothing to do with Hip Sing for the past three years and that he knew nothing about the shooting until after it happened. Charles added that he and his wife visited one another frequently.

The other nine defendants' testimony was not as dramatic as Charles's, but each denied any part in the shooting and each man claimed to be somewhere other than Chinatown when the murders occurred. Dong Bok Ling said he was at the Park Theater with friends; Joe Guey was having dinner with his cousin; and Yee Wat insisted he went to Worcester to collect a debt, not to avoid arrest. In each instance, defense witnesses corroborated these claims, directly contradicting testimony from the state's witnesses. "It was evident to all," the *Globe* remarked at the conclusion of testimony "that evidence grossly false has come from some of the witnesses." [22]

Bartlett placed corruption, bitter rivalry between the tongs, and anti-Chinese sentiment at the heart of his closing statement. During his eight-hour speech to the jury, Bartlett argued that the Boston police and an On Leong tong member eager to avenge the 1903 killings cooked up the story that Hip Sing members were responsible for the killings. With a "cunning only an Oriental mind could posses," Bartlett claimed, a corrupt bargain was made and put into effect. Unfortunately, the "able and honest" men in the district attorney's office were so "overwhelmed" with other work they failed to detect this scheme. Now it was the jury's responsibility to see the truth. "In God's name, be careful," he concluded.

Labeling the Chinatown murders the "most terrible ever committed in Massachusetts," District Attorney McGettrick attacked Bartlett's accusation that police corruption lay at the heart of the prosecution's case. Rather, McGettrick said, the police deserved praise for using "intelligence, industry and determination" to uncover Hip Sing's murderous plot and asserted that Bartlett's charge sprang from "desperation." To rebut Bartlett, McGettrick reviewed the evidence against each of the defendants. At the end of each summary, he posed a rhetorical question using a phrase introduced by Bartlett: "Is that 'Oriental imagination'?" As for those witnesses who provided an alibi for Warry Charles, McGettrick bluntly concluded, "They were lying."

Reporters covering the Chinese murder trial seemed genuinely perplexed and suggested the jury would find it difficult to sort out the truth from the welter of contradictory evidence. It is clear, the *Herald* wrote on

March 5, that some of the testimony is "grossly false." Aside from the fact that four men were shot dead, "all the rest is still in contest," the newspaper noted at the trial's conclusion. When the jury returned to the courtroom after just two hours of deliberation, reporters were shocked. The defendants were visibly anxious. Warry Charles's "eyes wandered from place to place, his hands and fingers were nervously twitched and twirled, and his mouth drooped dubiously at the corners." Each man was told by Judge Pierce to stand facing the jury foreman when his name was called. In a voice cracking with emotion, foreman Alfred Ziegler loudly proclaimed each man, "Guilty, in the first degree." Charles was found guilty as an accessory to murder. He sank to his seat in the cage with a look of "undisguised despair." Attorneys Bartlett and Pratt also were shaken. When asked what his next legal step would be, Bartlett could only shake his head and murmur, "I do not know." Five days later Bartlett filed a routine motion for a new trial.

Bostonians who had not paid much attention to the trial now confronted the "awful magnitude of the affair." Unless the court or the governor or the legislature acted, a mass execution would take place. "It will seem very much like leading animals to slaughter," Massachusetts senator James H. Vahey said in an interview quoted in the *Boston Globe* March 9. This trial, he added, "furnishes the most convincing proof I have yet known that the death penalty should be abolished." If, as the jury found, these men were guilty of murder, they were not deterred by the death penalty. Although they were aware capital punishment was "barbarously inflicted" in China and widely used in the United States, "they were still not thinking of that penalty when they committed the crime." Like all people who commit murder, the Chinese gunmen were thinking only about escaping. Executing these men "will be a terrible shock to the sensibilities of the Christian people of this state." It will "brutalize" individuals who support the legal process and undermine public morality generally. Vahey concluded by expressing the hope that the "history of Massachusetts will not be stained by the execution of these unfortunate Chinamen" and by urging passage of one of the anti–capital punishment bills before the legislature.

The Anti-Death Penalty League spearheaded the effort to enact a law abolishing capital punishment in Massachusetts. Florence Spooner, a native of Baltimore who abandoned a promising singing career for philanthropy and reform in Massachusetts, founded the league in 1899 in the aftermath of a successful prison reform campaign. Spooner's strategy was simple: enlist in the cause as many prominent men and women as possible, then lobby the legislature to abolish the death penalty or to enact laws reforming the process, if abolition could not be achieved. Among those whose names appeared under the league's banner were religious leaders Cardinal William O'Connell, Rev. Paul Revere Frothingham, Rabbi Charles Fleischer, Rev. Thomas I. Gasson, S.J., and Rt. Rev. Bishop Lawrence; former governors John D. Long, J. Q. A. Brackett, John L. Bates, Eugene Foss, and the current governor, David I. Walsh; women reformers Julia Ward Howe, Alice Stone Blackwell, Elizabeth Ballard, and Anita Wheelwright; and Yankee reformers Col. Thomas Wentworth Higginson, Robert Treat Paine, Montgomery Sears, Joseph Grafton Minot, and William Lloyd Garrison.[23]

Spooner articulated the league's argument against the death penalty when she testified before the Joint Judiciary Committee of the Massachusetts legislature in February 1900. First, she contended, the state has no warrant for taking human life. It is "certainly illogical" for the state to take a life "in order to impress men with the sacredness of human life." Second, Spooner argued, capital punishment is not a deterrent. There is no evidence that executing "an erring brother" will change the "murderous tendencies in delinquent wards, the misfortune of heredity or alcoholic habits." Knowing this, proponents of the death penalty resort to an emotional appeal. The "sentiment of revenge, wedded to ultraconservatism," is what keeps capital punishment "in the statute book." Spooner's third reason for opposing capital punishment was the damaging effect executions have on society. "If dime-novel accounts of horrible things have a demoralizing influence on society," she asked, "how much more brutalizing must be the influence of accounts of these legalized horrors, emphasized as they are, by reality!" Fourth, the language of Genesis—"Whoso sheddeth man's blood by man shall his blood be shed."—Spooner pointed out, is anachronistic. The passage was written at a time when blood feuds were common and used by ancient governments to rationalize their control of societies very different from our own. Surely, capital punishment is not a "law designed for all ages and for the whole world," she asserted. Indeed, the Very Reverend William Byrne, Vicar-General of the Catholic Archdiocese of Boston, spoke to just that point, Spooner noted, when he told the committee, "We are living under the Christian dispensation of grace and mercy and not under the Mosaic code." Finally, Spooner argued, because jurors "dread to judge a human soul" guilty men often have been turned loose.[24]

Several of Spooner's arguments were consistent with the position taken by Attorney General Hosea Knowlton. Shortly after the league was founded, in 1899, Knowlton independently recommended to the legislature that it enact a law exempting minors and women from the death penalty if convicted of first-degree murder. "Public sentiment would not tolerate the execution of a boy" under the age of eighteen, he wrote. The argument for exempting women from capital punishment stood "upon different considerations, mostly sentimental." But the proof of Massachusetts's rejection of the death penalty for women was plain: no woman convicted of murder had been executed in more than a century. The legislature should recognize the wide acceptance of these cultural imperatives, Knowlton concluded, and enact this reform.[25]

While some legislators praised Knowlton's modest proposal for reforming the law of murder, others chided the attorney general for "not following out the logic of [his] convictions, by recommending not a partial but a total abolition of the death penalty." In response to that criticism, Knowlton—who had prosecuted more capital cases than any other Massachusetts lawyer—bluntly and briefly spelled out his views.

> The punishment of murder by death does not tend to diminish or prevent that crime; that a man who is so far lost to reason as to conceive the commission of murder with deliberate and premeditated malice aforethought does not enter into a discussion with himself of the consequences of the crime; that the infliction of the death penalty is not in accord with the present advance of civilization; and that it is a relic of barbarism, which the community must surely outgrow, as it has already outgrown the rack, whipping post and the stake.

Knowlton added: "I think I am justified in saying that the majority of those who have been or are engaged in the trial of capital cases share these same views."[26]

Influenced by Knowlton and pressured by Spooner, the House divided almost equally in 1900 on whether to abolish capital punishment. The vote was 103 in favor of abolition and 105 against. Surprisingly, following this narrow defeat, the league all but abandoned its effort to abolish capital punishment and focused instead on a bill that would permit a

jury to qualify its verdict of murder in the first degree by adding the words
"without capital punishment." During a long, acrimonious debate held before packed galleries in the spring of 1907, the bill's opponents argued that
providing the option would effectively abolish capital punishment, and
they were not ready to do that. Supporters of the measure contended that
the sentencing option would have the effect of determining the extent to
which the people were opposed to capital punishment, and of discovering whether or not the death penalty was a deterrent. The proposal was a
splendid piece of "self-correcting experimental legislation." Senator Vahey
carried the debate in the upper house and he also spent considerable time
on the House floor. With Spooner and her allies looking on from the gallery, the Senate voted 20 to 17 to support the bill, but the House rejected
the proposal 93 to 92. Speaker of the House John N. Cole, a Republican
from Andover, cast the deciding vote.[27]

The league continued to fight, using the convicted men's plight to
arouse opposition to the death penalty. Spooner and Vahey worked hard
to bring bills before the House and Senate abolishing capital punishment
or permitting the jury to qualify its verdict. The fate of the "poor ignorant
Chinamen," as they were described in the *Globe* February 14, was routinely
bemoaned by proponents of anti-capital punishment legislation, but without success. The pending execution of the Chinese aroused little sympathy. No bill abolishing the death penalty came to a recorded vote in either
chamber for the next four decades.[28]

While the league's anti-capital punishment bills were bottled up in
committee, attorneys for the nine convicted Chinese initiated a series of
legal moves to save their clients' lives. Bartlett and Pratt filed a motion for
a new trial, arguing that the verdict was against the weight of the evidence,
and on April 13, 1908, filed a short list of exceptions to rulings made by
trial judges Pierce and Brown. In July, for the first time in the commonwealth's history, a trial court set aside the verdict in a capital case, finding there was not sufficient evidence to convict Wong Duck, Wong How,
Dong Bok Ling, and Yee Jung. At the same time, the court ruled that the
guilty verdicts stood for the other five defendants and disallowed the most
important defense exception—a witness should be allowed to testify that
a police officer and a Chinese interpreter had conspired to bribe prosecution witnesses to give perjured testimony. The court claimed that the defense motion had not been properly saved during the trial. Bartlett and

Pratt immediately asked the Supreme Judicial Court (SJC) to appoint a special commissioner to hear arguments "to settle the truth of said exception disallowed by the Superior Court." In September, the SJC appointed Professor Samuel C. Bennett of Boston University Law School to hear evidence and to report to the court.[29]

The hearing was held on November 19 and 20, 1908. The format was simple: under oath, each of the three defense attorneys was questioned by attorney Joseph Bartlett (Charles's son) about his recollection of the colloquy that took place between the defense and Judges Pierce and Brown during the contested bench conference. Assistant District Attorney Felix McGettrick cross-examined each witness. Commissioner Bennett was to determine the validity of the defendants' claim to an exception to the trial court's adverse ruling on the defense's effort to explore the matter of perjured testimony. Everyone acknowledged that the controversy began when defense attorney Pratt asked John Feeney, a prosecution witness, to explain his relationship with police officer John Linton. Before Feeney spoke a word, Assistant District Attorney Dwyer shouted, "Objection." Judge Pierce upheld the objection, ruling that as an officer of the commonwealth, Linton, "like the King, could do no wrong." Unless Feeney's testimony directly contradicted some fact to which officer Linton had testified earlier, it was not admissible, the judge added.[30]

A long bench conference followed, during which Pratt and Bartlett explained the bribery scheme that was to have been used to bolster the prosecution's case. Witnesses were paid by Yee Wah—an interpreter and On Leong leader who worked closely with officer Linton—to testify that they saw Warry Charles and two other defendants at a trolley stop on the day of the murders. The false testimony was intended to link Charles more closely to the murders, to show that he conspired with the gunmen as charged. Judge Pierce listened but insisted the evidence was inadmissible. At this point, Bartlett motioned for the court stenographer to approach the bench so that he might formally record the defense's exception to Judge Pierce's ruling. Pierce then said: "No, you needn't do that; your rights are saved; you can trust me; put it in writing." A few days later, Pratt submitted a written summary of his argument to the court, believing that the court had allowed his exception and that he had laid the basis for a successful appeal for a new trial. But, without informing counsel, the judges rejected

Pratt's written presentation. Therefore, Judge Pierce did not include the contested defense motion in the bill of exceptions he sent to the SJC.[31]

After hearing the full story, Bennett ruled that "the words of the court gave the [defense] counsel reasonable cause to believe that their right was saved." The SJC accepted Bennett's finding, but the defendants' victory was short-lived. On May 20, 1909, the SJC ruled that while the trial court should have saved the exception, its ruling excluding evidence about alleged police corruption, bribery, and perjury was correct. Specifically, the SJC rejected Pratt and Bartlett's argument that their evidence about Yee Wah's perjury scheme should be accepted on the "broad ground that any attempt on the part of any person connected with either party to a suit, to procure false testimony" undermined the defendants' right to a fair trial. Speaking for a unanimous court, Chief Justice Marcus P. Knowlton pointed out that neither Yee Wah nor any of the four men allegedly bribed testified during the trial. Moreover, officer Linton's testimony "was wholly immaterial to any disputed point in the case." Therefore, "the defendants were not harmed by the [trial court's] ruling." There would be no new trial for the five defendants.[32]

On July 3—following a second failed attempt to win a new trial—Min Sing, Hom Woon, Leong Gong, Warry Charles, and Joe Guey were sentenced to death. The first three men were to be executed during the week of October 10, and the remaining two prisoners were scheduled to die during the week of October 17, 1909. Twenty-two days before the date set for their execution, Min Sing, Hom Woon, and Leong Gong decided not to petition for commutation of their sentence, "preferring execution to imprisonment for life." Attorney Julius Woodman, a partner of Bartlett and Pratt, hurried to the Charles Street jail to talk to the men about their decision. They were firm. "A great many people hold the theory that death is preferable to life imprisonment," the *Globe* editorialized, "but few of them are ever called upon to make the choice, and probably few indeed would stay with the theory with the cold-blooded calm exhibited by our friends Min Sing, Leong Gong and Hom Woon, whom we are going to kill."[33]

Twelve days after the men made their fateful decision, they were moved quietly and quickly from the Charles Street jail to the state prison at Charlestown and placed in the "condemned cells in the death house." Warden Benjamin F. Bridges set in motion the last movements of the machinery of death. Frank Davis, state electrician of New York, tested the electric chair. Those state agencies whose responsibility it was to provide official witnesses to an execution were notified. Warden Bridges also arranged for Chinese food to be brought to the condemned men and gave permission to Rev. Fr. Augustine Malley, the prison's Roman Catholic chaplain, to visit Hom Woon, Min Sing, and Leong Gong. Fr. Malley spent days and nights in the men's cells, instructing them in the Catholic faith. On Sunday, October 10, they were baptized and received into the Catholic Church. Just before midnight on the following day Fr. Malley administered Holy Communion to the three men and gave them the last rites. He chanted prayers for the dying before their cells until Warden Bridges came to take them to the iron-doored death chamber.

At 12:07 A.M. the witnesses to the executions left the warden's office, where they had been waiting nervously, and marched two by two along the north wall of the prison until they came to the death chamber. Once inside the small room, the seven men were seated on plain wooden chairs that faced the electric chair. A nod from the electrician to Warden Bridges sent him and Deputy Warden Nathan Allen to the cell door where the three prisoners were being held. Warden Bridges rapped on the wooden door separating the cells from the death chamber. Carrying a cross in his hand, Fr. Malley stepped out, followed by two guards, one on either side of the prisoner. Hom Woon walked firmly toward the electric chair.

Fr. Malley knelt before the death chair and with the cross held before Hom Woon's face, repeated aloud the Lord's prayer as the guards strapped the condemned man in the chair and attached the electrodes, one at the top of the head and the other to the calf of his left leg, bared from the knee. Hom Woon stiffened slightly but moved easily when he was shoved back into the chair.

The guards finished their work and stepped back just as Fr. Malley completed his prayer. Warden Bridges raised his staff of office and as he saw Hom Woon exhale, the electrician turned on the current. Hom Woon surged against the heavy leather straps. After a minute the current was shut off. A physician listening for signs of life shook his head, stepped back, and the current was turned on again. When it was shut off, Hom Woon was pronounced dead. His body was removed from the chair and dragged out of the sight of the witnesses.

Min Sing was brought into the death chamber next and fourteen minutes after Hom Woon had been pronounced dead, Min Sing was dead. When Min Sing was strapped into the chair the guards neglected to buckle the strap that should have held his left forearm down on the arm of the chair. The force of the current caused his arm to fly up toward his head and his index finger point straight up. The hand and finger remained in that grotesque position until the current was turned off.

Leong Gong, the youngest of the three men at nineteen years of age, was the last to be executed. The current surged through his body and he was pronounced dead fourteen minutes after Min Sing. As Leong Gong died, Fr. Malley groaned. That was the only sound from any of the spectators. Not one of the condemned men spoke a word in the death chamber

At 1:45 A.M. Bridges and the witnesses returned to the warden's office to sign a certificate verifying that the three Chinese men had been executed according to law. A quiet, orderly crowd of about 150 people, chiefly young men and boys, waited outside the prison gate until the executions were completed. Extra police officers that were assigned to Chinatown reported that the streets were "deserted and unusually quiet." But "every backroom was crowded by gleeful On Leong tong men who smoked and speculated on the manner of the execution at Charlestown."

Three days after Leong Gong, Min Sing, and Hom Woon were executed Warry Charles and Joe Guey were moved to the state prison in preparation for their executions. Just as Warden Bridges began the process leading to Charles's and Guey's executions, however, Governor Draper granted a sixty-day respite so that the Council might hear the prisoners' application for a pardon. The hearing before the "court of last resort," as defense attorney Pratt called the Council, began on November 5. Freed from the constraints of courtroom procedure and decorum, Pratt and Bartlett argued passionately in language often laced with racial epithets that their clients were victims of an elaborate, carefully planned conspiracy. Charles and Guey were "marked for death" by the On Leong tong, whose members were deeply involved in criminal activities. Charles had worked with the New York City police to smash On Leong's smuggling and gambling operations. For that reason, Charles "was hated with the great hatred of which the race is capable." When he moved to Boston a price was put on his head. Guey also incurred On Leong's hatred, Pratt asserted. Two members of that tong brought a bogus criminal charge against Guey. It was not coincidence that the same men testified against him during his murder trial. In fact, Pratt contended that On Leong staged the shootout in Boston's Chinatown, told the police Charles and Guey were responsible, and so used the police to do On Leong's "dirty work." At the trial, On Leong arranged for Chinese witnesses who lied, and Yee Wah—the On Leong leader who worked with officer Linton—bribed several white men to give perjured testimony supporting On Leong's version of the crime.[34]

In his closing statement to the committee, Assistant District Attorney Dwyer angrily dismissed the defense's conspiracy claims and denounced Pratt and Bartlett. "Not a scintilla of evidence has been offered here," Dwyer argued, "which has not previously been considered by the proper legal tribunal and in each case decided against the defendants." He added, Pratt is "so much bound up in [this case] he is unable to make a fair statement." Finally, Dwyer made a moving personal statement:

> I am sorry I am here at all having witnessed with my own eyes the infliction of the penalty of death on three co-defendants of these men, my ideas have undergone, if not a complete change, at least a considerable modification, in regard to capital punishment.
>
> But it would be a terrible thing, it would be a stain upon the fair name of our Commonwealth, if these two men were sent innocent to their death, but my belief in their guilt leads me to say it would be a public calamity if they should be freed altogether or benefit by modification of their sentence. It would be an injustice to those three compatriots of theirs who have already paid the penalty for their crime.[35]

Bartlett closed for the defense. During a long, rambling speech, he brushed aside the guilty verdicts, noting that the jury deliberated only long enough to consider each of the nine defendant's case for about twelve or fourteen minutes. He spoke about conspiracy, invoked the names of two popular law enforcement officials, and argued that popular hatred of Chinese had shaped the trial's outcome. None of the defendants "should have been convicted on the evidence which was produced in this case," Bartlett began. "It smells foul. It was wicked evidence. It was manufactured evidence." District Attorney John Moran acknowledged the situation by freeing one defendant and scheduling new trials for three others. Even if the evidence were compelling, Bartlett continued, he and the late Attorney General Knowlton had concluded that capital punishment "had to be done away with." Certainly, Charles and Guey should not be put to death.

They were innocent men "set up" by On Leong. Remember, Bartlett said to the committee, the Chinese are "a subtle cunning race" who systematically lie, manipulating our courts to serve their own vengeful purpose. Bartlett begged the committee not to be so used.[36]

The *Globe* agreed with Bartlett's assessment, but the *Herald* took an opposite point of view. On one hand, a mass of testimony about perjury and bribery made it clear, the *Globe* wrote, "that the Chinese are utterly regardless of western standards and that any trial of them for crimes under western methods is likely to result in miscarriages of justice." On the other hand, the *Herald* said that "while a doubt had been raised as to the guilt of the Chinamen, there was too much positive evidence of guilt to warrant allowing them to go free." Both papers pointed out that in the past fifteen years only two commutations of death sentences had been granted.[37]

On November 30, 1909, sixteen days before their scheduled execution, Governor Draper announced that he had accepted the recommendation of the Executive Council to commute the death sentences of Charles and Guey to life imprisonment. Following the announcement, Lt. Governor Louis Frothingham, who chaired the Council's pardons committee, revealed how narrowly the committee had defined its responsibility. The defense argued that the committee should retry the case, but according to Frothingham, "there was no question of pardoning the Chinamen, since the court had passed on the question of guilt." The committee focused strictly on the penalty.[38]

Reaction to Draper's decision varied widely. Guey was "so overcome by the news of the commutation that he sank to his knees when told." Warry Charles was "disappointed." "Up to the very last minute," he said, "I confidently expected a full pardon." Members of the Anti-Death Penalty League held a self-congratulatory meeting, "rejoicing" that the sentences of death had been commuted. But the league's happiness seemed prompted more by Assistant District Attorney Dwyer's personal turn against the death penalty than by the fact that the lives of two of five men sentenced to death in 1908 had been spared. Years later, Spooner wrote that the execution of Min Sing, Hom Woon, and Leung Gong had "blighted my courage to even stand up for religion in a world of so little love."[39]

The league's hollow cheer for commutation marked the beginning of the end for its campaign to abolish the death penalty in Massachusetts. In addition to the enormous difficulty of overcoming the arguments supporting the death penalty, the league undoubtedly lost public support by linking its cause to the Chinese murder defendants. Boston newspapers commonly placed the Chinatown murders within a context framed by a general fear of social turmoil and racial conflict. The *Herald* contended that the danger of violence was greater in 1907 than it had been in 1903, because "more Chinese are armed," and the *Globe* darkly predicted that tong rivalry would lead to "wholesale killing." Perhaps to make its frightening point more powerful, the *Globe* compared the 1907 Chinatown shootout to the 1886 Haymarket riots and the danger of anarchy. The *Evening Transcript* seemed to believe the collapse of law and order had happened already when it warned its readers, "criminal law has become with us an unworkable machine." Given this climate of opinion, capital punishment could be justified as a necessary response to the need for greater law and order.[40]

With the exception of Fr. Malley, who ministered to the three men while they awaited execution, even their supporters rarely acknowledged the humanity of the Chinese. Racist attitudes shaped the debate over whether the Chinese should live or die, sapping it of much of its humanitarian and emotional content. During the trial and the appeals process, defense attorney Bartlett regularly focused on alleged racial differences, referring to the "cunning Oriental mind," mocking the testimony of Chinese prosecution witnesses, and insisting that Chinese were peculiarly capable of lying and of hatred. Neither Bartlett nor the league referred by name to the condemned men. Min Sing, Hom Woon, and Leung Gong were the "three Chinamen," or the "unfortunate Chinamen," not individual human beings each with a name and a personal history. These same beliefs dominated the press coverage of the execution. According to the *Herald*, for example, the "three Celestials" manifested a "stolid indifference" to the impending execution. Within days after the execution the *Globe* was laughing at Chinese. It reported the streets of Chinatown were empty. "Scarcely a Chinaman could be seen" and when a man did appear, the *Globe* mockingly noted, he "scurried across the street as fast his little legs could carry him."[41]

New laws and court decisions added legitimacy to popular racism. Three years after the execution of Min Sing, Hom Woon, and Leung Gong, the Massachusetts legislature debated a law making it a criminal offense for a white woman under the age of twenty-one to enter a hotel or restaurant owned or managed by Chinese. At about the same time, Congress renewed the Chinese Exclusion Act, tightening legal loopholes and extending its restrictive provisions without a time limit. Under the guise of preventing a tong war, immigration officers used the law to raid Boston's Chinatown, rounding up men who could not produce a certificate of residence or whose claim to be sons of U.S. citizens of Chinese descent was tangled.[42]

While Boston's Chinese community struggled to survive, the league staggered and collapsed. The same year Min Sing, Hom Woon, and Leung Gong were executed, James Vahey left the Massachusetts Senate after an unsuccessful run for governor. Three years later Father Byrne, the most articulate Catholic spokesman against the death penalty, died. Without Vahey's machinations or Byrne's voice, Spooner's league was unable to move the machinery of government. The onset of World War I dealt another blow to the league's campaign. Spooner acknowledged the obvious: the "wanton destruction" of World War I "greatly delayed" the effort to abolish capital punishment in Massachusetts. The anti–death penalty bills the league introduced never got out of the Judiciary Committee. In fact, no bill came to a recorded vote in either legislative chamber until 1947.[43]

Other political and social changes indirectly affected the league, narrowing its base of support and further weakening its influence. When John F. Fitzgerald took office as Boston's first American-born Irish Catholic mayor in 1906, the city's politics were changed permanently. The Brahmin's worst fears were soon realized. Irish Catholic Democrats gained firm control not only of Boston's most heavily populated wards but of the newly strengthened mayor's office as well. When the pugnacious James Michael Curley swept into office, therefore, the battle lines were clearly drawn. What Boston needs, Curley said, taking aim at the city's proud tradition of voluntarism, is "men and mothers of men, not gabbing spinsters and dog-raising matrons in federation assembled." One of the incidental victims of Curley's aggressive ethnic politics was the Anti-Death Penalty League, which asked its members to put aside ethnicity, politics, and religion for the cause.[44]

Although Archbishop O'Connell initially had supported the league, joining with Protestant clergy to push the campaign against the death penalty, he backed away from the group soon after he took control of the Boston archdiocese in 1908. Emphasizing the theme of a "church militant," he urged Catholics to adopt an independent attitude and to focus on their own distinctive culture. He encouraged Catholics to avoid all forms of and practices of Protestantism, including volunteer groups dominated by Protestants. In 1912, when the league made another attempt to persuade the legislature to abandon capital punishment, O'Connell did not join with Protestant clergy who testified before the judiciary committee. He told Spooner he saw no reason to acknowledge publicly his support for the abolition of the death penalty. In short, O'Connell's strategy of building a "church triumphant" further undermined the league's effectiveness.[45]

From its inception, the Anti-Death Penalty League was a loose coalition with a long shot at success. Yet the league manifested its influence in two close votes in the legislature to abolish capital punishment and when significant numbers of potential jurors stated they would not sentence to death even men from the despised Chinese minority. However, the league was not able to build on these successes and stood by helplessly while three men were executed. A few years later, the league disappeared, a victim of a complex dynamic that included anti-Chinese sentiment, proponents of capital punishment, and the political and social struggle between Yankees and Irish, Catholic and Protestant. The humanitarian standard to which the hope for abolition of the death penalty was pinned would not be held so high again until mid-century.

Nothing about the Sacco and Vanzetti case is uncontested except its notoriety. It is the most famous murder case in Massachusetts history and it may legitimately lay claim to being one of the most famous murder trials of the twentieth century. From the summer of 1921, when Nicola Sacco and Bartolomeo Vanzetti were tried and found guilty of murdering a paymaster and a guard in South Braintree, until the two Italian immigrants were executed on August 23, 1927, people in Massachusetts and around the world were divided over whether they were guilty or innocent and whether they had received a fair trial. Likewise, during the past eighty years a legion of polemicists and historians have picked over every facet and fact of the case without reaching consensus: a handful of scholars have argued that Sacco and Vanzetti were guilty as charged; some historians have concluded that a wave of antiradicalism strongly influenced the outcome of Sacco and Vanzetti's trial, and others have determined that one or the other of the two men, or both, were innocent.[1]

The Massachusetts Supreme Judicial Court (SJC) to which Sacco and Vanzetti appealed their murder conviction had a long history as one of the preeminent state supreme courts in the nation, but throughout most of the twentieth century it did little more than pay lip service to the rights of the accused rather than aggressively seeking justice. At the time of Sacco and Vanzetti's trial the SJC's review of capital appeals extended only to points of law, not the evidence, and under Chief Justice Arthur P. Rugg, a conservative Republican who occupied the court's center seat from 1911 to 1938, the SJC gave broad discretionary power to trial judges to rule on points of law, creating a procedure that sharply limited the SJC's ability to correct injustice even if it wanted to. Coincidently, popular anxiety about radicalism, immigration, and a "crime wave" buttressed the court's reluctance to change lower court decisions. For these reasons, the SJC very rarely reversed a death sentence. Harvard Law professor Felix

Frankfurter's controversial 1927 book condemning District Attorney Frederick Katzmann's cross-examination of Sacco and Judge Webster Thayer's conduct of the trial highlighted other alleged shortcomings of Massachusetts's capital procedure. Frankfurter contended the Sacco-Vanzetti jury pool was tainted by a deep, communitywide prejudice against political radicals, a fault made more egregious by the trial court's unwillingness to conduct extensive pretrial questioning of potential jurors. That meant, according to an argument Frankfurter made thirty-four years later when he was an associate justice of the Supreme Court of the United States, that jurors exposed to prejudicial material or who held a preconceived opinion about a particular group or class or race were predisposed to find a defendant guilty.[2]

These procedural flaws, together with other alleged shortcomings in the conduct of Sacco and Vanzetti's trial, cast a shadow over the Massachusetts criminal justice system. In the half-century following the two men's execution, the legislature, the courts, and a grass-roots movement slowly reacted to the barrage of criticism by reforming major aspects of capital procedure and by initiating a campaign to abolish the death penalty. Just twelve years after Sacco and Vanzetti were executed the Massachusetts legislature granted the SJC the power to review fact and law and to reverse a death sentence "for any reason justice may require," a change that increased the number of death sentences reversed by the court. Several decades later the Supreme Court of the United States tackled the issue of what, if anything, should be done about communitywide prejudice, or presumed juror bias, but ultimately the Court failed to establish a single clear standard. In 1973, however, the Massachusetts legislature enacted a statute mandating extensive questioning of prospective jurors in an effort to discover whether a potential juror held firm prejudicial opinions that would taint the outcome of a case, and four years later—fifty-three years after Sacco's and Vanzetti's executions—the Massachusetts court abolished the death penalty. These significant legal changes were triggered by Sacco and Vanzetti's trial.[3]

About three o'clock on the afternoon of April 15, 1920, Frederick A. Parmenter, paymaster for the Slater and Morrill shoe company, and Alessandro Berardelli, an armed guard, were shot dead as they crossed Pearl Street in South Braintree, Massachusetts, en route from one Slater and Morrill factory building to another with the weekly payroll totaling $15,776.51. The assailants grabbed the two steel payroll boxes and jumped into a car driven by an accomplice. (Two other men also may have been in the car.) The bandits' car paused briefly at a railroad crossing before speeding past Slater and Morrill's business office and several stores lining the street. Two days later police found the car believed to have been used in the holdup in a wooded area near West Bridgewater and identified it as a car reported stolen a few months earlier.[4]

Twenty days after the crime two police officers boarded a trolley en route to Brockton from West Bridgewater and arrested Sacco and Vanzetti. The police had been led to the two men by Ruth Johnson, an automobile garage owner's wife, who had acted on a police request to report any attempt to pick up a car owned by Mike Boda, an alien suspected of political radicalism. Bridgewater chief of police Michael E. Stewart questioned Sacco and Vanzetti. He asked about their movements that day, whether they were anarchists or communists, and whether they believed in the overthrow of the United States government. On the following day, May 6, 1920, Norfolk-Plymouth County district attorney Frederick G. Katzmann questioned Sacco and Vanzetti. Born in Roxbury, Katzmann graduated from Harvard College in 1896 and from Boston University Law School six years later. Following his admission to the bar in 1902, Katzmann joined the Norfolk-Plymouth County district attorney's office and won election as district attorney in 1917. He asked Sacco about the gun he was carrying when arrested and about his whereabouts on the day of the South Braintree holdup and murders. Katzmann asked Vanzetti many of the same questions. Perhaps because they believed their arrest was part of the U.S. government's post–World War I campaign against political dissidents, Sacco and Vanzetti gave Katzmann evasive and false answers.[5]

Katzmann concluded that Sacco and Vanzetti had taken part in the South Braintree robbery and murder. He also charged Vanzetti with participating in an attempted payroll robbery in Bridgewater on December 24, 1919, and elected to try him for that crime first. On June 11, 1920, a grand jury returned an indictment against Vanzetti for attempted robbery and intent to murder. Trial began eleven days later. Sixty-three-year-old Plymouth Superior Court judge Webster Thayer heard the case against Vanzetti. Circumstantial evidence presented by District Attorney Katzmann tied Vanzetti to the car used in the attempted holdup and eyewitnesses identified Vanzetti as the man standing in the middle of the street firing a shotgun at the truck carrying the L. Q. White Shoe Company's payroll. Katzmann also introduced into evidence a shotgun shell found at the crime scene said by experts to be similar to shells Vanzetti carried in his pocket the night of his arrest. Defense attorney John P. Vahey presented more than two dozen witnesses—mostly Italian neighbors of Vanzetti—who placed him in Plymouth peddling fish on the morning of the attempted robbery, but Katzmann's sharp cross-examination effectively lessened the impact of their testimony. Vanzetti did not testify on his own behalf. A jury brought in a verdict of guilty on July 1, 1920, and six weeks later Judge Thayer sentenced Vanzetti to twelve to fifteen years in prison.[6]

A few weeks after Vanzetti's sentencing, he and Sacco were indicted for the murders of Parmenter and Berardelli. By the time Sacco and Vanzetti took their seats in the Dedham courthouse prisoner's dock—a four-foot-square wood and metal enclosure situated just in front of the bar so that the defendants when seated could see the court but not be seen by the audience behind the bar—their background and political views had become widely known. Born in 1891, Sacco was seventeen years old when he arrived in Boston from southern Italy. He worked on a road gang and at an iron foundry before learning shoe edging, a skill that led to steady employment in Massachusetts shoe factories after 1910. In 1912 he married, and the following year his wife, Rosa, gave birth to their son, Dante. In addition to working long hours at the Milford Shoe Company, caring for his family, and tending his vegetable garden, Sacco committed time and energy to an anarchist group. He supported striking workers in nearby Hopedale, and he distributed anarchist literature. He opposed World War I and either to evade the draft or to be prepared to return to Italy in anticipation of a revolution, he and about one hundred other anarchists fled from the United States to Mexico in May 1917. Sacco remained there until September, when he returned to Massachusetts under a false name. At the conclusion of the war he resumed his true identity and took a job at 3K Shoe in Stoughton.[7]

Vanzetti's life in the United States was at once more footloose and studious than Sacco's. Born in 1888, near Turin in northern Italy, he immigrated to New York City in 1908 shortly after the death of his mother. For eight months he washed dishes in a New York restaurant. In the spring of 1909, Vanzetti left the city for the Connecticut countryside, hoping to find outdoor work, but by the fall he was back in New York working as a pastry chef, a skill he had learned as an apprentice in Italy. Sometime in 1912 he again fled from the city. He held a construction job in Springfield, Massachusetts, before moving to Plymouth, where he found work at a cordage factory until an unsuccessful strike in which he participated led to his being placed on an employer blacklist. As he drifted from job to job, Vanzetti educated himself, reading a great number and variety of ancient and modern authors. His reading and life experiences led him to embrace anarchism, and in May 1917 Vanzetti traveled to Mexico with Sacco and a band of his fellow believers. He subsequently crossed back into the United States with Sacco, but while his friend set a course straight for Massachusetts, Vanzetti slowly and circuitously wandered across the nation's heartland before returning to Plymouth. During the two years prior to his arrest, he peddled fish door to door in the town's Italian neighborhoods.[8]

The process of choosing jurors began May 31, 1921, in the Norfolk Superior Court, Dedham. As they had at Vanzetti's Plymouth trial, Judge Webster Thayer presided and District Attorney Frederick Katzmann led the prosecution team. Three-term Republican governor Samuel W. McCall had appointed Thayer, an 1879 Dartmouth College graduate and a good amateur baseball player, to the Superior Court in 1917. Fred H. Moore, the chief defense lawyer for the defendants, worked closely with two experienced Norfolk County criminal lawyers, Jeremiah J. and Thomas F. McAnarney. Moore specialized in labor defense cases, chiefly in California, but he had successfully defended two Italian radicals charged with murder during a textile strike organized by the IWW, the radical Industrial Workers of the World, in Lawrence, Massachusetts, in 1912.

In opening remarks he made to each group of potential jurors after they crowded into the courthouse, Judge Thayer spoke of duty. "It is not a sufficient excuse that the service [of a juror] is painful, confining, and distressing," the judge told the assembled men.

It is not sufficient excuse that a juror has business engagements and other duties more profitable and pleasant that he would rather perform, for you must remember the American soldier had other duties he would rather have performed than those that resulted in his giving up his life upon the battlefields of France, but he with undaunted courage and patriotic devotion that brought honor and glory to humanity and the world rendered the service and made the supreme sacrifice. He answered the call of the Commonwealth.

Of course, Thayer continued,

In this age of freedom of thought and of speech an individual is entitled to have his own private views upon all social, religious, political
and economic questions, but he should never bring them into the jury
room, especially when they might operate in the least possible degree
to the prejudice of either party . . . for the majesty of the law and obedi-
ence to the law must be supreme and must control the individual opinion as well as the individual will.[9]

Thayer's rhetorical linking of soldiers and jurors has been portrayed as
a manifestation of patriotic gore intended to bias the jury against alien radicals. In fact, the duty/rights distinction had roots in Anglo-American law
that stretched at least to Oliver Wendell Holmes Jr.'s celebrated *Common
Law* (1881). The distinction became a commonly used social-legal concept
that emphasized that a person's social obligations and duties preceded his
rights. Law imposes duties, according to Holmes, and therefore, "logically
precede[s] rights." A citizen's duty to military service or to jury service
takes precedence over an individual's right to liberty. Following this formulation, Thayer's speech to the Sacco-Vanzetti jurors distinguished between a person's public duty to the state and his personal or private right
to hold and express opinions on the issues of the day. He warned jurors
they must subordinate their personal rights to their public duty.[10]

Following Thayer's lecture the potential jurors were ushered into waiting rooms before being summoned for individual questioning by the court
and possible challenge by the prosecution or the defense. Judge Thayer
asked each juror the required statutory questions: Are you related to either party; that is, to either of the defendants or to either of the deceased?
Have you any interest in the trial or its results; do you hope to gain finan-
cially by its outcome? Have you expressed or formed an opinion on the
issue before the court? Are you aware of any bias or prejudice that will
prohibit you from being fair and impartial? In capital trials the court also
asked each potential juror about his opinion in regard to the death penalty.
"Are your opinions of such a character as to preclude you from finding a
defendant guilty of a crime punishable by death?" The court could ask
follow-up questions and if a juror's answers suggested he did not "stand
indifferent," he would be dismissed for cause. According to a law in effect at the time of Sacco and Vanzetti's trial, unless directed by the court

neither the district attorney nor the defense was permitted to question the jurors, although the judge could permit either party to suggest additional questions to be asked a juror. More than thirty years earlier, however, the SJC had ruled that a judge's refusal to comply with counsel's request to ask additional questions would not be considered an abuse of a judge's discretionary authority.[11]

Despite Thayer's clarion call to unselfish service only 7 of the 500 men summoned to the courthouse were accepted as jurors during the first three days. One by one hundreds of potential jurors were eliminated. "The greatest number of those men who were excused" by the court for cause, the *Boston Daily Globe* reported, stated that "no matter what the law was their own repugnance to voting for a verdict that meant condemnation of a defendant to death was greater and they would convict nobody of murder in the first degree." Increasingly frustrated at the snail's pace at which the jury was being assembled despite daily twelve-hour sessions, Judge Thayer aggressively and erroneously demanded of every potential juror who expressed opposition to capital punishment whether "he had ever done anything to get the law changed or to get his name taken from the jury list on the ground he was not qualified to serve." In addition to those men eliminated for cause by the court, more than 100 potential jurors also were challenged peremptorily—struck by the defense or the prosecution without having to state a reason, although the lawyers probably had picked up bits of information or a suspect opinion during Thayer's questioning of each juror. When the prosecutor struck the last juror from a second large pool of potential jurors, Judge Thayer ordered the sheriff to summon 200 additional men "from the bystanders or from the County at large" who were "qualified and liable to be drawn as jurors" and to order these additional potential jurors to report to the Dedham courthouse in the morning. That night sheriff's deputies fanned out across Norfolk and Plymouth counties, serving notices to men they found, among other places, at a Needham Masons' meeting, a band concert in Braintree, and on their way to work in the early morning. In this way, an additional 175 "indignant" men stood before Judge Thayer in the morning. The final 5 men were chosen from this group and at 1:20 A.M. on June 4 the 12 tired jurors were sworn.[12]

The jurors chosen to hear the murder charge against Sacco and Vanzetti were ordinary men, "neither too high nor too low on the social scale," as the *New Bedford Standard-Times* put it in its 1950 retrospective. Two real estate agents, two machinists, a foreman of Quincy's water-meter repair shop, a shoe worker, a mill worker, a mason, a farmer, a grocer, a clothing salesman, and a photographer composed the jury. All but one were married and had children. Repairman Walter H. Ripley, a seventy-year-old former Quincy police and fire chief and the oldest juror, was appointed foreman, but the youngest juror, twenty-eight-year-old John F. Dever, a U.S. Army veteran working as a salesman at Filene's and a self-described "defendants' man" suggested an informal ballot that stimulated the jury's initial discussion about the guilt or innocence of Sacco and Vanzetti. "We started discussing things, reviewed the very important evidence about the bullets and everybody had a chance to speak his piece," Dever recalled. "There never was any argument, though. We just were convinced Sacco and Vanzetti had done what the prosecution had charged them with." During the jury's discussion, John E. Ganley recalled, he stressed the testimony of Austin Reed, the Medfield railroad crossing guard who identified Vanzetti as a passenger in the bandit car, and Frank D. Marden highlighted Louis Pelser's eyewitness account of looking out a half-open window above his factory workbench to see an armed man shoot another man kneeling in the street. When asked whether he could identify the gunman, Pelser pointed to Sacco. Although the ballistic experts for the prosecution and the defense gave dense, confusing testimony, the surviving jurors told the New Bedford reporter the evidence that most impressed them was that of the old-fashioned Winchester bullets, one of which was taken from Berardelli's body and duplicates of which were found on Sacco when he was arrested. Dever remembered that District Attorney Katzmann asked the defense ballistics expert, James Burns, why he had not used Winchester bullets in his tests with Sacco's gun. Burns replied he had not been able to find any of the rare old-fashioned bullets. "But do you know who had some of them," Dever rhetorically asked the *Standard-Times* reporter, "Sacco." Finally, Dever concluded, "there was no single piece of evidence that determined the verdict. Various pieces fitted into chains of evidence."[13]

At the close of the trial Judge Thayer had instructed the jury. As he had in his opening remarks, he used the soldier-juror analogy to emphasize the importance of the duties imposed on a juror. "Like the true soldier," he said, a man who answers the state's call to serve as a juror fulfills his duty "to God, to country, to his state, and to his fellowmen." Once selected, a

juror has the "solemn duty" to apply the law fearlessly and without prejudice and to insist the law be applied fairly and equally "to all classes of
society, the poor and the rich, the learned and the ignorant, the most powerful citizen as well as the most humble, the believer as well as the unbe-
liever, the radical as well as the conservative, the foreign-born as well as
the native-born." "I therefore beseech you," Thayer added, "not to allow
the fact that the defendants are Italians to influence or prejudice you in the
least degree. They are entitled, under the law, to the same rights and considerations as though their ancestors came over in the Mayflower." Following a review of the evidence, Judge Thayer concluded his instructions by
stating: "My duties, gentleman, have now closed and yours begun." Seven
and a half hours later the jury announced it had found the two men guilty
as charged.[14]

A few days after their conviction Sacco and Vanzetti submitted a motion to the court for a new trial on the ground the verdicts were "against
the weight of the evidence," a boilerplate motion routinely made following
a capital conviction that was leavened in this instance with an argument
about the jury's alleged prejudice against radicals. According to Massachusetts criminal procedure, Judge Thayer heard the defendants' argument. About a month and a half later, on December 24, 1921, he denied the
motion, characterizing the defense claim that the jurors' judgment "was
unduly warped by prejudice" as an unwarranted "attack" on the jurors'
integrity. The law, Thayer wrote, spells out an explicit division of responsibility: a jury determines the facts and the court rules on the law. If a trial
judge can set aside a jury's verdict as against the evidence because the facts
presented are complex and contradictory, "no action can be tried which
may not be brought in review before the court upon the facts and the trial
by jury will be virtually superseded." Therefore, for the court to take the
extraordinary step of setting aside a jury verdict, a judge must find that
a jury "mistook or abused their trust." In fact, Thayer noted, the twelve
men empanelled to hear the case had been selected carefully, sequestered
from the moment they were sworn until the trial concluded, and based on
their best reading of the disputed facts and the opportunity they had to
observe the witnesses, they found the defendants guilty. For these reasons,
Judge Thayer concluded "I cannot—as I must if I disturb these verdicts—
announce to the world that these twelve jurors, violated the sanctity of
their oaths, threw to the four winds of bias and prejudice their honor,

judgment, reason, and conscience, and thereby abused the solemn trust reposed in them by the law as well as by the Court."[15]

While Thayer drafted his initial ruling, the defense filed several "supplementary" motions that were not argued until November 1923. A little less than a year later, Thayer also denied those motions and Sacco and Vanzetti appealed to the SJC. At this point Fred Moore left the case and sixty-two-year-old William G. Thompson, a prominent civil attorney and a long-time member and officer of the Boston Bar Association, assumed responsibility for Sacco and Vanzetti's defense. Thompson sincerely believed that the two men were innocent and that he, and other men of his class, had an obligation to prevent the commonwealth from making a fatal mistake. When he stood before the SJC on January 11, 1926, he had been practicing law for more than thirty years and had earned a reputation as a supremely self-confident, dominant courtroom attorney.[16]

The five justices who listened to Thompson were a remarkably homogeneous—though not an elite—group. Associate Justices Henry K. Braley, James B. Carroll, George A. Sanderson, and William C. Wait and Chief Justice Arthur P. Rugg all had been born during the Civil War era and, with the exception of Judge Carroll, who had been born the only son of Irish immigrant parents in the mill town of Lowell, each man had come of age in a small Massachusetts town. Their lives there had been far from bucolic. Each man had faced and overcome adversity. Judge Braley's father, a whaling captain, died when his son was still in his teens. Young Braley shouldered responsibility for the family farm and still managed to complete school by rising early, feeding the livestock, walking five miles to the train, attending school, and returning home in time to complete his chores and then to study late into the night. Judge Wait suffered from infantile paralysis as a child and as an adult was "noticeably lame," but a lifelong regime of exercise allowed him to row and to play golf. Judge Carroll paid his way through the College of the Holy Cross by working as a Worcester evening high school administrator, and Sanderson and Rugg paid part of their Boston University Law School tuition by shelving books in the library. With the exception of Braley, who "strove incessantly to repair" his lack of formal education, all of the judges who heard Sacco and Vanzetti's appeal had graduated from college and law school. Every one of the judges—three Republicans and two Democrats—had rejected the lure of political office in favor of the law and, with the exception of Rugg, each man had served on the lower Superior Court before being appointed to the SJC.[17]

The SJC's justices also shared fundamental values. According to their contemporaries each man—including the Irish Catholic Judge Carroll—manifested "Puritan" characteristics: ethical, religious, hard working, with a simple life-style and a commitment to fulfilling his social-legal duties. Judges Braley and Wait, who wrote for the court in Sacco and Vanzetti's 1926 and 1927 appeals, respectively, won praise for their commitment to "duty" and the "stern code of the Puritan," and for the pride they took in the "judicial traditions of Massachusetts." Similarly, Chief Justice Rugg said at Judge Sanderson's death in 1933 that he was a "true product of the original settlers of the Massachusetts Bay Colony," and like those hardy people, Sanderson "was disciplined by a life of industry, frugality and simplicity." He "carried his full share of the court's work," completing just days before his death the last of the 498 opinions he wrote during his eight years on the SJC. Former Superior Court Judge Frederick Chase praised Sanderson's social and personal characteristics. "In an uneasy and unstable age," Sanderson and his brethren on the court were "driven by an abiding sense of DUTY." In addition to their work on the court, the justices served their communities as selectman, school committeeman, university trustee, bar association officer, and church official. At Rugg's death in 1939, the president of the Suffolk Bar Association linked his personal and social characteristics to a judicial philosophy shared by all of the court's judges: "He gave short shrift to any doctrine of the rights of man which was not also a doctrine of man's duties."[18]

The social background and intellectual values shared by the judges of the SJC sustained a theory of judging based on duty rather than power. It began with their assumption that human nature is unchanging, and, therefore, the principles of conduct that guided the Puritans were appropriate guides for the twentieth century. The law codifies society's controlling principles by delineating governmental power, articulating a citizen's duty to society, and defining a citizen's rights against the state. A judge has a responsibility to follow the law's commands; he has no power to make law. For this reason, appellate judges ordinarily defer to the legislature, but when the court states what the law means, its power transcends that of the other branches of government. By asserting they were not acting to accrue political power, but merely carrying out their duty to the law, the judges who sat on the SJC during the first half of the twentieth century justified their theory of judging.

In addition to the judges' fundamental belief that the law privileges duties over rights, the SJC's review of Judge Thayer's trial rulings was bound by legal rules, none more important than those laid down by Chief Justice Rugg in *Davis v. Boston Elevated Ry. Co.* (1920). In that case, Wilfred W. Davis was standing on a platform in the center of Washington Street, Brookline, at a regular streetcar stop about six feet from an approaching train at 10:30 P.M. on July 6, 1912, when a piece of lead struck him in the left eye. He brought suit against Boston Elevated, claiming his injury resulted from an explosion in a fuse box aboard the streetcar. Boston Elevated argued the streetcar fuse box did not contain lead and that a bullet, perhaps fired by a striking transit worker, caused Davis's injury. At trial before Superior Court judge John D. McLaughlin, a jury found for Davis, awarding him $1,000; but in January 1914 McLaughlin set aside the verdict as "against the weight of the evidence." A second trial followed in October 1914 presided over by Superior Court judge Richard W. Irwin. A Norfolk County jury returned a verdict for Davis, awarding him $15,000. Boston Elevated filed a motion for a new trial on the ground the jury's verdict was against the weight of the evidence. Judge Irwin denied the motion and Boston Elevated appealed to the SJC, which heard oral argument in January 1916. The SJC rejected the streetcar company's argument that a bullet caused Davis's injury. That claim "was not supported by the evidence," and a jury "might well regard the theory as incredible." Judge Charles A. DeCourcy, who had taken his seat on the high court in 1911, held a jury could find by drawing inferences from the circumstantial evidence presented at trial that a fuse box aboard the streetcar had exploded, projecting a piece of lead into Davis's eye. The conclusion the jury reached, DeCourcy wrote, "was not based on mere conjectures; it was the result of logical reasoning from established facts." The court overruled the exceptions filed by Boston Elevated and Davis's $15,000 settlement seemed secure.[19]

Several months later, however, Boston Elevated filed a motion for a new trial on the grounds of newly discovered evidence. A newspaper story about the case had come to the attention of William Liebman, an x-ray technician at Massachusetts Charitable Eye and Ear Infirmary. Liebman told an attorney for Boston Elevated that x-rays he had taken two days after the accident clearly showed the object lodged near Davis's eye to be a bullet. Judge Irwin ruled the x-ray evidence did not meet the legal definition of newly discovered because it merely added to testimony already given at the two trials. In comments made during the hearing, Judge Irwin also suggested Liebman might have altered the pictures. Irwin denied Boston Elevated's motion, insisting his ruling fell within the bounds of judicial discretion and, therefore, he would not set aside the jury's verdict.[20]

Boston Elevated appealed Irwin's rulings to the SJC. Attorney William G. Thompson, who six years later represented Sacco and Vanzetti, called Judge Irwin's denial of the defense motion for a new trial following the discovery of the x-rays "an abuse of judicial power" and labeled the judge's conduct during the hearing "wholly arbitrary and capricious." Daniel J. Gallagher, attorney for Davis, essentially repeated Irwin's rulings, adding that the so-called newly discovered x-ray evidence was introduced too late to be credible.[21]

Chief Justice Rugg spoke for a unanimous court in the spring of 1920. Although the *Davis* decision received little notice, it had an extraordinary impact on the Massachusetts criminal justice system generally and the outcome of the Sacco-Vanzetti trial in particular. Rugg's three rulings greatly expanded a trial judge's power and made it far more difficult for a defendant to successfully appeal lower court rulings. According to the first ruling, a trial judge is not obligated to make certain findings of fact. Judge Irwin did not need to accept as fact that the x-ray plates had been adequately authenticated or that the testimony of Dr. Liebman was sufficiently convincing to conclude definitively that the object in Davis's eye was a bullet, as Boston Elevated insisted. To permit the judge's ruling on a factual issue to be contested would be "to put on trial the magistrate instead of the case." According to the second ruling, a trial judge has broad discretionary authority in regard to a motion for a new trial on the ground of newly discovered evidence and that ruling would not be reviewed even if erroneous, barring an egregious abuse of judicial discretion. For evidence to qualify as newly discovered, three criteria must be fulfilled: it must be "weighty," "credible," and "pertinent to fundamental issues" presented in the case; the new evidence must be more than cumulative; and there must be a probability that the new evidence would be a major factor in the jury's reaching a decision. And according to Rugg's third ruling, even if all three criteria in regard to newly discovered evidence were met, a trial judge would not be bound to grant a motion for a new trial. Furthermore, when a trial judge denied a motion for a new trial based on newly discovered evidence, his ruling would not be regarded as an abuse of judicial discretion, or be open to review by the SJC. "The question is not whether we should take a different view of the evidence or should have made an opposite decision from that made by the trial judge," Rugg wrote, but to sustain the defendant's objections "it is necessary to decide that no conscientious judge, acting intelligently, could honestly have taken" Judge Irwin's view. "We are not prepared to decide that." Finally, Rugg's rulings bolstered the authority of trial judges by limiting the appeals process. "When a case has been fairly and fully tried upon correct principles of law and a verdict has been rendered," the chief justice wrote in *Davis*, "it is in the interest of the commonwealth that there should be an end of the litigation." [22]

The court's rulings in *Davis* had a direct and devastating impact on the outcome of Sacco and Vanzetti's two appeals before the SJC. Attorney Thompson said he wished *Davis* "had never been heard of." "[If I] had known what the effect of taking that case to the [Massachusetts] Supreme Court was going to be," he added, "I would have refused to argue it." Among the dozens of exceptions to Judge Thayer's rulings made by the defendants, the most important to their appeal were the following: the court was bound to accept as fact certain admissions made by the district attorney; the court was obligated to grant a new trial on the basis of newly discovered, credible, weighty evidence; the trial judge's denial of the defendants' motion for a new trial based on the discovery of new evidence was an abuse of judicial discretion. All three of these defense arguments clashed with the SJC's ruling in *Davis*. [23]

The defense argued Judge Thayer had erred when he refused to accept as illegal and prejudicial the fact that jury foreman Walter Ripley brought into the deliberation room some 38-caliber shells like those found in Vanzetti's revolver. At a preliminary hearing the prosecution accepted as fact Ripley's act and in their motion Sacco and Vanzetti argued the district attorney's admissions were binding on the court. Thayer denied the Ripley motion and made two findings of fact: the district attorney's admissions of fact were not binding on the court; and Ripley "never intended to prejudice in any manner the rights of the defendants." Thayer contended that most of the jurors could not recall Ripley's showing or talking about the bullets. With an eye on the appeal he knew would follow, he ruled:

"The mere production of the Ripley cartridges and the talk and discussion about them did not create such disturbing or prejudicial influence that might in any way affect the verdict or operate in any way whatsoever to the prejudice of the defendants." But Thayer did not stop with a legal opinion. With a flash of emotion clearly aimed at his critics inside and outside the courtroom, Thayer lashed out: "At any rate, I am not willing to blacken the memory of Mr. Ripley and to pronounce those eleven surviving jurors as falsifiers under oath by claim of counsel that are so weak, so fragile, and so unsatisfactory; for it should be borne in mind that jurors, whose work is greater and whose responsibility under the law, is far more important than that of the presiding justice have rights that even he [William Thompson, Sacco and Vanzetti's counsel] should honor and respect." Relying on *Davis*, the SJC upheld Thayer's rulings on two other crucial points and reiterated its support for the broad use of judicial discretion. First, Justice Braley wrote for a unanimous court, the trial judge alone can determine from the evidence the facts and his decision is final. Second, the court rejected the defendants' argument that Thayer's rulings on these and related issues were an abuse of judicial discretion. A trial judge, the SJC had ruled in *Davis*, could not act arbitrarily or whimsically or with unchecked power, but if his rulings are characterized by "intelligence and learning, controlled by sound principles of law, of firm courage combined with the calmness of a cool mind, free from partiality, not swayed by sympathy nor warped by prejudice nor moved by any kind of influence save alone the overwhelming passion to do that which is just" judicial discretion has been used properly. Measured by this standard, Judge Thayer did not "exercise his judicial discretion in such a manner as to constitute a denial of justice." For these reasons, together with the court's oft-expressed belief that "successive motions for a new trial might easily be converted into an obstruction of public justice and become an abuse," the SJC affirmed Sacco and Vanzetti's conviction.[24]

Early in 1927 Sacco and Vanzetti were before the SJC again. On October 23, 1926, Judge Thayer had denied the defendants' motion for a new trial based on the discovery of new evidence. Specifically, the defendants contended that Celestino Madeiros, a convicted eighteen-year-old murderer jailed in Dedham while awaiting a decision on his appeal, had passed to Sacco a slip of paper on which Madeiros had written: "I hear by confess to being in the south Braintree shoe company crime and Sacco and Vanzetti was not in said crime." In an affidavit attached to Sacco and Vanzetti's motion, Madeiros stated he met four Italians, later tentatively identified as members of the Morelli gang, at a bar in Providence, Rhode Island, and they invited him to join them in robbing the Slater and Morrill payroll. Madeiros claimed he sat in the bandit car nervously clutching a handgun while the robbery and murders took place. Neither Madeiros nor anyone from the Morelli gang appeared before Judge Thayer during the motion hearing; the defendants and the prosecution relied on dozens of affidavits. In his affidavit, young Madeiros claimed he confessed simply to save the lives of two innocent men. Thayer did not believe Madeiros.[25]

"Madeiros is, without doubt," Judge Thayer wrote, "a crook, a thief, a robber, a liar, a rum-runner, a 'bouncer' in a house of ill-fame, a smuggler, and a man who has been convicted and sentenced to death for the murder of . . . a cashier of the Wrentham Bank." Thayer also pointed out how few details about the crime Madeiros was able to recount. His failure to recall accurately any details of the crime, Thayer said of Madeiros "would seem to be more consistent with the fact that he was not there, rather than that fear benumbed his sight and memory." Finally, if Madeiros had been double-crossed by the Morelli gang as he said, why would he refuse to divulge the names of the gang members responsible for murdering Parmenter and Berardelli?[26]

In its brief to the SJC the defense aggressively attacked Judge Thayer's ruling, pointing out his errors and assaulting his logic, as well as his "prejudice and personal hostility" toward the defendants. The defense brief was tied together with phrases such as "he pays no attention to the fact," "he ignores the undisputed fact," "he entirely ignores the undisputed fact" and concluded by asserting that Judge Thayer "ignores every agreed fact, every undisputed fact, and every statement in any affidavit, tending to establish the truth of Madeiros' confession." Defense attorney Thompson especially objected to Thayer's charge that he had slipped information about the case to Madeiros in order to bolster the credibility of his confession. Further, Thompson charged that Thayer's findings "grossly violated" the "judicial traditions of this Commonwealth" and were a "reflection of the still lingering public excitement caused by the campaign of [U.S. Attorney General] Mitchell Palmer in 1920 against the so-called 'Reds.'" For these reasons, Thompson asked the SJC—"the ultimate tribunal for the administration of justice according to law"—to give Sacco and Vanzetti "all the protection that the common law affords, not merely the protection of its technical rules, but the protection of that fundamental spirit of fairness upon which all lesser rules are based." [27]

Without acknowledging the validity of a single claim made by the defense, the SJC affirmed Judge Thayer's ruling denying Sacco and Vanzetti's motion for a new trial based on newly discovered evidence. As it had in the defendants' initial appeal, the SJC leaned heavily on its ruling in *Davis v. Boston Elevated* (1920), a decision that broke with the court's tradition of judicial restraint and legislative deference and denied capital defendants substantive appellate review. (As late as the 1930s only seven state supreme courts had rule-making power and it was used infrequently.) Although it was highly unusual for the SJC to initiate change or to apply recently articulated rules of civil procedure directly and immediately to a capital case, the practice of integrating civil and criminal procedure had deep common law roots. Early English criminal law allowed legal actions by the crown and by a private party so that an aggrieved party might bring a civil action against the same person for the same transgression charged by the crown with a public wrong. In the United States the line between these overlapping courses of action, and the rules that governed them, remained ill defined for some time. Private litigants, for example, enjoyed a common law right to discovery—the pretrial exchange of information. The discovery rule's success in speeding up civil proceedings eventually led to the adoption of a similar rule in Massachusetts criminal cases, but not until 1974 after years of debate. That the Rugg court would use a decision in an ordinary civil case to greatly expand a criminal trial judge's discretionary authority and apply to a capital case a rule adopted to expedite the termination of civil litigation was extraordinary. [28]

Yet, that is exactly what the SJC did when, in a short businesslike decision issued on April 5, 1927, it upheld every one of Judge Thayer's rulings denying Sacco and Vanzetti a new trial. First, despite an elaborate defense argument to the contrary, the court upheld Judge Thayer's ruling that no reliance could be placed upon Madeiros's alleged confession, because the trial judge's ruling on that issue was, according to court rule, a matter of fact and, therefore, "final." Second, the court upheld Thayer's denial of the defense motion for a new trial based on the discovery of new evidence, finding the trial judge's ruling within the nearly limitless bounds of his discretionary authority as established in *Davis*. "It is not imperative," Justice Wait wrote for a unanimous court, "that a new trial be granted even though the evidence is newly discovered, and, if presented to a jury, would justify a different verdict." Nor was the court obligated to order a new trial even if there were "actual errors of law" in the trial judge's explanation of his ruling. Third, citing *Davis* again, the SJC rebuffed Sacco and Vanzetti's contention that Thayer's refusal to grant a new trial on the basis of solid newly discovered evidence constituted "an abuse of discretion amounting to denial of due process." To permit the defense to contest the arguments put forth by the trial judge in his decision denying the motion "would be to put on trial the magistrate instead of the case." "It is not for us to determine what is to be believed. The question for us is: Could the judge conscientiously, intelligently and honestly have reached the result he has reached." To answer that question in favor of the defense, it would be "necessary to decide that no conscientious judge, acting intelligently, could honestly have taken the view expressed by [Judge Thayer]." For these reasons, the court concluded, a new trial was not necessary to prevent a failure of justice.[29]

On Saturday morning, April 9, 1927, Sacco and Vanzetti were sentenced to death. Judge Thayer read the formulaic orders. Before he completed reading Vanzetti's sentence, Sacco cried out: "You know I am innocent. That is the same words I pronounced seven years ago. You condemn two innocent men." Without repeating the words he had spoken before Sacco interrupted, Thayer hurriedly concluded, "by the passage of a current of electricity through your body within the week beginning on Sunday, the tenth day of July, in the year of our Lord, one thousand nine hundred and twenty-seven. This is the sentence of the law."[30]

This chilling legal ritual intensified the divisive debate within the Massachusetts legal community. The *Boston Herald* reporter F. Lauriston Bullard summed up the situation as follows: "Probably four in five, perhaps nine in ten, of the lawyers of the city [Boston] are anti-Sacco on the ground chiefly that nothing must be permitted to damage the reputation of the judicial system of Massachusetts. To which the minority, including not a few lawyers of eminence, reply that nothing can do the courts more harm than to proceed to the end on the assumption of their infallibility." While most practicing attorneys said nothing publicly, some law professors were less reticent about entering the fray. In May 1925, Roscoe Pound, dean of Harvard Law School, wrote to Sacco and Vanzetti's appellate attorney William Thompson suggesting how he might handle the identification evidence on which Sacco and Vanzetti's conviction seemed to depend. About a month later, Pound bluntly told Thompson: "I would not hang a dog on the evidence" and proposed "the whole trial ought to be written up thoroughly" by someone with the "courage and the sense of justice to speak out vigorously about these cases." Pound begged off taking a partisan public position. But a number of Harvard law professors did speak or write publicly about the case, none more vociferously and aggressively than Felix Frankfurter. Before his appointment to Harvard Law School in 1914, from which he had graduated eight years earlier, Frankfurter had served as an assistant U.S. attorney and helped found the *New Republic* and the American Civil Liberties Union. He had also become an intimate friend of Justice Louis Brandeis. Frankfurter was forty-four years old in 1927 when he spoke out for Sacco and Vanzetti.[31]

Shortly before Judge Thayer sentenced Sacco and Vanzetti to death, and before the appeals process had run its course, Frankfurter published a scathing attack, exposing what he argued were the weaknesses of the prosecution's case and the legal irregularities that had marred the trial and the SJC's decision to allow the convictions to stand. Frankfurter's enormously influential *Atlantic Monthly* article and subsequent book, *The Case of Sacco and Vanzetti: A Critical Analysis for Lawyers and Laymen*, tar the Dedham judge, prosecutor, and jury with the brush of prejudice and bias. Frankfurter paints a vivid picture of the greater Boston area as awash in "political passion and patriotic sentiment" that the prosecutor "systematically" used, and in which the judge "connived" in order to allow "Red hysteria" to "dominate" the courtroom and to "divert and pervert the jury's mind." According to Frankfurter, the Sacco-Vanzetti jurors' pledge to impartiality was compromised to begin with and then overwhelmed by patriotic zeal and by District Attorney Katzmann and Judge Thayer's unconscionable effort to stoke the fires of prejudice so that the two Italian radicals would be found guilty regardless of the evidence. In this way, Frankfurter concluded, the "ample safeguards against perversions of justice" were fatally undermined.[32]

Despite this inflammatory thesis, Frankfurter claims his book is a "disinterested summary" of the trial. To make his case for Sacco and

Vanzetti's innocence and for the likely guilt of Celestino Madeiros and the Providence-based Morelli gang, Frankfurter focuses on three major areas of the trial and appeals process: eyewitness testimony; the so-called mortal bullet; and "consciousness of guilt." He begins with Mary Splaine's uncontradicted eyewitness identification of Sacco. Based on a brief, distant look at the speeding bandit car, Splaine, an employee of Slater and Morill, gave a remarkably detailed description of Sacco as one of the bandit car's passengers. According to Frankfurter, Splaine's feat resulted from the unethical police practice of allowing Splaine to view Sacco alone rather than in a lineup. "Everyone knows," Morton Prince, a Harvard psychologist quoted at length by Frankfurter, explains, that following a face-to-face meeting between an eyewitness and a suspected criminal "the image of [that] person later develops, or may develop, in an observer's mind and becomes a false memory." In other words, according to Prince's controversial theory, when, at trial more than a year later, Splaine saw Sacco seated inside the prisoner's docket, the sight triggered a "false memory," leading her to believe she had first seen him in the speeding get-away car. She then filled in the descriptive details simply by looking across the courtroom at Sacco. In this way, Frankfurter argues, Splaine's "false memory" produced an erroneous identification.[33]

Frankfurter used a more conventional lawyer's technique to undermine the credibility of the other eyewitnesses who placed Sacco and Vanzetti at the crime scene. He compresses and highlights the testimony of eyewitnesses for the defense whose accounts contradicted the men and women the prosecution put on the stand. To discredit the testimony of Louis Pelzer, a shoe cutter who identified Sacco as the man he saw standing over the fallen body of Berardelli, for example, Frankfurter briefly excerpts and exaggerates the clarity of testimony given by three of Pelzer's fellow workmen who said he took cover under a workbench when the shooting began. Contradictory eyewitness testimony is commonplace, and experts argue that it may simply be that some people can make accurate observations or identifications and others cannot. Likewise, jurors tend to believe eyewitnesses who appear credible and likable, and who seem not to have a motive to distort the truth. For one or more of these reasons, the Sacco-Vanzetti jurors apparently believed Pelzer, and not the defense witnesses.[34]

What Frankfurter regarded as duplicitous testimony about the mortal bullet forms the second part of his argument. At trial, four ballistics experts testified: Massachusetts State Police captains William Proctor and Charles Van Amburgh for the commonwealth and James E. Burns and Henry J. Fitzgerald for the defense. Their lengthy testimony was contradictory, highly technical, and often confusing. In his critique of the trial Frankfurter focuses on a single phrase Proctor used. He charges that District Attorney Katzmann and Judge Thayer deliberately manipulated and misinterpreted Proctor's testimony to make it appear he believed one of the bullets taken from Berardelli's body had been fired from the Colt automatic found on Sacco the night of his arrest. When Katzmann asked Proctor whether he had an opinion "as to whether bullet No. 3 was fired from the Colt automatic," Proctor answered that in his opinion the mortal bullet was "consistent with being fired from [Sacco's] pistol." At the trial's conclusion, as Frankfurter tells it, Thayer highlighted Proctor's response, instructing the jury: "it was his [Sacco's] pistol that fired the bullet that caused the death of Berardelli." "Naturally," Frankfurter writes, "the Court's interpretation became the jury's."[35]

Following Sacco and Vanzetti's conviction, the defense filed a number of motions for a new trial, one of which was based on its discovery of the pretrial arrangement between Katzmann and Proctor and Thayer's jury instruction on the meaning of Proctor's testimony. In an affidavit Proctor (who died shortly after the conclusion of the trial) stated he and Katzmann had created language that masked the police captain's doubt that the mortal bullet had been fired from Sacco's gun. Proctor insisted he "repeatedly" told Katzmann he would have to answer negatively if he were asked directly whether he had concluded that the mortal bullet had been fired from Sacco's gun. Therefore, according to Proctor, the two men worked out a compromise that allowed him to seem to support the prosecution's position without explicitly saying so. At the motion hearing, Katzmann denied he had repeatedly asked Proctor whether he could testify that the mortal bullet came from Sacco's gun. The district attorney also pointed out that Proctor had framed the question asked in court and that the words " 'consistent with' were often used by witnesses in court." Thayer denied the defense motion, ruling that the district attorney's questions to Proctor were clear, fairly interpreted, and answered honestly. Frankfurter vehemently disagreed.[36]

As a law professor Frankfurter knew that all expert testimony is prearranged, yet he heatedly charged that the pretrial arrangement between

Katzmann and Proctor "shake[s] one's confidence in the whole course of the proceedings and reveal[s] a situation which in and of itself undermines the respect usually to be accorded to a jury's verdict." Frankfurter also objected to Thayer's denial of that part of the defense motion asserting that he had given a misleading interpretation of Proctor's testimony. "In his charge," Frankfurter writes, referring to his abbreviated version of the judge's instructions about the bullet and implying a conspiracy between the district attorney and the judge, "Judge Thayer misled the jury by maximizing the Proctor testimony as the prearrangement intended it should be maximized."[37]

In fact, Frankfurter exaggerates the significance of Proctor's statement. He strips away the context and qualifiers in Thayer's charge to the jury and belittles Thayer's "moral exhortations" and his praise for the "ideals of justice." Roughly halfway through his thirty-four-page charge, Thayer noted that the commonwealth made "claims" about evidence, including that the fatal bullet had been fired by Sacco's pistol. "If that is true," he pointed out, it would be evidence "tending to corroborate" the testimony of eyewitnesses who placed Sacco at the scene of the crime. "On the other hand," Thayer said at the conclusion of his paragraph-length summation of the ballistics testimony, two experts for the defense testified the fatal bullet did not come from Sacco's pistol.[38]

The third part of Frankfurter's critical analysis focuses on Judge Thayer's use of consciousness of guilt, a legal concept that assumes persons guilty of a crime act guilty. John H. Wigmore, a professor of law who later engaged in a newspaper battle of words with Frankfurter, explains the concept in his *Treatise on the Anglo-American System of Evidence*: "A criminal act leaves usually on the mind a deep trace, in the shape of a consciousness of guilt, and from this consciousness of guilt we may argue to the doer of the deed by the bearer of the trace." Although the concept of consciousness of guilt was used widely, critics pointed out that its manifestations were equivocal. "Almost anything," Robert Hutchins and Donald Slesinger argue in the *University of Pennsylvania Law Review*, "if to the popular imagination it denotes a sense of shame, may be introduced to prove, inferentially, the commission of a crime." According to the legal rule and the commonsense notion on which it rested, indications of consciousness of guilt include flight, silence under accusation, lying, carrying a gun, resisting arrest, and nervousness. However, Wigmore and other lawyers acknowledge, the "same symptom is often the result of exactly opposite psychological conditions" than guilt. For that reason, Hutchins and Slesinger warn, "since the lay and legal view is that consciousness of guilt is a fact and an extremely impressive fact, it would seem that this is one of the cases where there is a grave danger that the jury will be misled." [39]

Judge Thayer's charge to the Sacco-Vanzetti jury defined consciousness of guilt and explained that in order to give legal meaning to the concept it had to be based on facts. "The entire record of every person's life," Thayer instructed, somewhat simplistically, "is safely locked up in the vault of the human brain." A jury may gain access to a criminal defendant's mind by interpreting the "speech, physical acts, movements and manifestations of the body." In this case, Thayer noted, the jury must determine whether the conduct of the defendants on the night of their arrest indicated they were "conscious of having committed some crime." Did the behavior of the defendants when they hastily departed from the Johnson garage after being told the car they sought could not be driven away because it did not have the proper license plate manifest guilt or resignation? The commonwealth argued the men's retreat from Johnson's garage, the fact both men carried guns, the threatening moves they allegedly made when police approached them on board the trolley, and the lies the two suspects told when they were interrogated at the Brockton police station, manifested consciousness of guilt for the murders of Berardelli and Parmenter. The defense contested, or interpreted differently, these same facts. The jury's task, Thayer stated, was to determine the truth. If Sacco and Vanzetti's behavior or their statements to authorities "were made for the purpose of deception in regard to the facts relating to the murders of Berardelli and Parmenter," then the jury may consider those facts as evidence of consciousness of guilt. If their behavior may be explained as unrelated to the murders or their statements to the police were made for any purpose other than the concealment of the facts relating to the murders—because they feared arrest for their radical political activities—Thayer concluded, you must "give the evidence no further consideration whatsoever." [40]

Frankfurter elaborates on the defense position. If specific aspects of Sacco and Vanzetti's behavior manifested consciousness of guilt its origins lay in their fear of being arrested or deported for political radicalism and had nothing to do with murder. First, although Thayer made much of the episode, Sacco and Vanzetti's behavior at Johnson's garage did not manifest consciousness of guilt. Friends of Sacco and Vanzetti asked whether they could claim their car. Johnson said no, because it did not have the proper license plate. There was a brief conversation and the four Italian men left the scene. Second, Frankfurter offers an alternative explanation for why the men were carrying pistols and he flatly rejects the claim the two men made threatening gestures when they were confronted by a Brockton police officer aboard the trolley. Carrying a gun is not unusual in these turbulent times, Frankfurter writes. Sacco "acquired the habit of carrying a pistol while a night watchman" and Vanzetti carried a gun because in his fish-peddling business he often carried large amounts of cash. (Frankfurter failed to mention that Sacco lied to the officer on board the trolley, saying, "I ain't got no gun." A search carried out at the police station discovered Sacco's Colt automatic tucked into his waistband.) Third, Frankfurter admits Sacco and Vanzetti lied to police, but, he argues, they were trying to conceal their movements and the identity of their friends, because they "were not innocent of the charge on which they *supposed* themselves arrested," namely, their radical beliefs and activities. But, according to Frankfurter, District Attorney Katzmann "adopted" Sacco and Vanzetti's "confession of radicalism, exaggerated and exploited it," making it appear to manifest a consciousness of guilt for the murder of the paymaster and his guard. Thayer's instructions to the jury pounded the same theme.[41]

Frankfurter mutes his critique of the SJC's decision issued May 12, 1926 upholding Thayer's denial of the defense motions for a new trial. He laments that the SJC's scope of review did not include issues of fact but focused solely on questions of law. According to Frankfurter, the defense presented Judge Thayer with solid factual evidence for why he should order a new trial, but he brushed it aside. He did not act impartially, calmly, or without prejudice. Therefore, Thayer's ruling was an abuse of judicial discretion. However, because the SJC's appellate review focused narrowly on questions of law, the court upheld Thayer's rulings on matters of fact as within his discretionary power. These "rulings are puzzling in the extreme," and "contrary to the standards of Anglo-American justice," Frankfurter insists.[42]

Frankfurter's argument may have seemed objective and professional. He had skillfully reduced thousands of pages of testimony to a readable, authoritative 14-page magazine article and a short book of 118 pages. Everyone who believed in Sacco and Vanzetti's innocence or that the government had deliberately denied them a fair trial adopted Frankfurter's argument, examples, and conclusions. Indeed, his argument framed the opposition narrative for several generations.

Perhaps at the invitation of the conservative *Boston Evening Transcript*, John Wigmore, former dean of Northwestern University Law School and, at sixty-four, the nation's preeminent authority on the law of evidence, responded to Frankfurter. About a month after *The Case of Sacco and Vanzetti* appeared, the *Transcript* published Wigmore's rebuttal. He wrote, he said, to show that Frankfurter's argument was "neither fair nor accurate nor complete," and "to vindicate Massachusetts Justices." But Wigmore's obvious political conservatism and a handful of factual errors undercut his effort. Snidely referring to Frankfurter as "a prominent pundit in a leading law school," Wigmore attempted to brand the Harvard professor as a radical. Criticism of Sacco and Vanzetti's trial and appeals, Wigmore asserted, began among "various alien communist circles" and "was extended to the general public" by Frankfurter.[43]

Wigmore made at least three significant factual errors. To counter Frankfurter's argument that Sacco had lied to an interrogator because of his fear he would be arrested and or deported for his radical beliefs, Wigmore insisted that when cross-examined at trial, Sacco stated he already had a passport. Therefore, he would have no need to lie. In fact, Frankfurter pointed out in a rebuttal published the next day in the *Transcript*, "a careful search of the record of Sacco's cross-examination discloses no such questions and answers." That erroneous assertion had come from Thayer's mistaken ruling and not from the trial transcript. Wigmore stated also that Frankfurter had failed to mention Sacco's cap, calling it a damning omission. In fact, Frankfurter had included the conflicting testimony about the cap recovered from the crime scene. Finally, Wigmore argued that the SJC could and did review both law and facts. Citing cases and law touching on that point, Wigmore insisted that the SJC's April 1926 opinion affirmed Thayer's rulings on the law and, furthermore, that the court found "sufficient evidence to justify the verdict of guilty of murder." Every Massachusetts lawyer knows, Frankfurter wrote in his rebuttal, the SJC cannot pass on the guilt or innocence of Sacco and Vanzetti or any other criminal conviction. Only errors of law may be before the court and, according to the court's decision, the trial judge's findings of fact were final. Frankfurter successfully closed the issue in his favor by quoting the court's recent decision: "It is not imperative that a new trial be granted even though the evidence is newly discovered, and if presented to a jury, would justify a different verdict." [44]

Wigmore did get it right when he said the defense had introduced the issue of radicalism, but he missed the point of Frankfurter's thesis. As though he were delivering a telling blow, Wigmore triumphantly pointed out that Sacco and Vanzetti's trial attorneys introduced the issue of radicalism because they had to explain why the two men lied to their interrogators following their arrest. "Of course, the defense introduced radicalism," Frankfurter impatiently fired back. District Attorney Katzmann and Judge Thayer "utilized this unavoidable disclosure by the defendants of their hated views to excite the passions of the jury against them."

The two lawyers' duel ended with Frankfurter's sharp rejoinder. To contemporary readers, his arguments seemed accurate, straightforward, and nonpartisan, whereas Wigmore's piece was full of obvious factual errors, cynicism, and political conservatism. Most important, Wigmore had not effectively summarized the prosecution's case. Instead, he had attempted unsuccessfully to refute Frankfurter's main points piecemeal. Harvard president A. Lawrence Lowell spoke for many. "Wigmore's ridiculous article" he told Chief Justice Howard Taft, "looked as if there was nothing serious to be said on the side of the courts." [45]

Ironically, it was Boston's legendary civil rights attorney and activist, Moorefield Storey, who defended the legal process and the verdict against Sacco and Vanzetti. In a brief letter printed in the *Boston Herald* the day after the paper published an editorial calling for a new trial, Storey, the former president of the N.A.A.C.P. and the American Bar Association, warned his fellow citizens that "a man who has not heard the evidence, who has not seen a witness, and whose opinion is formed only from loose and irresponsible talk has no right to express an opinion on the question whether the verdict is right or not." The Sacco-Vanzetti case was tried before a good jury and the postconviction motions for a new trial were "carefully considered and overruled" by Judge Thayer. Although he did not mention Frankfurter by name, Storey dismissed his central argument. "Nothing could be more preposterous," Storey wrote, "than the suggestion that officers representing the attorney general's office of the United States, conspired with the officers charged with the duty of enforcing law in Massachusetts to convict two innocent men of murder, and when to that amazing claim is added the testimony of a convicted murderer, it only shows how desperate is the defendant's position when he must resort to such material." Storey concluded: "Our system of administering the law in Massachusetts is on trial," and if Sacco and Vanzetti are freed on the basis of Madeiros's confession, "the lives and property of Massachusetts citizens are no longer safe."[46]

Storey's plea for informed judgment and support for the Massachusetts criminal justice system was overshadowed by the *Herald*'s Pulitzer Prize–winning editorial, "We Submit," that appeared the day before Storey's letter. F. Lauriston Bullard's powerful argument that sufficient doubt about the verdict existed for the SJC to grant a new trial and Frankfurter's scathing attack carried the day and created pressure on Governor Alvan T. Fuller to intervene in the case. The possibility some sort of rehearing would be forthcoming did nothing for Sacco's spirits; he plunged into despair and refused to sign a petition for clemency carried to the governor by defense attorneys Thompson and Herbert Ehrmann. In a letter dated May 4, 1927, Vanzetti echoed Frankfurter's primary arguments. With help from his lawyers, Vanzetti charged in his petition that Katzmann's cross-examination of Sacco "was designed to excite the utmost prejudice and hostility against us at a time when the public mind was most abnormally excited against such men as we are" and that Judge Thayer's bias caused his discretionary rulings to go consistently against the defendants. In the name of justice, Vanzetti asked for a public investigation by "able and disinterested men." Governor Fuller, a forty-nine-year-old Republican and former automobile dealer, rejected the idea of public hearings, but on June 1, he announced in connection with his investigation of the case the formation of an advisory committee consisting of Judge Robert Grant, Harvard President Abbott Lawrence Lowell, and Massachusetts Institute of Technology president Samuel W. Stratton. The committee examined witnesses, with the notable exceptions of Thayer, Katzmann, and ten available jurors, in the presence of defense counsel and attorneys for the commonwealth.[47]

Two general questions guided the committee's work during its hearings: Was the trial fair? and, Is there reasonable doubt about Sacco and Vanzetti's guilt? Following two weeks of testimony about the law and the facts, at 10:30 A.M. Monday, July 25, attorney Thompson stood to deliver a closing statement. As he had throughout the appeals process, Thompson argued the trial was fundamentally unfair, but this time he leveled his criticism at Judge Thayer personally. Thompson divided his argument into four parts. First, the conditions surrounding the trial—the national and local hunt for Reds, the breathless, patriotic newspaper coverage, and the presence of armed guards at the courthouse—prejudiced the jury, even though they may not have been "conscious of it." Second, Thompson argued that Judge Thayer's "state of mind and conduct" prejudiced the defendants at trial and during the appeals process. "He is a narrow-minded man; he is a half educated man; he is an unintelligent man; he is full of prejudice," Thompson said of Thayer. He is not intentionally wicked, but because of his beliefs he thought he was "rendering a great public service" by seeing that two radicals were found guilty. To substantiate his charge, Thompson highlighted the testimony of several witnesses who stated Thayer had made prejudiced remarks about radicals outside of court and that manifested prejudice shaped Thayer's in-court rulings. "Do you think," Thompson asked the committee, "that Thayer's prejudiced feeling did not enter into any of the decisions adverse to the defendants? Unless you can really say that you ought not refuse relief to these two men. There has been an unfair trial." Third, Thompson argued that Katzmann had not played fair; he had withheld information and witnesses who might have been useful to the defense, and his cross-examination of Sacco had no purpose other than creating hatred of radicals. Fourth, and most important, Thompson appealed to the committee's class bias. Massachusetts courts, he told the three committeemen, had a well-earned reputation for being fair, especially in regard to poor, friendless defendants. Thayer's loose, vulgar talk outside court and his bullying attitude in the courtroom badly damaged that reputation. But, Thompson continued, the SJC has never granted a motion finding a lower court judge has abused his discretionary power. Therefore, the defendants' only hope and the state's only hope to remove the stain from its record is for the committee to recommend a pardon. "You are the only people standing between Sacco and Vanzetti and the electric chair." [48]

Assistant District Attorney Dudley P. Ranney (Katzmann had left the district attorney's office for private practice) wasted no time coming to the commonwealth's primary point. There was nothing in the record to support the accusation that Judge Thayer's alleged prejudice was manifested at the trial or in his postconviction rulings. Ranney made the same show-me argument in response to the defendant's contention that radicalism permeated the trial. Acknowledging that people coming into the Dedham courthouse were searched by police, he insisted there was no evidence to suggest that anything other than "wise police protection" prompted that procedure. And, Katzmann's aggressive cross-examination of Sacco stayed within the bounds of the law. Finally, Ranney dismissed as "pure speculation" the notion that someone had tampered with the mortal bullet and as a "mere play on words" the defense claim that Proctor's use of the word "consistent" meant anything other than the fatal bullet might have come from Sacco's pistol. In closing, Ranney begged the committee to ignore public opinion and to report to the governor only the facts.[49]

Within days after closing arguments were made, the Advisory Committee sent its report, largely written by Lowell, to Governor Fuller. On August 3, 1927, he denied Sacco and Vanzetti's plea for a pardon. Fuller found no credible evidence that Judge Thayer or the jurors were prejudiced. Sacco and Vanzetti had a fair trial. The governor also agreed the jury had sufficient evidence to convict and that none of the postconviction motions "presented any valid reason for granting the accused men a new trial." Judge Thayer's postconviction rulings were free of bias. Fuller acknowledged that "many sober-minded and conscientious men and women" harbored doubts about the "guilt or innocence of the accused and the fairness of the trial," but he hoped the fact that he and the Advisory Committee independently came to the conclusion that Sacco and Vanzetti had received a fair trial and that the two men were guilty as charged would help quiet public discontent.[50] Despite a renewed outburst of public anger, Sacco and Vanzetti were executed on August 23, 1927.

More than three-quarters of a century later, though bits and pieces of new evidence have surfaced, and new interpretations have been put forth, for many people a definitive conclusion about Sacco and Vanzetti's guilt or innocence is still an elusive goal. But the flaws in the law privately recognized by the majority of the Massachusetts legal community and publicly articulated by Frankfurter slowly have been reformed. A 1939 statute allowed the Massachusetts SJC to review the law and the facts, a change that not only gave the SJC greater power to review capital convictions but limited a trial judge's discretionary power as well. During the second half of the twentieth century the Supreme Court of the United States and the SJC also enacted rules designed to filter out prejudice from a jury pool.

Supreme Court justice Frankfurter had a hand in that change as well. These reforms were Sacco and Vanzetti's positive legal legacy.[51]

With a handful of exceptions, the Massachusetts legal community had been silent about the specific issues swirling around the Sacco-Vanzetti case and firmly committed to defending the Massachusetts criminal justice system. When defense attorney Thompson attempted to win the Boston Bar Association's support for a new trial, for example, the president, George R. Nutter, forbade any discussion. But, without mentioning the Sacco-Vanzetti case by name, in 1925 Attorney General Jay R. Benton successfully persuaded the legislature to enact a law accelerating the appeals process. The law abolished the bill of exceptions, an ancient and contentious method of appeal, in favor of simply sending an official record from the trial court to the SJC along with the defendant's assignment of errors. In June 1927, Governor Fuller privately told the owner and publisher of the Boston *Traveller* and the Boston *Herald* that he found it "abhorrent" that responsibility for life and death decisions fell on one man, trial Judge Thayer. Attorney General Arthur K. Reading, lamenting the "misrepresentations and propaganda" that had besmirched the "fair name of the Commonwealth" as a result of Sacco-Vanzetti, proposed to the legislature a bundle of modest reforms designed to streamline the criminal justice system. At this point, Nutter reversed his earlier stand and told the *New York Times* that the "Sacco-Vanzetti case showed serious imperfections in our methods of administering justice."[52]

Almost immediately after Sacco and Vanzetti's execution, the legal community launched an effort to reform the criminal justice system. The Judicial Council of Massachusetts, an appointive, advisory body created three years earlier and charged with "the continuous study of the organization, rules and methods of procedure and practice of the judicial system of the Commonwealth," proposed that the legislature enact a law allowing the SJC to order a new trial "if satisfied that the verdict was against the law or the weight of the evidence, or because of newly discovered evidence, or for any other reason that justice may require." The Judicial Council of Massachusetts was one of more than a dozen such judicial advisory councils formed throughout the United States in the 1920s. Each of the chief judges in the Massachusetts court system—the SJC, the Superior Court, and the Land Court—appointed a representative to serve on the council for an unspecified term, and the governor, with the advice and consent of his Council, appointed one judge of the probate court, one district court judge, and four members of the bar to serve four year terms. The enabling legislation called for the Judicial Council to report annually to the governor and allowed it to make recommendations for rule changes to the courts.[53]

In a report published within months after Sacco and Vanzetti were executed, the Judicial Council proposed legislation designed to transform capital procedure. "The extraordinary length of time which elapsed between conviction of Sacco and Vanzetti and their execution, as well as certain of the proceedings in the case," the report began, "illustrated in a striking way some serious defects in our methods of administering justice in murder cases." To speed up the appeals process, the council recommended that motions for a new trial be filed within one year after the defendant is found guilty and that a convict has a right to one appeal to the SJC, unless a single justice rules a new and substantial question ought to be heard by the full court. The SJC also should be granted the power to review substantive issues of fact so that it can remedy a trial judge's error. If the trial judge's ruling is correct, the SJC's review would "establish the fact that he is right" and convince the people that justice had been done. "It is vital that our Courts do justice," the report added. "It is also vital that people know that they do justice." Finally, the SJC also should be empowered to pass on the weight of the evidence to determine whether the jury's verdict was justified by the facts.[54]

Although they had followed very different career paths and had been appointed to the council by four different state officials, all nine men serving on the Massachusetts Judicial Council in 1927 unanimously agreed about what needed to be done to remedy the criticism aimed at the courts during the Sacco and Vanzetti case. Chief Justice Arthur Rugg, author of the decision responsible for expanding the trial court's discretionary power and restricting the SJC's ability to review capital appeals, appointed to the council William Caleb Loring. A vocal advocate for legal reform, Loring was "born in the purple" at Beverly, Massachusetts, entered Harvard College as a member of the class of 1872, graduated from Harvard Law School three years later, and served as an associate justice of the SJC from 1899 to 1919. He helped found the Boston Bar Association, a professional group he and his elite colleagues believed should take the lead in regulating the bench and bar and lobbying the legislature for or against bills affecting the administration of justice. Other former judges appointed to the council included Franklin G. Fessenden, a seventy-eight-year-old Harvard-trained lawyer who sat on the Superior Court bench for thirty-one years; Frank A. Milliken, a longtime District Court judge in New Bedford, a textile manufacturing city that was home to thousands of recent immigrants; Charles T. Davis, a graduate of Harvard College admitted to the bar in 1886 who practiced in Boston for a decade before being appointed a Land Court judge, a post he held for thirty-eight years (1898–1936); and William M. Prest, from the Suffolk County Probate Court. Conservative Republican Governor Channing Cox appointed four attorneys: forty-seven-year-old Frederick W. Mansfield, a distinguished Irish-Catholic lawyer and Democrat who unsuccessfully ran for governor in 1916 but won election as mayor of Boston in 1933; Robert G. Dodge, a Harvard Law School graduate who joined Moorefield Storey's Boston law firm in 1910 and, like his mentor, also earned a reputation as a public advocate against injustice; Frank W. Grinnell, a member of the Boston Bar and secretary of the Massachusetts Bar Association from 1915 to 1960, who performed the council's secretarial duties; and a lawyer from Holyoke, Addison L. Green, who served as the council's chairman from 1924 to 1929.[55]

Year after year, despite changing personnel, the council argued that the existing procedure of allowing a single trial judge to pass on the law and the facts of a capital case put too much pressure on that judge. The council's *Fourteenth Report* spelled out its position.

> In substance this means there is no review of the discretion of the single judge. This a matter of life or death, once treated with utmost care, even beyond the requirements of the law, has now been committed to a single judge of the Superior Court, with no review whatever on its most vital aspects. Such a situation places an unfair responsibility upon the trial judge and upon the Governor, is a potential threat to justice and is not reassuring to the public who have a right to demand that judicial consideration should be exhausted before a man is condemned to death.

After more than a decade of being thwarted by timid legislators, the council's proposed legislation quietly passed through the legislature and on July 12, 1939, Republican Governor Leverett Saltonstall signed it into law. The *New Republic* applauded the law but also warned that "'it could happen again—either in Massachusetts or anywhere in the United States—in spite of the rules of the courts regarding appeals in capital cases, if the psychology that prevailed in Boston after the war is allowed to reemerge."[56]

The SJC was less than enthusiastic about the new law. The court had long been hesitant to reverse a trial court and until the 1960s and the onset of a new national legal culture, the SJC reversed only a handful of murder convictions. From 1892, when the SJC ceased to be a trial court and became strictly an appeals court for capital offenses, to 1939, the court reversed only three murder convictions, or 4.6 percent of all the murder appeals it heard. After 1939 a growing number of convicted murderers asked the court to exercise its extraordinary power to review questions of fact and well as law, but the justices interpreted the new law narrowly. In *Commonwealth v. Gricus* (1944) Judge Henry T. Lummus, writing for a unanimous court, acknowledged that the 1939 statute allowed the court to review the facts of a murder conviction, but, he lectured, "it does not convert this court into a second jury, which must be convinced beyond a reasonable doubt of the guilt of a defendant by reading the reported evidence, without the advantage of seeing and hearing the witnesses." For this reason, Lummus added, the court must decide the verdict "was so greatly against the weight of the evidence as to induce in his mind the strong belief that it was not due to careful consideration of the evidence, but that [the guilty verdict] was the produce of bias, misapprehension or prejudice." Only in such "rare instances" would the SJC grant a new trial. In *Commonwealth v. Bellino* (1947), the court made the eye of the needle through which the defendant had to pass to win a new trial even smaller. "The statute does not require us to review all questions of evidence and of procedure at the trial to which exceptions have not been duly saved," Justice Stanley E. Qua wrote. From 1940 to 1996 the SJC heard 1,033 homicide appeals, nearly ten times the number it heard in the period 1892–1939. Of the total number, 729 were appeals made by defendants convicted of first-degree murder. The SJC reversed 126 first-degree convictions, or 17.2 percent, chiefly after 1970. Although the court did not exercise its extraordinary power granted to it by the 1939 statute in all of these cases, there is no question that the law enacted in the wake of Sacco's and Vanzetti's executions changed the face of Massachusetts justice.[57]

The other major reform in Massachusetts capital procedure that may be attributed to the reaction against the Sacco and Vanzetti verdict dealt with curbing the impact of popular bias on jury selection. Frankfurter, it will be recalled, cast much of the blame for the guilty verdict on jurors who carried their prejudice against radicals into the jury room. For the remainder of his professional life, Frankfurter argued that one way to prevent popular prejudice from tainting jury verdicts is to root out jurors who, because of deep community bias, could not render a fair verdict.

Frankfurter borrowed the central premise of his argument about tainted juries from his longtime friend and Supreme Court justice Oliver Wendell Holmes Jr.'s dissent in *Frank v. Mangum* (1915). In that case, Leo Frank, a Jew charged with the murder of a young girl, came to trial in an Atlanta courtroom surrounded by a hostile, howling mob. The mob's threats prompted the trial judge to publicly state that if "one juryman yielded to reasonable doubt . . . neither prisoner nor counsel would be safe from the rage of the crowd." But he did nothing to protect the jury from the "passions of the mob." For this reason, Holmes concluded, the trial judge had adhered to the form, but not the substance of a fair trial and, therefore, Frank had been deprived of due process of law because a mob had dominated his trial.[58]

Without doubt many Massachusetts Yankees rejected the political values embraced by Sacco and Vanzetti, but the evidence does not support Frankfurter's charge that the Dedham jurors mindlessly and prejudicially reflected the area's alleged fanatical patriotism or that the district attorney and the trial judge successfully manipulated them into disregarding the evidence. In all likelihood, the Dedham jurors had been exposed to prejudice against aliens and radicals. Beginning in the late nineteenth century some Massachusetts Republicans and Democrats campaigned for immigration restrictions. Non-English-speaking immigrants, the so-called Restrictionists argued, were a major source of political corruption and crime and they could not be assimilated into the American republic. During World War I, Congress and state legislatures, including Massachusetts, also enacted draconian laws aimed at choking off political dissent from alien-radicals already in the United States. And in the war's turbulent wake, the politically ambitious U.S. attorney general A. Mitchell Palmer coordinated a series of New Year's Day raids against suspected alien-radicals in major urban centers across the country, leading to the arrest and imprisonment of thousands. In greater Boston, FBI agents and local police rounded up more than five hundred men and women suspected of violating the Alien Act's prohibition against affiliation with "any organization that entertains a belief in, or advocates the overthrow by force or violence of the government of the United States."[59]

Not everyone was of one mind about the government's anti-Red campaign, however. Several suburban Boston newspapers cheered the FBI's sweep, but when some of the suspected alien-radicals were brought into court, Federal District Court judge George W. Anderson (a Yankee Democrat) blasted the government's action as ill conceived and contrary to the defendants' constitutional right to due process. The Massachusetts chapter of the Daughters of the American Revolution and the Massachusetts Public Interest League condemned Judge Anderson, but the *Boston Globe* and *The Nation* hailed his courageous stand. About the same time the F.B.I. and Judge Anderson clashed, the Norfolk-Plymouth County district attorney charged a Norwood man with violating a Massachusetts statute prohibiting anyone from speaking, counseling, or advocating the overthrow of the commonwealth. There seemed to be plenty of evidence to convict Sergis Zakoff. Two police officers testified Zakoff had told them he was a "Bolshevik" who believed in revolution, a fact the accused freely admitted on the witness stand. But the jury found the accused alien-radical not guilty. A stunned Judge Thayer asked two questions of the jurors before they filed out of the courtroom. "Didn't you listen to my instructions? Didn't you consider the testimony given by the police officers?" In what seems like a clear case of jury nullification, the foreman replied the jurors thought the accused had to have done something to overthrow the government and not simply talk about it.[60]

The Sacco-Vanzetti jury also claimed to be uninfluenced by the threat of radicalism. In 1927 ten of the original jurors told Governor Alvan Fuller and the Adivsory Commission their decision finding Sacco and Vanzetti guilty as charged was not affected by the talk about radicalism. Nearly thirty years after the trial the *New Bedford Standard-Times* interviewed the seven surviving jurors and asked, among other questions, to what extent they were influenced by Sacco and Vanzetti's radicalism. John Dever, a Catholic U.S. Army veteran, insisted that "talk of radicalism is absurd. Radicalism had nothing whatsoever to do with it." Harry King, a retired sixty-four-year-old shoemaker, had a similar memory. "Propaganda about their being radicals and about their being framed on the charges did not reach me before the trial," he said. "I was just a man in the street, minding my own business." King thought the "defense put the radical element in the trial to hide the issue of murder," but he denied the strategy's effectiveness. "As jurors, such talk did not concern us." Other jurors praised the way in which Judge Thayer managed the trial. Alfred L. Atwood, a Norwood realtor, recalled that Thayer "never showed any bias [or] favoritism. If I remember anything with absolute clarity," Atwood added, "it was the judge's fairness." Dever also believed Thayer had acted without prejudice. "He may have expressed his opinion outside of court. But he didn't indicate his preference to the jury."[61]

As reported by Governor Fuller and the Advisory Commission, each juror testified that the "fact that the accused were foreigners and radicals had no effect upon his decision and that native Americans would have been equally certain to be convicted on the same evidence." Thirty years later none of the surviving jurors had changed his mind. A juror's memory cannot be taken as conclusive proof of the court's impartiality; but together with testimony before the governor and Advisory Commission it certainly warrants the inference that the bias with which the jury and Judge Thayer were charged by the defense and by supporters of Sacco and Vanzetti did not blind the jury to the facts. Modern court decisions about jury bias also have cast serious doubt on Frankfurter's assertion that pretrial publicity necessarily prejudices a jury and taints its verdict. Frankfurter certainly was not the first to focus on the issue of jurors' bias. As far back as Aaron Burr's treason trial, U.S. Supreme Court Chief Justice John Marshall ruled that jurors did not need to be ignorant of the issue to qualify as unbiased or impartial. He created a distinction between light and fixed opinions, a rule that allowed jurors to serve who had read newspaper accounts of Burr's planned foray down the Mississippi River but had not made up their minds and barred those who had formed a fixed opinion on the basis of that same information. Judge Thayer used this same distinction when he instructed would-be jurors in regard to two of the standard questions posed by the court in an effort to determine whether a juror was impartial, or in the language of the court, "stood indifferent": "Have you expressed or formed any opinion upon the subject matter alleged in either or both of these indictments?" "Are you sensible of any bias or prejudice?" For a juror to be disqualified, the judge explained, his opinion about the case "must be something more than a vague impression" derived from reading newspaper accounts or from casual conversation. It must be something more than a "light opinion." If, however, Thayer explained, a juror held an opinion that was "so strong and so deeply rooted that [he] will close his mind against the testimony that may be offered and will combat and resist such testimony," he properly would be disqualified by the court from serving on the jury.[62]

Making a judgment about whether an individual juror held a light or a fixed opinion often proved difficult enough, but in the 1960s several criminal defendants argued that communitywide prejudice arising from inflammatory pretrial publicity made empanelling an impartial jury impossible. The Supreme Court seemed to support that argument in *Irvin v. Dowd* (1961), when it ruled, "widespread and inflammatory publicity had highly prejudiced the inhabitants" against the defendant. In fact, 62 percent of the men and women in the jury pool were excused for cause because they had formed a fixed opinion about Irvin's guilt and eight of the twelve jurors who served on the jury admitted during voir dire (pretrial questioning) they thought the defendant guilty. In a concurring opinion, Justice Frankfurter, who had been appointed to the Supreme Court twelve years after Sacco and Vanzetti's execution, made the same argument he had in his 1927 book about their trial: jurors' prejudice can be presumed when a crime has aroused the "passions of the community." The jurors in *Irvin* and many other criminal trials, Frankfurter asserted, entered the jury box with "their minds saturated by press and radio for months preceding by matter designed to establish the guilt of the accused. A conviction so secured obviously constitutes a denial of due process of law in its most rudimentary conception." Within a decade, however, the Court backed away from this view, rejecting Frankfurter's argument that "actual prejudice on the part of the jury might be inferred from pretrial publicity." In rejecting Frankfurter's twice-made argument for presumed prejudice the Supreme Court reinforced the ancient ideal that indifferent jurors may be found regardless of community sentiment and, according to the oath taken by Massachusetts jurors, "well and truly try, and true deliverance make . . . according to the evidence."[63]

Chiefly in reaction to public expressions of racial prejudice, the Massachusetts legislature in 1973 amended the rule for determining whether potential jurors stood indifferent. The new rule allowed a trial judge to question potential jurors about a broad range of "attitudes, exposure, opinions or any other matters which may cause a decision or decisions to be made in whole or in part upon issues extraneous to the issues of the case, including, but not limited to, community attitudes, possible exposure to potentially prejudicial material or possible preconceived opinions toward the credibility of certain classes of persons." Two years later, by changing "may" to "shall" the legislature made the rule mandatory. In *Commonwealth v. Sanders* (1981) the SJC determined that the law required a trial judge to question each potential juror "individually and outside the presence of other persons about to be called as jurors" with respect to racial prejudice in cases involving interracial rape. But, in a number of cases involving other types of bias the court ruled that unless there was a "substantial risk that the jury would be influenced by extraneous issues" the trial judge need not interrogate potential jurors. In short, fifty-four years after Frankfurter made an impassioned argument about how completely community political bias had tainted the Sacco-Vanzetti jury, the Massachusetts court still refused to adopt the notion that a fair trial must begin with a presumption of prejudice.[64]

Sacco and Vanzetti's trial and execution stands as a metaphor for an era of intolerance and anxiety, but that does not necessarily mean the trial judge and jury failed in their responsibility to be as fair and impartial or that the jury succumbed to bias in reaching its guilty verdict. Without doubt, as defense attorney Thompson insisted, Judge Thayer spoke loosely and prejudicially outside the courtroom. Did his biased opinions determine his rulings in court? No lawyer successfully made that argument. Did the jury come to a verdict of guilty because they were swept up by a wave of patriotism? Governor Fuller's personal investigation and the Advisory Committee's interviews led them to believe the jurymen were honest and had come to the conclusion Sacco and Vanzetti were guilty as charged because that was the way they read the evidence. Fifty years later the surviving jurors clung to that story.

That the Massachusetts legal community began working to reform the criminal justice system almost immediately after the execution came as no consolation to Sacco and Vanzetti. In the long run, however, the legacy of injustice, or the perception of injustice, led to important changes in due process. Changes in capital procedure made by the legislature and the court improved Massachusetts justice. As a result criminal justice became fairer and more exacting and more just. Did the new rules eliminate the possibility of prejudice or mistake? No. But, ironically, because of fear of another possible mistake, Sacco and Vanzetti opened the door to the abolition of capital punishment in Massachusetts.

The legal defense for murder of not guilty by reason of insanity has a venerable and controversial history. One of the basic assumptions of Anglo-American law is that a defendant must have the capability to exercise free will to be held responsible for a criminal act. The legal term *mens rea*—a state of mind that renders the accused and his act culpable—is a reflection of the fundamental belief that it would be morally reprehensible to execute a person who does not know or understand what he or she did was wrong. The controversy over the insanity defense stems mainly from the formulation of the test to determine criminal responsibility, but the question whether there should be an insanity defense at all also has been debated from the early nineteenth century to the present.[1]

Once thought to be a panacea, the mixture of science and law that constitutes the basis for the modern insanity defense often has failed to temper justice with mercy or to curb public outrage when a heinous murderer has been found not guilty by reason of insanity. In the intellectual and emotional melee that follows a contentious verdict based on the insanity defense, courts and psychiatrists and politicians compete over who should shape and control the reforms said to be needed. In part, the quarrel between psychiatrists and lawyers is a result of the ferment within psychiatry that began in the early twentieth century. Increasingly, psychiatrists looked beyond the mental asylum to which they had been linked in the nineteenth century to the pathology, diagnosis, and treatment of mental disease. Modern psychiatry was desperate to be a hard science, but it remains reliant on symptoms as a basis for analysis. Because psychiatry lacks cognitive and professional unity, legislators and courts have sought to balance the claims made by science and the demands made by the law with the public's perception of insanity. Understandably, the results have been mixed.

Before the advent of modern science—the idea that physical and emotional causes, rather than moral wickedness, explained human behavior—

courts applied the "wild beast" standard. This test exempted a defendant from punishment only if he were "totally deprived of his understanding and memory, and doth not know what he is doing, no more than an infant, than a brute or a wild beast." As psychiatry's scientific status became established, however, the wild beast standard was denounced as too narrowly drawn and as missing the essence of insanity. In 1843 an English court chased the wild beast from the courtroom but opened up new avenues of controversy when it found the Scottish woodcutter Daniel McNaughten not guilty by reason of insanity for the murder of Prime Minister Robert Peel's secretary.[2]

The uproar that followed McNaughten's trial led to an extraordinary meeting of all fifteen high court judges. They approved the change in the legal definition of insanity from the wild-beast symptoms to a more inclusive cognitive test, but the judges amplified the trial court's rules beginning with the so-called right-from-wrong test. A defendant was required to prove beyond a reasonable doubt that while committing the criminal act he "was laboring under such a defect of reason, from disease of the mind, as not to know the nature and quality of his act; or, if he did know it, that he did not know what he was doing was wrong."[3]

The year following the English court's ruling, the Massachusetts Supreme Judicial Court (SJC) sought to improve on its insanity rules. Dr. Isaac Ray, the Massachusetts-born American founder of forensic psychiatry whose work was quoted authoritatively in the McNaughten trial, guided Chief Justice Lemuel Shaw's ruling in *Commonwealth v. Rogers* (1844). Ray aggressively advocated legal reform. Before his appearance in *Rogers*, he had charged the legal profession with being woefully ignorant of insanity, ignorance that he claimed "led to frightfully numerous cases of judicial homicide." Ray testified that Abner Rogers could tell the difference between right and wrong but that he was driven by an "irresistible impulse" to murder Charlestown State Prison warden Charles Lincoln. Rogers believed Lincoln was part of a conspiracy to persecute him and the only way he had to protect himself was to murder the warden. Within Rogers's delusional framework, Ray argued, the killing seemed right.[4]

Attorney George Bemis begged a skeptical jury to accept Ray's expert analysis and to put aside the "common opinion" that a plea of not guilty by reason of insanity was nothing more than a clever excuse for getting away with murder. The prosecutor countered Bemis's plea by attacking the medical experts who had testified to the defendant's insanity. "Can mere opinions of medical men, founded on representation of facts not seen by themselves, representations coming through partial, contradictory, suspicious and doubtful channels, be a sure or a safe foundation for a judicial verdict?" he asked. In other words, the methods used by psychiatry could not lead to the truth.[5]

Coming just eight years after the Massachusetts legislature nearly abolished capital punishment and in the midst of a string of capital jury nullifications, Shaw's charge to the jury grafted Ray's irresistible impulse argument onto the McNaughten right-from-wrong test. Once it has been established that the mind of the accused is diseased, Shaw wrote, the question becomes "whether the disease existed to so high a degree, that for the time being it overwhelmed the reason, conscience and judgment, and whether the prisoner acted from an irresistible impulse." The McNaughten-Shaw test invited jurors to make a link between the alleged existence of a mental disease and a defendant's criminal behavior or between the uncontrollable emotional aspects of a defendant's behavior and his ability to form a rational intent. Shaw's carefully crafted instructions to the jury—the first opinion delivered by a U.S. court of last resort on the criminal responsibility of the insane—led the jury to a verdict of not guilty by reason of insanity.[6]

The ink was barely dry on Shaw's opinion, however, before psychiatrists insisted that the McNaughten-Shaw rule failed to reflect accurately the available knowledge about the human mind. Lawyers also were divided about the worth of psychiatric testimony. Prosecutors, on one hand, believed a psychiatrist's testimony was useful only if it focused exclusively on the legal question whether the defendant knew his or her conduct was wrong. Defense attorneys, on the other hand, wanted to enlarge that focus to include expert testimony about the causes of a defendant's mental state. Politicians and the public also weighed in on the issue. Despite these fissures, the Massachusetts test to determine criminal responsibility remained substantially unchanged well into the twentieth century. As late as 1958, for example, a special Massachusetts committee created to study the death penalty acknowledged there were major problems with the insanity defense. "There can be no doubt," the committee wrote, "but that the psychiatric unsoundness of the present Massachusetts law on legal responsibility for criminal behavior has imposed an almost impossible task upon psychiatrists testifying in court. They are called upon to testify in terms of a completely erroneous conception of mental responsibility." Still, the committee said, because modern psychiatry "is far from an exact science," it intended to stick with McNaughten-Shaw.[7]

Shortly after the SJC adopted Ray's 1844 formula for determining whether a defendant is sane, Ray identified contradictory psychiatric testimony as the single biggest obstacle to widespread acceptance of McNaughten-Shaw. Professionals and outside observers alike believed scientific truth should point to one conclusion about a defendant's sanity. Ray argued the problem lay with lawyers, not psychiatrists. He warned his colleagues who testified in court to be prepared "to have his sentiments travestied and sneered at, his motives impugned and pit-falls dug in his path by lawyers feigning cordiality and fellow-feeling." To withstand courtroom assaults, Ray stressed the need for psychiatrists to prepare carefully and to avoid the traps set by lawyers. Don't be drawn into giving an "unqualified reply," but express "modest doubt," he said. Don't go along with a general hypothetical question but insist on "even the minutest of circumstances" about the homicide and the defendant's state of mind. Don't link insanity to a single factor. And above all, don't try to define insanity, because lawyers will use your answer "to perplex and embarrass." Alas, even if psychiatrists followed his advice, Ray admitted he and colleagues were the butt of a popular joke told in courthouse corridors and taverns. "If you have an uncontrollable impulse to commit crime," the storyteller would say of a murder defendant pleading not guilty by reason of insanity, "we have an uncontrollable impulse to punish you."[8]

Dr. L. Vernon Briggs was Ray's intellectual heir. During the first half of the twentieth century Briggs made it his goal to end the courtroom spectacle of dueling psychiatrists. Boston-born, he was an active participant in the turn-of-the-century transformation of American psychiatry. Some American psychiatrists developed a more analytic psychiatry incorporating Freudian insights and experimented with new therapeutic approaches. Briggs, and a handful of others, looked beyond the boundaries of medicine to create a mental hygiene movement that aimed to demonstrate the social usefulness of modern psychiatry. Convinced that mental disease was a product of environmental, hereditary, and individual deficiencies, Briggs believed that psychiatry and progressive politics should work together to identify and treat mentally ill people as one step toward creating a new social order. In fact, Briggs predicted, until society acted "to stop the swelling stream of defectiveness and mental illness," there would be more crime and murder.[9]

Briggs was an indefatigable advocate of the psychological links between mental illness and murder. He believed that mental illness and moral degradation were the root causes of crime and violence. Therefore, he advocated that potential criminals be identified early in life by compulsory scientific testing so that the proper cure might be applied "before the disease becomes chronic" and so render "the defective a harmless member of society." Briggs insisted that the "real offender is society and not the children in the form of men, not the mentally diseased" who commit violent crime.[10]

In 1880, at age seventeen, Briggs left Harvard College to take a fashionable sea voyage for reasons of health. Arriving in Honolulu during a smallpox epidemic, he successfully completed the government examination for a physician's license and went to work helping the sick. Later in the decade Briggs interned in a mental hospital in San Francisco. When he returned to Boston he studied at Tufts University and the Medical College of Virginia. In 1899, he befriended Boston's most eminent physician, Walter Channing, and accepted an offer of a supervisory position at his private mental hospital. After only a year on the job, however, Briggs left for a more lucrative position at Boston City Hospital, a move that caused Channing to think Briggs ungrateful and unprofessional and Briggs to believe he had been undervalued and underpaid by Channing. Their personal and professional quarrel festered for more than a decade, each man recruiting allies from within the Boston medical and political communities. Briggs talked about suing Channing for libel and Channing managed to block for a time Briggs's appointment to the state board of insanity.[11]

Although his quarrel with Channing seemed to preoccupy Briggs, he simultaneously pursued his own professional advancement and the transformation of mental health policy and practice in Massachusetts. He established and administered two psychiatric hospitals, managed a large private practice in Boston, pushed for a law abolishing the use of physical or chemical restraint in private and public mental hospitals, and vigorously defended his ideas and reputation by privately publishing several books. Briggs was especially eager to promote mental hygiene, but unlike others in the movement he did not focus exclusively on children. Mentally ill adults, especially murderers, were his targets. He believed that mentally ill people either were born without a sense of moral responsibility or are "warped by the environment" so that they manifest personality and character defects that make it impossible for them to adapt to their social environment or to compete with other people. Unless these "handicapped" people are identified and helped early in life they will be "knocked from pillar to post," and "punished in their homes, in the schools, and in prisons." Unless society cares for them by making an "intelligent effort to direct their energies" in a positive direction, some mentally ill men and women will become destructive and dangerous, Briggs predicted.[12]

When mentally ill people landed in court, Briggs believed that the law's adversary procedures undermined scientific truth and the legal protection provided a defendant. He wanted to bridge the gulf between law and psychiatry by intervening in the process before a mentally ill defendant appeared in court. He was especially critical of the "spectacle in our courts of two or more physicians pitted against one another, testifying to diametrically opposite opinions as to the mental condition and responsibility" of the defendant. Such a procedure, he said, not only humiliates the mentally ill defendant but increases the likelihood that a mentally ill capital defendant will be sentenced to death and executed. Against the opposition of the Massachusetts Psychiatric Association and Attorney General J. Weston Allen, Briggs lobbied the public and the legislature for a law that required all capital defendants to undergo a psychiatric examination by neutral experts as soon as they were taken into police custody.[13]

Briggs launched his campaign for transforming Massachusetts's criminal insanity laws in his 1921 book *The Manner of Man That Kills*. One of the book's three case studies focuses on Briggs's testimony as an expert witness in the murder trial of Bertram G. Spencer.[14] Early on the evening of March 31, 1910, a masked man boldly walked into the parlor of a Springfield home where Martha Blackstone, a thirty-nine-year-old school teacher, and three female friends sat piecing together a puzzle and talking about a series of unsolved neighborhood robberies. One of the women glanced up, saw the intruder, and cried out. All four women bolted from the room screaming. The masked man fired several shots, one of which killed Blackstone. Mass meetings were held demanding police action and Governor Eben Draper offered a $500 reward for information leading to the murderer's arrest. About a week later, Springfield police arrested Spencer, a

twenty-nine-year-old packinghouse clerk. A search of his West Springfield home where he lived with his wife and child uncovered a revolver,
two black handkerchiefs that police believed had been used as masks, and
more than one hundred pieces of inexpensive jewelry and other personal
items, many of which were later identified as stolen. Spencer initially denied any responsibility for the robberies and murder and complained of a
headache. The morning following his arrest, however, he confessed to the
robberies and to the murder of Martha Blackstone.

On the day of Spencer's arrest, the *Springfield Republican* distinguished Spencer's crime spree from that of other robbers. The newspaper
suggested Spencer was motivated by a "daredevil bravado, a love of the
spectacular and a lack of pecuniary calculation which strongly suggested
either the monomania of an unbalanced mind or a romantic vanity fed on
by penny dreadfuls." On April 8, the *Republican* reiterated this hypothesis, suggesting that crime novels "exert a powerful influence on minds not
positively resistant to such influences."

While Spencer was confined to jail awaiting trial, the court appointed
three psychiatrists to examine him. During their interviews, they learned
that mental illness was common to Spencer's extended family, that his father had abused him, and that throughout his life Spencer had suffered
fits of uncontrollable rage and bouts of deep depression. Other pieces of
Spencer's troubled personal history also emerged during his examination. His erratic behavior had caused him to be expelled from school, to
be abruptly discharged from the U.S. Navy, and to be fired from two jobs.
These facts, together with observations of his behavior, led the examining
psychiatrists to conclude that Spencer's "mental deficiency and the obliq-
uity of his moral nature is so great that it constitutes real insanity." Acting
on that judgment, the court committed Spencer to the Bridgewater Institute for the Criminally Insane, "pending the determination of his sanity."
The court ordered Dr. Alfred Elliott to submit monthly reports describing
Spencer's behavior and treatment.

The people of Springfield were not convinced of Spencer's insanity.
The *Springfield Republican* gave voice to the popular belief that Spencer
should stand trial so that lawyers and a jury and not psychiatrists might
determine the question of his sanity. Democrat Christopher T. Callahan
made this argument the centerpiece of his successful campaign against the
incumbent district attorney, Stephen Taft, a Republican. Although he in-

sisted he was not criticizing Taft's handling of Spencer's case, Callahan denounced both the law permitting the use of state-paid psychiatrists to buttress a defendant's insanity plea and the way in which the experts reached their conclusion about Spencer's insanity. According to Callahan, echoing prosecutors in *Rogers* more than a half-century earlier, the psychiatrists had not gathered their facts correctly. "How were these facts brought to the minds of the experts? As facts established by evidence from the witness stand? Not at all. They were furnished by the defendant's family and friends, and accepted by the experts without legal proof. These facts, in my opinion, should have been submitted under oath in open court and should have been subjected to the test of careful cross-examination." [15]

Although there may have been other reasons for Callahan's election as district attorney in 1910, it is clear voters' dissatisfaction with Taft's handling of Spencer's insanity plea played a major part. "In the public mind the fact that Spencer was allowed to go to the Hospital without a trial, either rightly or wrongly, was, according to an editorial in the *Springfield Republican*, "a very effective political argument against Mr. Taft." The voice of the people also may have caused Elliott to change his evaluation of Spencer. Beginning a month after Callahan's election, Elliott no longer used the term "insane" to describe Spencer's mental condition as he had in his first court report. Rather, from December to May he diagnosed Spencer as a "moral imbecile of a rather low order." Then, following a meeting with Callahan, Elliott told the court that he now believed Spencer was sane and that his crimes were "for gain, revenge or to satisfy his passion, or to protect himself when overtaken in criminal deeds, and were not the result of an irresistible impulse or obsession or the reaction of a delusion or hallucination, or the result of some acute mental observation." The court promptly ordered Spencer transferred from Bridgewater to the Springfield jail preparatory to his trial for murder. [16]

Trial began in the Hampden County Superior Court on November 13, 1911. Attorney General James M. Swift and newly elected District Attorney Callahan represented the state. Spencer's court-appointed counsel, Richard P. Stapleton and Colonel Charles M. Young, asked Judge John Crosby to probe jurors' attitudes about the insanity defense during voir dire. Judge Crosby denied the request, stating he believed his instructions to the jury at the close of the trial would clear up any confusion. Of the 125 men called, nearly one-quarter (30) of the potential jurors stated that their opposition to capital punishment would prevent them from finding Spencer guilty regardless of the evidence and they were dismissed. A larger number of men admitted they had formed an unshakeable opinion about Spencer's guilt. Not until late afternoon was a jury of 12 men empanelled.[17]

District Attorney Callahan opened for the state. He outlined the details of the murder and defined legal insanity:

> In our Commonwealth simple insanity, a word which can and is stretched to cover a multitude of mental imperfections, does not excuse a criminal. It is not sufficient for the defense to show that he is a moral pervert, or that he is mentally defective. There are few of us who are wholly free from those imperfections. It is not enough that the alienists may pronounce him insane. The evidence must go further and show that he was so far insane that at the time he committed the crime he did not know the difference between right and wrong.

When Callahan began to speak, the *Boston American* noticed that Spencer sat well back in the open-top steel cage where criminal defendants were confined during trial and seemed oblivious. "His head tilted back slightly and a pair of large eyes, almost round, stare fixedly and vacantly ahead." But, according to the *New York World*, Spencer's vacant passivity was exceptional. He "jerks and twists his body, [and] his spasmodic movements of the neck, his ceaseless, crazily rapid teetering of the upper foot of his crossed legs" seem to signal an impending outburst. Several times during the trial Spencer did explode. His "hair flying, his big eyes wild with fury, his mouth dripping," Spencer shouted, flew into a rage, and lunged forward as if to burst out of the defendant's box.[18]

Near the end of the third day of testimony, Colonel Young, Spencer's white-haired lead counsel, made his opening statement. "We have but one defense," he acknowledged, "mental defectiveness, mental incapacity, mental unsoundness." Spencer was not able "to distinguish right from wrong to the extent that the law requires in order to constitute capacity to commit crime; that he is the victim of impulses and desires which he is unable to control." During the next eight days, Young and co-counsel Stapleton used every opportunity to pound the facts of Spencer's legal insanity. Following testimony from Spencer's relatives and co-workers in which terms such as "queer," "wild-eyed," "nervous," "enraged," and "hysterical" were used to describe Spencer's behavior, Stapleton asked Elliott to define insanity. Elliott could not be pinned down. Despite his lack of scientific precision, Elliott believed that Spencer was not legally insane, that his cognitive ability was normal. Therefore, "my opinion," he testified of Spencer, "was that he knew right from wrong; he knew his act was wrong. He knew there was a penalty connected; he knew what the penalty was, and he was not governed by an irresistible impulse."[19]

When Briggs was summoned to testify, he walked from the defense table to the witness stand wearing a tweed suit, a fashionable flat collar and necktie, and a Van Dyke goatee. He flatly contradicted Elliott. Without hesitation, Briggs, who was testifying in his first capital trial, stated that he believed Spencer to be legally insane, that it was not possible for him to distinguish between right and wrong, and that his criminal acts were driven by an irresistible impulse. Under fierce cross-examination by Attorney General Swift, Briggs insisted Spencer's mind "broke up" because of inherited mental defects and a brutal childhood. Briggs could not explain why some people who experience similar childhood trauma are sane adults. Finally, Swift asked Briggs to explain the apparent conflict between his diagnosis of insanity and Spencer's rational actions on the fatal night. Briggs answered that he did not "understand the question," since it was possible for a person to be both rational and insane. Swift derisively dismissed the doctor.[20]

On the eleventh day of the trial Stapleton closed for the defense. He reiterated his argument that Spencer should be found not guilty by reason of insanity. To make his point Stapleton emphasized Spencer's "heredity," and "the veritable hell" of his boyhood home life that created a "diseased and disordered brain that has been defective from birth and twisted toward a criminal life by impulse, training and treatment." Stapleton also highlighted Elliott's early diagnosis of Spencer's insanity and accused Elliott of changing his diagnosis because of political pressure.[21]

Late on Friday afternoon, November 24, 1911, Attorney General Swift made his closing statement to the jury. He poked fun at Spencer's defense of not guilty by reason of insanity. "My father struck me on the head when I was nine years old and that was why I did it," Swift mockingly intoned. Swift insisted there was nothing wrong with Spencer. He had feigned insanity to save his life and for a time he had fooled the experts. Eventually, however, all but one of the examining psychiatrists concluded Spencer was legally sane. Only Briggs—that "wonderful expert"—clung to the diagnosis that Spencer was insane. But Briggs was "foolish," "deceptive," and "gullible," the attorney general told the jury. There was "nothing the matter with [Spencer] except a quick temper" and Swift urged the jury to use the law to avenge the "foul murder" of Martha Blackstone.[22]

Judge Crosby's lengthy charge emphasized the jury's responsibility to determine whether Spencer was criminally responsible for his acts and he carefully distinguished between legal insanity and "mere inferiority of intellect." The jury retired at 9:50 P.M. Four hours later the jury came back into court to ask three questions. None was about insanity. At 3:08 A.M. a weary group of jurors filed back into the courtroom and announced that it had found Spencer guilty of murder in the first degree.[23]

One month later, the court heard arguments for a new trial based on several procedural objections made by the defense during the trial. Stapleton maintained the jury willfully had disregarded the evidence. Six state-employed psychiatrists had testified that Spencer was "mentally defective." As a matter of law the "jury were at liberty to disregard expert testimony," but the court should not permit the jury to decide both the facts and the law, to reject without consideration a defendant's right to a plea of not guilty by reason of insanity. Stapleton asked the trial court not to permit jury nullification. A few days later, Judge Crosby denied the defense motion for a new trial. Following futile appeals to the SJC and to Governor Noble Foss, Spencer was sentenced to death.[24]

During his time on "Murderers' Row," Spencer wrote a barrage of letters to Briggs and sent childlike illustrated love poems to his mother. He complained about his wife and the ill treatment he allegedly received from several prison guards and said he thought his lawyer had conspired against him. He told Briggs he had embraced the Christian Science religion. He would soon "be in the next world with God, and oh, how happy I shall be ever after." Briggs thought Spencer did not understand the permanency of death. When Spencer walked into the execution chamber, he nodded to the witnesses, said "Good night," and smilingly took his seat in the electric chair.[25]

Briggs was appalled. He contended that all of the psychiatrists who examined Spencer knew he was insane at the time of the murder and at the trial. Some thought he was medically insane but not legally insane. Briggs denounced the distinction between medical insanity and legal insanity as without a difference. The awful result of the confusion between psychiatry and the law was the unnecessary execution of an insane person. "The whole legal machinery of the State," he wrote angrily, "had been put in motion to crush this defective and uphold the Majesty of the Law and so it came about that Bertram G. Spencer, a defective from birth, with the mind of a child, was tried for his life and sentenced to death and executed with a smile upon his lips."[26]

Aside from Briggs's bitter remarks, Spencer's execution at Charlestown prison on September 17, 1912, created little public comment. But within legal and medical circles the sensational trials of the wealthy New York playboy Harry Thaw, who claimed a "brainstorm" drove him to murder the architect Stanford White, caused both local and national legal and medical communities to reassess the insanity defense. John H. Wigmore, Northwestern University Law professor and president of the American Institute of Criminal Law and Criminology, for example, created a national blue-ribbon committee to tackle the problem of criminal responsibility. The committee's charge was to draft a law that would address the concerns of lawyers and psychiatrists and give credibility to the insanity defense. In 1916 the institute's proposed law on insanity and criminal responsibility appeared in the *Harvard Law Review*. The model statute contained four major provisions. One, it incorporated the fundamental principle that a defendant may not be held criminally responsible if the "necessary mental element is lacking": "No person hereafter shall be convicted of any criminal charge, when at the time of the act or omission alleged against him, he was suffering from mental disease and did not have by reason of such disease the particular state of mind which must accompany such act or omission in order to constitute the crime charged." Two, according to the committee member and law professor Edwin Keedy, the model statute eschewed psychological theories, hoping therefore that "changing views as to the nature and scope of mental disease" would not affect the law. Similarly, section three eliminated legal definitions of insanity. Building on this separation, section four assigned to each of the key participants in an insanity trial a restricted role. Medical experts called by the court were to state an opinion about a defendant's mental condition at the time of the alleged offense. Lawyers were to work within the rules defining criminal responsibility, and the court was to describe to the jury "the mental element in the crime charged." It was the jury's task to determine whether the defendant's mental condition caused the "particular state of mind" described by the judge.[27]

The *Harvard Law Review* gave the institute's model statute a tepid reception. "It is difficult to see," the editor wrote, "wherein the proposed legislation would materially change the existing legal situation." Among other shortcomings, the proposal failed to cover the irresistible impulse that under the McNaughten-Shaw rule supplied the "element of power of choice." Massachusetts legislators apparently agreed with the *Review*'s criticism of the model statute and ignored the call to reform existing insanity laws.[28]

While the discussion went on within legal circles about what, if any, reforms to make in the insanity defense law, Briggs plunged into the controversy by testifying for the prosecution in the murder trial of Jennie Zimmerman. The twenty-six-year-old Springfield woman pleaded not guilty by reason of insanity to the shooting death of a man who had reneged on his promise of marriage. After several frustrated attempts to contact him, Zimmerman flagged down a car driven by her cousin and former lover, Dr. Henry Zimmerman, in the summer of 1919. The doctor was wearing his U.S. Navy uniform when he approached Jennie. They spoke heatedly for a few moments before the young woman fired four shots, killing the doctor instantly. Several eyewitnesses watched Jennie throw down the revolver and run a short distance from the scene before a passerby apprehended her. Trial began on May 10, 1920.[29]

Anticipating a defense of not guilty by reason of insanity, District Attorney Charles H. Wright told the jury that Zimmerman made careful plans to murder her cousin. She purchased a revolver at a neighborhood hardware store, told friends of her intention, and stalked the victim for several days before firing the fatal shots. After her arrest, Zimmerman freely and voluntarily confessed to the murder, alleging that Dr. Zimmerman "had dishonored her." In fact, the prosecutor told the jury, the young woman stated that the doctor had performed two illegal abortions on her, one in 1916 and another in 1918. But when she later begged the doctor "to make good" on his promise of marriage, he said "Forget it." Scorned, Zimmerman murdered the doctor.

Defense counsel William G. McKechnie's opening statement to the jury sketched out Jennie Zimmerman's difficult and troubled personal history. On the fourth day of trial, while Briggs and other psychiatrists watched and listened, Zimmerman took the stand in her own defense. Red-eyed, shaking, and sobbing hysterically as she spoke, Zimmerman told of her childhood in a "house of poverty." Because her mother was confined to an insane hospital and her father was an alcoholic, she said, the responsibility for caring for her six young siblings fell to her. Largely dependent on charity and the money she earned delivering newspapers, she was forced to leave school after the seventh grade. A few years later she opened a small store that provided her with a stable income for the first time in her life. But, in 1915 she became ill and went to see Dr. Zimmerman. While she was under the influence of a drug he administered, Dr. Zimmerman raped her, she told the court in a barely audible voice.

At this point in her story, a *Boston Globe* reporter noted sympathetically, Zimmerman had to be helped from the courtroom. She was unable to continue the following day. It was apparent, according to the newspaper, that "her night of deep anguish had completely unnerved her." After a restful weekend, Zimmerman resumed her story. She looked much stronger, the *Globe* reporter noted, but as soon as she took her seat on the witness stand "she wilted and became limp as a rag." Her "heart-breaking sobs were audible in all parts of the courtroom."

While women in the packed courtroom wept and jurymen with "pained looks on their faces" leaned forward to catch her words, Jennie Zimmerman continued the story of her ill-fated relationship with Dr. Zimmerman. She said he frequently came to her store at closing time and drove her home. Although she noted he carefully avoided the main streets of Springfield when they were together, she swallowed her pride and eagerly consented to an intimate relationship. When she discovered she was pregnant, Dr. Zimmerman performed an abortion. Jennie asked when they would marry and Dr. Zimmerman answered by saying that they "were man and wife for all intents and purposes, just the same as if a ceremony had been performed." Jennie dismissed such an idea as "socialist." On numerous other occasions, she testified, she unsuccessfully implored Dr. Zimmerman to marry her.

Defense attorney McKechnie now introduced psychiatric testimony. A Northampton psychiatrist stated that Jennie's mother suffered from a manic-depressive condition. Making use of a seven-thousand-word hypothetical question, another psychiatrist, Dr. Paul Waterman, stated that Zimmerman was "mentally unsound at the time of the shooting." She could not distinguish between right and wrong at the time she shot Dr. Zimmerman, he said. A third psychiatrist, Dr. Thornton Vail, testified that Zimmerman's actions were those of an insane person. On cross-examination, the district attorney wanted to know how Zimmerman's actions might be distinguished from an angry jilted woman who was sane. Vail answered vaguely that it was the "ideology of the case."

Briggs completely disagreed with his colleagues' insanity diagnosis. He told the court that the "shooting was the act of a jealous, emotional woman." Defense attorney McKechnie sharply cross-examined Briggs. He tarred Briggs with his testimony in the Spencer case and with his lack of objectivity. "Are you the same Dr. L. Vernon Briggs who pronounced Bertram Spencer insane?" McKechnie asked. "I am the man," Briggs replied. McKechnie asked Briggs a few more questions but then concluded that he thought the psychiatrist displayed "altogether too lively an interest in the outcome of this case" and dismissed him.[30]

In closing, McKechnie rehearsed the facts of Zimmerman's difficult childhood and, what he called, her "betrayal" by Dr. Zimmerman. "Don't you want your women folk to be protected in this community from men like Dr. Zimmerman?" the defense attorney asked. McKechnie claimed he was not going to appeal to the "'unwritten law' [of self-defense] or to the jurors as men of families to find the shooting justified on the ground that Jennie had been cruelly wronged," but he did argue that her mind was clouded when she shot Dr. Zimmerman. And, he added, there were "good and honorable" women "who believed in Jennie Zimmerman and were ready to offer her a new start in life." District Attorney Wright countered weakly, suggesting that the "story of insanity has but one purpose, to blind you to your straight out duty to the people of Massachusetts."

After deliberating briefly, the jury returned a verdict of not guilty by reason of insanity. The court allowed Zimmerman to choose to which of the state's mental hospitals she would prefer to be committed. Although she had previously "expressed a horror of the place" she chose Northampton Insane Hospital so that she would be close to her new friends. A Boston support group already had raised $400 to assist Zimmerman to begin a new life when she was released from the hospital.[31]

Briggs's general commitment to the mental hygiene movement and his specific experience in the Spencer and Zimmerman trials led him to initiate an energetic campaign to reform Massachusetts laws governing criminal insanity. His argument for change was at once personal and professional. He empathized with the mentally ill defendant who was subjected to days of testimony about "delusions and hallucinations, before a jury of laymen decided whether he was mentally ill or not." A psychiatrist was of little use in such a situation. Far from being able to give an "unbiased scientific opinion," psychiatrists were subjected to "ridicule" by lawyers eager to make a point rather than to discover the truth. Not only did the rough courtroom treatment of psychiatrists cause them professional embarrassment and unfairly stigmatize their profession, but by denigrating psychiatric testimony lawyers tended to cause jurors to disregard "all the medical evidence," and that "opened the door to the possible execution of mentally ill persons," according to Briggs.[32]

Using his extensive political and professional connections, Briggs vigorously pursued a four-pronged strategy designed to change the way in which Massachusetts courts identified mentally ill criminal defendants. He sounded out his professional colleagues about the usefulness of a new law. He consulted with lawyers about the constitutionality of his proposal to require all capital defendants to be examined by state psychiatrists shortly after indictment "to determine his mental condition and the existence of any mental disease or defect which would affect his criminality." To rally public support, Briggs published *The Manner of Man That Kills*, the book that argues for change by analyzing three recent capital trials in which the defense of not guilty by reason of insanity was made unsuccessfully. Finally, he lobbied the Massachusetts legislature to pass the bill he had carefully crafted. Briggs's initial efforts to build support for his proposal uncovered far more skeptics and critics than supporters.[33]

Although his professional outlook closely resembled that espoused by Dr. William Healy, Boston's leading mental hygienist, Briggs failed to gain his support for state-mandated psychiatric testing of capital defendants. Healy was the leading child-welfare activist in the United States. He had authored *The Individual Delinquent* (1915) and he directed the Judge Baker Foundation, a private Boston clinic concerned with improving juvenile justice through psychological testing and analysis. Healy insisted that no child should be approached with a priori assumptions about the cause of delinquency. In place of overly simplistic and deterministic theories of delinquency and criminality, Healy offered a complicated web of casual factors unique for each child. For this reason, he condemned the "formulation of criminal law based on pure assumptions and advocated an intensive and widespread study of the crime question rather than the making of new and more drastic legislation based on old and unproved theories of crime." In short, Healy privileged his brand of psychiatry over the law and refused to endorse Briggs's proposed bill. Healy called the quickly administered examination by state psychiatrists who did not share his views inadequate and impractical.[34]

Briggs also asked members of the legal community to review his proposed law designed to resolve the question of a defendant's sanity before trial. The president of the Boston Bar Association, Henry Hurlbert, endorsed it, but Judge Frederick Pickering Cabot abruptly declared Briggs's proposal unconstitutional. To require that a psychiatrist's report be made available to the court would violate a defendant's constitutional right against self-incrimination, the judge told Briggs. Several district attorneys warned that psychiatrists would find a greater number of capital defendants not criminally responsible before trial. Finally, Harvard law professor Joseph H. Beale publicly cautioned against enacting a new law. Although acknowledging some flaws in the insanity defense rules, Beale contended that most lawyers thought the existing system worked well enough. It's true, Beale told a conference on psychiatry and the law in which Briggs was a participant, the law is far from perfect. "But," he challenged the participants, "can you lay down any better exact rule than the rule which the law now lays down as to the criminal responsibility of persons of unsound mind?" Only careful "research, study, and experiment" will gradually improve the law governing insanity, he concluded.[35]

Briggs's effort to win political support for his bill also seemed likely to fail. He had long been identified with the Democratic party. He attended the 1911 Democratic national convention, cheering Woodrow Wilson's presidential nomination, and he publicly allied himself with Democratic governors Eugene N. Foss and David I. Walsh. But in 1920–21 when Briggs urged the Massachusetts legislature to embrace his insanity reform bill, Republicans dominated the statehouse. Governor Channing Cox easily held sway over a heavily Republican legislature. Of 40 state senators only 5 were Democrats, and there were 188 Republicans in the House to a mere 52 Democrats. Not surprisingly, the bill had "rough sledding" in the legislature, but it was eventually passed and Governor Cox signed it into law in the spring of 1921.[36]

But political machinations and bureaucratic lethargy made Briggs's victory a hollow one. Hoping to scuttle the reform, the legislature's leadership deliberately omitted funds to implement the law and the trial court clerks, whose responsibility it was to alert the department of mental diseases to a triggering indictment, refused to cooperate. Briggs responded to these roadblocks with characteristic initiative and energy. He invited to his home every Boston psychiatrist he knew and asked if they would examine the targeted defendants without charge. Although many in this group had been "earning part of their livelihood doing the very work, of which this law would virtually deprive them," everyone agreed. Two years later the legislature relented and amended the original law to include a professional fee. And, in 1925, Briggs pushed through an amendment subjecting court clerks to a fine for failing to report a targeted defendant to the Massachusetts Department of Mental Diseases.[37]

Although controversial and far-reaching, the Briggs law was remarkably simple and straightforward. It provided impartial psychiatrists appointed by the Massachusetts Department of Mental Diseases to examine all persons indicted for a capital crime or for repeated felonies. The court, the prosecutor, and the defense attorney had access to the psychiatrists' report, but it was not admissible as evidence at trial. Briggs believed this procedure would spare the mentally ill defendant the bewildering experience of a trial, or, if a trial occurred, the neutral psychiatric report would eliminate the confusing courtroom spectacle of dueling psychiatrists. The reform, he boasted, "practically does away with the necessity of expert testimony or the trial of mentally ill persons in criminal cases." A defendant found to be insane was committed to a state mental hospital until he or she was determined fit to stand trial and if acquitted at trial by reason of insanity was sentenced for life to a state hospital. The governor might pardon the prisoner only if state psychiatrists certified that he or she was no longer dangerous.[38]

Lawyers were slow to credit the Briggs law with bringing about significant changes, but Boston psychiatrists trumpeted its beneficial effects. Attorney Frank W. Grinnell, secretary of the Massachusetts Bar Association, for example, claimed that the "public and the professions were still ridiculing the absurdities of expert testimony in general and that of alienists in particular." Most lawyers, he wrote in the *Massachusetts Law Quarterly* in 1928, believe that psychiatry "is the study of 'nuts' and that some psychiatrists and their enthusiastic adherents are 'nuts' themselves who need study."[39]

The psychiatrist Winfred Overholser presented a completely different picture of the Briggs law. According to Overholser, co-director of the Massachusetts Department of Mental Diseases, the law transformed not only the legal treatment of mentally ill defendants but criminal justice in general. It all but ended the possibility that a mentally ill defendant would be put to death or imprisoned. For this reason, humanitarianism flourished, "vindictive justice" waned, and the mentally ill defendant received the medical treatment he or she needed. Overholser generated data meant to support his generalizations. From 1921 to 1934, 5,172 indictments for murder and various felonies were reported to Department of Mental Diseases, according to the Briggs law provisions. Of that total, 429, or 8 percent of the indictments reported were for first-degree murder. State psychiatrists found 66 (15 percent) of these capital defendants "insane." Overholser touted these data as showing that contrary to the public's perception psychiatrists did not find "all criminals insane." And, he pointed out, the average annual number of capital defendants found insane steadily declined from 1921 to 1934. Overholser suggested that this trend reflected the examiner's tendency to avoid speculating about the "exceedingly tenuous and metaphysical topic of 'criminal responsibility.'" Despite this obvious flaw, Overholser concluded on an upbeat note, praising the Briggs law as the "most significant step yet taken toward a harmonious union of psychiatry with the criminal law."[40]

Among other shortcomings, however, Overholser's claim about the relatively low number of capital defendants found insane by state psychiatrists masked a serious systemic bias toward women murdered by men. Of the 1,253 indictments for murder from 1900 to 1940, 49 defendants (4 percent) raised the issue of inanity, 31 of whom were men indicted for murdering their wives or sweethearts. Of the 31, 18 were found to be insane before trial and committed to an asylum and 10 men were found not guilty by reason of insanity at trial, of whom several pleaded guilty to a lesser crime.[41]

Although the law's gender bias did not lead to public criticism, a sensational 1934 robbery-murder trial severely undermined the Briggs law's effectiveness. A bank heist and two machine-gun murders committed by the fleeing robbers eventually led to a trial in which the sanity of the three defendants became the central issue. Irving and Murton Millen and Abraham Faber, the latter a recent graduate of the prestigious Massachusetts Institute of Technology, burst into a suburban Boston bank and grabbed nearly $15,000 in cash. The fleeing robbers gunned down a policeman answering the bank alarm and a firefighter standing nearby. Captured after a bruising fight in a New York City hotel lobby, the Millen brothers and Faber were returned to Massachusetts under heavy guard. Defense attorneys William R. Scharton and George S. Harvey announced that all three men would plead not guilty by reason of insanity.[42]

An examination administered by Briggs and Dr. Earl Holt found each of the three men to be sane. At trial, Briggs, whom the *Globe* described as the "picturesque patriarch of the courtroom," testified that the Millen brothers were "perfectly sane." But Briggs astonished the prosecution and the packed courtroom when he stated that the evidence he heard in court about Faber's family tree, his upbringing, and his adult behavior changed his mind. He now concluded that Faber's "judgment as to right and wrong, or his resistance to outside domination might be impaired." Holt stuck by his original diagnosis, insisting that Faber and the Millen brothers were sane and should be held criminally responsible.[43]

Scharton and Harvey challenged the Briggs law's constitutionality as well as the accuracy of Briggs and Holt's diagnosis of the Millen brothers and Faber. Scharton insisted the Briggs law was a violation of the defendants' right against self-incrimination, because information they divulged during their examination might be disclosed during the psychiatrist's trial testimony. Judge Nelson Brown overruled the defense motion and Scharton excepted, hoping to make the trial court's ruling the basis for an appeal to the SJC. To counter the state's psychiatric report, the three capital defendants enlisted their own mental health team, the first time such a move had been made since passage of the Briggs law thirteen years earlier. The three defendants were insane according to Dr. Ely Jellife and Dr. Evelyn G. Mitchell. Jellife, famous for his persuasive courtroom arguments describing Harry Thaw and Leopold and Loeb as insane, began his testimony in Millens-Faber by contending that "four-fifths of all men who go out with guns to rob and kill are mentally diseased." Then, using easily understood language, Jellife focused on the Millens' insanity. "Nature handed them both a lemon," he said, and their home environment "increased the difficulties that nature imposed." Every move the brothers made during and after the bank robbery and murders "was a symptom of [their] insanity."[44]

In his closing argument to the jury, District Attorney Edmund Dewing ridiculed the trio's insanity defense. Their defense of not guilty by reason of insanity is "bunk, it is rot," he said. The psychiatrists assigned under the Briggs law found the three men perfectly sane. Remember, the prosecutor shouted, Faber graduated from M.I.T. and the gang depended on his brains. His actions before, during, and after he had committed robbery and murder were those of a "normal human being." Faber and the Millens wanted money and they "worked together, ruthlessly and efficiently" to get it. "So that you can go home and face your neighbors with a clear conscience," Dewing concluded, "find these three murderers guilty."

Leaning comfortably on the mahogany railing framing the jury, Scharton spoke directly and quietly to the jurors. Faber lived a blameless life for twenty-four years, he began, but Murton Millen "exerted the maniacal force of the diseased mind" on the impressionable young man, causing him to rob and murder. Murton also psychologically tortured and twisted his younger brother, driving him to the same murderous goal. You should find them not guilty by reason of insanity, Scharton told the jurors. "In a place like Bridgewater, full of insane men, there can be no happiness. The sun seldom shines there," he concluded in a whisper.

After six hours of deliberation the jury returned a verdict of guilty of first-degree murder for each man. Murton and Irving Millen and Abraham Faber stood impassive, while their family members wailed or silently wept. Outside the courtroom a crowd cheered the guilty verdicts. The jurors sat tired and motionless, not knowing what to do next. The district attorney smiled and shook the hand of each juror. The defense attorneys followed. "You don't have to sit there any longer, Mike," a court officer said to the jury foreman. At that the foreman stood. "It's the Red Sox tomorrow afternoon," he said, smiling.

By the time twenty-three-year old John Charles McCann pleaded not guilty by reason of insanity for the attempted rape and murder of nine-year-old Anna Marie Magnuson in 1949, psychiatry had undergone substantial and sophisticated changes, largely due to research conducted during World War II. Yet, neither state-employed psychiatrists nor the SJC seem to have assimilated the changes that had occurred in the profession.

Following the Millen-Faber case, psychiatrists employed to examine capital defendants under the Briggs law consistently filed brief general reports that avoided the question of criminal responsibility and, therefore, invited conflicting testimony at trial about the nature and extent of the defendant's mental disease or deficiency. The promise and effectiveness of the Briggs law vanished. In fact, the Briggs law had become something of a deterrent to reform by permitting the court to rest comfortably on the notion that a cursory pretrial examination settled the question of a defendant's criminal responsibility. McCann's trial illustrated the bankruptcy of the Briggs law and the difficulties inherent in linking psychiatry and the law.[45]

Two state psychiatrists testified at McCann's trial. They told the jury that the young army veteran had been under a psychiatrist's care for "certain psychotic disorders" before the murder but that in their opinion he was not criminally insane. During cross-examination McCann's attorney asked one of the doctors whether the hospital staff had difficulty in making a decision about McCann's sanity. Testimony from the defendant's stepmother prompted the question. She earlier had stated that a doctor told her the hospital staff was divided about the sanity of her son. Under oath, the doctor not only denied making such a statement to McCann's mother but also repeated his opinion that John MCann was sane when he murdered the little girl and stuffed her partially nude body into a cedar chest in the attic of his home.[46]

Although psychiatrists for the defense and prosecution agreed that McCann was a psychopathic personality, they differed on the fundamental question whether McCann suffered from a mental disease that affected his criminal responsibility. An expert for the defense testified that at the time of the crime McCann probably could tell the difference between right and wrong, but that he was "unable to control his impulses." On one hand, if the jury accepted this characterization, McCann would have come under the umbrella of protection offered by Massachusetts's McNaughten-Shaw rule. He would not have been criminally responsible for his acts. On the other hand, experts called by the prosecution stated that McCann easily distinguished between right and wrong and fully controlled his impulses. Nothing more than "an lewd and lascivious urge to have sexual intercourse" drove McCann's behavior, a prosecution expert testified. Finally, in an effort to broaden the insanity rule according to which the jury would make its decision about McCann's sanity, the defense asked for a special instruction to the jury. It wanted the jury to be told that it must find McCann had "more than a superficial awareness of his deeds" in order to find him capable of distinguishing between right and wrong. Judge Eugene Hudson refused the defense request and the jury quickly found McCann guilty of murder in the first degree. On appeal, the SJC refused to second-guess the trial judge and it found no reason to overturn McCann's death sentence or to revisit its insanity rules.[47]

Just a few years later, however, insanity rules came under sharp attack as enthusiasm for the death penalty waned. In 1948 the Universal Declaration of Human Rights affirmed that "everyone has the right to life" and that "no one shall be subjected to torture or to cruel, inhuman or degrading treatment or punishment," and three years later Massachusetts enacted a so-called mercy law. The alternative sentencing law allowed a capital jury to reach a verdict of first-degree murder but sentence the defendant to life imprisonment rather than death. In 1953 a British Royal Commission on Capital Punishment raised serious questions about the efficacy of capital punishment generally and attacked the insanity defense in particular. The commission published testimony from U.S. Supreme Court justice Felix Frankfurter, among others, that labeled the McNaughten rules "in large measure shams." Frankfurter told the commission he did "not see why the rules of law should be arrested at the state of psychological knowledge of a time when they were formulated." Likewise, the American Committee on Forensic Psychiatry concluded that the right-from-wrong test was "based on an entirely obsolete and misleading conception of the nature of insanity." Every person, the committee insisted, possess an integrated personality of which reason is only one element and not the sole determinant of his or her conduct. A 1958 Massachusetts commission came to a similar conclusion, but clung to the McNaughten-Shaw rule simply because it did not know what else to do.[48]

U.S. District Court Judge David Bazelon took up the challenge of bringing insanity rules into conformity with contemporary psychiatric knowledge. In *Durham v. United States* (1954) he flatly rejected both the right-from-wrong test and the irresistible-impulse test as outdated and inadequate. Peppering his opinion with citations to psychiatric literature, Bazelon ruled, "an accused is not criminally responsible if his unlawful act was the product of mental disease or mental defect." The jury's task is to weigh the facts and the expert opinions to determine whether there was a casual connection between the defendant's criminal act and his mental abnormality. Such a test would go far toward upholding the best legal and moral traditions of the western world, Bazelon grandly concluded. He was convinced that his new rule was solid and that it would usher in a new era of harmony between psychiatrists and lawyers and be beneficial to mentally ill criminal defendants.[49]

In fact, the *Durham* rule was not adopted; nor did it restore peace. It did stimulate an acrimonious public debate, which in turn eventually caused some state courts and the American Law Institute to redefine legal sanity. The solicitor general of the United States, Simon E. Sobeloff, applauded *Durham*. To restrict psychiatrists to testimony simply about a defendant's ability to reason as dictated by *McNaughten* bars the "most advanced and enlightened thought from the witness stand," Sobeloff wrote in the American Bar Association's *Journal* in 1955. "The whole point," he added, "is not to restrict the test [for sanity] to particular symptoms, but to permit as broad an inquiry as may be found necessary according to the latest accepted scientific criteria." Of course, Sobeloff admitted, the *Durham* rule does not articulate precisely what symptoms would lead an expert to find a defendant mentally incompetent, but the rule's greatest strength is its invitation to inclusiveness. Rather than focusing solely on the discredited right-from-wrong test, a jury would have the opportunity to weigh all of the psychiatric evidence and come to a conclusion as to whether a defendant's "lack of control over his emotions has deprived him of control over his acts." Finally, Sobeloff sought to quiet *Durham*'s critics. The new rule would not coddle criminals, or undermine the law's deterrent effect. A person found not guilty by reason of insanity would be committed to a mental hospital for an indefinite period, certainly "no more inviting a prospect than a fixed term in jail." And, detention and treatment in a hospital offered society greater protection than a prison warden's certificate that a prisoner had served his time and been discharged regardless of his medical condition.[50]

The law professor Jerome Hall sharply disagreed with Sobeloff's brief for *Durham*. He denounced *Durham* as an assault on the "very foundation of Anglo-American law" and hailed the right-from-wrong test as "fundamental in our standards of morality." As Hall saw it, *McNaughten* had endured precisely because of its "common sense" emphasis on the "normal functions of perceiving and interpreting ordinary phenomena as a test of normal competence." *Durham*, in contrast, embraced the absurd idea that a "rational person may be insane." Pity the poor jury. Told to forget evidence of a defendant's normal intelligence, jurors were to sort through confusing and contradictory expert testimony to figure out whether the defendant had a mental disease and whether the criminal act was the product of that disease. Under these criteria nothing but "blind faith" could lead jurors to make "a causal connection between the act and the 'disease,'" Hall contended. For this reason, so-called psychiatric experts would dominate a trial in which a plea of not guilty by reason of insanity was made. Jurors, lawyers, and the law would be pushed aside and our system of law would be replaced by a "tyranny of experts," a move that was characteristic of communist dictatorships, not of the rule of law favored by western nations.[51]

Although not every critic of *Durham* forced the product rule into a Cold War mold, state courts universally rejected Bazelon's argument. Still, its expansiveness tempted defense lawyers everywhere to make use of the product rule. In 1958, for example, Massachusetts attorney Louis Goldstein used the product rule to frame a defense for Jack Chester, a tactic that pushed the SJC into including *Durham* in its review of the available methodological options for interpreting a defendant's sanity. Chester murdered his eighteen-year-old girlfriend after their marriage plans collapsed. Although his statements sometimes belied his argument, Chester pleaded not guilty by reason of insanity.

Psychiatric evidence offered by the defense at trial highlighted the cumulative effect of Chester's troubled childhood, his adolescent attempts at suicide, and his inability throughout his young life to deal with frustration or to control his anger. Three experts concluded that Chester "had suffered from a serious mental illness since he was twelve years old" and that he was in the grip of that illness when he shot to death his girlfriend as she stood in the doorway of her home. To counter this interpretation, the prosecution relied on the testimony of two psychiatrists who had examined Chester shortly after his arrest. They found him "perfectly sane," "normal," and without "any mental disease or defect which would affect his criminal responsibility." Chester's own impromptu speech deepened the confusion about his sanity. Speaking in staccato bursts, he told the jury, "I am not looking for your sympathy. I am not denying what I did to Beatrice Fishman. It was premeditated. It was cold-blooded murder."

Later, Chester made another remarkable statement. "It is my opinion that any decision other than guilty, guilty of murder in the first degree, with no recommendation for leniency, is a miscarriage of justice," he shouted as the jurors filed out of the courtroom.[52]

Were these the words of a mentally disturbed person or a remorseful, guilt-ridden defendant? The jury puzzled over this dilemma. After several hours of deliberation the jury asked the judge about irresistible impulse. Quoting from *McCann*, Judge Eugene Hudson did his best to describe someone whose illness made him "incapable of resisting and controlling an impulse which leads to the commission of a crime." Apparently satisfied that Chester was not suffering from a mental disease that caused him to be in the grip of an irresistible impulse, the jury found Chester guilty of first-degree murder. He appealed to the SJC, arguing that if allowed to stand, the verdict "would work a miscarriage of justice."[53]

Essentially, Chester asked the SJC to assess a jury verdict based on contradictory psychiatric opinions by plunging into the vast literature on insanity and criminal responsibility. Noting that the subject of criminal responsibility was receiving more attention at the time "than any other subject in the criminal law," the court reviewed and evaluated three methodological options for finding insanity. First, joining the chorus of *Durham*'s critics, the court noted that the product rule left key words undefined, such as "disease," "defect," and "product." Second, the court acknowledged that its own 114-year-old McNaughten-Shaw insanity rule was not perfect. But, at least, the combination of right-from-wrong and irresistible impulse provided a jury with "a standard." The *Durham* rule provided nothing. Third, acknowledging that a new rule proposed by the American Law Institute (ALI) promised to bring greater clarity to the issue, the court said, however, "no question touching that rule is before us." In the end, the court stuck by its ancient rule and upheld Chester's death sentence.[54]

Nine years later in *Commonwealth v. McHoul* (1967), the "troublesome" issue of criminal responsibility again was before the SJC. James McHoul was a mental patient at Boston State Hospital. On March 29, 1966, he appeared in the ward without his trousers. He told a male nurse who asked about the whereabouts of his clothing, "I want to tell you something. I did something wrong. I raped a woman." At trial, McHoul pleaded not guilty by reason of insanity, but a jury convicted him of assault with intent to rape, chiefly on the testimony of a state psychiatrist. "According to the M'Naghten rule," Dr. Malcom Rosenblatt stated, McHoul "was legally sane." Defense counsel moved to strike the doctor's entire statement, but the trial judge struck only that part about the McNaughten rule, allowing the jury to believe that a qualified expert had decided McHoul was sane according to Massachusetts law. The trial judge also refused a defense request to charge the jury using the ALI's wording on mental disease and criminal responsibility. The ALI statement read: "A person is not responsible for criminal conduct if at the time of such conduct as a result of mental disease or defect he lacks sufficient capacity either to appreciate the criminality of his conduct or to conform his conduct to the requirement of law." McHoul appealed.[55]

The SJC reversed McHoul's conviction and adopted the ALI standard. A unanimous court held the trial judge's ruling on Rosenblatt's *McNaughten* opinion constituted error. A defendant's ability to distinguish between right and wrong was only one part of the Massachusetts rule used to determine sanity. In addition to the right-from-wrong test the jury must decide whether mental disease had overwhelmed a defendant's "reason, conscience and judgment" and rendered him incapable of resisting and controlling "an impulse that leads to the commission" of a criminal act. To mitigate future problems of interpretation, the SJC announced it was adopting the ALI model code. Justice Arthur Whittemore termed the ALI definition of criminal responsibility "an evolutionary restatement of our rule." The court believed the ALI code improved on the McNaughten-Shaw test in several significant respects. First, it allowed experts to "testify fully as to the nature and extent of impairment of defendants' mental faculties as well as their observations or other bases for their conclusions." Second, the code modified the classical wording: it qualified "capacity" by adding "substantial"; it used the word "appreciate," rather than "know"; and it rejected the words "irresistible impulse," in favor of stating the defendant's lack of capacity to control his or her conduct. These subtle changes created a modern, flexible definition of insanity, according to the SJC. "We believe [the ALI code] will tend to minimize misunderstanding," sustain the "principle of criminal irresponsibility," uphold the "deterrent effect of criminal penalties for wrong conduct," and recognize the "injustice of punishing those lacking the capacity to appreciate the wrongfulness of their behavior." The court also thought the new definition would lessen "semantic dueling between attorneys and experts and [put an] end to the confusing debate on the issue of 'Does he know right from wrong?'" Still, the court was not naïve enough to believe the newly worded test would create unity among expert psychiatric witnesses.[56]

The architect of McHoul's successful insanity appeal came before the SJC in the fall of 1975 to argue for additional changes in the insanity defense. In the intervening eight years, however, the climate of opinion about the insanity defense had changed drastically. Public skepticism about the value of psychiatric justice had resurfaced, linked chiefly to fear generated by a sharp increase in violent crime and the feeling that criminals were escaping the punishment they deserved, sometimes by falsely claiming insanity. Data generated in the District of Columbia supported this argument. The year *Durham* was adopted only 0.4 percent of all cases tried resulted in a verdict of not guilty by reason of insanity. By 1961, the figure had shot up to 14.4 percent. Not surprisingly, therefore, in 1972, the District of Columbia federal appeals court junked *Durham* in favor of a slightly modified version of the ALI rule.[57]

In *Commonwealth v. Mutina* (1975) Boston's legendary criminal defense attorney William Homans Jr. successfully bucked this national conservative trend. He asked the SJC to reverse Harry J. Mutina's first-degree-murder conviction and to make significant changes in the procedural rules for insanity trials. Homans faulted the prosecution's reliance on the "presumption of sanity" and the trial court's refusal to instruct the jury about what would happen to Mutina if he were found not guilty by reason of insanity. Although the SJC specifically rejected both arguments, the court decided unanimously the verdict was "against the weight of the evidence" and reversed Mutina's conviction. Chief Justice G. Joseph Tauro also wrote for a slim majority, arguing that at the option of a defendant who raised the defense of not guilty by reason of insanity the trial judge must instruct the jury regarding the consequences of a verdict of not guilty by reason of insanity.[58]

Tauro's controversial *Mutina* opinion buttressed his newly won reputation as a bold but difficult leader. Following his admission to the bar in 1927, Tauro practiced law in Lynn for more than thirty years before accepting a political position in the statehouse. Governor Francis Sargent appointed Tauro Chief Justice of the SJC in 1970. Surprisingly, Tauro emerged as a leader, brushing aside the SJC's traditional deference to the legislature and to precedent and staking out the court's constitutional and inherent power. In *Commonwealth v. O'Neal* (1975) the Tauro court abolished the mandatory death penalty for murder committed in the course of rape, a decision that foreshadowed the court's abolition of capital punishment.[59]

Tauro's majority opinion about the insanity defense was as bold and controversial as his condemnation of capital punishment. The facts of Mutina's case were straightforward. About midnight on March 16, 1971, Harry Mutina confronted his former girlfriend Ruth Achorn on the front steps of her home as she returned from a date. He stared at Achorn and her companion for a full minute before he fired two shots. One shot killed Achorn and the second wounded her friend. Mutina fled. About ninety minutes later Boston police found him crouching in a corner at McLean Hospital, a psychiatric facility. When police read a Miranda warning to him he "just grunted," and he made no response at all to questions asked of him. For several hours he sat rigidly in a chair with his eyes tightly closed.[60]

At trial, two psychiatrists testified there was a history of mental illness on both sides of Mutina's family and that he suffered from an "acute schizophrenic illness." Using the ALI standard adopted by the SJC in *McHoul*, the experts stated that Mutina was not able to "conform his conduct to that which he knew was wrongful by virtue of his mental disorder." Assistant District Attorney Terence M. Troyer did not introduce any independent evidence touching on the issue of criminal responsibility but instead relied on the "presumption of sanity" and his sharp and detailed cross-examination of the two psychiatrists. Neither doctor wavered from his original diagnosis, a fact that led the SJC to remand the case to the Superior Court for a new trial.[61]

The court might have stopped here. But, over the vigorous dissent of Justices Francis Quirico, Paul Reardon, and Herbert Wilkins, Chief Justice Tauro insisted on addressing the issue of whether a jury should be told what would happen to a defendant found not guilty by reason of insanity. The traditional practice against instructing juries about the legal consequences of their verdict has deep roots. In the mid-nineteenth century Chief Justice Lemuel Shaw articulated the rule that jurors were to come to a verdict on the factual evidence presented in court, the arguments made by the defense and the prosecution and the judge's instructions on the law. To do otherwise, Shaw had contended, would lead to result-oriented verdicts that might well undermine the basic question of the defendant's guilt or innocence and usurp the court's responsibility for deciding what the penalty should be.[62]

While acknowledging the general validity of Shaw's argument, Tauro insisted on an exception when the defendant's sanity was the issue. He argued that jurors were not "sterile intellectual mechanisms purged of all those subconscious factors which have formed their characters and temperaments" but flesh-and-blood citizens with a myriad of concerns, biases, prejudices, fears, and frustrations. Knowing this, the court has established procedural and evidentiary rules designed to mitigate the likelihood of a juror coming to a verdict primarily on the basis of an emotional reaction. At the same time, however tightly drawn and clearly explained the court's procedural rules, it is not possible, or desirable, for the court to block completely a juror's experiences and emotions from entering into his or her deliberations. Jurors often wisely applied their personal concept of justice "to blunt the sometimes sharp cutting edge of the law." Of course, understanding and tolerating this reality does not permit jurors to disregard the law, or to consider facts and issues not properly introduced at trial.[63]

A criminal trial involving the plea of not guilty by reason of insanity further complicates jury deliberations. If the verdict is not guilty, the jury understands that the defendant will be free. If the verdict is guilty, jurors understand that punishment will follow. Only in those rare cases when the insanity defense is raised is the jury given a third choice whose "legal consequences they may not know or fully understand." Yet, inevitably during their deliberations jurors will discuss the issue. In the absence of correct information from the court about the outcome of a verdict of not guilty by reason of insanity, jurors will rely on their biases and emotions. Such an unguided procedure easily may lead to an erroneous verdict.[64]

For this reason, Tauro concluded for the court's slim majority, "we believe it is best to entrust jurors with a knowledge of the consequences of a verdict of not guilty by reason of insanity." Jurors have responsibility for a defendant's life and liberty and for the safety of society. Therefore, they are entitled to know that if they reach a verdict of not guilty by reason of insanity the defendant will be confined in a secure mental hospital and that by statute society will be protected from a "killer who [is] not legally responsible for his acts." Lacking those assurances, the Mutina jury ignored "overwhelmingly persuasive evidence that the defendant was insane at the time of the killing" and found Mutina guilty of first-degree murder. The evidence and the law "clearly played little part in their final verdict." They mistakenly applied their own emotional standard of justice. Had the judge instructed the jury about the consequences of a verdict of not guilty by reason of insanity, "we believe the jury might not have arrived at a guilty verdict."[65]

On the basis of the outcome in *Mutina* and his belief that a trial judge's instruction about the consequences of a verdict of not guilty by reason of insanity would have a positive effect on a jury's deliberations, Tauro articulated a new rule governing an insanity defense. The defendant, or the jury, if the defendant did not object, was entitled to an instruction from the trial judge regarding the consequences of a verdict of not guilty by reason of insanity.[66]

A few months after delivering the court's opinion in *Mutina*, Tauro was forced by the state's mandatory retirement statute to leave the SJC at age seventy. Governor Michael Dukakis asked fifty-six-year-old Associate Justice Edward Hennessey to assume leadership of the court. Although Chief Justice Hennessey was more cautious and politic than Tauro, the two agreed that the court's independence from the legislature and, as far as possible, from the new conservatism of the U.S. Supreme Court was all-important. In *Commonwealth v. Kostka* (1976), an insanity defense brought the latter issue squarely before the court.

Paul Kostka was indicted in 1973 for murdering a convenience-store clerk in the course of a robbery. At trial Kostka plead not guilty by reason of insanity, but despite considerable evidence of long-standing mental illness a jury found him guilty of murder in the first degree. In 1976 he appealed that conviction to the SJC. Kostka's primary contention was that the trial judge had erred in denying his motion for a directed verdict of not guilty by reason of insanity, because the commonwealth had failed to prove him sane beyond a reasonable doubt. He argued that a recent Supreme Court decision prohibited the commonwealth from relying on the presumption of sanity in a case where there has been uncontradicted expert testimony that the defendant was insane at the time the crime was committed.[67]

Speaking for the court, Hennessey explained how Massachusetts courts differed from other state and federal courts in its handling of the presumption of sanity rule. In every jurisdiction the law presumed that everyone charged with a crime was sane and therefore had the capacity to commit crime. After the defendant introduced evidence of insanity most jurisdictions shifted the burden of proving the defendant's sanity beyond a reasonable doubt to the prosecution. Only a handful of states, including Massachusetts, allowed the jury to weigh the presumption of sanity against evidence of insanity presented by the defendant. These historic differences suggest that the "purpose and nature of the presumption [of sanity] have traditionally been considered to be matters to be defined by courts . . . rather than by the Constitution," Hennessey concluded. Specifically, because the Massachusetts rule incorporates both the presumption and the facts that underlie it in any particular case, it falls within "generally accepted concepts of basic standards of justice" and does not violate constitutional due process.[68]

Just one year after Kostka the court revised its insanity defense procedure again. At issue in *Blaisdell v. Commonwealth* (1977) was the constitutionality of the revised Briggs law. The Massachusetts legislature had divided the Briggs law into two parts. The first part of the new statute allowed the court to order a psychiatric examination to determine a defendant's competency to stand trial. The second part required a defendant who declared his or her intention to plead not guilty by reason of insanity to undergo a psychiatric examination to shed light on whether the defendant was criminally responsible by reason of mental illness or defect. Charles Blaisdell was indicted for murder and three Essex County psychiatrists found him competent to stand trial. Blaisdell entered a plea of not guilty by reason of insanity and the commonwealth asked that he submit to a psychiatric examination that would provide the court with expert opinion about his criminal responsibility. Blaisdell refused. The trial judge told him if he did not cooperate he would be prohibited from making the defense of not guilty by reason of insanity. Blaisdell asked the SJC to rule on the question, arguing that the statute and the procedure constituted an "impermissible 'chill'" on the exercise of his privilege against self-incrimination.[69]

A divided court ruled that a court-ordered psychiatric examination was a form of compelled self-incriminatory testimony, because it was likely to result in disclosure of information that would constitute a confession or provide the commonwealth with leads to other damning evidence. To bring the revised Briggs law into conformity with the privilege against self-incrimination, Justice Paul Liacos outlined detailed procedural steps to prevent the prosecution from having access to the psychiatric report unless the defendant elected to testify himself or to present expert testimony based on his statements to the psychiatrist.[70]

Three years after *Blaisdell* the SJC focused on a mentally ill defendant's ability to premeditate murder. Following a breakup with his girl friend in the spring of 1973, Dennis L. Gould was in and out of various institutions for the mentally ill. On one occasion he was treated with drugs and psychotherapy after he had intentionally placed his right arm under the path of a trolley car. Despite a court order prohibiting any contact with his former girl friend, Gould stalked the young woman for more than two years. He suffered from constant, fixed delusions that led him to believe he was the savior of the Jewish people. In that role Gould believed his divine mission on earth was to kill his girl friend because she was "impure." On July 17, 1978, he brutally stabbed the young woman to death as she left the nursing home where she worked. After his arrest Gould said he would not go to jail or to a hospital, but he would allow authorities to take him to Israel and there be tortured or nailed to a cross.[71]

Every psychiatrist who examined Gould diagnosed him as a "paranoid schizophrenic." Two doctors testified at trial that his long-standing mental illness made it a clear-cut case of "lack of criminal responsibility." But one doctor stated that Gould knew that murder was wrong and that he was capable of controlling his behavior. This testimony, of course, echoed the ALI standard adopted by the SJC in *McHoul* (1967). Using that standard a jury found Gould guilty of murder in the first degree. Gould appealed the verdict.[72]

The SJC used the opportunity to transform its rule about mental impairment and criminal responsibility. *Gould* overruled longstanding precedent forbidding a jury to consider a defendant's abnormal state, short of insanity. The court invited a jury to consider the effect of mental illness on a defendant's ability to consciously and rationally form a plan to commit murder. The court held that psychiatric testimony may properly be offered to distinguish between intent expressed as a conscious desire and premeditation as expressed by a critical evaluation of the pros and cons of a criminal act. In Gould's case experts agreed that his intent to murder his girl friend was the result of a "long-standing, constant delusional belief system" and not a well-thought out premeditated plan. Because a defendant's diminished capacity bore only on the question of degree of guilt, Justice Ruth Abrams insisted that the court's new rule was not tanta-mount to adopting a doctrine of diminished responsibility, a slippery slope the court wanted to avoid. Five years later, however, the court took a giant stride in just that direction when it decided *Commonwealth v. Henson*.[73]

Albert Henson, Regina DiBlasio, and Lori Newton were parked curb-side at John's Lounge in Brockton early in the morning of July 21, 1981. DiBlasio was driving the car and Henson was seated in the front passen-ger seat. Newton sat alone in the rear. When Ernest Hill walked out of the club, Henson called to him. As Hill approached the car Henson shot and wounded him and DiBlasio sped away. Four months later Newton made a statement to the police that led to Henson's arrest. At trial Henson was convicted of assault with intent to murder.[74]

On appeal, Henson insisted the trial judge was required to instruct the jury on the element of specific intent to kill. Henson contended the jury should have been allowed to consider the effect of his intoxication—Newton had testified that Henson had been drinking nonstop for nearly twenty-four hours. The SJC agreed with Henson's argument. Speaking for a nearly unanimous court, Justice Herbert Wilkins stated that a jury should be instructed to consider whether a defendant's mental state pre-vented him from forming a specific intent for assault with intent to mur-der. *Henson*, like *Gould*, focused on a necessary state-of-mind element and planted the seed from which the court's subsequent decisions about the relationship between a defendant's mental state and the question of intent flourished.[75]

The SJC's carefully calibrated reforms were threatened by two national events. In November 1978, Dan White, a former member of the San Fran-cisco Board of Supervisors ran amok in city hall, shooting to death Mayor George Mascone and Supervisor Harvey Milk. White was arrested and charged. He pleaded diminished capacity, not insanity, but the distinction was lost on the general public. The supposed cause for White's inability to control his actions was the so-called Twinkie defense. White sometimes stuffed himself with junk food and there was testimony that excessive sugar consumption tended to impair his mental clarity. The jury found White guilty of voluntary manslaughter, not murder. The verdict touched off riots in San Francisco and howls of outrage throughout the state and nation. Reacting quickly, the California legislature abolished the defense of diminished capacity and irresistible impulse.[76]

Additional animus against the insanity defense was stimulated by the trial of John Hinckley Jr. On March 30, 1981, Hinckley stood waiting and alert outside a Washington, D.C., hotel. As President Ronald Reagan left the Hilton Hotel and walked toward his waiting limousine, Hinckley fired six shots, seriously wounding Reagan and his press secretary, James Brady. Hinckley's self-professed goal in shooting Reagan was to impress the actress Jodie Foster, a woman Hinckley had never met. At trial in federal district court, his defense was not guilty by reason of insanity. There occurred the predictable battle between psychiatrists. The trial lasted eight weeks and the jury deliberated for three and a half days before reaching a verdict of not guilty by reason of insanity.

It was a reasonable verdict, but understandably it stirred up a storm of protest. The day after the trial concluded, a news poll found that 75 percent of the public disapproved of the verdict and that 70 percent wanted to get rid of the plea of not guilty by reason of insanity altogether. President Reagan contributed to the public's misunderstanding of the insanity defense when he commented that the defense was "used more and more in murder trials." These people "found innocent by reason of insanity," he said, are put into a mental hospital but then quickly "turned loose" as "cured," a practice that allows them to "go right out in the street and commit the same crime over again." Other public officials called it a "rich man's defense," one that permits murderers to use "confusing procedures to their own advantage." Driven by this sort of overblown rhetoric, Congress restructured the federal rules regulating an insanity defense. A defendant may use the defense only if "at the time of the commission of the act" he or she "as a result of a severe mental disease or defect" is "unable to appreciate the nature and quality or the wrongfulness of the act." The rule omits the possibility of "irresistible impulse" and stipulates that insanity did not include psychopathic or sociopathic behavior. Finally, the 1984 Insanity Defense Reform Act placed the burden of proving insanity on the defendant rather than making the prosecution prove sanity.[77]

The SJC did not succumb to the popular hysteria. Rather than abolishing or restricting the insanity defense the Massachusetts court aggressively extended its decisions in *Gould* and *Henson* that had articulated new rules allowing a jury to consider a defendant's mental state on the question of his intent or knowledge that the victim's death will follow his acts. In *Commonwealth v. Grey* (1987) the SJC ruled that evidence of mental impairment, short of criminal insanity, was relevant to a jury's determination of whether a defendant accused of murder possessed the capacity to act with malice. Four years later in *Commonwealth v. Sama* (1991) the court held that a defendant's mental impairment also might be part of a jury's assessment of the accused's intent, or his knowledge that his actions likely would cause a death.[78]

Both *Grey* and *Sama* departed markedly from the traditional view of malice as judged by the objective standard of the reasonable person. Malice aforethought is an essential element of both first- and second-degree murder. If the prosecution proves the killing was the result of cool reflection—a process that may take but a few seconds—a jury may find the defendant guilty of murder in the first degree. A conviction of murder in the second degree requires proof that the killing was committed with malice aforethought, but without the aggravating factors of deliberate premeditation, or cool reflection, extreme cruelty, or felony-murder. Malice is the element that separates murder from manslaughter.[79]

Malice "is the requisite mental element" of murder and includes "any unexcused intent to kill, to do grievous bodily harm, or to do an act creating a plain and strong likelihood that death or grievous harm will follow." The first two parts of this tripartite definition of malice focus on a defendant's specific intent and spell out a subjective standard based on proof of a defendant's actual state of mind. This did not mean, the court made plain, that malice aforethought requires any actual intent to kill, or any foresight of such consequences by the defendant, "if the jury thought them obvious." In other words, it is not a legitimate excuse for a murder defendant to argue he could not have predicted the fatal consequences of his actions.[80]

In 1983, fifteen-year-old Terry Grey worked for a summer youth program cleaning Franklin Park in the Dorchester area of Boston. He and some of the other teenaged workers were fearful that persons within the group might attempt to steal their paychecks. On August 8, Grey brought to work a switchblade knife that he showed off to his co-workers by flicking the blade in and out. One of Grey's co-workers asked to hold the knife, but Grey refused, saying he believed the co-worker intended to steal his paycheck. When the co-worker stepped toward Grey, the youngster pulled the knife from his pocket, flicked the blade open, and stabbed the boy in the chest, killing him.[81]

Before trial, two psychiatrists examined Grey and later testified that he was of borderline retarded intelligence and suffering from paranoid traits. They also believed Grey's mental impairment might cause him to act impulsively and aggressively when confronted with a stressful situation. Other witnesses contradicted the experts, stating that Grey stabbed the victim with the intention of killing him. The defense asked the trial judge to instruct the jury that Grey's mental state at the time he stabbed the victim was relevant to questions about the defendant's ability to form a specific intent to kill. The judge denied the request. On appeal, Grey, who had been convicted of murder in the second degree, argued that the denial of the requested instruction was an error.[82]

The SJC reversed Grey's conviction, noting that the trial judge should have instructed the jury on the issue of intent so that it might "consider the defendant's mental status on the day in question." In fact, given Grey's mental condition, he may not have formed a specific intent to kill his co-worker. "We reach this conclusion," Justice Herbert Wilkins wrote, "because we do not know on what possible basis the jury concluded that the defendant killed the victim with malice." Wilkins insisted the court's decision did not mean it had embraced a diminished-capacity defense.[83]

In *Sama* the SJC turned its attention to the third part of the malice definition. Daniel Sama and his friend were living in a halfway house for recovering alcoholics. On December 20, 1989, the two violated their pledge of sobriety and consumed large quantities of alcohol and Xanax, a prescription drug that affects the central nervous system. The two men ended up in Waltham near the Amtrak railroad tracks, where Sama slashed and stabbed his friend nearly two dozen times in the face and neck. An Amtrak worker reported the fight to the Waltham police and, acting on a tip from a young boy who witnessed the murder, they arrested Sama.[84]

Sama was represented by William Homans, who sixteen years earlier had won two major victories: the abolition of the death penalty and the right to have a jury instructed about the consequences of a verdict of not guilty by reason of insanity. At trial, Sama did not contest the murder of his friend, but he claimed his uncontrolled alcohol and drug consumption that day caused him to black out, to lose all memory of the incident. An expert witness testified that Sama might have been hallucinating when he slashed his friend to death. Homans asked the trial judge to tell the jury it could consider the effect of the defendant's mental state on the question of "what he knew." Judge Hiller Zobel refused and a Middlesex County jury returned a verdict of murder in the first degree against Sama.[85]

The SJC concluded that Zobel's refusal to issue the instruction asked for by the defense constituted reversible error. The court ruled that under the third part of the definition of malice a jury should examine the "nature and extent of the defendant's knowledge of the circumstances at the time he acted" and whether a reasonable person "would have recognized that the defendant's conduct would create a plain and strong likelihood of death." To establish the third part of malice the prosecution must show the defendant knew he was stabbing the victim and that a reasonable person would know that such an act could lead to the death of the victim. In other words, a murder defendant will not be found guilty without the requisite guilty *mens rea*.[86]

The SJC's innovative and far-reaching decisions in *McHoul, Mutina, Gould, Grey,* and *Sama* seemed to usher in a new era, but the popular turmoil stimulated by the trial of Kenneth Seguin turned back the clock. In the spring of 1992 Seguin, a thirty-five-year-old software designer, lived in suburban Holliston with his wife, Mary Ann, and the couple's two children, Daniel, age seven, and Amy, age five. On the morning of April 29, police found Seguin wandering in the Hopkinton State Forest, where he said two unidentified men had left him after assaulting him. He told police the masked men had burst into his home late the previous night and "whacked" his wife in the head with an axe as she lay sleeping next to him and forced his two children to take pills. There were superficial wounds on Seguin's left wrist, left ankle, left temple, and the right side of his neck. A search by police led to the discovery of Mary Ann's body in the Sudbury River and the children's bodies in a Franklin pond. The children's throats had been slashed. The police dismissed Seguin's story about masked intruders and charged him with three counts of murder. At trial Seguin plead not guilty by reason of insanity.[87]

After describing the crimes in general terms, Judge Robert Barton asked each prospective juror whether he or she would have difficulty returning a verdict of not guilty by reason of insanity if the commonwealth failed to prove Seguin's guilt beyond a reasonable doubt and that he was legally sane. Ten prospective jurors stated they did not believe in the concept of insanity as a defense. "I just think if there's a crime committed someone should pay for what they've committed," one potential juror said. Five potential jurors expressed the opposite view: "Well, as far as I'm concerned he's definitely insane to do something like that to his wife and kids." The jurors who were chosen answered Barton's question by indicating they were open to a verdict of not guilty by reason of insanity.[88]

Psychiatric testimony presented by the defense and the district attorney differed sharply. Experts called by the defendant argued that Seguin was not criminally responsible, that his "mental illness made it impossible for him to conform his conduct to the requirement of law." They told the jury Seguin had a history of chronic depression, made worse by work-related stress, and that he had manifested some of the dangerous side effects of the drug Prozac. For these reasons, the psychiatrists testified, Seguin believed the only solution to his problems was "to take his family to a better and safer place, heaven." To counter the defense, Assistant District Attorney Marguerite Grant called three psychiatrists, two of whom had testified for the prosecution in the trial of John Hinckley. They said that on April 28 and 29 Seguin was able to appreciate the wrongfulness of his actions. A state psychiatrist, Nancy Gregg, added that she examined Seguin within a few days following the murders and she formed the opinion then that he had the capacity to control his conduct.[89]

Opinions outside the courtroom also were divided sharply. The *Boston Globe* columnist Bella English thought Seguin's insanity defense was nothing more than a cynical attempt to escape punishment for his horrible murders. "If Hitler were tried today, he'd wage an insanity defense," she wrote, adding, "How do the judge and jury keep a straight face?'" The Los Angeles *Times* expressed the opposite point of view. "If Kenneth Seguin wasn't mad, what other explanation could there be?" *USA Today* put the case in a larger context. A 1992 study found that nearly 75 percent of female murder victims knew their killer intimately. Twenty-six Massachusetts women were murdered by their husbands or boyfriends, up from fourteen in 1990.[90]

After six days of deliberation, a jury found Seguin guilty of murder in the second degree. That is, applying the court's *Gould* rule, the jury concluded Seguin's psychosis undercut his ability to premeditate the murders of his wife and children, but that he was not insane. Standing on the courthouse steps following the announcement of the verdict, Seguin's attorney blasted the media for "pandering to people's fears about mental illness."

He also lamented "all of the prejudices and biases that are built into people through years of simplistic and ignorant commentary on the nature of mental illness." Boston defense attorney John P. White Jr. added, "It's difficult to convince a jury that a person who is an ordinary-looking human being, who is not frothing at the mouth and throwing himself on the floor, suffers from a mental illness so severe that it overpowers his ability to discern right from wrong."[91]

Critics of the insanity defense, including Republican Governor William Weld, used the public's dissatisfaction with the Seguin verdict to call for reinstating the death penalty and for abolishing the insanity defense. The *Globe*'s Bella English was among those who called for such action. She applauded the U.S. Supreme Court's approval of Montana's abolition of the insanity defense. But, she lamented, it is not likely Massachusetts will adopt the Montana scheme, "because many legislators are defense lawyers and others are pretty nutty themselves and some are both." *Boston Herald* commentator Howie Carr said he believed the insanity defense was nothing but a way for murderers to avoid the punishment they deserved. "Granted, Seguin didn't beat the rap this time," Carr wrote in September 1995, "but someday, sooner or later, and probably sooner, Seguin will run this jive past a particularly stupid court, or an even dumber-than-usual Governor's Council or parole board. And he'll walk." Given this "reality," how can the attorney general "still think we don't need a death penalty in Massachusetts?" Both Carr and English cheered when Governor Weld filed a bill calling for the abolition of the insanity defense. The *Globe* editorial page, however, rebuffed the governor's proposed law. "Weld's bill proposes a solution not to a genuine problem but to a constellation of perceptions that are understandable, perhaps, but false. Abolition of the insanity defense answers no true social need. On the contrary, it deprives society and the criminal justice system of a choice that affirms free will and responsibility as guiding values for the American rule of law."[92] The Democratic-controlled legislature voted down the governor's bill.

While Weld's bill was before the House, the SJC heard Seguin's appeal. He made one major argument: Judge Barton's questioning of potential jurors did not dig deep enough to uncover their true attitudes about the insanity defense. The court made short work of that argument. First, Justice Herbert Wilkins noted that the court frequently had rejected the claim that "there is such a widespread prejudice against psychiatrists and the concept of criminal irresponsibility" that the SJC should mandate questioning of potential jurors about their bias against the use of an insanity defense. Second, Judge Barton did question each prospective juror and he found no basis for thinking that additional probing would have changed the mind of any juror about the validity of the insanity defense. Finally, Wilkins ruled that in future cases in which the defendant raised the issue of a lack of criminal responsibility trial judges would be required to use Barton's technique. Potential jurors were to be asked whether they held an opinion that would prevent them from returning a verdict of not guilty by reason of insanity if the commonwealth failed to prove the defendant criminally responsible.[93]

The public furor created by Seguin's trial and verdict eventually subsided, but the contentious debate about the rules governing the insanity defense continued to be heard in the courtroom. In *Commonwealth v. McLaughlin* (2000) the SJC revisited the insanity defense's fundamental questions. Who should assume the burden of proving whether a capital defendant is sane or insane? What level of proof is required? Can a jury rely on a "presumption of sanity" when weighing a defendant's plea of not guilty by reason of insanity? George McLaughlin's mad, murderous rampage in the winter of 1995 brought these questions to the SJC.[94]

McLaughlin believed that two of his nursing home co-workers and several unidentified residents in the apartment building where he lived were harming him with high-frequency beams. To escape the punishment they were inflicting on him, McLaughlin murdered his two co-workers and set fire to his apartment building, causing the death of a resident. McLaughlin told the police he thought the building's fire alarm would alert all the tenants to the fire. The only issue at trial was whether McLaughlin was criminally responsible at the time of his acts. He was found guilty of involuntary manslaughter and arson and not guilty by reason of insanity of two charges of murder in the first degree.[95]

The SJC granted review and affirmed McLaughlin's convictions but took the occasion once again to alter the rules governing an insanity defense. The court argued that Chief Justice Shaw's classic charge to the jury in *Commonwealth v. Rogers* (1844) had been modified by the SJC when, without reason, it shifted the burden to the government of proving a defendant's sanity beyond a reasonable doubt. This latter formulation may well have confused the jury, because jurors also were told that in determining whether the government met its burden they could rely on the "presumption of sanity." "The juxtaposition of these statements," Justice Francis X. Spina noted, "may lead jurors to conclude that the reasonable doubt standard, as applied to potentially insane defendants, means something less than what we have clearly said it means in all other contexts." To allay potential confusion, to make it simpler to explain to jurors, the court barred any future mention of the "presumption of sanity." Rather, the new *McLaughlin* rule called for the defendant to show the absence of criminal responsibility by a preponderance of the evidence and for the prosecution to prove all elements of a criminal act, including *mens rea*, beyond a reasonable doubt.[96]

The rule changes introduced by the SJC in *McLaughlin* mirror the long history of the insanity defense in Massachusetts: the SJC promoted reform by extending its commitment to the principle that to be culpable a capital defendant must have the capability to exercise free will. In 1844 the court had pioneered the nation's first insanity instruction and ushered in a new era in the late twentieth century by allowing a jury to assess a criminal defendant's subjective mental state and the element of malice within the offense of murder. By basing guilt on personal liability rather than dated presumptions of law, the Massachusetts court brought the law into closer conformity with the science of psychiatry and with the noblest moral and legal principles. But the court's rules have not eliminated popular bias against the insanity defense for murder. The prospect that someone committing a particularly repellent murder may be found not guilty by reason of insanity because a jury determined that a mental defect impaired the defendant's ability to act with malice aforethought or to form a criminal intent continues to stir public anger. Likewise, opposition to the insanity defense also surfaces under the *Gould* rule allowing a jury to find that a defendant's mental impairment short of insanity is a basis for a verdict of murder in the second degree.

During the last quarter of the twentieth century, in the face of public opposition, the SJC worked hard to improve the law in regard to insanity and mental impairment. The defense still must prove beyond a reasonable doubt that the accused was not responsible for his actions or unable to form a clear intent to murder. The question whether the enlightened reforms enacted by the Massachusetts court finally have succeeded in harnessing psychiatry to the law remains unanswered. It is clear the court's commitment to the fundamental principle that all criminal defendants have a right to a fair trial distinguishes its procedure in insanity trials from other state and federal courts. The SJC's long history shows that it is convinced a jury must find a defendant mentally competent to stand trial and capable of acting with malice and of forming a criminal intent in order to be held responsible for his or her act. However susceptible to bias or to misunderstanding, there is no other choice in a humane democratic society.

EIGHT

THE RIGHT TO AN ATTORNEY AND CRIMINAL DISCOVERY

In the decades following the enactment in Massachusetts of a mercy law, criminal procedure was transformed and the way opened to abolishing the death penalty. Led by Chief Justice Earl Warren, the Supreme Court of the United States ended legally enforced racial discrimination and strengthened the rights of criminal defendants. The Court fleshed out and extended to the states the code of criminal procedure outlined in the Fourth, Fifth, and Sixth Amendments of the Bill of Rights as well as in the Fourteenth Amendment's admonition that no one shall be deprived of life or liberty without due process of law. Specifically, the Court curbed unreasonable searches and seizures, ensured that the accused had the pretrial assistance of effective counsel, prevented a suspect's self-incriminatory statements from being used in court, redefined the parameters of a voluntary confession, and guaranteed a public trial by an impartial jury. In addition to implementing these rights, state criminal courts also adopted additional new procedures, including a "discovery" rule that requires prosecutors and defendants to share specific information before a trial begins. Death penalty trials held in Massachusetts during the last quarter of the twentieth century offer dramatic examples of the impact of these changes.[1]

Until the Warren Court turned its attention to the rights of the accused in the 1960s, Massachusetts's criminal due process—fair and reasonable rules consistently applied—was roughly the same as it had been a century earlier. The rights of capital defendants were narrowly defined at trial and successful postconviction appeals to the Supreme Judicial Court (SJC) were rare. From 1892 to 1939, for example, the court heard 108 murder conviction appeals—only a handful of which hinged on an alleged violation of a defendant's constitutional right—and reversed just 3. As late as its

1960 term the SJC heard just 3 homicide appeals and in each case allowed the conviction to stand. For this reason, among others, when the Supreme Court began to impose national criminal due process standards, the SJC and many other state courts protested that the Supreme Court was interfering with the state's traditional control of criminal trials. SJC chief justice Raymond S. Wilkins, for example, joined with nine other state supreme court justices to complain publicly that the Warren Court was "adopting the role of policy maker and failing to exercise proper judicial restraint." [2]

By 1970, however, the SJC not only had embraced the changes initiated by the Warren Court but had accelerated the pace of procedural change by using the Massachusetts Declaration of Rights. The SJC "currently appears more outspoken concerning the significance of rights under the Declaration of Rights than at any time in its history" Justice Herbert P. Wilkins observed in 1980. Despite Chief Justice Warren's retirement in 1969, rising murder rates throughout the nation, a legal and political outcry that the courts were "soft on crime," and occasional public hysteria, the SJC used state constitutional provisions to establish higher procedural safeguards for capital defendants than were required by the Supreme Court. In 1975 the court linked due process and capital punishment by finding unconstitutional the mandatory death sentence for rape-murder. Five years later, the SJC held the death penalty for murder unconstitutional. [3]

The rights of the accused protected by the federal Bill of Rights were extended to state criminal defendants very slowly. Not until *Powell v. Alabama* (1932), a case involving nine young black men sentenced to death for the alleged rape of two white women, did the Supreme Court rule that the Fourteenth Amendment's due process clause includes the right to effective counsel in state capital trials and on that ground reversed the Scottsboro Boys' convictions and death sentences. The decision breached the jurisdictional wall separating state and federal criminal procedure, but for the next three decades the Court struggled to determine whether it should incorporate the Bill of Rights through the Fourteenth Amendment and make those rights routinely applicable to state criminal proceedings. Some members of the Court argued that the Fourteenth Amendment's due process clause incorporates all of the Bill of Rights, and therefore state criminal trials should be held to a single national standard. In the name of federalism, other justices contended the Court should require noth-

ing more than conformity to a fundamental principle of fairness, leaving
to the states the precise definition and application of due process. By the
1960s a solid core of liberal activists dominated the Court and in *Gideon
v. Wainwright* (1963) declared that the Sixth Amendment is incorporated
through the Fourteenth Amendment's due process clause and therefore
state criminal defendants have a constitutional right to counsel. The right
to *effective* counsel—the issue that had drawn the Court to state criminal
trials in 1932—proved more difficult to define and posed greater problems
in capital trials, as I show later in this chapter.[4]

Beginning in colonial times, Massachusetts courts adopted the practice
of appointing an attorney to represent a capital defendant at trial, a rule
written into Article 12 of the Declaration of Rights in 1780, acknowledged
in 1805 by the SJC, and codified in 1820. Until 1890 and the siren call of
industrialization, the bar took that responsibility seriously, but when the
legislature transferred original jurisdiction for capital cases from the SJC
to the lower Superior Courts, elite lawyers who had previously accepted
appointment by the SJC to represent an indigent capital defendant began
a headlong rush away from such assignments. In a speech to the American
Bar Association in 1896, Joseph B. Warner, founder of one of Boston's
most successful law firms, rationalized the elite bar's break with its traditional commitment to public service. The practice of law has become "so
specialized" and so "lucrative," Warner argued, that many lawyers are unprepared "to go outside a given range of work" and unwilling to put aside
their own profitable practice to defend without pay an accused murderer.
For this reason, among others, between 1892 and 1911 the capital defense
lawyers appointed by the Superior Court tended to have less formal training and criminal trial experience than those attorneys who previously had
been appointed by the SJC. This trend accelerated after 1911 when by statute an accused murderer was permitted to petition the court to appoint an
attorney of his or her choosing. Approved by the elite Boston Bar Association, the law offered modest payment to lawyers willing to represent indigent defendants. The pool of attorneys from which the defendant usually
chose—so-called jailhouse lawyers who frequented the courthouse looking for such an assignment—often had limited time, training, and skills to
devote to a capital trial. For this reason, the law signaled the end of two in-
terrelated century-old ideals: that the state has a responsibility to provide

an accused murderer with the best possible defense, and that the bar's best and brightest has a professional and civic duty to serve the bar and the state without compensation.[5]

By undercutting these ideals the 1911 law implicitly recognized the existence of a deep divide within the Massachusetts bar, a growing gulf between elite corporate and appellate lawyers and those who made their living in the lower civil and criminal courts. While Harvard-trained lawyers joined State Street firms geared to meet the needs of corporations and financial institutions, graduates from Boston's newer law schools scrambled to represent less affluent clients, including criminal defendants. Recognizing this split could weaken the criminal justice system, the Boston Bar Association lobbied for higher admission standards. The legislature, however, fought to keep admission to the legal profession open and easy. There were no formal rules at all for admission to the Massachusetts bar until the creation of a Board of Bar Examiners in 1897. Over the next three decades the board administered a perfunctory examination that rarely included criminal law. In 1934 the SJC ruled that admission to the bar was a judicial, not a legislative function, and it imposed tough criteria. To qualify for the bar examination candidates were required to have graduated from a "public day high school" and to have completed at least two years of college and three years at a "full-time" law school. The Board of Bar Examiners also recommended that applicants complete a criminal law course, but no specialized training existed for capital defense lawyers. Therefore, as they had since 1911, death penalty lawyers learned on the job either as a court-appointed attorney or as an assistant district attorney.[6]

The 1911 law allowing an indigent murder defendant to choose from among a limited pool of untrained jailhouse lawyers was challenged in 1923. Paul Dascalakis, a recent Greek immigrant to Boston convicted of murdering Alice Arsenault, his landlady and lover, appealed his death sentence on the grounds that his court-appointed attorney, John W. Schenck, had conducted an incompetent defense.[7]

At a motion hearing before trial Judge Patrick Keating, Dascalakis's new attorney, John Patrick Feeney, attacked Schenck, one of a handful of African American attorneys practicing in Massachusetts in the 1920s. Born in Medford to parents who had fled from South Carolina slavery, Schenck had not attended college or law school but he had read the law while working as a statehouse messenger. He was fifty-three years old and had been admitted to the Massachusetts bar just eight years before Dascalakis came to trial in 1922. Schenck's home and office were located far from the white professional world, and his practice was centered in Boston's lower criminal courts.[8]

Dascalakis testified at the hearing that he met Schenck in the Charles Street jail when the lawyer approached him, saying the court sent him "to take [Dascalakis's] story." When Dascalakis looked puzzled, Schenck said, "You know I am a lawyer." "I don't know what he mean he is a lawyer," Dascalakis recalled. "I think it funny because I never saw in my life colored people like this." During Schenck's follow-up visit, Dascalakis said he told the lawyer, "You don't have any right to talk to me, you are a colored man." Schenck responded, "What is the difference?" According to Dascalakis's testimony, he told Schenck, "I want an American lawyer." When asked why, given his hostility, he had petitioned the court to appoint Schenck, Dascalakis claimed he had tried to contact another lawyer, but Schenck had blocked him from doing so. Dascalakis told Judge Keating that Schenck ignored his request to accompany the jury to the murder scene and refused to allow him to take the stand in his own defense at trial. Dascalakis also insisted Schenck failed to explain that he could address the jury at his trial's conclusion.[9]

After Dascalakis waived attorney-client privilege, Schenck took the stand. District Attorney Fielding briefly questioned Schenck, but Feeney subjected the black attorney to a withering cross-examination. Feeney sought to establish whether Schenck told Dascalakis that he might testify on his own behalf. Schenck's initial answer was evasive, but after repeated prodding he said he had told Dascalakis he could testify. Feeney demanded to know exactly what Schenck had said to Dascalakis. Schenck equivocated. "In substance, [I told him] it was entirely within his province" to take the stand in his own defense. Feeney shot back: "Don't you know that [Dascalakis] can't understand the words, 'entirely within your province.'" "I have not said that those were the exact words," Schenck retorted; "I can't remember the exact words." Feeney would not let go. He demanded to know when Schenck told Dascalakis he could testify. Schenck replied that he and the defendant had discussed the question after the prosecution had completed its case. "Well, Mr. Witness," Feeney asked contemptuously, "as a trial lawyer do you say that was the time to determine whether a man should take the stand or not?" Schenck said nothing.[10]

Judge Keating denied the defense motion for a new trial and in June 1923 the SJC heard Dascalakis's appeal. Chief Justice Arthur P. Rugg, who held the center seat from 1911 to 1938, had earned praise for his knowledge of the law, his commitment to legal craftsmanship, and his love for the legal profession. But perhaps because he had no doubt about Dascalakis's guilt or because he preferred to defer to the trial judge's ruling that Schenck's conduct of Dascalakis's trial had been acceptable or because he realized any attempt to define professional behavior would open a Pandora's box of legal challenges, Rugg avoided articulating a standard of competence for a practicing attorney.

"Much stress has been put upon the alleged incompetence or negligence of the counsel assigned by the court," Rugg began, adding that it was not clear the court held the power to set aside a verdict "because of the insufficiency of counsel." It is true, he acknowledged, "that evidence was admitted in examination of witnesses by the counsel for the defendant [Schenck] which could not have been introduced against his objection," but that "is a matter of slight consequence." To buttress his point Rugg offered a hypothetical example that assumed Schenck's courtroom behavior had been driven by a carefully crafted legal strategy. Skilled criminal attorneys, the chief justice contended, often allow immaterial or irrelevant evidence to become part of the trial record in the hope of learning something that might be beneficial to the defendant. The fact that in Schenck's hands the strategy did not work "is neither error in law nor incompetence." After all, examining and cross-examining witnesses is a difficult art and "methods differ." No one was in a better position to observe Schenck's courtroom strategy than Judge Keating and he denied the defense motion.[11]

Rugg also brushed aside other accusations leveled against Schenck by the defense. Schenck's failure to object to an improper remark by the district attorney cannot be labeled "negligence or incompetence." Nor may Schenck be blamed because Dascalakis did not accompany the jury to view the scene of the crime. A defendant does not have a right to accompany jurors; the matter is up to the judge. Judge Keating, Rugg speculated, "may have believed the defendant waived his right to go on the view." The judge also may have thought Dascalakis waived his right to make an unsworn statement at the trial's conclusion. By shifting the focus from Schenck's missteps to what Keating may have thought and to a trial judge's discretionary authority, Rugg was able to conclude that Dascalakis's court-appointed counsel had conducted "a faithful and proper defense."[12]

Finally, Rugg cautiously listed a handful of characteristics that distinguish a good trial lawyer: "experience, capacity, industry, alertness, faithfulness, learning and character." But, the chief justice quickly backpedaled away from these very general markers of effectiveness. "Perfection cannot be demanded," he noted, "even if a standard of perfection could be formulated"; nor may all lawyers "be held to the same standard of excellence."[13]

Chief Justice Rugg did not state which, if any, of the general characteristics he listed Schenck possessed or how far from perfection his performance had drifted. In fact, Rugg avoided establishing a standard of competency by which an attorney's performance in a capital case might be measured. Therefore, his *Dascalakis* opinion stopped far short of defining, or even suggestively outlining, what kind of behavior by a trial attorney might signal that a defendant had not been faithfully and properly defended. Nor did the chief justice acknowledge that a capital defense attorney might need to possess a higher degree of skill and commitment than an ordinary trial lawyer. Rugg's formulation was sentimental, a nostalgic reflection of a nineteenth-century legal world where well-educated elite lawyers voluntarily participated in the criminal justice system when called upon by the state. His decision left the trial courts without guidance and future defendants caught in such a bind largely without recourse, a combination that helped lower the standard to which court-appointed capital attorneys were held.

For this reason, the issue of attorney competence did not surface again for more than two decades after Rugg left the SJC in 1938. This hiatus did not mean the quality of court-appointed attorneys had improved. In fact, in 1952 the Boston Bar Association reported with alarm that "there was reason for serious question as to the competence and diligence of the defense conducted by counsel appointed by the court" in recent capital cases. Among other first-degree murder trials in which the defense was conducted poorly by a court-appointed attorney, the Bar committee pointed to the murder trial of Marshall Cox as an especially egregious example.[14]

Fifty-nine-year-old Marshall Cox murdered his wife, Helen, in 1948. Married in 1933, the couple lived in a modest home near Concord Center.

They had friends and they took part in the affairs of their church. Helen played the piano and read a good deal. Marshall had graduated from Harvard College in 1911 and completed a Master's degree in chemistry the following year. He taught chemistry at Tufts University until 1929 when he resigned to launch a small candy manufacturing business. A few years later he inherited the Stow Country Club. The business was moderately successful, but in 1948 a heavy snowstorm caused the roof of the clubhouse to collapse and the cost of repair strained Cox's financial resources. He feared he would no longer be able to provide for his wife. Knowing Helen dreaded the thought of being old and poor, Cox came to the conclusion that he should murder her as an act of "kindness." [15]

On the morning of February 21, 1948, he asked Helen to play a Mozart piece. While she sat at the piano, Cox approached her from behind and repeatedly struck her on the head with a hammer. When she fell to the floor he plunged an ice pick into her chest. He ended his brutal assault by strangling Helen with a length of copper wire. He then made two phone calls, one to his broker and a second to the Concord police. When he opened the door of his home to admit a police officer sent to the scene, Cox was covered in blood. He told the officer, "I have just done a most terrible thing. I killed my wife." At police headquarters, Cox voluntarily made a detailed statement admitting guilt. He said he thought he "did a good job and the state would take his life and that [he and his wife] would both meet in the next world." [16]

While held at the Concord jail, Cox petitioned the court to appoint Francis W. Juggins to represent him. On March 3, Cox was indicted for first-degree murder and ten days later the court assigned two psychiatrists to examine him. On their recommendation Cox was admitted to Bridgewater State Hospital for observation. In a letter to the court, the hospital's medical director reported that Cox manifested a "morbid state of mind." Dr. Warren Stearns concluded that Cox was "insane and in need of care in a hospital for mental disease," and, therefore, unfit to stand trial. Two years later, Stearns informed the court that Cox had recovered his sanity and, therefore, he could be brought to trial. [17]

When attorney Juggins began his defense of Cox in April 1950, he had been practicing law since 1932, when he left Harvard Law School after completing his first year. He spent very little time with Cox before the trial. Juggins and Cox had spoken briefly at the Concord jail, for a few minutes at Bridgewater when Cox was admitted for treatment, and for about thirty minutes on the eve of the trial nearly two years later. Not surprisingly, therefore, Juggins' trial strategy gave every indication of being hastily prepared and ill conceived. First, he argued that according to law, Dr. Stearns should be called as a prosecution witness and that his uncontradicted testimony "required a directed verdict of not guilty by reason of insanity." Second, Juggins insisted it was "improper" for Assistant District Attorney Lyman Sprague to cross-examine the only witness called by the defense—a psychiatrist who had examined Cox. The court made it clear that Juggins' arguments were incorrect, contrary to the law and to established criminal procedure. Despite this obvious setback, Juggins asked the jury to find Cox not guilty by reason of insanity. "No person in their right mind could have done such a thing," Juggins told the jury during his brief closing remarks.[18]

District Attorney Sprague argued that Cox was legally responsible for the premeditated murder of his wife, an act he committed with "extreme atrocity and cruelty." The prosecutor told the jurors it was their responsibility to determine the importance of the psychiatric testimony, adding that none of the doctors who examined Cox concluded he could not distinguish right from wrong, the shorthand legal test for insanity. Sprague also read to the jurors a letter written by Cox a short time after he arrived at Bridgewater hospital. Referring to the mental state that had caused him to murder his wife, Cox lightheartedly told his sister that he "snapped out of it almost immediately." Sprague asked the jury to reject Cox's insanity plea and to find him guilty of first-degree murder.[19]

After deliberating less than three hours the jury found Cox guilty. Judge Joseph Hurley asked Cox if he had anything to say as to why the penalty of death should not be imposed. Cox made a long, coherent argument for his insanity at the time of the crime and in the process exposed Juggins' shoddy performance. Cox pointed out there existed plenty of evidence to support his claim of insanity other than psychiatric testimony. My family history, Cox told the jurors, was riddled with mental illness, but "nothing of that kind was brought out" and my court-appointed attorney also slighted my personal mental health record. Finally, he insisted, a "normal person" would have lied or fled after committing a murder, "but I didn't do anything like that. I wasn't normal." Perhaps, now, after hearing me, Cox said, some jurors might say, "I don't think he got a very good deal at this trial." He added: "This verdict does not redound to the glory of Massachusetts."[20]

Three months after Judge Hurley had sentenced Cox to "suffer the punishment of death by the passage of a current of electricity through your body," the one-time country club owner and his court-appointed attorney appeared before Hurley to argue a motion for a new trial. Juggins had not prepared a bill of exceptions nor had he entered a formal objection to the district attorney's absurd closing syllogism: since most men were sane there was a rational probability that the defendant was sane and, therefore, Cox was criminally responsible for his wife's murder. Juggins simply re-peated the same wrong-headed argument he had made at trial. During a rambling, largely incoherent argument almost completely lacking specific details, he insisted psychiatric testimony must be accepted without ques-tion. He blamed the trial jury for failing to understand his interpretation and for returning a guilty verdict. Judge Hurley denied the motion and Cox appealed the ruling to the SJC.[21]

Justice Raymond S. Wilkins, whom Republican governor Leverett Saltonstall had placed on the SJC in 1944, once again explained that Juggins's argument about allowing uncontested psychiatric testimony had no merit and that Judge Hurley had not erred in denying Cox's motion for a new trial on that issue. But the trial's outcome shocked the court and it took the rare step of reviewing the facts as well as the law to determine whether "there was a miscarriage of justice." Indeed, the court found the trial "an extraordinary affair" and without elaborating, Wilkins ordered a new trial.[22]

Because the issue of Juggins's competency was not specifically before the court, Wilkins simply provided a remedy for Cox, leaving unanswered specific questions about Juggins's effectiveness as well as the broad issue implicitly raised by the case of what criteria should be used to insure the competency of court-appointed attorneys. The year after the Cox deci-sion, however, a special committee of the Boston Bar Association charged with investigating the performance of court-appointed criminal attorneys issued a report decrying the lack of specific standards for appointing law-yers and it found shoddy performance by court-appointed lawyers to be all too common. Based on interviews with Charlestown prisoners incarcer-ated between 1941 and 1951, the committee also concluded that an alarming number of court-appointed attorneys had failed to meet their professional obligation to their clients. To meet this crisis, the Bar Association offered two simple remedies: the bar's assistance in evaluating potential court-appointed attorneys; and, to discourage "jailhouse lawyers," the committee recommended that the court weigh more heavily "other criteria" than a prisoner's petition to appoint a specific attorney. These reforms, the committee stated, will help ensure that lawyers appointed to represent criminal defendants are "fully qualified by training, experience, reputation and character" and that an attorney has not "solicited such employment." [23]

Within two years after the Bar committee's report, the Massachusetts legislature and the court acted on its recommendations. The legislature put into law what had been common practice for some time: the court was required to appoint an attorney for an indigent person indicted for capital murder who pleaded not guilty at arraignment. The new law also mandated "reasonable compensation" and payment of "reasonable expenses" incurred by a court-appointed lawyer. For its part, the Superior Court adopted Rule 95, a provision that seeks to improve the quality of attorneys appointed by the court. Specifically, the trial court's rule states that "no person shall be assigned as counsel in a murder case unless he had been a member of the Bar for more than ten years and the court has satisfied itself that he was fully qualified by training, experience, reputation, and character to discharge the responsibility imposed upon him." The court's rule also seeks to eliminate "jailhouse lawyers" by prohibiting an attorney from soliciting employment as counsel for the accused and by forbidding a court-appointed lawyer from receiving any compensation other than that allowed by the court. [24]

These modest changes bolstering a criminal defendant's right to effective counsel were reinforced and extended by the U.S. Supreme Court. In a series of controversial decisions the Warren Court removed the barrier between state criminal procedure and the Bill of Rights. In 1963, for example, the Court declared the Sixth Amendment right to counsel applies to the states under the due process clause of the Fourteenth Amendment. Although Massachusetts, like many other states, already required capital defendants to be represented by an attorney, the Court ruled in *Gideon v. Wainwright* (1963) that the Sixth Amendment as applied to the states through the Fourteenth Amendment requires that counsel must be appointed to represent indigent defendants charged with serious offenses in state criminal trials. The decision not only signaled the doctrinal triumph of the incorporation of the Bill of Rights but extended a constitutional right to state criminal defendants. The Court also ruled that a defendant's right to counsel extends to every "critical" stage of a criminal proceeding, including a preliminary hearing, and in *Douglas v. California* (1963) that "fairness and equality" mandate that the court appoint an attorney for indigent defendants during the appeals process. "There can be no equal justice," Justice William O. Douglas wrote for a divided Court, "where the kind of an appeal a man enjoys depends on the amount of money he has." Three years later, in *Miranda v. Arizona* (1966), the Court extended to all criminal suspects under police custodial interrogation the right to an attorney, overturning the SJC's earlier position that there is "nothing in the statutes of Massachusetts giving a person accused of a capital crime or any other crime a right to counsel before being brought into court." Finally, speaking for a Court divided five to four in *Stovall v. Denno* (1967), Justice William Brennan concluded the right to counsel is retroactive, that "no distinction is justified between convictions now final and convictions at various stages of trial."[25]

The convicted murderer Henry Arsenault was among the first Massachusetts prisoners to seize on the Court's new ruling permitting a retroactive appeal. He argued that his 1955 conviction should be overturned because counsel did not represent him when he pleaded guilty to murder at a preliminary hearing. Arsenault and two other armed men planned to rob a wealthy dress manufacturer by forcibly entering his Newton home, but the men entered the wrong house and in the ensuing confusion shot to death its occupant. The gunmen fled on foot, but they were quickly captured and placed under arrest by police. The following morning at a probable cause hearing in Newton District Court, Arsenault appeared without a lawyer and spontaneously pleaded guilty to murder and assault with intent to rob. A grand jury subsequently returned an indictment charging Arsenault with murder. At his arraignment several days later—still without a lawyer—Arsenault changed his plea to not guilty. At trial, his court-appointed attorney allowed Arsenault to take the stand in his own defense. He admitted firing the fatal shot but insisted it was not intentional. Not surprisingly, on cross-examination, the district attorney reminded Arsenault that he voluntarily had pleaded guilty at his probable cause hearing. The trial jury found Arsenault guilty of first-degree murder and he appealed.[26]

Carefully parsing the Supreme Court's holding in *White v. Maryland*

(1963) that the aid of counsel is necessary at all stages of pretrial criminal proceedings for the accused to mount an informed defense, SJC justice Paul G. Kirk rejected Arsenault's appeal. As Kirk, a Democrat appointed to the court in 1960, saw it, the question was "whether the rule of the *White* case should be retroactive." Speaking for a unanimous court eager to defend its power to define state criminal procedure free from Supreme Court interference, Kirk presented an argument that was defensive and strained. There was no reason for Arsenault to enter any plea at his probable cause hearing, Kirk wrote, but once he uttered the damaging guilty plea it could be used against him at trial. The rule that a guilty plea constitutes an admission that could be used against the defendant has roots extending at least as far back as 1874. Not until *White*, Kirk continued, was that rule of evidence found "constitutionally unacceptable." For the Supreme Court to initiate change at this point "would have a serious impact upon the administration of justice in this Commonwealth and elsewhere." Therefore, he said, "it is our conclusion that *White v. Maryland* is not retroactive."[27]

The famous Boston attorney F. Lee Bailey represented Arsenault before the Supreme Court of the United States. In a *per curiam* opinion the Court swept aside the SJC's tortured reasoning and Attorney General Elliot Richardson's tepid oral argument. The right to counsel at every critical stage of a criminal proceeding—custodial interrogation, pretrial hearings, trial, and appeal—is retroactive. Denial of counsel, the Court concluded, "invariably deny a fair trial." The SJC's ruling was reversed.[28]

As sweeping as was the Court's decision about the right of the accused to counsel, it left unresolved the issue of the *effective* assistance of counsel. As far back as *Powell v. Alabama* (1932), the Court had acknowledged the importance of appointing effective counsel for a criminal defendant, so that the trial did not become a meaningless ritual. After less than a decade of experience with *Gideon*, however, the post-Warren Court came to believe defendants increasingly raised the issue of attorney competence simply because they were disappointed with the outcome. The difficult task facing state courts was to articulate a standard that preserved the right to effective counsel while distinguishing claims of ineffectiveness founded simply on the notion that a different legal strategy would have produced a different result.[29]

In Massachusetts, the convicted murderer Leonard Lussier brought the issue of effective counsel before the SJC in 1971, arguing he had been denied that constitutional right at his 1954 trial. Lussier, a twenty-one-year-old sailor home on leave, shot and killed a bystander during an attempted robbery of a Springfield, Massachusetts, liquor store. Following his arrest, Lussier led police on a tour of the route he had taken from his foster parents' home to the liquor store where the crime had occurred, and without benefit of counsel at his arraignment Lussier pleaded guilty to murder. Several days later, he petitioned the court to appoint as his counsel James L. Vallely, a criminal trial lawyer with eighteen years' experience. At trial, Vallely argued that Lussier's gun had fired accidentally when he slipped on a patch of ice running from the store to a getaway car following the aborted robbery. The jury did not find that story convincing and found Lussier guilty of first-degree murder. In accordance with the mercy law, however, the jury recommended he not be executed and the trial judge sentenced Lussier to life imprisonment.[30]

Seventeen years after his conviction and sentencing, Lussier, prompted by the changed legal climate initiated by the Warren Court, offered two specific examples of attorney Vallely's alleged ineffectiveness during his 1954 trial. Lussier contended that his court-appointed attorney should have objected to the introduction of his confession and that he should not have revealed to the jury that Lussier pleaded guilty to murder at his arraignment. Before focusing on Lussier's specific argument, Justice Jacob J. Spiegel, the first Jew to serve on the SJC, defined the "standard of representation to which a criminal defendant is entitled." First, he quoted from a recent Federal Circuit Court of Appeals decision, *Scott v. United States* (1970). "Only if it can be said that what was or was not done by the defendant's attorney for his client made the proceedings a farce and a mockery of justice, shocking to the conscience of the Court, can a charge of inadequate legal representation prevail." Second, Spiegel added language drawn from a noncapital case heard by the SJC in the same term as Lussier's. Effective assistance of counsel, he pointed out, does not mean "counsel was ineffective because of retrospective differences of opinion about judgments formed, or tactics used by the trial lawyer during the trial; because of the failure to offer, or the failure to object to the offer of evidence; because of retrospective opinions that different tactics or strategy might have been more successful than those used by the trial lawyer; or because a different or better result might have been obtained by a different lawyer."[31]

Spiegel found that, measured by these standards, the defense provided by Lussier's court-appointed attorney met the court's test of effectiveness. The problems confronting Lussier's counsel were "exceedingly difficult and grave." At trial, Lussier's confession was offered in evidence by the prosecution. After a full hearing on the question of the admissibility of Lussier's confession, the trial judge ruled it was voluntary and should be admitted into evidence. Subsequently, Vallely correctly pointed out that the arraignment judge did not accept Lussier's guilty plea because he was not represented by counsel and that Lussier was a young man with a ninth-grade education whose "mind was so malleable or yielding that he would easily agree with whatever some one might say to him just to be agreeable." It seems plain, Spiegel concluded, that Vallely did the best he could to minimize the impact of Lussier's guilty plea. It was not a manifestation of Vallely's ineffectiveness that his effort to mitigate the confession's damage was not successful and that Lussier was found guilty at trial. For these reasons, the SJC denied Lussier's appeal.[32]

Three years later the court wrestled again with the question of how to gauge a court-appointed counsel's effectiveness. On the basis of very strong evidence, John J. Saferian had been convicted of armed robbery and sentenced in 1967 to Walpole Sate Prison for twelve years. About a year later the trial judge denied Saferian's motion for a new trial on the claim of ineffective representation, and a single SJC justice upheld that ruling. In the summer of 1974, however, the issue came before the full court.[33]

Justice Benjamin Kaplan, who had come to the court after nearly three decades on the faculty of Harvard Law School, acknowledged that Saferian's lawyer should have done much more in the way of pretrial preparation and that at trial he relied too heavily on cross-examination alone. "Counsel did not go over facts with the defendant, or seek to interview the prospective witnesses, or ask the prosecutor for material, or make routine pretrial motions apart from the motion to suppress," Kaplan noted. "He relied on cross-examination and argument," and depending on improvised cross-examination alone, even if "of virtuosic quality, is not to be recommended." At the same time, evidence of Saferian's guilt "was overwhelming" and his court-appointed attorney did "everything that could be done for him." Specifically, Kaplan found that Saferian's appeal failed to show that his trial attorney's mistakes or omissions had cost the defendant a "substantial defense."[34]

Having denied Saferian's appeal, Kaplan addressed the larger issue of counsel-effectiveness. Rather than offering general bromides about the character of a defense attorney, Justice Kaplan articulated a two-part rule. A defendant's appeal alleging a subpar performance by a defense lawyer would trigger a "discerning examination and appraisal of the specific circumstances of the given case to see whether there has been serious incompetency, inefficiency, or inattention of counsel—behavior falling measurably below that which might be expected from an ordinary fallible lawyer." If examples of incompetence were found the court would then determine whether the lawyer's flawed performance had "deprived the defendant of an otherwise available, substantial ground of defense." It was up to the defendant to demonstrate both the trial attorney's ineffectiveness and the resulting damage to the defense.[35]

In 1984, the Supreme Court adopted a standard similar to *Saferian.* The Court held a convicted defendant must show that his lawyer's performance "fell below an objective standard of reasonableness" and that but for his counsel's errors the result would have been different. Justice Thurgood Marshall dissented, writing that the standard adopted by the Court was so malleable it would be of no use at all. In fact, while the group of decisions establishing a defendant's right to counsel is now unassailable, the criteria to measure an attorney's effectiveness clearly favor the prosecution.[36]

In the same year the SJC laid down its conservative criteria for measuring an attorney's effectiveness, the court took a bold step toward safeguarding a defendant's rights by adopting a criminal discovery rule. Beginning in the 1930s the states and the federal government extended pretrial discovery—the exchange of information between contending parties—in civil cases, but discovery was not available in criminal cases at common law. In fact, most observers believed criminal defendants had too many advantages as it was. Therefore, criminal trials were characterized by what Harvard Law School Dean Roscoe Pound called the "sporting theory of justice," a battle of wits between two lawyers in which concealment was a major part of their strategy. A discovery rule was first incorporated into federal rules of criminal procedure in 1944, and the American Bar Association helped accelerate its use by recommending in 1970 that states adopt a version of the federal rule allowing defendants to see "books, papers, documents, or tangible objects" if they were "material to the preparation" of a defense. In Massachusetts, the rule's adoption was directly linked to Ella Mae Ellison's dramatic appeal of her murder conviction in 1978.[37]

The roots of modern criminal discovery lie in common law pleading rules and their corollary, the bill of particulars. Common law pleading rules are lengthy and detailed—sometimes absurdly so—but their formalism and strictness were designed to provide the defendant with information about the alleged crime so that an informed defense could be mounted. To some, however, the ancient common law rules were perceived as a means of elite control, and beginning in the 1830s reformers launched a campaign to simplify the law so that it would express a democratic "public voice." In Massachusetts, defenders of the common law fended off reform of common law pleading until 1899 when the state adopted a short form of the criminal indictment. Under the new statute a murder indictment no longer needed to allege the manner or specific means of the cause of death. At the same time, to compensate for the brevity of the indictment and to protect the defendant's right to due process under Article 12 of the Declaration of Rights, the law allowed the defendant to file a motion for "more specific information as to the exact nature of the crime which he is alleged to have committed."[38]

In *Commonwealth v. Jordan* (1911) the SJC upheld the constitutionality of the short-form indictment and of a defendant's right to details about the alleged crime, but Justice Marcus Morton refused to restrict a trial judge's discretionary authority to deny the defendant access to information beyond what the court considered essential to a defendant's understanding of the crime. There is "no rule of law which requires the commonwealth" to "disclose the evidence on which it relied." For the next six decades capital defense attorneys hammered away at the *Jordan* rule, initially trying to pry loose grand jury testimony so that a defendant could demonstrate differences in a witnesses' testimony or obtain a copy of a confession.[39]

Reformers won a small concession in 1966. In response to a motion by the convicted murderer Robert Cook that he be allowed access to grand jury minutes, the SJC revealed it had read Cook's trial record and the minutes in question and decided he did not have a "particularized need" for the information. The implication of the ruling was clear: the court might allow a defendant access to grand jury proceedings. Five years later the convicted cop killer Benjamin De Christoforo challenged that rule.

Sixty-two-year-old Justice Paul C. Reardon wrote for a divided court. He acknowledged "the difficult burden" the particularized need rule "places on a defendant seeking to impeach a witness," but he defended the trial court's decision denying De Christoforo access to grand jury minutes. Reardon contended the defendant had not shown that the inconsistencies between the arresting officer's grand jury testimony and his trial testimony were adequate to overturn De Christoforo's first-degree murder conviction. On the more controversial issue of when and how the particularized need rule should be changed, Reardon's argument was equivocal. He noted weakly that "it may be desirable that we give further consideration to this rule," but he insisted that nothing should be done until the "rule making power of this court" could be brought to bear on the problem.[40]

Justice Spiegel and Chief Justice G. Joseph Tauro vigorously dissented. Spiegel began by questioning the logic of the particularized need rule. It imposes an "intolerable burden" on the defendant and is "out of touch with the 'growing realization that disclosure, rather than suppression, of relevant materials ordinarily promotes the proper administration of justice.'" How can a defendant possibly show that access to grand jury minutes will support his contention about a witness's inconsistencies, "unless perchance he is possessed of supernatural powers?" Next, Spiegel pointed out the cases on which the majority relied to uphold the particularized need rule had been interpreted differently by other jurisdictions. Many federal courts, for example, had interpreted *Dennis v. United States* (1951) as repudiating the particularized need standard and at least one federal appeals court had held that the need was shown as soon as the defense stated that it wished to use the grand jury transcript to impeach a witness. The American Bar Association and other commentators also have advocated the position that "once a witness has testified at trial, the reasons for preserving grand jury secrecy simply fade away." Finally, Spiegel noted, there is no reason to follow a rule "which does not stand the light of logical analysis" simply because the court is committed to the principle that cases under adjudication are governed by earlier decisions. "The principle of *stare decisis* is not absolute because no court is infallible." We should hold that after a witness has testified at trial or at any preliminary hearing the relevant portion of his or her grand jury testimony should be turned over to the defendant.[41]

The split within the court over the particularized need rule was mended in 1974, and four years later a new criminal discovery rule was adopted unanimously in *Commonwealth v. Ellison*. Speaking for a unanimous court in *Commonwealth v. Stewart* (1974), a noncapital criminal case, Justice Kaplan argued that requiring a defendant to show a particularized need in order to gain access to grand jury testimony is "faulty" and "intrinsically unsound." Not only was a defendant forced to guess in order to show a need for grand jury testimony, but also the trial judge on whom the burden of determining whether the particularized need test had been met was placed in an impossible position. To fulfill his role a trial judge had to assume "vicariously and uncomfortably the role of counsel." To end this dilemma Kaplan crafted a temporary solution. The court will "routinely order" the prosecution to hand over the defendant's grand jury testimony and that of any trial witness called by the commonwealth. For a permanent solution to the discovery issue, Kaplan deferred to the Committee on Criminal Rules, a body created by the Massachusetts Judicial Conference and composed of a diverse group of legal professionals, including prosecutors, defense attorneys, law professors, and judges.[42]

A few months before the Rules Committee began its work, three young African Americans walked into Boston's Suffolk Jewelers, waved handguns at the employees, and demanded they hand over cash and jewelry and open the safe. While twenty-year-old Nathaniel Williams and seventeen-year-old Anthony Irving scooped money and jewelry into a bag, Terrell Walker, seventeen years old, stood guard. At a moment when the gunmen's attention seemed focused on the loot, John Schroeder, an off-duty Boston police officer who happened to be in the store, attempted to stop the robbery. Walker shot him dead. The three men fled in a getaway car. They divided the cash and jewelry at Walker's girlfriend's Columbia Point apartment.[43]

With a portion of their loot, Williams and Irving bought and used heroin before boarding a six o'clock bus bound for Atlanta, Georgia. Meanwhile, store employees identified Terrell Walker as the assailant. Boston police arrested Walker, his girlfriend, Darlene Freeman, and Terrell's brother and brought them to police headquarters for questioning. Freeman told police the identity of the other two men involved in the robbery-murder and their plan to flee to Atlanta, information that allowed Virginia police to board the southbound bus and to arrest Williams and Irving. After a few hours of questioning, both men signed statements, confessing their part in the robbery and naming Walker as responsible for the murder of officer Schroeder. Irving also confessed to stealing a Mercury car used in the robbery. Neither man mentioned a female accomplice.[44]

The following day, Boston police officers arrived in Virginia and questioned Williams and Irving. The interviews were tape-recorded. Irving's account of the robbery-murder was unchanged, but Williams now said that a "light-skinned" African American woman about eighteen years old drove the getaway car. He also told police that following the robbery she accompanied the three men to Freeman's apartment, where she accepted some money and rings. Williams and Irving were returned to Boston and indicted on charges of armed robbery and murder in the first degree. In April 1974, the men proposed a plea bargain, but the district attorney refused to negotiate until Williams and Irving agreed to testify at trial against Walker and reveal the identity of the woman who drove the getaway car. Four months later, the district attorney accepted a guilty plea to second-degree murder from Williams and Irving in exchange for information about the woman they now said drove her car (not a stolen car) during the robbery-murder and for identifying Walker as Schroeder's assailant.[45]

In May, Boston police arrested Ella Mae Ellison, a twenty-seven-year-old dark-skinned African American woman, and charged her with armed robbery and murder. She told police she had moved to Boston from Rochester, New York, with her four children and her common-law husband in the spring of 1973. She admitted knowing Williams and Irving and occasionally giving them a ride in her car, a 1969 Ford, but she denied any involvement in the robbery-murder, a claim supported by Freeman's testimony at the Walker trial. Nevertheless, a grand jury indicted Ellison for murder and armed robbery on May 15, 1974.[46]

William P. Homans, scion of an old Massachusetts family and a Harvard Law School graduate who specialized in civil rights and criminal law, represented Ellison. At a pretrial hearing, Homans filed a discovery motion asking the commonwealth to disclose any exculpatory evidence, information that would tend to support Ellison's innocence. Although the prosecution agreed to comply with the motion, Assistant District Attorney Newman Flanagan withheld the taped and written statements made by Williams and Irving in Virginia. Shortly before Ellison's trial on November 18, 1974, Homans repeated his request for exculpatory evidence held by the district attorney. Homans told the trial judge he believed exculpatory evidence existed, but Flanagan denied it, adding "he would not consider exculpatory the mere omission of mention of the defendant from a witness statement about the crime." Judge Robert Sullivan denied the defense motion.[47]

At trial, Williams and Irving testified that Ellison had driven the getaway car, but under cross-examination both men admitted they had not mentioned Ellison when they were questioned in Virginia. At this point, Flanagan offered to put into evidence the documents Homans had sought. When Homans listened to the taped interviews of Williams and Irving, he asked the court to declare a mistrial because the prosecution had withheld exculpatory evidence. Judge Sullivan denied the motion and Homans excepted, laying the basis for an appeal. A jury found Ellison guilty and the court sentenced her to two concurrent life sentences.[48]

In May 1976, however, Williams and Irving recanted their trial testimony and Ellison moved for a new trial. At a hearing, Williams said he invented a woman driver to minimize his friend Irving's part in the crime and to meet the plea-bargain terms set by District Attorney Flanagan. Irving stated he felt compelled to testify against Ellison, because he feared he would face the death penalty if he did not accept the district attorney's deal. Both men said they named Ellison because she was not a friend and because she had returned to Rochester, where they believed the police would not find her. To Williams and Irving's flip-flop, Ellison's new attorney, Max Stern, added that Flanagan's suppression of exculpatory evidence—the Virginia statements—had changed the shape of Ellison's trial. Judge Roger J. Donahue (Judge Sullivan died in June 1976) denied the defense motion for a new trial, declaring he did not believe Williams and Irving's recantations and that the prosecution's failure to turn over the Virginia statements was not an error serious enough to warrant a new trial. Ellison appealed the ruling to the SJC.[49]

The SJC unanimously reversed Ellison's conviction and ordered that she be freed. Specifically, the court held the commonwealth's "failure to produce the Virginia statements favorable to the defendant violated the rule that suppression by the prosecution of requested material evidence which is favorable to the accused is a denial of due process." Therefore, to conform to Article 12 of the Massachusetts Declaration of Rights the defense must be allowed access to exculpatory evidence that tends to furnish aid to the defendant's case or corroborates the defendant's version of the facts or calls into question an element of the commonwealth's version of events or challenges the credibility of a key prosecution witness. By tying the discovery rule to due process in this way, Justice Kaplan's *Ellison* ruling underscored the principle that procedural rules are a significant part of a defendant's fundamental rights.[50]

Shortly after *Ellison*, the SJC ordered the commonwealth's trial courts to adopt the new rules drafted by the Committee on Criminal Rules. In its report to the court outlining its work, the committee acknowledged the "highly volatile atmosphere of the criminal adversary system" and the "polarized" controversy over the criminal discovery rule in particular. Defense attorneys and prosecutors clashed repeatedly, each side "pressing for only a one-sided liberalization, while raising countless objections to freer discovery on a mutual basis." For this reason, a great many lawyers initially rallied around the status quo. But the SJC's path-breaking decision in *Ellison,* together with two years of debate within the committee, won over a substantial majority of the legal community to the belief that criminal discovery would be beneficial to the criminal justice system: more defendants would plead guilty; trials would be completed faster; the presumption of innocence would be bolstered; and prosecution and defense would be more honest.[51]

Beginning in the 1960s, the Supreme Court of the United States extended the guarantees of the Bill of Rights to state criminal defendants. Although initially reluctant to follow the Court's lead, the SJC took major steps on its own initiative to extend greater protection to criminal defendants. Among other rights made available to state criminal defendants, the accused had a right to a reasonably effective attorney and access to exculpatory evidence held by the prosecution at an early stage of the proceeding. The SJC made these changes effective in the 1970s and altered the imbalance of power between the state and the accused. Although far from perfect and still open to being manipulated by aggressive prosecutors, these changes had a profound impact on the administration and the perception of capital punishment.

Together with the changes described above, reforms focusing on the admissibility of a defendant's confession also helped to create an "expectation of justice" that far exceeded the pre-Warren Court standard and eventually led the SJC to reject the death penalty as inherently unjust.

By the sixteenth century a criminal suspect in England could invoke the common-law right against self-incrimination, and about a century later an English court ruled a coerced confession inadmissible as evidence in court. Together, these two aspects created a shield to protect the accused. The privilege against self-incrimination was a legitimate defense against a judge's questions, but also against all government authorities inside or outside court. Contemporaries linked the right not to give evidence against oneself to freedom of speech, religion, and political liberty. For this reason the right against self-incrimination made its way into the bills of rights attached to the U.S. Constitution and to U.S. state constitutions. Judges and legislators subsequently added due process—fair and reasonable rules consistently applied—to the common law and constitutional prohibition against self-incrimination or a confession not freely given. Until the mid-twentieth century, state courts defined these aspects of due process and for this reason confession rules varied widely from state to state. The "due process revolution" initiated by the U.S. Supreme Court during the 1960s and 1970s created a national standard by fusing the privilege against self-incrimination and confession rules.[1]

Throughout its long history the Massachusetts Supreme Judicial Court (SJC) crafted rules designed to prohibit a murder suspect's illegally obtained confession from being used in court without undermining the community's need to be safe from violence. The court's efforts to achieve this balance were shaped by four major strands of legal thought: the English common law rule that an admissible confession must be voluntary—freely given without fear or favor; a Progressive Era effort to make the courts more efficient by restricting the appeals process; a series of twentieth-century decisions by the U.S. Supreme Court extending the Fifth and

Sixth Amendments of the U.S. Constitution to state criminal defendants; and state constitutionalism, a jurisprudence based on the Massachusetts Declaration of Rights with the goal of establishing a higher standard of voluntariness and fairness for the admissibility of confessions than articulated by the Supreme Court. The SJC embraced state constitutionalism when the Supreme Court's commitment to reform waned.[2]

Each generation uses the law to bolster the social values and moral principles it believes are important. In the wake of the American Revolution, for example, the courts' role in protecting liberty was profoundly enhanced, and two centuries later the Supreme Court's civil rights decisions spurred the nationalization of the Bill of Rights and the extension of rights to the accused. Still, in the face of an escalating murder rate or in the wake of a heinous murder, it is not unusual for the public to clamor for a speedy conviction. A confession is the surest path to that end. Therefore, the police use interrogation techniques designed to obtain a suspect's confession, techniques so effective that occasionally innocent persons have confessed. At trial, courts and juries have struggled to match neat legal rules against the messy reality of murder and sometimes have permitted confessions obtained by trickery or by persons other than police officers. Some state legislatures (not including Massachusetts) have legitimized confessions obtained outside the rules if supported by corroborative evidence from other sources. Over the past several centuries these methods—foul and fair—have raised questions about the integrity of criminal due process and, therefore, about the imposition of the death penalty triggered by a confession.[3]

Massachusetts Puritans sought to control man's sinful and passionate nature by creating religious institutions that would help the righteous achieve salvation and laws that would punish those who wandered from the straight and narrow while simultaneously safeguarding an individual's right to due process. Confession was at the heart of this culture. In church, men and women confessed their shortcomings, bringing out into the open sins hidden from their neighbors. The same process figured in Massachusetts criminal courts. But to be admissible a suspect's confession had to be voluntary. For this reason, the colony's laws prohibited the use of torture to extract a confession and information obtained from the folk belief that blood would flow from a corpse touched by a person guilty of murder was not admissible in court. To warn the community about the dangers of sin and to erase any doubt of the condemned person's guilt, authorities encouraged a convicted person to confess while standing on the gallows.[4]

The origins of these cautious colonial Massachusetts practices were rooted in the English prohibition of torture and in the Puritans' special hatred for the arbitrary procedures used by the English Court of High Commission. This ecclesiastical court required a suspected religious dissident to take an oath to tell the truth at the outset of an interrogation before charges were revealed. In this way, Puritans were entrapped, forced to confess to dissident behavior that carried a severe penalty. While an explicit privilege against self-incrimination did not exist in colonial Massachusetts, the court's commitment to the common law and to due process created a protective envelope within which the defendant was relatively safe from self-incrimination or a coerced confession.[5]

In the run-up to the American Revolution, religion gradually lost its vise grip on Massachusetts criminal procedure, and the arguments of professional lawyers schooled in the common law dominated capital trials. In the summer of 1773, for example, John Adams and Josiah Quincy Jr. defended a poor young fisherman charged with piracy and murder. Ansell Nickerson claimed to be the sole survivor of a bloody assault by armed men who boarded the small fishing schooner on which he worked. Advocate General Samuel Fitch argued that Nickerson's account of what allegedly had happened aboard the schooner simply was not believable and, he strongly implied, the young man had confessed as much. Adams attacked the admissibility of Nickerson's confession as "extrajudicial," meaning that neither the examining justice of the peace nor Governor Thomas Hutchinson, a commissioner for the Trial of Piracy, had a legal right to hear a confession of murder. Adams also contended that if a defendant's confession were admitted into evidence, a "Principle Rule of Law" required the defendant's exculpatory as well as his incriminating statements to be admitted. The commissioners deliberated for nearly three hours before freeing Nickerson. Adams believed his arguments about the inadmissibility of Nickerson's alleged confession accounted for the court's decision.[6]

Nickerson's close call with death at the hands of a prerogative court was but one of the stimuli causing the postrevolutionary generation to insist on trial by jury and greater protection against the admissibility of self-incriminating statements or coerced confessions. Indeed, in the early republic there emerged a heightened concern for the preservation of liberty that elevated the power of the law. Judges were urged to act "with that anxious regard for personal liberty and to prevent vexatious oppression." Rules of criminal procedure "established in arbitrary times" and "expedient under a government of prerogative," the SJC stated, "[are] not suited to the spirit of our free institutions." Often the court's commitment to republicanism simply meant legitimizing the common law. In 1804, for example, the court explicitly assimilated the common law rule that a confession must be voluntary to be admissible at trial as evidence.[7]

Embracing voluntariness was a significant step toward extending greater protection to the accused, but as Chief Justice Lemuel Shaw noted, "the great variety of facts and circumstances, attending particular cases, renders the application [of the confession rule] difficult, and each case must depend much on its own circumstances." The 1830 trials of Francis and Joseph Knapp for the murder of the wealthy Salem sea captain Joseph White amply demonstrate Shaw's point. By virtue of his marriage to White's grandniece, twenty-seven-year-old Joseph Knapp believed he would inherit the captain's estate. Unwilling to wait until the old man died, Knapp hatched a plan to murder White. Joseph brought his younger brother Frank into the scheme and he recruited Richard and George Crowninshield to kill Captain White. After the killing, a Salem vigilante group eventually gathered evidence that led police to the four men, and they were charged with murder.[8]

While the Knapps and the Crowninshields awaited trial before the SJC the case changed dramatically. First, Attorney General Perez Morton accepted Joseph Knapp's offer to testify against the Crowninshields in exchange for a grant of immunity. Second, confronted by certain conviction and execution, Richard Crowninshield knotted together two silk handkerchiefs and committed suicide in his cell. His death seemed to destroy the state's case, because under the law accessories to a criminal act could not be tried as such unless the principal defendant was convicted first. Third, keenly aware of the legal difficulties the case now presented, Morton added the nationally recognized Massachusetts lawyer and U.S. Senator Daniel Webster to the prosecution team. Fourth, the state charged young Frank Knapp as principal, although he stood in a street nearly three hundred feet from White's home while Crowninshield stabbed the captain. Webster aggressively and brilliantly argued that Frank could be charged as a principal in "this bloody drama," because he had hired the Crowninshields and because by standing in the street and acting as a lookout Frank had aided and abetted the murder. At this point, Joseph reneged on his plea bargain and refused to testify against his younger brother.[9]

At trial, Webster and defense attorney Franklin Dexter clashed over the admissibility of Frank's alleged confession. Webster contended that Frank's jail-cell conversation with his brother Phippen and Rev. Henry Colman constituted a voluntary and admissible confession from Frank. Dexter rebutted Webster's argument. Even if Frank's statement were a confession, it was not admissible because Phippen had held out the chance of a pardon to Frank, an illegal encouragement rendering Frank's statement involuntary.[10]

A voluntary confession may be used in evidence against a defendant, Justice Samuel Wilde wrote for a slim majority, but the court must use "great caution" in assessing a confession's voluntariness. "Hasty confessions may be easily extorted by threats or promises from a person accused of a crime, when in a state of agitation and alarm; and therefore all such confessions are excluded from the consideration of the jury. The slightest influence is sufficient to exclude them." Without doubt, Phippen sought to influence Frank with the hope of a pardon.[11]

Without Frank's incriminating statement and without his brother Joseph's testimony, Frank's first trial ended in a hung jury. He was retried in August on the same evidence, found guilty, and hanged before a crowd of five thousand people on Salem Common, September 28, 1830. One month later, Joseph stood trial for White's murder. During a pretrial hearing, special prosecutor Webster and defense attorney Dexter clashed over the admissibility of Joseph's confession. As a result of a plea bargain brokered by Rev. Colman with the attorney general's approval, Joseph made an oral confession to Colman and then signed a written confession that was delivered to the attorney general in which Joseph agreed to testify against his accomplices if he were granted immunity from prosecution. He broke that agreement when he refused to testify against his younger brother. Dexter now argued that Joseph lost the state's promise of immunity as a result of his refusal to testify, but that the confession was inadmissible because he had made it on the promise of favorable treatment. Webster countered that Joseph's confession was credible and admissible because his immunity depended on his telling the truth. If Joseph's confession cannot be used against him, Webster said, "the government is trifled with and the course of justice impeded." A prosecutor would not be able to offer immunity to an accomplice in exchange for his testimony at trial for the government.[12]

Sixty-two-year-old Salem native Justice Samuel Putnam spoke for a unanimous court. Rev. Colman encouraged Knapp to believe he would receive a pardon if he confessed and, therefore, that oral confession was not admissible. But Knapp made his written confession after he had won a grant of immunity. According to that bargain Knapp would not be prosecuted if he remained "true and faithful in the performance of his engagement." According to an English rule Putnam now applied to Knapp's case, however, if "the prisoner does not conduct himself truly, he is not at liberty to take back the confession which he deliberately made." For this reason, the court held Knapp's written confession "is competent evidence for the consideration of the jury."[13]

In his closing argument to the jury Dexter made one last attempt to blunt the force of Knapp's confession. The defense attorney told the jurors they were competent to judge both law and fact and he encouraged them to use their power to reject Knapp's confession as incompetent evidence. When Justice Putnam instructed the jury at the close of the trial he countered Dexter's argument. It is true, Putnam said, that to determine a defendant's guilt or innocence questions of law and fact often are intertwined and a jury must interpret both. But it is the court's responsibility to decide questions of law during a trial, and a jury may not review those matters. Once the court has ruled evidence admissible a jury cannot reject it as incompetent, but it is free to decide how much weight to give the evidence. Specifically, Putnam reminded the jury the court had determined Knapp's confession had been given voluntarily and admitted it into evidence, but "the weight and credit of it" was now the jury's decision. The jury had no trouble sorting out the legal questions swirling around Knapp's confession and returned a guilty verdict. Joseph Knapp was hanged for the murder of Captain Joseph White on December 31, 1830.[14]

For more than a century, the SJC upheld the formal criteria of voluntariness outlined in *Knapp*, only occasionally taking sympathetic notice of the aggressive methods used by police to obtain a suspect's alleged voluntary confession. Massachusetts courts assimilated the English common-law rule of voluntariness, because they believed it a principled and fair rule that would protect an individual's rights and insure the community's

safety. Certain of the rule's correctness, state court judges largely were un-
concerned with its practical consequences in any particular case. On rare
occasions, however, in the name of justice, judges allowed their conscience
to shape their decision, or at least, added dicta that manifested a concern
for the poor and disadvantaged. Until the 1960s, this dialogue between
what legal historians have labeled the "jurisprudences of head and heart"
or "formalism and fairness" framed the SJC's approach to the admissibility at trial of an alleged confession.[15]

Chief Justice Ruben A. Chapman's decision rejecting an appeal from
thirteen-year-old Charles Cuffee, an African American convicted and sentenced to death in 1871 largely on the basis of incriminating statements he
made to New Bedford police about the bludgeoning death of Benjamin
Howard, a Westport farmer, manifested aspects of both formalism and
fairness. Two days after Howard's murder police took Cuffee from school
without a warrant and led him to the scene of the crime. Judging the boy's
reactions at the murder scene to be signs of guilt, the officers took Cuffee
to the police station, searched him, stripped off his clothing, and placed
him in a cell. Without advising him to remain silent or allowing him to
consult with a lawyer or friends, officers questioned Cuffee continuously
until midnight and for several hours the following day. The boy's statements were confused and contradictory, but the attorney general argued
they tended to show his guilt.[16]

At trial, Cuffee's court-appointed counsel objected to admitting into
evidence the boy's incriminating statements, because he had not been
warned that anything he said could be used against him. However, both
the trial court and the SJC ruled the statements admissible in the absence
of any evidence of threats or promises by the police and reminded defense
counsel that authorities were not required to warn Cuffee. In fact, until the
mid-1960s the privilege against self-incrimination did not protect a suspect during an interrogation conducted by police. According to this interpretation, compelling a suspect to give evidence against himself meant
legal compulsion, and since a suspect could not be charged with perjury
for testifying falsely, or contempt for refusing to testify, there was no legal
pressure for a suspect to give self-incriminating testimony. The police had
no legal authority to make a suspect answer their questions—although
they were not obligated to tell him or her that—and, therefore, the privilege against self-incrimination did not apply.[17]

Although the SJC denied Cuffee's appeal, the court heaped praise on the trial judge for "instructing the jury that if, upon the whole evidence in the case, it appeared to them that these statements had been induced by threats or promises, they should not be allowed any weight or effect against the prisoner." Likewise, according to the trial judge, a jury could also sort out Cuffee's contradictory statements made to his several interrogators. But "it is not to be presumed," the seventy-year-old Chapman noted, implicitly legitimizing the police tactic of late-night rotating interrogators, "that if one officer makes threats or promises, their influence will lead the prisoner to accuse himself falsely to another officer." As Chapman's final remark suggests, voluntariness was less a tool of analysis than a conclusion teased from the circumstances of a suspect's treatment.[18]

On occasion, the trial court and SJC seemed convinced of a defendant's guilt despite the fact that a confession had been ruled involuntary. A string of unsolved sexual assaults against young Boston women began in December 1873 and continued into the summer of 1875. A break in the investigation finally came when a passerby saw twenty-two-year-old Thomas W. Piper, sexton of the Warren Avenue Baptist Church, jump to the street from a window in the church's bell tower and reported what he saw to the police the day after the discovery in the belfry of the badly battered body of five-year-old Mabel Young. Piper was arrested, strip-searched, and jailed, awaiting arraignment. Assistant Deputy Chief of Police John Ham entered Piper's cell. "How could you do such a dreadful thing?" Ham asked. Piper turned away and said nothing. "Do you think you could be in your right mind when you killed her?" Piper broke his silence, saying he did not know but that he "hadn't felt right for some time." He asked officer Ham whether he thought his colleagues at the church believed him guilty. "I'm sure they do, as all the circumstances point directly at [you]," Ham replied. As he left the cell, Ham told Piper "it would go better if you confessed." By prearrangement, Hamm then ushered into Piper's jail cell Rev. George Pentecost.[19]

At trial, defense counsel E. P. Brown made no objection to Ham's testimony recounting his conversation with Piper, but Brown protested vigorously to Pentecost's testimony that Piper had confessed to murdering Young. Brown argued that officer Ham brought Piper and Pentecost together for the sole purpose of encouraging Piper to confess. Therefore, since there had been an "inducement" from Ham, the incriminating statements made by Piper to Pentecost were not admissible. SJC justices Otis Lord and James D. Colt, who were sitting as a trial court in this capital case, agreed and ruled the confession inadmissible. But Attorney General Charles Train, a wily veteran prosecutor, insisted he had not offered the testimony of Ham and Pentecost as evidence of a confession but intended Pentecost's testimony to show the defendant's "consciousness of guilt," that Piper's conduct and statements were manifestations of his guilt. The court permitted this argument and admitted into evidence Piper's incriminating statements. A jury found Piper guilty of murder in the first degree and the court sentenced him to death. The SJC heard Piper's appeal but upheld the trial court's interpretation. A few weeks before his execution in 1876, Piper confessed to the murder of Mabel Young and to assaulting and raping three other women.[20]

Three years later, the SJC added an important provision to its confession rule. In *Commonwealth v. Culver* (1879) the court held a trial judge had erred when he refused to hear evidence from the defendant intended to rebut the presumption that his confession was voluntary. Simply accepting the arresting officer's denial that he had not made any offers of favor to the defendant was not acceptable. George Culver's defense witnesses should have been permitted to offer evidence to show the police improperly induced his confession. Finally, Justice Lord suggested that the discretionary practices used by trial courts to test the voluntariness of a confession be brought together under a single rule.[21]

The SJC took up Lord's suggestion when it adopted a comprehensive confession rule in *Commonwealth v. Preece* (1885). Richard Preece, James Burns, and Erick Guerin were juveniles arrested by Northampton police and charged with feloniously setting fire to a warehouse. Three police officers questioned Burns while he was in custody, and he confessed to the crime. The other boys initially denied their guilt, but when confronted with Burns's statement, they too confessed. At a pretrial hearing, the defendants challenged the admissibility of the confessions, offering evidence to show the officers exacted the confession by threatening Burns. Burns insisted the officer angrily shouted at him: "You had better tell the truth." The officer, however, testified he merely asked the boy to tell the truth. The trial judge admitted the boy's confession and the SJC upheld his ruling, admitting it could not sort out the conflicting testimony. Still, the SJC had serious misgivings about the interrogation methods used by the police, to which Chief Justice Marcus Morton gave voice. "Whether it is just and humane to take into custody young boys suspected of a crime, and, apart from their parents and friends, and without warning them that they are not obliged to criminate themselves, to worm out of them a confession," Morton said, "is not for our consideration."[22]

Although the SJC did not rule for the boys, Morton's statement may have helped spur the creation of an expanded confession rule intended to offer a defendant greater protection. Reaching back to *Knapp* and *Culver*, the court held that after a trial judge hears evidence from both the prosecution and the defendant he should decide whether a confession is voluntary and admissible. When there is conflicting testimony about a confession's voluntariness, however, the "humane practice" calls for a judge to instruct a jury that it can consider all the evidence in order to decide whether the defendant voluntarily confessed.[23]

The SJC's *Preece* reform did not stimulate other changes in Massachusetts criminal procedure. Although Oliver Wendell Holmes Jr. argued as early as 1881 in *The Common Law* that "the felt necessities of the time" should shape the law rather than logic or axioms, few changes were made in criminal law or procedure despite the social-economic transformation of Massachusetts in the wake of the Civil War. By 1900, more than three-quarters of the state's 2.8 million people lived in a city. Nearly half of the state's population was foreign born. Four decades later, on the eve of Franklin D. Roosevelt's third term, the population of Massachusetts had increased by 34 percent, to 4.3 million people, more than half of whom worked in manufacturing. To keep pace with these changes civil law was transformed during this period, but despite a 54 percent increase in murder indictments during the first four decades of the twentieth-century, criminal procedure remained largely unchanged. The number of appeals in which the SJC found that the trial court made a serious procedural error during a murder trial ending in conviction suggests how little change occurred in criminal procedure: from 1892, when the SJC stopped functioning as a capital trial court, to 1939 the SJC found reversible error in just 3 of 103 murder convictions.[24]

Chief Justice Arthur P. Rugg, who occupied the SJC's center seat from 1911 to 1938, was the chief architect of the jurisprudence that increased the trial court's importance. He believed the law should not be changed quickly or easily, especially at a time when he perceived society's basic institutions and values to be under assault. For that reason, he articulated a procedural rule in *Davis v. Boston Elevated* (1920) that increased the likelihood the appeals court would defer to the trial court and, therefore, decreased the likelihood the appeals court would initiate procedural change. In fact, during Rugg's tenure the SJC denied the appeals of forty-two of forty-four men sentenced to death.[25]

Together with the court's previous decisions allowing the police wide latitude in obtaining a suspect's confession, the rules Rugg promulgated meant a criminal suspect was caught in a vise grip. First, a suspect need not be warned of his or her right to remain silent. Second, a defendant could not expect a trial court judge to find a confession inadmissible simply because the police used manipulative or duplicitous techniques. Third, Rugg's *Davis* rule allowed a trial judge to deny a defense motion for a new trial on either of these grounds with almost complete confidence the SJC would uphold the ruling.[26]

Six months before Rugg retired from the SJC, the court heard an appeal from Stephen Mabey, a fifty-five-year-old Boston man convicted of murdering Mildred L. Bosse, a twenty-eight-year-old married woman with whom Mabey admitted being alone with in her apartment drinking liquor on the day of her death. During a long, late-night interrogation by police, Mabey confessed to poisoning Bosse, but at a pretrial hearing he argued his confession was involuntary. He argued confinement had made him "hungry, ill and weak, the officers had called him foul names and threatened him with a club." To end his torment he confessed to the killing. Mabey's story did not sway Judge Frederick W. Fosdick and he ruled the confession voluntary and admissible. A jury convicted Mabey of second-degree murder. He appealed the verdict. Speaking for a unanimous court, Justice Henry T. Lummus, who had been appointed to the SJC in 1932, denied Mabey's appeal. Citing Rugg's decision in *Commonwealth v. Russ* (1919), Lummus ruled the trial judge did not need to credit Mabey's testimony about the alleged circumstances in which he gave his confession and brushed aside the fact Mabey had not been warned that anything he said would be used against him. Finally, Lummus upheld the trial judge's ruling that although some of the language used by police during Mabey's interrogation bordered on an improper inducement, when taken within the context of the entire interrogation "the words in question are not suggestive of any promise."[27]

The SJC's decision in *Mabey* followed a template whose outlines were being sketched out by the Supreme Court. The Court, along with the U.S. Congress and state legislatures across the nation, reacted to the Roaring Twenties with dozens of laws intended to curb a rising national murder rate, combat organized crime, and fix a criminal justice system that allegedly allowed criminals to escape punishment. President Herbert Hoover created a national commission headed by former U.S. Attorney General George W. Wickersham that sought to understand the causes of crime and to expose corruption, brutality, and inefficiency in the criminal justice system. Little came of the commission's recommendations until President Lyndon Johnson took office more than three decades later, when the nation believed it was about to be swamped by another crime wave. Prior to Johnson's declaration of a war on crime, the Supreme Court had taken only a few cautious steps toward intervening in state criminal trials, the most important in *Brown v. Mississippi* (1936) when a unanimous Court reversed the convictions of three African American men whose confession had been obtained following repeated brutal beatings administered by police officers. Chief Justice Charles Evans Hughes held that a criminal conviction based on confessions extorted by torture violates the fundamental right to a fair trial guaranteed by the due process clause of the Fourteenth Amendment.[28]

The major flaw in the voluntariness standard from a defendant's perspective was its subjectivity. The Court had not developed an objective test but, rather, sought to determine case by case whether the totality of circumstances offended fundamental fairness. Under this test, no one feature of an interrogation made a confession inadmissible. Instead, the court examined all of the facts leading to a suspect's confession and then made a judgment of whether the confession was made voluntarily. Fifteen-year-old Peter Makarewicz's confession to the murder of Geraldine Annese provides a case in point. Norwood police officers brought Makarewicz to the station around midnight on November 5, 1954. A rotating team of officers questioned the boy without a parent or counsel present during three lengthy sessions from midnight to ten o'clock the next morning. The first session lasted from 12:15 A.M. to 1:45 A.M. At 2:00 A.M. officers ordered Peter to remove all of his clothing and a police chemist applied a liquid used to discover the presence of blood to Peter's arms, neck, and groin and to his clothing. The second interrogation session began when the chemist's test was completed at 3:15 A.M. At 4:00 A.M. Peter was given coffee and a doughnut and allowed to rest. An officer woke the boy at 8:30 A.M. and brought him into the chief's office for a third round of questioning. He was told the chemist's test revealed that the traces of blood found on his clothing were consistent with Geraldine's blood type. Peter broke down. He sobbed for some time and then confessed to committing the murder.[29]

At a pretrial hearing to determine the voluntariness of the boy's confession, Makarewicz claimed he was exhausted by the ordeal and "did not know what replies he gave to the police," that his confession was involuntarily induced by fear and psychological coercion. To the contrary, the police told the trial judge that Peter showed no sign of any physical or mental weakness during the interrogation. An officer also stated that after Peter's confession, he told the boy's father his son had admitted killing the girl. When the father said, "Junior, you didn't do that. You were tired and they made you say it." Peter answered, "No. I did it." The trial judge ruled the confession voluntary and admissible and at trial a jury found Makarewicz guilty of first-degree murder but recommended the death sentence not be imposed.[30]

Before the SJC, Makarewicz argued the fact of his youth, the ten-hour interrogation to which he was subjected, and the absence of a parent or lawyer to advise him made the confession unfairly coerced and inadmissible. The court disagreed, finding that Makarewicz's treatment had been within acceptable limits. Citing two recent Supreme Court decisions, Justice Edward A. Counihan found the totality of the circumstances of Makarewicz's interrogation were "proper and reasonable." Finally, the SJC held that an implied threat of force made by one of the officers during the interrogation should not have been made "but that the coercive effect of all the circumstances leading to the confession did not render the confession inadmissible." On this point, Counihan cited a nineteenth-century decision by Justice Oliver Wendell Holmes Jr..[31]

The SJC's *Makarewicz* ruling also conformed to the court's long-standing resistance to limiting police interrogation practices and to declaring voluntary and admissible confessions obtained under problematic circumstances. Aggregate data on reversible error makes this point clear. From 1805 to 1964 the SJC found reversible error in only five first-degree murder convictions, and not one was reversed on a finding of an involuntary confession until after the Supreme Court's decision in *Massiah v.*

United States (1964). *Massiah*, according to Yale Kamisar, is an "oddball Sixth Amendment–'confession' case." The Court held that the postindictment use of an informant to obtain incriminating statements from Winston Massiah violated his right to counsel. Speaking for the majority, Justice Potter Stewart emphasized that Massiah thought he was speaking to a friend, not to a government agent whom he had reason to fear. "Any secret interrogation of the defendant . . . without the protection afforded by the presence of counsel, contravenes the basic dictates of fairness in the conduct of criminal causes and the fundamental rights of persons charged with crime," Stewart concluded.[32]

Within weeks after Stewart's opinion, F. Lee Bailey, a young, aggressive Boston attorney already nationally known for his defense of Dr. Samuel Sheppard, a Cleveland osteopath convicted of murdering his wife, made a similar argument before the SJC on behalf of Robert and William McCarthy. The McCarthy brothers had been convicted in 1963 for the shooting death of Irving Sandman, a real-estate investor the two men had lured to a vacant Roxbury house owned by Robert McCarthy. After a violent struggle, William shot Sandman. At trial, Bailey moved to suppress an incriminating statement William made to two Boston police officers who had captured William in Oak Park, Illinois, several months after the brothers had been indicted for murder. The court denied the motion, but when the prosecution tried to put the statement into evidence, Bailey renewed his motion to suppress. The judge excused the jury and held a hearing on the confession's admissibility.[33]

Without the jury being present, the officers testified they talked with William McCarthy for about an hour before they took his statement. They claimed they had not coerced William or promised him anything in return for his statement and that he spoke voluntarily. One of the officers admitted he knew a Boston attorney represented William, but the officer insisted William did not ask for an attorney until after he confessed. At the hearing, McCarthy disputed the officer's testimony, contending he had asked for a lawyer during the interrogation before making a formal statement. Judge Felix Forte ruled the statement voluntary, despite McCarthy's claim he was denied counsel, but in conformity with "humane practice," Forte instructed the jury to disregard the statement if they found it had not been voluntarily given. A jury found Robert and William McCarthy guilty of murder in the second degree.[34]

The McCarthy brothers appealed the verdict, arguing the confession had been obtained in violation of a constitutional right. In the light of *Massiah*, Justice Arthur E. Whittemore wrote for the SJC, "it may no longer be assumed that the absence of counsel prior to the time when the defendant is 'brought into court' may be disregarded." Therefore, he concluded, William McCarthy's confession was obtained contrary to a constitutionally protected right. Because the defendants had been indicted and had retained counsel, they could not be interrogated without counsel. The judgments for murder against Robert and William McCarthy were reversed and set aside.[35]

Suffolk County District Attorney Garrett Bryne was outraged at the Supreme Court's and the SJC's decisions, and the liberal *Boston Globe* was left searching for a new legal balance. Bryne gave voice to the view widely held by law enforcement officials that questioning suspects without informing them of their rights is indispensable to police work. According to this view McCarthy's confession was voluntary and admissible. Bryne denounced the Court's latest decision and the constitutional basis on which it rested. If five men sat down "to think carefully how to destroy the country, they couldn't do more harm to law enforcement than the present U.S. Supreme Court." He added: the only adherents to the Court's philosophy "are the thousands of murderers, rapists, and narcotics peddlers behind prison walls who hope to go free because of recent decisions." The *Globe*'s rhetoric was much more temperate than Bryne's, but no less anxious. The newspaper's editorial page hoped a balance might be struck between a defendant's rights and the need of police to interrogate a suspect.[36]

Two years later, as part of its campaign to extend all of the procedural guarantees of the Bill of Rights to state criminal proceedings, the U.S. Supreme Court ruled on the admissibility of confessions obtained during police interrogations. In *Miranda v. Arizona* (1966) Chief Justice Earl Warren, speaking for a badly divided Court, extended the Fifth Amendment's protection against self-incrimination and the Sixth Amendment's right to counsel to state criminal proceedings. Warren was critical of police methods; he quoted from manuals that described various tricks of the police trade, ranging from simple flattery to logically persuasive appeals to get a defendant in custody to confess. For this reason, Warren insisted, at the outset of questioning initiated by police after a person has been taken into custody, the suspect must be informed in unequivocal terms of a constitutional right to remain silent and that anything said during an interrogation could be used in court. In addition, the Court required police to tell a suspect of a right to counsel during interrogation and that if he or she were unable to employ an attorney the state would provide one. If the police question a suspect without a lawyer present, Warren warned, "a heavy burden rests on the Government to demonstrate that the defendant knowingly and intelligently waived his privilege against self-incrimination and the right to counsel."[37]

The deeply critical tone of the Court's dissenters in the *Miranda* decision helped unleash a storm of criticism of the Court for its alleged coddling of criminals. In every part of the country police complained that *Miranda* would handcuff their investigative abilities. Reaction in Massachusetts was muted, however, because the legal community had debated and discussed the confession issue extensively in the two years since *Massiah* and *McCarthy*. The American Law Institute (ALI) committee to draft a model code for prearraignment procedures, which included, among others, SJC Justice Ammi Cutter and Harvard law professor James Vorenberg, had embraced the *Escobedo v. Illinois* (1964) guidelines: a suspect had the right to invoke the Fifth Amendment and to remain silent during questioning; the police were required to advise the suspect of that right; and a lawyer must be given access to his or her client at the station house. With these existing guidelines and "the ancient and honorable right not to be compelled to incriminate oneself," the *Boston Globe* concluded, the "Supreme Court did not create any new rights" with *Miranda*.[38]

Massachusetts police officers and prosecutors were less certain about *Miranda* than the ALI or the *Globe*, but here too reaction was mixed. Boston police commissioner Edmund McNamara cynically commented that the new *Miranda* rules "make it very easy for us to protect the rights of the accused, but very difficult to protect the rights of the public when the obviously guilty are allowed to go free on a technical error." But the police chief of nearby Somerville thought the ruling would "not interfere with normal police investigations." Likewise, District Attorney William T. Buckley played down *Miranda*'s impact. Middlesex district attorney John J. Droney's comment bordered on hysteria: "It's going to be a cruel summer for innocent people and the police, and it's going to mean witnesses will be killed, or otherwise intimidated by hoods, gangsters and rapists."[39]

The Supreme Court's decision not to apply *Miranda* retroactively, and

the fact that the outcome of relatively few cases then before the Massachusetts courts turned on a defendant's confession, also helped delay the public impact of the new rules. Although prosecutors opposed to *Miranda*
insisted that confessions are an integral part of obtaining homicide convictions, of the 68 homicide appeals made to the SJC from 1948 to 1966, only
9 (13 percent) raised the issue of confession. The court refused to reverse
a single one, ruling all 9 confessions voluntary and admissible. In the wake
of *Miranda*, from 1967 to 1992, the SJC heard appeals of 858 homicide
convictions, of which 80 (9 percent) raised the issue of confession. Of that
number 12 were reversed. In other words, 0.014 percent of the total number of homicide appeals made to the SJC in the post-*Miranda* era were
reversed because the confession was determined to have been illegally
obtained.[40]

Commonwealth v. McKenna (1969) was the first murder-confession case
to come before the SJC in the post-*Miranda* era and the result seemed to
deliver what the court had promised. Although SJC chief justice Raymond
S. Wilkins, a long-time critic of the Warren court's activism, found reversible error in *McKenna*, the tactics used by police suggest how quickly
they had adapted to *Miranda*'s constraints. In the winter of 1968, Jack
Landau, a Boston television producer, was robbed and murdered in his
home. An eyewitness's report of two young men carrying a television set
from Landau's apartment building, an abandoned car containing some of
the stolen goods, and fingerprints inside the apartment where the body
was found led police officers to two Revere teenagers, Michael Riley and
Eugene McKenna. At the home of the latter, an officer arrested the boy and
read him a *Miranda* warning. Before leaving home for the Revere police
station, McKenna asked his aunt, who was present, to call an attorney. At
the station, police again advised McKenna of his rights to counsel and to
silence. However, after being told his fingerprints had been found at the
murder scene, McKenna stated he would "tell the story."[41]

At some time during McKenna's interrogation, his lawyer telephoned
the Revere police station. He spoke to the police officer in charge of the
investigation, who said McKenna would be taken to Boston police headquarters. The officer did not say that McKenna's interrogation had begun.
McKenna had confessed by the time he saw his lawyer in Boston. During a pretrial hearing, McKenna's counsel challenged the admissibility of
the confession, but Judge Cornelius J. Moynihan found that McKenna had

"knowingly and intentionally waived his right to be silent and his right to the assistance of counsel at his interrogation" and, therefore, the teenager's confession was admissible at trial.

Shortly after police officers took McKenna into custody, another team of officers arrested Riley at his home. An officer told Riley he did not have to answer any questions. Riley asked his father to call an attorney. At the Revere police station Riley was booked on a charge of murder and again advised of his rights. Riley's interrogation did not begin until McKenna had confessed. The two boys were then brought together and McKenna repeated his story of the killing. An officer then asked Riley if he had anything to say. Riley said nothing. At that moment, Riley's attorney appeared outside the interrogation room and asked to see his client. As an officer started toward the door to speak with the boy's attorney, Riley said, "I just want you to understand one thing. I wasn't in the room when the man was stabbed." Judge Moynihan found that Riley's statement was voluntary. A jury found both young men guilty of first-degree murder but recommended the death sentence not be imposed.

The SJC reversed the judgment and set aside the verdicts. Justice Paul Kirk's opinion made it clear that neither the police nor the trial court had fulfilled its obligation under *Miranda*. First, in addition to warning the defendants, the "person in custody must be told of his right to the assistance of counsel and be afforded the opportunity to exercise these rights throughout the interrogation." Therefore, despite McKenna's written waiver and Riley's implied waiver of the right to counsel, the police were obligated to stop the interrogation and allow the boys to consult with a lawyer. Second, the trial court must look beyond the fact that the police "punctiliously adhered to the verbal formula" of *Miranda* and expose the "tactics which effectively prevented or forestalled the exercise of the defendants' rights." Finally, with a nod to the court's critics, Kirk commended the "speed and skill shown by the police in gathering evidence of a direct or circumstantial nature." But, he added, the *Miranda* procedures "are part of the law of the land and must be obeyed."

The court's admonition did little to change how Boston police operated or to appease the public's fear about crime generally or to lessen its specific outrage about *Miranda*. Anecdotal evidence suggests that when interrogating a suspect Boston police behaved like law enforcement officials in other major U.S. cities, usually complying with the letter but not the spirit of the required fourfold warnings propagated by *Miranda*. Still, the public continued to believe *Miranda* tied the hands of the police, making it likely that violent crime would go unpunished, or, as Police Commissioner McNamara put it, a guilty person would be released on a technicality. The impact of this misperception certainly was heightened by a soaring crime volume, a fourfold increase in murders in Massachusetts from 1950 to 1980, and by outspoken advocates for a tougher criminal justice system. Superior Court Chief Judge Walter H. McLaughlin, for example, echoed public sentiment when he told the Massachusetts House of Representatives in 1970 that it "was a sad commentary that the lawless of society . . . deny to the decent people of the Commonwealth the right to move freely about our streets because of stark fear [and yet] are entitled to priority on our judges and our courtrooms."[42]

The heated controversy among the Massachusetts public, the police, and the courts about admitting into evidence confessions made by suspects without the presence of an attorney boiled over during the trial of twenty-two-year-old George W. Mahnke for the murder of Rhonda Bornstein, nineteen, of Newton Center. Bornstein, a part-time dental assistant and student at the University of Massachusetts, Boston, was murdered on September 15, 1970, but her body was not found until December 10, 1971. Twenty-seven-year-old Daniel J. O'Connell, one year out of Boston College Law School, represented Mahnke at trial. Following a month-long voir dire aimed at determining the voluntariness of Mahnke's incriminating statements made to a group of vigilantes and later to the police, Judge McLaughin ruled inadmissible everything Mahnke said to his vigilante kidnappers while he was held captive, but the judge held Mahnke's statements made to his captors later in the day about where Bornstein's body was buried manifested "a complete change of attitude" and were made of his own "free will." McLaughlin held inadmissible the incriminating statements Mahnke made to the Boston police during an interrogation that took place at Massachusetts General Hospital, because the police had knowingly denied the defendant the benefit of counsel. A jury found Mahnke guilty of murder in the second degree. The verdict was at once popular and controversial.[43]

In February 1975, Mahnke appealed his conviction. Eight months later, a badly divided SJC set aside his murder conviction and life sentence and reduced the sentence to manslaughter. Chief Justice G. Joseph Tauro, who was scheduled for mandatory retirement at the close of the court's 1975 term, wrote for a majority that included justices Paul C. Reardon, Francis J. Quirico, and Robert Braucher. Tauro made three arguments. First, he rejected the defense argument that the Bornstein vigilante group and the police had created an illegal alliance. Second, he accepted the trial court's distinction between a confession and an incriminating statement and the lesser degree of protection the latter provided the defendant. Using the "totality of circumstances" test the chief justice found Mahnke's incriminating statements were voluntary. Third, Tauro held the SJC could not review Judge McLaughlin's ruling about the admissibility of Mahnke's statements, nor could the appellate court draw inferences contrary to the trial judge that were derived from his findings.[44]

Just two years after *Mahnke* the SJC expanded a defendant's right against self-incrimination and revisited the question of its responsibility as an appellate court to weigh credibility and to review findings of fact that had divided the court in *Mahnke*. Justice Ruth Abrams, the first woman to sit on the SJC, wrote for the majority in *Commonwealth v. Haas* (1977). Abrams found that incriminating statements made to the police by the defendant Gordon Haas after he had been given full *Miranda* warnings and had intelligently and knowingly waived his rights were not admissible because they followed so closely an illegal interrogation carried out by the police. A belated warning could not put the cat back in the bag. And, drawing on Justice Edward Hennessey's dissent in *Mahnke*, Abrams argued, "Our appellate function requires that we make our own independent determination on the correctness of the judge's 'application of constitutional principles to the facts as found.'"[45]

Abrams wrote again for the court on the issue of confession in *Commonwealth v. Tavares* (1982). Seventeen-year-old David Tavares and two friends had been drinking heavily for several hours on the evening of May 24, 1979, when they accosted Jesse Aranjo and asked him for some money. He refused and a fight ensued that left Aranjo badly beaten and unconsciousness. He later died from his injuries. The New Bedford police asked Tavares whether he would voluntarily answer questions about Aranjo's death. The young man agreed and during the course of the conversation he made some incriminating statements. After the police advised him of his *Miranda* rights, Tavares admitted he fought with Aranjo but he denied killing him. The police charged Tavares with murder and he later stood trial. At a pretrial hearing, Tavares argued his youth and inexperience undercut the waiver of his rights and, therefore, his statements were not voluntary and should not be admitted at trial. The trial judge, however, concluded that Tavares had knowingly and voluntarily waived his rights and admitted the statements at trial. A jury found Tavares guilty of second-degree murder.[46]

Exercising its appellate function to make an independent determination of the trial judge's ruling and applying the standard that voluntariness must be shown beyond a reasonable doubt (not by the lesser standard, a preponderance of the evidence) the SJC concluded the trial court had not erred on these issues. Still, the court's decision widened the humane practice requirement in three ways: a voir dire must be conducted on the voluntariness of a defendant's incriminating statements, as well as an alleged confession; the prosecution must prove beyond a reasonable doubt the voluntariness of any statement made by the defendant to law enforcement officers; and a trial judge must "instruct the jury that the Commonwealth has the burden of proving beyond a reasonable doubt that the statement was voluntary and that the jurors must disregard the statement unless the Commonwealth has met its burden."[47]

Justice Abrams's ruling in *Tavares* completed the reversal of the Tauro court's decision in *Mahnke*. From 1975 through the 1990s the SJC extended greater protection to criminal defendants against self-incrimination by coupling an expanded voluntariness standard to the nineteenth-century humane practice rule. At the same time, Chief Justice Hennessey publicly encouraged criminal attorneys to make greater use of the Massachusetts Declaration of Rights, and his successor, Chief Justice Paul Liacos, promised in 1989 that he also would use the Massachusetts Constitution to protect the rights of the accused. These statements—touting the benefits of state constitutionalism—were, in part, a reaction to Chief Justice Warren Burger's drive to limit the Court's role to make procedural rules or new law. "To try to substantially change civil or criminal procedure by judicial decision," Burger wrote, "is the worst possible way to do it." Reform is the responsibility of the legislature, the chief justice added. The Court not only deferred to the legislature but, beginning with *Harris v. New York* (1971), it steadily reduced *Miranda* protection. In *Oregon v. Elstad* (1985), for example, the Court held that a failure to administer the required warnings before a suspect's first incriminating statement does not make statements made after a warning inadmissible. This ruling allowed the police to get a useable statement from a defendant even though they "lost" the first statement because of a *Miranda* violation.[48]

In *Commonwealth v. Smith* (1992), the SJC rejected the Court's ruling in *Elstad*, as it had in 75 percent of criminal procedure cases from 1969 to 1989. Relying on the principles previously articulated in *Commonwealth v. Haas* and *Commonwealth v. Tavares*, the SJC ruled as a "matter of State common law" that an incriminating statement made by John F. Smith, an eighteen-year-old, ill-educated farm hand, before his Miranda warnings tainted his subsequent confession to a double murder. "To allow that statement to be used at his trial," Justice John M. Greaney wrote for the majority, "would countenance precisely the kind of police interrogation that the presumption of taint was intended to deter." Together with *Harris*, *Haas*, and *Tavares*, the SJC's decision in *Smith* further enhanced its humane practice rules, crafting a higher standard of protection against self-incrimination than under the rules of the Supreme Court.[49]

The court's determination to extend greater protection against an involuntary confession to a capital defendant often came in the face of hostile political criticism and contrary Supreme Court decisions. Although the SJC's humane practice rules were founded on common law grounds, a constitutional concept of fairness underlay the rules, and for that reason, they dovetailed easily with the Supreme Court's early rulings. And, when the Supreme Court's effort to enlarge the rights of criminal defendants was slowed after 1970, the SJC turned to the Massachusetts Constitution. The court became "more outspoken concerning the significance of rights under the Declaration of Rights than at any time in its history," Justice Wilkins observed in 1980.[50]

The effectiveness of the courts' confession rules depended, of course, on suspects' invoking their right to silence or to an attorney and the degree to which police adhered to the rules. The presence of an attorney usually led to a plea bargain rather than the suspect's freedom. Likewise, as many of the cases discussed in this chapter show—and this is consistent with the national picture—suspects commonly waive their right to remain silent or to have an attorney present and police officers trained in the use of the law's loopholes and in interrogation techniques often succeed in inducing suspects to give incriminating statements despite the rules. (Informed estimates are that confessions are obtained in roughly 40 percent of all criminal arrests and that in about a quarter of all prosecuted cases the defendant would not be convicted if it were not for his own incriminating statements.)

For more than 370 years the Massachusetts SJC articulated rules for determining the voluntariness and fairness of a defendant's confession. The SJC's postrevolutionary commitment to voluntariness was coupled in the late nineteenth century with the humane practice of allowing a jury to determine the weight to be given to a defendant's confession. The Supreme Court's *Miranda* decision and, after 1969, the SJC's innovative use of the Massachusetts Declaration of Rights established a bulwark against police and prosecutorial efforts to undermine a defendant's right to remain silent and to be represented by counsel. These confession rules are at the heart of the criminal justice system, edging Massachusetts closer to achieving an "accusatorial as opposed to [an] inquisitorial system."[51]

A suspect's protection against self-incrimination, together with his or her right to a reasonably effective attorney, and access to exculpatory evidence held by the prosecution at an early stage of the proceeding, dramatically changed the capital trial. Although far from perfect and still open to manipulation by aggressive police officers and prosecutors, these procedural reforms had a significant impact on the conduct of a capital trial.

TEN

THE RIGHT OF
THE ACCUSED TO
AN IMPARTIAL
JURY

For roughly two decades following the resignation of Chief Justice Earl Warren from the Supreme Court of the United States in 1969, a handful of state appellate courts stimulated a resurgence in both the activism and impact of state courts. The Massachusetts Supreme Judicial Court (SJC) was at the forefront of this development, using the Massachusetts Constitution to rule on a cluster of key constitutional questions. The SJC linked procedural activism to a string of substantive decisions that expanded the rights of the accused beyond those acknowledged by the Supreme Court. In 1979, for example, the SJC prohibited discrimination practiced under the guise of selecting an impartial jury in a capital trial, a position that the Supreme Court accepted only partially as late as 1994.[1]

The right to an impartial jury is stated in Article 12 of the Massachusetts Declaration of Rights and in the Sixth Amendment of the U.S. Constitution, and, in 1947, it was made binding upon the states by the Fourteenth Amendment. Giving concrete application to this common law mandate, however, proved especially difficult when it came into conflict with the Supreme Court's call for making the jury a "body truly representative of the community." To implement this ideal, Congress enacted legislation in 1968 requiring federal courts to randomly select the names of potential jurors to create a jury pool that is a fair, representative cross section of the community. In *Taylor v. Louisiana* (1975) the Supreme Court extended the ideal of the cross-sectional jury to state courts.[2]

Traditionally, the process of empanelling an impartial jury began with the court posing questions to potential jurors during voir dire ("to speak the truth"). Since 1648, Massachusetts law defined an impartial juror as being capable of putting aside personal interests and preconceptions and of deciding the case solely on the evidence presented in court. If the court found the juror did not "stand indifferent," the law required that the person be excused for bias and another juror selected. The defendant also was permitted to challenge jurors. The purpose of challenges was to eliminate jurors who were biased toward the defendant, the prosecution, or the case, and who, therefore, might threaten the jury's impartiality. Prospective jurors might be challenged in two ways: challenge for cause and peremptory challenges. In *Commonwealth v. Mutina* (1975), the SJC recognized the interrelationship of the exercise of challenges as a system designed to produce an impartial trial jury.[3]

The system to which the court referred was created in 1836. In that year, the Massachusetts legislature added a statutory question requiring a trial judge to excuse potential jurors for cause who held firm opinions against the death penalty. At the same time, it re-enacted a provision allowing a capital defendant to use a limited number of peremptory challenges to strike jurors on no more than the "sudden impressions and unaccountable prejudices we are apt to conceive upon the bare looks and gestures of another," as the English common law jurist William Blackstone put it. In 1869, the legislature extended to prosecutors the right to use a limited number of peremptory challenges. For more than a century, challenges for cause were used by the court and peremptory challenges by a prosecutor to create a "death qualified" jury—one from which opponents of capital punishment had been purged. Prosecutors also were keen to strike prospective jurors who were of the same race or ethnic group as a defendant. Capital defendants used peremptory challenges to eliminate jurors thought to be "conviction prone." In short, both sides struggled for an advantage at the crossroads where the death penalty intersected with the rules that governed the court's effort to empanel an impartial jury.[4]

The precise origins of the statutory question that permitted the court to challenge for cause potential jurors who held an opinion that precluded their finding a defendant guilty in a capital case are obscure. But it seems clear that the confluence of two seemingly unrelated early nineteenth-century Boston social-political movements contributed significantly to the law's adoption. Both opposition to the death penalty and anti-Catholicism attracted large numbers of committed and noisy adherents in the 1830s. Anti-Catholicism crested in the summer of 1834 when an angry mob burst into the Ursuline Convent in Charlestown, forced the resident nuns to flee for their lives, and then burned a building to the ground. At about the same time, Robert Rantoul, a Gloucester Democrat elected to the Massachusetts House following a sensational murder trial in which two of his young friends were condemned to death, launched a movement to end capital punishment. The trial of eight men accused of torching the Ursuline Convent brought these two very different movements together in the fall of 1834.[5]

Attorney General James T. Austin, who had served for twenty-five years as Suffolk County district attorney before becoming the state's chief law officer, prosecuted the case against John Buzzell and the others indicted for capital arson. Austin labored under a severe disadvantage in empanelling an impartial jury, because he had very limited means to challenge potential jurors who had formed an opinion about the case. He wanted to exclude two types of juror: those who shared the defendants' anti-Catholicism and those who were opposed to the death penalty. Austin won the first round. Chief Justice Lemuel Shaw ruled that at the attorney general's request, the court would ask a potential juror whether he believed it a crime to destroy a Catholic convent. But the court denied Austin's second motion, which would have had the court ask potential jurors whether they believed arson should be punished by death as the law required. Moreover, Shaw ruled that exceptions to the court's rulings could not be taken, "that a decision, when once made, was so far final, as not to be open to exceptions to be taken as of right."[6]

After a tumultuous trial, Buzzell and his co-defendants were found not guilty—a verdict greeted with cheers by their friends who had packed the courtroom. Although it is not clear that Shaw's ruling denying Austin the right to ask potential jurors about their views on capital punishment determined the outcome of the trial, Austin certainly had cause for concern because of the growing strength of the anti–capital punishment movement. He grumbled that Suffolk County juries in particular refused to convict defendants indicted for capital crimes. Shaw's *Buzzell* ruling meant that jurors' views on capital punishment would be off limits to the attorney general, making his goal of empanelling a jury that would convict much tougher to achieve.[7]

In 1836 the legislature came to Austin's rescue by adding a third statutory question to those routinely posed by the court to prospective jurors. After narrowly defeating a bill to abolish capital punishment, the legisla-

ture enacted a statute that required the court to challenge for cause a potential juror if he held an opinion that would "preclude him from finding
any defendant guilty of an offense punishable with death." Chief Justice
Shaw subsequently gave the statute a broad interpretation that endured
for more than a century. The "usual interrogatories" put to potential jurors
prior to a murder trial, Shaw noted, were to discover whether a person had
"conscientious scruples or such opinion on the subject of capital punishment as to preclude him from finding a defendant guilty."[8]

Lysander Spooner, a self-made lawyer from central Massachusetts, publicly challenged Shaw's ruling following John Webster's controversial conviction for murder in 1850. Eliminating jurors who were opposed to the
death penalty was unconstitutional, because such a procedure "*destroyed
the trial by jury itself.*"[9]

Spooner's argument rested on a distinction between the government
and "the country," or the people. Jurors are drawn at random from the mass
of the people, he contended, "for the very purpose of having all classes
of minds and feelings that prevail among the people at large represented
in the jury." A jury drawn from a cross section of the people will be "a
more just, impartial, and competent tribunal, than the government itself,"
he argued. Even if a potential juror who opposes the death penalty should
want to be excluded, or even if a juror refuses to serve because he could
not conscientiously render a verdict according to the evidence if the verdict were followed by the death penalty, "*still the court could not discharge
him.*" A jury trial from which people had been excluded because of their
feelings and opinions about the death penalty was no longer a trial "by the
country" as required by the Constitution but a trial by that "portion only
of the country, which had been selected by the government, on account of
their having no opinions or feelings different" from the prosecution. Only
a jury made up from a true cross section of the community will be impartial and properly fulfill the requirement that its verdict be unanimous. The
concurrence of the "*whole* country" as a condition of conviction and punishment is required from motives of both "justice and caution toward the
life, liberty, property, and character of the person accused." Therefore, if
"*any portion* of 'the country,'" as represented in the jury, dissent from the
conviction or punishment, that is "sufficient reason to doubt the propriety
or justice of such a conviction or punishment."[10]

But it will be argued, Spooner wrote, that to exclude a juror on the basis of his position on the punishment that will be inflicted on conviction by the government "is a difference . . . with which the juror has nothing to do." Spooner proposed two answers to this objection. First, the guilt or innocence of a defendant is determined mainly with a view to his punishment, if found guilty. "Punishment or no punishment is the practical question at issue," he insisted. There may be a theoretical distinction between the determination of a defendant's guilt or innocence and his conviction, but "there can hardly be said to be any practical, or even legal difference between them." The second reason conviction and punishment are inextricably bound together is that death is different. No court tells a jury that they are to try a capital case with the same indifference to consequences that they would a case where the results are less important. "On the contrary," Spooner wrote, "courts impress upon jurors the solemn, fearsome duty they are undertaking and urge caution."

In so doing, however, the court acts on an entirely different principle from that which it used to exclude potential jurors for their opposition to capital punishment. Because those excluded jurors manifested more sensibility about the consequences of their decision, the government strikes them. At the same time, the government instructs those who remain on the panel that they are to keep the serious consequences of their decision in the forefront of their mind and "act with corresponding caution." In short, the government establishes a "standard of sensibility" that biases the outcome and deprives a defendant of a trial by the "whole country"—by persons who represent "all degrees of sensibility, which prevail among the people at large."

Finally, Spooner argued, if a jury drawn from the "whole country" includes men absolutely opposed to the death penalty, the court must postpone the trial, rather than illegally striking them. If after repeated attempts, a jury representing a genuine cross section of the community cannot be empanelled that will agree to render a verdict if the defendant is to be executed, "the statute proscribing the punishment of death must be repealed, and such a penalty substituted as jurors will all consent to aid in enforcing."

Spooner's brilliant argument against the government's use of challenge for cause to remove potential jurors opposed to capital punishment had no immediate impact on the Massachusetts legal community. For more than a century, the court routinely dismissed potential jurors who expressed qualms about the death penalty. Still, widespread public sentiment against capital punishment caused prosecutors to appeal for new tools. In the wake of the Civil War, therefore, Massachusetts attorneys general sought to bolster their power to shape capital juries by winning legislative approval for their right to exercise peremptory challenges.[11]

English and American common law had long restricted use of peremptory challenges to the defendant. The Massachusetts colonial law code had permitted a defendant to "challenge any of the Jurors, and if the challenge be found just and reasonable by the Bench, or the rest of the Jurie, as the Challenger shall choose, it shall be allowed him." Prior to the American Revolution, the law allowed a capital defendant thirty-five peremptory challenges, giving statutory life to Blackstone's dictum that from a sense of "tenderness and humanity" the defendant should not "be tried by any one man against whom he has conceived a prejudice, even without being able to assign a reason for such dislike." Perhaps to bring Massachusetts into conformity with federal law, in 1793 the legislature set a limit of twenty on the number of peremptory challenges a defendant might use in a capital trial. Significantly, neither the federal statute nor Massachusetts law extended the right of peremptory challenges to the government.[12]

In 1865, however, Congress extended to prosecutors a limited number of peremptory challenges in federal criminal trials. Four years later, Massachusetts followed with a similar statute allowing the attorney general five peremptory challenges in capital cases for which he had exclusive jurisdiction. Both Attorney General Charles Allen (1867-72) and Attorney General Charles Train (1872-79) tied their arguments for the use of peremptory challenges to the death penalty. Allen told the legislature in 1868 that he was convinced a murderer had escaped conviction because he was unable to keep two men off the jury who were opposed to capital punishment. He recommended larger jury pools and a prosecutorial right to exercise peremptory challenges. Train pushed for a greater number of peremptory challenges, claiming that an 1858 statute allowing a jury to distinguish between first- and second-degree murder made it very difficult to win a first-degree conviction. "Experience has demonstrated," Train told the legislature in 1873, "that juries will return a verdict of guilty of murder in the second degree, instead of in the first degree, where there is the slightest ground, and sometimes when there is not, since such a verdict does not involve a possibility of taking the life of a prisoner." The legislature responded by increasing the number of peremptory challenges allowed the prosecutor to ten. Now, although it was possible to create a "death-qualified" jury, Train still believed that "the danger that the innocent may be executed instead of the guilty, presses upon the juryman with fearful power" and might lead him to vote for an acquittal when a conviction was warranted.[13]

Capital defendants only rarely contested the procedural advantages gained by the government during the latter half of the nineteenth century. Only two cases involving challenge for cause came before the SJC from 1870 to 1970. In *Commonwealth v. Wong Chung and [Charley Chin]* (1904) the defendants appealed their conviction of murder in the second degree on the grounds that one of the jurors should have been challenged for cause by the court. The juror to whom the defense objected was a convicted felon and an alleged army deserter. Defense attorney Joseph F. Paul, who had been admitted to the bar in 1878 after studying at Boston University Law School, as well as in Paris and Berlin, argued that the juror's felony conviction meant he was not "of good moral character" as the law required and that his flight from the army during the Civil War deprived him of his rights as a citizen of the United States, including the right to vote and to serve on a jury in Massachusetts. Paul also contended that limitations placed on his examination of potential jurors during voir dire prevented the defendant from discovering the juror's checkered past.[14]

Chief Justice Marcus Knowlton found the defendants' argument without merit. First, Massachusetts law did not bar an ex-felon from jury service. "Our law," the chief justice noted, "is more humane and charitable. . . . and recognizes the possibility of repentance and reformation." Second, the juror in question was not found legally guilty of desertion, although his name appeared on a list of men who had fled from the army. Even "if the facts shown in this case would have been a ground of challenge for cause," Knowlton ruled, it was within the discretion of the trial judge to permit the juror to be sworn. Finally, while voir dire is an important means of acquiring information about potential jurors, Knowlton reminded the defense, it is not the only means. In a capital trial, the defendant is provided with a list of potential jurors and he has the right to use a peremptory challenge to strike anyone he suspects is not qualified or impartial. Besides, Knowlton concluded with remarkable candor: "It would be most unfortunate, if for an accidental error or omission hardly more than technical, it should be necessary to set aside a correct verdict."[15]

Justice Arthur P. Rugg succeeded Chief Justice Knowlton in 1911 and held the center seat for the next twenty-seven years. Born during the Civil War on a western Massachusetts farm his ancestors had settled in the seventeenth century, Rugg was educated at Amherst College and Boston University Law School. Following his admission to the bar in 1886, he practiced law in Worcester, served four years as assistant district attorney and nearly ten years as city solicitor of Worcester. Republican Governor Curtis Guild appointed Rugg to the SJC in 1906. Like many other state court judges during the early twentieth century, Rugg presided over a court that decided cases by applying iron rules established to maintain age-old principles underlying the law. Rugg believed the primary purpose of the law is to "guide and control people."[16]

During his long tenure, Rugg heard fifty-one appeals of homicide convictions, including thirty-three defendants who had been sentenced to death. He found reversible error in only two cases: *Commonwealth v. Retkovitz* (1915) and *Commonwealth v. Madeiros* (1926). Both defendants were retried, sentenced to death, and executed, Madeiros after the court rejected a second appeal. Only Daniel Cooper's failed appeal touched on the question of challenge for cause. Cooper was tried and convicted in the summer of 1914 for the shooting death of Alfred Bradish, a rival for the affection of a woman who lived near Cooper's Upton home. During voir dire Judge Hugo Dubuque asked a potential juror: "Are your opinions such as to prevent you from returning a verdict of guilty against the defendant for an offense punishable by death?" The venireman answered yes. Judge Dubuque pressed him, asking if he "would not be willing to do your duty as a juror under your oath." He answered, "I wouldn't want to send a man to the chair." "None of us want to," Judge Dubuque shot back, "but the question is whether we are willing to do what the law stands for, and be counted to do our duty, if the evidence and the law justifies it—that is the question." When the juryman hesitated again, Judge Dubuque added within the hearing of the nine jurors already chosen: "You must understand that it isn't a desirable task for a judge or jury to sit upon capital cases. Now, the question is whether you have such a settled opinion as to capital punishment that it would prevent you from giving a just verdict

upon the law and the evidence in the case?" Plainly chagrined, the juror
answered, "No." "Then you stand indifferent," the judge snapped. District Attorney James Stiles immediately used one of his peremptory challenges to strike the juror. A few minutes later, defense attorney James E.
Swift entered an exception to the judge's remarks. Judge Dubuque denied
the defense motion and Cooper appealed to the SJC.[17]

The defense argument on this issue was very weak. Although Judge
Dubuque had tongue-lashed the juror for his views about capital punishment, he had found the man indifferent. Therefore, in his brief to the
SJC, Cooper argued simply that Judge Dubuque's remarks were prejudicial. Any expression of opinion by a trial judge in the hearing of the jury is
grounds for reversal, he said.[18]

The commonwealth countered by arguing that the judge's remarks
were casual and did not affect the course of the trial. After all, Dubuque's
charge to the jury was full and clear and the juror to whom the judge's remarks were directed was not sworn. Therefore, even if Judge Dubuque's
comments were prejudicial, they were "cured by the charge."[19]

Speaking for a unanimous court, Justice Henry Braley, a Fall River
lawyer who had served on the Superior Court for eleven years before his
appointment to the SJC in 1902, brushed aside Cooper's argument that
the trial judge's remarks about capital punishment undercut the goal of
achieving an impartial jury. The judge's words must not be "wrenched
from the context," Braley began, without specifying to what context he referred. Ironically echoing Lysander Spooner's argument, Braley defended
Judge Dubuque's lecture to the juror who expressed conscientious scruples about the death penalty as necessary to sustain the law:

> The judge manifestly desired to impress upon the juror the necessity of
> a due and proper administration of the laws, and to make clear to him
> that his refusal to perform the duty for which he had been summoned
> because performance might be disagreeable and against his conception
> of what the law ought to be, would prevent, if a sufficient number of the
> community eligible for service as jurors adhered to a like opinion, the
> conviction and punishment of those guilty of the crime charged.

Borrowing from the prosecutor's argument, Judge Braley concluded that
if the trial judge had exceeded his discretionary power, he repaired any
possible damage by making it clear in his instructions to the jury that the

determination of the defendant's guilt or innocence was solely within their power.[20]

The Rugg court's deference to the discretionary authority of the trial judge in homicide cases was the mainstay of the SJC's capital jurisprudence through the 1960s. In *Commonwealth v. Ladetto* (1965), Justice Paul C. Reardon, who had served seven years as chief justice of the Superior Court before joining the SJC in 1962, at age fifty-three, ruled that Superior Court judge Reuben Laurie was well within the bounds established by the court when he refused the defendant's request during voir dire to ask potential jurors whether they held "any opinion that would prevent or preclude [them] from recommending life imprisonment for a defendant found guilty of the first degree murder of a police officer." Defense attorney Joseph J. Balliro argued that by not permitting this or other related questions and by erroneously telling the entire panel of potential jurors that "it is the law of this Commonwealth that murder in the first degree is punishable by death," the trial judge made it impossible for the defendant to be judged by an impartial jury. Balliro pointed out that since 1951, Massachusetts law had allowed a jury to find the defendant guilty of murder in the first degree "and after consideration of all the evidence, recommend that the sentence of death be not imposed, in which case [the defendant] shall be punished by imprisonment in the state prison for life."[21]

The constitutional issues raised in *Ladetto* arose from the 1964 conviction and sentencing to death of Peter Ladetto for murdering a police officer. On the evening of September 14, 1963, Peter and Louis Ladetto attempted to rob at gunpoint the A&P grocery store in Malden, Massachusetts, while their accomplice, Lawrence Guerra, waited nearby in a getaway car. A customer in the store observed the robbery in progress and flagged a passing police cruiser. As Officer Edward Callahan entered the store, Peter Ladetto fired a shot at him, which ultimately was fatal, and the officer slumped to the floor. Officer George Hood came to his partner's aid, but a flurry of gunshots from the Ladettos hit Hood in the mouth, knee, and thigh and he fell face down in the street.[22]

When the getaway car failed to start, a passerby grabbed Guerra, but Louis Ladetto fled from the scene on foot. Peter Ladetto commandeered a passing car and forced the driver to take him to the home of a girlfriend in Watertown. The next day, Ladetto made his way to a small town near Lewiston, Maine, where he took a job on a farm. Four days later, FBI agents arrested Ladetto. Before his appearance in a Bangor court, and before he was informed of his right to an attorney, Ladetto confessed to a Massachusetts state trooper that he shot Officers Callahan and Hood during the botched Malden grocery store holdup. At trial, a jury convicted Ladetto of murder in the first degree and sentenced him to death.[23]

On appeal before the SJC, Ladetto raised dozens of procedural points, including, for the first time in more than a hundred years, the question whether persons holding scruples against the imposition of the death penalty should be allowed to sit on a capital jury. Defense attorney Balliro argued that the 1951 statute giving a jury power to choose the penalty for a defendant found guilty of first-degree murder ended the judicial imperative for challenging jurors for cause because they expressed reservations about capital punishment. The court's procedure conflicted with the statute. Therefore, the court wrongly dismissed sixteen potential jurors and denied Ladetto his right to an impartial jury. Balliro used the following colloquy between the court and a potential juror to illustrate his point:

Q. Have you any opinion—
A. Well, since His Excellency, the Governor has made an issue of that [capital punishment], it's caused a little doubt in my mind as to whether it should be so, whether the law should be changed.
Q. Well, is your state of mind—
A. It is unsettled Your Honor.
Q. So at the present time you cannot say that you have an opinion one way or the other?
A. That is right.
The court: This juror, in my opinion, is not indifferent, and may be excused.[24]

Balliro argued neither this venireman nor others who were ambivalent about the death penalty should have been dismissed. Since 1951, a juror's refusal to impose the death penalty was no longer irreconcilable with voting guilty to first-degree murder, "because his views may be ameliorated by virtue of his being permitted to recommend that a life sentence be imposed." The law was based on the legislature's "recognition that many citizens had an inherent repugnance to sentencing their fellow human being to death." Given this motivation, why should jurors not be given the opportunity "to intelligently determine within their own conscience whether they still have opinions which would conflict with their returning a verdict of guilty?" Moreover, Barillo insisted the legislature's recognition that many of our citizens are "possessed of merciful considerations is subverted by a procedure which . . . excludes from a jury all those who may so feel."[25]

The 1951 mercy law, according to Barillo, is an instruction manifesting the legislature's intent to define an impartial jury as representing a cross section of the community and not "composed solely of people who feel that because a man killed, he, too should be killed." The defendant must be granted the opportunity of having one person chosen who may persuade eleven others to show mercy. Of course, every defendant in a capital case runs the risk of having "hearts of stone sit on his judgment," but the Sixth Amendment of the U.S. Constitution and Article 12 of the Massachusetts Declaration of Rights "mandates that the alternate punishment provisions be explained to prospective jurors and otherwise be made an integral part of the selection of a petit jury."[26]

The SJC rejected Balliro's eloquent and original argument for constitutionally changing the way Massachusetts capital juries were selected, but the court did open the door to reform a crack. Surprisingly, Justice Reardon, known as "a stern adherent of the right and the good and the lawful," encouraged trial courts to use their discretionary power to expand the rights of the accused. Excusing for cause a potential juror whose "opinions are such as to preclude him from finding a defendant guilty of a crime punishable with death" did not deny Ladetto his constitutional right to an impartial jury. A juror must stand indifferent, be open to the evidence presented, and be prepared to carry out the law of the commonwealth. Seating jurors who are opposed to capital punishment, Reardon said, quoting *People v. Riser* (1956), "would in all probability work a de facto abolition of capital punishment, a result which, whether or not desirable of itself, it is hardly appropriate for this court to achieve by construction of an ambiguous statute." But, Reardon added, with a casual but significant nod to Balliro's call for reform, it would be a "wise exercise of discretion" for the trial judge to inquire of potential jurors during voir dire whether they had any opinion that would prevent them from recommending life imprisonment for a defendant convicted of first-degree murder.[27]

Two presumptions about the role and purpose of the judiciary that Reardon shared with a majority of the court over which Chief Justice

Raymond Wilkins presided from 1956 to 1970 motivated Justice Reardon's recommendation for changing the criteria by which capital jurors were selected. First, in the area of criminal procedure, Reardon, an advocate of judicial self-restraint, firmly believed that neither the Supreme Court nor the SJC should usurp the legislative function, especially in regard to an issue as divisive as capital punishment. Therefore, in *Ladetto* he recommended that trial judges use their discretionary power to resolve questions about which capital jurors stood indifferent. Refusing to make a constitutional issue about whether potential jurors held an opinion for or against capital punishment that would preclude their making an impartial decision allowed Reardon to defer to existing statutes defining impartiality and possibly ward off a Supreme Court interpretation that would permit seating jurors opposed to capital punishment. Second, Reardon believed that a defendant's rights must be balanced against the community's demand to be protected from hardened criminals. At the same time, he acknowledged that the state's right to prosecute "bad eggs" had to be balanced against a defendant's unalienable rights spelled out in the Declaration of Rights of the Massachusetts Constitution. In short, for Reardon, rule making in a capital case amounted to an exercise in determining whether a defendant's rights secured by fundamental law had been unmistakably infringed by the state's conduct of the trial.[28]

The practice of disqualifying potential jurors who held conscientious scruples about the death penalty came before the court three years after *Ladetto*. In 1968, the SJC considered two cases focusing on the impartiality of jurors selected to try first-degree murder charges. In each case, the trial judge excused for cause jurors who, because of opposition to capital punishment, stated they would not join in a verdict that would require the imposition of the death penalty.[29]

In *Commonwealth v. Nassar*, defense counsel argued that excluding those persons who hold conscientious scruples against the death penalty results in a jury that is not representative of a cross section of the community and is not impartial because it is more disposed to convict than is a jury from which potential jurors with such beliefs are not excluded. The defendant, George Nassar, was a familiar figure to the SJC; he had been convicted of murder in the first degree and sentenced to death in 1965. A 1966 appeal led to the reversal of Nassar's death sentence. After a new trial, Nassar was found guilty of murder in the first degree, but the jury recommended that the death sentence not be imposed. He was sentenced to life imprisonment. In 1968 Nassar appealed that conviction, contending a number of errors, including an argument challenging the use of a death-qualified jury.[30]

Nassar was convicted of shooting to death Irvin Hilton, a gas station manager. The trial jury heard chilling testimony from Rita Buote and her fourteen-year-old daughter Diane. Trembling and sobbing, the two women told the court that when they drove into Hilton's Andover gas station and stopped at the pumps they saw Hilton on his knees in front of the grease rack, looking up at a man, whom they later identified as Nassar, holding a gun in his hand. He fired several shots into Hilton, who fell over on his side. According to Buote, Nassar then turned and walked rapidly to the driver's door of her car. He tried to open the door, but Buote had locked it. As she cowered on the seat, she testified, Nassar pointed the pistol at her and pulled the trigger twice. When the gun failed to fire, he banged on the window, shouted something, and then walked away. Other witnesses, arriving at just that moment, saw a man, whom they were unable to identify, climb into a car and drive away.[31]

Before the SJC, District Attorney John Burke rejected Nassar's claim that he had been denied an impartial jury because the trial judge had systematically excluded all potential jurors who were opposed to, or held conscientious scruples against, the death penalty. In fact, it would not have been an error to exclude those persons whose opinions would prevent them from finding a defendant guilty of a crime punishable by death. Burke also lauded trial Judge Donald Macaulay for telling prospective jurors that they might be dismissed for cause if they held opinions that would prevent them from making a recommendation that the death penalty not be imposed. For these reasons, the commonwealth concluded that Nassar had been tried before an impartial jury.[32]

The smart, aggressive, thirty-four-year-old attorney F. Lee Bailey—already something of a household name—made Nassar's appeal before the SJC. Although lacking the statutory ten years of trial experience necessary to qualify for court-assignment in a capital case, Bailey was well prepared. In 1961, at age twenty-seven, less than three months after he was admitted to the Massachusetts bar, Bailey won his first murder case. That same year he took up the cause of Dr. Samuel Sheppard, the affluent thirty-year-old Ohio osteopath convicted of murdering his wife in 1954. Eventually,

Bailey convinced the Supreme Court of the United States that the carnival atmosphere in which Sheppard's trial took place fell far below the minimum requirement for due process. A new trial in 1966 found Sheppard not guilty.[33]

The heart of Nassar's second appeal was an argument borrowed from *Witherspoon v. Illinois* (1968), a case in which the Supreme Court had granted certiorari in the spring of 1967. A jury in Cook County, Illinois, found William Witherspoon guilty of murder and fixed his penalty at death. At the time of his trial, the law permitted the prosecutor to death-qualify the jury, to exclude those jurors who "might hesitate to return a verdict inflicting [death]." Early in the voir dire, the trial judge set the tone for the process of selecting a jury. "Let's get these conscientious objectors out of the way, without wasting any time on them," he said. In rapid succession, forty-seven veniremen were successfully challenged for cause on the basis of their attitudes toward the death penalty. In a brief to the Supreme Court, Witherspoon contended that the state could not confer on a jury selected in such a manner the power to determine guilt. Along with the American Civil Liberties Union and the NAACP Legal Defense Fund, Bailey filed an *amicus curiae* brief on Witherspoon's behalf. Not surprisingly, therefore, Bailey's argument in *Nassar* relied heavily on *Witherspoon*.[34]

Bailey told the SJC that the systematic exclusion from a capital jury of people who were opposed to, or held conscientious scruples against, capital punishment deprived the defendant of a jury that represented a cross section of the community and insured the prosecution of a jury whose members were "conviction prone." Such a procedure violated the Sixth and Fourteenth Amendments to the U.S. Constitution, which guarantee an impartial jury.[35]

A slender body of authorities supported Nassar's argument. Bailey relied chiefly on *Smith v. Texas* (1940), *Glasser v. U.S.* (1942), and a 1961 *Texas Law Review* article by Walter Oberer. In *Smith v. Texas,* Justice Hugo Black blasted racial discrimination in the selection of juries and asserted that to be constitutionally acceptable a jury must be a "body truly representative of the community." In *Glasser*, the Court concluded that choosing women jurors only from a list made available by the Illinois League of Women Voters violated the "traditional requirements of jury trial." Bailey argued that although these admonitions did not mean that every jury has to contain representatives of all economic, social, religious, and political groups, they must be held to mean that prospective jurors should be selected without systematic and intentional exclusion of members of these groups.[36]

Smith and *Glasser* addressed the systematic disqualification of black people and women from juries and not jurors who were opposed to, or expressed conscientious scruples about, capital punishment. But Bailey extended the argument, insisting there can be "no question that people opposed to capital punishment also are an identifiable group." Indeed, he added, a 1966 Gallup Poll showed that more people in the United States opposed capital punishment than supported it. For this reason, when the trial court excluded all potential jurors opposed to or expressing conscientious scruples against the death penalty, it excluded an identifiable community group and denied Nassar the equal protection of the law.[37]

Citing Oberer's short, provocative article, Bailey next challenged the old and widely accepted Massachusetts practice of challenging for cause jurors who expressed opposition to capital punishment. Oberer asserted that "a jury qualified on the death penalty is more apt to convict" and, therefore, "a defendant tried before such a jury is denied a fair trial on the basic issue of guilt or innocence." He produced scattered evidence to show that jurors routinely were challenged for cause merely because they were hesitant or ambivalent about the death penalty. To sustain his argument that this process resulted in a "conviction prone" jury, Oberer used data drawn from general psychological and sociological studies purporting to show that individuals will "tend to run to a coherent, discernible pattern with respect to attitudes and values" and called on trial courts to inform their decisions about jury selection with the enlightened testimony of psychologists and psychiatrists. Although neither Oberer nor Bailey cited any data specifically referring to jurors, the latter concluded that death-qualified juries unfairly prevented "community conscience" from playing a part in a capital case. The SJC now had a historic opportunity, Bailey concluded, to nullify a procedure that "results in a trial by a partial and prejudicial jury."[38]

Speaking for the SJC, Justice Ammi Cutter, whom the Republican governor Christian A. Herter appointed to the court when Justice Raymond S. Wilkins was elevated to chief in 1956, rejected Nassar's argument for three closely related reasons. First, the practice of excusing prospective jurors if their views about capital punishment precluded them from joining in a verdict resulting in a death sentence had deep roots in Massachusetts law. Second, jurors assigned to capital cases must be prepared to examine evidence impartially and to enforce capital punishment when the evidence convinces them of the defendant's guilt beyond a reasonable doubt and they find no mitigating or other circumstances to find otherwise. Third, following this historic practice "does not impair any constitutional right to an impartial jury." While Cutter acknowledged that the Massachusetts court's opinion might be affected by the Supreme Court's decision in *Witherspoon* and a companion case, *Bumper v. North Carolina* (1968), he chose not to take up Bailey's invitation to place the SJC on the forefront of change.[39]

In *Commonwealth v. Sullivan*, which was argued on the same day as *Nassar* but not decided until two months later, the court cited to the defendant's disadvantage the Supreme Court's decision in *Witherspoon*. Tried and convicted of the shooting death of a railway express guard during a payroll holdup in December 1966, William Sullivan argued that striking potential jurors who stated they did not "believe" in capital punishment was an error that deprived him of his Fourteenth Amendment right to an impartial jury properly selected from a cross section of the community. Although there was no prejudice to the commonwealth by including jurors who did not believe in the death penalty, defense attorney John Zamparelli argued that Sullivan was disadvantaged. Persons who oppose capital punishment are an identifiable group within the community and, therefore, should not be excluded. Moreover, recent studies show that people who favor capital punishment are not impartial but conviction-prone. The SJC seized on this last point, noting, "there are no data before us tending to show that jurors not opposed to the death penalty tend to favor the prosecution."[40]

In fact, the *Witherspoon* ruling had no specific impact on the outcome of either *Nassar* or *Sullivan*, because the jury in each of the Massachusetts cases had recommended life imprisonment, not death. Narrowly interpreted, *Witherspoon* did not change the state's right to challenge prospective jurors "who state that their reservations about capital punishment would prevent them from making an impartial decision as to the defendant's guilt." Although the court sometimes blurred the line between a juror's determination of a defendant's innocence or guilt and his decision about the penalty to be imposed, *Witherspoon* held unconstitutional only the court's right to strike for cause those who were unable to act as impartial arbiters "of the punishment to be imposed." *Witherspoon* articulated a narrow rule.

> Nothing we say today bears upon the power of a State to execute a defendant sentenced to death by a jury from which the only veniremen who were in fact excluded for cause were those who made unmistakably clear (1) that they would *automatically* vote against the imposition of capital punishment without regard to any evidence that might be developed at the trial of the case before them, or (2) that their attitude toward the death penalty would prevent them from making an impartial decision as to the defendant's *guilt.*[41]

During the SJC's 1970 term, the last year Chief Justice Ray Wilkins guided the court, six defendants raised questions related to the selection of jurors in capital cases in the light of *Witherspoon.* In *Ladetto v. Commonwealth* the court was asked to reconsider its decision in *Commonwealth v. Ladetto* (1965). The defendant argued that the court failed to recognize two constitutional errors. First, Ladetto contended that the trial court violated *Witherspoon* by excusing three potential jurors who expressed moderate reservations about the morality of the death penalty. In their answers to the trial judge none of the three veniremen made it "unmistakingly clear" that he would "automatically" vote against the imposition of capital punishment "without regard to any evidence." The trial judge did not attempt to determine whether the venireman were willing or able to make an impartial decision of guilt.[42]

Defense attorney Balliro argued that under *Witherspoon* even definite opposition to capital punishment is not a constitutionally valid basis for excluding jurors for cause. It must be shown, he contended, that the juror cannot make an impartial determination of guilt or innocence. Ladetto's second contention was that the trial court was constitutionally in error for not asking potential jurors the following question: "Have you any opinion that would preclude or prevent you from recommending life imprisonment for a defendant found guilty of murder in the first degree?" Defense attorney Balliro argued that *Commonwealth v. Ladetto* (1965) recommends, and *Witherspoon* mandates, such a question in order to insure an impartial jury.[43]

The SJC refused to budge from the position it had taken on the selection of jurors five years earlier. As he had in *Commonwealth v. Ladetto* (1965), Justice Reardon wrote for the court. There was no error, he said, in the trial judge's excusing for cause three potential jurors whose occasionally ambiguous answers manifested an "attitude" about capital punishment that would have made it "difficult for them to engage in an unprejudiced determination of guilt." Reardon reiterated his earlier view: asking a question about a potential juror's views about life imprisonment would have been a "wise exercise of discretion" on the part of the trial judge, but failure to do so was not a constitutional error. In other words, the court read *Witherspoon* and its earlier decision in *Ladetto* as permitting the exclusion of jurors who would automatically vote against the death penalty but not as requiring the striking of jurors who would automatically vote for the death penalty. According to the SJC, neither *Witherspoon* nor *Ladetto* required the trial court to take affirmative action to insure impartiality.[44]

Like the court's opinion in *Ladetto*, its decisions in *Commonwealth v. Connolly* (1970), *Commonwealth v. Mangum* (1970), *Commonwealth v. Flowers* (1970), *Commonwealth v. French* (1970), and *Commonwealth v. Robertson* (1970) addressed the question whether the trial court had properly applied Massachusetts law by excluding only those potential jurors whose opposition to capital punishment would have affected their ability to make an impartial judgment of a defendant's guilt or innocence. The defendants highlighted the responses by several veniremen, arguing that jurors were excluded merely because they held a personal belief against capital punishment.[45]

In *Connolly* and *Mangum*, for example, a number of potential jurors declined, or were unable, to answer specifically the statutory question whether they held any opinions that would preclude them from finding a defendant guilty of a crime punishable by death. "I wouldn't want to put any one to death," one would-be juror replied to the question put by Superior Court Judge George Thompson. Not altogether reassuringly, Judge Thompson stated: "You wouldn't be putting him to death. Somebody else would take care of that." When the statutory question was repeated, the venireman again hesitated and was excused. During voir dire in *Mangum*, Elise Reynolds declared she was "undecided in my mind; I don't really believe in capital punishment," she added. "I understand your right to such a belief," Judge Eugene Hudson, a twenty-four-year veteran on the bench replied, "but is your feeling so firm that you would not vote for a conviction?" Reynolds simply repeated her view: "I don't believe in capital punishment." Declared Judge Hudson: "This lady does not stand indifferent."[46]

Connolly and Mangum argued before the SJC that dismissing jurors solely because they held an abstract or general opinion against the death penalty was precisely what the Supreme Court ruled unconstitutional. Not so, retorted the *Mangum* court. "The impartiality or indifference of a prospective juror under interrogation is an attribute which must appear affirmatively," Justice Francis Quirico wrote. "If the juror is unable or unwilling to say whether he could, or could not, judge the case on its merits, he should not be allowed to serve." The court also rejected Connolly's argument that excluding veniremen without attempting to relate their opinions against capital punishment to either guilt or sentencing denied him the right to an impartial jury drawn from a cross section of the community. Connolly contended that the exclusions denied him equal protection and, by creating a conviction-prone jury incapable of rendering a fair verdict, violated due process. The SJC rejected the due process argument, relying on *Witherspoon*, *Bumper*, and *Commonwealth v. Sullivan* and concluding that "there was not sufficient evidence to show that juries culled of those opposed to the death penalty are more likely to convict." And, while recognizing that "a substantial segment of the community was opposed to capital punishment," the court found that excluding jurors who were generally opposed to capital punishment does not violate the integrity of the jury's fact-finding process.[47]

Because neither the Supreme Court nor the SJC seemed open to expanding the guidelines for capital jury selection articulated in *Witherspoon* (1968) and *Commonwealth v. Sullivan* (1968), questions about the constitutionality of death-qualified juries came before the SJC less frequently after 1970. Although Chief Justice G. Joseph Tauro took the SJC in bold new directions during his five-year tenure (1970–75), he was not prepared to change the ground rules for challenging potential jurors for cause. In *Commonwealth v. Lussier* (1973), the defendant, Alan Lussier, argued that in the light of the recent decision in *Furman v. Georgia* (1972) declaring the death penalty to be unconstitutional, it was reversible error for the trial judge in his case to question potential jurors about their views on capital punishment unless the commonwealth tried him for rape-murder, the only crime that still carried the death penalty. Therefore, Lussier maintained, excluding jurors who were opposed to capital punishment unnecessarily deprived him of "scrupled jurors." The chief justice brusquely dismissed this argument. "We think this attenuated argument entirely misses the point," Tauro wrote, quoting *Witherspoon*: "We simply cannot conclude, either on the basis of the record now before us or as a matter of judicial notice, that the exclusion of jurors opposed to capital punishment results in an unrepresentative jury on the issue of guilt or substantially increases the risk of conviction."[48]

One year later, James McAlister, convicted of the robbery and first-degree murder of a taxicab driver taking him from one Boston nightclub to another, contended that excluding for cause prospective jurors because of their answers to questions about the death penalty created a jury composed chiefly of men and women "who possessed social and personal characteristics which made them more likely to be favorably disposed to the prosecution." William Homans Jr., known in Boston as a "right-on lawyer" because he defended blacks, Vietnam war protesters, and poor people, argued that a "death-qualified" jury was biased on the question of punishment and the question of guilt or innocence. Homans admitted that no study can perfectly replicate the situation confronted by a capital jury, but he contended that new, "solid and convincing" data supported his argument that a jury from which potential jurors who hold scruples against capital punishment are excluded is nothing more than a jury "organized to convict."[49]

Justice Reardon carefully reviewed the record as well as Homans's contention that a death-qualified jury deprived the defendant of a jury that could fairly and objectively determine his guilt or innocence on the evidence. The questions put to the veniremen by the trial judge, Reardon wrote, "dealt not with their general attitudes toward capital punishment but with the influence of those attitudes on their ability to appraise the evidence fairly." Trial judge Walter McLaughlin "took pains" to ensure that "the attitudes expressed were more than just personal convictions and that they would interfere with the jurors' capacity to perform their duty." It may be argued, Reardon continued, that the trial court's inquiries eliminated those jurors whose opinions about the death penalty were strongest, and, therefore, the jury was "still skewed toward conviction." The SJC did not accept this view, Reardon declared.[50]

The studies presented do not demonstrate a conviction-prone bias in death-qualified juries, Reardon argued. Also, the studies are flawed, because they rely on data drawn from simulated trials, which cannot reproduce the great responsibility which exists "in the solemnity of a courtroom" when a defendant's life is at stake. Futhermore, the evidence presented does not shake the court's "fundamental conviction that juries generally are capable of impartially carrying out their tasks of evaluating the evidence and arriving at verdicts without regard to personal opinions."[51]

For Judge Reardon and the other members of the Tauro court, an impartial jury could be achieved by pursuing a balancing strategy. By strongly encouraging the trial court to exclude those potential jurors who hold opinions that would preclude their recommending mercy, as well as those whose repugnance of capital punishment would not permit them to find a defendant guilty however strong the evidence, it would be possible to achieve a neutral jury. Reardon claimed that if attitudes toward the death penalty correlated with conviction-proneness, a balancing strategy would eliminate potential jurors at both extremes. Finally, by silencing extreme expression of opinion about capital punishment, the court believed it might preserve the ideal of the impartial jury.[52]

By carefully articulating new guidelines for using challenge for cause to empanel an impartial capital jury, the SJC sought to silence extreme expressions of opinion for and against capital punishment. At the same time, the court sought to bring the common law definition of an impartial juror into conformity with reality without sacrificing the noble principle that a juror can stand indifferent.

Both the state and the defendant were still free, of course, to use peremptory challenges to eliminate would-be jurors perceived to be biased about capital punishment, the defendant, the state, or the case. Unlike challenges for cause, peremptory strikes historically required no explanation. Lawyers commonly used peremptory challenges to eliminate potential jurors simply because they belonged to, or were hostile to, the same identifiable group as the defendant. It was common, for example, for prosecutors to strike black veniremen if the defendant was black.

The use of racially motivated peremptory challenges came under attack in 1965. Robert Swain, a black man convicted by an all-white jury of raping a white woman, argued that the Talladega County, Alabama, prosecutor used his peremptory challenges to strike all of the blacks who were potential jurors, a violation of the equal protection clause of the Fourteenth

Amendment. Swain demonstrated that no black person had served on a local jury in fifteen years. In fact, the state court acknowledged, "Negroes are commonly on trial venires but are always struck by attorneys in selecting the trial jury." Still, the Supreme Court of Alabama ruled against the defendant's constitutional challenge and Swain appealed to the U.S. Supreme Court.[53]

Speaking through Justice Byron White, the Supreme Court concluded that there is nothing in the Constitution that requires a trial judge to inquire into the motives behind a prosecutor's use of peremptory challenges, as long as he is using them in the ordinary give and take of a trial. "The presumption in any particular case must be that the prosecutor is using the State's challenges to obtain a fair and impartial jury to try the case," White insisted. Only if the defendant proved systematic removal of blacks by the prosecutor "in case after case . . . with the result that no Negroes ever serve on petit juries" might a court conclude that the prosecutor had kept black people off juries "for reasons wholly unrelated to the [trial] outcome." Any other presumption, White maintained, "would establish a rule wholly at odds with the peremptory challenge system as we know it." True, in Swain's case, black veniremen were challenged because the defendant was black; but the Court was confident that in other trials lawyers were just as likely to strike "Catholics, accountants or those with blue eyes."[54]

Because the Supreme Court was keen to insulate the use of the peremptory challenge as a trial tool, it placed an enormous burden on the defendant to demonstrate racial discrimination. Not surprisingly, therefore, despite "extensive and biting criticism" every defendant who tried to meet the standard set by *Swain* "found it to be an illusory goal." In the two decades following *Swain* not a single federal court found that a prosecutor had used race-based challenges in violation of the equal protection clause. Rather, the attack against *Swain* came from the state courts. California in 1978, and Massachusetts the year following, imposed on their state prosecutors a heavier burden than that imposed by *Swain*.[55]

In *Commonwealth v. Soares* (1979), the SJC rejected the *Swain* standard for determining whether peremptory challenges were used in a racially discriminatory manner. Justice Paul J. Liacos, who served from 1989 to 1996, found that three black men were wrongly convicted of murder in the first degree. Liacos's decision placed the SJC in the forefront of constitutional change in the United States and helped stimulate an effort by several state courts to sustain the momentum initiated by the Warren Court's revolutionary work in criminal procedure. In addition to his commitment to judicial activism, Liacos's personal experience also made him sensitive to the court's role in protecting individual rights. As a second-generation Greek American whose family law firm built a reputation representing ethnic working-class immigrants in a dying factory town, Justice Liacos was keenly aware of the damaging effects of racial discrimination.[56]

In the 1970s Boston boiled with racial animosity and violence that was fueled by an increase in violent crime, a series of brutal killings, and the implementation of a court order that required the city to bus school children from one racially homogeneous neighborhood to another in order to bring about racial integration in the city's public schools,. From 1958 to 1974 the number of criminal and murder cases that came before the Superior Court nearly tripled. Several widely reported murders involving black assailants and white victims also grabbed the public's attention in the early 1970s. Desperate white residents in the city's South End formed street patrols to rid their neighborhood of crime, convinced that it was "us against them," white against black. The legislature reacted to the rising tide of violence and the popular fear accompanying it by enacting a series of tough crime bills. At the height of this crisis, a group of Harvard football players and some black men clashed violently.[57]

At the conclusion of its 1976 season, the Harvard College football team met for dinner and an award ceremony at the Harvard Club in downtown Boston. Alcoholic beverages were served before, during, and after the meal and ceremony. Shortly after midnight, about fifty football players left the Harvard Club for a bar in Boston's "combat zone," a seedy, six-square-block area pockmarked with bars, strip joints, and street-walking prostitutes. It was an area where blacks often were the retailers and whites the customers. When the bar closed at 2:00 A.M. the players scattered to their cars for the drive back to Cambridge. As one group of six young men walked toward their car, they encountered two black women, with whom the players traded crude remarks about sexual favors while the women alternately grabbed at the students' genitals and wallets. The talk ended when the players arrived at their car and the women continued walking. Just then, however, one of the players discovered that his wallet was missing. Suspecting the women, the players gave chase. The women ran into an alley adjacent to the Carnival Lounge, but a slightly built, thirty-three-year-old black man, Richard Allen, blocked the players' path. The players returned to their car and drove toward the Carnival Lounge.[58]

Within a few minutes, one of the players in the car spotted one of the black women walking. "There she goes," he shouted and another young man jumped out of the car and ran after the woman. A second group of players was standing nearby and joined in the chase. The woman was caught, fell to the street, scrambled to her feet, and ran again. At this point, Edward Soares, a stocky, thirty-three-year-old bearded black man, joined the fray, knocking down one of the Harvard men. Realizing he was outnumbered, Soares slowly backed away toward Boston Common. The football players inched toward Soares, confronting him near a kiosk on the edge of the Common.[59]

From somewhere behind the group, Allen yelled, "You came to the Zone, you got burned. Now clear out of here. Get the hell out of here." But, motioning to the encircling players, Soares taunted them: "Come on. I've been waiting for this," he said. The players hesitated. Glancing around, looking for a safe way to retreat, one of the players spotted a black man in a leather coat armed with a knife. Before the players turned and ran, Leon Easterling lunged forward and stabbed Thomas Lincoln, one of the players.[60]

As the players retreated toward their parked car, Easterling, Allen, Soares, and three other men ran after them, shouting insults and threats, including, "We're going to cut you white motherfuckers." In the parking area next to the players' car, Soares and Easterling fought with Andrew Puopolo, one of the Harvard men. Easterling struck over Soares's shoulder with his knife, cutting Puopolo in the chest. "I'm all right," Puopolo said to a teammate. "Let's get out of here." But as they moved to leave, Soares and then Easterling stabbed Puopolo in the chest. One of the blows caused a massive wound from which he died on December 17, 1976.[61]

Easterling, Allen, and Soares were indicted for murder in the first degree and their trial opened March 8, 1977, amidst a deluge of publicity that often located the crime within the context of Boston's recent history of racial hostility. During the jury empanelment, Judge James Roy found thirteen black veniremen indifferent. Assistant District Attorney Thomas Mundy peremptorily challenged twelve of these potential jurors. The remaining black man was seated and subsequently designated as foreman of the jury by Judge Roy. Each time a prospective black juror was challenged by the prosecution, defense attorney Henry Owens III noted for the record the race of the person, objected to the prosecutor's use of the peremptory challenge, and took exception to Judge Roy's refusal to sustain his objection.[62]

When Owens, one of a handful of black criminal defense attorneys practicing in Boston, tried to explain to the court what he was doing when he objected to the prosecutor's use of peremptory challenges aimed at potential black jurors, the following colloquy occurred: "If it develops during the course of the selection of the jury that [the prosecutor] systematically challenges black jurors through the use of peremptory challenges, your Honor, I would like to make an offer of proof at that time," Owens began. Judge Roy interrupted: "Well, you're familiar with the decisions in that area?" "Correct," Owens said and again attempted to explain his position. "Wait a minute," Judge Roy blurted out. "So far as I'm concerned, if I were sitting down there, either on the prosecution or the defense, I would have challenged that person on the basis of his lack of intelligence." Owens tried to explain. "I don't care what your position is," the judge fired back. "You've noted your exception, and that's it. I'm not going to have any more speeches about that, and I'll see you in the lobby at one o'clock."

At the lobby conference, Judge Roy was blunt. "Now, you look here, Mr. Owens. Sit down for just a moment. I've got something to say to you on the record. I'm not going to have any injection of racial prejudice into this case if I can prevent it, and I want you making no speeches out there. The law is clear in recognizing the purpose of peremptory challenges. You've already got it on the record in respect to your position, and I don't want it repeated any more."

After twelve of the thirteen black veniremen called were challenged by the commonwealth, Owens requested a hearing on the matter. "Your Honor," he said, "if the Court were to conduct a hearing at this time directed to the District Attorney to find out if any of the peremptory challenges exercised by him were in any manner used to exclude black people from this jury." Judge Roy asked Assistant District Attorney Mundy whether he wanted to reply to Owens's motion. "No, your Honor," the prosecutor said. "Very well," the judge replied and ruled that the defendant's motion was denied and the exception saved.

Less than two weeks later, a jury returned guilty verdicts of murder in the first degree for each defendant and the court imposed a sentence of life imprisonment. The defendants appealed, arguing numerous errors but focusing chiefly on the prosecution's use of peremptory challenges.[63]

Before the SJC, Mundy argued that the court should adhere to the *Swain* standard and pointedly referred to Judge Roy's warning to the defense about "injecting racial prejudice into the jury selection process." To bolster his defense of *Swain*, Mundy made two brief points. The defense, he noted, used several of its peremptory challenges to strike veniremen with Italian surnames, thus removing potential jurors with the same ethnic identity as the victim. Also, the defense did not cite a single case in which a state court had rejected the *Swain* standard, and, Mundy concluded, there was no reason for the SJC to do so.[64]

Owens, in contrast, urged the court to grant the defendants "a greater degree of protection under our [state] constitution than may be available under our federal constitution," to use the state constitution to prohibit what *Swain* allowed. He began his argument by assailing the district attorney's use of "racially inflammatory epithets" during the trial and concluded by ridiculing the *Swain* standard as showing "a total lack of understanding as to the nature of racism and how it can operate in jury selection." Between these bookends, Owens stacked a variety of specific and general points. First, he said, there are no data to support the rationale that black jurors would be more biased toward black defendants than whites. Second, a review of federal data show the *Swain* standard to be "unreasonably high." Third, the defendant had no access to state data of the sort *Swain* proposed as necessary to demonstrate that the prosecutor's peremptory challenges were racially motivated. These specific points led Owens to assert that the *Swain* rule "does not merely permit abuse" of prosecutorial peremptory challenges; "it invites it." Finally, Owens concluded, *Swain* all but abandons "the minority defendant's right to an impartial jury." In the name of "reason and the humane concept that informs our Declaration of Rights," Owens pleaded with the SJC to use Article 12 of the Massachusetts Constitution as a bulwark "to uphold the accused's right to an impartial jury."[65]

"We accept the invitation to reexamine the issue" within the framework of Article 12, a divided court announced on March 8, 1979. By a 4-to-3 vote the SJC brushed aside *Swain*'s weak protection of a defendant's right to a fair trial, created a new standard for the use of peremptory challenges in Massachusetts courts, found that Soares, Easterling, and Allen had been deprived of their "constitutionally protected right to a trial by a jury fairly drawn from the community," and reversed the trial verdict. The minority concurred in the result but "saw no occasion for the decision of any constitutional question, State or Federal, [or] for critical review of decisions of the Supreme Court of the United States." Justices Braucher, Quirico, and Wilkins also rejected the majority's use of the Massachusetts Declaration of Rights to determine the constitutional issues surrounding the prosecutor's use of peremptory challenges. "It may be wise to defer to any guidance which may come from the United States Supreme Court on the basis of the United States Constitution," Braucher wrote. "Holdings involving interpretation of the Massachusetts Constitution seem gratuitous and premature," he added, revealing a deep split within the court over the legitimacy of state court activism.[66]

Writing for the majority, Justice Liacos unhesitatingly thrust the SJC into the forefront of the movement to supplement federal constitutional rights with an expanded interpretation of state constitutional guarantees of the rights of the accused. While he acknowledged a legitimate use for peremptory challenges, Liacos wasted little time on *Swain*. In three short paragraphs and as many footnotes, Liacos concluded that *Swain* offers "negligible protection . . . to a defendant asserting the right to trial by a jury of peers" as called for in Article 12. Previous decisions of the SJC and the U.S. Supreme Court had articulated the crucial characteristic of an impartial jury: it must be drawn randomly from a fair and representative cross section of the community. Although every jury need not mirror the community, a trial jury should be as near an approximation of the ideal cross section of the community as random selection allows. For this reason, Liacos wrote, the court will not permit peremptory challenges to be used to "exclude prospective jurors solely by virtue of their membership in, or affiliation with, particular, defined groupings in the community." Allowing members of discrete groups to be excluded by peremptory challenges "would leave the right to a jury drawn from a representative cross section of the community wholly susceptible to nullification through the intentional use of peremptory challenges to exclude identifiable segments of that community." Article 1 of the Declaration of Rights of the Massachusetts Constitution delineates those groups that may not permissibly form the basis for striking potential jurors: sex, race, color, creed, or national origin.[67]

The remedy proposed by Liacos for the misuse of peremptory challenges was a rule that applied to the defendant and to the commonwealth. Either party might rebut the presumption that peremptory challenges were used legitimately to eliminate prospective jurors whose special relationship to the case raised the possibility of individual bias. Drawing on their extensive experience with jury empanelment, their knowledge of local conditions, and their familiarity with the contending attorneys, trial judges would weigh the arguments made by both sides to determine whether the peremptory challenges in question had been used to exclude would-be jurors on the basis of a bias presumed to derive from a person's sex, race, color, creed, or national origin. If a trial judge drew the "reasonable inference" that peremptory challenges were used improperly to strike members of protected groups, the offending attorney had the opportunity to defend his strikes. Then, the judge's task was to sort out "bona fide reasons for such peremptories [sic] from sham excuses belatedly contrived to avoid admitting facts of group discrimination."[68] If the trial judge then found that peremptory challenges were used unjustifiably to eliminate members of protected groups, the court might then conclude that the jury as constituted failed to fulfill the representative cross-section requirement, dismiss the jurors previously selected, and begin the process of jury selection anew.[69]

The SJC's path-breaking decision in *Soares* gave rise to both procedural and substantive problems associated with judicial review of peremptory challenges, which had traditionally been final and unreviewable. In the seven years between *Soares* and the Supreme Court's decisions in *Batson v. Kentucky* (1986), which finally held that using race as the reason for striking a juror is a violation of the Equal Protection Clause and *J.E.B. v. Alabama* (1994), when the logic of *Batson* was extended to gender, the SJC refined the evidentiary standard and the remedy laid out in *Soares*.[70]

In *Commonwealth v. Walker* (1979), the SJC found that Assistant District Attorney Timothy O'Neill had not used his peremptory challenges to systematically exclude black jurors and thereby deny Walker a fair trial by an impartial jury. Of the sixty-four prospective jurors interviewed during voir dire, nine were African American and one Hispanic. Thirty-five, including two who were black, were excused for cause. The defendant peremptorily challenged eight prospective white jurors, and the prosecutor used seven peremptory challenges, eliminating five blacks, one Hispanic, and one white. Two blacks were sworn as jurors and were among the twelve who later found Walker guilty of assault and battery. The jury concluded that on July 4, 1976, Walker, a young black man, deliberately drove his car into a group of white people, seriously injuring three persons.[71]

In Walker's defense, Edward Berkin argued that the commonwealth's use of peremptory challenges violated Article 12, as interpreted by the court in *Soares*. Speaking for a unanimous court, Justice Braucher disagreed. He deferred to the trial judge's conclusion that there was not systematic exclusion of any discrete group. Challenges of five out of seven blacks presents a "less compelling showing than challenges of twelve out of thirteen in the *Soares* case," Braucher concluded, adhering to the fine distinction between the two cases drawn by the trial court.[72]

The following year the Massachusetts Appeals Court rejected Lawrence Kelly's argument that the trial judge should have dismissed the entire pool of potential jurors because only five of the fifty prospective jurors were African American. The trial court ruled that Kelly, a black man convicted of that kidnap and rape of a white woman, failed to present any evidence to substantiate his claim that the underrepresentation of African Americans was due to systematic exclusion. To support his claim that the commonwealth used its peremptory challenges to keep blacks off the jury in violation of the *Soares* principles, Kelly pointed to the prosecutor's exclusion of two black veniremen. But the Appeals Court ruled that the commonwealth had accepted without objection three black jurors who, along with eight other, white jurors, voted to convict Kelly. Therefore, the Appeals Court concluded, these facts do not reveal "a pattern of systematic exclusion of blacks through the use of peremptory challenges."[73]

Three years later, the SJC heard two additional cases that turned on the court's definition of permissible peremptory challenges. Gregory Robinson, an African American drug addict, was convicted of armed robbery and murder in 1976. The trial court denied the defendant's motions for a new trial. In 1981, however, the SJC agreed to hear Robinson's appeal. He contended that during the process of empanelling an impartial jury, the prosecutor had used his peremptory challenges in a racially biased manner, contrary to the *Soares* standard. Assistant District Attorney John A. Kiernan successfully challenged two African Americans and one Puerto Rican, resulting in an all-white jury.[74]

Speaking for the court, Justice Benjamin Kaplan began by criticizing the trial record. He noted that the *Soares* standard presumed that peremptory challenges were used properly with a wealth of specific data needed to counter that presumption. The record presented by Robinson, however, lacked relevant information about the number of peremptory challenges used by the prosecutor to exclude white jurors, as well as a comparison of the numbers and percentage of black and white jurors who were excluded. Moreover, Kaplan pointed out, the victim of the crime was Asian and no member of that group sat on the jury. In short, Kaplan concluded, the trial judge was perfectly correct in ruling that Robinson had not satisfactorily countered the presumption of proper use of peremptory challenges.[75]

In *Commonwealth v. Reid* (1981), however, the SJC found that the defendant had improperly used her peremptory challenges when she excluded all six men chosen for the jury. Ultimately, a jury of six men and six women convicted Lucille Reid of murder in the second degree in the stabbing death of her neighbor Danny Harris. When asked by Judge Sullivan during a bench conference to explain her challenges, defense attorney Joyce Poulin refused. The remaining potential jurors were dismissed without objection. The following day, Reid objected to the disallowance of her challenges, claiming that she had a constitutional and a statutory right to use her peremptory challenges for whatever reason she saw fit without explanation. She insisted her right to use peremptory challenges was not subject to judicial control.[76]

Before the SJC Reid elaborated on her argument made during trial. Relying on *Swain*, Reid labeled *Soares* a "radical departure" from past practices governing the use of peremptory challenges. She believed the court had gone too far toward leveling the playing field by making the defendant as responsible as the prosecution for empanelling an impartial jury. Reid contended that the defendant should never have the burden of guaranteeing a fair trial to the commonwealth. Moreover, she said, *Soares* is too inclusive because only "historically excluded groups" who are the focus of prejudice should be protected from the prejudicial use of peremptory challenges and not white men, who need no constitutional protection.[77]

Justice Ruth Abrams wrote for the court in *Reid*. To be sure, the court recognized the importance of peremptory challenges, she said, but their use is not required by either the state or the federal constitution. In fact, the court stated in *Soares* that the presumption of proper use is rebuttable with a showing that prospective jurors are being excluded solely by reason of their group membership. Reid's attempt to strike all the men from the jury, Abrams pointed out, certainly gives credence to the trial judge's conclusion that Reid was using her peremptory challenges to create a biased and homogeneous jury. Finally, an experienced trial judge may implement the prohibition against striking persons on account of their group affiliations in a variety of ways. By refusing to permit the defendant to strike without reason all of the men on the jury, Abrams concluded, the trial judge salvaged an impartial jury.[78]

From 1979 to 1986, the SJC applied the *Soares* standard broadly to both the prosecution and the defense and to issues arising from race and gender, but the court's commitment to state constitutionalism failed to inspire other state courts or to silence critics who either attacked the state courts' "evasion of the Burger Court" or bemoaned the use of peremptory challenges under any circumstances. After *Soares*, and a similar decision by the California Supreme Court, some observers thought that those state court decisions might lead to the widespread disavowal of *Swain*'s extremely limited restriction of the racially motivated use of peremptory challenges. Yet, in the seven years between *Soares* and the Supreme Court's prohibition of race as the reason for striking a juror, no states other than California and Massachusetts imposed constitutional limits on peremptory challenges that exceeded *Swain*. Indeed, during that same period, at least nineteen jurisdictions decided to follow *Swain*.[79]

Critics of *Soares*, and of state court activism generally, voiced concern about state courts breaking loose from Supreme Court interpretations. Prophetically speaking for those state courts that subsequently followed *Swain*, Justice Braucher in his dissent in *Soares* scorched the majority for dismissing the values of constitutional uniformity and unity to be achieved by states adhering to decisions made by the "United States Supreme Court on the basis of the United States Constitution." Off the bench, a handful of law professors countered the proponents of state constitutionalism by supporting the principles of old federalism. Activist state courts, they cautioned, should pause and consider the important principles of constitutional hierarchy and propriety and the dangers that might follow from a state court's "insulating" its decision from Supreme Court review or from evading the guidelines laid down by the Court to explore new terrain where there were no standards to guide the judge.[80]

Although the Supreme Court was divided along procedural lines, it was not quite as cautious as many of its observers. Justices Stevens, Blackmun, and Powell applauded the SJC's *Soares* decision and urged their brethren "to allow the various States to serve as laboratories" in which the issue of peremptory challenges received further study before being addressed by the Supreme Court. Justices William Brennan and Thurgood Marshall also encouraged state court activism, refusing to sit by while the Court and most states clung to *Swain*. For this reason, Marshall and Brennan repeatedly dissented from the Court's denial of certiorari in capital cases in which prosecutors used peremptory challenges to remove all black people from the jury. The most troubling aspect of *Swain* for Marshall was that it permitted *some* racial discrimination. "Since *every* defendant is entitled to equal protection of the laws and should therefore be free from invidious discrimination," Marshall puzzled, "it is difficult to understand why several must suffer discrimination because of the prosecutor's use of peremptory challenges before any defendant can object."[81]

Marshall's argument finally bore fruit. In *Batson v. Kentucky* a divided Supreme Court revisited the rules governing the use of peremptory challenges and held that using race as the reason for excluding a potential juror was a violation of the equal protection clause. Although its scope was narrower, the remedy adopted by the Court was similar to that used by the SJC: an allegation by the defendant supported by facts that the prosecutor used his peremptory challenges in a racially discriminatory manner forced the state to give a convincing nonracial explanation for its challenges.[82]

While Burger and Rehnquist argued that the Court had gone too far, Marshall contended that *Batson* had not gone far enough. In a concurring opinion, he charged that the California and Massachusetts experiences illustrate the limitations of the approach allowing defendants to challenge the racially discriminatory use of peremptory challenges. Marshall cited, among other cases, *Commonwealth v. Robinson* (1981), in which the SJC denied the defendant's claim that his right to an impartial jury had been violated by the prosecutor's use of peremptory challenges. Marshall asserted that the *Soares-Batson* solution still left prosecutors free to discriminate against blacks in jury selection "provided that they held that discrimination to an 'acceptable' level." The only way to end discrimination, according to Marshall, was to ban entirely the use of peremptory challenges.[83]

Eight years after *Batson*, and fifteen years after *Soares*, the Supreme Court prohibited the use of peremptory challenges to eliminate jurors simply because of their sex. In *J.E.B. v. Alabama* (1994), Justice Harry Blackmun found that "intentional discrimination on the basis of gender" is based on "gross generalizations," invites "cynicism respecting the juror's neutrality," and violates the equal protection clause. Some lower federal courts also have used *Batson* to invalidate peremptory challenges based on ethnicity, but no state court other than Massachusetts specifically prohibited the use of peremptory challenges to eliminate jurors simply because of their religion. Clearly, in *Soares*, the SJC had played the "republican schoolmaster," teaching other courts the meaning of democracy.[84]

Following a long history of legally sanctioned bias with regard to jurors' views about the death penalty and the discriminatory use of peremptory challenges, two landmark decisions by the SJC about challenge for cause and peremptory challenge greatly expanded the right of a capital defendant to an impartial jury and went far toward reconciling the tension between those who argued that capital juries must be death qualified and those who argued juries must not be conviction prone. *Ladetto* (1965) was a legal wedge that opened the court to scrutiny of the death penalty, and *Soares* (1979) marked the path that led to the court's abolition of capital punishment.

By regulating challenges, the SJC sought to curtail prejudice and to increase the likelihood that a cross-sectional jury properly drawn would be impartial. At the same time, the court acknowledged that "no juror enters into his temporary judicial service stripped of his background and emotions. To hold otherwise would be to defy human experience." Applying its insight about the nature and pervasiveness of prejudice led the court to conclude that there is reason to believe that a capital jury cannot be impartial, no matter how fine the procedural sieve through which jurors are required to pass. Drawing on this conclusion, among others, the SJC found capital punishment unconstitutional according to the Massachusetts Declaration of Rights. In short, due process was the engine driving the argument for abolition.

---- ELEVEN ----
"SUCCESS—
AT LONG LAST"

At a noon rally on May 10, 1947, Massachusetts governor Robert Brad-ford, who had vaulted into the governor's office after winning a national reputation as a tough-on-crime Middlesex County district attorney, told a cheering crowd on Boston Common that providing subsidies for veter-ans' housing was his top priority. Later in the day the governor spoke to reporters about his proposed sales tax. Neither Bradford nor the report-ers following the governor that chilly spring day said anything about the executions of Philip Bellino and Edward Gertson. The two men had been electrocuted at the Massachusetts State Prison shortly after midnight for the murder of nineteen-year-old Robert "Tex" Williams, a former U.S. Marine.[1]

In a little more than two decades the callous indifference manifested by the public silence about the execution of Bellino and Gertson disap-peared. A loud and vigorous debate about capital punishment eventually led to a temporary national halt in executions and to the abolition of the death penalty in Massachusetts. Bellino and Gertson were two of one hun-dred fifty-three persons executed in the United States in 1947, and in the twentieth century, the sixty-fourth and sixty-fifth—and last—persons to be executed in Massachusetts to date. Although the signs of change were not then apparent, Bellino's and Gertson's executions came on the cusp of a social and legal transformation of attitudes and practices in regard to the death penalty on which Massachusetts abolitionists had been working for two decades. During the 1950s the number of executions began to decline throughout the United States, falling steadily until they were stopped alto-gether between 1968 and 1977.[2]

The murder for which Bellino and Gertson were executed was not es-pecially gruesome, nor did the Boston press give the story much coverage when it occurred on August 7, 1945. Williams was shot in the back of the head and his body left in an ocean marsh not far from the main road connecting Boston to a string of North Shore suburbs. Four days earlier, Williams had led Bellino, Gertson, and Charles Mantia to a Newton, New Hampshire, summer camp where they robbed an illegal dice game at gunpoint. Williams had promised a haul of at least $10,000, but when the gang met to divide up the loot there was only a few hundred dollars. Angry and fearful that Williams would "squeal" to the police, Bellino, Gertson, and Mantia took Williams for a "ride." Just before midnight the four men crowded into a taxi, stopping at an isolated spot along the road to Lynn. Mantia remained with the cab driver while the three others walked out toward the ocean. Only Gertson and Bellino returned. When Mantia asked where Williams was, Gertson said he decided to "stay with his girl." A few days after the discovery of Williams's body, Mantia led police to Gertson and Bellino.[3]

At trial, Mantia and the taxi driver, James Salah, were District Attorney Hugh Clegg's star witnesses. Gertson and Bellino testified in their own defense. According to the defendants, the four men were heading for a nightclub when Williams insisted on stopping at the Lynn marshes to recover a stolen license plate he had hidden there. An argument ensued. Williams allegedly accused Bellino of withholding his share of the loot from the crap-game robbery. The young man then supposedly pulled a revolver and fired two wild shots at Gertson, who fired a single shot in self-defense, killing Williams. The jury dismissed this unconvincing tale and found both Gertson and Bellino guilty of first-degree murder after deliberating less than six hours on June 18, 1946. Judge Joseph L. Hurley sentenced the two men to death.[4]

Gertson and Bellino appealed the verdict to the Supreme Judicial Court (SJC). According to a recently enacted statute, the trial court had empanelled fourteen jurors at the outset of the trial but dismissed two just before submitting the case to the jury. Gertson and Bellino contended this procedure violated their right to trial by jury guaranteed by Article 12 of the Massachusetts Declaration of Rights. The SJC rejected the argument. "We see nothing in this statute that contravenes the provisions of the Declaration of Rights for the preservation of trial by jury," Justice Stanley Qua wrote for a unanimous court. Moreover, anticipating the defendants' appeal to the U.S. Supreme Court, the SJC added, the Sixth Amendment to the U.S. Constitution has "never been held to extend so far as to control the action of the States."[5]

Originally scheduled to die February 28, 1947, Gertson and Bellino received a stay of execution, pending their appeal to the Supreme Court on the constitutionality of the fourteen-person jury. The defense contended that the fourteen-person jury, which heard the case in June 1946, was unconstitutional because the extra jurors system did not become law until October 1945, after their crime had been committed. As the SJC predicted, however, the Supreme Court denied certiorari. Shortly after the Court's refusal to review the convictions, Governor Bradford and the Council granted the two men a reprieve, a gesture that was extended until May 8.[6]

While Gertson and Bellino awaited execution, the Massachusetts legislature debated a bill that would have permitted juries to recommend life imprisonment for persons convicted of first-degree murder. The mercy bill, as well as a proposal for the outright abolition of capital punishment, was the work of the Massachusetts Council Against the Death Penalty (MCADP). Although the Massachusetts group had a grudging, paper relationship with the American League to Abolish Capital Punishment, the MCADP acted independently from the New York–based national organization, distinguishing itself from the left-wing politics that drove both the American League and the Sacco-Vanzetti Defense Committee.[7]

Directed initially by a Quaker activist, the MCADP soon turned for its leadership to Sara Rosenfeld Ehrmann, a thirty-three-year-old Brookline housewife and mother of two young children, whose husband, Herbert, had been on the Sacco-Vanzetti defense team. Born in Bowling Green, Kentucky in 1895, Sara Rosenfeld moved with her parents, Abram and Helen, to Rochester, New York, when she was three years old. Because Sara's father was a liquor salesman who spent a great deal of time on the road, Sara's mother assumed major responsibility for raising Sara and her two brothers. She taught the children the "fundamentals of Judaism," but she also encouraged a belief in a homespun universal religion, in pacifism, and in the Democratic politics of William Jennings Bryant. For this reason, perhaps, when Sara enrolled at the University of Rochester in 1912 she joined a sorority that previously had excluded Jews and prepared herself for a career as a reform worker, drawing political inspiration from her mother as well as the professor and later Democratic congressman Meyer Jacobstein.[8]

During the summer following her freshman year, Sara joined her family on their annual visit to their Kentucky relatives. At her cousin's home, Sara met Herbert Ehrmann, who had just completed his first year at Harvard Law School. They talked and went on a hayride with friends, but they made no plans to meet again. At the end of the summer, Sara returned to Rochester, but rather than continue her college education she worked for the women's suffrage movement. She loved the work, especially her first job chauffeuring Eleanor Garrison, a prominent Massachusetts suffragist, on a speaking tour of New York state. At each stop Sara Rosenfeld, a "petite, brown-eyed" young woman, jumped on the hood of the car shouting, "Votes for Women," and traded barbs with hecklers until a crowd gathered. I "was never a rebel," she later recalled, but thought it only "fair and right" that women should vote. As this comment suggests, Ehrmann was—and remained—a "social feminist," a term historian William O'Neill coined to describe women whose primary concern was service to others and to society, in contrast to feminists whose goal was the achievement of individual opportunities.[9]

On a fall 1914 visit with friends at Wellesley College, Herbert and Sara met again. For the next three years they shuttled back and forth between Rochester and Boston and later between Smith College in Northampton, Massachusetts, where Sara spent her junior year (1915–16), and Boston, where Herbert worked as a Legal Aid lawyer. They were married in Rochester on May 12, 1917, shortly after Sara graduated from the University of Rochester and just about a month after the United States entered World War I. Their first son, Bruce, was born in Boston the following June. A few months later, Herbert left for Washington, D.C., accepting a position as staff attorney with the government shipping board. The war ended by the time Sara and their baby moved to a rented farmhouse in Chevy Chase, Maryland, to be with Herbert. Rather than returning directly to Boston, the Ehrmanns moved to Ohio, where Herbert was part of a team of young progressive lawyers Felix Frankfurter, then a professor at Harvard, recruited to study the criminal justice system in Cleveland. The team shared the belief that urban crime might be ameliorated through improved training of local police, more efficient courts, and the elimination of political corruption. The result was a landmark study, *Criminal Justice in Cleveland*.[10]

Sara welcomed the temporary move to Cleveland. Like many college-educated young women of her generation, she found the housewife's traditional role unfulfilling and she seized an opportunity to help compile the Cleveland criminal justice data. Back in Boston, Sara took courses at Radcliffe College, volunteered at an immigrant aid agency, and put her legal research skills to good use. Working pro bono with William Thompson, appellant attorney for Sacco and Vanzetti, Herbert became convinced that a Providence gang was responsible for the robbery and murders for which Sacco and Vanzetti were convicted. Sara dug out data from federal court records to bolster Herbert's theory. Of course, neither Herbert Ehrmann's alternate scenario nor defense motions raising serious due process questions stopped the executions of Sacco and Vanzetti. Many years later, Sara privately commented, "I saw the details of the Sacco-Vanzetti case close up, including the judicial hesitancy to explore exculpatory routes, the media's hysteria, the emotional outcry for their lives. I knew there was something wrong with the death penalty because there were too many questions unresolved when the men were executed. Their deaths signified a finality inappropriate in terms of the finality one could feel with respect to the evidence." Sara Ehrmann's public silence about Sacco-Vanzetti, her proven legal research skills, and her commitment to social reform led Zechariah Chafee, a Harvard law professor and MCADP board member, to offer Sara the position of executive director of MCADP. She accepted and agreed to a annual salary of $1,200, a contractual arrangement that "melted away" at the onset of the Great Depression. It is hard to imagine a more inauspicious time to assume a leadership role in an unpopular cause. In addition to Sacco-Vanzetti, a string of highly publicized murders captured national attention during the 1920s and 1930s and boosted public support for the death penalty. Nathan Leopold and Richard Loeb's "thrill murder" of young Bobby Franks, Al Capone's Chicago gangland killings, and the Lindbergh kidnap-murder, among other sensational homicides, led national magazines and newspapers to conclude that a "crime wave" was pounding the people of the United States.[11]

Richard W. Child asserted in the *Saturday Evening Post* that an overly indulgent criminal justice system allowed most murderers to escape punishment. In fact, the opposite seemed true. From 1930 to 1940, states executed nearly eighteen hundred death row inmates nationwide, including eighteen in Massachusetts. At no time during this gruesome decade did a significant number of Massachusetts citizens, the legislature, or the SJC speak out against capital punishment. Public rallies for some men condemned to death were vociferous but often sparsely attended. Until 1951 when Governor Paul Dever signed a mercy bill and set in motion a twenty-four-year period in which no prisoner was put to death, Massachusetts governors and members of the Council supported the death penalty and routinely denied clemency appeals. At the same time, the SJC rejected dozens of motions for new trials brought by men convicted of capital murder. Under Chief Justice Arthur P. Rugg, who came to the court in 1906, moved to the center seat in 1911, and served until 1938, Massachusetts' criminal due process changed very little. The court offered the accused little constitutional protection and a bare handful of options for postconviction appeal. During Rugg's long tenure, the SJC reversed only two capital convictions and on retrial both men were found guilty and subsequently executed.[12]

While lawyers hammered at the court's constricted view of criminal due process, the MCADP forged a three-pronged strategy to overcome legislative support for capital punishment. Rather than campaign around an abstract—for or against capital punishment—referendum question as advised by the American League to Abolish Capital Punishment, Ehrmann focused on the Massachusetts legislature. She inundated legislators with data about capital punishment and sought to make it as easy as possible for lawmakers to embrace some manifestation of opposition to the death penalty. Specifically, she and others she recruited appeared each year before the Joint House-Senate Judiciary Committee, urging lawmakers to enact a bill abolishing the death penalty or a law permitting jurors to recommend mercy, or to support a resolution establishing a commission to study the pros and cons of capital punishment.

The second prong of her strategy was to focus on specific capital cases in order to illustrate to legislators and fix public attention on the glaring imperfections of murder investigations and capital procedure. Of course, she also wanted to bring as many people as possible into the abolition campaign, but she was interested chiefly in recruiting political, religious, and civic leaders, men and women whose names might flank the MCADP's letterhead. Third, Ehrmann brought pressure to bear on sitting governors not to sign execution orders.

The MCADP left to lawyers the effort to change capital procedure. Working separately from Ehrmann, Zechariah Chafee and a handful of attorneys repeatedly asked the Boston Bar Association to study the question of capital punishment. Chafee and Francis Russell, who was working on a book about Sacco-Vanzetti, also urged the Judicial Council—the appointive advisory group established in 1924—to recommend to the legislature a law permitting the SJC to review matters of fact as well as questions of law as part of a capital appeal.[13]

With a burst of energy she sustained for almost four decades, Ehrmann plunged into her work in 1928. Her long campaign against capital punishment began with the simple act of hosting a public dinner-speech by E. Roy Calvert, an English criminologist and author of *Capital Punishment in the Twentieth Century*. Calvert told his Boston listeners that the "problem of capital punishment must be approached in a scientific manner unbiased by any sentimental reasoning." He produced data that showed the death penalty is not a deterrent to homicide. Meeting privately with Ehrmann, Calvert suggested ways to administer efficiently the flow of paper created by the campaign. A short time after Calvert's appearance, Ehrmann issued a press release noting that state senator Angier Goodwin's bill to abolish the death penalty had the support of a number of locally prominent people. Next, she and small, energetic band of young MCADP members spoke face-to-face with each member of the Judiciary Committee. Every legislator received a flyer listing ten reasons for abolishing capital punishment that had the personal endorsement of the current Massachusetts commissioner of corrections, Warren A. Stearns, who stated, "I am unalterably opposed to capital punishment. It does more harm than good." About a month later, Ehrmann and dozen other opponents of capital punishment testified before the Judiciary Committee in favor of Goodwin's bill. She stressed two arguments. First, she said society ought to feel safe sentencing murderers to life imprisonment. "There is no danger that Life Prisoners are wantonly pardoned" or that those few who are pardoned will murder again. For emphasis Ehrmann added, "no life prisoner has ever murdered a guard in Massachusetts" and "no life prisoner [has] ever escaped." Second, she pointed out that those states and countries that had abolished capital punishment had lower homicide rates.[14]

Gleason Archer, dean of Suffolk Law School, spoke bluntly for proponents of the death penalty. Without the death penalty, Archer contended, the "criminal element" will seize control of society. To support this frightening assertion, he cited the general chaos—though there were no reported homicides—accompanying the 1919 Boston police strike. Life imprisonment is not an acceptable alternative, he said, because imprisonment does not crush the killer's spirit. "Lifers are rosy with the hope" they might be paroled or pardoned, Archer claimed. They also are likely to escape and become "beasts of prey" again. Executing a murderer rids the world of a "human mad-dog," Archer told the legislators. The Judiciary Committee rejected Goodwin's abolition bill 11 to 5, a margin that remained unchanged for the next decade.[15]

In addition to articulating the arguments against capital punishment, Ehrmann focused on a controversial murder case, the first in a long string of accused and convicted murderers she sought to save from death. The case against Gangi Cero seemed slight, but before justice had run its course, Cero was tried twice for murder and came within a few hours of being executed for a crime he did not commit. For many years afterward, Ehrmann would cite the Cero case as evidence that the criminal justice system was flawed and, therefore, that capital punishment should be abolished lest the wrong person be executed by the state.[16]

On June 11, 1927, Joseph Fantasia was shot in the back at close range as he walked along a crowded street in Boston's North End. Guided by two eyewitnesses, the police arrested Cero, a Brooklyn, New York, native who six weeks earlier had moved to Boston to work for Samuel Gallo, a clothing salesman. At trial, an eyewitness testified that he saw Cero drop "something" as he ran from the murder scene. Another witness stated that he saw an unidentified man fire the fatal shot, toss away the revolver, and slowly walk away from the chaotic scene. Under oath Cero denied that he had murdered Fantasia and claimed that he accidentally had dropped nothing more sinister than his hat as he pushed his way through the panic-stricken crowd. Despite Cero's statement and other contradictory evidence, the jury found Cero guilty of first-degree murder on November 17, 1927. Judge Louis S. Cox denied three defense motions for a new trial. Cero appealed the rulings.[17]

William R. Scharton, one of the best criminal lawyers in Boston, represented Cero before the SJC. In the spring of 1928, Scharton argued, as he had before trial began, that the entire jury empanelled to hear Cero's case was tainted because police officers had interviewed potential jurors listed for the November 1927 sitting of the criminal court and forwarded the results to the Suffolk County district attorney. At trial, Judge Cox had refused to allow Cero to ask each potential juror whether the police had questioned him or his family members. The judge ruled that potential jurors were to be asked only the statutory questions during voir dire. Was the juror related to the prisoner or to the deceased? Did the potential juror have any interest in the case? Was he conscious of any bias about the case? Did the potential juror hold an opinion that would preclude him from finding the defendant guilty of an offense punishable by death if the evidence satisfied him beyond a reasonable doubt? [18]

Judge Edward P. Pierce, who had been appointed to the SJC in 1914, spoke for a unanimous court in rejecting the defendant's appeal for a more far-ranging round of questions during voir dire. "There is not a word, not a phrase, in the statement of counsel for the defendant, which, if proved, would have the slightest evidential value in establishing that the list of jurors was not prepared according to law or that the jurors were not legally drawn," Pierce gruffly wrote, missing the point. Judge Cox was not obligated to permit the defense to ask potential jurors questions, despite an 1887 statute designed to open that possibility. The statute provided that examination "may be made by the parties or their attorneys under the direction of the court." In *Commonwealth v. Poisson*, however, Justice Oliver Wendell Holmes Jr. held that the statute did not mean what it seemed to mean. The trial judge still had discretionary power over the voir dire proceeding, Holmes argued, "and it is exercised wisely by not going beyond the usual questions." Applying this precedent, Judge Pierce found that the trial court had acted properly in prohibiting the defense from asking potential jurors about their interrogation by police and, therefore, "no legal harm had resulted." Further, Pierce found that the police questionnaire potential jurors were required to complete was benign. Potential jurors and their family members were asked about their "life style," their "politics," their "affiliations," and if they were related to any "former Boston officer" who had abandoned his duty during the 1919 police strike, among other questions. But, because the questionnaire "was prepared for general use and was not directed to the case at bar," Pierce was "unable to see how such an investigation, properly conducted, can be interpreted, as the defendant contends, to be an 'attempt to influence the jurors in favor of the Commonwealth.'" Cero's jury was impartial and indifferent, Pierce concluded.[19]

Having brushed aside the constitutional questions Cero raised, Pierce also upheld Judge Cox's denial of the defendant's motion for a new trial on the basis of newly discovered evidence. Specifically, the SJC ruled that Cox was not obligated to hear evidence that another person had murdered Fantasia. Following the SJC's ruling, Judge Cox sentenced Cero to be executed during the week of November 4, 1928. Cero was moved into a death row cell at Charlestown prison.[20]

About a month before Cero's scheduled execution, Samuel Gallo, Cero's former employer, was arrested and charged with contempt of court for offering a bribe to a crucial government witness if he would change his testimony about Cero. Gallo was found guilty and sentenced to two years at Charlestown, the prison in which Cero was being held. Gallo befriended Cero, providing him with money, cigarettes, and food. But on Columbus Day 1928, Cero attempted to murder Gallo, plunging a kitchen knife into his chest as the two men walked in the prison exercise yard. After his violent act, Cero told prison authorities that if he was to die for murder then so too should Gallo, but Cero stopped short of accusing Gallo of committing the murder and of proclaiming his own innocence.[21]

But as his execution day drew closer, Cero had second thoughts about maintaining his silence. Just two days before his scheduled execution, his older brother Cosimo arrived at Charlestown prison from New York. After several hours of emotional conversation, Cosimo pried from his brother the names of several people who could save him. Cosimo bolted from the prison and ran through Boston's North End shouting, "Help me! Help me!" On the second day of his search, just nine hours before Cero was to be executed, Cosimo was introduced to Philomina Romano, a young woman who said she saw Gallo fire the shot that killed Fantasia. Cosimo grabbed Romano's hand and the two rushed through the North End's crowded streets to the Massachusetts statehouse, where Governor Alvan T. Fuller sat in vigil, as he did prior to all executions. After hearing Romano's story shifting guilt from Cero to Gallo, the governor brought Judge Cox into the discussion. In addition to repeating her eyewitness account, Romano added details that supplied the missing motive for Fantasia's murder. She had been Gallo's mistress until she fell in love with Fantasia. To show his scorn for Gallo, Fantasia ordered Romano to slash Gallo's cheeks as he stood on a North End street corner. It now seemed possible that Gallo murdered Fantasia to revenge the humiliation he had suffered at the hand of Fantasia. Fuller and Cox agreed that Cero's execution must be stopped. A murder indictment was returned against Gallo.[22]

At this point the MCADP became directly involved in Cero's defense. The group raised money to provide Cero with additional legal help and an investigator to aid in building a case against Gallo. The investigator's first job was to find Philomina Romano, who, since Gallo's arrest, had repudiated her statement exonerating Cero and then disappeared. At trial, Romano—who was found a few days before trial and held in Charles Street jail—and Cero testified that Gallo murdered Fantasia. Gallo denounced Cero and Romano as liars and claimed he was in East Boston at the time of the murder. Following Judge Cox's instructions, the jury was ushered out of the courtroom at about six o'clock in the evening. While the jury deliberated, Gallo anxiously paced the detention room above their heads. Just before 1:00 A.M. the jury came back into the courtroom to announce that it had found Gallo guilty of murder in the first-degree.[23]

This bizarre finding meant two men, each alone and independently of the other, were charged with the murder of the same man by separate indictments found at different times, and each had been separately convicted and sentenced to death. Arguing that this was untenable and unconscionable, counsel for Cero explored the possibility of a gubernatorial pardon and then filed a motion with Judge Cox, who had presided over both trials, to dismiss the guilty verdict against Cero. At the motions' hearing late in March 1929, Ehrmann served as the MCADP's eyes and ears. She felt Judge Cox was "exceedingly hostile" toward Cero and that he did not believe in Cero's innocence. In the witness box, Cero explained that he had initially not named Gallo as the murderer because, "I don't want to be a stool pigeon." When asked by Judge Cox to define the term, Cero said, "one who tells on another." Whether this statement convinced Cox or not, he did set aside both guilty verdicts and ordered a new trial for Cero and Gallo.[24]

While Cero's attorneys prepared for a fall trial date, Ehrmann and Zechariah Chafee worked behind the scenes to have the district attorney drop the charge against Cero. In the summer of 1930, for example, Ehrmann went to see Frank Brooks, chairman of the Parole Board and a friend of Suffolk County assistant district attorney F. M. Sheehan, to urge Brooks to intervene with Sheehan on Cero's behalf. But Brooks refused, telling Ehrmann there was good reason—though no concrete evidence—to believe that Cero and Gallo were accomplices in the murder of Fantasia. Dismayed, Ehrmann turned her attention to Cero, who once again had been moved to death row. In the month before the trial Ehrmann visited Cero two or three times a week.[25]

In the fall of 1930, Cero and Gallo were tried together on the original separate murder indictments. This curious decision by the prosecution was one of several unusual procedures that distinguished their trial. The commonwealth insisted that both men were guilty as charged, arguing that each man acted independently to produce a single criminal result, the murder of Fantasia. At the same time, the state relied on Cero's testimony—"a murderer and a confessed perjurer," as Gallo's defense counsel put it—to convict Gallo but failed to extract an accusation against Cero from Gallo, because the latter insisted that he was elsewhere at the time of the murder. Another handicap with which Assistant District Attorney Sheehan struggled was the disappearance—again—of his star witness, Philomina Romano. In the absence of the mystery woman, Sheehan read from the transcript of her testimony at Cero's second trial in which she accused Gallo of the murder of her lover. Given these obstacles, the Boston press saw it as a foregone conclusion that Sheehan would fail to convict both Cero and Gallo and bring this "strange murder case" to a conclusion. The MCADP was especially critical of Sheehan's closing statement. Cero's defense attorney, Thomas Bresnahan, for example, claimed that Sheehan too often used language intended to prove conspiracy or joint motive rather than adhering to argument designed to show that each man acted separately to effect the murder of Fantasia. Somehow the jury sorted out the facts despite this confusing procedure, acquitting Cero and finding Gallo guilty of first-degree murder.[26]

Cero returned to Italy a free man and Gallo appealed his conviction to the SJC. In the spring of 1931 Gallo argued that the trial court had erred in denying his two motions for a new trial. Gallo contended that the trial court's rejection of his motion for a separate trial violated his right to due process guaranteed by Article 12 of the Massachusetts Declaration of Rights and the Fourteenth Amendment of the U.S. Constitution. Furthermore, Gallo argued, his right to "to meet the witnesses against him face to face" was violated because when Romano could not be found the court allowed the district attorney to read from Romano's damning testimony given against him at a previous trial.[27]

Writing for a unanimous court, Chief Justice Rugg rejected Gallo's bid for a new trial. In doing so he revealed much about how the SJC thought about criminal procedure generally and specifically about the relationship between due process and justice. Rugg's formalist approach emphasized *stare decisis* and the discovery of underlying legal principles. He routinely deferred to the trial judge's discretionary powers and rejected defense arguments he found contrary to "our system of criminal procedure as disclosed in the decisions of this court." He paid lip service to social and political change, but he supported without question traditional law enforcement techniques and rules of evidence that placed a criminal defendant at a severe disadvantage. As he saw it, contemporary government's formal commitment to safeguarding the rights of a criminal defendant had rendered meaningless the "traditional tenderness for persons accused of crime," a sentiment with roots in arbitrary government. For this reason, he saw little reason to explore the relationship between procedural and substantive rights. All of these views were present in Rugg's *Gallo* decision.[28]

Gallo objected to being tried with Cero, and before the SJC, he demanded the right to be tried alone. He argued quite reasonably that there was an enormous temptation for co-defendant Cero to perjure himself by testifying that Gallo was the sole perpetrator of the murder for which both men were tried. Rugg cast Gallo's argument for a separate trial as old fashioned and not a procedural right to which the defendant had a legitimate constitutional claim. "The tendency in recent years," he wrote in April 1931 of judicial decision-making, "has been away from formalities in the conduct of criminal trials." To substantiate that generalization Rugg pointed to the simplification of criminal indictments, a reform enacted by Massachusetts in 1876. For Rugg, Gallo's argument about due process was nothing but a quibble harking back to a rigid system of common law rules. Therefore, the prosecution's decision to try both men at the same time on separate indictments and the trial judge's compliance with this procedure did not violate basic fairness or a substantial right. Rugg closed this issue by articulating a general rule: a criminal defendant has no "vested rights in matters merely procedural, bearing no vital connection with a real defense." In short, although the procedural system might be seriously flawed, the court would not consider a challenge legitimate unless a capital defendant was able to show that a specific and egregious violation of due process had led directly to an erroneous finding of guilty.[29]

Gallo's second major argument for a new trial centered on the oft-disappearing Romano. Gallo argued that allowing a transcript of Romano's testimony from a previous trial to be read to the jury in her absence at his second trial violated his right "to meet the witnesses against him face to face." Rugg acknowledged that Article 12 of the Massachusetts Declaration of Rights states a "general principle of government for the security of liberty and the ascertainment of truth in prosecutions for crime," but, he argued, a constitutional guarantee carries with it "well-recognized common law exceptions." The common law rule about testimony "is that its credibility shall be tested by cross-examination." That rule was followed in Gallo's first trial when Romano was present and testified. Although the defense argued that new issues and questions were raised at Gallo's second trial to which the transcript of Romano's earlier testimony did not speak, Rugg brushed that contention aside. "The indictment was the same. The plea was the same," he snapped. Gallo's conviction was affirmed and he was sentenced to death.[30]

Rugg's long tenure on the SJC ended just as the U.S. Supreme Court began to take a more expansive view of the relationship between the Bill of Rights and criminal procedure, and he cannot be faulted for not embracing that doctrine in the 1920s and 1930s. But it is also true that Rugg never publicly worried about executing an innocent person or found that the police had abused their power or that a defendant's confession had been anything other than voluntary and admissible. As Rugg made clear in *Gallo*, his general presumption was that the legal principles discovered and applied by modern courts had ended any threat to criminal defendants from an arbitrary and powerful government.[31]

Although Ehrmann and the MCADP had helped shift the blame for Fantasia's murder from Cero to Gallo, as soon as the latter was sentenced to death Ehrmann successfully lobbied Governor Joseph Ely to commute Gallo's sentence to life imprisonment. Flush with their first victories, the MCADP held a celebratory public meeting at Boston's Ford Hall. Although all of the speeches given that night were upbeat, the ambivalence built into the MCADP's legal-political strategy was evident. Cero's attorneys praised the justice system for ultimately exonerating their client, but

Ehrmann highlighted the flaws inherent in a system that had brought Cero within a few hours of being wrongfully executed. "Have there been others not so fortunate as Cero Gangi?" she asked. "Who can say? This case seemed in no respect unusual until the appearance of the Romano girl." In a follow-up pamphlet intended for state legislators, Ehrmann emphasized the system's fallibility: "It should be clearly understood that the last minute affidavit which stayed the execution was secured through no effort of the government nor of Cero's attorneys. The evidence was obtained by Cosimo Gangi." Her point was plain. It was not the legal system but investigative work and intervention by a rank amateur that saved Cero's life.[32]

The MCADP's approach to achieving the abolition of capital punishment evident at the Cero victory party guided the group throughout the 1930s and 1940s. Ehrmann worked to win passage of a law abolishing or weakening capital punishment while Chafee sought to change criminal procedure by providing a greater degree of legal protection for a capital defendant. Each year, carrying an armload of pamphlets and data meant to answer all questions about abolition, Ehrmann personally lobbied everyone from rank-and-file members of the legislature to the governor, while Chafee worked behind the scenes to influence members of the Massachusetts bar. Ehrmann rarely antagonized someone with whom she disagreed. Still, the work was filled with difficulties over which she and her colleagues had no control. Ehrmann and Chafee contended with widespread public support for capital punishment, an opinion often hardened by a brutal murder or a sensational trial. Often, too, their single issue was swept aside by national and world events, including the Great Depression, Prohibition, crime waves, and World War II, that dominated the legislature's agenda. Early in 1941, for example, a friendly legislator told Ehrmann that she should "transfer her drive and energy to one of the organizations providing aid for Great Britain," and, near the war's conclusion, some MCADP members criticized Ehrmann for continuing to advocate abolition when Nazi war criminals were to be executed. The Rosenbergs' executions were also divisive within the organization. Without regard to any or all of these obstacles and opinions Ehrmann doggedly pursued the goal of abolition.[33]

In the spring of 1934 while Ehrmann prepared MCADP testimony to support Governor Ely's modest proposal to limit capital punishment to first-degree, rationally premeditated murder, several murders committed in the course of a series of robberies seized the public's attention. In De-

cember 1933 an employee of a Fitchburg sporting goods store was murdered during a botched hold-up and on January 2, 1934, two armed men
shot and killed a Lynn movie theater worker and fled with about $200.
During a bank robbery in Needham a month later a man wielding a machine gun murdered a police officer and a firefighter. Three days after
the Lynn robbery-murder two Boston cab drivers, Clement Molway and
Louis Berrett, were arrested and charged with the murder. At trial, eight
eyewitnesses identified the two men as the assailants. Each defendant took
the witness stand on his own behalf. Berrett insisted he spent the morning
of the crime aimlessly looking for his business partner, and Molway told
the jury he cruised around Boston looking for fares without success. Essex
County district attorney Hugh A. Cregg sharply cross-examined the two
defendants, exposing holes and inconsistencies in their alibis. After two
weeks of trial, a juror later reported, it seemed likely the two men were
going to be found guilty. But, on February 27, in a special evening session
at the old Salem courthouse a "tired looking" Cregg asked Judge Thomas
F. Hammond to allow the evidence against the two men to be reviewed.
"Shamefacedly, but manfully," the eight eyewitnesses then acknowledged,
one by one, they had been mistaken when they identified Molway and
Berrett as the men who murdered their co-worker. Calling it an "act of
Providence," Cregg apologized to Molway and Barrett and Judge Hammond set them free. Cregg explained to the jury that the three men apprehended for the Needham bank robbery also had confessed to two other
crimes, including the murder committed at the Lynn movie theater.[34]

The *Christian Science Monitor* called the defendants' last-minute reversal of fortune a "dramatic victory for justice" and Ehrmann worked the
case into her presentation to the Judiciary Committee. She emphasized
how close Molway and Berrett had come to being wrongfully convicted
and sentenced to death. But, in the immediate aftermath of the Needham
bank robbery and murder, Ehrmann's argument against capital punishment lost much of its power.[35]

In addition to emphasizing the possibility of a fatal mistake, Ehrmann
eagerly enlisted leading Massachusetts politicians in the campaign to abolish capital punishment. It was a strategy filled with disappointments. Early
in her tenure as executive secretary she was surprised and delighted, for
example, when Boston's four-term mayor, the legendary James Michael
Curley, accepted an invitation to serve as vice-chairman of the MCADP.

But every time Ehrmann asked him to speak in favor of abolition Curley danced away. He was unable to testify before the Judiciary Committee in February 1929 because he would be "out of town." He begged off addressing the Lowell Kiwanis Club because of a "previous engagement." In May 1929 "Mrs. Curley's illness" made it impossible for him to attend the annual meeting of MCADP. Finally, Ehrmann sent a tersely written letter to Curley. "Enclosed please find a membership blank which you may return with your check" if you wish to remain in MCADP. Ehrmann eventually received a letter instructing her to remove Curley's name from the masthead of the organization. Six years later, during Curley's one term as Massachusetts governor, he signed death warrants for four men, including the Needham gang.[36]

State representative Christian Herter, a young Beacon Hill Republican who came to Massachusetts from New York in 1927 when he married Mary Pratt, an heir to the Standard Oil fortune, was a staunch, if moderate, ally of Ehrmann's. In 1932 Herter volunteered to steer MCADP's mercy bill through the House. The mercy law allowed a jury to make a binding recommendation to the court that a defendant found guilty of first-degree murder be sentenced to life imprisonment rather than to death. Allowing juries to decide on a sentence other than death for first-degree murder signaled a weakening of jurors' commitment to the death penalty. Beginning in 1867, when Illinois empowered juries to decide whether life or death was the appropriate sentence, state after state eliminated the mandatory death penalty. Herter's freshman status and the nationwide furor over the Lindbergh kidnapping caused the Massachusetts mercy bill to go down to defeat. He felt responsible for the loss and he apologized to Ehrmann. "You must feel I have been a very weak reed to lean on. I feel I mishandled things badly," he wrote. Ehrmann was touched by his apology, but she would have none of it. The bill's defeat, she wrote, was due to "deep seated prejudice and ignorance" and politicians' "fear of being recorded on a controversial measure." Next time, she promised, we will be better organized. Herter and Ehrmann continued to talk amicably and to work together constructively during the next two decades as Herter moved up the political ladder. For this reason, perhaps, when Herter became governor (1952–56) he refused to sign death warrants for convicted murders for which a jury did not recommend life imprisonment as the mercy law allowed.[37]

Governor Joseph B. Ely and Ehrmann became friends and political allies at the same time Herter entered the Massachusetts House. Ely was a Yankee Democrat from Hampden County, where he built a lucrative legal practice ("What's the matter with being a high-priced lawyer?" he asked during the campaign) and served as district attorney before he was elected governor in 1930. Using speeches written by Ehrmann, Governor Ely introduced bills to study the usefulness of capital punishment and to exempt from first-degree murder charges men and women who were "blinded by sudden passion" when they murdered. Capital punishment did not deter emotional murderers or hardened criminals, Ely told the legislature. He cited the example of the convicted murderer Joseph Belanski, who when sentenced to death said, "What of it," adding, "electricity isn't such a bad way to die." The governor also used statistics to make his point. From 1920 to 1930 there were 91 murders in Suffolk County, for which 122 defendants were indicted. But only 2 men were electrocuted. The conclusion was obvious: Capital punishment "leads to bargaining with guilty men." Despite Ehrmann's powerful data and the governor's persuasive speech, the legislature looked askance at both bills. In part, legislators were eager to distance themselves from the governor's widely criticized use of the pardoning power. The *Boston Herald*, for example, pointed out that in three years the governor had issued an unprecedented 127 pardons, including 12 for men convicted of first-degree murder. "The penologists, not the people are getting the benefit of the doubt," the *Herald* fumed. Ely chose not to run for reelection in 1934.[38]

James Michael Curley and Charles Hurley held the governorship for single terms before Leverett Saltonstall, a Republican patrician with a "South Boston face," occupied the governor's corner office for three terms from 1939 to 1944. Saltonstall seemed open to Ehrmann's arguments for enacting a mercy law. As early as 1933, during his tenth term in the Massachusetts House, Saltonstall suggested that his views regarding capital punishment were changing and he promised Ehrmann he would support a death penalty study. Another promising sign occurred during the 1935 House debate on a mercy bill; Saltonstall left the Speaker's chair, freeing his Republican colleagues to vote as their consciences dictated. When he took office as governor in 1939, one of the first meetings he held was with a Chafee-led lawyers' committee lobbying for a mercy bill.[39]

Although Governor Saltonstall hesitated to endorse the mercy bill, he signed a bill expanding the SJC's appellate duties in capital cases. The bill had been in the making for twelve years. In the aftermath of the Sacco-Vanzetti case, the advisory Judicial Council began the drum beat against allowing a single trial judge to pass on "mixed questions of law and fact arising from motions for a new trial." Because such questions often involved matters of life and death, "we think the responsibility too great to be thrown upon one man," the councilors argued. Even if the trial judge was correct, there is no tribunal to establish the fact that he was right. "It is vital that our Courts do justice," the council's report concluded in 1927; "it is also vital that people know that they do justice." Initially, only a handful of legislators dared take up the council's recommendation with its implicit criticism of Judge Webster Thayer and the SJC's handling of the Sacco-Vanzetti case. But, in 1939, following Thayer's death and Chief Justice Rugg's retirement, the legislature required the court to consider the whole case and not just the questions of law raised.[40]

A few months later Saltonstall confronted the grim reality of putting someone to death. He rejected a petition to commute the death sentences of two young men convicted of the murder of a Somerville shopkeeper from whom they took $3.50. Wallace W. Green, age twenty-one, and Walter St. Sauveur, age nineteen, were originally scheduled to be electrocuted in May 1939, but the state's official executioner reported that the chair was not functional and the needed repairs took four months to complete. On August 1, Governor Saltonstall rejected a plea for clemency, stating that there were "no mitigating circumstances presented to me sufficient to alter the operation of the statutes of the Commonwealth as expressed through the jury's findings of fact and the court's ruling of law." With that formulaic pronouncement, the state of Massachusetts set in motion the machinery of death. The two men were moved into separate death cells at Charlestown State Prison, where they received religious counseling and consumed "hearty last meals." At one minute after midnight Green was handcuffed between two guards and led from his cell to the execution chamber singing the hymn "Jesus Saves." Five shocks of electricity surged through Green's body. The electrodes on his body were removed and replaced three times and twenty minutes passed before Green was pronounced dead at 12:23. St. Sauveur followed. Rev. Ralph Farrell heard St. Sauveur's confession before the condemned man was strapped into the chair. Three shocks of electricity, the first of eighteen hundred volts, the second of fifteen hundred volts, and the third of twenty-one hundred volts surged through St. Sauveur's body. After fifteen minutes he was pronounced dead. The prolonged agony to which the men were subjected caused the official witnesses to writhe and the chaplains to flee the room. In the grim aftermath angry officials and editorials condemned the "hideous bungling" of the executions and called for an end to the barbarous use of capital punishment.[41]

Publicly Ehrmann said nothing specific about the brutal executions. As usual, she prepared carefully for the next legislative session, firmly believing she had Saltonstall's support for death penalty reform. During his campaign for a second term as governor, Saltonstall told Ehrmann that capital punishment was a matter for the people's representatives. "If I am [re-elected] Governor and a [mercy] bill reaches my desk," he told her, "I shall expect to approve it." She reminded him of his pledge the following year, but, like many other measures, the mercy bill was sidetracked by the outbreak of war in Europe. In the winter of 1943, however, Ehrmann's intense effort seemed likely to pay off. Governor Saltonstall sent a mercy bill to the legislature. Ehrmann followed up with a "Dear Senator" letter sent to every member of the upper chamber in which several former district attorneys called the governor's proposal "a very moderate and reasonable one." She prodded to action a long and eclectic list of supporters. She asked Charles Sprague, a Lynn box manufacturer and member of the Republican State Committee, to write to Republicans on the Judiciary Committee, and she urged a cluster of Boston lawyers sympathetic to the cause to write key Democrats. Ehrmann also organized a parade of witnesses to speak in favor of the bill before the Judiciary Committee. Initially, it looked as if there would be smooth sailing, but the Judiciary Committee divided over whether the mercy bill should allow jurors or the judge to make the sentencing decision. Late in May, Ehrmann wrote Governor Saltonstall urging him to intervene. The "Senate situation is serious," she said. Although senators on the Judiciary Committee have been told the governor favored a bill, "the ones to whom I have spoken are under the impression that you don't really care if the Bill is defeated." This rumor encourages the opponents of change. "Only word from you will save the Bill," she wrote following a "stormy session." The governor said nothing, but a bill permitting a trial judge to sentence a capital defendant found guilty of first-degree murder to life imprisonment squeaked through the

Senate and passed the House by a vote of 113 to 94. Ehrmann and the MCADP stood on the threshold of success. But Saltonstall unexpectedly and without explanation decided not to sign the bill into law, using a pocket veto to kill it. It seems likely that his cautious support for liberal ideas generally, two narrow electoral victories and his hope to be elected to the U.S. Senate caused Saltonstall to back away from the controversial bill. Ehrmann felt betrayed.[42]

As promising but ultimately deeply disappointing as her relationship was with Saltonstall, Ehrmann knew from the outset that Republican governor Robert Bradford would not be likely to embrace any part of abolition. Their relationship began during his 1940 campaign for Middlesex County district attorney. Bradford had remarked that too many juries failed to convict a capital defendant simply because they did not want to be responsible for executing a fellow human being. Ehrmann jumped on Bradford's comment and asked whether he would be willing to speak at the MCADP's 1941 meeting. Without making clear his views on the death penalty, Bradford politely begged off, leaving Ehrmann to believe he was "definitely interested." She next asked whether he would testify in favor of abolition before the Judiciary Committee. Bradford replied that there had been "some misunderstanding." He believed "it would be unwise and unnecessary to remove the death penalty." In fact, just a few months after his exchange with Ehrmann, District Attorney Bradford successfully prosecuted two young men for a murder committed during a gas station hold-up. According to defense attorney Henry Avery, the trial judge agreed to a plea bargain that would have permitted James Nickerson, age twenty, and Paul Giacomazza, age seventeen, neither of whom had a prior criminal record, to plead guilty to second-degree murder. Bradford insisted on first-degree murder and the death penalty. The two youths were convicted, sentenced to death, and executed on June 30, 1942. Giacomazza was the first person in the history of the commonwealth under the age of eighteen to be executed for murder.[43]

Despite Bradford's rebuff to her overtures and his string of capital convictions as district attorney, Ehrmann clung to the hope that Governor Bradford would sign into law a mercy bill passed by the Massachusetts legislature in 1948. The bill allowed a jury finding a defendant guilty of first-degree murder to submit to the court a written statement outlining its reasons for recommending the defendant be sentenced to life imprisonment. Bradford did not respond directly to Ehrmann, but on April 26, 1948—oddly enough on the very day the U.S. Supreme Court validated an 1897 federal law allowing a jury to find a defendant guilty of first-degree murder but qualify the verdict by adding "without capital punishment"— he vetoed the bill. While Bradford acknowledged that "the idea of punishment by death is abhorrent," he insisted that "all the veneer of civilization had not lessened the savagery, brutality, or frequency of murder" and, therefore, of the need for capital punishment. The existing law, he said, divides responsibility, giving to the jury the task of determining the defendant's guilt or innocence and to the judge the burden of sentencing the convicted. By requiring a jury to determine both a defendant's guilt or innocence and an appropriate sentence, the mercy bill would "fasten in the jury a far greater share of the total responsibility." Bradford was unhappy with the bill's form but also fearful of its outcomes. Because the probability of "mitigating circumstances" was high, Bradford believed no jury would support a death sentence. In short, the mercy bill would end the "deterrent effect of the death penalty" and, he predicted, the number of murders would climb. The mercy bill, the governor concluded, "pays lip-service" to capital punishment, but "effectively destroys it by providing that the penalty should be imposed not by law, but by a jury of twelve men groping in the dark to agree on a reason for choosing between life and death." [44]

Reaction to Bradford's veto of the mercy bill varied. The *New Bedford Standard Times* cheered the governor's action, adding that Massachusetts should be proud to be one of only five states that did not provide for some kind of alternative capital sentencing. We should not be influenced by "what some other countries or States have done." This was the kind of reasoning Harvard Law School dean Erwin Griswold found "unfortunate and indicative of the provincialism associated with New England." Alexander Forbes told Ehrmann he agreed with much of Bradford's legal argument but still felt that the "death penalty is archaic and barbarous." Forbes questioned MCADP's strategy and urged Ehrmann to work for outright abolition. The *Boston Evening American* and the *Boston Herald* condemned Bradford's veto. "In his ill-becoming role of defender of legalized killing," the *Evening American* editorialized, "Mr. Bradford rejects the lessons of history which prove beyond any reasonable doubt that the death penalty does not prevent acts of violence, but is more apt to prompt them." The *Herald* added that the governor's frightening presumption about a link between the death penalty and rising violent crime rates might well be unfounded. Crime rates "may not bear any relation to the severity of the legal penalty." For her part, Ehrmann wrote, "At this moment I am very tired and cannot think of the next step."[45]

In the fall of 1948, however, she plunged back into the battle, organizing "Independent Democrats for Dever," writing a League of Women Voters pamphlet that explained the upcoming referendum issues, and helping to save Miriam Van Waters's job as superintendent of the Massachusetts Reformatory for Women. Democrat Paul Dever's November gubernatorial victory marked a watershed in Massachusetts politics and tilted the balance in the abolitionists' favor. On the campaign trail Dever loudly promised jobs for veterans and a massive road-building program. He whispered to liberals that he opposed capital punishment and that he would sign into law a mercy bill. To complement Dever's victory, a "fighting fund" directed by Thomas "Tip" O'Neill helped the Democrats take control of the House for the first time since before the Civil War. The Democrats also won half the State Senate seats and swept all the statewide offices. The *Boston Herald* celebrated the Democratic victories by predicting that the abolition of capital punishment was not far off.[46]

Just as Ehrmann began to prepare for the MCADP's annual campaign to abolish capital punishment, her long-time ally Van Waters came under attack for her management of the Women's Reformatory. The commissioner of corrections, who had been appointed by former governor Bradford, ousted Van Waters from the superintendency, a position she had held for seventeen years. The commissioner charged Van Waters illegally allowed women prisoners to work outside the facility and, more explosively, that she permitted homosexuality to flourish inside the prison. Although the commissioner never publicly accused Van Waters of homosexuality, his aggressive investigation into her private life helped fuel the rumor that "something queer was going on." Ehrmann immediately came to Van Waters's aid, helping to organize the Friends of the Framingham Reformatory, lobbying legislators, and encouraging positive stories about Van Waters. A national newsmagazine, for example, praised Van Waters for her dedicated work at the prison and argued that her progressive political and professional views were the real story behind her firing. By March 1949 a host of volunteers, including Eleanor Roosevelt, succeeded in restoring Van Waters to her position. But that victory cost Ehrmann dearly.[47]

The mercy bill everyone thought certain to pass was swamped in the wake of the Van Waters affair. Scurrilous rumors and innuendoes circulated that abolitionists were the "same crowd" who came to Van Waters's defense. The *Herald* columnist "Billy" Mullins acknowledged the damaging link, but he attributed the defeat of the 1949 mercy bill to the "fundamentalist" opposition by the Judiciary Committee chairman, state senator John Mackay, to "any tampering with the law," and to an "atrocious murder" that caused two Bristol County senators to become "embittered against any relaxation of the capital punishment law." As a result, a mercy bill passed in the House but lost by a single vote in the Senate.[48]

Neither the Senate defeat nor the political risk of opposing capital punishment shook Governor Dever's commitment to abolitionism, however. Although he once stated publicly that he favored use of the death penalty under certain circumstances, during his two terms in office Dever commuted to life imprisonment the death sentence of every convicted murderer. Among others, Dever acted to save the life of Frederick Pike, a nineteen-year-old Charlestown youth sentenced to death for the murder of another boy during a robbery in the Bolton home of a man who previously had befriended Pike. The governor commuted to life imprisonment the death sentence of Joseph Galvin, a mentally troubled Dorchester man who beat to death a forty-one-year-old Dorchester woman from whom he stole a handbag and then fled to a New York mental institution. At Ehrmann's urging, Governor Dever also commuted the death sentence of Edward Lee, an African American railway cook convicted of murdering a Roxbury pawnbroker. Ehrmann gathered information clearly showing Lee's court-appointed counsel as exploitative and unprepared. Because of their obvious mitigating factors, Pike, Galvin, and Lee were relatively easy decisions for the governor and the Council. But Dever also commuted to life imprisonment the death sentences of Charles McNeill, convicted of the roadside shooting death of an insurance salesman, and two men convicted of sexually assaulting and murdering girls of ages seven and eight years.[49]

Dever's actions drew praise and sharp criticism from the press, but neither friend nor foe correctly gauged his commitment to abolition. "Billy" Mullins cheered Dever's fairness and commitment to due process. The governor recognized that Pike's youth and troubled upbringing cried out for mercy and that inadequate court-appointed attorneys placed poor capital defendants at a severe disadvantage. Other newspapers contended, however, that regardless of the mitigating circumstances Dever had no right to "thwart the wishes of the courts, the legislature and the people, no one of whom has ever indicated a desire to eliminate capital punishment." It's true, the *Boston Herald* admitted, that Dever was "nullifying the capital punishment law instead of seeking its repeal" but, with its eye on the electoral prize for which Dever had announced, the paper contended that the governor's actions were not likely to become a campaign liability because many Republicans and independents silently supported the governor. In fact, neither an abstract commitment to due process nor a political calculus fully explains Dever's motivation. Sitting on a park bench with the *Boston Traveler* columnist Clem Norton, Dever revealed his deep personal feelings about the death penalty. "I question whether I or any human has the power to take a life. If I let a person die, I could see his mother crying at the grave, hear the clods of earth as they were shoveled onto the coffin. I woke up a couple of times at night in a sweat when I felt that I had to let a man die, but I am glad that I never did."[50]

Dever's commitment to abolition opened the way to passage of the mercy law in 1951. "Success—At Long Last!" Ehrmann proclaimed when the bill breezed through the Democratic House and the Republican-controlled Senate and was signed by Governor Dever April 3. 1951. With the exception of murder committed in the course of a rape or an attempt to commit rape, the new Massachusetts law stipulated that whoever is found guilty of murder in the first degree "shall suffer the punishment of death, unless the jury shall by their verdict, and as a part thereof, upon and after consideration of all the evidence, recommend that the sentence of death be not imposed," in which case the person shall be sentenced to life imprisonment without the possibility of parole.[51]

Ehrmann publicly praised the "clear thinking and sense of justice" the majority of legislators had shown and Governor Dever's "enlightened understanding and human sympathy." Although some abolitionists believed the law eliminated capital punishment de facto, Ehrmann quickly put the victory into perspective. The statute rid the state of an "archaic mandatory law," and brought Massachusetts into conformity with the vast majority of other states. The mercy law was a step toward abolition. Therefore, against the advice of some MCADP members who counseled "a considerable interlude" before mounting an abolition effort, Ehrmann immediately launched a campaign to end capital punishment in Massachusetts.[52]

TWELVE

THE ABOLITION OF
THE DEATH PENALTY

During the fifteen years following passage of the mercy bill, Sara Ehrmann fought to win abolition of the death penalty chiefly using the same tactics that had led to the successful passage of alternate sentencing. Generally speaking, the political-social landscape she and abolitionists confronted after 1951 was markedly different from that of the first half of the century. Fewer and fewer people were put to death, especially in the northern states, and by 1966 the number of people supporting the death penalty had fallen to 42 percent, a record low. In Massachusetts, from 1948 to 1972, an unbroken string of governors chose not to sign any death warrants. This trend was bolstered by the transformation of criminal due process—fair and reasonable rules consistently applied—beginning in the 1960s.

Before the Warren Court set in motion revolutionary changes, the Supreme Court had shied away from applying the Bill of Rights to state criminal procedure. Therefore, few Americans thought that a state's death penalty laws might be affected by the Eighth Amendment's prohibition against "cruel and unusual punishment." The Eighth Amendment, like the rest of the Bill of Rights, was understood to restrict only the federal government and then only to block torture or some other barbarous means of inflicting a lingering death. This being said, the Court did take a few tentative steps toward redefining the Eighth Amendment before its landmark decision finding capital punishment unconstitutionally cruel and unusual in *Furman v. Georgia* (1972).[1]

Between 1910 and 1972 the Court heard four cases that pointed the way to *Furman*, as well as to the SJC's abolition of capital punishment. The first case in which the Court changed its interpretation of the Eighth Amendment involved a minor U.S. official working in the Philippines convicted in 1910 of falsifying a customs record. American control of the Philippines gave the Court the opportunity to define the relationship between the Bill of Rights and local legislative authority. Officer Paul A. Weems was sentenced to fifteen years at hard labor while shackled and the permanent loss of his civil rights. A majority of the Court held the sentence violated the Eighth Amendment because it was disproportionate to the crime. What is cruel and unusual, Justice Joseph McKenna wrote, should be determined by current sensibilities and not by "impotent and lifeless formulas."[2]

Nearly half a century later, Justice Frank Murphy reinvigorated the argument that the Court's understanding of the Eighth Amendment was subject to change. A fifteen-year-old African American boy, Willie Francis, sentenced to death in Louisiana for murder survived the punishment of death. (The state's portable electric chair worked poorly.) The question before the Court was whether Francis could be strapped into the electric chair a second time. Attorneys argued that the attempt to execute Francis again would constitute double jeopardy and cruel and unusual punishment. "More than any other provision in the Constitution," Murphy wrote in 1947, "the prohibition of cruel and unusual punishment depends largely, if not entirely, upon the humanitarian instincts of the judiciary. We have nothing to guide us in defining what is cruel and unusual apart from our own consciences." The Court refused to block a second execution and one year later Francis was executed successfully.[3]

Eleven years later the Court fully embraced the argument that the framers' understanding of the Eighth Amendment was subject to revision. Writing for a majority in *Trop v. Dulles* (1958), Chief Justice Earl Warren argued that depriving a soldier convicted of desertion during World War II of his citizenship constituted cruel and unusual punishment. "The words of the Amendment," he began, "are not precise and their scope is not static. The Amendment must draw its meaning from the evolving standards of decency that mark the progress of a maturing society." Just four years later, the Eighth Amendment was incorporated through the Fourteenth and applied to the states. The Court's *per curiam* decision in *Furman* flowed from these cases. When the Court reversed *Furman*, the Massachusetts SJC held the death penalty violated the Declaration of Rights prohibition against cruel or unusual punishment.[4]

Trop was followed by two decades of murderous tumult. The headlines focused on the assassinations of President John F. Kennedy, Martin Luther King Jr., and Robert Kennedy and the murders committed by the Boston Strangler, but "ordinary" homicides climbed steadily throughout the

1960s, peaking in 1973. Not surprisingly, 1968 was the last year in which a bare majority of Americans, when polled, opposed the death penalty. In Massachusetts, however, where an execution had not taken place since 1947, a sizeable majority of voters favored the death penalty. But Massachusetts officials and the court were out of step with the people. Unlike President Richard M. Nixon, who mused publicly about the need for a death penalty to fight "crime in the streets," seven consecutive Massachusetts governors—Republicans and Democrats alike—refused to sign a death warrant. When that string came to an end with the election of a Democratic maverick in 1978, the SJC struck down every attempt to enact a new death penalty law.

On the broad coattails of Dwight Eisenhower, Massachusetts Republicans briefly regained control of the House and Senate and Christian Herter narrowly defeated incumbent Governor Dever. Given Herter's warm personal relationship with Ehrmann and his sympathy, if not outright support, for abolition, his victory was not a major setback for the campaign to end capital punishment in Massachusetts. But the attorney general's office went to George Fingold, the first Jew to win statewide office and a crusader "against crime, graft and Communism." From 1952 to 1958, Attorney General Fingold called for the vigorous use of the death penalty, while Herter—and his six successors in the governor's office—refused to carry out court-ordered death sentences. The fact that Massachusetts capital juries used the mercy law to recommend life imprisonment without parole in 100 of the 132 convictions for first-degree murder from 1951 to 1972 lessened the public pressure on Massachusetts governors, but prior to the SJC's landmark ruling declaring unconstitutional the death penalty for felony murder-rape in *Commonwealth v. O'Neal* (1975), they were often under severe pressure to carry out a death sentence.[5]

In the spring of 1956 Governor Herter and the governor's Council vigorously debated whether to commute to life imprisonment the death sentence of Kenneth Chapin, an eighteen-year-old Springfield high-school boy convicted of murdering fourteen-year-old Lynn Ann Smith and four-year-old Steven Goldberg, one of the two children under Smith's care on the night of September 25, 1954. There were thirty-eight stab wounds on Smith's upper body and her neck was broken. Steven Goldberg's skull was fractured and he had been stabbed more than twenty times. Police launched a citywide manhunt for a "powerful maniac." Two weeks after the murders, however, Chapin freely confessed to Springfield police. He said he had no reason for murdering Lynn Ann Smith. When she opened the Goldbergs' door in response to his knock, he was wearing his father's hat and jacket and holding a knife. "She just screamed and I stabbed her; it was intended as a joke but it backfired," he told police. Chapin "went after the boy with the knife" because he was afraid the boy, who awoke during the melee, would recognize him. After the slaying, Chapin ran to his own house just a few doors away, where he washed the blood from his shirt and hid the knife in his bedroom. A few days later he acted as one of the pallbearers at Smith's funeral.[6]

The primary issue at trial and before the Superior Court and the Council was Chapin's sanity. Hampden County Superior Court Judge Charles Fairhurst rejected repeated defense motions for additional psychiatric testing and a jury convicted Chapin of murder in the first degree. Judge Fairhurst sentenced Chapin to death, but deferred execution, pending motions for a new trial and an appeal to the state's highest court. Before the SJC, defense counsel contended, among other arguments, that the means by which the trial court determined that Chapin was criminally responsible were inadequate and erroneous. Specifically, defense attorney Samuel Sears, a former president of the Massachusetts Bar Association and working pro bono, argued the jury did not recommend mercy because the perfunctory state-mandated psychiatric examination—governed by just six and a half lines of text—led the jury to privilege that testimony to the exclusion of more detailed and significant defense testimony about Chapin's lack of criminal responsibility. The SJC found no merit in this argument, pointing out that the jury heard a defense psychiatrist testify at length that Chapin's "personality structure involved a lack of sufficient ego controls" and "a lack of adequate comprehension of the 'wrongness' of his [anti-social] behavior." The jury weighed that defense testimony against the opinions of four experts who testified that Chapin "was legally responsible on the evening when he killed the two children." The SJC sustained the jury's guilty verdict and the sentence of death.[7]

Following Chapin's failed SJC appeal, Governor Herter asked Jack Ewalt, Massachusetts commissioner of mental health, to examine the boy. Ewalt's report found Chapin legally sane, but the doctor concluded he "appeared to be a schizoid, isolated, emotionally flattened individual." On the basis of Ewalt's report, Herter recommended that the Council commute

Chapin's death sentence to life imprisonment. "There is no rational explanation for the two horrible crimes committed by Chapin," Herter stated on April 26, 1956, but "society would not be benefited by the execution of Chapin because of his abnormal characteristics and questionable personality condition, as well as his youth and complete lack of prior criminality." His decision did not mean he was prepared to abandon the death penalty altogether. After a month's study, the Council rejected Herter's clemency recommendation. Councilor Endicott "Chub" Peabody declared he could not vote for commutation because Chapin was sane at the time of the murder. A week later, however, the Council granted another six-month respite to allow defense attorneys to pursue an appeal to the Supreme Court of the United States.[8]

Efforts to save Chapin were carried on against a pro–death penalty backdrop aggressively painted by Attorney General Fingold. Although Fingold said nothing publicly during the Council's deliberations, he had made his position clear. Gearing up for a gubernatorial run, he had made a number of speeches about "killers and commutation." The *New Bedford Standard Times* cheered the attorney general for calling attention to murderers who escaped the death penalty because of executive clemency, and the *Boston Independent Democrat* quoted Fingold as blaming the "current reign of terror" on the fact that Massachusetts was not enforcing the death penalty. He told a Boston audience that the state should "dust away the cobwebs which have grown over the electric chair at Charlestown." And in a speech to the Beverly Women's Republican Club he said, "No one goes to the chair in Massachusetts is becoming the slogan among criminals." Although the attorney general did not name names, he had forced the issue of capital punishment into the next governor's race.[9]

Fingold's popular demand to "dust off the chair" and the Council's opposition to commutation was capped by the Supreme Court's denial of certiorari in Chapin's appeal on October 8, 1956. Chapin was moved to the Walpole prison's death house and his execution scheduled for December 1. Attorney Sears and Governor Herter asked the Council to hear testimony from Dr. Frederick Wertham, a distinguished New York psychiatrist who had examined Chapin. On November 28, speaking in heavily German-accented English, Wertham confidently stated that Chapin "didn't know right from wrong—he didn't have the capacity to know." To deliberately take the life of a mentally ill person, Wertham told the Councilors, would "compound the wrong." Of course, we all want to prevent future murders, he said, but "we won't accomplish that end by sending a sick boy to the electric chair." The day following Wertham's argument a group gathered at Ehrmann's Brookline home to await the Council's decision. Shortly after 11:30 A.M. Attorney Sears called Ehrmann with the good news. The Council voted 6 to 3 in favor of commutation. One angry councilor publicly claimed that commuting Chapin's death sentence "declared open season on children." But Chub Peabody reversed his earlier negative vote and approved commutation. The process also led Peabody to change his mind about capital punishment, a transformation for which he credited Ehrmann.[10]

The *Boston Herald* praised everyone who had worked to save Chapin and concluded that Massachusetts was the better for their effort. "What stands out vividly today," the *Herald* editorialized, "is the fact that Massachusetts has finally decided to keep a life rather than take one. An unimportant life, too, a warped and crippled life, a life of little value to the boy himself, a life that will now fritter away in the bleak inconsequence of prison existence. But Massachusetts has chosen to keep even such a lesser life, and by that choice has imbued all human life with a special consecration. Even the affront of murder of two children has not moved us to execute."[11]

Governor-elect Foster Furcolo said nothing about Chapin, but during his campaign he had used information supplied by Ehrmann to call for a commission to study the question of capital punishment. An affable, approachable politician, Furcolo worked his way through Yale College and Yale Law School before enlisting in the U.S. Navy during World War II. When he returned home, he opened a law practice in Springfield and won election to Congress in 1948, only the second Democrat in Massachusetts history to win a congressional seat from western Massachusetts. He served in the House until 1952 when Governor Dever appointed him state treasurer. Following an unsuccessful run for the U.S. Senate, he swept into the governor's office with 53 percent of the votes cast. He was the first Italian American to be elected chief executive of the commonwealth. In his 1957 inaugural address he railed against political corruption and championed the idea of what became the Special Commission Established for the Purpose of Investigating and Studying the Abolition of the Death Penalty in

Capital Cases. In April a House-Senate joint resolution created the fifteen-member commission, which began meeting in the summer of 1957.[12]

For more than eighteen months the commission listened and debated the efficacy and desirability of the death penalty in Massachusetts. The commission heard dozens of passionate and reasoned arguments from lawyers, law enforcement officials, legislators, lobbyists, religious leaders, and interested citizens. Its report was thoughtful and carefully drafted, but divisive all the same. After sketching out the comparative history of the use of the death penalty in the United States, the report addressed three broad questions. What is the relationship of the death penalty and its use to the rate of murder in Massachusetts? What effect does the death penalty have on the administration of justice? What are the moral arguments for and against capital punishment?

The commission's comparative analysis revealed that from 1933 to 1956 Massachusetts executed twenty-four persons and that the average per capita murder rate for Massachusetts was low, just 1.5 per one hundred thousand population. By comparison, in southern states where capital punishment was most frequently used the rates of murder were far higher. Still, the commission acknowledged, comparative data alone did not answer the question whether abolition of the death penalty would be likely to increase the number of murders, generally, or increase the danger to police officers, specifically. The Massachusetts police chiefs who testified before the commission insisted that warning an armed felon that if he killed someone he would "burn" had a deterrent effect. But, a police chief from Rhode Island, where capital punishment had not been practiced since 1852, stated that public safety was not enhanced by capital punishment. Fr. Donald Campion, S.J., buttressed this point of view with a systematic comparative study. He concluded there was no "empirical support to the claim that the existence of the death penalty in the statutes of a state provides a greater protection to the police than exists in states where that penalty has been abolished."

Conceding, for the sake of argument, the right of the state to take a life, the commission expressed the concern that an innocent person might be put to death. While no systematic study of erroneous executions existed, there was evidence that raised serious doubts about the guilt of some persons who had been put to death in other states. No such mistakes were known to have been made in Massachusetts, but the commission pointed out that innocent men, such as Gangi Cero and Louis Barrett and Clement Molway, had come perilously close to being executed, and a handful of men imprisoned for second-degree murder were subsequently exonerated of guilt. Therefore, the commission concluded, capital punishment caused juries to move too slowly for fear of making a fatal mistake, and it was too risky.

A sentence of life imprisonment for first-degree murder not only avoided the risk of executing an innocent person but also, according to available data, raised no risk to the community should the prisoner be pardoned or paroled. Of the thirty-five persons convicted of first-degree murder in Massachusetts between 1900 and 1958 who were serving a life sentence either as a result of commutation or jury recommendation, twenty-five were still in prison or had died, the commission reported. Parole or pardon released ten "lifers" after serving an average of twenty-two years in prison. None of the men released was subsequently convicted of any crime.

The commission also weighed the moral arguments for and against capital punishment. Rabbi Roland B. Gittelsohn and the Unitarian minister Rev. Dana Greeley, whom Ehrmann had enlisted in the abolitionist cause, argued that "the only moral ground on which the state could conceivably possess the right to destroy human life would be if this was indispensable for the protection and preservation of other lives. This places the burden of proof," the clergymen insisted, "on those who believe that capital punishment exercises a deterrent effect on the potential criminal. Unless they can establish that the death penalty does, in fact, protect others at the expense of one, there is no moral justification for the State to take a life." Those who support the death penalty by referring to the biblical injunction to take an "eye for an eye" overlook the fact that "this represented a limitation upon the then existing practice of unlimited vengeance." These people also forget that the New Testament challenges all people to "Love your enemies," Gittelsohn and Greeley concluded.[13]

A majority of the commission concluded that capital punishment does not offer the community better protection against murder than life imprisonment and that it does more harm to the legal and social order than good. There was reason to believe, the commission report said, that if the death penalty were not a part of the process, murder trials would be shorter and "conviction more swift and certain if life imprisonment rather than death were the maximum penalty." Not only is capital punishment contrary to the ideal goal of individual rehabilitation, but the death penalty tends to cheapen human life and to encourage adults and children to believe that violence is the proper way to resolve social and personal problems. For all these reasons, the majority urged enactment of a law providing for a mandatory life sentence without parole for murder in the first degree.

Three commission members dissented from the majority's call for abolition of the death penalty. State senator Mary Fonseca said the people ought to make any decision about abolition, and House member John Sennott said he did not believe the "mere possibility of error can be urged as a reason why the right of the State to inflict the death penalty can be questioned in principle." The most damaging dissent to the abolitionist cause—because of the commonwealth's very large and politically powerful Roman Catholic population—came from Monsignor Thomas J. Riley. He spelled out the Catholic Church's position on capital punishment in absolute terms. The supreme and all-perfect God created man and he is, therefore, capable of self-determined activity during his earthly existence. While man is on earth he operates within God's moral law, which establishes Christian society's social parameters. Within that frame, the purpose of the state is to provide for man's temporal needs, a goal that implies divine authorization to take whatever steps are necessary to protect and preserve society. For that reason, the state may "claim the right in the name of God, to take away human life in circumstances in which this would appear clearly to be in accord with God's own will." [14]

Not all Catholic clergy adhered to the orthodox position so clearly articulated by Monsignor Riley. In the months preceding and following the commission's final report, Ehrmann orchestrated an effort to spotlight Catholics who supported abolition of the death penalty. Shortly after Governor Furcolo's call for a commission to study capital punishment, Rev. Edward Hartigan, chaplain at Norfolk State Prison, published an argument against capital punishment in the *Pilot*, the official newspaper of the Boston archdiocese. Hartigan agreed the state received its authority from God through natural law and that the state was empowered to punish crime, including the taking of human life, if that were necessary to protect society. But, Hartigan emphasized, the state's right to take life is not absolute. If it could be shown that life imprisonment is just as effective a deterrent to murder as capital punishment, then "the State is morally wrong to use the death penalty." Hartigan left no doubt where he stood on the issue. He thought the deterrent effect of the death penalty was "overestimated" and " very poor." [15]

Rev. John Grant, the Boston editor of a popular devotional magazine, *Ave Maria*, Fr. Robert Drinan, S.J., a professor at Boston College Law School, and Rev. Charles E. Sheedy, dean of the College of Arts and Sciences at the University of Notre Dame, also spoke out against capital punishment. Grant rehearsed the orthodox argument but insisted that every other means of deterring murder must be exhausted before the state may resort to capital punishment. If investigation shows that life imprisonment is "just as effective as the electric chair for the protection of society, then the State must employ the lesser punishment to attain its end," he argued. Drinan took opposition to the death penalty a step further. In a widely circulated leaflet, he argued that the Catholic Church had no official position on the death penalty. "While the Church has never condemned capital punishment," Drinan wrote in December 1957, "the tendency of the last century in predominately Catholic countries has been to abolish the death penalty." In short, abolitionism and Catholicism are not necessarily contradictory. Sheedy echoed Drinan's call for abolition. In a blunt, passionate speech Sheedy told the Massachusetts legislature's Judiciary Committee:

> So much slaughter has been done in the name and under the cover of religion that it is time the goodness and mildness of Jesus had their say. The cloak of religion has covered both the just and the unjust. The false priests buzzed about the martyrs; the prison chaplain hears the last confession of the condemned murderer. I can see where a person might hold the view, reluctantly, regretfully, sorrowfully, that the miserable state of society requires the penalty of death for crime. But to put this under God, to connect it up with His will and His law, is intolerable. I think God wants it out. [16]

Before the commission's majority report calling for the abolition of capital punishment was published, the Republican party united behind the gubernatorial candidacy of Attorney General Fingold, an advocate of the death penalty. The son of a Russian-born shoe factory worker, Fingold attended Malden public schools. "I haven't had the Ivy League opportunities of the governor," Fingold declared after he received his party's nomination. "I am a product of Boston's streets and a night law school." An overweight, chain-smoking, hard-hitting prosecutor who first came to public attention in 1948 when, as an assistant attorney general, he investigated political corruption in Revere, Fingold stayed on the job as attorney general while he ran for governor. On Saturday, August 30, 1958, he kicked off his campaign with a rally at the Sons of Italy hall in East Boston. He gave a rousing speech condemning Governor Furcolo. The following morning, while reading the newspaper in his Concord backyard, Fingold suffered a stroke and died instantly. Just two months before the general election the Republicans were without a gubernatorial candidate. Although tainted by bribery scandals within his administration, the Democratic incumbent Foster Furcolo easily won a second term by defeating his hastily chosen opponent, Charles Gibbons. The Republican candidate for governor chose not to beat the drum for capital punishment or make an issue of the fact that Furcolo had commuted the death sentences of Domenick L. Bonomi, convicted of murdering his wife, and three men convicted of robbing and murdering a Newton man.[17]

Furcolo's victory and that of other legislators thought to be favorable to abolition led Ehrmann to be optimistic about the chances of ending capital punishment when the legislature met in 1959. "My over-all view," Ehrmann said of the fall election results, "is that although we have lost a few good friends who supported our cause, it looks like we have gained a good deal of support in both houses." The results of a questionnaire she had sent to every candidate for political office in Massachusetts, together with the commission's report, strongly suggested an abolition bill had a good chance of passage. In fact, the Judiciary Committee favorably reported a bill and the Senate embraced it. But, as the session wound down the House rejected abolition, dashing Ehrmann's hopes once again.[18]

At the conclusion of his second term, Governor Furcolo chose to run for the U.S. Senate, and the political newcomer Republican John Volpe finished ahead of Joseph Ward, a Fitchburg Democrat, in the wide-open race for the governor's office. A devout Catholic, Volpe had climbed from hod carrier to C.E.O. of his own national construction company and to the post of federal highway commissioner under President Eisenhower before winning the governor's race in 1961. The chief issues of the campaign had been the "elimination of corruption and scandal" and the sales tax, but for the eight years during which Volpe, Chub Peabody, and then Volpe again held the governor's office, far more sweeping and contentious issues demanded the governor's attention. National and international issues forced their way into nearly every political decision made in Massachusetts. The civil rights movement, the Supreme Court's due process revolution, and the decline in the number of executions nationwide complicated the debate over capital punishment. At the same time, the Massachusetts murder rate rose, a Boston serial killer was on the loose, and the murder of a police officer by a radical political gang created a loud public outcry for use of the death penalty.[19]

Volpe's and Peabody's handling of the issue of the death penalty were completely different. During his 1960 campaign for governor Volpe repeatedly said he believed the question of what to do about capital punishment was a matter for the legislature. "I don't believe the governor should have any more right to determine the outcome of the decision as to whether or not the death penalty should be abolished than any other citizen," he said whenever asked about his position in regard to capital punishment. He added, however, that unlike the hard-liners, he was not convinced that capital punishment is a deterrent. One month into his second term—in the wake of Peabody's politically damaging 1963 statement that if the Boston Strangler were caught and convicted he would not sign a death warrant— Volpe stunned a packed press conference by announcing that he would allow the death penalty to be carried out. In fact, Volpe's strategy, which he undertook on the advice of his old friend and executive legal counsel G. Joseph Tauro, was to delay in the hope that the electorate or the legislature would resolve the issue. In the meantime, when a defendant's appeals were exhausted the condemned man was granted a ninety-day "respite" so that his case might be restudied. Tauro's legal assistant James O'Leary negotiated delays and reprieves with the Council, juggling one then another. By early 1966 there were eight men on death row, but when Volpe left the governor's office for his appointment in the Nixon administration in 1969, he had not sent a single man to his death.[20]

Volpe had performed well enough during his first term to cause many Democrats to believe his reelection was certain. Peabody's challenge was written off as the "last hurrah" of the old-stock Yankees. Volpe was a hard-working son of immigrants, a self-made man, who counted Cardinal Richard Cushing as a personal friend. He also had tarred the Democrats with the brush of political corruption. Peabody, a Yankee by birth, the son of an Episcopal bishop, and an All-American football player at Harvard, had served on the Council from 1954 to 1958 but was considered too liberal to be elected. But Volpe coasted, while Peabody campaigned hard, pumping for a graduated income tax, constitutional reform, and an end to the death penalty. As a result, Peabody not only carried the traditional Democratic urban strongholds but also ran well in the suburbs. And he benefited from the larger than usual number of voters who turned out to send young Edward Kennedy to the U.S. Senate. Peabody squeaked into the State House and for two tumultuous years the debate about capital punishment occupied center stage.[21]

For hopeful MCADP members and abolitionists generally, the governor's initial step toward ending the death penalty hardly seemed promising. Even before Peabody's inaugural ceremony on January 4, 1963, he clashed with his fellow Democrats, including House Speaker John "Iron Duke" Thompson. The governor wanted to oust Thompson and install his own man as the Democratic leader of the House, but after six ballots and mounting bitterness, Thompson was reelected Speaker. Ironically, the Speaker and Governor Peabody made peace and as soon as the dust from the Speaker's battle settled, work began on an abolition bill. In letters and meetings Ehrmann and the governor's legislative aides sketched out a "plan of action," and on January 30, the governor publicly introduced his bill to end capital punishment in Massachusetts. Although he spoke in his signature wooden style, his announcement was explosive—even more explosive than it should have been—because the governor gratuitously added three more charges to his bombshell. One, Peabody stated he had recommended commuting to life imprisonment the death sentence of John Kerrigan, a convicted "cop killer." Two, he declared he intended to recommend clemency for all convicted murderers sentenced to death; and, three, in response to a reporter's question, he stated he would not sign a death warrant for the Boston Strangler, if and when he was caught and convicted.[22]

John Joseph Kerrigan, a forty-seven-year-old ex-convict, had been sentenced to death September 24, 1961, for the fatal shooting of Cambridge patrolman Lawrence W. Gorman. According to testimony at trial, Kerrigan and an accomplice, Edgar Cook, were trying to break into a Kendall Square restaurant in the early morning of September 3, 1960, when

Officer Gorman surprised them. As they ran from the scene, Kerrigan fired three shots, one of which struck Gorman in the back. As he lay dying the officer emptied his gun at the fleeing pair, wounding Cook. Kerrigan escaped, but Cook was captured. On May 14, 1961, however, Cook escaped from the East Cambridge jail, killing the jail master in the break. Cook hid in an apartment belonging to John Fratus, a friend of Kerrigan's. Fratus, partly out of fear and partly to collect the reward money, tipped off the authorities to Cook's whereabouts. As Boston police and FBI agents closed in on the apartment, Cook killed himself. Fratus became the chief prosecution witness at Kerrigan's trial, testifying that he overheard Kerrigan tell Cook he fatally shot Gorman.[23]

Kerrigan took the stand in his own defense and insisted he was at the Dorchester home of his sister at the time of the shooting. Kerrigan's alibi was corroborated by his sister and by her friend. After deliberating just one hour and twenty minutes a jury found Kerrigan guilty of murder in the first degree. Judge Charles Fairhurst sentenced Kerrigan to die in the electric chair but stayed the sentence pending appeal. When the clerk asked Kerrigan whether he had anything to say, he stood silent for a moment then said, "I wasn't on Kendall Square that day." The SJC heard Kerrigan's appeal on February 4, 1963.[24]

On the same day the SJC heard Kerrigan's arguments for a new trial, the Massachusetts Chiefs of Police Association mailed a letter to every legislator, urging them to vote down Governor Peabody's call for abolition of the death penalty. The MCADP also began its lobbying effort. Six weeks later, James Lawton, Governor Peabody's legislative secretary, appeared before the Judiciary Committee to launch the governor's abolition bill. "Surely no piece of legislation to be considered by the General Court this year," Lawton began, "will evoke more violent or emotional reaction than the matter of capital punishment we consider today." He hoped, however, that by focusing on the "relative merits of the law as it now stands," the committee might avoid the usual "confused excitement." Having paid lip service to the benefits of rational discourse, Lawton then bluntly and threateningly laid out the governor's position. First, murderers "do not stop to consider the legal consequences before committing murder." Second, states without the death penalty have not experienced an increase in the number of murders. Third, our capital justice system can make and has made mistakes. Finally, if the legislature does not abolish capital punishment, the governor will use his power to commute the death sentence of every convicted murderer.[25]

By early April several slightly different versions of an abolition bill were being debated in the House and Senate. On the eighteenth the Senate passed a bill that abolished the death penalty for all convicted first-degree murderers, except for someone serving a life sentence who killed a prison guard, or an imprisoned felon who in the course of an escape killed a guard. One week later, at the weary conclusion of an all-night session as Ehrmann watched from the gallery, the House passed a similar bill. Speaker Thompson warned that a celebration was premature; parliamentary procedure required the House and Senate to take enactment votes. On Friday morning, May 4, Governor Peabody and Speaker Thompson convened a meeting of abolitionists at the Parker House to map strategy and to count House members for Monday's showdown vote. Because he was suffering from a badly infected knee caused by wartime shrapnel, Thompson was confined to a wheelchair. For that reason he telephoned House members rather than roaming the House corridors in search of votes. Governor Peabody used his influence as well and publicly vowed "a last-ditch fight" to enact a bill. At the same time, police officers knocked on legislators' office doors, urging them to hold firm against abolition. When the House vote was tabulated the abolition bill lost by twelve votes.[26]

Peabody's legislative aides brought him the bad news. The governor walked down to Speaker Thompson's office and thanked him for his effort. The Speaker, who sat with his leg propped up on a sofa, shook hands with Peabody and then left for home. He later issued a statement saying that although the governor lost his fight for abolition, he "proved to those who were with him that he doesn't quit on them." Peabody vowed, "the fight will go on." Not everyone believed him. The *Boston Post-Gazette*, for example, predicted the governor would run away from abolition "as fast as his All-American feet can carry him." In fact, Peabody stayed the course, running against the tide of public opinion once again by pressuring the Council to commute to life imprisonment the death sentence of John Kerrigan, who had lost his appeal to the SJC.[27]

In the winter of 1963, in the wake of President John F. Kennedy's assassination, Peabody altered his abolitionist rhetoric, trying to make his position more politically palatable. His opposition to capital punishment had not wavered, he told the *Springfield Union*, but people should understand he had a constitutional responsibility to carefully study and consult with the Council about commuting a convicted murderer's death sentence if the facts led to that conclusion. He also emphasized that no governor since 1947—Democrat or Republican—had signed a death warrant. Despite Peabody's softer rhetoric, Ehrmann was certain the governor's controversial position on capital punishment would be the most important campaign issue in November's gubernatorial race against Republican John Volpe, who sought to regain the office he had lost in 1962. In fact, in an unprecedented turn of events, Lt. Governor Francis Bellotti defeated Peabody in the Democrat primary. Both Bellotti and Volpe opposed the death penalty, but voters did not perceive either as a zealous abolitionist. The candidates differed over whether to impose a sales tax, but whispers about Bellotti's alleged Mafia ties probably made the difference. Although Lyndon Johnson swept to a huge victory over Barry Goldwater, Volpe edged out Bellotti by twenty-three thousand votes in a ballot of nearly 2.4 million.[28]

After taking office in January 1964, Volpe took two public steps intended to push the issue of capital punishment off the front page. First, he announced he would not stand in the way of an execution ordered by the court; and, second, about a year later, he abruptly fired commissioner of corrections George F. McGrath. McGrath was a forty-nine-year-old Irish American who had worked his way up from the streets of South Boston. He attended Boston University, worked at Charlestown State Prison during the late 1930s, and later won a job as an executive assistant to the Harvard law professor Sheldon Glueck. In 1953, at age thirty-six, McGrath entered Boston College Law School, evening division. When he graduated six years later, Governor Foster Furcolo appointed him commissioner of corrections, an appointment extended by Peabody and briefly by Volpe. Just one year into his new term, however, Volpe dismissed McGrath because his outspoken stand against capital punishment did not fit with the governor's sought-after low profile on this issue.[29]

"Two years ago," the *Boston Traveler* wrote on the eve of McGrath's dismissal, a bill to abolish the death penalty lost by a scant margin, "but today even abolitionists concede such a bill is dead." At the same time, Volpe worked to defuse the death penalty issue. He encouraged adroit legal maneuvering to prevent the eight convicted murderers on "death row" from being executed and he pressured the legislature to pass a death penalty moratorium while a commission determined whether the death penalty was a deterrent to murder. Finally, when Charles Tracy, a "convicted cop killer" ran out of options, Volpe granted him a respite from the electric chair.[30]

In the early morning of May 25, 1962, Tracy, a twenty-nine-year-old African American short-order cook, entered the basement of the Kenmore Square office of the National Shawmut Bank of Boston and set off an alarm. Boston police responded to the call. Several officers searched the main floor of the bank but discovered no one. They went to the basement, which was a maze of small rooms connected by two narrow corridors. The officers spread out and slowly searched the basement. One shot was fired, followed by three more shots in rapid succession. Running toward the sound, the officers reached an opening to a supply room, where they saw Officer John J. Gallagher lying wounded on the floor. When his fellow officers tried to reach Gallagher, they came under fire from a "light-skinned colored male" who was standing wedged between two metal lockers in the supply room. One of the officers shouted, "I am Sergeant Barry of the Boston Police. Put your gun out. Give yourself up. We are only interested in the wounded officer." Tracy did not respond. Whenever the police officers tried to reach Gallagher they came under fire. Nearly two hours passed before police officers were able to subdue Tracy and rescue their comrade. Officer Gallagher died at approximately 6:00 A.M.[31]

At each of his two trials—the first ended in a hung jury—Tracy took the stand. He testified he did not remember entering the bank, but he did recall squeezing into a locker, where he found a loaded revolver and gun belt. At the instant he emerged from the locker, Gallagher called out to drop the gun. Officer Gallagher, according to Tracy, then fired a shot, hitting him in the wrist and a reflex action caused the revolver to fire. Tracy also said he could not let go of the gun and that he did not hear Sergeant Barry call to him to throw the gun out. Finally, Tracy testified that before he arrived at the bank he drank a grape-colored soft drink someone at his workplace gave to him, causing him to become "numb" and "blank." The first jury, in May 1963, disagreed, but seven months later in an atmosphere charged by the assassination of President John F. Kennedy, the jury found Tracy guilty of murder in the first degree and he was sentenced to die. The SJC upheld the verdict by a split decision, and the Supreme Court declined to accept the case for review.[32]

In September 1966, Tracy filed a petition asking Governor Volpe for mercy, to commute his sentence to life imprisonment. The first stop in this process was the Parole Board, chaired by Joseph F. McCormack. A Democrat publicly opposed to capital punishment, McCormack figured Tracy would be best served by delaying a decision. To force Governor Volpe to tackle Tracy's commutation request a few weeks before the gubernatorial election, as some Democrats wanted, would force the governor to alienate either abolitionists or proponents of the death penalty. Volpe did not want to be put in that position. More important, McCormack feared that politicizing the case would jeopardize Tracy's chances of winning the Council's favorable recommendation. Not all the Parole Board members agreed with McCormack's strategy. Democratic Councilor George Cronin Jr. sought to use the issue to push Volpe off the political tight wire he was walking. Since the governor sought the power to make these life and death decisions, Cronin argued, he "now must assume that responsibility of decision completely divorced from any political significance or motivation." Board member John T. Lane also urged McCormack to get Tracy's case to Volpe as soon as possible. Lane, the only African American on the board, wanted Volpe to confront the racial bias of capital punishment. Speaking for the growing number of Boston blacks demanding full civil rights, Lane asserted that Tracy's sentence and the effort to postpone his hearing also were prompted by racial bias. In the end, McCormack prevailed, and Tracy's case was not forwarded to Volpe until after he won a new four-year term.[33]

In the waning days before Tracy's scheduled execution during the week beginning December 14, 1966, the *Boston Globe*, among other newspapers, weighed in against the execution. There "is a substantial possibility that Tracy is NOT guilty of first-degree murder." Quoting liberally from Justice Arthur E. Whittemore's SJC dissent, the *Globe* argued against the majority's conclusion that Tracy had committed premeditated murder. Tracy entered the bank without tools or a weapon and he shot Officer Gallagher in the presence of other police officers, a "foolhardy act," not a planned, thoughtful act. Tracy's story that he drank a strange concoction and became "numb" reads like a "cock and bull story," but it must be read with the "officer's testimony and with the testimony of other witnesses" who said that Tracy "looked, acted and talked 'funny'" before he walked into the bank. The *Globe* also cheered that part of Justice Whittemore's dissent championing the argument that Tracy was deprived of his constitutional rights by the police interrogation. For the state to invoke the death penalty against a man who "may not be guilty of first degree murder and is not even a hardened criminal would be vicious beyond description. It would also have the most grievous consequences for the reputation of Massachusetts in the nation and the world," the *Globe* concluded.[34]

The MCADP and a substantial number of Boston College faculty also petitioned Governor Volpe, asking that he and the Council commute Tracy's death sentence. Prompted by Ehrmann, attorney John G. S. Flym, of Foley, Hoag and Eliot, sent an "urgent" circular letter to Boston-area lawyers asking for their support in the campaign to save Tracy. Two days later, at nine o'clock in the morning on December 7, Fr. William Kenealy, S.J., a former dean and current Boston College Law School professor, personally carried a petition signed by eighty-five Law School and Boston College faculty to Governor Volpe, asking him to "extend executive clemency to Charles E. Tracy." "With profound sorrow and heartfelt sympathy with the family, the friends, and the colleagues of Officer John J. Gallagher," the college faculty began, "we believe that the commutation of this death sentence will prevent the compounding of private and personal tragedy, and promote the public interest of the Commonwealth." Like the *Globe*, the Boston College faculty sided with Justice Whittemore in finding Tracy's "conduct in this tragedy was unplanned, bewildered, impulsive and irrational, rather than conduct inspired by '*deliberately premeditated malice aforethought*.'" The signers were "appalled" by the omission of this important and critical reference in the trial judge's charge to the jury. Fr. Kenealy and the others insisted this "critical omission in the charge to the jury constitutes a clear challenge to the conscience of the Executive Department to exercise that merciful clemency which, in our benign jurisprudence, is available to mitigate in particular instances the unforeseen horror of sheer legality."[35]

Volpe acted the day after receiving the Boston College petition. On the governor's recommendation, the Council voted 6 to 2 for a six-month respite for Tracy. Volpe told the Council he intended to file a bill in the next legislature calling for a death penalty moratorium so that a commission might determine whether capital punishment is a deterrent to murder.

Allowing Tracy to die before the legislature acts, Volpe declared, would be unfair to Tracy since others on death row would benefit if a moratorium were granted. The governor added the usual political caveat: he had not changed his position on the death penalty. "I see it as my clear duty," he said at his weekly news conference on December 8, 1966, "to enforce the laws of the commonwealth, including the death penalty, as they presently exist in as fair and impartial manner as is humanly possible."[36]

In the spring Volpe threw the political hot potato of capital punishment to the legislature. He asked for a special study commission to determine whether the death penalty is a deterrent. The bill was killed in the House by nine votes, largely in reaction to the Boston Strangler's escape from the state's hospital for the criminally insane at Bridgewater. Some minor changes were made and the bill refiled, but it failed by an even larger margin. On the third attempt in August Volpe's staff used every weapon in the governor's arsenal, including an especially welcome statement from Cardinal Richard Cushing. For the first time since he assumed control of the archdiocese in 1945, the crusty, popular spiritual leader of Boston's Roman Catholic population revealed that he did not believe capital punishment is a deterrent and that he personally regretted capital punishment was the law of the commonwealth. The bill sailed through the legislature. Although the MCADP opposed it, a referendum on capital punishment also was planned for 1968.[37]

On the eve of the scheduled referendum, following her thirty-eighth consecutive appearance before the Joint Judiciary Committee of the legislature, Sara Ehrmann stepped down as president of the MCADP and of the American League to Abolish Capital Punishment (ALACP). "No matter how anyone feels about capital punishment," Charles W. Bartlett, president of the Boston Bar Association, wrote, "he can't have anything but admiration for the one-woman crusade that Mrs. Ehrmann has put on over the years." Of course, she had plenty of help, Bartlett continued, but year after year, it "has been she, who rounded up the speakers for the hearings, sent out the appeals for funds and generally rallied anyone and everyone who might conceivably assist." The MCADP and the ALACP are "high sounding names but pretty largely no more nor less than Sara Ehrmann," Bartlett concluded.[38]

New faces and tactics characterized the Massachusetts abolitionist effort after 1968. Attorney William Homans Jr. and Harvard Law School professor Laurence H. Tribe were most prominent among those lawyers who sometimes acted in cooperation with the Massachusetts Civil Liberties Union when the focus of the abolitionist movement shifted to the courts. Likewise, Tufts University philosophy professor Hugo A. Bedau revived the ALACP and produced scores of scholarly publications zeroing in on the death penalty's legal and social inequities. In addition, Boston University president John Silber, who had earned his spurs in the Texas abolitionist movement, assumed responsibility for educating the public.[39]

Despite Ehrmann's tireless effort and the infusion of new blood into the abolitionist movement, the results of the death penalty ballot question put to voters in 1968 was a huge—but not unexpected—disappointment. "Shall the commonwealth of Massachusetts retain capital punishment for crime," the plebiscite unambiguously asked voters. The total yes votes were 1,159,348; the total no votes 730,649; and there were 458,008 blanks. Of 351 Massachusetts cities, only 12 voted negatively. Within a month after voters expressed their preference for capital punishment Volpe left the governor's office for his position in the Nixon cabinet. Lt. Governor Francis W. Sargent served as acting governor from 1969 through 1970 before winning a full four-year term of his own in 1971. An affable, lanky, lantern-jawed, low-key Yankee from Cape Cod, Sargent had made his name as an environmentalist and as head of the Department of Public Works. Before 1970 he said nothing publicly about the death penalty, but during his campaign for governor made clear his opposition to capital punishment, though he tacked on the caveat that he would sign a bill providing the death penalty for murderers of law enforcement officers.[40]

Sargent's remark was prompted by the shooting death of Officer Walter A. Schroeder during the September 23, 1970, robbery of the State Street Bank in Brighton. Police charged William "Lefty" Gilday, a forty-one-year-old ex-convict, with first-degree murder and two counts of armed robbery. Also indicted were Stanley R. Bond, Robert J. Valeri, Susan E. Saxe, and Katherine A. Power. Valeri, Saxe, and Bond, all armed, entered the bank while Gilday, armed with a semiautomatic rifle, remained in a car parked outside the bank to protect the trio in making their getaway. Power was waiting nearby in a "switch" car. The three robbers left the bank with more than $23,000 and sped off in the getaway car. Just at that moment, Officer Schroeder arrived on the scene, and from across the street Gilday began shooting at him, fatally wounding the officer. All five members of the gang made their way to Bond's Beacon Street apartment where, according to a witness, Saxe and Power accused Gilday of being "trigger happy" for murdering Schroeder. Captured within hours, Valeri confessed, sending the others running. Gilday fled from Boston, driving to several Massachusetts cities before forcing his way into a Haverhill home and holding a family hostage for nearly twenty-four hours. At gunpoint, he forced two family members to drive him to Worcester, where he was later arrested.[41]

Gilday and Valeri, twenty-one years old, met while serving time in Walpole State Prison. Bond was the third male member of the Revolutionary Action Force-East, as the gang called itself. He was a Vietnam veteran who had flown thirty-six combat missions before he was honorably discharged. Bond "came home well, but everything else he did went wrong," a friend said later. Convicted of armed robbery and sentenced to Walpole, Bond befriended Valeri and "Lefty" Gilday. The three men enrolled in STEP (Student Tutor Educational Project), a program designed to help inmates further their education. Because of their success in the program, Valeri, Bond, and Gilday were paroled and admitted to Boston-area colleges. Valeri and Gilday enrolled at Northeastern University and Bond began attending Brandeis, where he met Susan Saxe and Kathy Power.[42]

Power, a Catholic deacon's daughter and former high school valedictorian from Denver, Colorado, entered Brandeis in 1967. Fervently opposed to the Vietnam War, Power joined the Brandeis Sanctuary Community and helped organize a refuge for an AWOL army private in 1968. As the war escalated, Power abandoned her nonviolent beliefs and in May 1970, when four Kent State students were killed by National Guard troops, Bond, Power, and Saxe helped organize the National Strike Information Center at Brandeis, which promoted student strikes nationwide. When the strike information center needed money, Bond, Power, and Saxe robbed banks in Illinois, Pennsylvania, and California. After the Brighton murder, Bond, Saxe, and Power drove to Philadelphia, then to Atlanta, where they split up. Police captured Bond in a Colorado motel several days later. But Saxe and Power remained free. Saxe was arrested in Philadelphia in 1975, and Power turned herself in to authorities in 1993. Justice Edward F. Hennessey labeled the entire episode "an odyssey of violence against the background of political revolution, or at least pretensions of revolution."[43]

Valeri testified for the prosecution in Gilday's trial after pleading guilty to manslaughter at a separate trial. Gilday was convicted of first-degree murder and robbery and sentenced to death. On March 10, 1972, he joined twenty-three other men in Walpole Prison awaiting execution.[44]

One hundred eleven days later, the U.S. Supreme Court held capital punishment as then practiced unconstitutional. In *Furman v. Georgia* (1972), a patchwork majority noted tersely "that the imposition and carrying out of the death penalty in these cases constitute cruel and unusual punishment in violation of the Eighth and Fourteenth Amendments." Abolitionists, defense lawyers, and the more than six hundred inmates under sentence of death across the nation loudly celebrated. Sara Ehrmann was joyous. "I feel victorious. I appreciate every ounce of success. I feel triumphant. Yes, I feel triumphant," she told the *Boston Record-American*.[45]

Lawyers for the Legal Defense Fund who had brought the historic cases to the Court and a handful of abolitionist veterans soon realized *Furman* was less than it seemed. Each justice wrote a separate opinion. None of the five justices in the majority joined any part of their brethren's argument. Justices Thurgood Marshall and William Brennan believed the death penalty was unconstitutional under any circumstances, but each justice reached that conclusion by a different route. Marshall insisted capital punishment serves no legitimate purpose and therefore it is cruel and unusual, a violation of the Eighth Amendment. Brennan drew on Chief Justice Earl Warren's interpretation of the Eighth Amendment in *Trop v. Dulles* (1958) to argue that the amendment's meaning had changed since its passage. "The words of the Amendment are not precise and their scope is not static," Warren wrote. "The Amendment must draw its meaning from the evolving standards of decency that mark the progress of a maturing society." The fact that infliction of the death penalty by a state has become increasingly rare, Brennan argued, suggests there is "a deep-seated reluctance to inflict it." For that reason it is imposed arbitrarily in violation of the Eighth and Fourteenth Amendments.[46]

Justice William O. Douglas focused on the discriminatory impact of the death penalty. He acknowledged there are a host of factors that play into a court's decision to sentence a defendant to death, but Douglas pointed to statistical evidence showing that African Americans convicted of rape or of the murder of a white person were far more likely to be sentenced to death than a white person convicted of the same crime. The Eighth Amendment requires legislatures "to write penal laws that are even-handed, nonselective, and nonarbitrary." Because death penalty statutes are imposed in a discriminatory fashion, Douglas concluded, they are unconstitutional.[47]

The concurring opinions of Justices Potter Stewart and Byron White were more narrowly tailored. They focused on the arbitrary manner in which the death penalty was imposed. Sentencing in death penalty cases, in Stewart's famous phrase, is "cruel and unusual in the same way that being struck by lightning is cruel and unusual." For all the people convicted of capital crimes in 1967 and 1968, Stewart wrote, only a "capriciously selected random handful" was sentenced to death. White also emphasized the infrequency with which the death penalty was imposed, adding that it was used so seldom it was not a "credible deterrent."[48]

Furman's dissenters also raised a variety of issues, but they all expressed the view that the Court was infringing on legislative turf and that Americans had not repudiated the death penalty in the name of an "evolving standard of decency," as Justices Brennan and Marshall had insisted. Noting that the majority had not found the death penalty unconstitutional under all circumstances, Chief Justice Warren Burger sketched a roadmap for states that wanted to rewrite death penalty legislation to meet the objections raised by the Court. States "may seek to bring their laws into compliance with the Court's ruling by providing standards for juries and judges to follow in determining the sentence in capital cases or by more narrowly defining the crimes for which the penalty is to be imposed."[49]

Proponents of the death penalty seized on Burger's broad hint. Within days after *Furman*, legislators in several states announced their intention to introduce bills to reinstate capital punishment, and just four months later California voters amended the state constitution to permit the death penalty. About the same time, a nationwide Gallup Poll showed 57 percent of the American people favored capital punishment. In Massachusetts, the chief justice of the Superior Court, Walter H. McLaughlin, darkly predicted a surge of violent crimes and called for a constitutional amendment supporting the death penalty.[50]

In the meantime, the Supreme Court and state courts around the nation took steps to implement *Furman*. In a series of *per curiam* decisions the Court ordered resentencing in 118 death penalty cases from twenty-six states that were before the Court along with *Furman*. Consistent with its ruling in *Furman*, for example, the Court ordered the Massachusetts court to resentence John S. Stewart and John H. Kerrigan, both of whom were under sentence of death for murdering a police officer. Stewart had been sentenced to death less than a year before Furman. Kerrigan had been awaiting execution since September 23, 1961. All but two of the remaining Massachusetts inmates under sentence of death would eventually claim a reversal on the grounds of *Furman* and *Stewart*. However, dicta in Justice Stewart's concurring opinion in *Furman* suggested that Massachusetts's mandatory death penalty for felony rape-murder might satisfy constitutional requirements. Two black youths, Alphonso Pickney and Robert O'Neal, were under sentence of death for that crime.[51]

The Supreme Court's ambivalence about the death penalty's constitutionality gave rise to a flurry of capital punishment legislation in the states. Florida restored its death penalty just four months after *Furman* and within four years thirty-eight states enacted new death penalty statutes. In Massachusetts an intense struggle over the death penalty engaged the courts, the legislature, a series of governors, and the people of the commonwealth for more than a decade.[52]

The SJC was the first branch of Massachusetts government to react to the Supreme Court's abolition of the death penalty. By its July 23, 1973, ruling in *Commonwealth v. LeBlanc,* the SJC applied *Furman* to the death sentenced convicts not mentioned in the Court's *per curiam* holding in *Stewart*. David LeBlanc had been sentenced to death in the winter of 1971 for the shotgun murder of his stepfather. In a unanimous opinion, the SJC decided "in the light of the *Furman* case," LeBlanc's death sentence "may not remain." The court ordered LeBlanc and all prisoners under sentence of death for murder to be resentenced to life imprisonment. In addition, the statute allowing a capital jury to decide whether a convicted murderer would be sentenced to life imprisonment or to death was declared unlawful because of that discretionary provision.[53]

Three weeks later in *Commonwealth v. A Juvenile* (1973), the SJC overturned Alphonso Pickney's death sentence for felony murder-rape. Pickney, a black Roxbury teenager, had been found guilty of the "brutal and heinous" rape-murder of a forty-seven-year-old white woman. On appeal, defense counsel William Homans argued that the statute governing Pickney's trial allowed a judge unconstitutional discretionary authority. Because Pickney was just sixteen years old at the time of the crime and seventeen years old when he was sentenced to death on February 15, 1972,

Judge Allan M. Hale could have tried Pickney as a delinquent child or instituted adult criminal proceedings. Judge Hale also had the option of trying Pickney as an adult, but sentencing him as a juvenile. By making the initial determination to try Pickney as an adult, Homans insisted, the trial judge placed Pickney "in irreversible jeopardy [*sic*] of being 'among a capriciously selected random handful upon whom the sentence of death has been imposed.'" Hale also chose to sentence Pickney as an adult. Those two statutory provisions, Homans concluded, allowed a trial judge unconstitutional discretionary authority; therefore, Pickney's death sentence must be reversed.[54]

Writing for a unanimous court, Justice Paul C. Reardon agreed. In the light of the Supreme Court's finding in *Furman*, "we hold that imposition of the death penalty [in Pickney's case] left as it was within the discretion of the judge, is invalid, and that the penalty is therefore limited to life imprisonment." In holding that the capital sanction could not be constitutionally applied to a juvenile, despite the mandatory provision of the felony rape-murder law, the court noted that it was "theoretically possible" for a trial judge to handle such a case under the juvenile code, despite the "enormity of the crime." "We do not voice any opinion," the court added prophetically, on the constitutionality of the law mandating a death sentence for murder-rape if the defendant is an adult at the time of the crime. In short, the fate of nineteen-year-old African American Robert O'Neal, whose February 1973 conviction for rape-murder had led to a mandatory death sentence, was yet to be decided. This hint of the court's openness to argument against a mandatory death penalty was not shared by the legislature.[55]

Well before the *LeBlanc* ruling, House members filed five different death penalty bills. In the spring of 1973, the Joint Judiciary Committee held a two-hour public hearing. Spokespersons for and against the death penalty gave emotional speeches, but none as grotesque as that of Representative George Sacco (D-Medford). Speaking in favor of his bill calling for a mandatory death penalty for the murder of a police or correctional officer, Sacco loudly and proudly proclaimed, "I believe in two chairs and no waiting." Early in August the Judiciary Committee reported out favorably a mandatory death penalty bill for all first-degree murder convictions, a proposal modeled on the state's pre-1951 statute. Opponents argued that the bill's mandatory provision was fictional, because under the proposed law a jury still might exercise considerable discretion by finding the defendant guilty of either second-degree murder or manslaughter. After vociferous and divisive debate, the House voted 130 to 89 in favor of the bill. Death penalty opponents slowed final enactment of the bill by asking the SJC for an advisory opinion about its constitutionality.[56]

On September 25, Attorney General Robert H. Quinn filed a brief with the SJC. Prepared with the assistance of Harvard Law School professor Lloyd Weinreb and attorney William Homans, the brief argued that the bill violated the Massachusetts constitutional prohibition against "cruel or unusual punishment." The attorney general defined "cruel" as "excessive in relation to the offense punished, no matter how heinous," an interpretation drawn from *Trop v. Dulles* (1958). A mandatory death penalty, Quinn claimed, demeans "the dignity of man" and causes the "total destruction of the individual's status in organized society" and therefore is "cruel." Taking a statement from Justice Brennan's concurrence in *Furman* one step further, Quinn concluded that capital punishment "is not merely different in degree of severity but different in kind from every other penal sanction and therefore 'unusual' within the meaning of the Eighth Amendment."[57]

As the legislative session drew to a close, the House grew too impatient to wait for the court's advisory opinion. On October 1, the House forged ahead, passing a mandatory death penalty bill by a vote of 143 to 82. Before the Senate could take up the bill, two especially brutal murders occurred in Boston. Gangs of black youths allegedly burned to death a young white woman in Roxbury and near Columbia Point assaulted and stabbed to death a white fisherman. Riding that wave of emotion, the Senate passed a slightly different mandatory death penalty bill by a vote of 20 to 11. After some haggling, a bill specifying the types of criminal homicide subject to the mandatory death sentence passed the Senate and the House just after Thanksgiving 1973.[58]

Just four days after the legislature passed the bill and three years almost to the day after "Lefty" Gilday gunned down his brother Walter, Detective John D. Schroeder was murdered while investigating a holdup. Amidst a storm of public outrage, opponents of capital punishment rallied to oppose the mandatory death penalty bill now sitting on Governor Sargent's desk. At a State House news conference Boston University president John Silber solemnly observed, "It is difficult to control our instinct to avenge the cruel and senseless murder of detective Schroeder. Capital punishment cannot return to life detective Schroeder or any other victim. Tragically, the most we can do for those who are killed is to show our concern for the sanctity of life." Silber also presented the governor's secretary with a MCADP petition signed by ten thousand people urging Sargent to veto the bill. The following day the Massachusetts Chiefs of Police Association countered with a letter demanding the governor sign the bill into law. On December 6, six hundred police officers, returning from Detective Schroeder's funeral, marched on the governor's office demanding an interview. Governor Sargent agreed to talk with a small delegation of the officers and during an hour-long meeting punctuated by angry shouts, the police officers urged the governor to sign the bill.[59]

The day before the bill would be automatically pocket-vetoed (the legislative session would end before the governor signed the bill) Sargent told State House reporters of his intention. He wanted to help the "cops," he said, but he felt the death penalty was "imagined help." Sargent added, "I'm amazed at the number of people who think the electric chair would end violence. I really don't." The following day, December 10, the governor issued a somewhat more formal press release outlining his reasons for vetoing the bill. Sargent acknowledged, "We live in times of alarming violence" and bowed to the tough job performed by the police, but he criticized the mandatory death penalty bill as of "doubtful constitutionality, because it is both too broad in scope and too loosely drawn." He also shared his "personal and moral compunctions about the taking of human life by the state" and articulated a political position that seemed to allow the governor to appease both sides. "I will sign a capital punishment measure that is limited to killers of law enforcement officers," the governor stated forcibly, hastily adding that before signing such a bill he would "insist it be considered by our Supreme [Judicial] Court on the question of constitutionality."[60]

Governor Sargent's pocket veto drew criticism from capital punishment opponents and proponents. Opponents felt Sargent had "knuckled under" because he suggested he would sign some sort of death penalty bill. At the same time, the chairman of the Boston Police Patrolmen's Association decried the governor's decision, labeling it "craven" and "politically motivated." Not surprisingly, therefore, the battle reignited in the spring of 1974. On March 5, the House passed the same death penalty bill the governor had vetoed the preceding session, but this time the legislature figured there would be time to attempt to override Sargent's expected veto. The Senate also passed the mandatory death penalty bill, though by a narrow margin. As predicted, Governor Sargent vetoed the bill within hours after it reached his desk. The House quickly and easily overrode the veto, but the Senate vote fell one shy of the requisite two-thirds needed to override.[61]

Capital punishment was a nonissue in the 1974 gubernatorial campaign, since both Sargent and the eventual winner, Democrat Michael Dukakis, opposed the death penalty. The youngest son of Greek parents, Dukakis graduated from Swarthmore College and Harvard Law School. Following admission to the bar in 1955 he practiced law, but his chief interest was politics. Elected to the Massachusetts legislature in 1963, he earned a reputation as a "tough, honest maverick," or as "cold and compulsive," depending on who was asked. He proudly embraced the first label when he took office as governor in January 1975. Just four months later, under intense pressure from citizens angry about rising crime and murder rates, the legislature immediately tested Governor Dukakis's resolve on capital punishment. A bill mandating the death penalty in nine categories of murder landed on the governor's desk April 29, 1975. He already had prepared a veto message. Dukakis told the legislature that he could not "reconcile the willful taking of a human life by the state with his own moral and ethical beliefs." He added, that he had never seen "any convincing evidence that the death penalty is a deterrent to crime" and that he had "grave doubts about the constitutionality of the legislature's bill." Two days later the House voted 156 to 68 to override the governor's veto, but by a single vote the Senate failed to override the veto, briefly ending political debate on the issue. The death penalty continued to be a divisive political issue, but the spotlight shifted to the court.[62]

On the morning of March 27, 1972, Robert O'Neal, a nineteen-year-old African American, forced his way into a Roxbury apartment occupied by Gladys Mercadel, a fifty-eight-year-old white woman and her thirty-four-year-old son, Earl. Once inside the apartment O'Neal drew a gun, grabbed Gladys's wrist, and dragged her to the rear of the apartment. Earl, who suffered from muscular dystrophy, lay helpless in his bed. About twenty minutes later, O'Neal returned to Earl's room and assaulted him, stabbing him in the neck and stomach with a kitchen knife. O'Neal then took money and other items and fled. Shortly thereafter, Mercadel's nephew came to the apartment and alerted the police. When the police arrived they found Earl lying in a pool of blood, seriously injured. Gladys Mercadel had been strangled to death. Her partially clothed body lay on her bed with a wad of tissue stuffed in her mouth. There was evidence she had been raped before she had been murdered. O'Neal surrendered to Boston police a few days after the homicide. He made voluntary statements admitting he had entered the apartment, stabbed a man lying in bed, and taken money. A jury found O'Neal guilty of rape-murder. Before sentencing O'Neal to death, Judge Allan Dimond stated his belief that *Furman* "did not annul the Massachusetts statute that makes the death penalty mandatory for murder committed in the commission of rape." On appeal, attorney Bill Homans took aim at this premise.[63]

Briefs were filed and oral arguments were made before the SJC. In April 1975, Chief Justice G. Joseph Tauro delivered what turned out to be the first of two decisions in *Commonwealth v. O'Neal.* Born and educated in Lynn, Massachusetts, the son of an immigrant shoemaker, Tauro worked his way through Boston University Law School and was admitted to the bar in 1927. He hung out a shingle in his hometown and slowly created a busy and lucrative private practice. He built a professional and personal relationship with one of his clients, Volpe Construction, that led him to Beacon Hill as Governor Volpe's legal counsel in 1961. A short time later, Volpe appointed Tauro chief justice of the Superior Court, a position he held until Governor Sargent moved him to the SJC's center seat in 1970. The *Boston Globe* greeted Tauro's appointment to the SJC with derision. Tauro's "most distinguished feature in the legal world," the *Globe* wrote, "has been his pompous, self-important manner. He is also known for his vindictive attitude toward his critics." In case anyone missed the point, the *Globe* added: "The state's highest court needs new blood, new talent, new thinking, new force. The Tauro appointment brings none of this."[64]

Almost immediately after taking his seat on the court, Chief Justice Tauro began to prove his critics wrong about his professional qualifications and motivation. In a heated dissent, he blistered the SJC's ancient policy of legislative deference. "I do not believe we should look to the legislature for change," he wrote. "To do so is a distortion of the concept of judicial review." A year later, Tauro assaulted the court's "slavish adherence to stare decisis." In criminal procedure, too, the Tauro court swept aside old rules and added new protections for the accused.[65]

Tauro's drive for judicial independence thrust the SJC into the forefront of a post-Warren court movement to supplement federal constitutional rights with an expanded interpretation of state constitutional guarantees. Although the Bill of Rights and the Fourteenth Amendment provide the most important provisions for the defense of a capital defendant, each state supreme court is the final authority on the meaning of its own constitution. For this reason, a state court may decide the death penalty violates a provision of its state constitution, even though the Supreme Court of the United States has ruled the death penalty does not violate any provision of the federal constitution. In 1972, for example, the California Supreme Court became the first appellate court to find the death penalty unconstitutional. Although nine months later a public referendum spearheaded by Governor Ronald Reagan amended the constitution to declare that none of its provisions was inconsistent with capital punishment, the California court's action spurred the Massachusetts SJC.[66]

During the decade following the resignation of Chief Justice Earl Warren from the Supreme Court in 1969, the SJC was "more outspoken concerning the significance of rights under the Declaration of Rights than at any time in its history," according to Justice Herbert Wilkins. Tauro's colleagues and successors on the bench publicly encouraged lawyers to make greater use of the Massachusetts Declaration of Rights and insisted that "the duty of maintaining constitutional rights of a person on trial for his life rises above mere rules of procedure." For this reason the SJC's bold and controversial decisions about capital punishment not only had deep roots within Massachusetts law and culture, but were a manifestation of a new shift toward state constitutionalism as well.[67]

Within this context, in April 1975 Tauro spoke for a narrow, divided majority in *O'Neal*. He rejected both of the defense's major arguments. Homans had argued the statute imposing a mandatory death penalty for rape-murder was unconstitutional under *Furman* either because it allowed the jury to have discretion in determining whether the death penalty should be imposed, or because the death penalty itself was cruel and unusual punishment in violation of the Eighth Amendment. The discretion analysis "appears plausible at first glance," Tauro wrote, but "there are serious problems connected with its use." Specifically, when a jury finds that a murder was committed in the course of a rape, the death penalty is automatically imposed. Juries, "if properly charged, have no discretion to find mitigating circumstances or a lesser degree of culpability." Of course, it is possible a "'rogue'" jury may disregard the evidence to avoid subjecting the defendant to the death penalty. However, such an argument cannot be accepted without discrediting of "our entire criminal jury system."[68]

Alternatively, Homans argued the death penalty violates the Eighth Amendment and Article 26 of the Massachusetts Declaration of Rights, which prohibit cruel or unusual punishment. The judicial and scholarly literature on this issue, Tauro noted, is immense, but ultimately inconclusive. Therefore, he chose another route arguing that the due process clause of the Fourteenth Amendment—and he added in a footnote, the "fundamental constitutional principles enshrined in our State constitution dictate an identical result"—protect a fundamental right to life. "Life is a constitutionally protected fundamental right," he asserted. Therefore, an infringement of that right "triggers strict scrutiny under the compelling State interest and least restrictive means test." For this reason, to take a life by statute, the state must show that "such action is the least restrictive means" to achieve a "compelling government end." Tauro then ordered the Commonwealth and O'Neal to respond to the court's argument in thirty days.[69]

Justices Wilkins, Hennessey, and Kaplan concurred with Tauro, but Justices Reardon, Quirico, and Braucher dissented. Wilkins and Kaplan were dubious about Tauro's due process–compelling state interest argument, but they agreed with the need for additional argument. Wilkins urged that "particular attention should be paid to art. 26." He acknowledged that at the time of its adoption Article 26 "was not intended to prohibit capital punishment." However, when the prohibition against "cruel or unusual punishment" was interpreted in the light of the "evolving standards of decency that mark the progress of a maturing society," as suggested by *Trop v. Dulles* (1958), Article 26 may establish higher standards than the Eighth Amendment. Without foreclosing the validity of either Tauro's or Wilkins's position, Hennessey invited wide-ranging argument, including the idea that "new standards of compassion have made the death penalty unconstitutional."[70]

The commonwealth's supplemental brief, signed by the district attorneys of Suffolk, Middlesex, and Bristol counties, argued that capital punishment is a deterrent to rape-murder and that the state has a compelling interest in protecting its citizens from this heinous offense. First, the Commonwealth argued that life imprisonment is an insufficient punishment to deter a rape-murderer. In fact, absent the death penalty there would be an incentive for the rapist to murder his victim to improve his chances of "escaping apprehension while not substantially increasing his penalty if he were caught." To buttress this argument, the commonwealth cited the economist Isaac Ehrlich's 1975 study of the deterrent effect of capital punishment. Using multiple regression analysis, Ehrlich concluded that each execution might have resulted in seven or eight fewer murders. Finally, the commonwealth reminded the court of women's "desperate need" for protection and the people's call for capital punishment.[71]

Homans's supplemental brief asserted that "the punishment of death operates to preclude regular, predictable, evenhanded application of capital punishment and there can be no compelling governmental interest which cannot be served by means less drastic than the killing of an inevitably small number of convicted, incarcerated felony rape-murderers." To justify the infringement on the fundamental right of life, the government must show the death penalty is "necessary to promote a compelling governmental interest" and that death is "precisely tailored" to achieve this interest. Homans conceded that some murderers might be deterred by the death penalty, but since the overwhelming majority of crimes committed are not the result of rational choice, death is not a deterrent. Finally, Homans concluded that life imprisonment for rape-murder would properly satisfy the community's need for safety and justice.[72]

Speaking three days before Christmas for a bitterly divided court, Chief Justice Tauro declared unconstitutional the state's mandatory death sentence for murder committed in the course of a rape or attempted rape. Tauro also broadly hinted that no death penalty statute would pass constitutional muster. His argument relied primarily on the Massachusetts Constitution, letting his Fourteenth Amendment argument slip into a footnote. He also changed his mind about entering the "morass" surrounding the question whether capital punishment is cruel and unusual punishment, because he wanted to resolve the question of the "constitutionality of capital punishment under the cruel or unusual test." He merged two constitutional strands from the Massachusetts Declaration of Rights, an analysis of Article 26 prohibition against cruel or unusual punishment and a due process argument based on Articles 1, 10, and 12.[73]

Tauro rejected the state's argument that capital punishment is a more effective deterrent to murder than life imprisonment. Two special commissions of the Massachusetts legislature and virtually every contemporary criminologist have concluded that capital punishment does not deter murder. Studies comparing homicide rates in states without capital punishment to similar contiguous states with the death penalty show that homicide rates "are conditioned by other factors than the death penalty." Scientific studies also show that a mandatory death penalty is not a greater deterrent to homicide than discretionary use of capital punishment. "My review of the available studies," Tauro stated, "reveals no firm indication that capital punishment acts as a superior deterrent to homicide than other available punishments." Therefore, he said, the commonwealth has not demonstrated that its compelling interest in deterrence "cannot adequately be served by other less restrictive means of punishment, nor did it show that the need to hold together the social compact required serious crimes to be punished by death."[74]

Based on these arguments, Tauro concluded the commonwealth had not met the heavy burden of demonstrating that in pursuing its legitimate goal of protecting citizens from the crime of rape-murder it had chosen means that did not "unnecessarily impinge on the fundamental constitutional right to life." For this reason, the mandatory death penalty for murder committed in the course of rape violates the due process clause and the cruel or unusual punishment clause of the Massachusetts Constitution. Moreover, in footnote 23 he extended the court's analysis beyond rape-murder. The state should be aware, Tauro wrote, that any new death penalty statute must meet the "compelling state interest" test. Justices Hennessey and Wilkins concurred with the chief's opinion while stressing Massachusetts's "unique" past and recent death penalty history and the importance of Article 26. Wilkins noted, for example, that Massachusetts "should be particularly conscious of the seriousness" of imposing the death penalty, because of the "inordinate attention, not all of it favorable" that the Salem witch trials and the execution of Sacco and Vanzetti brought to the state.[75]

His argument completed, Tauro lashed out at Justices Braucher and Reardon for disagreeing with him. Perhaps his attack was a parting shot—at age seventy Tauro was compelled to retire from the court—in a long-festering quarrel. Perhaps it was simply another manifestation of his irascible personality or perhaps his rhetoric was heightened by the importance of the death penalty issue before the court. Whatever the reason, his verbal assault on two men with whom he had served nearly his entire tenure on the bench was personal and gratuitous. He accused Braucher of trying to avoid the important constitutional issues by resorting to "doubtful" and "strained" statutory construction and of violating his constitutional obligation as a judge. He next savaged Reardon's "novel suggestion" that the SJC "refrain from construction and application of our State Constitution" and wait for the Supreme Court to offer guidance. Reardon's point was "utterly without merit," Tauro declared. "This court—not the Federal courts—bears ultimate responsibility for construction of our State Constitution. Our interpretation," Tauro crowed, "of the State Constitution is final and cannot be challenged in the Federal courts." Finally, Tauro fired back at the charge that he allowed his personal views rather than the law to shape his opinion. On the contrary, Tauro retorted, he was motivated by the need to uphold the Constitution and to maintain the SJC's "independence and impartiality."[76]

Overlooking Tauro's jabs at his colleagues, Governor Dukakis hailed the majority decision as "the crowning achievement of his judicial career" and a "brilliant work of exposition." In an editorial headlined "Ending the Death Penalty," the *Globe* sang the praises of an evolving constitution. "Standards of human justice have changed—for the better, we think—and both [the U.S. Constitution and the Massachusetts Constitution] were intended to serve more as general guides than as hard and fast rules." The SJC's *O'Neal* decision, the *Globe* concluded, brought the law into conformity with contemporary Massachusetts values. In fact, the *Globe*'s assessment of popular beliefs about the constitutionality of the death penalty was far too optimistic. Although Massachusetts citizens were somewhat more ambivalent than Americans generally, a 1974 Gallop poll showed roughly two-thirds of all Americans favored the death penalty for murder.[77]

For this reason, among others, the SJC's *O'Neal* decision did not end controversy over the death penalty in Massachusetts. In fact, just seven months after *O'Neal*, death penalty proponents in Massachusetts and across the nation received a boost when the Supreme Court found a new Georgia death penalty statute constitutional. A majority of the Court was satisfied that Georgia's statute, and by implication the death penalty laws of thirty-seven other states, had substituted guided discretion for arbitrariness. One year later, the Massachusetts legislature asked the SJC for an advisory opinion on the constitutionality of a proposed death penalty bill. Shaped by the Court's decision in *Gregg v. Georgia* (1976), the Massachusetts bill provided that in a murder trial a jury would first determine a defendant's guilt or innocence; if it found the defendant guilty, the jury would then vote separately on punishment. To arrive at a sentence, the jury would take into account mitigating as well as aggravating circumstances and the SJC would automatically review all death sentences. In its Advisory Opinion, the SJC told the legislature that its view of the constitutionality of the death penalty had not changed since *O'Neal*. The House bill might meet the standard set by the Supreme Court, but "it does not meet the *O'Neal* objection, that capital punishment violates Article 26 of the Declaration of Rights prohibiting a court or magistrate from inflicting cruel or unusual punishment." The legislature also failed to show the death penalty's "peculiar efficacy in comparison with other punishment." In short, the court held firm to its state constitutional analysis.[78]

With the death penalty issue seemingly settled, Governor Dukakis launched his bid for reelection in May 1978. A poll showed the governor trouncing his Republican challenger by nearly forty percentage points. Dukakis held a similarly wide lead over his chief Democratic primary opponent, Edward J. King, a conservative businessman and former Boston College football star. But as the summer wore on, Dukakis's advisers grew worried. During a televised debate on August 31, Dukakis aloofly reminded viewers of his record, while King hammered home his agenda—tax cuts, a return to the law setting the minimum age for drinking at twenty-one years of age, and an end to state-funded abortions, mandatory jail sentences for drug pushers, and the reinstatement of capital punishment. Follow-up polls showed Dukakis was more popular than King, but that a majority of people were desperate about growing inflation and furious about crime. By the afternoon of primary day it had become clear that King had defeated the incumbent governor by nearly ten percentage points. King cruised to an easy victory in the November election.[79]

On August 15, 1979, Governor King delivered on his campaign promise to sign into law a death penalty bill. A solemn King set the stage for another court test of the death penalty. He told a group of supporters at the State House that he considered the death penalty to be "a fitting punishment that will provide a 'deterrent' to murder." King added, "All you have to do is read the list of crimes for which capital punishment is called for here and I think they deserve it." The law permitted a sentence of death for those convicted of first-degree murder in cases involving rape, hijack, kidnap, murder on contract, the murder of a police officer, fire fighter, or corrections officer, and the second conviction for first-degree murder. Once a prisoner was sentenced to death, the law stipulated that the sentence be reviewed by the SJC. Finally, the law's preamble declared the people's "duly elected representatives must not be shut off by the intervention of the judicial department on the basis of a constitutional test intertwined with an assessment of contemporary standards." Suffolk County district attorney Newman Flanagan, who also had campaigned for the death penalty, stood by the governor's side. He was the first prosecutor to make a test case out of the new law.[80]

Two days after the law went into effect, two young black men were charged with murdering a white, twenty-eight-year-old Boston cab driver. Because of Boston's volatile racial climate, drivers were instructed by their supervisors not to pick up two or more young men "of the opposite race," but just after 4:00 A.M. on November 16, 1979, cabbie Jeffrey Boyajian agreed to take three leather-jacketed young black men to a housing project in Roslindale. After directing Boyajian to a dead-end street, James Watson and Frederick Clay pulled him from his cab. "Take what you want, but let me live," he begged. But after beating and robbing Boyajian, Clay shot him to death, according to an eyewitness. Two of the assailants were arrested and indicted for murder. District Attorney Flanagan asked the SJC for a declaratory judgment to determine the constitutionality of the 1979 death penalty law before he went to trial.[81]

Framed in this novel way, the issue came before the SJC in May 1980. The court's composition and its personality had changed since its *O'Neal* decision five years earlier. Governor Dukakis had made three appointments; he replaced Reardon and Tauro with Paul J. Liacos and Ruth Abrams, and he promoted Associate Justice Edward F. Hennessey to the center seat. Hennessey graduated from Northeastern University in 1941, just in time to enlist in the U.S. Army "for the duration." He served primarily in Italy, where he earned six battle citations and promotion to the rank of captain. As the war wound down, Hennessey's commanding officer assigned him to defend soldiers charged with serious crimes. On one such occasion, he witnessed the execution of three men convicted of rape. When the war ended, Hennessey went straight to Boston University Law School. Admitted to the bar in 1949, he served briefly as an assistant district attorney in Middlesex County, practiced with a private law firm, edited the *Massachusetts Law Quarterly*, and in 1966, accepted an appointment to the bench. Together with his wartime brush with "rough justice," these experiences deepened Hennessey's love for the order, rationality, and fairness of the law and may have stiffened his opposition to capital punishment.[82]

By a 6-to-1 vote, the SJC concluded in *District Attorney v. Watson* (1980) that the new death penalty statute violated Article 26, the cruel or unusual punishment clause of the Massachusetts Declaration of Rights. Chief Justice Hennessey acknowledged that all punishment is cruel; but the court's focus in *Watson*, he said, was on punishment that "is too cruel under constitutional standards." In making such a distinction, "contemporary moral standards" guide the court and not the definition used by the framers of the Massachusetts Constitution and frozen in time. Rather, the court applies the "evolving standards of decency that mark the progress of a maturing society." Contemporary public opinion about the death penalty is relevant to the process of defining Article 26, but a judicial conclusion about the constitutional validity of the death penalty cannot rest on opinion polls. "We think that what our society does in actuality," Hennessey wrote, "is a much more compelling indicator of the acceptability of the death penalty than the responses citizens may give upon questioning."[83]

Two examples buttressed the chief justice's argument. First, Hennessey insisted that the fact that no one had been executed in Massachusetts since 1947 spoke more persuasively about the acceptability of the death penalty than opinion polls and passionate rhetoric. Successive governors "who bore the responsibility for administering the death penalty" found it "unacceptable." Second, Hennessey branded the death penalty unconstitutionally cruel because it was applied arbitrarily and discriminatorily. The court accepted the "wisdom of *Furman*," but without being restricted by it. Statutes acceptable under *Furman*'s guidelines were not free—and could not be free—from racial bias and capriciousness and, therefore, offend Article 26. For these reasons, the SJC held the death penalty unconstitutionally cruel.[84]

Justices Reardon, Wilkins, and Liacos wrote concurring opinions.

Reardon had difficulty with the "evolving standards of decency" argu-ment. He could not rid himself of the doubt that applying such a standard was simply a rationalization for enforcing his own private view rather than a standard enjoined by the Constitution. But he was certain that evidence accumulated since *Gregg* demonstrated that "death sentences will rarely be carried out" and then, only after "agonizing months and years of uncer-tainty." For that reason, Reardon concluded, "the punishment is cruel and unusual and violates art. 26 of the Declaration of Rights." Wilkins con-curred with the majority's opinion, but he objected to the court passing on the constitutionality of the death penalty statute without considering an actual case and he would have preferred to avoid a confrontation with the legislature.[85]

In his concurring opinion, Justice Paul J. Liacos, who came to the court in 1976 and who once described the death penalty as "torture in the guise of civilized business," passionately amplified the court's reasons for find-ing the death penalty "impermissibly cruel when judged by contemporary standards of decency." Liacos wrote movingly of how the imposition of the death penalty was "disguised by the language and technique of ab-straction," how a "ritual language reduced to stereotyped phrases" masked our "shame" and the "degrading" business of deliberately putting some-one to death. Indeed, the clear purpose of the prohibition against cruel or unusual punishment, Liacos argued, "is to guarantee a measure of human dignity even to the wrongdoers of our society" and to preserve the dignity of government. Capital punishment, Liacos concluded, is "antithetical to the spiritual freedom that underlies the democratic mind."[86]

Two years later, in his "State of the State" address, Governor King asked the legislature to defy the court once again. He condemned "judicial leniency" and demanded that "the restoration of the death penalty be put before the voters" in November 1982. King also announced his intention to seek reelection, fully aware that his primary opponent would be former governor Michael Dukakis, whose opposition to capital punishment was well known. Massachusetts voters would have two opportunities to evalu-ate the court's opposition to the death penalty, the Democratic primary race in September and a referendum question on the November ballot. Po-litical pundits characterized the death penalty issue as "extremely volatile" and predicted it would "polarize the Democratic primary race." Because King framed the issue as a "litmus test for those who are soft on crime versus those who want to enforce the law," nearly everyone believed King would be the political beneficiary of the referendum.[87]

In fact, by late summer Governor King had cut Dukakis's early lead almost in half and campaign polls indicated he had seized the momentum in the Democratic primary battle. On the eve of the primary election King announced he had filed a bill that would allow the state to quickly implement capital punishment if voters approved the proposed constitutional amendment. A week later, King challenged Dukakis to tell voters what he would do if the referendum were to pass. "Will he sign it or will he veto it; he should give the people a straight answer," King demanded. Dukakis's answer came quickly: "Yes, governor, I'd veto your bill," he said, adding, "but what a pathetically transparent political maneuver in the final days of this campaign."[88]

Dukakis completed his four-year odyssey to personal vindication by squeaking out a narrow victory over King, winning the right to face Republican John W. Sears in the general election. In the run-up to that election the issue of capital punishment received less attention than it had in the primary. The debate between Dukakis and Sears was more rational and less visceral. A *Globe* editorial promoted this spirit when it argued that "the wise and humane course would be to reject" the ballot question restoring capital punishment in Massachusetts. But the ghost of Ed King prevailed and voters cleared the way for legislative enactment of a death penalty statute by approving the referendum question by a margin of 60 to 40. The issue now was whether proponents could force a death penalty bill through the legislature quickly enough to be signed by outgoing governor King, a death penalty supporter, or whether opponents could delay it until after the inauguration of governor-elect Dukakis, who had vowed to veto any capital punishment legislation.[89]

Nine days after the election, shortly before 3:00 A.M., by a vote of 17 to 14, the Massachusetts Senate approved a bill restoring capital punishment. The bill differed markedly from a House version passed a few days earlier. The House rejected the Senate's death penalty bill on November 29, paving the way for a conference committee. Senate president William Bulger took charge of the secret negotiations, and after brief debate in the Senate and House, a death penalty bill was approved just six weeks after voters had approved a constitutional amendment. Seven years to the minute after the SJC found a death penalty unconstitutional in *O'Neal*, lame-duck governor King signed the death penalty bill into law. He assured his listeners that the statute "will meet all constitutional requirements," and he warned "would-be murderers that if they break the law they will pay the full price." Max Stern, a lawyer who was chair of Massachusetts Campaign Against Restoration of the Death Penalty, branded the law "bloodbath legislation."[90]

The revised law called for a two-step process. A defendant charged with first-degree murder who pleaded innocent would go to trial. If the defendant were convicted, a judge would weigh aggravating and mitigating circumstances and decide whether the death penalty was justified. The law allowed the death penalty for ten kinds of aggravating circumstances, including the murder of a police officer, prison guard, judge, juror, or witness, and murder for hire or during an escape from jail or during a rape, robbery, arson, bombing, or torture. The judge must consider the defendant's age, criminal record. and any mental illness as a mitigating factor.[91]

About 8:30 P.M. February 26, 1983, fifty-seven days after the state's death penalty statute went into effect, Massachusetts state trooper George L. Hanna Jr. was shot to death after he stopped a red Vega in the parking lot of a liquor store on Route 20 in Auburn. An eyewitness saw three men in addition to Hanna standing between the trooper's cruiser and the Vega. One man was spread-eagle across the Vega's hood. The other two were standing toward the rear of the car. One of those men shot Hanna and he fell forward. When he struggled to get to his feet, the two men wrestled him to the ground and one of them fired six bullets into Hanna's chest and back. "Let's get out of here," one of the men yelled in Spanish, and the car sped away. Twenty-four hours later the police arrested Abimael Colon-Cruz, José Colon, and Miguel Angel Rosado. Shackled and surrounded by eleven heavily armed state troopers, the suspects were arraigned in Worcester Central District Court. In June 1983, a grand jury indicted each of the defendants for Hanna's murder. Following hearings on a series of pretrial motions, prosecutor Daniel F. Toomey announced that he intended to ask the SJC to determine the death penalty's constitutionality before going to trial. Hearings before the court began in April 1984.[92]

The court could not rely on the cruel or unusual punishment clause as it had when it declared capital punishment unconstitutional in *Watson* (1980). Voters had added the following language to Article 26 in 1982: "No provision of the Constitution, however, shall be construed as prohibiting the imposition of the punishment of death. The general court may, for the purpose of protecting the general welfare of the citizens, authorize the imposition of the punishment of death by the courts of law having jurisdiction of crimes subject to the punishment of death."[93]

Speaking for a razor-thin 4-to-3 majority, Justice Liacos, a former Boston University Law School professor whom Governor Dukakis had appointed to the court during his first term, acknowledged that the amendment "now prevents this court from construing any provision of the Massachusetts Constitution, including art. 26 itself, as forbidding the imposition of the punishment of death." He disagreed, however, with the commonwealth's argument that the Article 26 amendment prohibited the court from invalidating any capital punishment statute under any article of the Massachusetts Constitution. "We do not see anything in the new language of art. 26 which prevents us from invalidating a particular death penalty statute under the Massachusetts Constitution on a ground other than the imposition of the punishment of death is forbidden." He noted, for example, that although the Supreme Court had held the imposition of the death penalty is not invariably cruel and unusual punishment, it struck down as unconstitutional a number of death penalty statutes on other grounds. In short, Liacos interpreted the voter-approved amendment to Article 26 as prohibiting the court from finding a death penalty statute unconstitutional simply because it clashed with the cruel or unusual punishment clause. In this same vein the court found the 1982 death penalty statute violated Article 12 of the Declaration of Rights because it provided that only those defendants who pleaded not guilty and demanded a jury trial were at risk of being put to death. Those who pleaded guilty avoided the death penalty. "The inevitable consequence," Liacos wrote, "is that defendants are discouraged from asserting their right not to plead guilty and their right to demand a trial by jury."[94]

The SJC's controversial decision in *Colon-Cruz* marked the last time the issue of capital punishment was before the Massachusetts court. Although politicians continued to exploit the issue and the legislature debated it several times after 1984, no law was enacted and Massachusetts remains one of the twelve states without a death penalty.

After more than fifty years of struggle by death penalty abolitionists, the Massachusetts Supreme Judicial Court found capital punishment unconstitutional in 1980 and in 1984. The court's decisions capped an unofficial moratorium in effect since 1947, when two convicted murderers were executed. In addition to citing the long list of elected governors who refused to implement the law, the court noted the discriminatory impact of race, the Massachusetts Constitution's prohibition against "cruel or unusual punishment," and the need to protect a defendant's right to due process. In the aftermath of the court's action, several Republican governors eager to pad their "tough on crime" credentials sought to restore the death penalty. Democrat legislators easily turned back their initial efforts. In 1997, however, following the brutal murder of a ten-year-old boy, a divisive, emotional struggle to reinstate the death penalty cut across party lines and only an intense lobbying effort by Cardinal Bernard Law prevented the restoration of the death penalty in Massachusetts. Six years later, in the wake of revelations that over the past decade courts across the nation had sentenced more than a hundred wrongly convicted men to death, Massachusetts Republican governor Mitt Romney introduced one of the most strictly limited death penalty bills in history. The governor claimed his proposal was legally airtight and scientifically unassailable.

Within less than a month after the court's October 18, 1984, decision in *Colon-Cruz*, Michael Dukakis regained the governor's office. His pledge to veto any new death penalty bill coupled with his appointment to the Supreme Judicial Court's center seat of an outspoken opponent of capital punishment prevented any further effort to reinstate the death penalty in Massachusetts until Republican William F. Weld became governor in 1991. Weld had deep New England roots (although he was born in New York), breezed through Harvard College and Harvard Law School, and served on the House Judiciary Committee's legal staff for the Watergate investigation. When Ronald Reagan vaulted into the White House, Weld was appointed U.S. attorney and later assistant U.S. attorney general. He won the Massachusetts governor's office by being far more charming than Boston University president John Silber and by promising to be tough on crime and flexible on social issues. (He favored affirmative action for minorities and women and also supported abortion rights for women.) Each year he held office he filed a death penalty bill.[1]

Weld argued there was a pressing need for a Massachusetts death penalty law. He insisted capital punishment works as a "deterrent and as the only fitting punishment for certain types of first-degree murder." Under Weld's bill, the state would be permitted to seek the death penalty if any of twelve aggravating circumstances were present, including killing of police officers, judges, prosecutors, or jurors, killings by previously convicted murderers, and murder in connection with rape, robbery, or drug dealing. Weld's running mate, Lt. Governor Paul Cellucci, shocked many by asserting that the benefits of capital punishment outweighed the risk of executing those unjustly convicted. Attorney General Scott Harshbarger, a Democrat, denounced Cellucci's "inhumanity" and branded Weld's proposal "a simplistic, arbitrary, misguided, ineffective and costly response, cloaked in the guise of a remedy to the brutalizing violence that angers us all." The state's Roman Catholic bishops also weighed in against the death penalty. Still, Lou DiNatale, senior fellow at the McCormack Institute for Public Affairs, pointed to the growing number of Massachusetts House and Senate races in which the death penalty figured largely. "At this point," DiNatale said in the summer of 1994, "you can only get hurt [politically] by coming out against the death penalty." The roadside slaying of state trooper Mark Charbonnier a few months later increased the political heat on those candidates opposed to the death penalty. In fact, the Massachusetts Senate approved a Republican-sponsored rider to a budget bill that would have restored capital punishment by lethal injection for twelve kinds of first-degree murder. However, the House rejected a death penalty bill 88 to 70.[2]

When Weld's death penalty bill failed again in 1995, he proposed a ballot initiative to reinstate the death penalty. His proposal was much the same as the bill he had introduced in the legislature previously, but the ballot measure contained specific safeguards for the accused, including an

exemption for minors and the mentally incompetent from a death sentence
and the establishment of a separate sentencing jury apart from the one
that handed down the conviction. Attorney General Harshbarger spoiled
Weld's plan. He ruled against placing the proposal on the ballot because
Article 48 of the Massachusetts Constitution limits the kinds of law citizens can enact through the ballot process. Specifically, Article 48 prohibits any proposal relating to the courts' powers. "It is difficult to imagine,"
the Boston *Globe*'s editorial page argued, "a matter better kept out of the
hands of the populace and reserved to the deliberative branches of government than the state's right to put another person to death." After Weld was
reelected, his commitment to the ballot initiative evaporated.[3]

After serving less than one year of his second term as governor, Weld
announced he intended to challenge U.S. Senator John Kerry. In the meantime, Weld dove into the polluted Charles River to celebrate the passage of
the Rivers Protection Act, abruptly withdrew from his speaking slot at the
Republican national convention, and whispered to everyone who would
listen that he was bored with the governor's office. Shortly after Kerry
soundly defeated him, Weld resigned as governor in the forlorn hope of
winning Senate confirmation as the U.S. ambassador to Mexico. In July
1997, Lt. Governor Paul Cellucci became acting governor of Massachusetts. He vowed publicly he would sign a death penalty statute during his
tenure as governor.[4]

Three months later, on October 1, Salvatore Sicari and Charles Jaynes
lured ten-year-old Jeffrey Curley into their car from the sidewalk in front
of the boy's Cambridge home with the promise of a bicycle. The two men
smothered Curley to death with a gasoline soaked rag, raped him, and
stuffed his lifeless body into a concrete-filled tub. A week later the boy's
body was pulled from the Great Works River in Maine. Horrified by the
grisly murder, on October 21 the Massachusetts Senate focused its debate
not on whether to reinstate the death penalty but on how broad to make it.
By a vote of 20 to 17 the Senate approved a bill former governor Weld and
Acting Governor Cellucci had advocated for years. In a debate punctuated
by highly charged rhetoric, the Senate did not stop with police officers,
judges, multiple murders, and drug trafficking, but with each vote increased the types of first-degree murder for which death would be the penalty prescribed by law. By a 22 to 14 margin, for example, the Senate voted

to permit capital punishment for the murderer of a child under the age of fourteen who was kidnapped and sexually assaulted. A few amendments were designed to extend greater legal protection to capital defendants.[5]

Under enormous pressure, House Speaker Thomas Finneran, a Democrat and an opponent of capital punishment, announced on October 23 he would allow the Senate bill to come to a vote in the House within two weeks. In the meantime, experts and advocates on both sides aggressively lobbied House members. James A. Fox, dean of Northeastern University's College of Criminal Justice, told legislators that of the 188 prisoners who were convicted of first-degree murder and paroled after the Supreme Court struck down capital punishment in 1972 only one man from that group was imprisoned for killing again. Data handed to legislators by another Northeastern professor, William Bowers, showed that only a tiny number of Massachusetts residents surveyed knew that the penalty for first-degree murder was life imprisonment without parole. "You don't have to execute people to make sure they don't kill again," Bowers said. "You just don't let 'em out."[6]

Jeffrey's parents, Robert and Barbara Curley, along with a cluster of relatives, all wearing yellow ribbons with the boy's name, also talked with legislators. Echoing the strategy embraced by Acting Governor Cellucci, Robert Curley was overheard telling a legislator: "The people want it. The people are the ones who put you in here and if it doesn't get done today, then enjoy your time in the Statehouse, because you may be gone the next time." One Democrat legislator shot back: "A vote to reinstate the death penalty would be a step back into the darkness and would be another step in furtherance [sic] of isolating our country from the civilized world." A Boston Herald poll seemed to provide evidence for both viewpoints: the poll showed that 74 percent of Massachusetts voters backed a death penalty for those who murdered a child. However, only a bare 51 percent thought it would be a deterrent and only 40 percent said they would be less likely to re-elect their representative if he or she voted against a death penalty bill.[7]

Bernard Cardinal Law, Archbishop of Boston, wielded the moral authority of the Roman Catholic Church in opposition to the death penalty. Sometimes accompanied by Sr. Helen Prejean, author of the best-selling Dead Man Walking, Law worked the halls of the State House, quietly talking to legislators and lobbyists. The Massachusetts Catholic Conference

had previously circulated to all 160 members of the House a column written by Law. A horrible, violent crime, the cardinal began, "has rendered us
numb, frustrated, and angry. To call for capital punishment in such a climate is understandable." But "support for capital punishment is not a litmus test for revulsion at Jeffrey's murder. Those of us who oppose capital
punishment are not soft on murder." The Catholic Church, he explained,
believes the best way to protect potential victims from a similar crime is
to put the convicted murderer behind bars for life without the possibility
of parole. Capital punishment is not the answer. It is nothing more than a
collective act of revenge. Of course, violence and murder are wrong and
the Church must address the social problems within the contemporary
culture that contribute to the current "epidemic of sexual crimes and domestic violence." The Church "do[es] not need quick fixes like capital
punishment," Law concluded. "We need the patience to seek out answers
to more profound questions and the will to rewrite our cultural script." [8]

One day later, on October 28, after twelve hours of contentious debate,
the House voted 81 to 79 to resume capital punishment, fifty years after
the last murderer was executed in Massachusetts. "I won't vote against
my conscience," Representative William J. McManus, an opponent of the
death penalty during the debate, said. Donna Cuomo, another Democrat,
countered, "The people really want the death penalty and I felt I didn't
want to deny the people their voice." Supporters of the death penalty
in the House gallery cheered and shouted "Thank you!" when the final
vote was cast. Standing rumpled and unshaved on the front lawn of the
State House, bathed in television's bright light, Acting Governor Cellucci
hailed the vote as a "victory for justice and for the people of Massachusetts." House Speaker Finneran attributed support for the death penalty
bill to nearly three decades of frustration over increasing violence. "We live
in a time in society when our culture is coarse, it is violent, and it has unacceptable, unspeakable levels of conduct that are not always condemned
and almost condoned," he said. He quietly noted that the fight was not
over, because the measure passed by the House differed from the bill enacted by the Senate and a conference committee would have to hammer
out a mutually acceptable version of the proposed law. [9]

Nine days later, in a stunning reversal, the House refused, on a tie vote,
to reinstate the death penalty. Under parliamentary rules, the 80-to-80 vote
killed the bill, which would have allowed capital punishment for fifteen

categories of first-degree murder. Representative John P. Slattery, a Democrat from suburban Peabody, who had voted for the House version of the death penalty bill, voted against the conference-committee version of the bill. Moved by the fear that an innocent might be executed, Slattery said, "I don't want to be lying in my bed at 12:01 A.M. fifteen years from now knowing that somebody is being put to death, [and] that I helped create the mechanism for putting that person to death." The tie vote blocked the proponents of the death penalty from bringing the issue back before the legislature until 1999.[10]

Slattery's switch and the realization that Speaker Finneran had outmaneuvered him caused Acting Governor Cellucci nearly to explode with anger. Yelling, red-faced, Cellucci declared, "This battle is not over!" He accused Speaker Finneran of using "dirty tricks" to block the will of the people. "The people of Massachusetts wanted a death penalty," Cellucci shouted at the television cameras. "Last week they had it, and tonight Speaker Finneran stole it away." The governor let it be known that Republican activists would recruit a candidate to oust the Peabody Democrat in the 1998 election. Speaker Finneran acknowledged the death penalty could become a major issue in some legislative races, but, he added, "I think most people, look for greater breadth, a greater scope in their candidates. They'd like to know what somebody's position is on education, economic development, taxes, the environment, housing, a whole host of issues." Attorney General Harshbarger, widely believed to be positioning himself to challenge Cellucci in the upcoming race for governor, defended a representative's right to vote his or her conscience.[11]

Governor Cellucci handily defeated Harshbarger in November 1998, but his desire to oust legislators opposed to capital punishment failed. Undeterred, Cellucci used his political power in an effort to change the outcome of the vote on capital punishment to be held in the 1999 legislature. He rewarded two Republican legislators who had voted against the death penalty with political plums (a judgeship and an administrative post) and thereby opened the way to special elections he hoped his hand-picked death penalty proponents would win. The results were mixed. In the meantime, Jeffrey Curley's killers, Sicari and Jaynes, were convicted in federal court of first-degree murder and sentenced, respectively, to life imprisonment without parole and life imprisonment plus ten years for kidnapping. For these reasons, Cellucci's capital punishment drive lost momentum and on March 29, 1999, the Massachusetts House defeated a new death penalty bill by an 80-to-73 margin. Two years later Jeffrey Curley's father announced he too opposed the death penalty.[12]

Before he completed his first elected term as governor, Cellucci resigned, and Lt. Governor Jane Swift served as acting governor until January 2003, when Republican Mitt Romney took office. A son of the former Michigan governor and Republican presidential hopeful George Romney, Mitt graduated from Brigham Young University in 1971 and Harvard Law School four years later. His Utah roots and a successful business career led to Mitt's selection as CEO of the 2002 Winter Olympic committee, a highly visible position that brought him back to Massachusetts and the governor's office. He made support for the death penalty a priority during his campaign, but despite polls showing most Massachusetts voters favoring capital punishment, the legislature opposed reinstating it by a wide margin. A number of legislators, for example, pointed to recent revelations in Illinois that thirteen death row inmates had been wrongly convicted as evidence that ordinary jurors operating in the present flawed legal system cannot make valid life-and-death decisions. Rumored to be harboring presidential aspirations, Romney was undeterred by the predicted uphill fight in the legislature.[13]

On September 23, 2003, Governor Romney named the eleven-member Council on Capital Punishment and charged it with "crafting a proposal to reinstate capital punishment in Massachusetts for a narrow set of crimes." At the press conference announcing his council, the governor stated that DNA technology and other advances in forensic sciences meant that an "error free" and "air-tight" death penalty law could be crafted. "Just as science can be used to free the innocent," he said, "it can also be used to identify the guilty." House Democrats and death penalty opponents were critical of the governor's proposal. Former House member and criminal defense attorney John Slattery predicted little would come from Romney's effort. "He is bucking the popular trend," Slattery said. I don't think he has a chance of convincing the House that the system is foolproof." James Alan Fox, a professor at Northeastern University, pooh-poohed the notion that the use of science can create an infallible criminal justice system. "Science is performed by scientists and scientists are human beings and they are not infallible," Fox said. "Science is irrefutable, but scientists can make mistakes. How can the governor guarantee whether evidence is planted or mishandled or incorrectly tested?"[14]

Although Romney claimed the members of the Council on Capital Punishment were chosen solely because of their backgrounds in law and science, all of the lawyers and judges were Republicans with records that suggested they favored the death penalty. Council co-chair Joseph L. Hoffman, an Indiana University Law School professor, for example, had clerked for U.S. Supreme Court Chief Justice William Rehnquist and served as a consultant to Republicans on the U.S. House of Representative's committee on death penalty legislation. Hoffman insisted Romney's effort had the potential for breaking new legal ground in the contentious and emotional debate over the death penalty. Dr. Henry C. Lee, known for his testimony in the O. J. Simpson murder trial, headed the council's forensic section. Before the council's work began, he applauded Romney's "responsible approach" to "the issue of capital punishment," adding, "every state in the nation should look to the example he is setting in this area."[15]

In May 2004 the council issued its report. Co-chair Frederick R. Beiber, a Harvard Medical School pathologist, said that if the council's recommendations were adopted in their entirety by the legislature a "fair," "narrowly tailored," and "as infallible as humanely possible" death penalty statute could be enacted in Massachusetts. The cornerstone of the council's recommendations was that the death penalty be applied only to a narrow list of cases (political terrorism, torture murders, murders of police officers and others in the criminal justice system, and murders of multiple victims) and that each case include scientific evidence, such as DNA, fingerprints, or footprints. The physical evidence would have to "strongly corroborate" the defendant's guilt and the trial judge would be required to instruct the jury that nonscientific evidence can be unreliable. Moreover, the bar for establishing the guilt of a capital defendant would be raised from "beyond a reasonable doubt" to a finding of "no doubt." The council also proposed that a capital defendant be given the option of facing two separate juries: one for trial and, if convicted, one for sentencing. Finally, the council recommended that courts have broad authority to set aside wrongful death sentences, that the state attorney general review every decision by a district attorney to bring a capital case, and that a separate review board investigate claims of error in capital cases. "There's no system that [is] remotely like this," Hoffman said. He added: "The death penalty ought to be reserved for only the most clear-cut, sure-thing cases."[16]

Opponents and proponents alike expressed dissatisfaction with the council's proposals. Boston criminal defense and civil liberties attorney Harvey Silvergate told the press that the proposal "doesn't hit at enough of the real problems in the system that causes false convictions." He also was critical of two key assumptions made in the council's plan: that DNA evidence is as useful in proving guilt as it is in proving innocence; and that merely instructing a jury to use "human evidence" carefully is adequate. "Jurors are going to go by their gut, the attorney said, "and their gut is that eyewitness testimony is very effective, even though we know it is very prone to error." Columbia University law professor James S. Liebman, author of a nationwide study of the rate of error committed in death penalty cases, pointed out to the Boston Globe that DNA evidence can be used to prove a suspect's presence at the scene of a murder, but it tells nothing about motive, intent, the presence of another suspect, or the plausibility of a self-defense argument. Proponents of capital punishment also expressed doubts about the efficacy of the council's proposals. Kent Scheidegger of the Criminal Justice Legal Foundation, a pro–death penalty group, said the proposal was worded so narrowly it would not cover the recent murder of a seven-year-old New Jersey girl who was abducted, raped, and murdered by a convicted sex-offender. Likewise, a U.S. Justice Department attorney told the New York Times that the Romney recommendations were indeed innovative but ran the risk of making the criteria so narrow that "no one is going to be executed under this law."[17]

The Boston Herald columnist Peter Gelzinis highlighted Romney's presidential aspirations as the driving force behind the "cumbersome piece of retribution." It was, he said, a "death penalty bill made in Massachusetts, but designed to be carried through a valley of red states." Former Massachusetts governor Michael Dukakis also emphasized the bill's political purpose, branding Romney's effort a "charade." Finally, the Globe editorial page noted that human error, shoddy work, and politics recently had caused Virginia governor Mark Warner to order a review of more than 150 capital murder convictions involving DNA evidence.[18]

For most of its history Massachusetts executed men and women convicted of murder, but reform and abolitionism often competed for cultural, political, and legal dominance. Thirty-three years after the last executions for murder in Massachusetts the Supreme Judicial Court found the death penalty unconstitutional. During the quarter-century following the court's ruling, Republican governors and Democratic legislatures repeatedly have faced each other down.

To date, the SJC's historic decision that the death penalty violates a fundamental right to life protected by the Massachusetts constitution has stood as a bulwark against the passions that murder and the legal proceedings that follow arouse. For this reason, if and until an especially brutal killing creates an emotional call for revenge that may drive the legislature to enact a death penalty law that the Supreme Judicial Court would find constitutional, Massachusetts will remain one of twelve states where the death penalty is not permitted.

NOTES

PREFACE

1. *Commonwealth v. Hardy*, 2 Mass. 302 (1807).

2. J. S. Cockburn, "The Nature and Incidence of Crime in England 1559–1625," in *Crime in England, 1550–1800*, ed. Cockburn (Princeton, N.J., 1977), 49–58; Douglas Hay et al., eds., *Albion's Fatal Tree: Crime and Society in Eighteenth-Century England* (London, 1975), 17–22.

3. *Commonwealth v. Colon-Cruz*, 393 Mass. 150 (1984).

4. *Malinski v. New York*, 324 U.S. 401, 414 (1945).

5. Felix Frankfurter, *The Case of Sacco and Vanzetti: A Critical Analysis for Lawyers and Laymen* (Boston, 1927); *District Attorney v. Watson*, 381 Mass. 648, 650, 661 (1980).

6. *Trop v. Dulles*, 356 U.S. 86, 101 (1957).

1. MURDER AND DUE PROCEEDING IN COLONIAL MASSACHUSETTS

1. Justice John Cushing, "Charge to the Nantucket Grand Jury," August 1746, William Cushing Family Papers, vol. 1, Massachusetts Historical Society, Boston. Bradley Chapin, *Criminal Justice in Colonial America, 1606–1660* (Athens, Ga., 1983), 77, reports that homicides accounted for 2.4 percent of all serious crime tried by the Court of Assistants from 1630 to 1643.

2. Nathaniel Ward's *Body of Liberties* (1641) did not make a clear distinction between murder and homicide committed in self-defense or accidentally. The Laws and Liberties of Massachusetts (1648) corrected this mistake. There is a rich literature outlining the key features of Massachusetts colonial law. See, among others, George Haskins, *Law and Authority in Early Massachusetts* (New York, 1960); Barbara A. Black, "The Concept of a Supreme Court: Massachusetts Bay, 1630–1686," in *The History of the Law in Massachusetts: The Supreme Judicial Court, 1692–1992*, ed. Russell K. Osgood (Boston, 1992), 43–79; David H. Flaherty, "Criminal Practice in Provincial Massachusetts," in *Law in Colonial Massachusetts, 1630–1800*, ed. Russell Osgood (Boston, 1984), 191–242. Chapin, *Criminal Justice in Colonial America*, provides a basis for comparing Massachusetts law with that of other colonies. But see also Lawrence H. Gipson, "The Criminal Codes of Connecticut," *Journal of the American Institute of Criminal Law and Criminology* 6 (1915): 177, and "The Criminal Codes of Pennsylvania," *Journal of the American Institute of Criminal Law and Criminology* 6 (1915): 323; and Herbert W. K. Fitz-

[NOTES TO PAGES 2–3]

roy, "The Punishment of Crime in Provincial Pennsylvania," in *Courts and Criminal Procedure*, ed. Eric H. Monkkonen (Westport, Conn., 1991), 69.

3. Samuel Sewall, *The Diary of Samuel Sewall, 1674–1729*, ed. M. Halsey Thomas, 2 vols. (Boston, 1973), 2:714. Until 1639 the Court of Assistants was part of the General Court, whose members were legislators, magistrates, and judges. A 1639 statute separated the Court of Assistants from the General Court and made the governor, deputy governor, and magistrates a court to "hear and determine all and only actions of appeal from the inferior courts, all causes of divorce, all capital and criminal causes extending to life, member and banishment." The *Colonial Laws of Massachusetts* (Boston, 1889), 28–29. The Massachusetts Act of 1692 created the Superior Court of Judicature with both appellate and original jurisdiction and consisting of a chief justice and four other justices appointed by the governor with the advice and consent of the Council, a legislative and advisory body elected annually by the House of Representatives. The Constitution of 1780 provided for the Council to be elected by joint ballot of the House and Senate. Roscoe Pound, *Organization of Courts* (Boston, 1940), 66.

4. For the history of infanticide, see Peter C. Hoffer and N. E. H. Hull, *Murdering Mothers: Infanticide in England and New England, 1558–1803* (New York, 1984). Chap. 30 of Magna Charta is the source of modern procedural and substantive due process. Carl Stephenson and Frederick G. Marcham, eds., *Sources of English Constitutional History* (New York, 1972), 1:121. Mary Sarah Bilder, "The Origin of the Appeal in America," *Hastings Law Journal* 48 (1997): 913. In Massachusetts, until 1692, an appeal could be made either by the jury or by the court. *The Colonial Laws of Massachusetts* (Boston, 1889), 47–48. The New Haven colony and Connecticut radically reduced a defendant's right to a jury trial and allowed magistrates far more discretion than in Massachusetts (Gipson, "Criminal Codes of Connecticut," 333–35).

5. David Allen Hearn, *Legal Executions in New England, 1623–1960* (Jefferson, N.C., 1999), 5–6.

6. John Noble, ed., *Records of the Court of Assistants of the Colony of Massachusetts Bay, 1630–1692*, 3 vols. (Boston, 1904), 2:25–26; *The Book of the General Laws and Libertyes Concerning the Inhabitants of the Massachusets* (1648; facsimile edition, Cambridge, Mass., 1929), 29, 13, 28, 32, 36, 54.

7. J. S. Cockburn, *A History of English Assizes, 1588–1714* (Cambridge, 1972), 121–22, 141; John H. Langbein, "The Criminal Trial before Lawyers," *University of Chicago Law Review* 45 (1978): 263. Article 26 of Ward's *Body of Liberties* permits "every man that findeth himselfe unfit to plead his own cause in any Court shall have Libertie to imploy any man to help him, provided he give him noe fee or reward for his paines." The prohibition against fees to lawyers was repealed in 1648. *The Colonial Laws of Massachusetts*, 39. Julius Gobel Jr. and T. Raymond Naughton, *Law*

Enforcement in Colonial New York, A Study in Criminal Trials, 1664–1776 (New York, 1944); Gipson, "Criminal Codes of Connecticut," 177, and "Criminal Codes of Pennsylvania," 322. The Pennsylvania court records are not complete, but existing records show only one recorded execution before 1715 (Fitzroy, "Punishment of Crime in Provincial Pennsylvania," in Monkkonen, *Courts and Criminal Procedure*, 81–83). Cotton Mather, *Bonifacius, An Essay upon the Good*, ed. David Levine (Cambridge, Mass., 1966), 122–27.

8. *Laws and Libertyes*, 87. The General Court had appellate jurisdiction in criminal cases until 1865 (Pound, *Courts*, 29). Flaherty, "Criminal Practice," notes that lawyers played an increasingly important role in the appeals process by the early eighteenth century (212–14). William E. Nelson, *Americanization of the Common Law: The Impact of Legal Change on Massachusetts Society, 1760–1830* (Cambridge, Mass., 1975), 226–27. See Mary Sarah Bilder, "Salamanders and Sons of God: The Culture of Appeal in Early New England," in *The Many Legalities of Early America*, ed. Christopher L. Tomlins and Bruce H. Mann (Chapel Hill, N.C., 2001), 47–77.

9. Flaherty, "Criminal Practice," 205–9, 216

10. Noble, *Court of Assistants*, 2:69; James K. Hosmer, ed., *Winthrop's Journal, "History of New England," 1630–1649*, 2 vols. (New York, 1908), 1:235–36.

11. The Court of Assistants heard 290 criminal cases from 1630 to 1643, 2.4 percent of which were homicides (Hosmer, *Winthrop's Journal*, 1:235–36).

12. Ibid., 236.

13. Langbein, "Criminal Trial before Lawyers," 367, 301–2, 303, discusses the hearsay rule. See *Commonwealth v. Child*, 27 Mass. 252 (1829), in which the Supreme Judicial Court denied an appeal made on the ground that by commenting on the evidence in a criminal trial the trial judge had denied the jury its proper role.

14. Hosmer, *Winthrop's Journal*, 1:237, 238. Schooley was executed the same day, September 28, 1637, as John Williams (Noble, *Court of Assistants*, 2:69).

15. Hosmer, *Winthrop's Journal*, 1:282–83. When Talbye was excommunicated, she turned her back on the minister and tried to walk out of the church, but she was held in place by force. Essex County Court Records, April 27, 1637, in *Essex Insitute Historical Collections*, 129 vols. (1859–1993), 7:129, and August 25, 1638, ibid., 187.

16. Hosmer, *Winthrop's Journal*, 1:238; Noble, *Court of Assistants*, 2:78; Gail S. Marcus, " 'Due Execution of the Generall Rules of Righteous': Criminal Procedure in New Haven Town and Colony, 1638–1658," in *Saints and Revolutionaries: Essays on Early American History*, ed. David D. Hall, John M. Murrin, and Thad W. Tate (New York, 1984), 101.

17. Hosmer, *Winthrop's Journal*, 1:319–20. According to the *Laws and Libertyes*, jurors were permitted to "advise with any man they shall think fit to resolve or direct them, before they give their verdict" (32).

18. Carol F. Lee, "Discretionary Justice in Early Massachusetts," *Essex Institute Historical Collections* 112 (1976): 122.

19. John Winthrop, "On Arbitrary Government," in *Puritan Political Ideas*, ed. Edmund S. Morgan (Indianapolis, Ind., 1965), 151–53, 160.

20. *Laws and Libertyes*, vii.

21. Ibid., 5.

22. Noble, *Court of Assistants*, 3:24, 27–29, 30, 31, 32, 33.

23. The issue of a jury's right to decide fact and law was not resolved legally until *Commonwealth v. Anthes*, 5 Gray 185 (1855). Chief Justice Lemuel Shaw argued that if a jury decided the meaning and application of the law it could vary from case to case and in effect destroy the uniform administration of justice.

24. Noble, *Court of Assistants*, 3:24–25.

25. Ibid., 60, 63.

26. Ibid., 1:30, 32–33; Sewall, *Diary*, 1:10; Cotton Mather, *Pillars of Salt: An History of Some of the Criminals Executed in this Land for Capital Crimes*, in *Pillars of Salt: An Anthology of Early American Criminal Narratives*, ed. Daniel Williams (Madison, Wisc., 1993), 70; Noble, *Court of Assistants*, 3:63, 255–56; 1:51.

27. From 1637 to 1674 there were twelve adults murdered in Massachusetts, and ten adults murdered in 1675–76; twenty-one people were indicted and tried (Noble, *Court of Assistants*, 1:51, 52–54, 60, 71–73, 85–86). Four murders occurred in 1688–89; eighteen people were indicted (ibid., 303–4, 304–5, 306–7, 309–10; Noble, *Court of Assistants*, 1:52–54). Daniel Gookin, *An Historical Account of the Doings and Sufferings of the Christian Indians of New England* (1677), in *Archaeologia Americana: Transactions and Collections of the American Antiquarian Society* 2 (1836): 455, 466; Noble, *Court of Assistants*, 1:54.

28. Noble, *Court of Assistants*, 1:71–77; Gookin, *Historical Account*, 495–97.

29. Noble, *Court of Assistants*, 1:71–73; Lemuel Shattuck, *A History of the Town of Concord* (Boston, 1835), 62–63n, 374–75, 372. Jenny Hale Pulsipher, *Subjects unto the Same King: Indians, English, and the Contest for Authority in Colonial New England* (Philadelphia, 2005), 148–49, 155–56.

30. Massachusetts Historical Society, *Collections*, 88 vols. (Boston, 1792–1992), 5th ser., 5:5:17, 21–22, 24n; *Records of the Governor and Company of the Massachusetts Bay in New England*, 5 vols. (Boston, 1854), 5:136–37 (hereafter *Massachusetts Colonial Records*). Yasuhide Kawashima, "Jurisdiction of the Colonial Courts over the Indians in Massachusetts, 1689–1763," *New England Quarterly* 42 (1969): 532–50.

31. The legislature enacted a law against piracy in 1673. *Massachusetts Colonial Records*, 4, pt. 2, 563. Noble, *Court of Assistants*, 1:309–10. See, generally, G. F. Dow and J. H. Edmunds, *The Pirates of the New England Coast, 1630–1730* (Salem, Mass., 1923).

32. Noble, *Court of Assistants*, 1:320–21. Compare the court's handling of Coward's refusal to plea with the court's threat to Dorothy Talbye (ibid., 2:78). In entering a guilty plea for Coward the court may have been following the common law, rather than the English practice. William Blackstone, *Commentaries on the Laws of England*, 4 vols. (London, 1769; Chicago, 1979), 4:322–23. Blackstone cited the work of the seventeenth-century jurist Matthew Hale, *History of the Pleas of the Crown*, 2 vols. (London, 1736), 2:319, 322, to support his argument that the practice of punishing a defendant who stood mute was contrary to the common law and repugnant to the "humanity of the laws of England" and, therefore, should be abolished. Blackstone also stated that to "advise a prisoner to stand mute" was an "impediment to justice" for which a lawyer might be held in contempt of court and subjected to a fine and imprisonment (ibid., 4, 126).

33. Sewall, *Diary*, 1:248, 250. *Laws and Libertyes*, 24, provides that on the recommendation of any three justices, the governor may reprieve, but only the General Court can pardon a "condemned malefactor." The convicted person climbed a ladder that leaned against a horizontal beam from which a noose was hung. The hangman ascended another ladder, placed the noose around the neck of the person to be executed, climbed down, and standing on the platform, pulled, or turned, away the ladder on which the convicted person was standing.

34. Sewall, *Diary*, 1:250.

35. The exception occurred in the fall of 1673 when a Boston jury found Lodwick Fowler guilty of killing one of his shipmates, although he insisted at trial the musket discharged accidentally. Fowler appealed, and the court overturned his murder conviction and found him guilty of manslaughter (Noble, *Court of Assistants*, 3:255–56). This analysis is based on data included in ibid., vols. 1–3.

36. Ibid., 1:188, 295–96, 304; 3:222.

37. Convictions for infanticide remained high until the 1720s (Hoffer and Hull, *Murdering Mothers*, 39).

38. See, generally, John P. Demos, *Entertaining Satan* (New York, 1982); John Noble, ed., *Publications of the Colonial Society of Massachusetts*, 42 vols. (Boston, 1895–1956), 10:23–25. Thomas Brattle singled out Danforth for praise. G. L. Burr, *Narratives of the Witchcraft Cases* (Boston, 1914), 184. Sewall publicly recanted his part in the witchcraft craze in 1697 (*Diary*, 1:367).

39. Sewall, *Diary*, 1:316, 393. Riding circuit was often uncomfortable. In February 1741, for example, seventy-year-old Chief Justice Benjamin Lynde noted it was so cold that he walked on the frozen Charles River from Charlestown to Boston. At age seventy-one, Lynde commented he was "not so inclined to ride Circuit any longer." Lynde, *The Diaries of Benjamin Lynde and Benjamin Lynde Jr.* (Boston, 1880), 103, 199.

40. Lynde, *Diaries*, 111–12, 21. There are a great many examples of the court's being escorted; see, for example, Sewall, *Diary*, 1:332, 393; Lynde, *Diaries*, 113.

41. Lynde, *Diaries*, 166, 96–97.

42. Mather, *Pillars of Salt*, 1–10, 71–72; Sewall, *Diary*, 1:99–100, 2:727; Hosmer, *Winthrop's Journal*, 1:283. See, generally, Daniel A. Cohen, *Pillars of Salt, Monuments of Grace: New England Crime Literature and the Origins of American Popular Culture, 1674–1860* (New York, 1993).

43. Sewall, *Diary*, 1:509, 518.

44. Ibid., 2:626. Vetch may have argued that because Josias was drunk at the time he murdered his wife, the Native American could not have formed an intent to murder. Josias, Superior Court of Judicature [SCJ], 1700–1714, 242, Judicial Archives, Massachusetts State Archives, Boston. (All SCJ files, including Docket Books, are housed in the Judicial Archives.) Joseph Tanqua smashed his co-worker over the head with a hoe following an argument. Tanqua, SCJ, 1700–1714, 242. Lynde, *Diaries*, November 14, 1769, 193.

45. David B. Hall, *Worlds of Wonder, Days of Judgment: Popular Religious Belief in Early New England* (Cambridge, Mass., 1990); Hosmer, *Winthrop's Journal*, 2:218–19; Patience Boston, "A Faithful Narrative of the Wicked Life and Remarkable Conversion of Patience Boston," in Williams, *Pillars of Salt*, 124, 138–40.

46. Hosmer, *Winthrop's Journal*, 2:218–19. The woman was tried later and convicted of another crime, for which she was executed.

47. Sewall, *Diary*, 2:1046; following Sewall's death and until Lynde joined the court in 1728 the court functioned with only three judges. SCJ, reel 4, 42–43, 195–96; Rex v. Quasson (1726), SCJ, no. 19323; Rex v. Richardson (1728), SCJ, reel 4, 250–51. Lynde heard the following homicide cases: Rex v. Clenan (1729), SCJ, reel 4, 250–51; Rex v. Fuller (1730), SCJ, reel 4, 284; Rex v. Boston (1733), SCJ, reel 4, 122–23; Rex v. Julian (1733), SCJ Docket Book, Suffolk; Rex v. Lobb (1733), Lynde, *Diaries*, 26; Rex v. Quay (1733), SCJ, reel 4, 144–45; Rex v. Ralph (1733), SCJ Docket Book, Barnstable; Rex v. Orinsbury (1734), SCJ Docket Book, Suffolk; Rex v. Nottago (1736), SCJ Docket Book, Suffolk; Rex v. Nason (1736), Rex v. Stevens (1736), and Rex v. Wampum (1736), Lynde, *Diaries*, 70; Rex v. Stephen (1738), SCJ Docket Book, Barnstable; Rex v. Holmes (1738), SCJ Docket Book, Bristol; Rex v. Will (1739), SCJ Docket Book, Barnstable; Rex v. Hagar (1740), SCJ Docket Book, Middlesex; Rex v. Browne (1740), SCJ Docket Book, York; Rex v. Summer (1741), Lynde, *Diaries*, August 25, 1741, 116; Rex v. Pogonet (1742), SCJ Docket Book, Middlesex; Rex v. Fennison (1743), SCJ Docket Book, Middlesex; Rex v. Hunt (1744), SCJ Docket Book, Essex. By comparison, from 1715 to 1745 six Pennsylvania men were convicted of murder and sentenced to death (Gipson, "Criminal Codes of Pennsylvania," 332).

48. Rex v. Fuller (1730), SCJ, Docket Book, Barnstable; Rex v. Julian (1730);

Lynde, *Diaries*, May 1, 1736, 59; Rex v. Browne (1740); Rex v. Harding (1734), SCJ, case no. 37237; Rex v. Fitzpatrick (1744), SCJ, case nos. 58364, 59403, 59587; *Boston Newsletter*, March 22, 1744.

49. Lynde, *Diaries*, October 8, 9, 1734, 60.

50. Flaherty, "Criminal Practice," 236–37; SCJ Docket Book, Barnstable, 1733; SCJ, Minute Book, 23, 47, 35, 56, 51. For benefit of clergy, see George Dalzell, *Benefit of Clergy in America* (Winston-Salem, S.C., 1955). In 1732 the Massachusetts legislature attempted to abolish benefit of clergy. *House Journal* 10 (1731–32): 43. The privilege was abolished in 1785. *Acts and Resolves, 1785* (Boston, 1786), chap. 56.

51. Rex v. Fowles and Rex v. Warren, SCJ Docket Book, Suffolk, February 18, 1745. See, generally, John Lax and William Pencak, "The Knowles Riot and the Crisis of the 1740s in Massachusetts," *Perspectives in American History* 10 (1976): 179. Blackstone, *Commentaries*, 4:368–69, defines "arrest of judgment" as a court-ordered stay of judgment because a serious or reversible error was made during the arraignment or the trial; but Blackstone added that the defendant may be indicted and tried again. In fact, Fowles and Warren were indicted and tried a second time and found guilty, but the sentence of death was not carried out.

52. Lynde, *Diaries*, 89. Lynde does not record Barnes's punishment and there is no record of his execution.

53. Rex v. Stephens, SCJ Docket Book, Barnstable, April 26, 1737; Rex v. Eaton and others, SCJ Docket Book, Suffolk, August 11, 1741; Lynde, *Diaries*, August 25, 1741, 116.

54. Abner C. Goodell Jr., "The Murder of Captain Codman," *Proceedings of the Massachusetts Historical Society* 20 (1883): 122–23. In 1741 New York courts helped fuel a charge that black slaves were conspiring against whites, leading to the execution of thirty-four people. Thomas J. Davis, *A Rumor of Revolt: The Great Negro Plot in Colonial New York* (New York, 1985). The following account of the Codman murder is drawn from Goodell, "Codman," 122–26, 128, 131, 138–42.

55. *Boston Evening Post*, September 22, 1755. In Paul Revere's account of his famous ride, he notes that he headed north across the Charlestown neck, past Mark's remains still hanging in rusty chains. David H. Fisher, *Paul Revere's Ride* (New York, 1994), 106. In 1777, the Massachusetts legislature revised the penalty for treason, making the crime punishable by a simple hanging. *Acts and Resolves 1777* (Boston, 1778), chap. 32. In 1785 the legislature abolished the distinction between petit treason and murder, *Acts and Resolves, 1785* (Boston, 1786), chap. 69.

56. R. T. Paine to Eunice Paine, June 13, 1763, in *The Papers of Robert Treat Paine*, 2 vols., ed. Stephen T. Riley and Edward W. Hanson (Boston, 1992), 2:256–57; *Boston Evening Post*, June 13, 1763.

57. Riley and Hanson, *Paine Papers*, 2:257, 256; *Boston Evening Post*, June 13, 1763.

58. Riley and Hanson, *Paine Papers*, 2:257, 257n, 284, 285.

59. Ibid., 283–85.

60. Thomas Hutchinson to R. T. Paine, October 31, 1764, in Riley and Hanson, *Paine Papers*, 2:310, 311n; *Boston Gazette*, October 14, 1765. There was precedent for the court's permitting Shepardson bail. In 1726 the court allowed Robert Saco, a black sailor indicted for murder, released on bail. Rex v. Saco, SCJ Docket Books, Suffolk, August 9, 1726.

61. Riley and Hanson, *Paine Papers*, 2:359n, 365n.

62. Hiller B. Zobel, *The Boston Massacre* (New York, 1970), 182–93. My brief account of the Boston massacre trials is indebted to Zobel's superb narrative.

63. Ibid., 217–19.

64. Ibid., 241–44. As early as 1637 Margaret Weston had challenged three Salem jurors impaneled to hear a charge of defamation brought against her. G. F. Dow, ed., *Records and Files of the Quarter Courts of Essex County, Massachusetts*, 8 vols. (Salem, 1912): 1:7.

65. Zobel, *Boston Massacre*, 260–64. Adams's reminder to the Preston jurors about the dangers of capital punishment played to popular opinion. As early as 1761, in a speech to the Massachusetts legislature, former governor Francis Bernard acknowledged the "popular prejudices against capital punishments in this country." Bernard's speech quoted in William E. Nelson, "Emerging Notions of Modern Criminal Law in the Revolutionary Era: An Historical Perpective," *New York University Law Review* 42 (1967): 451.

66. Ibid., 264–65.

67. Barbara J. Shapiro, *Beyond Reasonable Doubt and Probable Cause: Historical Perspectives on the Anglo-American Law of Evidence* (Berkeley, Calif., 1991), 1–22; Zobel, *Boston Massacre*, 265.

68. William Molineux to Robert Treat Paine, March 9, 1770, in Riley and Hanson, *Paine Papers*, 2:463–64; Zobel, *Massacre*, 244–45, 271, 289, 294, 273. Adams owned a 1770 edition of Cesare Beccaria, *An Essay on Crimes and Punishment* (London, 1770). See L. H. Butterfield, ed., *Diary and Autobiography of John Adams*, 4 vols. (New York, 1964), 1:352–53.

69. Deborah Navas, *Murdered by His Wife* (Amherst, Mass., 1999), 5–7. This is a splendid narrative, containing valuable appendixes. *The Dying Declaration of James Buchanan, Ezra Ross and William Brooks, Who Were Executed at Worcester, July 2, 1778 for the Murder of Joshua Spooner* (Worcester, Mass., 1778) provides a great many details about the planning and execution of the murder.

70. Navas, *Murdered by His Wife*, 68–73.

71. For mention of Sprague and a sketch of Lincoln, see Conrad E. Wright and Edward W. Hanson, eds., *Sibley's Harvard Graduates, Biographical Sketches*

of Those Who Attended Harvard College in the Class of 1772-1774 (Boston, 1999), 121-28.

72. For a detailed analysis of Worcester County politics during the Revolution, see John L. Brooke, *Heart of the Commonwealth: Society and Political Culture in Worcester County, 1713-1861* (Amherst, Mass., 1989), 131-50.

73. Jabez Green was executed in Worcester, October 21, 1742 (SCJ, #56063). In December 1644 Goodwife Cornish was executed in York for the murder of her husband (Hosmer, *Winthrop's Journal*, 2:157).

74. Navas, *Murdered by His Wife*, 2, exaggerates the political split between Worcester County Loyalists and Patriots. Levi Lincoln, "Minutes in the Case of the Murder of Mr. Spooner," in ibid., 145.

75. Lincoln, "Minutes," 147. Defending all four defendants presented Sprague and Lincoln with a conflict of interest. The best defense for one client might very well involve compromising another's claim to innocence. Judge Zobel points out, for example, that the current American Bar Association Cannon of Ethics would not have permitted John Adams to defend both Preston and the soldiers because of obvious conflict of interest. To properly defend Preston, Adams might be forced to impugn the credibility of the soldiers or the reverse, or both (Zobel, *Massacre*, 242). Relying on memory, Chief Justice Cushing said that a motion for a jury of aliens had never been granted in Massachusetts. "Indictment of William Brooks, James Buchanan, and Ezra Ross, Notes of Associate Justice Nathaniel Peaslee Sargent," in Navas, *Murdered by His Wife*, 135.

76. Lincoln, "Minutes," 146-48. On this point, see also Blackstone, *Commentaries*, 4:119-21.

77. Lincoln, "Minutes," 149-51. Under normal circumstances a widow inherited one-third of her husband's real property to use during her lifetime.

78. Robert Treat Paine, "Minutes of Trial and Law Cases, 1777-1782," in Navas, *Murdered by His Wife*, 131-35.

79. The clerk's formulaic questions are cited in Zobel, *Massacre*, 294.

80. "Petition of Jabez and Johana Ross," in Navas, *Murdered by His Wife*, 160-61. Blackstone, *Commentaries*, 4:393, notes that a pardon for a murder committed "by laying in wait" or a murder for hire is prohibited under common law.

81. "Death Warrant," May 8, 1778, "Order for Suspension of Sentence," May 28, 1778, and "Return of the Sheriff," about the first midwives' exam, June 11, 1778, and "Opinion of the [Second] Midwives Exam," June 27, 1778, in Navas, *Murdered by His Wife*, 163-67. The councilors may have recalled the case of Margaret Fennison. She was sentenced to death for the murder of her illegitimately conceived child; but while awaiting execution, she claimed to be pregnant. A jury of matrons reported on February 7, 1743, that Fennison was not pregnant, but the governor hesi-

tated, granting a reprieve until April. By that time it was evident Fennison was not pregnant and she was executed April 14, 1743 (SCJ #56937).

82. *Massachusetts Spy*, August 6, 1778; Navas, *Murdered by His Wife*, 95–101.

83. Navas, *Murdered by His Wife*, 91.

84. Paine, "Minutes," 134; Zobel, *Massacre*, 289.

2. "HIDEOUS CONSEQUENCES" AND THE DECLARATION OF RIGHTS

1. The phrase quoted in the title, "hideous consequences," is from "Observations on Capital Punishments," *Boston Independent Chronicle*, February 7, 1793. The literature on republicanism is vast and contentious. See, especially, Gordon Wood, *Creation of the American Republic* (Chapel Hill, N.C., 1969); Robert E. Shalhope, "Republicanism and Early American Historiography," *William and Mary Quarterly*, 3rd ser., 39 (1982): 334–56; and Marc W. Kruman, *Between Authority and Liberty: State Constitution Making in Revolutionary America* (Chapel Hill, N.C., 1997). For the relationship between republicanism and the law, see G. Edward White, *The Marshall Court and Cultural Change, 1815–1835* (New York, 1991); and William E. Nelson, *Americanization of the Common Law: The Impact of the Legal Change on Massachusetts Society, 1760–1830* (Cambridge, Mass., 1975). See also Louis P. Masur, *Rites of Execution: Capital Punishment and the Transformation of American Culture, 1776–1865* (New York, 1989).

2. Constitution of the Commonwealth of Massachusetts (hereafter Massachusetts Constitution), pt. 1, arts. 24 and 30, and pt. 2, chap. 3 established the judiciary. In 1782 the Massachusetts legislature provided by statute for a court of five justices, including a chief justice, "each of whom must be an Inhabitant of this Commonwealth [and a person] of Sobriety of manners and learned in law." This statute also defined the jurisdiction of the court, provided for appellate review of certain matters, and gave the court power to regulate admission to the bar and to make "all other Rules respecting Modes of Trial and the Conduct of Business." *The General Statutes of the CommonWealth of Massachusetts, 1782* (Boston, 1783), chap. 9.

3. Samuel Checkley, *Murder a Great and Crying Sin* (Boston, 1733), 14–15; Gerard W. Gewalt, *The Promise of Power: The Emergence of the Legal Profession in Massachusetts, 1760–1840* (Westport, Conn., 1979), 3; Nelson, *Americanization of the Common Law*, 89–90. For the clergy's post-Revolutionary transformation, see Donald Scott, *From Office to Profession: The New England Ministry, 1750–1850* (Philadelphia, 1978), 52–75.

4. Massachusetts Constitution, Declaration of the Rights of the Inhabitants of the Commonwealth, arts. 12, 26, 29; Morton J. Horwitz, *The Transformation of American Law, 1780–1860* (New York, 1992), 16–30; Nelson, *Americanization of the Common Law*, 3–6; Neale to Robert Treat Paine, June 6, 1794, Paine Papers, Massachusetts Historical Society, Boston; *Commonwealth v. Foster*, 1 Mass. 488 (1805).

5. Aaron Bancroft, *The Importance of a Religious Education* (Worcester, Mass., 1793), 16–19. Frost had been found not guilty by reason of insanity for the murder of his father in 1783. Frost pleaded guilty to murdering a neighbor in 1793. The court held a hearing to determine whether there were mitigating factors that might encourage the governor to commute Frost's death sentence. *Massachusetts Spy*, October 2, 1783, September 26, November 6, 1793. George R. Minot, *The History of the Insurrection in Massachusetts* (Boston, 1788), 11–12; *An Address from the General Court to the People of the Commonwealth* (Boston, 1786), 34; Nathaniel Sargeant, Court Minutes, n.d., Essex Institute, Salem, Mass. Sargeant served on the court from 1775 to 1791. Historians argue that the postwar increase in property crimes was linked to changes in property relationships stimulated by the Revolution. See Nelson, *Americanization of the Common Law*; Daniel A. Cohen, *Pillars of Salt, Monuments of Grace: New England Crime Literature and the Origins of American Popular Culture, 1674–1860* (New York, 1993); and Alan Rogers and Edward Hanson, "Thieves, Rouges and Judges in Early Republican Massachusetts," *Massachusetts Legal History* 9 (2003): 109–27.

6. Paine to Elbridge Gerry, April 12, 1777, in James T. Austin, *The Life of Elbridge Gerry*, 2 vols. (New York, 1828), 1:220–21; James O. Horton and Lois E. Horton, *Black Bostonians: Family Life and Community Struggle in the Antebellum North* (New York, 1979), viii; *Massachusetts Centinel*, May 2, 1787.

7. Data compiled from the Docket Books of the Superior Court of Judicature and the Supreme Judicial Court [SJC], 1780–1788, Judicial Archives, Massachusetts State Archives, Boston.

8. *Boston Exchange Advertiser*, February 17, 1785. Before the Revolution, according to William Sumner, judges wore a black silk gown over a black suit, except when they heard a capital trial, for which they wore "scarlet robes with black velvet collars, and cuffs to the large sleeves, and black velvet facings to their robes." William H. Sumner, *Memoir of Increase Sumner* (Boston, 1854), 17. From 1792 until 1901 SJC judges did not wear robes.

9. Commonwealth v. Huggins and Mansfield (1783), SJC Records, case #153329; *Massachusetts Spy*, June 6, 1783; *Last Words of William Huggins and John Mansfield* (Worcester, Mass., 1783).

10. Papers of Increase Sumner, Criminal Cases, 1:15, Massachusetts Historical Society, Boston; *Boston Gazette*, November 10, 1783, January 19, 1784. The *Gazette* mistakenly identified Garcelli as "Portuguese," but Attorney General Robert Treat Paine recorded that Garcelli was Italian. Paine Diary, January 15, 1784, Massachusetts Historical Society.

11. *The Last Words and Dying Speech of Cassumo Garcelli* (Boston, 1783); *Massachusetts Spy*, January 22, 1784.

12. Commonwealth v. Grout (1784), SJC Records, case #103472; Commonwealth

v. Coven (1784), SJC Records, case #103477; *The Last Words and Dying Speech of Derick Grout and Francis Coven* (Boston, 1784); *Massachusetts Spy*, November 11, 1784.

13. Commonwealth v. Dixon (1784), SJC Records, case #1461332; *Massachusetts Spy*, November 24, 1784.

14. *Boston Independent Chronicle*, November 26, 1785, March 10, 1785; *Massachusetts Spy*, May 12, 1785.

15. Commonwealth v. Coombs (1786), SJC Records, case #133637; *Massachusetts Gazette*, May 29, 1786, December 23, 1786.

16. Stephen T. Riley and Edward W. Hanson, eds., *The Papers of Robert Treat Paine*, 2 vols. (Boston, 1992), 2:537n, identify Pynchon as a lawyer and one-time Loyalist who maintained a friendship with Paine.

17. Fitch Edward Oliver, ed., *The Diary of William Pynchon of Salem* (Boston, 1890), 261, 242.

18. Joshua Spalding, *A Sermon Delivered at Salem at the Execution of Isaac Coombs, an Indian* (Salem, Mass., 1787).

19. The best treatment of Shays' Rebellion is David P. Szatmary, *Shays' Rebellion: The Making of an Agrarian Insurrection* (Amherst, Mass., 1980).

20. *Independent Chronicle*, March 29, 1787; James R. Trumbull, *History of Northampton, Massachusetts from Its Settlement in 1654*, 2 vols. (Northampton, Mass., 1898–1902), 2:515–16.

21. Thomas G. Amory, *Life of James Sullivan*, 2 vols. (Boston, 1859), 1:205–7; *Massachusetts Centinel*, May 2, 1787; William V. Wells, *The Life and Public Service of Samuel Adams*, 3 vols. (Boston, 1866), 3:246, as quoted in Masur, *Rites of Execution*, 30.

22. *Last Words and Dying Speech of John Sheehan* (Boston, 1787); *Massachusetts Centinel*, November 24, 1787.

23. Papers of Increase Sumner, Criminal Cases, 3:287, Massachusetts Historical Society. Justices Sumner, Francis Dana, and William Cushing served as delegates to the Massachusetts ratifying convention from January 8 to February 6, 1788. *Acts and Resolves, 1784* (Boston, 1785), chap. 52. The punishment for highway robbery was less severe in 1711, when a new law called for a six-month prison sentence following conviction for the first offense and death if a person were convicted a second time of the offense. *The Act and Resolves, Public and Private, of the Province of Massachusetts Bay*, 21 vols. (Boston, 1869–1922), 1:674. (hereafter cited as *Province Laws*). In 1761 the law was changed so that a single conviction for highway robbery was punishable by death. *Province Laws*, 4:546. No one was executed for the offense until 1784. *Boston Independent Chronicle*, November 8, 1787; *Massachusetts Centinel*, May 10, 1788.

24. Data compiled from SJC Records, 1780–1790, Judicial Archives.

25. Commonwealth v. Smith (1789), SJC Records, case #105405; Commonwealth v. Denoffee (1789), SJC Records, case #105406.

26. *The Last Words and Dying Confession of Rachel Wall* (Boston, 1789). In her last words, Wall made no mention of either of her prior convictions—Commonwealth v. Ewers and Wall (1785), SJC Records, case #105405; and Commonwealth v. Nelson, Carter and Wall (1788), SJC Records, case #105406—but she claims two daring robberies for which she was not caught.

27. Robert Treat Paine, Trial Notes, Massachusetts Historical Society.

28. Ibid. In the immediate postwar period, two women were brought to trial charged with murdering their husbands. Rebecca Kerilly, of Boston, was acquitted of beating her husband to death in 1784, and Priscilla Woodworth, of Hampshire County, was acquitted of murder in 1782. Linda M. Kealey, "Crime and Society in Massachusetts in the Second Half of the Eighteenth Century" (Ph.D. diss., University of Toronto, 1981), 122. For sketches of Hughes and Gore, see William T. Davis, *A History of the Bench and Bar* (Boston, 1894), 521, 225.

29. Linda K. Kerber, *No Constitutional Right to Be Ladies: Women and the Obligations of Citizenship* (New York, 1998), 9, 23, notes the founding generation's ambivalence about women's right to equality before the law.

30. *Last Words and Dying Confession of Rachel Wall*; *Acts and Resolves, 1804* (Boston, 1805) chap. 143, sec. 7; *The Revised Statutes of the Commonwealth of Massachusetts* (Boston, 1836), chap. 125, sec. 15. For a brilliant discussion of the literature of thievery, see Cohen, *Pillars of Salt*, chap. 6.

31. Peter Forbes, *A Sermon; The Substance of which was Delivered at Taunton, November 11, 1784, Upon the Day of the Execution of John Dixon* (Providence, R.I., 1784), app., 7-8, 11-12; Cohen, *Pillars of Salt*, 104-10.

32. En route from Canterbury to London to join her husband, John, Abigail Adams learned that a young highwayman whose capture she witnessed was to be hanged. She thought the British exulted over executions while Americans had "commiseration for the wretched." Abigail Adams to John Adams, July 21, 1784, as quoted in David McCullough, *John Adams* (New York, 2001), 297.

33. Commonwealth v. Bailey (1790), SJC Records, case #105699; Commonwealth v. Edward V. Brown (1790), SJC Records, case # 105680; Commonwealth v. Edward Brown (1790), SJC Records, case #105739.

34. Data compiled from SJC Records, 1780-1784 and 1790-1794.

35. Robert Rantoul's 1836 argument for abolishing capital punishment in Massachusetts also argued that in creating government individuals do not surrender their right to life, nor can they. Alan Rogers, " 'Under Sentence of Death': The Movement to Abolish Capital Punishment in Massachusetts, 1835-1849," *New England Quarterly* 66 (1993): 27, 30.

36. *The Confession, Last Words, and Dying Speech of John Stewart* (Boston, 1797); *Columbian Sentinel*, April 8, 1797; *Boston Gazette*, April 7, 1797.

37. *Columbian Sentinel*, September 6, October 14, 1797; *The Life, Last Words, and Dying Speech of Stephen Smith* (Boston, 1797).

38. *Life, Last Words, and Dying Speech of Stephen Smith*.

39. Ibid.

40. *Biography of Mr. Jason Fairbanks and Miss Eliza Fales* (Boston, 1801), as quoted in Cohen, *Pillars of Salt*, 181.

41. Rev. Thomas Thacher, *The Danger of Dispising the Divine Counsel, Exhibited in a Discourse Delivered at Dedham, Third Precinct, September 13, 1801, The Lord's Day after the Execution of Jason Fairbanks* (Dedham, Mass., 1802), 23; Cohen, *Pillars of Salt*, 167–94. In "The Story of Jason Fairbanks: Trial Reports and the Rise of Sentimental Fiction," *Legal Studies Forum* 7 (1993): 119–30, Cohen argues that the publication of trial reports were intended primarily for a popular lay audience. Ferris Greenslet, *The Lowells and Their Seven Worlds* (Boston, 1946), 95–111.

42. *Report of the Trial of Jason Fairbanks on an Indictment for the Murder of Miss Elizabeth Fales* (Boston, 1802), 8; Thomas C. Amory, *Life of James Sullivan* (Boston, 1859), 17–18.

43. Jason Fairbanks, *A Solemn Declaration of the Late Unfortunate Jason Fairbanks, to Which Is Added Some Account of His Life and Character* [by Ebenezer Fairbanks] (Dedham, Mass., 1801), 6–8; Amory, *Sullivan*, 17–18; Charles Warren, *Jacobin and Junto, or Early American Politics as Viewed in the Diary of Dr. Nathaniel Ames, 1758–1822* (Cambridge, Mass., 1931), 134n.; *Report of the Trial of Jason Fairbanks*, 16–17, 22–25.

44. *Report of the Trial of Jason Fairbanks*, 16–17, 22–25.

45. Ibid., 21; Amory, *Sullivan*, 18–19.

46. *Report of the Trial of Jason Fairbanks*, 9; Amory, *Sullivan*, 19.

47. Warren, *Jacobin and Junto*, 127–128; *Report of the Trial of Jason Fairbanks*, 7.

48. *Report of the Trial of Jason Fairbanks*, 1–2; Davis, *History of the Bench and Bar*, 146. Dedham was sharply divided between Federalists and Republicans (Warren, *Jacobin and Junto*, 134–46).

49. *Report of the Trial of Jason Fairbanks*, 11; Fairbanks, *Solemn Declaration*, 6–8.

50. *Report of the Trial of Jason Fairbanks*, 11; *Columbian Centinel*, August 6, 1801.

51. *Report of the Trail of Jason Fairbanks*, 8–10; Warren, *Jacobin and Junto*, 131.

52. *Report of the Trial of Jason Fairbanks*, 11–21.

53. For the arguments by Otis and Lowell, see ibid., 37–64; for Sullivan's closing, see Amory, *Sullivan*, 20–35. *Boston Gazette*, August 11, 1801.

54. *Report of the Trial of Jason Fairbanks*, 37–41.

55. Ibid., 43, 46, 47–48.

56. Ibid., 64.

57. Sullivan's arguments here and in the following paragraphs are drawn from Amory, *Sullivan*, 3–8, 21–22, 25, 29–31.

58. *Report of the Trial of Jason Fairbanks*, 81.

59. Ibid., 82–83. *Boston Gazette*, August 11, 1801. Greenslet, *The Lowells and Their Seven Worlds*, suggests that Fairbanks's conviction and execution had a "catastrophic" effect on Lowell. Convinced of Fairbanks's innocence, Lowell retired from the practice of law in 1803 (111).

60. Warren, *Jacobin and Junto*, 133–41; *Report of the Trial of Jason Fairbanks*, 83–84. Cohen suggests that Otis's close friend and later the biographer of Fairbanks, Sarah Wentworth Morton, financed Fairbanks's escape (*Pillar of Salt*, 188–90).

61. *Report of the Trial of Jason Fairbanks*, 85.

62. Broadside issued by the Pandamonium Press, quoted in Warren, *Jacobin and Junto*, 142–43.

63. Ibid., 144–45.

64. Ibid., 144.

65. All quotations from Thacher's sermon are drawn from *Danger of Dispensing*, 8, 18–22, 23–26.

66. Data compiled from SJC Records. See also *Acts and Resolves, 1803* (Boston, 1804), chap. 981. Adam J. Hirsch, "From Pillory to Penitentiary: The Rise of Criminal Incarceration in Early Massachusetts," *Michigan Law Review* 80 (1982): 179.

67. For Tyng's comments, see 2 Mass. 3 (1805). William Cranch, reporter for the U.S. Supreme Court, also argued that publishing the court's decisions would buttress republicanism by ending that "servile recourse to the decisions of foreign judicatures, which since our revolution, we have been too much accustomed." Cranch's remarks are quoted in Charles Warren, *The Supreme Court in United States History*, 2 vols. (Boston, 1937), 1:289n. Ephraim Williams was the first person appointed by the governor to report the SJC's decisions, but he was overwhelmed by the task and resigned after one fruitless year. Born in Newburyport in 1760, Tyng graduated from Harvard College at age twenty-one, read the law in Virginia, and was admitted to the Essex County bar in 1784. Governor Caleb Strong appointed Tyng reporter in 1805.

68. *Commonwealth v. Battis*, 1 Mass. 94 (1805).

69. *The Confession of John Battus* (Dedham, Mass. 1805). There were two spellings of the defendant's last name. I use Battis, the spelling in SJC Records.

70. *Commonwealth v. Battis*, 1 Mass. at 94–95.

71. *Commonwealth v. Hardy*, 2 Mass. 302, 308 (1807). Massachusetts appointed counsel for capital defendants from an early date, as outlined in Chapter 1, but Hardy spelled out the rule. See Alan Rogers, "'A Sacred Duty': Court Appointed Counsel in Massachusetts Capital Cases," *American Journal of Legal History* 61 (1997): 440.

72. Commonwealth v. Hardy, SJC Records and Briefs, November 1806, 2:686–88, Judicial Archives; *Boston Courier*, December 18, 1806.

73. *Commonwealth v. Hardy*, 2 Mass. at 308, 312. Davis, *History of the Bench and Bar*, 633 (Thatcher), 436 (Blake).

74. *Commonwealth v. Hardy*, 2 Mass. at 315–16. For a sketch of Chief Justice Parsons, see 10 Mass. 507 (1813). Throughout his brief tenure on the SJC (1806–13) Parsons insisted on "strict and almost punctilious" adherence to the rules of criminal procedure. 10 Mass. 507, 529 (1813).

75. *Commonwealth v. Hardy*, 2 Mass. at 316; SJC, Records and Briefs, March Term, 1807, 233.

76. Unless indicated, all details from the following account of the Phillips case are drawn from *Report of the Trial of Henry Phillips for the Murder of Gaspar Denegri, Heard and Determined in the SJC at Boston on the 9th and 10th January 1817* (Boston, 1817), 6–9, 14–29, 33–35, 43–45, 46–47.

77. For sketches of George Sullivan, Davis, and Parker, see Davis, *History of the Bench and Bar*, 145, 186, 244. For Shaw, see Leonard W. Levy, *The Law of the Commonwealth and Chief Justice Shaw* (New York, 1957), 8–9.

78. Nelson, *Americanization of the Common Law*, 114.

79. During the Boston Massacre trials, the colonial court made an exception to the common law rule and provided jurors with lodging, food, and drink, including an alcoholic punch, wine, and rum. Hiller B. Zobel, *The Boston Massacre* (New York, 1970), 250.

80. William Blackstone, *Commentaries on the Laws of England*, 4 vols. (London, 1769; repr., Chicago, 1979), 4:199–200.

81. *Columbian Sentinel*, March 15, 1817.

82. Caldwell v. Jennison and Commonwealth v. Jennison (1783), as quoted in Nelson, *Americanization of the Common Law*, 101–2.

83. *Report of the Trial of Jason Fairbanks*, 87.

3. "UNDER SENTENCE OF DEATH"

1. *Boston Daily Advertiser*, March 26, 27, 28, 29, 30, 1846. The Supreme Judicial Court had original jurisdiction over all capital crimes. Capital cases were tried by a jury presided over by at least three judges, usually the chief justice and two associates. See William T. Davis, *A History of the Bench and Bar* (Boston, 1894), 72. Following his acquittal for murder, Terrill was tried and found not guilty of arson,

also a capital crime. Justices Samuel Wilde, Charles Dewey, and Samuel Hubbard heard the murder charge; Chief Justice Lemuel Shaw and Justices Wilde and Hubbard presided over Terrill's arson trial in January 1847.

2. *The Life and Death of Mrs. Maria Bickford* (Boston, 1846). Recent historians have placed the murder and trial within a framework that includes the demise of community morality and the rise of consumerism. See, for example, Barbara Hobson, "A Murder in the Moral and Religious City of Boston," *Boston Bar Journal* 22 (November 1978): 2; Daniel A. Cohen, "The Murder of Maria Bickford: Fashion, Passion, and the Birth of Consumer Culture," *American Studies* 31 (1990): 5.

3. Robert D. Bulkley Jr., "Robert Rantoul Jr., 1805–1852: Politics and Reform in Antebellum Massachusetts" (Ph.D. diss., Princeton University, 1971), 16–20.

4. Bulkley, "Robert Rantoul," 152–70, 245–46.

5. *Boston Post*, January 13, 23, February 24, 1836.

6. Robert Rantoul Jr., "Report on the Abolition of Capital Punishment," in *Memoirs, Speeches and Writings of Robert Rantoul, Jr.*, ed. Luther Hamilton (Boston, 1854), 439–50. The following discussion of Rantoul's argument draws from ibid., 446, 460–61, 476–80.

7. *Boston Post*, March 19, 21, 25, 1836, February 2, 5, 1839.

8. Ibid., January 23, February 10, 1840.

9. Charles Spear, *Essays on the Punishment of Death* (Boston, 1845). See also Louis Masur, *Rites of Execution: Capital Punishment and the Transformation of American Culture, 1776–1865* (New York, 1989), 124–32.

10. *Hangman*, January 1, May 21, August 13, 1845. Each issue of the paper listed those "Under Sentence of Death."

11. Ibid., November 5, December 17, 1845, January 2, 1846.

12. Briggs's speech was published in the *Prisoner's Friend* (the new name for the *Hangman*) January 21, 1846. In 1794 Pennsylvania became the first state to enact a law dividing murder into degrees. Edwin R. Keedy, "History of the Pennsylvania Statute Creating Degrees of Murder," *University of Pennsylvania Law Review* 97 (1949): 759.

13. *Boston Times*, February 4, 6, 10, 12, 14, 17, 1846; *Prisoner's Friend*, February 18, 25, March 4, 14, 25, April 1, 1846.

14. *Prisoner's Friend*, February 25, 1846.

15. *North American Review* 62 (1846): 40–44, 51–53, 62–63, 66.

16. J. P. Weeks, *The Trial of Albert Terrill Charged with the Murder of Mrs. Maria Bickford Before the Supreme Court in Boston, Boston Daily Mail Report* (Boston, 1846).

17. *Boston Daily Advertiser*, March 26, 1846.

18. Ibid., March 29, 1846.

19. Edward G. Parker, *Reminiscences of Rufus Choate* (New York, 1862), 29–33;

Clement Hugh Hill, "Memoir of the Honorable Rufus Choate," in *Proceedings of the Massachusetts Historical Society* 11 (1896-97): 124-28.

20. Jean Matthews, *Rufus Choate: The Law and Civic Virtue* (Philadelphia, 1980) 147-48; Parker, *Reminiscences of Choate*, 162, 216, 288.

21. *Boston Daily Advertiser*, March 26, 27, 1846; *Prisoner's Friend*, April 1, 1846.

22. *Boston Daily Advertiser*, March 26, 1846.

23. Ibid., March 27, 1846.

24. Ibid.; Parker, *Reminiscences of Choate*, 222.

25. *Prisoner's Friend*, April 8, 1846; *Boston Courier*, March 31, 1846.

26. *Prisoner's Friend*, April 15, 1846; *Boston Evening Transcript*, April 1, 1846.

27. *Boston Herald*, January 11-20, 1847; *Prisoner's Friend*, January 20, 27, 1847.

28. *Boston Evening Transcript*, January 19, 1847; *Prisoner's Friend*, March 1849. In September 1848 the *Prisoner's Friend* changed from a weekly to a monthly newspaper.

29. Wendell Phillips, *Speeches, Lectures and Letters* (Boston, 1863), 254; *Prisoner's Friend*, January 27, 1847.

30. *Boston Herald*, January 2, 3, 1849. Masur, *Rites of Execution*, 9-19, is especially insightful about Goode's trial and its aftermath.

31. Davies, *History of the Bench and Bar*, 248, 178.

32. *Boston Herald*, January 4, 1849.

33. Ibid.

34. Ibid., April 9, 1849.

35. Ibid., April 10, 1849.

36. *Prisoner's Friend*, May 1849.

37. Ibid., April and May 1849.

38. *Liberator*, May 4, 1849, as quoted in Masur, *Rites of Execution*, 17.

39. *Prisoner's Friend*, May 1849.

40. *Boston Daily Evening Transcript*, May 25, 1849.

41. Rantoul, *Report on the Abolition of Capital Punishment*, 439-50; Masur, *Rites of Execution*, 94. For a brilliant survey of the New England crime literature, see Daniel A. Cohen, *Pillars of Salt, Monuments of Grace: New England Crime Literature and the Origins of American Popular Culture, 1674-1860* (New York, 1993), 26. For the burning of the Ursuline Convent, see Thomas H. O'Connor, *The Boston Irish: A Political History* (Boston, 1995), 46-48.

42. *Boston Herald*, May 25, 26, 1849; *Prisoner's Friend*, July 1849. The newspaper referring to Spear was not identified.

43. Cummings was hanged in Taunton on August 7, 1839. Barrett was hanged in the Worcester County jail, among the first convicted murderers in Massachusetts to be hanged privately (*Hangman*, January 1, 15, 1845). For the number of men tried for murder, see *Annual Report of the Attorney General's Office*, 1835-1843; and *Ab-*

stract of the Annual Reports of the District Attorneys for 1844–1849. In 1852 the legislature voted to punish treason, rape, and arson with life imprisonment rather than death. *General Laws of the Commonwealth of Massachusetts*, passed subsequently to the revised statutes [1836–1859], 2 vols. (Boston, 1854–[1859]), vol. 1, chap. 259. A statute defining degrees of murder was passed in 1858; ibid., vol. 2, chap. 160.

44. Webster's confession appeared in several Boston newspapers, including the *Boston Daily Mail*, July 3, 1850.

45. Among several accounts of the Webster-Parkman murder case, see Cleveland Amory, *The Proper Bostonians* (New York, 1947), 207–27.

46. Professor Cornelius Felton visited Webster on December 22 and passed on his impressions to Edward Everett. Everett Diary, December 23, 1849, Massachusetts Historical Society, Boston. For the ancient practice in Massachusetts of appointing attorneys for capital defendants, see Alan Rogers, "'A Sacred Duty': Court Appointed Attorneys in Massachusetts Capital Cases, 1780–1980," *American Journal of Legal History* 61 (1997): 440; *General Statutes of the Commonwealth of Massachusetts* (Boston, 1821), chap. 14, sec. 8; William T. Davis, *A History of the Bench and Bar* (Boston, 1894), 211–12, 290–91; and George Bemis, Diary, January 27, 1850, Massachusetts Historical Society.

47. *Boston Evening Transcript*, March 19, 1850; George Bemis, *Report of the Case of John W. Webster* (Boston, 1850), 8.

48. Bemis, *Report*, 82, 101–17.

49. Ibid., 229–66.

50. *Commonwealth v. Webster*, 59 Mass. 295 (1850); *Boston Evening Transcript*, April 1, 1850.

51. Lysander Spooner, *Illegality of the Trial of John W. Webster* (Boston, 1850), 3–16. Massachusetts first allowed prosecutors peremptory strikes in 1869. *Acts and Resolves, 1869* (Boston, 1870), chap. 151. The U.S. Supreme Court acknowledged a portion of Spooner's argument in *Witherspoon v. Illinois*, 391 U.S. 510 (1968). For a complete discussion of the uses of challenges for cause and peremptory challenges, see Alan Rogers, "'An Anchor to the Windward': The Right of the Accused to an Impartial Jury in Massachusetts Capital Cases," *Suffolk University Law Review* 33 (1999): 35.

52. A Member of the Legal Profession, *A Statement of Reasons Showing the Illegality of that Verdict upon Which Sentence of Death Has Been Pronounced against John W. Webster* (New York, 1850), 22–23; "The Webster Case," *Monthly Law Reporter* 13 (1850): 13; Joel Parker, "The Law of Homicide," *North American Review* 72 (January 1851): 178–204.

53. *Commonwealth v. Webster*, 59 Mass. at 304–5. This paragraph and the two following draw on Leonard W. Levy, *The Law of the Commonwealth and Chief Justice Shaw* (New York, 1957), 220–25. Levy points out that Shaw had made an

identical argument about implied malice in *Commonwealth v. York*, 9 Metc. 93 (1845).

54. *Commonwealth v. Webster*, 59 Mass. at 305, 325. After the trial and his failed bid for commutation, Webster confessed. He told of a quarrel and of hitting Parkman in the head. But, even if believed, this story would not have freed him from the charge of murder. As Shaw pointed out, provocation by words alone did not mitigate an intentional homicide (ibid. at 305).

55. Ibid. at 317–20. Delegates to the 1853 Massachusetts Constitutional Convention held a lengthy debate over the jury's right to decide both the law and the facts; see *Official Report of the Debates and Proceedings in the State Convention to Revise and Amend the Constitution* (Boston, 1853), 437–63. In *Commonwealth v. Anthes*, 5 Gray 185 (1855), Shaw ruled that a legislative act giving a criminal jury the right to decide both the law and the facts was unconstitutional.

56. *Commonwealth v. Webster*, 59 Mass. at 295, 320.

57. Ibid. See also Frank R. Hermann, S.J., and Brownlow Spear, "To a Moral Certainty: The Historical Context of the Webster Charge on Reasonable Doubt," *Boston Bar Journal*, March–April 1992, 22.

58. Cesare Beccaria, *On Crimes and Punishment* (London, 1785; repr., Indianapolis, Ind., 1963), 21.

59. Speaking at the 1853 Massachusetts Constitutional Convention, Benjamin Butler, who rose to the rank of general during the Civil War and was elected governor in 1882, defended Shaw's unpopular *Webster* ruling. Butler believed Webster's execution "may be the last to take place in Massachusetts." *Official Report of the Debates*, 462.

60. *Acts and Resolves, 1852* (Boston, 1853), chaps. 259, 274. *Prisoner's Friend*, November, April, 1853. For details of Clough's crime, see *Boston Daily Journal*, April 29, 1854.

61. *Prisoner's Friend*, May 1854. All descriptions and quotations from the witnesses for and against the death penalty in the following discussion are drawn from this issue.

62. *Senate Document*, no. 103 (1854).

63. Marvin Bovee to Wendell Phillips, as quoted in Masur, *Rites of Execution*, 160.

64. *Green v. Commonwealth*, 94 Mass. 155 (1866). In April 1864, following his confession in open court to the murder of a bank teller, Edward Green was sentenced to death. For two years Governor Andrew refused to issue a death warrant, but when a new governor, Alexander H. Bullock, took office in 1866, he signed Green's execution order. Green was hanged April 13, 1866. Wendell Phillips was an exception; he wrote an article against the death penalty, in *North American Review* 133 (December 1881): 534.

4. "THE MONSTER PETITION"

1. "Governor A. W. Gilchrist on the Law's Delay," *Journal of Criminal Law and Criminology* 2 (1911): 294. The *Journal* reported that the governor of Florida was outraged that more than a year commonly elapsed between the sentencing and execution of a convicted murderer.

2. Moorfield Storey, "Some Practical Suggestions as to the Reform of Criminal Procedure," *Journal of Criminal Law and Criminology* 4 (1914): 495, 510, 513. In support of his argument that "the defenses of society against criminals have broken down," Storey quotes Harvard president Charles W. Eliot, among others. Cornelius Dalton, John Wirkkala, and Anne Thomas, *Leading the Way: A History of the Massachusetts General Court* (Boston, 1984), 166–72.

3. *Journal of Criminal Law and Criminology* 2 (1912): 742. Among many such articles, the *Journal* published one by SJC judge DeCourcy, "On Delays in the Administration of Justice," *Journal of Criminal Law and Criminology* 2 (1911): 100. See also *Acts and Resolves, 1939* (Boston, 1940), chap. 341.

4. E. J. McDermott, "Delays and Reversals on Technical Grounds in Criminal Trials," *Journal of Criminal Law and Criminology* 2 (1911): 28, 36.

5. Harvard law professors Sam Bass Warner and Henry B. Cabot spoofed readers in "Changes in the Administration of Criminal Justice during the Past Fifty Years," *Harvard Law Review* 50 (1937): 583, by describing as contemporary a murder trial that occurred in 1883. The literature on criminal procedure is sparse. Two books by Lester B. Orfield are old but indispensable: *Criminal Appeals in America* (Boston, 1939) and *Criminal Procedure from Arrest to Appeal* (New York, 1947). See also Lawrence M. Friedman, *Crime and Punishment in American History* (New York, 1993).

6. Richard W. Wilkie and Jack Tager, eds., *Historical Atlas of Massachusetts* (Amherst, Mass., 1991), 39–40.

7. *Annual Report of the Attorney General for the Year Ending 1892* (Boston, 1893), vi–xiii. Attorney General Hosea M. Knowlton noted in 1897 that popular opinion held that the number of murders had increased, but he insisted that the number of murders relative to the population of Massachusetts had declined each year after 1875. *Annual Report of the Attorney General for the Year Ending 1897* (Boston, 1898), xv. Roger Lane, *Policing the City, Boston, 1822–1885* (Boston, 1967), 205, suggests that improved investigative methods helped Boston police solve murders. Of the twenty-one men executed for murder from 1901 to 1920, fifteen were recent immigrants. See Daniel A. Hearn, *Legal Executions in New England, 1623–1960* (Jefferson, N.C., 1999), 301–43. The last woman executed in Massachusetts was Rachel Wall in 1789.

8. For executions in the United States, see James W. Garner, "Crime and Judicial Inefficiency," *Annals of the American Academy of Political and Social Science*

29 (March 1907): 162. In 1885, 108 persons were legally executed in the United States as compared with 116 in 1904. The number of persons illegally lynched exceeded the number of legal executions each year from 1885 to 1889 (ibid.). Philadelphia's murder rate may be found in Roger Lane, *Murder in America* (Columbus, Ohio, 1997), 185. In Alameda County, California, from 1870 to 1910, crime rates fell. Lawrence Friedman and Robert V. Percival, *The Roots of Justice: Crime and Punishment in Alameda County, California, 1870–1910* (Chapel Hill, N.C., 1981), 32. Charles Loring Brace, *The Dangerous Classes of New York and Twenty Years Among Them* (New York, 1872); Storey, "Some Practical Suggestions," 495, 496.

9. These data compiled from Hearn, *Legal Executions in New England*, 243–348. Andrei Ipson and Wasili Ivanowski were executed on March 7, 1911, for the murder of two police guards protecting a Lynn shoe factory's payroll. *Boston Globe*, June 6, 1910, March 7, 1911.

10. *In re Kemmler*, 136 U.S. 436 (1890); *Storti v. Commonwealth*, 175 Mass. 549 (1900); *Commonwealth v. Storti*, 177 Mass. 339 (1901).

11. *Boston Daily Bee*, December 1, 1849; George Bemis, ed., *Report of the Case of John W. Webster* (Boston, 1850), 369. Webster's confession and the Report of the Executive Council, *Boston Courier*, July 20, 1850.

12. *New York Tribune*, April 6, 11, 1850.

13. *The General Statutes of the Commonwealth of Massachusetts, Enacted December 28, 1859* (Boston, 1860), chap. 158 (hereafter *Massachusetts General Statutes, 1859*).

14. Leonard Levy, *The Law of the Commonwealth and Chief Justice Shaw* (New York, 1957), 224; *Commonwealth v. Webster*, 5 Cush. 293, 305 (1850); *Webster v. Commonwealth*, 59 Mass. 386 (1850). According to the *Monthly Law Reporter*, March 1846, 484, in 1794 Pennsylvania, in 1819 Virginia, in 1824 Ohio, and between 1824 and 1846 Maine, New Hampshire, New Jersey, Alabama, Mississippi, Louisiana, Tennessee, Missouri, and Michigan broke with English common law and divided murder into degrees.

15. *Massachusetts General Statutes, 1859*, chap. 160; *Boston Herald*, March 27, April 13, 1858. The legislature gave consideration to adopting degrees of murder when the criminal code was under review in 1840. *Monthly Law Reporter*, March 1846, 484.

16. *Monthly Law Reporter*, July 1858, 136. Ten years after passage of the statute creating degrees of murder, Chief Justice Ruben Chapman noted that the legislature regarded the old common law rule of implied malice "as too severe." *Commonwealth v. Andrews*, 97 Mass. 543 (1868). For more than a century Massachusetts trial judges quoted Shaw's explanation of the phrase "deliberately premeditated malice aforethought." *Commonwealth v. Webster*, 5 Cush. 293.

17. Until 1891 the SJC acted both as a trial court and as an appeals court in homicide cases.

18. *Commonwealth v. Desmarteau*, 82 Mass. 1, 6–7 (1860).

19. Ibid. at 10–15; *Springfield Republican*, April 26, 1861.

20. *Annual Report of the Attorney General for the Year Ending 1867* (Boston, 1868), 4; *Annual Report of the Attorney General for the Year Ending 1873* (Boston, 1874), 8–9.

21. *Acts and Resolves, 1899* (Boston, 1900), chap. 409. The SJC upheld the new law in *Commonwealth v. Snelling*, 189 Mass. 12 (1905). For a full discussion of criminal discovery, see Alan Rogers, "Murder in Massachusetts: The Criminal Discovery Rule from *Snelling* to Rule 14," *American Journal of Legal History* 60 (1996): 438.

22. *Springfield Republican*, April 26, 1861; *Annual Reports of the Attorney General* for 1861–65; *Commonwealth v. Hersey*, 84 Mass. 173 (1861); "James Callender Hanged," *Berkshire County Eagle*, September 18, 1862.

23. *New York Times*, October 3, 1865; *Boston Daily Evening Transcript*, October 16, 1865; "An Act in Relation to Evidence in Criminal Prosecutions," *Journal of the House of Representatives of the Commonwealth of Massachusetts* (Boston, 1866), 46. The bill became law May 26, 1866; *Acts and Resolves, 1866* (Boston, 1867), chap. 245. In 1864, Maine became the first state to permit state criminal defendants to testify on their own behalf. George Fisher, "The Jury's Rise as Lie Detector," *Yale Law Journal* 107 (1997): 575. Gradually every state (except Georgia) conceded to a defendant the right to testify under oath. Lester B. Orfield, *Criminal Procedure from Arrest to Appeal* (New York, 1947), 459.

24. *American Law Review* 1 (April 1867): 443–50.

25. *Annual Report of the Attorney General for the Year Ending 1874* (Boston, 1875), 9–10.

26. *Commonwealth v. Nicholson, An Abstract of the Argument of Edgar J. Sherman, Attorney General* (Boston, 1885), 16–18.

27. At a Massachusetts criminal trial a potential juror might be challenged for cause if he or she (women were permitted to serve on a jury after 1951) had a personal or professional relationship with one of the trial's participants, a personal interest in the outcome, or an antipathy to capital punishment that would prevent him or her from weighing the evidence fairly. The 1869 law gave the prosecutor five peremptory challenges. *Acts and Resolves, 1869* (Boston, 1870), chap. 151. Because the original statute granted prosecutors fewer peremptory challenges than allowed the defendant, Attorneys General Allen (1866–71) and Train (1872–79) urged the legislature to increase the number prosecutors were permitted to use. *Attorney General's Report, 1872* (Boston, 1873), 9–10. The legislature responded to Train's request by increasing the number of peremptory challenges a prosecutor might use to ten. *Acts and Resolves, 1873* (Boston, 1874), chap. 317, sec. 2.

28. The SJC's jurisdiction is spelled out in *The Public Statutes of the Commonwealth of Massachusetts, Enacted November 19, 1881* (Boston, 1886), chap. 150. Holmes's address to the Boston Bar Association, March 7, 1900, as quoted in G. Edward White, *Justice Oliver Wendell Holmes: Law and the Inner Self* (New York, 1993), 253. As late as 1971 the court rendered 421 opinions, a caseload several judges considered "intolerable." *Report to the Supreme Judicial Court of the Executive Secretary* 43 (Boston, 1972).

29. *Commonwealth v. Hardy*, 2 Mass. 302, 303 (1807). Nathan Dane, *General Abridgement and Digest of American Law*, 8 vols. (Boston, 1823–1824), 7:210–18, cites several unreported murder cases tried between 1780 and 1802 in which the SJC assigned counsel to a capital defendant.

30. *Commonwealth v. Hardy*, 2 Mass. at 316.

31. *The General Statutes of the Commonwealth of Massachusetts* (Boston, 1821), chap. 14, sec. 8. From 1832, when the attorney general began to keep systematic records, to 1891, when original jurisdiction for capital crimes was transferred from the SJC to the Superior Court, there were 533 murder indictments. *Annual Report of the Attorney General*, 1832–91; SJC Docket Books, 1873–83, Judicial Archives, Massachusetts State Archives, Boston. My collective portrait is based on biographical data drawn from William T. Davis, *History of the Bench and Bar* (Boston, 1894) and *History of the Massachusetts Judiciary* (Boston, 1900). Michael E. Hennessy, *Twenty-five Years of Massachusetts Politics* (Boston, 1917). Searle was born in Salem in 1826 and read the law after graduating from Phillips Andover Academy; he was admitted to the Suffolk bar in 1847 (Davis, *History of the Bench and Bar*, 240). The junior counsel appointed by the court to represent a capital defendant averaged thirty years of age and had about four years of legal experience. Fifteen of the eighteen on whom I have data attended law school.

32. *Annual Report of the Attorney General for the Year Ending 1892* (Boston, 1893), xiii; *Report of the Commission to Inquire into the Expediency of Revision of the Judicial System of the State, December 1876* (Senate Document no. 50), 17. Roscoe Pound, *Organization of Courts* (Boston, 1940), 226–40, lists fifteen states that created intermediate appeals courts during the late nineteenth and early twentieth centuries.

33. *Annual Report of the Attorney General, 1876* (Boston, 1877), 7–8.

34. *Annual Report of the Attorney General, 1887* (Boston, 1888), 16; *Annual Report of the Attorney General, 1889* (Boston, 1890), 14.

35. *Address of His Excellency John J. Q. Brackett*, January 2, 1890 (Boston, 1890), 15; *Acts and Resolves, 1890* (Boston, 1891), chap. 379. The 1891 statute transferring capital jurisdiction to the Superior Court from the SJC required that murder trials be heard by three Superior Court judges; in 1894 the number of judges required became two or more; and in 1910 one justice of the Superior Court was empowered

to preside at a homicide trial. *Massachusetts General Laws Annotated*, 49 vols. (St. Paul, Minn., 2005), 34–35:233. See also Alan Dimond, "The Transfer of Capital Cases from the Supreme Judicial Court to the Superior Court," in Supreme Judicial Court Historical Society, *Annual Report*, 1991.

36. *Annual Report of the Attorney General for the Year Ending 1892* (Boston, 1893), xiii.

37. Three murder convictions were appealed to the SJC between 1881 to 1891, and twelve between 1892 and 1902, despite the fact that there were fewer murders committed in the decade after 1892. *Annual Report of the Attorney General* for 1881–1902 (Boston 1882–1903).

38. SJC Docket Books, 1892–1939; *Trial of James Trefethen and William Smith for the Murder of Deltena J. Davis* (Boston, 1895), 9, 11–12, 33, 37, 91, 114, 231. The second court-appointed attorney to be drawn from the elite pool of lawyers was William Doherty.

39. *Commonwealth v. Trefethen*, 157 Mass. 180, 189, 194, 195 (1892). The hearsay rule on which the trial court relied, *Commonwealth v. Felth*, 132 Mass. 22 (1882).

40. *Commonwealth v. Trefethen*, 157 Mass. at 189, 194, 195. Two other capital convictions were appealed unsuccessfully in 1892, *Commonwealth v. Coy*, 157 Mass. 200 (1892), and *Commonwealth v. Holmes*, 157 Mass. 233 (1892).

41. *Trial of James Trefethen*, 287, 292, 393.

42. *Commonwealth v. Madeiros*, 25 Mass. 304 (1926); at a new trial, *Commonwealth v. Madeiros*, 257 Mass. 1 (1926), Madeiros was convicted of first-degree murder and executed. *Boston Globe*, August 23, 1937. *The General Statutes of the Commonwealth of Massachusetts* (Boston, 1940), chap. 341, required the SJC to review the entire capital case, not just questions of law.

43. *Commonwealth v. Howard*, 205 Mass. 128, 149 (1910), *Commonwealth v. Williams*, 171 Mass. 461, 462 (1898), *Commonwealth v. Holmes*, 157 Mass. 233, *Commonwealth v. O'Neil*, 169 Mass. 394 (1897), and *Commonwealth v. Howard*, 205 Mass. 128, are rulings about marital discord. *Commonwealth v. Robertson*, 162 Mass. 90 (1894) and *Commonwealth v. Howard*, 205 Mass. at 148, are about the admissibility of photographic evidence. *Commonwealth v. Best*, 180 Mass. 492 (1902) established a rule about ballistic tests.

44. *Commonwealth v. Chance*, 174 Mass. 245, 248–49 (1899). At his arraignment Chance pleaded not guilty to the charge of murder, but at trial a jury returned a verdict of guilty of murder in the second degree and the SJC denied his subsequent appeal. In *Commonwealth v. Preece*, 140 Mass. 276 (1885), the court created what it called a "humane practice" rule for the admission of confessions. The rule allowed the defendant to present evidence that a confession was not voluntary as argued by the prosecution; the issue was left to the jury to be weighed and considered.

45. *Boston Globe*, April 1, 2, 1904.

46. Ibid., April 4, 1904; *Boston Herald*, March 20, 1906.

47. *Boston Globe*, April 4, 5, 10, 11, 12, 22, 1904.

48. Ibid., September. 19, 20, 1904.

49. *Globe Newspaper Company v. Commonwealth*, 188 Mass. 449, 452, 454 (1905).

50. *Boston Globe*, January 3, 1905. The test applied to juror Nason followed court practice established by Chief Justice Shaw in *Commonwealth v. Webster*, 59 Mass. 295, 298 (1850). Details from the following discussion of the Tucker trial are drawn from *Boston Globe*, January 2–22, 24–27, 1905.

51. *The Official Report of the Trial of Charles Louis Tucker*, 2 vols. (Boston, 1907), 1:46.

52. *Commonwealth v. Tucker*, 189 Mass. 457, 467–86 (1905).

53. Ibid. at 486–98. The court's humane practice, *Commonwealth v. Preece*, 140 Mass. 276.

54. *Boston Herald*, January 14, 18, 28, 1906. The defense request for Supreme Court review, *Boston Herald*, February 28, 1906; the court's denial of certiorari, *Boston Herald*, March 16, 1906. The Fourth Amendment protection against unreasonable searches was extended to state criminal proceedings in *Mapp v. Ohio*, 367 U.S. 643 (1961). According to the *Boston Herald*, March 31, 1906, the petition campaign was financed by Vahey's law firm and sent to every newspaper in Massachusetts.

55. *Boston Herald*, March 31, 1906.

56. Ibid., April 1, 9, 1906. The Boston Building Laborers' Union adopted a resolution endorsing commutation of Tucker's death sentence.

57. Ibid., April 6, 1906. The vote against the bill was 132 to 68. In his statement following Tucker's execution, Vahey sought to refute rumors about Tucker's alleged "unnatural" behavior. *Boston Globe*, June 12, 1906.

58. Ibid., May 22, 1906. The population of Massachusetts in 1906 was about 2.8 million people. Article 2, chap. 3, pt. 2 of the Constitution of the Commonwealth of Massachusetts declares: "Each branch of the legislature, as well as the governor or the council, shall have authority to require the opinion of the justices of the supreme judicial court, upon important questions of law, and upon solemn occasions." For a full discussion of the SJC's advisory role, see Cynthia R. Farina, "Supreme Judicial Court Advisory Opinions: Two Centuries of Interbranch Dialogue," in *The History of the Law in Massachusetts: The Supreme Judicial Court, 1692–1992*, ed. Russell K. Osgood (Boston, 1992), 353.

59. *Boston Globe*, June 9, 1906.

60. Ibid.

61. Details about the case in this paragraph and the following three are drawn from *Boston Herald*, June 8, 12, 1906.

5. A "TONG WAR" AND THE SECOND EFFORT
TO ABOLISH THE DEATH PENALTY

1. *Commonwealth v. Wong Chung and another,* 186 Mass. 231 (1903); *Commonwealth v. Min Sing and others,* 202 Mass. 121 (1908); *Boston Globe,* March 8, 9, 1908; *Boston Evening Transcript,* August 3, 1907.

2. State Library of Massachusetts, *Anti-Death Penalty League: The First League in America to Organize for the Abolition of Death as a Penalty for Crime* (Boston, 1912); Thomas H. O'Connor, *The Boston Irish: A Political History* (Boston, 1995), 175-80, 196-99; James O'Toole, *Militant and Triumphant: William Henry O'Connell and the Catholic Church in Boston, 1859-1944* (South Bend, Ind., 1992).

3. Frederick Rudolph, "Chinamen in Yankeedom: Anti-Unionism in Massachusetts in 1870," *American Historical Review* 53 (1947): 1; K. Scott Wong, " 'The Eagle Seeks a Helpless Quarry': Chinatown, the Police, and the Press: The 1903 Boston Chinatown Raid Revisited," *Amerasia Journal* 22 (1996): 81.

4. *Boston Chinatown* (Boston, 1976), 1-5.

5. Ibid.; Judge Emmons's visit to Chinatown, *Boston Globe,* June 28, 1903. For a sympathetic description of Chinese New Year, see *Boston Globe,* February 28, 1908; but for other less flattering views of Chinese men, see, for example, *Boston Globe,* September 9, 18, 1903, October 4, 1903; and Charles F. Holder, "The Chinaman in American Politics," *North American Review* 166 (February 1898): 226. Boston Police Captain Lawrence Cain used the term "the colony"; *Boston Globe* March 9, 1908.

6. *Boston Globe,* October 3, 1903. Several years later Boston police insisted they "raid members of each society with impartiality." *Boston Globe,* August 3, 1907.

7. Ibid., October 4, 14, 1903. For an analysis of the psychological barrier separating Chinese from white Americans, see Alexander Saxton, *The Indispensable Enemy: Labor and the Anti-Chinese Movement in California* (Berkeley, Calif., 1971).

8. *Boston Globe,* October 12, 1903.

9. Ibid., October 12, 13, 1903. Two white witnesses who testified on behalf of two suspected illegal Chinese immigrants were later arrested for perjury. Ibid., January 30, 1904.

10. Ibid., October 14, 1903. Hoar quoted in Lucy E. Sayler, *Laws Harsh as Tigers: Chinese Immigrants and the Shaping of Modern Immigration Law* (Chapel Hill, N.C., 1995), 16-17. See also J. Thomas Scharf, "The Farce of Chinese Exclusion Laws," *North American Review* 106 (January 1898): 85-93; Hon. John Russell Young, "The Chinese Question Again," *North American Review* 154 (May 1892): 596-602; James Phelan, "Why the Chinese Should Be Excluded," *North American Review* 173 (December 1901): 663-74. The following narrative of the trial is drawn from *Boston Globe,* December, 1-3, 4, 6, 1903, January 16, 1904.

11. *Commonwealth v. Wong Chung*, 186 Mass. at 234, 237, 238. The following description of the three-day visit by the Chinese delegation is drawn from *Boston Globe*, February 11, 12, 13, 1906.

12. For data illustrating the decline of the Massachusetts textile industry, see Richard Wilkie and Jack Tager, eds., *Historical Atlas of Massachusetts* (Amherst, Mass., 1991), 42. See also Sayler, *Laws as Harsh as Tigers*, 117–38; *Boston Globe*, September 9, 18, October 2, 10, December 3, 1906; *Boston Herald*, August 3, 1907.

13. *Boston Globe*, August 3, 1907; *Boston Herald*, August 3, 1907. On the day after the shooting, two of the wounded men died. The following description of the shooting and subsequent arrests is drawn from *Boston Globe*, August 3, 1907. The names of the suspects were often misspelled.

14. Ibid. *Boston Herald*, August 3, 1907.

15. *Boston Evening Transcript*, August 3, 1907. O'Brien left the *Transcript* for the *Herald* in 1910. Joseph Chamberlin, *The Boston Transcript: A History of Its First Hundred Years* (Boston, 1930), 191–200.

16. *Boston Globe*, January 20, 21, 1908.

17. *The Revised Statutes of the Commonwealth of Massachusetts* (Boston, 1836), chap. 137, sec. 6; Alan Rogers, "'Under Sentence of Death': The Movement to Abolish Capital Punishment in Massachusetts, 1835–1849," *New England Quarterly* 66 (March 1993): 27; *Sir Edward Coke Upon Littleton* (London, 1832), 155b. For the Massachusetts jurors' oath, see *The General Statutes of the Commonwealth of Massachusetts* (Boston, 1873), chap. 219, sec. 7. For a discussion of the modern jury system, see Jeffrey Abramson, *We the Jury: The Jury System and the Ideal of Democracy* (New York, 1994). The following narrative, unless otherwise indicated, is drawn from *Boston Globe*, January 20–22, February 3–5, 10, 18, 26, March 4, 6–9, 1908, and *Boston Herald*, August 3, 1907, January 23, March 5, 1908, November 30, 1909.

18. To provide a pool from which 12 would be selected, 111 potential jurors were called and examined.

19. For eyewitness testimony, see *Boston Globe*, February 4–17, 1908; for the court's ruling on evidence, see ibid., February 7, 1908.

20. Ibid., February 18, 1908.

21. For Bartlett's run for governor in 1905 and his "illegal" nomination in 1907, see Michael E. Hennessy, *Twenty-Five Years of Massachusetts Politics* (Boston, 1917), 147–50, 176–183. Pratt was the "illegal" Democrat nominee for attorney general in 1907 (ibid., 183).

22. On March 4, 1908, Yee Wat died in his cell, apparently from a heart attack.

23. *Woman's Who's Who of America* (New York, 1914–15), 771; State Library of Massachusetts, *Anti-Death Penalty League: The First League in America to Organize for the Abolition of Death as a Penalty for Crime* (1915).

24. *Capital Punishment: Some Reasons Why House Bill No. 381 Ought to Pass* (Boston, 1900), 17–21.

25. *Annual Report of the Attorney General for the Year Ending 1899* (Boston, 1900), xv–xvi.

26. *Annual Report of the Attorney General for the Year Ending 1900* (Boston, 1901), xviii–xix.

27. Ibid., xviii; *Boston Herald*, May 16, 24, 25, 1907; *Boston Globe*, May 15, 16, 24, 1907. The legislature defeated bills to abolish capital punishment by wider margins in 1901, 1902, 1903, and 1906. Hennessy, *Twenty-Five Years of Massachusetts Politics*, 101. The Tucker murder trial was mentioned frequently during debate on a House bill to abolish the death penalty in 1906, but the vote on a motion to substitute a minority report favorable to the bill was handily defeated, 132 to 68. *Boston Globe*, April 5, 1906. There were 28 Republicans and 12 Democrats in the Senate and 173 Republicans and 63 Democrats and 4 others in the House in 1907. The vote did not divide along party lines. *Journal of the House of Representatives of the Commonwealth of Massachusetts* (Boston, 1907), May 16–27, 1907, 992, 1003, 1005, 1018, 1045–47; *Journal of the Massachusetts Senate* (Boston, 1907), May 7–10, 1907, 808, 836–37.

28. For a Judiciary Committee hearing on a bill abolishing the death penalty, see *Boston Globe*, February 20, 21, 1912.

29. Hearing to Prove Exceptions in the Case of Min Sing, et al., November 19, 20, 1908, 2 vols., 1:1–3, Supreme Judicial Court, Judicial Archives, Massachusetts State Archives, Boston. In one of his first official acts District Attorney John B. Moran released Yee Jung from custody in August 1908. The other four defense exceptions to the trial court's rulings were trivial. *Commonwealth v. Min Sing*, 202 Mass. at 131–32; *The Revised Laws of the Commonwealth of Massachusetts*, 2 vols. (Boston, 1902), chap. 173, sec. 110, 2:1568. This marked the first time the law making possible a hearing to establish the truth of exceptions was used in a criminal case.

30. Hearing to Prove Exceptions, 1:1–3.

31. Ibid., 1:13–14, 18–19.

32. *Commonwealth v. Min Sing*, 202 Mass. at 128, 129, 132.

33. Julian Woodman to Governor Eben Draper, October 1, 1910, Memorandum on the Petition of Warry Charles and Joe Guey Before the Pardon Committee of the Executive Council, Massachusetts State Archives; *Boston Globe*, October 12, 1909. The following description of the executions of Min Sing, Leong Gong, and Hom Woon is drawn from *Boston Globe*, October 11, 12, 1909.

34. Hearing on Pardon of Warry Charles and Joe Guey, November 5, 6, 1909, 3 vols., 1:4–6, 12–16, 2:122–31, Massachusetts State Archives; Application for Pardon, No. 546, Joe Guey, Massachusetts State Archives.

35. Hearing on Pardon, 3:172–74.

36. Ibid., 3:197–98, 201–2, 213–18.

37. *Boston Globe*, November 8, 1909; *Boston Herald*, November 30, 1909. See also *Oregon v. Ah Lee*, 7 Oregon Reports 237 (1879), in which a trial judge instructed a jury to ignore the testimony of Chinese witnesses.

38. *Boston Globe*, November 30, 1909.

39. Ibid., December 1, 1909; *Boston Herald*, December 1, 1909. Draper's successor, Governor Eugene Foss, used the pardon power freely. An editorial cartoon showed the governor swinging open a prison door. The caption read: "The Open Door Policy—Wide Open." *Boston Journal*, December 12, 1912. Foss did not pardon either Charles or Guey. Both men died in prison. Francis Spooner to Cardinal William O'Connell, n.d., Cardinal O'Connell Papers, Archives of the Archdiocese of Boston.

40. *Boston Herald*, August 3, 1907; *Boston Globe*, August 4, 1907, March 8, 1908; *Boston Evening Transcript*, February 4, 1908.

41. *Boston Evening Transcript*, August 3, 1907. Bartlett's racially biased remarks were reported in the *Boston Globe*, March 4, 6, 1908. *Boston Globe* October 19, 1909.

42. The SJC told the Massachusetts legislature that its proposed anti-Chinese law was unconstitutional. *Opinion of the Justices*, 207 Mass. 601 (1912). Sayler, *Laws as Harsh as Tigers*, 110–11.

43. Father Byrne's obituary, *Boston Pilot*, January 13, 1912. For a typical Judiciary Committee hearing, see *Boston Globe*, February 20, 21, 1912. See also Sara Ehrmann to Members of the Massachusetts Council to Abolish the Death Penalty, November 2, 1947, Papers, 1845–1993, Sara R. Ehrmann, University Libraries, Archives and Special Collections Department, Northeastern University, Boston.

44. O'Connor, *Boston Irish*, 176–79, 183–88.

45. Ibid., 196–98; O'Toole, *William Henry O'Connell*; O'Connell to Spooner, February 28, 1913, O'Connell Papers, Archives of the Boston Archdiocese. Spooner also drifted away from the league. She converted to Catholicism and focused her attention on serving the Church.

6. SACCO AND VANZETTI

1. On the question of Sacco and Vanzetti's guilt or innocence, I agree with G. Louis Joughin and Edmund M. Morgan, *The Legacy of Sacco and Vanzetti* (New York, 1948), vii: "We do not believe that human judgment will ever be in a position to arrive at absolute certainty." Undeterred, many historians have tried to solve the puzzle. The most accessible books are Francis Russell, *Tragedy in Dedham* (New York, 1962) and *Sacco and Vanzetti: The Case Resolved* (New York, 1986). Russell argues in the later book that Sacco was guilty and Vanzetti innocent. Osmond K.

Fraenkel, *The Sacco-Vanzetti Case* (New York, 1931); Herbert Ehrmann, *The Case That Will Not Die* (Boston, 1969); William Young and David E. Kaiser, *Postmortem: New Evidence in the Case of Sacco and Vanzetti* (Amherst, Mass., 1985). Young and Kaiser make a case based on newly discovered evidence that "two innocent men, most probably were framed for a murder they did not commit" (9). Robert Montgomery, *The Murder and the Myth* (New York, 1960), argues that Sacco and Vanzetti were guilty. See also *The Sacco-Vanzetti Case: Transcript of the Record of the Trial of Nicola Sacco and Bartolomeo Vanzetti, 1920–1927*, 5 vols. (New York, 1928–1929).

2. Joughin and Morgan, *Legacy of Sacco and Vanzetti*, vii; Fraenkel, *Sacco-Vanzetti Case*, 12–13. Rugg served five years on the court before being appointed to the center seat. During Rugg's tenure as chief justice the SJC heard 108 appeals of homicide convictions and reversed 2, *Commonwealth v. Retkovitz*, 222 Mass. 245 (1916), and *Commonwealth v. Maderios*, 255 Mass. 304 (1927). Both men were retried, found guilty, and executed. About the crime wave, see *Annual Report of the Attorney General for the Year Ending 1926* (Boston, 1927), 7. In this report, Attorney General Jay Benton notes that experts have highlighted dozens of alleged causes for the increase in crime, but he thinks accelerating the pace of justice would be most beneficial. Felix Frankfurter, *The Case of Sacco and Vanzetti: A Critical Analysis for Lawyers and Laymen* (Boston, 1927). Frankfurter served on the Supreme Court from 1939 to 1962.

3. *The Laws of the Commonwealth of Massachusetts, Enacted 1939* (Boston, 1940), chap. 341, allows the SJC to review law and fact and to order a new trial "for any reason justice may require." The law regulating the examination of jurors may be found in *The General Laws of Massachusetts* (Boston, 1985), chap. 234; it was amended in 1973 to combat the prejudicial effects of "community attitudes" (chap. 219, sec. 7). The Supreme Court seemed to adopt Frankfurter's perspective on the issue in *Irvin v. Dowd*, 366 U.S. at 730, but backtracked in *Murphy v. Florida*, 421 U.S. 794 (1975). The SJC abolished the death penalty for murder in *District Attorney v. Watson*, 381 Mass. 648 (1980); the movement leading to the court's decision is discussed in detail in Chapter 12.

4. *Commonwealth v. Sacco and another*, 255 Mass. 369, 384 (1926); *Record of the Trial*, 1:64–70.

5. Sacco and Vanzetti met Mike Boda and Ricardo Orciani (the latter two men rode a motorcycle) at Johnson's garage to claim Boda's car. They left without the car because it did not have the proper registration. *Commonwealth v. Sacco*, 255 Mass. at 385. Sacco and Vanzetti knew that Andrea Salsedo, a New York City anarchist, had been arrested and either jumped or was thrown from a building to his death while in police custody. Prior to that incident, Sacco had collected money for Salsedo's defense and Vanzetti had traveled to New York, where he was told

by fellow anarchists to collect the Boston group's radical literature in anticipation of a government raid. (Joughin and Morgan, *Legacy of Sacco and Vanzetti*, 70–71; *Record of the Trial*, 1:1). Robert K. Murray, *Red Scare: A Study in National Hysteria, 1919–1920* (New York, 1955), outlines the post–World War I repression of civil liberties and the roundup of aliens and suspected leftists by the attorney general of the United States, A. Mitchell Palmer. More than six hundred men and women were rounded up in the greater Boston area. *Boston Globe*, January 5, 6, 1920.

6. Joughin and Morgan, *Legacy of Sacco and Vanzetti*, 26–57, details Vanzetti's trial for the Bridgewater attempted robbery. Vanzetti later angrily charged that attorney Vahey persuaded him not to testify. Among others, Elizabeth F. Loftus, *Eyewitness Testimony* (Cambridge, Mass., 1979), questions the reliability of eyewitness identification.

7. Sacco and Vanzetti were indicted for the South Braintree murders on September 11, 1920 (*Commonwealth v. Sacco*, 255 Mass. at 381). On the history of the prisoner's dock or cage, see Alan Rogers, "'In the Cage': The Prisoner's Dock and the Presumption of Innocence in Massachusetts Criminal Trials," *Massachusetts Legal History* 3 (1997): 89. On Sacco's background, see Fraenkel, *Sacco-Vanzetti Case*, 10–11, and Joughin and Morgan, *Legacy of Sacco and Vanzetti*, 456–57. Paul Avrich, *Sacco and Vanzetti: The Anarchist Background* (Princeton, N.J., 1991), argues that anarchists traveled to Mexico in 1917 in anticipation of a revolution in Italy.

8. For the highlights of Vanzetti's life, see Frankel, *Sacco-Vanzetti Case*, 11–12, and Joughin and Morgan, *Legacy of Sacco and Vanzetti*, 457–59.

9. *Record of the Trial*, 1:3. On April 10, 1920, at a naturalization ceremony held in Dedham, Judge Thayer commented on the dangers to American values posed by radical political ideology. Dedham *Transcript*, as quoted in Young and Kaiser, *Postmortem*, 22.

10. G. Edward White, in *Justice Oliver Wendell Holmes: Law and the Inner Self* (New York, 1993), 121–23, explores Holmes's idea that legal duties come before legal rights. White also points out that following publication of "The Theory of Torts," *American Law Review* 7 (1873): 652, Holmes discovered that an English jurist, Shadworth Hodgson, had articulated the same formulation in *Theory of Practice* (2 vols., London, 1870). Holmes, *The Common Law* (Boston, 1881), 219–20. White argues that the duty/rights distinction was peculiar to Holmes and other Brahmins, but clearly the idea had entered the mainstream.

11. *Record of the Trial*, 1:3. The five statutory questions may be found in *Annotated Laws of Massachusetts* (St. Paul, Minn., 1932–), chap. 234, sec. 28, and chap. 278, sec. 3. In Massachusetts, the practice of questioning jurors one by one began with *Commonwealth v. Min Sing and others*, 202 Mass. 121 (1908), according to the *Boston Globe*, February 3, 1908. As early as 1834 Attorney General James T. Austin presented a list of questions he wanted the court to ask potential jurors, but Chief

Justice Lemuel Shaw refused. *Commonwealth v. Buzzell*, 33 Mass. 153 (1834). *Commonwealth v. Burroughs*, 145 Mass. 252 (1887) upheld the trial court's refusal to ask additional questions of the potential jurors. The relative merits of the court as opposed to counsel conducting voir dire (the questioning of potential jurors) had long been a contentious issue in Massachusetts and other state courts and as late as 1974 there was no uniformity. See *Boston University Law Review* 54 (1974): 394.

12. *Record of the Trial*, 1:6–48, lists 153 of the potential jurymen questioned. *Boston Daily Globe*, May 31–June 4, 1921, describes the process in detail; the quotations are from a June 2, 1921, article. Judge Thayer mentioned that the strategy of herding all of the potential jurors in a room while a single person was questioned had become Massachusetts practice; in fact, the practice was first used during a 1908 murder trial of ten Chinese reported in the *Boston Daily Globe*, February 3, 1908. Although women were qualified to vote as a result of the Nineteenth Amendment, Massachusetts women were not permitted to serve on a state jury until 1951. Alan Rogers, "'Finish the Fight': The Struggle for Women's Jury Service in Massachusetts, 1920–1994," *Massachusetts Historical Review* 2 (2000): 27. The defense insisted it was entitled to receive a list of potential jurors, but the prosecution prevailed when it argued the process of rounding up additional men conformed to Massachusetts law. For a history of the use of challenges for cause and peremptory challenges in regard to capital punishment, see Alan Rogers, "'An Anchor to the Windward': The Right of the Accused to an Impartial Jury in Massachusetts Capital Cases," *Suffolk University Law Review* 33 (1999): 35. Sacco and Vanzetti each had twenty-two peremptory challenges for each of the two indictments against them, for a total of eighty-eight; the state had an equal number. Judge Thayer's remark to jurors opposed to capital punishment was inaccurate. In fact, only men who would not under any circumstances find a defendant guilty of a capital crime could be struck for cause by the court. Of course, a man who held such a belief was qualified to serve on a noncapital criminal jury and a civil jury. Moreover, since all men who were qualified to vote for representatives to the Massachusetts lower house were eligible for jury service, it was not possible for an eligible voter to avoid being summoned for jury service.

13. *New Bedford Standard-Times*, November 12, 1950. My point is that several jurors were impressed with the alleged scarcity of the Winchester bullets and together with eyewitness testimony created a body of evidence that led the jury to conclude Sacco and Vanzetti were guilty as charged. Joughin and Morgan report that Fred Moore told an anonymous Boston attorney that a juror said that the guilty verdict was based chiefly on expert testimony about the bullets (*Legacy of Sacco and Vanzetti*, 551 n. 48). Evidence about the bullets is still somewhat controversial. See Young and Kaiser, *Postmortem*, chap. 9 and p. 113, for the argument that Police Chief Michael Stewart and State Police Officer Albert Brouillard substituted a bul-

let they test-fired from Sacco's pistol for the original bullet III, the so-called mortal bullet. For the names and occupations of the jurors, see *Record of the Trail*, 1:48. A pretrial remark by Ripley, who died on October 10, 1921, was the subject of a defense motion alleging bias (see discussion later in the chapter).

14. Thayer's charge to the jury, *Record of the Trial*, 2:2239, 2262. SJC Associate Justice Henry T. Lummus, who served on the court from 1932 to 1955, wrote that charging a jury "is a great art. In essence it is advocacy; not partisan advocacy, but the advocacy of an honest and intelligent performance of duty, of giving justice to the law." Attorney General Edward J. McCormack quoting a lecture given by Lummus in, Henry Tilton Lummus, "Memorial," 344 Mass. 779 (1962).

15. *Record of the Trial*, 5:5547, 5548, 5563. Thayer quoted *Baker v. Briggs*, 8 Pick. 126 (1829) and noted that SJC Chief Justice Arthur Rugg had cited with approval the same case in *Edwards v. Willey*, 218 Mass. 366 (1914).

16. *Proceedings Before the Council and Members of the Association of the City of Boston, Memorial Read by Bentley W. Warren, Remarks by George E. Mears, and Herbert B. Ehrmann* (Boston, 1938), 2, 5. In a letter to Charles B. Rogers, November 19, 1926, Thompson wrote that if Sacco and Vanzetti were executed "violent and permanent antagonisms will be created which will certainly not be conducive to social peace and good order, and may lead to serious consequences" (quoted in Young and Kaiser, *Postmortem*, 76).

17. Following the death of a SJC justice he or she is memorialized before the court. For biographical information see the following memorials: Braley, 257 Mass. 586 (1931); Carroll, 280 Mass. 589 (1932); Sanderson, 281 Mass. 559 (1933); Wait, 297 Mass. 589 (1937); and Rugg, 302 Mass. 625 (1939) and *Arthur Prentice Rugg: Chief Justice of the Supreme Judicial Court of the Commonwealth of Massachusetts: A Memorial* (Worcester, Mass., 1939).

18. Rugg, *Memorial*.

19. *Davis v. Boston Elevated Ry. Co.*, 235 Mass. 482 (1920); Davis v. Boston Elevated (1920), SJC Records and Briefs, Archives of the Supreme Judicial Court, Boston, 1–3; *Davis v. Boston Elevated*, 222 Mass. 475, 479 (1916).

20. Davis v. Boston Elevated (1920), 2, 4–7, 26–27.

21. Ibid., Appendix, 2, 3, 36, 45, 60.

22. *Davis v. Boston Elevated Railway*, 235 Mass. at 494–95, 496, 502. The bullet or lead fragment had been destroyed during the chemical analysis (499).

23. "Argument on Behalf of Sacco and Vanzetti before Committee appointed by Governor Fuller," in *Record of the Trial*, 5:5263; *Commonwealth v. Sacco*, 255 Mass. 369; *Commonwealth v. Sacco*, 259 Mass. 128 (1927). A trial judge may not violate a defendant's rights, but in a criminal trial a judge has considerable latitude or discretion to rule what to permit and what not to permit. A judge's discretionary rulings

are subject to appellate review, but the standard applied by the SJC, as I show in a later discussion, gave the trial judge extraordinary flexibility.

24. *Record of the Trial*, 4:3583, 3593, 3598, 3603; *Commonwealth v. Sacco*, 255 Mass. at 381. The SJC defined discretion in *Davis v. Boston Elevated Railway*, 235 Mass. at 497. Ripley also was the focus of another defense motion. An affidavit claimed that when Ripley was summoned for jury duty he said to a friend who questioned Sacco and Vanzetti's guilt, "Damn them, they ought to hang anyway." Thayer did not explicitly address this defense argument, but the SJC ruled that Thayer had denied this motion when he rejected the first (*Commonwealth v. Sacco*, 255 Mass. at 380. Chief Justice Rugg spoke for the court in *Commonwealth v. Dascalakis*, 246 Mass. 12, 25 (1923).

25. Defendants Amended Bill of Exceptions, *Record of the Trial*, 5:4361–69.

26. *Record of the Trial*, 5:4726, 4738–39, 4741.

27. Ibid., 4851, 4859, 4861.

28. Sam Bass Warner, "The Role of Courts and Judicial Councils in Procedural Reform," *University of Pennsylvania Law Review* 85 (1937): 441, 442. Daniel J. Johnedis, in "Creation of the Appeals Court and Its Impact on the Supreme Judicial Court," *The History of the Law in Massachusetts: The Supreme Judicial Court, 1692–1992*, ed. Russell K. Osgood (Boston, 1992), 445, 449, argues that before 1970 the "court rarely reconsidered legal doctrines and only occasionally engaged in extensive discussion of the challenged law." To highlight how little criminal procedure had changed, Sam Bass Warner and Henry B. Cabot, in "Changes in the Administration of Criminal Justice during the Past Fifty Years," *Harvard Law Review* 50 (1937): 583, 584–85, 589, convincingly describe as contemporary a murder trial that had taken place in 1883. See also William Blackstone, *Commentaries on the Laws of England*, 4 vols. (1765; facsimile edition, Chicago, 1979), 4:308; Matthew Hale, *The History of the Pleas of the Crown* (London, 1778); William Hawkins, *A Treatise of the Pleas of the Crown* (London, 1716, 1728); Gerald Leonard, "Towards a Legal History of American Criminal Theory: Culture and Doctrine from Blackstone to the Model Penal Code," *Buffalo Criminal Law Review* 6 (2003): 691; Allen Steinberg, *The Transformation of Criminal Justice: Philadelphia, 1800–1880* (Chapel Hill, N.C., 1989). Private individuals in Philadelphia brought a majority of criminal prosecutions using a mix of criminal and civil procedures. Alan Rogers, "Murder in Massachusetts: The Criminal Discovery Rule from Snelling to Rule 14," *American Journal of Legal History* 40 (1996): 438.

29. *Commonwealth v. Sacco*, 259 Mass. at 136, 137, 138, 140, 142. The defense tried unsuccessfully to use *Davis* to its advantage by arguing that it was a "logical extension" of that ruling to conclude that if the new evidence introduced by the defense was "weighty," "material," and "relevant" and would lead a jury to find

Madeiros guilty of the crime for which Sacco and Vanzetti were charged a new trial
"must be granted as a matter of law" (*Record of the Trial*, 5:4809). Judge Wait also
cited Rugg's ruling on this issue in *Commonwealth v. Dascalakis*, 246 Mass. at 32.
In *Thayer v. Shorey*, 287 Mass. 76, 80 (1934), Rugg generalized his ruling in *Davis*:
"The courts of the Commonwealth constitute a single system for the administration of justice in conformity to law promptly and without delay."

30. *Record of the Trial*, 5:4895, 4904-5.

31. *New York Times*, June 26, 1927. For Pound's private musings to Thompson,
see N. E. H. Hull, "Reconstructing the Origins of Realistic Jurisprudence: A Pre-
quel to the Llewellyn-Pound Exchange over Legal Realism," *Duke Law Journal*,
1989, 1302, 1319, 1321. Hull also reveals that Pound drafted, circulated, and published a neutrally worded petition calling for a disinterested board to review the
Sacco-Vanzetti case; it was sent to Massachusetts governor Alvan T. Fuller in late
April 1927. Harvard law professors Zechariah Chafee Jr., Edmund Morgan, and
James Landis took a public position against the verdict (Joughin and Morgan,
Legacy of Sacco and Vanzetti, 258-62). See also Bruce Allen Murphy, *The Brandeis/
Frankfurter Connection: The Secret Political Activities of Two Supreme Court Jus-
tices* (New York, 1982), 34-39.

32. *Atlantic Monthly*, March 1927, 409; Frankfurter, *Case of Sacco and Vanzetti*,
46, 43, 59, 60. Justice Louis Brandeis encouraged Frankfurter to write the article
and book. See Murphy, *Brandeis/Frankfurter Connection*, 78-79. It is worth noting that Brandeis recused himself from participation in the case. For contemporary
reviews of Frankfurter's book, see *Texas Law Review* 5 (1926-27): 449; *Yale Law
Review* 36 (1926-27): 1192; *Cornell Law Quarterly* 12 (1926-27): 555; and *Harvard
Law Review* 40 (1926-27): 1031. Despite the mixed reviews of Frankfurter's book
by contemporary law professors, a number of journalists and historians followed
Frankfurter's lead. See, for example, Philip D. Strong, *The Aspirin Age* (New York,
1949); and Joughin and Morgan, *Legacy of Sacco and Vanzetti*, 204-5, 219. Russell,
Sacco and Vanzetti: The Case Resolved, 133-34, rejects Frankfurter's charges about
Judge Thayer's alleged bias among jurors, prosecutor, and judge as too general and
lacking specific substantiation. Jeffrey Abramson, *We, The Jury: The Jury System
and the Ideal of American Democracy* (New York, 1994), 53, points to a long list of
contemporary trials in which the outcomes were different than expected and not
apparently influenced by pretrial publicity.

33. Frankfurter, *Case of Sacco and Vanzetti*, 11-15, 33-34. The issue of false or re-
pressed memory remains controversial. See, generally, Elizabeth Loftus, *Eyewitness
Testimony* (Cambridge, Mass., 1996).

34. Frankfurter, *Case of Sacco and Vanzetti*, 17-20. When he was questioned immediately after the shooting, Pelzer said he saw nothing (*Record of the Trial*, 3:2421-
23, 2427, 2834-55). See also Loftus, *Eyewitness Testimony*, 17-19. Nearly thirty years

after the trial, juror Dever stated that Pelzer's testimony was very convincing because even though he was a reluctant witness, he seemed to be telling the truth. *New Bedford Standard-Times*, November 12, 1950.

35. *Record of the Trial*, 1:896, 3:3422.

36. Frankfurter, *Case of Sacco and Vanzetti*, 76; The Hamilton-Proctor Motions, *Record of the Trial* 4:3539–45, 3698–3704, 4120–23, 4127, 4259–60. Because Proctor died shortly after he gave the affidavit to the defense on October 23, 1924, Thayer was unable to question him at the motion hearing.

37. Frankfurter, *Case of Sacco and Vanzetti*, 76–77, 81–85.

38. Ibid., 65. For Thayer's charge to the jury, see *Record of the Trial*, 3:3407–31; for the full paragraph, see 3422. On one hand, Dever claimed to be unimpressed with Proctor's testimony, because the police captain admitted during cross-examination that he could not disassemble the Colt pistol, a feat Dever had mastered in the army. On the other hand, Dever stated that the defense ballistics expert, James Burns, "made a good impression. He was a man of fine appearance, apparently reliable and sincere." *New Bedford Standard-Times*, November 12, 1950. Finally, the 1983 Select Committee on Sacco and Vanzetti: Examination of Firearm-Related Evidence concluded the mortal bullet had been fired from Sacco's pistol (cited in Young and Kaiser, *Postmortem*, 95–96).

39. John H. Wigmore, *A Treatise on the Anglo-American System of Evidence at Trials at Common Law* (Boston, 1923), 544; Robert H. Hutchins and Donald Slesinger, "Some Observations on the Law of Evidence: Consciousness of Guilt," *University of Pennsylvania Law Review* 77 (1929): 725, 728, 740.

40. *Record of the Trial*, 3:3424–30.

41. Frankfurter, *Case of Sacco and Vanzetti*, 35–62, 38–39, 40, 62; *Record of the Trial*, 3: 2661–62.

42. Frankfurter, *Case of Sacco and Vanzetti*, 87–91.

43. Wigmore was also a past president of the American Institute of Criminal Law and Criminology. His reply to Frankfurter was published in the *Boston Evening Transcript*, April 25, 1927. The *Transcript* also published a rebuttal by Frankfurter, April 26, 1927, and a handful of letters about the Frankfurter-Wigmore debate, April 27, 1927.

44. Ibid., April 25, 26, 1927.

45. Henry A. Yeomans, *Abbott Lawrence Lowell, 1856–1943* (Cambridge, Mass., 1948), 494, as quoted in Joughin and Morgan, *Legacy of Sacco and Vanzetti*, 262.

46. *Boston Herald*, October 27, 1926.

47. "We Submit," *Boston Herald*, October 26, 1927. Russell claims Frankfurter "coached" Bullard (*Sacco and Vanzetti*, 132). *Record of the Trial*, 5:4907–47. Sacco refused to sign the petition, but Vanzetti spoke for both men. Several affidavits accompanied the plea.

48. *Record of the Trial*, 5:5257, 5266, 5258, 5267, 5269–5273, 5333, 5278–5279.

49. Ibid., 5334, 5341, 5340, 5339, 5344, 5347.

50. Ibid., 5378c–5378h. Thompson left the case after the governor's announcement, and attorney Arthur D. Hill assumed responsibility for a last ditch defense. *Boston Globe*, August 5, 20, 22, 1927.

51. Robert Lincoln O'Brien, owner and publisher of the Boston *Traveller* and the *Herald*, privately published a pamphlet in which he stated: "There arose in this state an intense demand that we should adhere to established legal procedure." *My Personal Relations to the Sacco-Vanzetti Case as a Chapter in Massachusetts History* (n.p., n.d.), as quoted in Joughin and Morgan, *The Legacy of Sacco and Vanzetti*, 333.

52. Douglas L. Jones, Alan Rogers, James J. Connolly, Cynthia Farr Brown, and Diane Kadzis, *Discovering the Public Interest: A History of the Boston Bar Association* (Canoga Park, Calif., 1993), 94; *Annual Report of the Attorney General for the Year Ending 1925* (Boston, 1926), 14–15; *General Laws of Massachusetts Enacted in 1925* (Boston, 1926), chap. 279; O'Brien, *My Personal Relations*, as quoted in Joughin and Morgan, *Legacy of Sacco and Vanzetti*, 333; *Annual Report of the Attorney General for the Year Ending 1927* (Boston, 1928), 122; *New York Times*, December 9, 1928.

53. "An Act Providing for the Establishment of a Judicial Council," *Acts and Resolves, 1924* (Boston, 1925), chap. 244; Sam Bass Warner, "The Role of Courts and Judicial Councils in Procedural Reform," *University of Pennsylvania Law Review* 85 (1937): 441, 445 n. 24.

54. *Third Report of the Judicial Council of Massachusetts* (Boston, 1927), 37–43. Harvard law professor Sam Bass Warner kept up a drum beat for reform. "Judges and Reform," a *New York Times* article about Warner's study published August 23, 1936, brands Boston's criminal justice system antiquated. Warner also published two law review articles: "The Role of Courts and Judicial Councils in Procedural Reform," *University of Pennsylvania Law Review* 85 (1937): 441; and, co-authored with Henry B. Cabot, "Changes in the Administration of Criminal Justice during the Past Fifty Years" (see n. 28).

55. 277 Mass. 589 (1931). Henry T. Lummus, "Statistics and Successions in the Supreme Judicial Court and the Superior Court of Massachusetts," *Massachusetts Law Quarterly* 8 (1923): 1, 48; *Fifth Report of the Judicial Council of Massachusetts* (Boston 1929), 3; Daniel L. Marsh, ed., *Story of Massachusetts*, 4 vols. (New York, 1938), 4:353; Thomas H. O'Connor, *The Boston Irish: A Political History* (Boston, 1995), 196; Jones, *History of the Boston Bar*, 179, 62, 73. Thompson and Ehrmann were appointed to the Council in 1931 and 1934, respectively. *Seventh Report of the Judicial Council of Massachusetts* (Boston, 1931), 3; *Tenth Report of the Judicial Council of Massachusetts (Boston, 1934)*, 4.

56. *Fourteenth Report of the Judicial Council of Massachusetts* (Boston, 1938), 14; *Journal of the Massachusetts House of Representatives*, June 21, 1939, 1499; *Journal of the Massachusetts Senate*, June 21, 1939, 1110. The bill passed the Senate by a vote of 22 to 10. *Boston Globe*, July 13, 1939. *The New Republic*, August 23, 1939, 68–69.

57. *Commonwealth v. Gricus*, 317 Mass. 406–7 (1944); *Commonwealth v. Bellino*, 320 Mass. 645 (1947). Data on the number of appeals and reversals made to the SJC was compiled by the author from *Massachusetts Reports*.

58. *Frank v. Mangum*, 237 U.S. 309 (1915). Holmes rejected Sacco and Vanzetti's application for habeas corpus in the days just prior to their executions. Holmes to Harold Laski, August 24, 1927, in *The Essential Holmes: Selections from the Letters, Speeches, Judicial Opinions, and Other Writings of Oliver Wendell Holmes, Jr.*, ed. Richard A. Posner (Chicago, 1992), 329.

59. Richard D. Brown and Jack Tager, *Massachusetts: A Concise History* (Amherst, Mass., 2000), 226–32; Murray, *Red Scare*. A May 1919 Massachusetts statute prohibited speech or publication advocating the overthrow by force or violence of the Commonwealth. *Acts and Resolves, 1919* (Boston, 1920), 115.

60. For editorial remarks hostile to anarchism and other radical beliefs appearing in suburban newspapers, see Young and Kaiser, *Postmortem*, 18–19. For reaction to Judge Anderson's decision in *Colyer v. Skeffington*, 265 F. 17 (1920), see *Boston Globe*, June 25, 1920; *New Republic*, July 14, 1920; and *The Nation*, July 3, 1920. Harvard law professors Frankfurter, Pound, and Chafee, along with nine other lawyers from outside Boston, signed a document condemning the Palmer raids. *A Report upon the Illegal Practices of the United States Department of Justice* (Washington, 1920), 3, as quoted in Joughin and Morgan, *Legacy of Sacco and Vanzetti*, 211–12. A full account of the Boston area round-up and Anderson's criticism of the Justice Department's strong-arm tactics may be found in Alan Rogers, "Judge George W. Anderson and Civil Rights in the 1920s," *Historian* 54 (1992): 289. The Dedham incident is reported by Young and Kaiser, *Postmortem*, 21–23.

61. *Record of the Trial*, 5:5378e (Governor Fuller's Report), 5378l (Lowell Commission Report); *New Bedford Standard-Times*, November 12, 1950.

62. 1 *Burr's Trial*, 416 (1807); *Record of the Trial*, 1:3–5.

63. *Irvin v. Dowd*, 366 U.S. 717, 718, 727, 730 (1961). The Court also seemed to embrace the idea of presumed prejudice in *Estes v. Texas*, 381 U.S. 532 (1965), and *Sheppard v. Maxwell*, 384 U.S. 333, 358 (1966), but explicitly rejected the argument in *Murphy v. Florida*, 421 U.S. at 798, and in *Patton v. Yount*, 467 U.S. 1025, 1028 (1984). Abramson, *We, the Jury*, 38–53, argues against the alternative of empanelling jurors with no knowledge of the circumstances of the crime. *General Laws of Massachusetts* (St. Paul, Minn., 1985–), chap. 219, sec. 7. In *Commonwealth v. Bonomi*, 335 Mass. 327, 333 (1957) the SJC quoted Article 13 of the Declaration of Rights

of the Constitution of Massachusetts: "In criminal prosecutions, the verification of facts in the vicinity where they happen, is one of the greatest securities of the life, liberty, and property of the citizen." The court also ruled it was within a trial judge's discretionary authority not to ask jurors any questions other than those four required by statute (334–35).

64. *General Laws of Massachusetts* (St. Paul, Minn., 1985–), chap. 234, sec. 28 (1973) and as amended 1975. In *Ham v. South Carolina*, 409 U.S. 524 (1973) the Supreme Court ruled that prospective jurors need not be questioned about race unless the defendant was a "special target for racial prejudice." Before the legislature made the rule mandatory, the court ruled in *Commonwealth v. Lumley*, 367 Mass. 213 (1975) that a trial judge should question jurors about possible racial prejudice. *Commonwealth v. Sanders*, 383 Mass. 637 (1981). For examples of the court's rulings in "other types of bias," see *Commonwealth v. Horton*, 376 Mass. 380 (1978) and *Commonwealth v. Shelly*, 381 Mass. 340 (1980). The relative merits of the court as opposed to counsel conducting voir dire (pretrial questioning) has been hotly debated; see, for example, *Boston University Law Review* 54 (1974): 394, 398.

7. THE INSANITY DEFENSE

1. The literature on the insanity defense is enormous. See, generally, Sheldon Glueck, *Mental Disorder and the Criminal Law* (Boston, 1927); Norman J. Finkel, *Insanity on Trial* (New York, 1988), and *Commonsense Justice: Jurors' Notions of the Law* (Cambridge, Mass., 1995); Senate Committee on the Judiciary, *The Insanity Defense* (Washington, D.C., 1982); Rita Simon, *The Jury and the Defense of Insanity* (Boston, 1967); "The Insanity Plea on Trial," *Newsweek*, May 24, 1982, 56; Dorothy O. Lewis, *Guilty by Reason of Insanity: A Psychiatrist Explores the Minds of Killers* (New York, 1999). As of 1991 two states have abolished the insanity defense and twelve states have adopted a guilty but mentally ill option. Norman J. Finkel, "The Insanity Defense: A Comparison of Verdict Schemas," *Law and Human Behavior* 15 (1991): 533.

2. Sir Matthew Hale articulates the "wild beast" theory in *The History of the Pleas of the Crown* (London, 1736), 34–35. *Reg v. McNaughten*, 10 Clark and Fin. 200, 8 Eng. Rep. 718 (1843). See, generally, Richard Moran, *Knowing Right from Wrong: The Insanity Defense of Daniel McNaughten* (New York, 1981); and Thomas Maeder, *Crime and Madness: The Origins and Evolution of the Insanity Defense* (New York, 1985). I use the term *psychiatrist* throughout, although Massachusetts courts and newspapers used *doctor* until about 1900 and then *alienist* until the 1930s to describe expert witnesses who testified about a defendant's mental condition. The Harvard Medical School established its first Chair of Psychiatry in 1920 and the American Medico-Psychological Association became the American Psychiatric Association in 1921.

3. Hale, *Pleas of the Crown*, 34-35.

4. *Commonwealth v. Rogers*, 7 Metcalf 500 (1844); Isaac Ray, "Criminal Law of Insanity," *American Jurist* 28 (1835): 254; George T. Bigelow and George Bemis, Esqs., *The Trial of Abner Rogers, Jr. for the Murder of Charles Lincoln, Jr.* (Boston, 1844), 43.

5. Bigelow and Bemis, *Trial of Abner Rogers*, 45.

6. *Commonwealth v. Rogers*, 7 Metcalf 500; Alan Rogers, "'Under Sentence of Death': The Movement to Abolish Capital Punishment in Massachusetts, 1835–1849," *New England Quarterly* 66 (1993): 27. Only a handful of states followed Massachusetts and added the "irresistible impulse" rule to its legal definition of insanity: Pennsylvania, Connecticut, Iowa, Kentucky, Minnesota, and Ohio. In 1849 the Massachusetts legislature passed a law that allowed the court to commit to an asylum a criminal defendant found to be insane before trial. *Acts and Resolves, 1849* (Boston, 1850), chap. 68. In 1904 the law was changed to permit the court to appoint two experts to determine a defendant's sanity and permitted defendants to be committed for observation. *General Laws of Massachusetts, Compiled Statutes, 1921* (Boston, 1922), chap. 123, sec. 100 (hereafter *General Laws, 1921*).

7. *Commonwealth v. Rogers*, 7 Metcalf 500; Bigelow and Bemis, *Trial of Abner Rogers*, 45, 224. In his 1850 inaugural address Boston mayor John Bigelow criticized the insanity defense, claiming that criminals escaped punishment by falsely pleading insanity. *Boston Herald*, January 7, 1850. *Report and Recommendations of the Special Commission Established for the Purpose of Investigating and Studying of the Death Penalty in Capital Cases* (Boston, 1958), 83. Henry Weihofen, *Insanity as a Defense in Criminal Law* (New York, 1933).

8. Only a relative handful of nineteenth-century capital defendants pleaded not guilty by reason of insanity. Of the 625 defendants indicted for murder from 1832 to 1899, 22 pleaded not guilty by reason of insanity and 8 were successful. Beginning in 1832, the attorney general published homicide data in the *Annual Report of the Attorney General*. For a full discussion of the insanity defense in nineteenth-century Massachusetts, see Alan Rogers, "Murderers and Madness: Law and Medicine in Nineteenth-Century Massachusetts," *Proceedings of the Massachusetts History Society* 106 (1995): 53–81.

9. Gerald N. Grob, *Mental Illness and American Society, 1875–1940* (New York, 1983). Clifford Beers's autobiography, *A Mind That Found Itself* (New York, 1908), usually is credited with launching the mental hygiene movement, but it should be noted that as early as 1906 Briggs promoted a Boston psychopathic hospital. L. Vernon Briggs, *History of the Psychopathic Hospital* (Boston, 1922). Briggs spells out his views in *The Manner of Man That Kills* (Boston 1922), 5–16. Briggs's membership in the National Committee for Mental Hygiene is found in L. Vernon Briggs, *History and Genealogy of the Cabot Family, 1475–1927*, 2 vols. (Boston, 1927), 2:776.

In a widely read series on American crime, Richard Child summarized popular attitudes about the insanity defense when he wrote that the odds were good that a murderer would not be brought to trial, but if that did happen he would likely "go to an insane asylum on the testimony of bought doctors." *Saturday Evening Post,* August 1, 1925, 8.

10. Briggs, *Manner of Man That Kills,* 13–14.

11. Briggs, *Cabot Family,* 2:774–76. Briggs describes his contentious relationship with Channing in *A Victory for Progress in Mental Medicine* (Boston, 1924). Briggs won a seat on the Massachusetts Board of Insanity and served from 1913 to 1916. *Boston Globe,* March 12, 1913.

12. Briggs, *Manner of Man That Kills,* 4–10. See Gerald R. Grob, *The Inner World of American Psychiatry, 1890–1940* (New Brunswick, N.J., 1985), 7–76, for Briggs's campaign against the use of restraints in mental institutions.

13. L. Vernon Briggs, "Conditions and Events Leading to the Passage of the Massachusetts Law Commonly Called the Briggs Law," *Bulletin of the Massachusetts Department of Mental Diseases* 12 (1927): 2–5; the Briggs law, *Acts and Resolves, 1921* (Boston, 1922), chap. 415; *Annual Report of the Attorney General for the Year 1922* (Boston, 1923), xxix–xxx.

14. The following discussion of Spencer's case is drawn from Briggs, *Manner of Man That Kills,* 23–28, 47–53, 59–60, 99–100, 102–8, 128–44.

15. As acting district attorney for Norfolk and Plymouth counties in 1902, Attorney General James Swift had applied the same strategy as advocated by Taft in *Attorney General's Report for the Year 1902* (Boston, 1903), xxi.

16. *Springfield Republican,* August 2, 1911.

17. *Trial of Bertram G. Spencer* (Boston, 1912), 6–18 (hereafter *Trial of Spencer*).

18. Ibid., 75–76; *Boston American,* November 15, 1911; *New York World,* November 16, 1911. For a discussion of the prisoner's dock, see Alan Rogers, " 'In the Cage': The Prisoner's Dock and the Presumption of Innocence in Massachusetts Criminal Trials," *Massachusetts Legal History* 3 (1997): 89.

19. *Trial of Spencer,* 503. Briggs claims that Elliott "hung his head" when he gave testimony at trial (*Manner of Man That Kills,* 148).

20. A picture of Briggs was published in the *Boston Globe,* March 12, 1913. For a contemporary summary of the cross-examination techniques used by lawyers to expose the weaknesses in forensic diagnoses, see John E. Lind, "The Cross-Examination of the Alienist," *Journal of Criminal Law and Criminology* 13 (1922): 228. See also *Trial of Spencer,* 673.

21. *Trial of Spencer,* 854–55, 857, 865. The contemporary psychiatrist Dorothy Lewis makes a roughly parallel argument in *Guilty by Reason of Insanity: A Psychiatrist Explores the Minds of Killers* (New York, 1998).

22. *Trial of Spencer,* 894–95, 903, 908–9, 912–18.

23. Ibid., 932, 942, 921, 952.

24. Briggs, *Manner of Man That Kills*, 204.

25. Ibid., 204–21, 228–29.

26. Ibid., 230.

27. Edwin R. Keedy, "Insanity and Criminal Responsibility," *Harvard Law Review* 30 (1917): 535, 724. Both Keedy and Wigmore were critical of Chief Justice Shaw's Rogers's rule. Keedy, "Insanity and Criminal Respopnsibility, II," ibid., 724–29; Wigmore, *A Treatise on the Anglo-American System of Evidence*, 2nd ed., 5 vols. (Boston, 1923), 2:sec. 242.

28. Note, "The Proposed Model Statute on Criminal Responsibility," *Harvard Law Review* 30 (1916): 179.

29. *Boston Globe*, May 10, 1920. In an article about jury selection, the *Boston Globe* noted that a "dramatic incident" occurred during the empanelling of the jury: Jennie Zimmerman challenged the potential juror of the "same religious faith" as she (May 11, 1920). The following narrative of the Zimmerman trial is drawn from ibid., May 12–15, 17, 18, 21, 24–26, 28–30, June 1, 2, 1920.

30. On the day following his testimony in the Zimmerman case, Briggs testified for the defense in the trial of Anna Tomaskiewicz, who pleaded not guilty by reason of insanity to poisoning her husband. Briggs stated she could not distinguish between right and wrong. A jury found Tomaskiewicz not guilty by reason of insanity.

31. I have not found a record indicating Zimmerman was released from Northampton. No woman has been executed in Massachusetts since 1789.

32. Briggs, "Briggs Law," 2–3.

33. *General Laws, 1921*, chap. 415.

34. Kathleen W. Jones, *Taming the Troublesome Child: American Families, Child Guidance, and the Limits of Psychiatric Authority* (Cambridge, Mass., 1999), 9, 30–34, 56–57. Judge Harvey Baker was Boston's first juvenile court judge and the clinic founded in his name opened in 1917. Healy's views on changes in criminal law, "Psychiatry, Psychiatrists and the Law," *Massachusetts Law Quarterly* 13 (1928): 30.

35. Henry Hurlbert served as Boston Bar Association president from 1921 to 1923. Winfred Overholser, "The Place of Psychiatry in the Administration of Criminal Law," *New Hampshire Medical Society* (1929), 488, "Psychiatry, Psychiatrists and the Law," *Massachusetts Law Quarterly* 13 (1930): 32, and "The Practical Operation of the Massachusetts Law Providing for the Psychiatric Examination of Certain Persons Accused of Crime," *Bulletin of the Massachusetts Department of Mental Diseases* 12 (1927): 35, 37; Briggs, "Briggs Law," 3. To Judge Cabot's consternation, Briggs claimed to be a member of the Cabot family (Briggs, *Cabot Family*, 653, 774).

36. Briggs, *Victory for Progress in Medicine*, 50–51, and "Briggs Law," 3; *General Laws, 1921*, chap. 415.

37. The 1923 amendment established a $4.00 fee payable to a psychiatrist conducting a mental exam for the court. *General Laws of Massachusetts, Compiled Statutes, 1923* (Boston, 1924), chap. 331; the penalty for a court clerk's failure to report a defendant who was covered by the legislation, chap. 169. The law was amended again in 1927 (chap. 59) and 1929 (chap. 105) to include probation officers in the reporting process.

38. Briggs, "Briggs Law," 4; *General Laws of Massachusetts, 1923*, chap. 123, sec. 100A, and, for provisions regarding commitment and release, secs. 90, 99–105.

39. Frank W. Grinnell, Editorial, *Massachusetts Law Quarterly* 13 (1928): 34. Grinnell added, "Most of us are still in doubt as to the correct pronunciation of 'psychiatry' and as to what it means."

40. Winfred Overholser, "The Briggs Law of Massachusetts: A Review and Appraisal," *Journal of Criminal Law and Criminology* 25 (1935): 859, 865, 873, 883.

41. These data were compiled from the *Annual Report of the Attorney General*, 1900 to 1940. In the latter year the attorney general ended the practice of reporting homicide statistics to the legislature. By contrast to the post-Briggs era, between 1844 and 1899, thirteen of the homicide defendants who raised the issue of insanity were men indicted for murdering their wives. The thirteen cases were disposed of as follows: the court sent nine men to an asylum before trial; one was found guilty of murder in the first degree and sentenced to death; a jury found another defendant guilty of murder in the second degree; and two men who pleaded not guilty by reason of insanity were found not guilty and sent to an asylum. For examples of gender bias, see the following three cases of men who murdered their wives and were declared insane: Christopher Cullen, *Boston Globe*, February 23, 26, 1929; Michael J. Walsh, *Boston Globe*, November 21, 1931; *Commonwealth v. Soaris*, 275 Mass. 291 (1931).

42. *Boston Globe*, February 3, 26, March 22, 1934.

43. Ibid., June 5, 1934.

44. Ibid., May 31, 1934. Scharton asserted that Faber was a "victim of overstudy at M.I.T." and that his "condition" was aggravated by his extraordinary concentration on the development of radio. *Boston Globe*, March 22, 1934. The SJC revisited Scharton's position in *Blaisdell v. Commonwealth*, 372 Mass. 753, 757 (1977). The following description of the Millens-Faber trial is drawn from *Boston Globe*, June 8, 1934.

45. *Boston Globe*, June 5, 1949; *Commonwealth v. McCann*, 325 Mass. 510 (1950). The United States did approve the International Covenant on Civil and Political Rights adopted by the UN General Assembly in 1966 until 1992 and excepted to those articles calling for the abolition of the death penalty for juveniles and preg-

nant women. Hugo A. Bedau, "International Human Rights Law and the Death Penalty in America," in *The Death Penalty in America: Current Controversies*, ed. Bedau (New York, 1997), 246.

46. *Boston Globe*, June 5, 1949; *Commonwealth v. McCann*, 325 Mass. at 513.

47. *Commonwealth v. McCann*, 325 Mass. at 515.

48. For a full discussion of the Massachusetts mercy, or alternative sentencing, law, see Alan Rogers, " 'Success—At Long Last': The Abolition of the Death Penalty in Massachusetts, 1928–1984," *Boston College Third World Law Journal*, Spring 2002, 281. Frankfurter's testimony, *United States v. Currens*, 290 F.2d 751 n. 5 (1961); *Royal Commission on Capital Punishment, 1949–1953* (London, 1953), 80. *Report and Recommendations of the Special Commission*, 83.

49. *Durham v. U.S.*, 214 F.2d 862, 870, 875–76 (1954); A. S. Goldstein, *The Insanity Defense* (New Haven, Conn., 1967), 83.

50. Simon E. Sobeloff, "Insanity and the Criminal law: From McNaghten to Durham and Beyond," *ABA Journal* 41 (1955): 793, 795, 796, 879.

51. Jerome Hall, "Responsibility and Law: In Defense of the McNaghten Rules," *ABA Journal* 42 (1956): 917, 919, 987, 988.

52. *Commonwealth v. Chester*, 337 Mass. 702, 708, 709 (1958).

53. Ibid. at 707–8, 703.

54. Ibid. at 711, 713–14. In jail awaiting sentencing, Chester committed suicide.

55. *Commonwealth v. McHoul*, 352 Mass. at 544, 546–47 (1967).

56. Ibid. at 544, 547, 551, 554.

57. Thomas Maeder, *Crime and Madness: The Origins and Evolution of the Insanity Defense* (New York, 1985), 92; *U.S. v. Brawner*, 471 F.2d 969 (D.C. Cir., 1972).

58. *Commonwealth v. Mutina*, 366 Mass. 811, 812 (1975).

59. For Tauro's obituary, see *Boston Globe*, October 7, 1994. Upon his retirement in 1957, Chief Justice Stanley Qua spelled out the court's traditional practices and philosophy. Qua, "A Few Reflections from the Experience of Twenty-two Years," *Boston Bar Journal* 1 (1957): 9. For Tauro's refusal to defer to the legislature and his denunciation of *stare decisis*, see *Lombardo v. D.F. Frangioso and Co.*, 359 Mass. 529, 536 (1971) and *United Factory Outlet Inc. v. Jay's Stores*, 361 Mass. 35, 52 (1972). *Commonwealth v. O'Neal*, 367 Mass. 440 (1975).

60. *Commonwealth v. Mutina*, 366 Mass. 811.

61. Ibid. at 814–17.

62. *Commonwealth v. Anthes*, 5 Gray 185 (1855); *Commonwealth v. Mutina*, 366 Mass. at 817, 824, 827.

63. *Commonwealth v. Mutina*, 366 Mass. at 818–21.

64. Ibid. at 821.

65. Ibid. at 822–23.

66. Ibid. at 823 n. 12.

67. *Commonwealth v. Kostka*, 370 Mass. 516 (1976); *In re Winship* 397 U.S. 358 (1970).

68. *Commonwealth v. Kostka*, 370 Mass. at 530–31, 537.

69. For revisions of the Briggs law, *General Laws of Massachusetts, Compiled Statutes, 1970*, (Boston, 1971), chap. 888; *General Laws of Massachusetts, 1971*, chap. 760; *General Laws of Massachusetts, 1973*, chap. 569. *Blaisdell v. Commonwealth*, 372 Mass. 753, 756–57 (1977).

70. *Blaisdell v. Commonwealth*, 372 Mass. at 772, 768.

71. *Commonwealth v. Gould*, 380 Mass. at 675–76.

72. Ibid., 677–79; *Commonwealth v. McHoul*, 352 Mass. 544.

73. *Commonwealth v. Gould*, 380 Mass. at 682–83; *Commonwealth v. Henson*, 394 Mass. 584 (1985).

74. *Commonwealth v. Henson*, 394 Mass. 584.

75. Ibid. at 592, 593. Chief Justice Hennessey concurred but added, "It's not in the public interest to conclude that a defendant's voluntary intoxication is relevant to most crimes of violence" (594).

76. *California Statutes, 1981* (Sacramento, 1981), chap. 404, 1592, penal code dec. 28 (b). White was paroled after serving five years of his sentence and shortly thereafter committed suicide.

77. William F. Lewis, "Power, Knowledge, and Insanity: The Trial of John Hinckley, Jr.," in *Popular Trials: Rhetoric, Mass Media, and the Law*, ed. Robert Hariman (New York, 1990), 114, 117, 127. See also 98 U.S. *Statutes* (Washington, D.C. 1984), 2057, 18 U.S.C.A. sec. 17.

78. *Commonwealth v. Grey*, 399 Mass. 469; *Commonwealth v. Sama*, 411 Mass. 293.

79. *General Laws of Massachusetts*, chap. 265.

80. *Commonwealth v. Huot*, 380 Mass. 403, 408 (1980); *Commonwealth v. Amaral*, 389 Mass. 184, 190 (1983); *Commonwealth v. McGuirk*, 376 Mass. 338, 346 (1978).

81. *Commonwealth v. Grey*, 399 Mass. at 472–73.

82. Ibid. at 471, 474.

83. Ibid. at 469, 472, 477, 478.

84. *Commonwealth v. Sama*, 411 Mass. at 294.

85. Ibid. at 295, 296; *Commonwealth v. O'Neal*, 367 Mass. 440; *Commonwealth v. Mutina*, 366 Mass. at 817.

86. *Commonwealth v. Sama*, 411 Mass. at 298.

87. *Boston Globe*, May 14, 1992.

88. *Commonwealth v. Seguin*, 421 Mass. 243, 246n (1995).

89. *Boston Globe*, January 27, 1993; *New York Times*, February 3, 1993.

90. *Boston Globe*, January 18, 1993; *Los Angeles Times*, April 18, 1993; *USA Today*, January 13, 1993.

91. *Commonwealth v. Gould*, 380 Mass. 672; *Boston Globe*, February 3, September 28, 1993.

92. *Boston Globe*, March 30, 1994; *Boston Herald*, September 13, 1995; *Boston Globe*, October 13, 1995.

93. *Commonwealth v. Seguin*, 421 Mass. at 245–49.

94. *Commonwealth v. McLaughlin*, 431 Mass. 506 (2000).

95. Ibid. at 507–9.

96. Ibid. at 529, 521–22, 534.

8. THE RIGHT TO AN ATTORNEY AND CRIMINAL DISCOVERY

1. Congress adopted new federal rules of "pleading, practices and procedure" in 1945. George H. Dession, "The New Federal Rules of Criminal Procedure," *Yale Law Journal* 55 (1946): 694; Fred P. Graham, *The Due Process Revolution* (Hayden Park, N.J., 1970); David J. Bodenhamer, *Fair Trial: Rights of the Accused in American History* (New York, 1992). Robert A. Kagan, Bliss Cartwright, Lawrence M. Friedman, and Stanton Wheeler, in "The Business of State Supreme Courts, 1870–1970," *Stanford Law Review* 30 (1977–78): 121, 147, report that the sixteen state supreme courts sampled in this study (not including Massachusetts) heard twice as many criminal appeals with constitutional issues between 1965 and 1970 as between 1955 and 1960, because of the Warren Court's due process revolution.

2. Data derived from *Massachusetts Reports*; "Memorial," 361 Mass. 912, 914 (1972); and *Massachusetts Law Quarterly* 53 (1958): 77, 88, 89.

3. Justice Herbert P. Wilkins, "Judicial Treatment of the Massachusetts Declaration of Rights in Relation to Cognate Provisions of the United States Constitution," *Suffolk University Law Review* 14 (1980): 887, 890–91. Massachusetts was one of four states to reject 75 percent or more of the Supreme Court's criminal procedure rulings from 1970 to 1980. Barry Latzer, *State Constitutions and Criminal Justice* (New York, 1991), 160–61. See also Justice William Brennan, "State Constitutions and the Protection of Individual Rights," *Harvard Law Review* 90 (1977): 489; *Commonwealth v. O'Neal*, 369 Mass. 242 (1975); *District Attorney v. Watson*, 381 Mass. 648 (1980).

4. *Powell v. Alabama*, 287 U.S. 45 (1932); Dan T. Crater, *Scottsboro: A Tragedy of the American South* (Baton Rouge, 1979); Edward Lazarus, *Closed Chambers: The Rise, Fall, and Future of the Modern Supreme Court* (New York, 1988), 83–85. For a sample of scholarly articles about the effectiveness of court-appointed capital defense attorneys, see Gary Goodpaster, "The Trial for Life: Effective Assistance of Counsel in Death Penalty Cases," *New York University Law Review* 58 (1983): 299; Ronald J. Tabak, "*Gideon v. Wainwright* in Death Penalty Cases," *Pace Law Review*

10 (1990): 491; Vivian Berger, "The Chiropractor as Brain Surgeon: Defense Lawyering in Capital Cases," *New York University Review of Law and Social Change* 18 (1990–91): 245; Bruce A. Green, "Lethal Fiction: The Meaning of 'Counsel' in the Sixth Amendment," *Iowa Law Review* 78 (1993): 433.

5. *Commonwealth v. Hardy*, 2 Mass. 302, 308 (1807); *Mass. General Statutes, 1820*, chap. 14, sec. 8; James Austin, *Annual Report of the Attorney General for the Year Ending 1834* (Boston, 1835), 29–30; Alan Rogers, "Court Appointed Attorneys in Massachusetts Capital Cases, 1780–1980," *American Journal of Legal History* 61 (1997): 440, 443–44; Joseph B. Warner, "The Responsibilities of the Lawyer," *ABA Reports*, 1896, 329; *Acts and Resolves, 1911* (Boston, 1912), chap. 432; *Commonwealth v. Dascalakis*, 246 Mass. 12 (1923). Dascalakis's name is spelled variously in the records.

6. Alan Rogers, "The Founders of the Boston Bar Association: A Collective Analysis," *Historical Journal of Massachusetts* 22 (1994): 93, 94–95; Douglas L. Jones, Alan Rogers, James J. Connolly, Cynthia Farr Brown, and Diane Kadzis, *Discovering the Public Interest: A History of the Boston Bar Association* (Canoga Park, Calif., 1993), 72–73; Gerald W. Gawalt, "The Impact of Industrialization on the Legal Profession in Massachusetts, 1870–1900," in *The New High Priest: Lawyers in Post–Civil War America*, ed. Gewalt (Westport, Conn., 1984), 288; *Massachusetts Reports*, 1934, 571–74.

7. Commonwealth v. Dascalakis, Transcript of the Trial held in Superior Court, June 7, 1922, Prepared for the Defendant's Motion for a New Trial, 2–3, 4–6, Supreme Judicial Court [SJC], Judicial Archives, Massachusetts State Archives, Boston (hereafter SJC Archives). The trial court and the SJC denied Dascalakis's original motion that the verdict was against the weight of the evidence. 234 Mass. 519 (1922). He was sentenced to death on January 17, 1923. *Boston Globe*, January 18, 1923.

8. *United States Census Tracts for 1920*; *Polk's [Boston] City Directory*, 1913 and 1922; SJC Docket Book, 1914, SJC Archives. In 1923 President Calvin Coolidge appointed Schenck assistant U.S. attorney for Massachusetts, a position he held until 1932, when he returned to private practice. He died in 1962.

9. Commonwealth v. Dascalakis, Transcript, 93–95.

10. Ibid., 94–97.

11. *Commonwealth v. Dascalakis*, 246 Mass. at 26–27. Rugg noted that in defense of John Webster in 1850, the court-appointed counsel Edward Sohier chose not to object to the prosecution's introduction of questionable evidence. Rugg did not mention that Sohier's inadequate defense was widely credited as an important reason Webster was found guilty and sentenced to death for murder. *Commonwealth v. Webster*, 59 Mass. 295 (1850). See also Joel Parker, "The Law of Homicide," *North American Review* 72 (1851): 178–204.

12. *Commonwealth v. Dascalakis*, 246 Mass. at 27, 28–29, 32.

13. Ibid. at 27.

14. "Representation by Counsel Appointed by the Court in Capital Cases," *Boston Bar Association Bulletin*, June 1952, 170–75.

15. Commonwealth v. Cox, Stenographic Record, Superior Court, Middlesex County, Motion for a New Trial, Hearing before Justice Hurley, July 14, 1950, 3 vols., 1:8–11, SJC Archives.

16. Ibid., 1:14–15.

17. "Report to Department of Mental Health on Marshall Cox, March 12, 1948," in Commonwealth v. Cox, "Summary of the Record," 5–7.

18. Commonwealth v. Cox, 3:255–57. The statutes misinterpreted by Juggins may be found in *Tercentenary Edition of the General Laws of the Commonwealth of Massachusetts* (Boston, 1932), chap. 123, sec. 100A, and chap. 125, sec. 48. (hereafter *General Laws, Tercentenary Edition*). For Juggins's closing remarks, see Commonwealth v. Cox, 2:181–82.

19. Commonwealth v. Cox, 2:190–99.

20. Ibid. 3:251, 258–59, 260, 263, 281.

21. Ibid., "Motion for a New Trial," July 14, 1950, 1:2–12.

22. *Commonwealth v. Cox*, 327 Mass. 609, 614–15 (1951). At a new trial Cox was found not guilty by reason of insanity and committed to a mental hospital.

23. "Representation by Counsel Appointed by the Court in Capital Cases," *Boston Bar Association Bulletin*, June 1952, 170–75.

24. *General Laws of Massachusetts, Compiled Statutes, 1954* (Boston, 1955), chap. 277, secs. 47, 56, chap. 276, sec. 37A. For the Superior Court's Rule 95, see Lee Silverstein, *Defense of the Poor in Criminal Cases in American State Courts*, 3 vols. (Chicago, 1965), 2:331, 348. Prior to the adoption of new rules, the SJC relied on *Betts v. Brady*, 316 U.S. 455 (1942), which holds that in the absence of special circumstances appointment of counsel in a noncapital case is not essential to a fair trial. In 1949 the SJC upheld Porthus Allen's 1932 second-degree murder conviction, although the ill-educated African American had represented himself at trial. Because he was not "mentally defective," the court was not obligated to appoint counsel, according to *Betts v. Brady*, 316 U.S. 455. *Allen v. Commonwealth*, 324 Mass. 558, 562 (1949).

25. *Gideon v. Wainwright*, 372 U.S. 335 (1963); *White v. Maryland*, 373 U.S. 59 (1963); *Douglas v. California*, 372 U.S. 353 (1963); *Miranda v. Arizona*, 384 U.S. 436 (1966); *Commonwealth v. McNeil*, 328 Mass. 436, 438 (1952). The SJC adopted Rule 10, providing for the assignment of counsel in noncapital cases, in 1964. Silverstein, *Defense of the Poor*, 348. *Stovall v. Denno*, 338 U.S. 293 (1967).

26. Francis Juggins represented Arsenault at trial. *Commonwealth v. Devlin and others* [Arsenault], 335 Mass. 555 (1957); *Arsenault v. Commonwealth*, 353 Mass.

575, 576-77 (1968). Governor Foster Furculo commuted Arsenault's death sentence to life imprisonment. *Boston Herald*, June 27, 1957.

27. *Arsenault v. Commonwealth*, 353 Mass. at 578, 582-83, 584; *White v. Maryland*, 373 U.S. 59; *Commonwealth v. Ayers*, 115 Mass. 137 (1874).

28. *Arsenault v. Massachusetts*, 393 U.S. 5, 6, 9 (1968).

29. *Ross v. Moffitt*, 417 U.S. 600 (1974) held that a state was not obligated by the Fourteenth Amendment's due process clause to appoint counsel for an indigent defendant's appeal to the state's highest court after a lower state court had ruled defendant's counsel was reasonably effective.

30. *Commonwealth v. Lussier*, 333 Mass. 83, 85-87 (1955); *General Laws, Tercentenary Edition*, chap. 265, sec. 2.

31. *Scott v. United States*, 427 F.2d 609, 610 (6th Cir) (1970), cert. denied, 379 U.S. 842 (1970); *Commonwealth v. Bernier*, 359 Mass. 13, 19 (1971).

32. *Lussier v. Commonwealth*, 393, 395-97 (1971). Reasonable as Spiegel's argument may have been, the "farce and mockery" phrase on which he relied was not the current standard for effectiveness of counsel. The federal court actually had stated in *Scott* that standard is "no longer valid as such but exists in the law only as a metaphor that the defendant has a heavy burden to show requisite unfairness."

33. *Commonwealth v. Saferian*, 366 Mass. 89, 94, 95-96 (1974).

34. Ibid. at 97, 93, 98. In *Commonwealth v. Geraway*, 364 Mass. 168, 184 (1969), the SJC notes an attorney's ineffectiveness can more readily be detected by "the trial judge than by appellate judges reading between the lines of a stale transcript."

35. *Commonwealth v. Saferian*, 366 Mass. at 96. Justice Edward Hennessey, "Constitutional Rights of the Accused," *Massachusetts Law Quarterly* 60 (1975): 19. The SJC upheld its rule in *Commonwealth v. Moran*, 388 Mass. 655, 658-59 (1983), and *Commonwealth v. Mamay*, 407 Mass. 412 (1990).

36. *Strickland v. Washington*, 466 U.S. 668 (1984); *ABA Standards Relating to the Administration of Criminal Justice: The Defense Function* (Chicago, 1971). For articles sympathetic to Marshall's point of view, see Berger, "The Chiropractor as Brain Surgeon: Defense Lawyering in Capital Cases," 245; and Bruce A. Green, "Lethal Fiction: The Meaning of 'Counsel' in the Sixth Amendment," *Iowa Law Review* 78 (1993): 433.

37. *Commonwealth v. Ellison*, 376 Mass. 1 (1974). Lawrence M. Friedman, *Crime and Punishment in American History* (New York, 1993), 386-87; Roscoe Pound, "The Causes of Popular Dissatisfaction with the Administration of Justice," *Report of the Twenty-ninth Annual Meeting of the American Bar Association* (Philadelphia, 1906), 404-5; American Bar Association, *Standards Relating to Discovery and Procedure before Trial* (1970); Robert L. Fletcher, "Pretrial Discovery in State Criminal Cases," *Stanford Law Review* 12 (1960): 293. My purpose in this section is to trace

the adoption of a discovery rule. The implementation of the rule is complex and open to interpretation about when, how much, and under what circumstances information must be shared.

38. Robert Rantoul Jr., "Oration at Scituate, Delivered on the Fourth of July, 1836," in *The Legal Mind in New England*, ed. Perry Miller (Ithaca, N.Y., 1962), 222–27; *Acts and Resolves, 1899*, (Boston, 1900) chap. 409. Article 12 of the Declaration of Rights states: "No subject shall be held to answer for any crime or offense, until the same is fully and plainly, substantially and formally described to him." For a full account, see Alan Rogers, "Murder in Massachusetts: The Criminal Discovery Rule from Snelling to Rule 14," *American Journal of Legal History* 60 (1996): 438.

39. *Commonwealth v. Jordan*, 207 Mass. 259, 265 (1911).

40. *Commonwealth v. Cook*, 351 Mass. 231, 233 (1966). *Commonwealth v. De Christoforo*, 360 Mass. 531, 533, 536 (1971). In *Commonwealth v. Galvin*, 323 Mass. 233 (1966), the SJC claimed the Massachusetts rule granting a trial judge discretionary authority in regard to a discovery motion asking for access to grand jury minutes conforms to the federal discovery rule in *Dennis v. United States*, 341 U.S. 494 (1951).

41. *Commonwealth v. De Christoforo*, 360 Mass. at 550–55.

42. *Commonwealth v. Ellison*, 376 Mass. 1 (1978); *Commonwealth v. Stewart*, 365 Mass. 99, 104–6 (1974); Committee on Criminal Procedure, Massachusetts Judicial Conference, *Proposed Rules of Criminal Procedure for the District and Superior Courts of Massachusetts* (1976), Archives of the Social Law Library, v–xi. Ohio, among other jurisdictions, continued to apply the particularized need rule. *State v. Tillman*, 2004 Ohio Court of Appeals 1030.

43. *Commonwealth v. Ellison*, 376 Mass. at 3, 2–4; *Boston Globe*, December 1, 1973.

44. *Commonwealth v. Ellison*, 376 Mass. at 5; *Boston Globe*, December 3, 1973.

45. *Commonwealth v. Ellison*, 376 Mass. at 5–6. Terrell Walker was tried separately from Williams and Irving. A jury found Walker guilty of murder in the first degree and armed robbery, and he was sentenced to life imprisonment on the murder charge and twenty-five years for each of several armed robbery indictments. *Commonwealth v. Walker*, 370 Mass. 548 (1976).

46. *Commonwealth v. Ellison*, 376 Mass. at 3, 6, 13–14. Freeman's testimony contradicted Williams's statement that the female driver of the getaway car had been given a share of the loot at Freeman's apartment.

47. Homans's obituary, *New York Times*, February 13, 1997; *Commonwealth v. Ellison*, 376 Mass. at 3, 8–9; Commonwealth v. Ellison, "Findings and Rulings; Exculpatory Evidence," Records and Briefs, 8, SJC Archives.

48. *Commonwealth v. Ellison*, 376 Mass. at 3, 9–13.

49. *Commonwealth v. Ellison*, "Defendant's Motion for a New Trial," Records and Briefs, 27, SJC Archives; *Boston Globe*, July 19, 1978.

50. *Commonwealth v. Ellison*, 376 Mass. at 23–26.

51. *Proposed Rules of Criminal Procedure*, xiii, 266–67, 268–69, 273; *Annotated Law of Massachusetts: Massachusetts Rules of Criminal Procedure*, chaps. 295–313. The most important difference between the federal rule of discovery and the Massachusetts rule is that it still lies within the Massachusetts court's discretion to issue a discovery order. Owen S. Walker, Esq., "The New Criminal Rules: Pitfalls for Prosecutor and Defense," *Massachusetts Lawyers Weekly*, December 25, 1978.

9. CONFESSION

1. An admission of guilt is a confession. A statement in which a suspect shows knowledge of a crime is an admission. Leonard Levy, *The Origins of the Fifth Amendment: The Rights against Self-Incrimination* (New York, 1968), 407, 409, 420; John Henry Wigmore, *A Treatise on the Anglo-American System of Evidence in Trials at Common Law*, 10 vols. (Boston, 1940) 8:sec. 2266; John V. Orth, *Due Process of Law: A Brief History* (Lawrence, Kans., 2003), ix. Article 12 of the Massachusetts Declaration of Rights prohibits a suspect from being "compelled to accuse, or furnish evidence against himself." Justice Felix Frankfurter highlighted the connection between rights and due process of law in *Malinski v. New York*, 324 U.S. 401, 414 (1945). In *Malloy v. Hogan*, 378 U.S. 1 (1964), the Supreme Court extended the privilege against self-incrimination to the states and added in dictum that the admissibility of a confession should be controlled by the Fifth Amendment.

2. The English common law rule of voluntariness, *Rex v. Warickshall* (1783); the "humane practice" rule, *Commonwealth v. Culver*, 126 Mass. 464 (1879). State constitutionalism is discussed in Robert A. Kagan, Bliss Cartwright, Lawrence M. Friedman, and Stanton Wheeler, "The Business of State Supreme Courts, 1870–1970," *Stanford Law Review* 30 (1977): 121, 147, and by Justice William Brennan in *Michigan v. Mosely*, 423 U.S. 96, 120 (1975) and "State Constitutions and the Protection of Individual Rights," *Harvard Law Review* 90 (1977): 489. For a survey of the SJC's role in the emergence of state constitutionalism, see Charles H. Baron, "The Supreme Judicial Court in Its Fourth Century: Meeting the Challenge of the 'New Constitutional Revolution,'" *Massachusetts Law Review* 77 (1992): 35. Two Supreme Court decisions bear directly on this topic, *Malloy v. Hogan*, 378 U.S. 1 (1964), and *Miranda v. Arizona*, 384 U.S. 457 (1966). Yale Kamisar, *Police Interrogation and Confessions: Essays in Law and Policy* (Ann Arbor, Mich., 1980); Leonard W. Levy, "The Right against Self-Incrimination: History and Judicial History," *Political Science Quarterly* 84 (1969): 1; John H. Langbein, "The Historical Origins of the Privilege against Self-Incrimination at Common Law," *Michigan Law Review*

92 (1994): 1047; Eben Moglen, "Taking the Fifth: Reconsidering the Origins of the Constitutional Privilege against Self-Incrimination," *Michigan Law Review* 92 (1994): 1086; Herbert P. Wilkins, "Judicial Treatment of the Massachusetts Declaration of Rights in Relation to Cognate Provisions of the United States Constitution," *Suffolk University Law Review* 14 (1980): 889, 922.

3. David J. Bodenhamer, *Fair Trial: Rights of the Accused in American History* (New York, 1992), 3–9; Kermit L. Hall, *The Magic Mirror: Law in American History* (New York, 1989), 3–8; David Fellman, *The Defendant's Rights Today* (Madison, Wis., 1976), 11.

4. See Chapter 1 for examples of how the court balanced the practice of the folk belief "murder will out" and due process. The Massachusetts Laws and Liberties (1648) prohibited torture except in specific, exceptional circumstances. Gail S. Marcus, " 'Due Execution of the Generall Rules of Righteous': Criminal Procedure in New Haven Town and Colony, 1638–1658," in *Saints and Revolutionaries: Essays on Early American History*, ed. David D. Hall, John M. Murrin, and Thad W. Tate (New York, 1984), 101, 121. See also preface to *The Book of the General Lawes and Libertyes Concerning the Inhabitants of the Massachusets* (1648; facsimile edition, Cambridge, Mass., 1929).

5. The origin of the privilege against self-incrimination is a contentious subject. Echoing Wigmore, *A Treatise on the Anglo-American System of Evidence*, 8:sec. 2250, Leonard Levy, in *Origins of the Fifth Amendment* (New York, 1968), 424–25, argues that common law courts assimilated the privilege against self-incrimination following the demise of the English Court of High Commission. In addition to Massachusetts, six other U.S. state constitutions guaranteed a privilege against self-incrimination before 1789: Maryland, North Carolina, New Hampshire, Pennsylvania, Vermont, and Virginia. Katharine B. Hazlett, in "The Nineteenth Century Origins of the Fifth Amendment Privilege against Self-Incrimination," *American Journal of Legal History* 42 (1998): 235, contends that in the United States the federal privilege against self-incrimination first emerged in *Boyd v. United States*, 116 U.S. 616 (1886).

6. William E. Nelson, *The Americanization of the Common Law: The Impact of Legal Change on Massachusetts Society, 1760–1830* (Cambridge, Mass., 1975); Ronald J. Pestrito, *Founding the Criminal Law: Punishment and Political Thought in the Origins of America* (DeKalb, Ill., 2000); L. Kinvin Wroth and Hiller B. Zobel, eds., *Legal Papers of John Adams*, 3 vols. (Cambridge, Mass., 1965), 2:335–337, 338 n. 11, 339, 340–44, 350, 350 n. 83. The *Boston Gazette*, August 9, 1773, printed a dramatic account of the trial. Four members of the court believed that their jurisdiction over piracy stopped short of murder (Wroth and Zobel, *Papers of John Adams*, 2:340).

7. See, generally, Nelson, *Americanization of the Common Law*; *Commonwealth*

v. Foster, 1 Mass. 488, 494 (1805); *Commonwealth v. Green*, 17 Mass. 515, 517 (1822); *Commonwealth v. John Chabbock*, 1 Mass. 143 (1804).

8. *Commonwealth v. Morey*, 67 Mass. 461, 463, 462 (1854); Daniel Webster, *The Works of Daniel Webster: Legal Arguments and Speeches to the Jury*, 6 vols. (Boston, 1854), 6:41, 46–47; *Commonwealth v. John Francis Knapp*, 26 Mass. 495 (1830). In *Commonwealth v. Curtis*, 99 Mass. 574, 578 (1867), an adultery trial before the SJC, Shaw held that Curtis's confession made to an officer who told the prisoner that "as a general thing it was better for a man who was guilty to plead guilty, for he got a lighter sentence" was inadmissible.

9. *Commonwealth v. John Francis Knapp*, 26 Mass. 495; *Commonwealth v. Joseph Jenkins Knapp*, 27 Mass. 478 (1830); *Appendix to the Report of the Trial of John Francis Knapp, on an Indictment for Murder* (Salem, 1830), American Antiquarian Society, Worcester, Mass.

10. *Commonwealth v. John Francis Knapp*, 26 Mass. at 501–5, 500, 501.

11. Ibid. at 506, 508. Because of Chief Justice Isaac Parker's death just before the Knapp trial, three members of the SJC sat as a trial court: Justices Wilde, Samuel Putnam, and Marcus Morton.

12. *Commonwealth v. Joseph Jenkins Knapp*, 27 Mass. at 477, 485–87.

13. Ibid. at 490, 491, 493–94. Lemuel Shaw was appointed chief justice of the SJC on August 31, 1830, but he did not take part in the trial of Joseph Knapp.

14. Ibid. at 495–96.

15. Peter Karsten, in *Heart versus Head: Judge-Made Law in Nineteenth Century America* (Chapel Hill, N.C., 1997), is concerned with the role of courts in the economic transformation of the United States, but I believe his insight is useful in understanding criminal law (4–5, 14–15).

16. *Commonwealth v. Cuffee*, 115 Mass. 285, 286 (1871). From 1780 to 1891 the SJC sat as a trial court and heard appeals in capital cases. Attorney General Charles Allen wrote to Governor William Claflin, November 20, 1871, that he was satisfied the verdict was proper, "but on account of [Cuffee's] youth and of his having been without full advantage of education and training" the attorney general recommended that Claflin commute Cuffee's sentence. On December 26, 1871, the Council commuted Cuffee's death sentence to life imprisonment. Pardon File, Archives of the Commonwealth of Massachusetts.

17. *Commonwealth v. Cuffee*, 115 Mass. at 287. Yale Kamisar, *Police Interrogations and Confessions: Essays in Law and Policy* (Ann Arbor, Mich., 1980).

18. *Commonwealth v. Cuffee*, 115 Mass. at 287–88.

19. *Boston Daily Globe*, May 24, 25, 1875; *Commonwealth v. Piper*, 120 Mass. 185 (1876). Ham's dialogue with Piper is quoted in James B. Muldoon, *You Have No Courts with Any Sure Rule of Law: The Saga of the Supreme Judicial Court of Massachusetts* (Peterborough, N.H., 1992), 147.

20. *Commonwealth v. Piper*, 120 Mass. at 188–89. Train had served as district attorney for Suffolk County from 1848 to 1853 before being elected attorney general in 1872. William T. Davis, *History of the Bench and Bar of Suffolk County* (Boston, 1894), 341. In *Commonwealth v. Tolliver*, 119 Mass. 312 (1876), the court held that an illegally obtained confession could be used to impeach a defendant's testimony if he took the stand in his own behalf.

21. *Commonwealth v. Culver*, 126 Mass. at 465, 466.

22. *Commonwealth v. Preece*, 140 Mass. 276, 277 (1885). In *Commonwealth v. Bond*, 170 Mass. 41 (1897), Justice Oliver Wendell Holmes Jr. undermined the SJC's "humane practice" rule when he ruled admissible the confession of a mentally retarded sixteen-year-old boy that had been dictated by authorities.

23. *Commonwealth v. Preece*, 140 Mass. at 277. John Wigmore, dean of Northwestern University School of Law, in what has become the standard work on evidence, states that the Massachusetts humane practice rule borders on "heresy," because it permits either party to challenge a judge's decision on the question of competency. According to Wigmore, the majority of jurisdictions divide the question of the admissibility of a confession into two parts: as a matter of law the court decides whether the confession is voluntary; the truth and evidentiary weight to be given to a confession is for the jury to decide, although it has no authority to reject a confession as incompetent. *A Treatise on the Anglo-American System of Evidence*, sec. 861.

24. Oliver Wendell Holmes Jr., *The Common Law* (Boston, 1881), 1; Richard W. Wilkie and Jack Tager, eds., *Historical Atlas of Massachusetts* (Amherst, Mass., 1991), 34–35. The data on murder indictments are from *Annual Report of the Attorney General*, 1892–1939. The data on reversible error are compiled from *Massachusetts Reports*, 1892–1939. In 1939 the legislature empowered the SJC to review facts as well as law in an appeal of a murder conviction. *General Laws of Massachusetts, Compiled Statutes, 1939* (Boston, 1940), chap. 341.

25. *Davis v. Boston Elevated Ry. Co.*, 235 Mass. 482 (1920).

26. *Commonwealth v. Russ*, 232 Mass. 58 (1919). Rugg cited *Commonwealth v. Bond*, 170 Mass. 41, the case in which Holmes ruled a confession dictated by authorities admissible. *Commonwealth v. Szczepanek*, 235 Mass. 411 (1920). The accused's confession is not inadmissible because he was not warned that he need not confess.

27. *Commonwealth v. Mabey*, 299 Mass. 96, 98–99 (1937); *Commonwealth v. Russ*, 232 Mass. 58.

28. *Brown v. Mississippi*, 297 U.S. 278 (1936). *Annual Report of the Massachusetts Attorney General for the Year Ending 1926* (Boston, 1927), notes that nearly one hundred bills aimed at curbing crime were filed in the Massachusetts legislature, many attempting to regulate criminals' use of guns and automobiles. Lawrence M.

Friedman, *Crime and Punishment in American History* (New York, 1993), 273-74. Justice Oliver Wendell Holmes Jr.'s dissent in *Frank v. Mangum*, 237 U.S. 309 (1915), opened the path to federal intervention in state criminal trials. Holmes spoke for the majority in *Moore v. Dempsey*, 261 U.S. 86 (1923), and marked the beginning of stricter scrutiny of state criminal trials by the Supreme Court.

29. *Commonwealth v. Makarewicz*, 333 Mass. 575, 580-81 (1956).

30. Ibid. at 581, 584, 585, 587, 589, 582. A 1951 law, *General Laws of Massachusetts, 1951,* chap. 203, allows a jury the option of not imposing a death sentence by a unanimous vote.

31. *Commonwealth v. Makarewicz*, 333 Mass. at 586, 588, 589. The defense relied on *Haley v. Ohio*, 332 U.S. 596 (1948), but the SJC rejected the argument, distinguishing *Haley* from *Makarewicz* by noting that Haley had been questioned continuously for five hours and held incommunicado for five days, during which time his attorney tried unsuccessfully to see him. The SJC cited *Watts v. Indiana,* 338 U.S. 49 (1949) and *Stein v. New York*, 346 U.S.146 (1953). In *Watts*, the Court stated that "any conflict in testimony as to what actually led to a contested confession is not this Court's concern" and in *Stein* that the question is "whether the circumstances leading to the confession were so coercive as to render it inadmissible." See, generally, Kamisar, *Police Interrogation and Confession.* Counihan cited *Commonwealth v. Bond*, 170 Mass. 41 (1879).

32. *Massiah v. U.S.*, 377 U.S. 201, 295 (1964);Yale Kamisar, *"Massiah* and *Miranda*: What Is Interrogation? When Does It Matter?" *Georgia Law Review* 67 (1978): 34.

33. *Commonwealth v. McCarthy*, 348 Mass. 7, 9-10 (1964). As late as 1952 Justice Lummus wrote in *Commonwealth v. McNeil*, 328 Mass. 436 (1952): "There is nothing in the statutes of Massachusetts," or any decision of the Supreme Court "giving a person accused of a capital crime or any other crime a right to counsel before being brought into court."

34. *Commonwealth v. McCarthy*, 348 Mass. at 11. The jury's verdict reveals the flaw in the "humane practice" rule: since juries deliberate in private it is impossible to know whether it found the confession coerced or whether other evidence led it to its conclusion.

35. Ibid.

36. *Boston Globe*, July 14, 17, 1964. The *Boston Globe*, July 16, 1964, reported that F. Lee Bailey had persuaded the Supreme Court to void Sam Sheppard's murder conviction.

37. *Miranda v. Arizona*, 483 U.S. 436, 444, 448-50 (1966). Justices Tom Clark, John M. Harlan, Potter Stewart, and Byron White dissented.

38. American Law Institute, *Model Code of Pre-Arraignment Procedures* (1966); *Boston Globe*, June 15, 1966.

39. *Boston Globe,* June 15, 1966.

40. *Johnson v. New Jersey,* 384 U.S. 719 (1966). The low number of confession reversals does not necessarily mean, of course, that police conformed to *Miranda* guidelines.

41. *Commonwealth v. McKenna,* 355 Mass. 313, 315–16, 319 (1969). The following discussion of the McKenna-Riley case is drawn from ibid. at 319–25, 327.

42. *Boston Globe,* June 15, 1966; *New York Times,* June 20, 1966; compare *Uniform Crime Report, 1950* (Washington, D.C., 1951), 90, and *Uniform Crime Report, 1980* (Washington, D.C., 1981), 52; Hon. Walter H. McLaughlin, "A Chief Justice's Dilemma," *Massachusetts Law Quarterly* 55 (1970): 203, 204.

43. *Commonwealth v. Mahnke,* 368 Mass. 662 (1975); *Boston Globe,* June 5, 6, 8, 9, 1973. George W. Mahnke lived with his mother, father, and brother in the Allston section of Boston, a community with an average annual per capita income of $10,774 in 1980. Rhonda lived with her mother, her father, an electrical contractor, and her brother in Newton, a community with an average annual per capita income of $20,601 (Wilkie and Tager, *Historical Atlas of Massachusetts,* 140, 142). Commonwealth v. Mahnke (1975), Summary and Findings, 9, 14, 21, 28, and Findings and Rulings on Motion to Suppress, 66–68, 75–76, Supreme Judicial Court Records and Briefs, Judicial Archives, Massachusetts State Archives, Boston. McLaughlin also ruled that Mahnke's statements were admissions only and not a confession; therefore, he was not entitled to the safeguards in respect to the admissibility of a confession.

44. *Commonwealth v. Mahnke,* 368 Mass. at 677–78, 679, 680, 681–83, 686–88. The *Boston Globe,* October 8, 1975, notes that Tauro aimed sharp, personal remarks at the dissenters. Under *Gen. Laws,* chap. 278, sec. 33E, the court decided that "justice required" the verdict of second-degree murder be vacated and a verdict of guilty of manslaughter be entered.

45. *Commonwealth v. Haas,* 373 Mass. 545, 550, 554 (1977). In *Commonwealth v. Harris,* 371 Mass. 462, 469, 470 (1976), the SJC ruled that when the voluntariness of a confession is contested the trial judge should not tell the jury his or her decision about its admissibility.

46. *Commonwealth v. Tavares,* 385 Mass. 140, 142–43 (1982).

47. Ibid. at 145, 152.

48. Hennessey's statement appeared in the *Boston Globe,* August 31, 1986; Liacos spoke to the *Globe* shortly after he was elevated to chief justice, September 1, 1989. Burger's statement about the Court's limited role, *New York Times,* July 4, 1971. *Oregon v. Elstad,* 470 U.S. 298 (1985). *Harris v. New York,* 401 U.S. (1971).

49. *Commonwealth v. Smith,* 412 Mass. 823, 824, 836 (1992).

50. Herbert P. Wilkins, "Judicial Treatment of the Massachusetts Declaration of Rights in Relation to Cognate Provisions of the United States Constitution," *Suffolk*

University Law Review 14 (1980): 889, 890. For state federalism, see Barry Latzer, *State Constitutions and Criminal Justice* (New York, 1991), 160–64; and Charles H. Baron, "The Supreme Judicial Court in Its Fourth Century: Meeting the Challenge of the New Constitutional Revolution," *Massachusetts Law Review* 77 (1992): 35.

51. Justice Frankfurter in *Watts v. Indiana*, 338 U.S. at 54.

10. THE RIGHT OF THE ACCUSED TO AN IMPARTIAL JURY

1. In addition to Massachusetts, the state appellate courts of Oregon, New Jersey, Michigan, and California were part of a movement to state constitutionalism—the use of state constitutions to extend criminal defendants greater protection than afforded by the Supreme Court. A. E. Dick Howard, "State Courts and Constitutional Rights in the Day of the Burger Court," *Virginia Law Review* 62 (1976): 873, 879, points out that state courts tended to focus their activism in a particular area. Mary C. Porter, "State Supreme Courts and the Legacy of the Warren Court: Some Old Inquiries for a New Situation," *Publius*, Fall 1978, 55, surveys the work of activist state courts in California, Michigan, New Jersey, and Alaska. Justice Stanley Mosk of the Supreme Court of California refers to the activist state court movement as "the new states' rights" in *California Law Enforcement* 10 (1976): 81, 82. Justice William Brennan encouraged the movement by inviting state courts to go further in protecting individual liberties than he found the Burger Court willing to go. See, for example, Brennan's dissent in *Michigan v. Mosely*, 423 U.S. 96, 120 (1975), in which he points out that "each State has power to impose higher standards governing police practices under state law than is required by the Federal Constitution," and also, Brennan, "State Constitutions and the Protection of Individual Rights," *Harvard Law Review* 90 (1977): 489.

2. *The Book of the General Lawes and Libertyes Concerning the Inhabitants of the Massachusets* (1648; facsimile edition, Cambridge, Mass., 1929), 51–52, provides for "tryall" by jury; under "General Priviledges," chap. 11, art. 1, the 1692 charter lists the right of every freeman to be tried by a jury of his peers; chap. 11, art. 7, states that in all capital cases the defendant "shall be allowed his reasonable challenges." Massachusetts Declaration of Rights, Article 12: "No subject shall be arrested, imprisoned, despoiled, or deprived of his property, immunities, or privileges, put out of the protection of the law, exiled, or deprived of his life, liberty, or estate, but by the judgment of his peers. . . . And the legislature shall not make any law, that shall subject any person to a capital or infamous punishment . . . without trial by jury"; *Fay v. New York*, 332 U.S. 261 (1947); *Smith v. Texas*, 311 U.S. 128 (1940). "The Jury Selection and Service Act," 28 U.S.C., secs. 1861–69, was enacted by Congress in 1968 and applied to federal courts. *Taylor v. Louisiana*, 419 U.S. 522, 528 (1975).

3. *Laws and Libertyes*, 51. The procedure for assembling a jury panel is described in L. Kinvin Wroth and Hiller B. Zobel, eds., *Legal Papers of John Adams*, 3 vols.

(Cambridge, Mass., 1965), 1:xlix; for an example, see 3:17-19. For the law governing modern jury selection procedures, see Nancy Gertner and Judith H. Mizner, *The Law of Juries* (Little Falls, N.J., 1997); and Jon M. Van Dyke, *Jury Selection Procedure: Our Uncertain Commitment to Representative Panels* (Cambridge, Mass., 1977). *Commonwealth v. Mutina*, 366 Mass. 810, 817-19 (1975). There is a considerable legal literature on challenge for cause and the use of peremptory challenges. See, for example, Mark Cammack, "In Search of the Post-Positivist Jury," *Indiana Law Journal* 70 (1995): 405, for a summary of arguments about challenge for cause; Randall Kennedy, *Race, Crime, and the Law* (New York, 1997), chap. 6, for the impact of peremptory challenges on the racial composition of juries; and Nancy S. Marder, "Beyond Gender: Peremptory Challenges and the Roles of the Jury," *Texas Law Review* 73 (1995): 1041. In *Commonwealth v. Ladetto*, 349 Mass. 237 (1965), the court encouraged the trial court to ask jurors their views about life imprisonment as well as the death penalty. *Witherspoon v. Illinois*, 391 U.S. 510 (1968). *Commonwealth v. Soares*, 377 Mass. 461. The court ruled against capital punishment on several occasions: *Commonwealth v. O'Neal*, 367 Mass. 440 (1975), *Commonwealth v. O'Neal*, 369 Mass. 242 (1975); "Opinion of the Justices," 364 N.E. Rep., 2d ser., 184 (1977); *District Attorney v. Watson*, 381 Mass. 648 (1980); *Commonwealth v. Colon-Cruz*, 393 Mass. 150 (1984).

4. The *Revised Statutes of the Commonwealth of Massachusetts* (Boston, 1836), chap. 137, sec. 6 (hereafter, *Revised Statutes, 1836*). William Blackstone, *Commentaries on the Laws of England*, 4 vols. (London, 1807), 4:353. *Acts and Resolves, 1869* (Boston, 1870), chap. 151, allowed the prosecutor two peremptory challenges. A 1736 statute stipulated that jurors who had a financial interest or other disqualifying interest in the outcome of the trial be challenged for cause. *Acts and Resolves, 1736–1737* (Boston, 1737), chap. 10, sec. 5. A defendant's right to an unlimited number of peremptory challenges was changed in 1795, when *Acts and Resolves, 1795* (Boston, 1796), chap. 45, sec. 3, limited a defendant's peremptory challenges to twenty. In 1873 the number of peremptory challenges allowed the prosecutor was increased to ten. *Acts and Resolves, 1873* (Boston, 1874), chap. 317. In *General Laws of Massachusetts, Enacted in 1932* (Boston, 1933), chap. 234, the number of peremptory challenges allowed the defendant and the prosecutor was fixed at twelve, where it remains at the present.

5. *Revised Statutes, 1836*, chap. 137, sec. 6: "No person whose opinions are such as to preclude him from finding any defendant guilty of an offense punishable with death, shall be compelled or allowed to serve as a juror, on the trial of any indictment for such an offense; see *Commonwealth v. Nassar*, 354 Mass. 249, 253 n. 3 (1968), wherein the SJC notes that "no explanation of its [1836 statute] adoption is set out in the *Report of the Commissioners on the Revision of the Statutes* (1836), part IV, 54–55." Alan Rogers, "'Under Sentence of Death': The Movement to Abolish

Capital Punishment in Massachusetts, 1835–1849," *New England Quarterly* 66 (1993): 27; Thomas H. O'Connor, *The Boston Irish: A Political History* (Boston, 1995), 46–47.

6. *Commonwealth v. Buzzell*, 16 Pick. 153, 155. Until 1892 the SJC sat as a trial court for capital crimes.

7. O'Connor, *Boston's Irish*, 47; *Annual Report of the Attorney General for the Year Ending 1839* (Boston, 1840), 6. Austin also asked the legislature to allow prosecutors to use peremptory challenges.

8. *Revised Statutes, 1836*, chap. 137, sec. 6; Rogers, "Under Sentence of Death," 29–32. Rantoul's bill abolishing capital punishment was defeated in 1835; it was passed by the House in 1836 but rejected by the Senate. Supreme Court justice Joseph Story was a member of the Massachusetts Commission to Revise the Laws in 1836, which made the challenge for cause aimed at jurors opposed to capital punishment part of Massachusetts law; six years later Story made it a part of federal procedure: in *U.S. v. Hewson*, 26 Fed. 303 (1844), a murder case tried in the U.S. Circuit Court of Massachusetts, Justice Story allowed the district attorney to ask each juror whether "he had any conscientious scruples as to finding a verdict of guilty in a capital case," adding that this had been the practice in "this court for the last twenty-five years, ever since the escape of two of the most atrocious men he ever knew in Rhode Island, through the scruples of two jurymen." George Bemis, ed., *Report of the Case of John W. Webster* (Boston, 1850), 5–6.

9. Leonard Levy, *The Law of the Commonwealth and Chief Justice Shaw* (New York, 1957), 218–24. Spooner read the law for about two years in the Worcester office of John Davis and Charles Allen, then in defiance of the law requiring a non-college graduate to study the law for five years before he might be admitted to the bar, Spooner publicly announced the opening of his own law office. At the same time, he published his reasons for defying the law in the *Worcester Republican*, August 26, 1835, a copy of which he sent to every Massachusetts legislator. The law was repealed in 1836. Spooner's publications are reprinted in their original form and pagination in Charles Shively, *The Collected Works of Lysander Spooner*, 4 vols. (Weston, Mass., 1971). Spooner, *Illegality of the Trial of John W. Webster* (Boston, 1850), 3–4.

10. Spooner, *Trial of John W. Webster*, 4–5. Quotations in the following discussion of Spooner's arguments are drawn from ibid., 4, 6–7, 8–9, 14, 15–16.

11. Chief Justice Shaw's interpretation of the statute that allowed the court to challenge for cause potential jurors who expressed scruples about capital punishment was carried to the U.S. Supreme Court. Horace Gray served as SJC reporter from 1854 to 1864, justice of the SJC from 1864 to 1873, and chief justice from 1873 to 1882, before he was appointed to the Supreme Court. In *Logan v. U.S.*, 144 U.S.

Reports 263, 298 (1892), Gray denied an appeal of a defendant convicted of murder in Texas Indian country, stating that those "jurors who stated on *voir dire* that they had conscientious scruples in regard to the infliction of the death penalty for crime were rightly permitted to be challenged by the government for cause."

12. *Laws and Libertyes*, 51; Nathan Dane, *General Abridgement and Digest of American Laws*, 8 vols. (Boston, 1823–29), 7:333. Blackstone, *Commentaries*, 4:353–54; Dane, *General Abridgement*, 7:274, citing Mass. Act, February 15, 1793. An Act for the Punishment of Certain Crimes Against the United States, chap. 9, sec. 30, 1 Stat. 119 (1790), had set the number of peremptory challenges allowed a defendant at twenty. As early as 1840 Attorney General Austin had complained that the state should be allowed peremptory challenges. *Attorney General's Report for the Year Ending 1840* (Boston, 1841), 6.

13. Act of Mar. 3, 1865, chap. 86, sec. 2 (v), 13 Stat. 500. A federal prosecutor was allowed five peremptory challenges and the defense twenty. *Acts and Resolves, 1869* (Boston, 1870), chap. 151. *Attorney General's Report for the Year Ending 1868* (Boston, 1869), 5–7. Train told the legislature that peremptory challenges would "aid him in securing an impartial jury." *Attorney General's Report for the Year Ending 1872* (Boston, 1873), 9–10; See also *Attorney General's Report for the Year Ending 1873* (Boston, 1874), 8–9.

14. *Commonwealth v. Wong Chung and another*, 186 Mass. 231, 233, 236–37 (1904); William T. Davis, ed., *History of the Bench and Bar of Suffolk County, Massachusetts* (Boston, 1894), 595.

15. *Commonwealth v. Wong Chung*, 186 Mass. at 234, 236, 237, 238; Alan Rogers, "Chinese and the Campaign to Abolish Capital Punishment in Massachusetts, 1870–1914," *Journal of American Ethnic History* 18 (1999): 37.

16. Rugg, "Proceedings in the Supreme Judicial Court for Arthur Prentice Rugg, Late Chief Justice," in *Arthur P. Rugg: A Memorial* (Worcester, Mass., 1939), 4–5; "Address to Association of the Bar of the City of New York" (1919), in ibid., 46.

17. James M. Rosenthal, "Reversible Error in Homicide Cases in Massachusetts, 1807–1927," *Massachusetts Law Quarterly* 13 (May 1928): 106, and "Reversible Error in Homicide Cases in Massachusetts, 1927–1949," *Massachusetts Law Quarterly* 34 (October 1949): 45; *Commonwealth v. Retkovitz*, 222 Mass. 245 (1915), and *Commonwealth v. Madeiros*, 255 Mass. 304 (1926) and *Commonwealth v. Madeiros*, 257 Mass. 1 (1926). *Commonwealth v. Cooper*, 219 Mass. 1 (1914); Commonwealth v. Cooper (1914), 1–2, Supreme Judicial Court [SJC] Records and Briefs, Judicial Archives, Massachusetts State Archives, Boston.

18. Commonwealth v. Cooper (1914), Defendant's Brief, 3.

19. Ibid., Commonwealth's Brief, 3–4.

20. Davis, *Bench and Bar*, 202; *Commonwealth v. Cooper*, 219 Mass. at 3.

21. *Commonwealth v. Ladetto*, 349 Mass. at 245. Biographical details about Reardon are drawn from Reardon, "Memorial," 405 Mass. 1703 (1989). Commonwealth v. Ladetto (1965), Defendant's Brief, 12, 16, SJC Records and Briefs.

22. *Commonwealth v. Ladetto*, 349 Mass. at 239-40.

23. Ibid. at 240-41.

24. Commonwealth v. Ladetto, Defendant's Brief, 14-16, 21.

25. Ibid., 21.

26. Ibid., 17-19.

27. Reardon's legal persuasion in Reardon, "Memorial," 405 Mass. at 1707. Reardon quoting *People v. Riser*, 305 P.2d 18 (Cal. 1956) in *Commonwealth v. Ladetto*, 349 Mass. at 246. In *Morgan v. Illinois*, 504 U.S. 719, 738-39 (1992), the Supreme Court ruled that a juror unalterably in favor of the death penalty cannot perform his or her duties in accordance with the law and may be challenged for cause.

28. See, for example, Reardon's comments in *Commonwealth v. Ladetto*, 349 Mass. at 245, 246, and his dissent in *Commonwealth v. O'Neal*, 369 Mass. at 285, 292; also Reardon, "Memorial," 405 Mass. at 1709, 1712, 1719.

29. *Commonwealth v. Nassar*, 354 Mass. 249; *Commonwealth v. Sullivan*, 354 Mass. 598 (1968).

30. *Commonwealth v. Nassar*, 354 Mass. 249; *Commonwealth v. Nassar*, 351 Mass. 37 (1966); Commonwealth v. Nassar (1968), Defendant's Brief, 14, SJC Records and Briefs.

31. *Commonwealth v. Nassar*, 354 Mass. at 251-52.

32. Commonwealth v. Nassar, Commonwealth's Brief, 2-6.

33. For the history of court-appointed attorneys in Massachusetts, see Alan Rogers, " 'A Sacred Trust': Court Appointed Attorneys in Massachusetts Capital Trials," *American Journal of Legal History* 41 (1997): 440-65. *General Laws of Massachusetts* (Boston, 1966), chap. 277, was the basis for Rule 95 of the Superior Court that in 1967 required an attorney appointed in a capital case to have a minimum of ten years' trial experience. Bailey filed a motion with the court excepting to Rule 95; the court allowed Bailey to continue with the defense until the close of the trial when it authorized his appointment and payment. Commonwealth v. Nassar, "Counsel in Capital Cases," 15-19; *Commonwealth v. Nassar*, 354 Mass. at 265-67. For Bailey's own account of his meteoric rise, see F. Lee Bailey, *The Defense Never Rests* (New York, 1971), 19-42, 67-114.

34. *Witherspoon v. Illinois*, 391 U.S. at 514, 516.

35. Commonwealth v. Nassar, Defendant's Brief, 14.

36. *Smith v. Texas*, 311 U.S. at 130; *Glasser v. U.S.* 60, 86 (1942); Walter E. Oberer, "Does Disqualification of Jurors for Scruples against Capital Punishment

Constitute Denial of Fair Trial on Issue of Guilt?" *Texas Law Review* 39 (1961): 545.

37. Commonwealth v. Nassar, Defendant's Brief, 35, 37.

38. Ibid., 14; Defendant's Brief, 38, 39; Walter Oberer, "Disqualification of Jurors," *Texas Law Review* 39 (1961): 545, 549, 549 n. 20.

39. *Commonwealth v. Nassar*, 354 Mass. at 256–57; *Witherspoon v. Illinois*, 389 U.S. 1035 (1968); *Bumper v. North Carolina*, 389 U.S. 1034 (1968). Cutter specialized in tax and insurance cases and rarely wrote on criminal cases during his tenure on the court (1956–72). However, Cutter was an active participant in the American Law Institute's Model Penal Code Project (1959) and that may have prompted Chief Justice Wilkins to assign *Nassar* to Cutter. Hon. Herbert Wilkins, "R. Ammi Cutter: A Personal Remembrance," *Supreme Judicial Court Historical Society Journal* 2 (1996): v, vii, ix, xi.

40. *Commonwealth v. Sullivan*, 354 Mass. at 608–9; Commonwealth v. Sullivan (1968), Defendant's Brief, 7, 9, 10, SJC Records and Briefs.

41. *Witherspoon v. Illinois*, 391 U.S. at 513, 518, 522 n. 21.

42. *Ladetto v. Commonwealth*, 356 Mass. 541 (1970).

43. Ladetto v. Commonwealth, Defendant's Brief, 6–7, 10, 15–16.

44. *Ladetto v. Commonwealth*, 356 Mass. at 547, 546.

45. *Commonwealth v. Connolly*, 356 Mass. 617 (1970); *Commonwealth v. Mangum*, 357 Mass. 76 (1970); *Commonwealth v. Flowers*, 357 Mass. 94 (1970); *Commonwealth v. French*, 357 Mass. 356 (1970); *Commonwealth v. Robertson*, 357 Mass. 559 (1970).

46. Commonwealth v. Connolly (1970), Defendant's Brief, 22, SJC Records and Briefs; Commonwealth v. Mangum (1970), Defendant's Brief, 12, SJC Records and Briefs.

47. *Commonwealth v. Mangum*, 357 Mass. at 79; *Commonwealth v. Connolly*, 356 Mass. at 622–23.

48. *Furman v. Georgia*, 408 U.S. 238 (1972). *Commonwealth v. Lussier*, 364 Mass. 414, 425. Chief Justice Tauro was the first person named to the center seat not already a member of the SJC. He was the first Italian American and one of a handful of Roman Catholics named to the court. A brief biography appears in *Boston Globe*, November 7, 1994.

49. *Commonwealth v. McAlister*, 365 Mass. 454, 458, 460–61 (1974); Commonwealth v. McAlister (1974), "Counsel for the G.I. Defense," *Time Magazine*, Oct. 19, 1970, www.time.com. Defendant's Brief, 6–8, SJC Records and Briefs. Homans cited: Bronson, "On the Conviction Proneness and Representativeness of the Death-Qualified Jury," *University of Colorado Law Review* 42 (1970): 1; Jurow, "New Data on the Effect of a Death Qualified Jury on the Guilt Determination

Process, *Harvard Law Review* 84 (1971): 567; White, "The Constitutional Invalidity of Convictions Imposed by Death-Qualified Juries," *Cornell Law Review* 58 (1973): 1176.

50. *Commonwealth v. McAlister*, 365 Mass. at 459, 460.

51. Ibid. at 460, 461.

52. Ibid. at 461.

53. *Swain v. Alabama*, 380 U.S. at 225, 231. For a historical survey of the relationship between black defendants, the Thirteenth Amendment, and the peremptory challenge, see Douglas L. Colbert, "Challenging the Challenge: Thirteenth Amendment as a Prohibition against the Racial Use of Peremptory Challenges," *Cornell Law Review* 76 (1990): 1.

54. *Swain v. Alabama*, 380 U.S. at 223, 224, 221–22. See also Randall Kennedy, *Race, Crime, and the Law* (New York, 1997), 193–204.

55. *Commonwealth v. Soares*, 377 Mass. at 476 n. 11, 475 n. 10; *McCray v. New York*, 461 U.S. 961, 963, 964–65 (1982), Justice Marshall dissenting from denial of certiorari; *Gillard v. Mississippi*, 464 U.S. 867, 871 (1983), Marshall dissenting from denial of certiorari; *Batson v. Kentucky*, 476 U.S. at 92–93. In *Commonwealth v. Soares*, 377 Mass. at 477 n. 12, the SJC acknowledged the aid it received from the California Supreme Court's decision in *People v. Wheeler*, 22 Cal. 3d 258 (1978).

56. Sketches of Liacos may be found in *Boston Globe*, August 31, 1986, and June 25, 1996; and Kay H. Hodge, "Hon. Paul J. Liacos: An Appreciation," *Massachusetts Law Review* 81 (1996): 134, 135.

57. The rate of murders in Boston declined steadily, if erratically, from 1850 to 1950, but then increased sharply after 1958. See Theodore N. Ferdinand, "The Criminal Pattern of Boston since 1849," *American Journal of Sociology* 73 (1975): 88–19; *Boston Globe*, June 14, 1975. The *Boston Herald*, October 4, 1973, reported the killing of a young woman by six black youths, and the *Boston Globe*, November 30, 1973, printed a story about the shooting death of a Boston police officer. For the busing story, see generally, J. Anthony Lukas, *Common Ground: A Turbulent Decade in the Lives of Three American Families* (New York, 1985). For the legislature's activity, see Cornelius Dalton, John Wirkkala, and Anne Thomas, *Leading the Way: A History of the Massachusetts General Court, 1629–1980* (Boston, 1984), 308.

58. Coverage of the incident often compared "Harvard athletes" and the "muggers and pickpockets [who] rule Combat Zone." *Boston Globe*, November 16, 17, 18, 1976. For the court's description of the crime, see *Commonwealth v. Soares*, 377 Mass. at 464–68.

59. *Commonwealth v. Soares*, 377 Mass. at 465–66.

60. Ibid. at 466.

61. Ibid. at 467–68.

62. *Boston Globe*, 8 March 1977. Attorney Wallace Sherwood's brief—one of

three filed by the defense—raised the issue of "extensive prejudicial pretrial publicity and the prosecutorial strategy of exploiting racial antagonisms." *Commonwealth v. Soares* (1979), Defendant's Brief, 20–22, and Appendix, SJC Records and Briefs. *Commonwealth v. Soares*, 377 Mass. at 473–74, 473–74 n. 8. The exchange that follows between Henry Owens and Judge James Roy is drawn from *Commonwealth v. Soares*, 377 Mass. at 473–74 n. 8.

63. *Commonwealth v. Soares*, 377 Mass. at 463; Commonwealth v. Soares, Assignment of Errors, 39–42.

64. Ibid., Commonwealth's Brief, 91–94.

65. Ibid., Defendant's Brief, 74, 29, 41, 77–83.

66. *Commonwealth v. Soares*, 377 Mass. at 463, 493–94.

67. Ibid. at 474–75, 477 n. 12, 478–81, 485–86, 488, 488 n. 33.

68. Ibid. at 489–91, quoting *People v. Wheeler*, 22 Cal. 3d 258, 282.

69. *Commonwealth v. Soares*, 377 Mass. at 491; although the court noted here that it was following the "suggestion" of the *Wheeler* court, the Massachusetts Appeals Court subsequently held that a trial judge need not dismiss the venire to remedy a claim of error. *Commonwealth v. Kelly*, 10 Mass. App. Ct., 811, 847 (1980).

70. *J.E.B. v. Alabama ex rel. T.B.*, 114 S.Ct. 1419. In *Batson v. Kentucky*, 476 U.S. at 108, Justice Marshall, in a concurring opinion, called for "banning peremptories entirely." Since *Batson*, the court has ruled that the equal protection clause is violated even when the jurors removed are not of the same race as the defendant. *Powers v. Ohio*, 499 U.S. 400 (1991). And, as in Massachusetts, the court prohibited the defense counsel from exercising peremptory challenges on the basis of race. *Georgia v. McCollum*, 112 S.Ct. 2348 (1992).

71. *Commonwealth v. Walker*, 379 Mass. 297, 300 (1979).

72. Ibid. at 301.

73. *Commonwealth v. Kelly*, 10 Mass. App. Ct. at 847.

74. *Commonwealth v. Robinson*, 382 Mass. 189, 194–95 (1981).

75. Ibid. at 195–96.

76. *Commonwealth v. Reid*, 384 Mass. 209, 251, 252 nn. 8, 9, 10 (1981).

77. Commonwealth v. Reid (1981), Defendant's Brief, 7, 11–12, SJC Records and Briefs.

78. *Commonwealth v. Reid*, 384 Mass. at 247, 253–54. In *Commonwealth v. Fruchtman*, 418 Mass. 8, 11–17 (1994), the court ruled that the defendant, convicted of "unnatural sexual intercourse with a child by force" was not denied a fair trial by the trial court's refusal to permit him to exercise peremptory challenges to exclude all women from the jury.

79. In 1980, SJC Justice Herbert P. Wilkins declared that the court "currently appears more outspoken concerning the significance of rights under the Declaration of Rights than at any other time in its history." Wilkins, "Judicial Treatment of

the Massachusetts Declaration of Rights in Relation to Cognate Provisions of the United States Constitution," *Suffolk University Law Review* 14 (1980): 887, 890–91. The California court held that peremptory challenges could not be used discriminatorily; *People v. Wheeler*, 583 P.2d 748 (1978). See also Donald E. Wilkes Jr., "The New Federalism in Criminal Procedure: State Court Evasion of the Burger Court," *Kentucky Law Journal* 62 (1974): 421. Justice John Paul Stevens rationalized the denial of certiorari in *McCray v. New York*, 461 U.S. 961, which raised questions about the use of peremptory challenges by arguing that "it is a sound exercise of discretion for the Court to allow various States to serve as laboratories in which the issue [of the procedural and substantive problems associated with judicial review of peremptory challenges] receives further study before it is addressed by this Court" (963). In *McCray* and *Gilliard v. Mississippi*, 464 U.S. 867 (1983), Justice Marshall dissented from the majority's denial of certiorari, pointing out that the issue was too important "to delay until a consensus emerges" (869).

  80. *Commonwealth v. Soares*, 377 Mass. at 494; Scott H. Brice, *"Anderson* and the Adequate State Ground," *Southern California Law Review* 45 (1972): 750; Edward L. Barrett Jr., *"Anderson* and the Judicial Function," *Southern California Law Review* 45 (1972): 739; see also Hans Linde, "Without 'Due Process': Unconstitutional Law in Oregon," *Oregon Law Review* 49 (1970): 125, and Book Review, *Oregon Law Review* 52 (1973): 325; and A. E. Dick Howard, "State Courts and Constitutional Rights in the Day of the Burger Court," *Virginia Law Review* 62 (1976): 873, 943.

  81. *McCray v. New York*, 461 U.S. at 963, denial of certiorari; ibid. at 964–65, Marshall dissenting from denial of certiorari. See also Marshall dissenting from denial of certiorari in *Gillard v. Mississippi*, 464 U.S. at 871.

  82. *Batson* applied only to prosecutors, but six years later, in *Georgia v. McCollum*, 112 S.Ct. 2348, the court extended its ruling to prohibit defense counsel from using race as the reason for striking a juror.

  83. *Batson v. Kentucky*, 476 U.S. at 105, 108.

  84. *J.E.B. v. Alabama ex rel. T.B.*, 114 S.Ct. 1419. Lower federal courts have extended *Batson* to cover Italian Americans, *United States v. Biaggi*, 673 F. Supp. 96 (E.D.N.Y. 1987), and Hispanics, *United States v. Alcanter*, 832 F. 2d 1175 (CA 9 1987). *Soares* limited use of peremptory challenges against any group specifically protected by state civil rights laws, including religious groups; in 1994 the appeals court threw out the conviction of a Roman Catholic priest after finding that the prosecution had used peremptory challenges to strike the only three presumably Roman Catholic potential jurors with Irish surnames. *Commonwealth v. Carleton*, 36 Mass. App. Ct. 137 (1994).

11. "SUCCESS—AT LONG LAST"

1. The chapter title is from a postcard Sara Ehrmann sent to members of the Massachusetts Council Against the Death Penalty (MCADP) to celebrate the signing of a mercy law, April 3, 1951. The postcard and other papers related to the activities of the MCADP are available in Papers, 1845–1993, Sara R. Ehrmann, University Libraries, Archives and Special Collections Department, Northeastern University, Boston (hereafter Ehrmann Papers). *Boston Herald,* May 10, 1947; *Boston Globe,* May 10, 1947. For a brief sketch of Gov. Robert Bradford, a descendant of William Bradford, second governor of the Plymouth colony over three centuries earlier, see Alec Barbrook, *God Save the Commonwealth: An Electoral History of Massachusetts* (Amherst, Mass., 1973), 55–56, 86. Bradford served as lieutenant governor under Governor Maurice Tobin, 1944–46. *Boston Herald,* May 10, 1947.

2. An enormous amount has been written about the death penalty in the United States; the following brief list is suggestive rather than exhaustive. The most recent study is Stuart Banner, *The Death Penalty: An American History* (Cambridge, Mass., 2002). See also Charles Black, *Capital Punishment: The Inevitability of Caprice and Mistake* (New York, 1981); Hugo A. Bedau, ed., *The Death Penalty in America,* 3rd ed. (New York, 1982); William Bowers, *Legal Homicide* (Boston, 1984); Welsh White, *The Death Penalty in the Nineties* (Ann Arbor, Mich., 1991); and Herbert Haines, *Against Capital Punishment: The Anti-Death Penalty Movement in America, 1972–1994* (New York, 1996).

3. *Boston Globe,* August 10, 1945. Details about Williams's slaying surfaced during the trial of Gertson and Bellino. *Boston Globe,* June 12, 13, 14, 15, 1946.

4. Ibid., June 15, 1946.

5. *Commonwealth v. Philip Bellino and another,* 320 Mass. 635, 639, 641 (1947). For the fourteen-person jury statute, see *Tercentenary Edition of the General Laws of the Commonwealth of Massachusetts* (Boston, 1932), c. 234, sec. 26B.

6. *Bellino et al. v. Massachusetts,* 330 U.S. Reports 832 (1946); *Boston Globe,* May 9, 1947. Relatives of Gertson and Bellino visited with Governor Bradford on May 8, 1947, but the governor refused to intervene. *Boston Herald,* May 8, 1947.

7. For the relationship between the American League to Abolish Capital Punishment and the MCADP, see Vivian Pierce to Glendower Evans, September 29, 1927, Ehrmann Papers. The American League began in 1925 and included among its founders Clarence Darrow. Pierce served as the league's executive secretary until the group's collapse and absorption by the MCADP in 1949. The "mercy bill" was a staple of the MCADP's campaign against capital punishment, introduced each year from 1928 to 1951.

8. William Ewing was the first executive director of MCADP. Details about Sara Ehrmann's early life are drawn largely from the first (and only) chapter of a 1977 draft of an unpublished biography by Michael Sussman, "The Movement against

Capital Punishment in Massachusetts: Origins and Lessons," 9–12, Ehrmann Papers. Jacobstein served in the U.S. House of Representatives from 1923 to 1929. In addition to her activity with MCADP, Ehrmann also served with dozens of volunteer groups, including the League of Women Voters, Women's City Club, United Prison Association, Norfolk Lifer's Group, and the American Jewish Committee.

9. Sussman, "Movement," 9–12, 10; William O'Neill, *Everyone Was Brave: The Rise and Fall of Feminism in America* (Chicago, 1969), 142–43.

10. Sussman, "Movement," 13–14. *Criminal Justice in Cleveland* (Cleveland, 1922; repr., Montclair, N.J., 1968). The Ehrmann's second son was named Robert Lincoln.

11. On the "subversive influence [of college education] upon the traditional conception of women and the family," see Carl N. Degler, *At Odds: Women and the Family in America from the Revolution to the Present* (New York, 1980), 314–15. Sussman, "Movement," 3, 13–15; *Commonwealth v. Sacco*, 255 Mass. 369 (1926); Herbert Ehrmann, *The Case That Will Not Die: Commonwealth v. Sacco and Vanzetti* (New York, 1969). Ehrmann's salary, Sara Ehrmann to Jack Rubinow, December 22, 1955, Ehrmann Papers; *Boston Globe*, April 26, 1963; Sussman, "Movement," 21. In fact, Ehrmann never received a salary but relied on donations to keep the organization afloat. Ehrmann to Hon. William Ramsdell, March 22, 1945, Ehrmann Papers. See also Francis Russell, *Tragedy in Dedham*, 2nd ed. (New York, 1971); Ehrmann, *Case That Will Not Die*; Arthur Weinberg, ed., *Attorney for the Damned: Clarence Darrow in the Courtroom* (Chicago, 1989), 16–89; Jim Fisher, *The Lindbergh Case* (New Brunswick, N.J., 1987). Sara Ehrmann opposed a Massachusetts bill, drawn up in the wake of the Lindbergh kidnapping, to make kidnapping a capital crime. Letter to the Editor, *Worcester Post*, March 21, 1932.

12. Richard W. Child, "The Great American Scandal: Our Crime Tide," *Saturday Evening Post*, August 1, 15, 29, September 12, 26, October 10, 24, 1925. The best source for homicide data is H. C. Brearly, *Homicide in the United States* (Chapel Hill, N.C., 1932). With Sara Ehrmann's direct influence, Governor Joseph B. Ely (1930–34) introduced a capital punishment study bill in 1931 and in 1934 a bill to redefine first-degree murder to except homicide motivated primarily by emotion. At the same time, Ely signed death warrants ordering the execution of seven convicted murderers.

13. Glendower Evans to Vivian Pierce, September 29, 1927, Ehrmann Papers; Ehrmann to Evans, January 12, 1931, Ehrmann Papers; Ehrmann to Editor Klaus, *Boston Transcript*, February 16, 1932, advocating a study of capital punishment but opposing a popular referendum; Francis Russell to Governor Saltonstall, December 21, 1938, Ehrmann Papers. *Third Report of the Judicial Council*, reprinted in *Massachusetts Law Quarterly* 13 (1927): 37, 40.

14. For Calvert's Boston visit, see *Boston Herald*, September 29, 1929; and Suss-

man, "Movement," 21. Ehrmann's press release was sent to Boston newspapers, January 8, 1930, and the leaflet sent to legislators of which Stearns's statement was a part, Ehrmann Papers. Ehrmann's testimony, Ehrmann Papers. Miriam Van Waters to Vivian Pierce, May 19, 1939, Ehrmann Papers, reports Ehrmann's desire to drive out the "old people."

15. Archer's argument was published in a leaflet by the National Civic Federation, January 15, 1931, Ehrmann Papers.

16. Among other reasons for abolishing capital punishment listed in MCADP leaflets dated 1931, 1934, and 1936 in Ehrmann Papers is the possibility of an "irrevocable miscarriage of justice." Cero's case is the accompanying example. Zechariah Chafee also testified, arguing that juries have difficulty in determining the dividing line between the several degrees of murder.

17. *Boston Globe*, November 16, 1927; *Commonwealth v. Cero*, 264 Mass. 264, 266 (1928).

18. Scharton established that police officers who questioned potential Suffolk County jurors were following orders issued by Boston police commissioner Herbert Wilson, but Scharton was not able to convince Judge Cox that he should be permitted to question jurors about the police visit. Commonwealth v. Cero, Motion for New Trial, 10–18, 20–34, 115–116, December 1, 1927, Supreme Judicial Court [SJC], Judicial Archives, Massachusetts State Archives, Boston.

19. *Acts and Resolves, 1887* (Boston, 1888), chap. 149. Holmes's interpretation of the 1887 statute, *Commonwealth v. Poisson*, 157 Mass. 510, 512 (1893).

20. *Commonwealth v. Cero*, 264 Mass. at 272. A MCADP member told Ehrmann that Cero was offered a five-year sentence if he would plead guilty to manslaughter, but he refused. Glendower Evans to Sara Ehrmann, January 30, 1931, Ehrmann Papers.

21. *New York Times*, October 11, 1931.

22. *Boston Herald*, January 10, 1929, and interview with Ehrmann in *Worcester Telegram*, December 25, 1966, provide details.

23. *Boston Herald*, March 1, 1929.

24. Ibid.; Sussman, "Movement," 29.

25. Sussman, "Movement," 30.

26. *New York Times*, October 11, 1931; *Commonwealth v. Gallo*, 275 Mass. 320, 323 (1931); Sussman, "Movement," 31.

27. *Boston Herald*, October 4, 1931; *Commonwealth v. Gallo*, 275 Mass. at 323, 328–29.

28. *Commonwealth v. Gallo*, 275 Mass. at 327, 326.

29. Ibid. at 325–26. Rugg gave two examples of the SJC's approval of the legislature's 1876 reform of criminal indictments: *Commonwealth v. Jordan*, 207 Mass. 259 (1911), and *Commonwealth v. Gedzium*, 259 Mass. 453 (1927).

30. *Commonwealth v. Gallo*, 275 Mass. at 329, 333–34.

31. Justice Harlan Fiske Stone's famous footnote in *United States v. Carolene Products Company*, 304 U.S. 144 (1938), proposes that the Court should impose higher standards of review in areas of civil liberties and civil rights. Rugg's public speeches are collected in Rugg, *Arthur Prentice Rugg: A Memorial* (Worcester, Mass., 1939).

32. Governor Ely's commutation of Gallo's death sentence, *Boston Globe*, October 13, 1931; Ehrmann's remarks, Sussman, "Movement," 32–33.

33. For a good summary of Massachusetts's politics during the 1930s and 1940s, see Alec Barbrok, *God Save the Commonwealth: An Electoral History of Massachusetts* (Pittsburgh, 1972), chaps. 3 and 4. For an outline of Chafee's work for MCADP, see Chafee to Sara Ehrmann, March 1, 1933; Raynor Gardiner to Sara Ehrmann, April 11, 1941, Ehrmann Papers. Long-time MCADP member Sheldon Glueck asked Ehrmann, February 2, 1954, whether she found it "embarrassing" to agitate for abolition "when the fate of the Nazi butchers will soon be at stake." Ehrmann to Glueck, February 10, 1945, Ehrmann Papers. On the Rosenbergs, see Ehrmann to Pierce, March 16, 1953, Ehrmann Papers.

34. Ehrmann sometimes wrote speeches for Governor Ely; see, for example, "Massachusetts Should Abolish Capital Punishment," prepared for Governor Ely, December 1931 by Sara Ehrmann, and "Address of His Excellency Joseph B. Ely to the Massachusetts General Court," January 5, 1933, Ehrmann Papers. For Molway and Berrett's ordeal, see *Boston Globe*, February 27, 1934.

35. *Christian Science Monitor*, March 1, 1934. Ehrmann to Berrett, March 27, 1941, Ehrmann Papers, thanking Berrett for testifying before the Judiciary Committee.

36. James Michael Curley to Executive Secretary, MCADP, February 9, 1928; Curley to Ehrmann, February 4, 1929; Curley to Ehrmann, April 16, 1929; Curley to Ehrmann, May 14, 1929; Curley to Ehrmann, September 28, 1929; Ehrmann to Curley, December 17, 1929; Curley to Ehrmann, May 26, 1930, Ehrmann Papers. Just one month into Curley's term, Alexander Kaminski was executed, and on June 7, 1935, three Needham bank robbers, Murton Millen, Irving Millen, and Abraham Faber, were executed.

37. Banner, *The Death Penalty*, 215, 354n15. Christian Herter to Ehrmann, May 10, 1932; Ehrmann to Herter, May 11, 1932; Herter to Ehrmann, December 13, 1938; Ehrmann to Herter, November 19, 1940, Ehrmann Papers.

38. Ely's speech, "Massachusetts Should Abolish Capital Punishment," December 1931, "by Sara Ehrmann," Ehrmann Papers. The *Herald* wrote twice about Ely's pardon policy, *Boston Herald*, October 26, 1932, and January 12, 1934. For a cautious endorsement of Ely's bill to distinguish passionate killers from "cold-blooded, clear-headed assassins," see *Boston Globe*, July 3, 1931.

39. Chafee to Ehrmann, March 1, 1933; Ehrmann Notes, 1935 legislative session; Russell and Chafee to Ehrmann, December 22, 1939, Ehrmann Papers.

40. *Third Report of the Judicial Council*, 37, 40. *General Laws of Massachusetts, Compiled Statutes, 1939* (Boston, 1940), chap. 341. The law expanding the court's review of capital appeals also reduced its jurisdiction over equity cases and allowed the SJC to send any case within its original jurisdiction to the Superior Court. Initially the SJC defined its new power of capital review narrowly. See *Commonwealth v. Gricus*, 317 Mass. 403 (1944), and *Commonwealth v. Philip Bellino*, 320 Mass. 635.

41. For the trial of Green and St. Sauveur, see *Boston Herald*, October 5, 1938. After the two men were sentenced Green cynically congratulated the prosecutor for his "personal victory," and St. Sauveur denounced Green as "too rotten and yellow to square me." Saltonstall's statement rejecting clemency, *Boston Globe*, August 1, 1939; details about the execution, *Boston Globe*, August 2, 1939. State Senator Charles Lane called use of the electric chair "barbaric and inhumane" and filed a bill substituting a gas chamber for the electric chair. *Boston Globe*, August 3, 1939.

42. Ehrmann to Saltonstall, February 19, 1941; "Dear Senator," May 13, 1943, Ehrmann Papers. Charles Sprague to Ehrmann, March 9, 1943, Ehrmann Papers, stating that he had written in support of the mercy bill. Sprague later agreed to become treasurer of MCADP, a position he held until 1951. Sprague to Ehrmann, November 2, 1951, Ehrmann Papers. Alford Rudnick to Edward Rowe, May 12, 1943; Ehrmann to Saltonstall, May 28, 1943, Ehrmann Papers. For an exchange of letters about the governor's pocket veto, see Herbert Ehrmann to Saltonstall, December 28, 1944, Ehrmann Papers. Miriam Van Waters, Superintendent of the Massachusetts Reformatory for Women, to Ehrmann, April 30, 1943, Ehrmann Papers, attributed the defeat to the murder of a Newburyport woman.

43. Robert Bradford to Sara Ehrmann, April 2, 1940; Ehrmann to MCADP Board, May 16, 1940; Ehrmann to Bradford, February 6, 1941; Bradford to Ehrmann, February 11, 1941; Herbert Avery to Sara Ehrmann, April 26, 1948, Ehrmann Papers. Avery also told Ehrmann he believed public criticism of Bradford's prosecution of young Giacomazza caused Bradford to actively oppose any modification of capital punishment from that time forward.

44. *Andres v. United States*, 333 U.S. 740, 748, 758 (1948). The Court pointed out that in only four states "is death the inevitable penalty for murder in the first degree: Connecticut, Massachusetts, North Carolina and Vermont." Bradford's veto message, *Boston Globe*, April 26, 1948.

45. *New Bedford Standard Times*, April 26, 1948. Griswold's public comment, Sara Ehrmann to Alexander Forbes, May 22, 1948, Ehrmann Papers; Forbes to Ehrmann, May 1, 1948, Ehrmann Papers; Ehrmann to James Donnoruma, April 28,

1948, Ehrmann Papers; *Boston Evening American*, April 28, 1948; *Boston Herald*, April 28, 1948.

46. The Schlesinger Library's collection of Ehrmann papers includes materials covering her work with the League of Women Voters and other volunteer activities (Barbrok, *God Save the Commonwealth*, 90–92). *Boston Herald*, March 23, 1949.

47. Estelle B. Freedman, *Maternal Justice: Miriam Van Waters and the Female Reform Tradition* (Chicago, 1996), chaps.14 and 15, covers the Van Waters case in detail. Van Waters served as president of the American League to Abolish Capital Punishment from 1938 to 1949 and as such she worked more closely with Vivian Pierce, the long-time executive secretary of the league, than with Ehrmann. Van Waters to Vivian Pierce, November 12, 1938, Ehrmann Papers. *The Nation*, February 12, 1949.

48. *Worcester Telegram*, April 13, 1949; Billy Mullins, "As I See It," *Boston Herald*, March 30, 1949. In a September 23, 1949, column Mullins worried that recent books about the Sacco-Vanzetti case would undermine young people's belief in the law. The scandal also caused Van Waters to resign as president of the struggling American League to Abolish Capital Punishment; the MCADP assimilated the organization and Ehrmann became director.

49. Dever stated he would not commute a death sentence for someone convicted of a murder for profit. *Daily Lynn Item*, July 26, 1951. Dever commuted to life imprisonment the death sentences of eight men. *Commonwealth v. Pike*, 324 Mass. 335, 336 (1949) and *Boston Herald*, June 30, 1949. *Commonwealth v. Galvin*, 323 Mass. 205 (1948); *Commonwealth v. Lee*, 324 Mass. 714 (1949); R. E. Lee to Sara Ehrmann, December 5, 1949; Wilbur Hollingsworth, Voluntary Defenders' Committee, to Ehrmann, November 28, 1949, Ehrmann Papers. Dever commuted the death sentences of Charles McGarty, who was convicted of the murder of an eight-year-old girl (*Commonwealth v. McGarty*, 323 Mass. 435) and of Vincent Delle Chiaie, a twenty-one-year-old man convicted of the murder of a seven year old girl (*Commonwealth v. Delle Chiaie*, 323 Mass. 615). Commonwealth v. McNeill, 328 Mass. 436 (1952); the *Southbridge News*, April 11, 1952, was not impressed with the mitigating evidence introduced at McNeill's commutation hearing to the effect that as a boy he had been beaten by his father and mistreated by juvenile authorities: "Had the jurors known all this, we assume they would have sent the judge to jail and the killer to the bench."

50. Billy Mullins, "As I See It," *Boston Herald*, June 30, 1949; Southbridge *News*, April 11, 1952; *Boston Herald*, April 13, 1952. Norton quoted Dever in an obituary in the *Boston Traveler*, April 14, 1958.

51. MCADP postcards proclaiming victory, Ehrmann Papers; mercy law, *Acts and Resolves, 1951* (Boston, 1952) chap. 203; *Commonwealth v. O'Neal*, 367 Mass. 440 (1975); *Commonwealth v. Colon-Cruz*, 393 Mass. 150 (1984); *Boston Globe*, April

4, 1951. The mandatory death penalty for rape-murder was added in the Senate and passed by one vote. *Massachusetts Senate Journal*, 1951, 611.

52. Ehrmann to Sprague, June 19, 1951; Sprague to Ehrmann, November 2, 1951, Ehrmann Papers.

12. THE ABOLITION OF THE DEATH PENALTY

1. *In re Kemmler*, 136 U.S. 436 (1890); *Furman v. Georgia*, 408 U.S. 238 (1972).

2. *Weems v. United States*, 217 U.S. 349 (1910).

3. *Louisiana ex rel. Francis v. Resweber*, 329 U.S. 459 (1947).

4. *Trop v. Dulles*, 356 U.S. 86 (1958); *Furman v. Georgia*, 408 U.S. at 238. The Eighth Amendment was incorporated through the Fourteenth Amendment and applied to the states in *Robinson v. California*, 370 U.S. 660 (1962). *District Attorney v. Watson*, 381 Mass. 648 (1980).

5. I do not mean to imply that Ehrmann's work was unimportant after 1951 but merely that the mercy law's success shifted the focus to the governor and the courts. Neil Vidmar and Phoebe C. Ellsworth, "Public Opinion and the Death Penalty," *Stanford Law Review* 26 (1974): 1245. Herter was Massachusetts governor from 1953 to 1956, when he accepted an appointment as U.S. under-secretary of state. Massachusetts Republicans held the House and Senate under Herter but not again thereafter. Fingold's comment, *New York Times*, September 1, 1958. The data on the number of capital jury recommendations of life imprisonment are compiled from *Masachusetts Reports*, 1948–72. In *Commonwealth v. O'Neal*, 369 Mass. 242, 267 (1975), Chief Justice Tauro noted that in the "great majority of non-rape murder cases juries have recommended that the death penalty not be imposed."

6. *Boston Globe*, April 27, 28, 1954; *Commonwealth v. Chapin*, 333 Mass. 610, 613–15 (1956).

7. *Commonwealth v. Chapin*, 333 Mass. at 620, 627.

8. *Boston Herald*, December 16, 1955, April 26, 1956; Jack Ewalt to Endicott Peabody, June 7, 1956, Papers, 1845–1993, Sara R. Ehrmann, University Libraries, Archives and Special Collections Department, Northeastern University, Boston (hereafter Ehrmann Papers); *Boston Globe*, June 1, 1956; *Boston Traveler*, November 29, 1956.

9. *New Bedford Standard Times*, April 23, 1955; *Boston Independent Democrat*, February 11, 1955; *Beverly Times*, April 7, 1953.

10. *New Bedford Standard Times*, April 23, 1955; *Boston Globe*, November 29, 1956. Many years later Ehrmann recalled the dramatic events of the Chapin case in the *Worcester Telegram*, December 25, 1966. Councilor Charles Gabriel expressed his disagreement with the Chapin decision. *Rockland Standard*, November 28, 1957. Chapin's Springfield neighbors were divided over the clemency decision. *Boston Globe*, November 30, 1956.

11. *Boston Herald*, November 30, 1956. The *Patriot-Ledger*, December 1, 1956, argued that the commutation of Chapin's death sentence to life imprisonment "makes it apparent that the use of capital punishment in Massachusetts has been suspended."

12. Tom Ehrlich [Furcolo's chief of staff] to Sara R. Ehrmann, July 25, 1956, Ehrmann Papers; *Boston Globe*, July 6, 1995; *Report and Recommendations of the Special Commission Established for the Purpose of Investigating and Studying the Abolition of the Death Penalty in Capital Cases* (Boston, 1959), preface (hereafter *Report on Abolition*; all quotations from the following discussion of the commission are drawn from this report, 15-16, 18, 21, 25-27, 29-31, 34-37, 44-47). Of the commission's fifteen members, three were appointed by the president of the Senate, five by the Speaker of the House, and seven by the governor. The Massachusetts Police Chiefs Association was angry that one of its members was not appointed by the governor to the commission. *Christian Science Monitor*, November 21, 1957.

13. Ehrmann and Gittelsohn had corresponded since at least November 9, 1955, when Gittelsohn told Ehrmann that he was "deeply interested in this work [abolition]" (Ehrmann Papers). Greeley also had a relationship with Ehrmann. See Dana McLean Greeley to Sara Ehrmann, July 17, 1955, Ehrmann Papers.

14. *Report on Abolition*, Minority Report, 64-65.

15. *Pilot*, January 21, 1956.

16. *Ave Maria*, May 4, 1957. Drinan's testimony before the commission was summarized in a leaflet and reported in many newspapers, including the *Springfield Union*, December 10, 1957. Sheedy made his statement February 19, 1964. "Rev. Sheedy Condemns Capital Punishment," Ehrmann Papers. It was reprinted and circulated by MCADP and the American League to Abolish Capital Punishment, which Ehrmann also guided. Excerpts from Sheedy's statement were published in the *Boston Globe*, February 20, 1964. In the March 1967 issue of *The Mentor: A Penal Publication*, Richard Cardinal Cushing, archbishop of the Boston archdiocese, said that his "personal reaction" was "to regret that capital punishment is a law on the books of the Commonwealth" (1-2).

17. Fingold's remarks, *Boston Globe*, August 28, 1958. *Commonwealth v. Bonomi*, 335 Mass. 327 (1957); *Commonwealth v. Devlin and others*, 335 Mass. 555 (1957). Commissioner of Corrections Arthur Lyman believed that Devlin, Arsenault, and LeBanc should be executed, but he publicly favored commutation of Bonomi's death sentence. *Boston Herald*, June 27, 1957; *Christian Science Monitor*, August 27, 1957.

18. According to Ehrmann's count, seventy-two of the ninety-two people who sought election to the Massachusetts House favored abolition. *Christian Science Monitor*, November 13, 1958. *Boston Herald*, March 20, 1959; *Boston Globe*, April 21, 1959.

19. Alec Barbrok, *God Save the Commonwealth: An Electoral History of Massachusetts* (Pittsburgh, 1972), 132–34. Kathleen Kilgore, *John Volpe: The Life of an Immigrant's Son* (Dublin, N.H., 1987). Volpe won a two-year term, 1961–62, gave way to Peabody, 1963–64, and then reclaimed the State House in 1965–66 and again, for a four-year term, 1967–70. Of this last term, Volpe served only two years before joining the Nixon administration as secretary of transportation; from 1969 to 1970 Lt. Governor Francis Sargent served as acting governor. The Massachusetts murder rate, as it did nationwide, more than doubled from 1950 to 1970. *Uniform Crime Report, 1950* (Washington, D.C. 1951), 90; *Uniform Crime Report, 1970* (Washington, D.C., 1971), 52.

20. *Boston Herald-Traveler*, September 3, 1960. Peabody's comment about the Boston Strangler, *Boston Globe*, January 21, 1963. Volpe's announcement that he would enforce the death penalty, *Boston Record-American*, February 4, 1965. *Boston Globe*, June 6, 1965. Following G. Joseph Tauro's appointment to the Superior Court in 1961, his son, Joseph L. Tauro, assumed the position of legal counsel to Governor Volpe. Volpe-Tauro delaying strategy, *Boston Globe*, February 20, 1969.

21. Barbrok, *God Save the Commonwealth*, 135–38.

22. Cornelius Dalton, John Wirkkala, and Anne Thomas, *Leading the Way: A History of the Massachusetts General Court, 1629–1980* (Boston, 1984), 339–41; Ehrmann to Lester Hyman [Peabody aide], January 21, 1963, Ehrmann to Peabody, January 21, 1963, James Lawton [Peabody's legislative secretary] to Ehrmann, January 25, 1963, Ehrmann Papers; *Boston Globe*, January 31, 1963. State senator Philip Graham argued that the governor's promise to commute all death sentences violated his oath of office because he was prejudging cases before the crimes were committed. *Boston Herald*, February 1, 1963. The *Berkshire Eagle*, March 1, 1963, downplayed "easterners'" alarm at the governor's "Strangler statement," noting that "westerners admire his courage, his image of 'damn the torpedoes' honesty."

23. *Boston Globe*, September 14, 1961.

24. Ibid., September 23, 1961. *Commonwealth v. Kerrigan*, 345 Mass. 508 (1963).

25. *Boston Record-American*, February 4, 1963. Lawton's statement to Judiciary Committee, Ehrmann Papers.

26. Senate's bill, *Lowell Sun*, April 18, 1963; initial House debate, *Springfield Union*, April 26, 1963; Parker House meeting, *Boston Herald*, May 4, 1963, and *Boston Advertiser*, May 5, 1963. The *Advertiser* reported that the governor's advisers urged him to drop the issue, but Ehrmann insisted the fight go on. Herbert Ehrmann blamed the police lobby for the bill's failure. "Speech by Herbert Ehrmann," n.d., Ehrmann Papers.

27. *Boston Globe*, May 7, 1963; *Medford Mercury*, May 7, 1963; *Boston Post-Gazette*, August 9, 1963. Early in September a Medford man killed a police officer

and the wave of outrage caused the Council to vote 6 to 3 against Kerrigan's commutation. *Worcester Telegram*, September 25, 1963; *Boston Record-American*, November 8, 1963. *Commonwealth v. Kerrigan*, 345 Mass. 508 As a result of *Furman v. Georgia*, 408 U.S. 238, Kerrigan was resentenced to life imprisonment.

28. Peabody's softer abolitionist position, *Springfield Union*, December 2, 1963. During the Democrat primary Bellotti often raised the question of capital punishment; see, for example, *Springfield Union*, April 20, 1964. Ehrmann feared that Bellotti would make Peabody's opposition to the death penalty the central issue, but, in fact, Bellotti's position was very similar to Peabody's. Ehrmann to Edward McCormack, May 11, 1964, Ehrmann Papers. Election results, Barbrok, *God Save the Commonwealth*, 140–43.

29. Volpe's 1964 death penalty declaration, Kilgore, *John Volpe*, 146–47. *Boston Globe*, February 4, 1965; *Boston Record-American*, February 25, 1965. McGrath was appointed commissioner of corrections for New York City. *New York Times*, March 3, 1966.

30. *Boston Traveler*, February 17, 1965; *Boston Globe*, June 6, 1965. In addition to Charles Tracy, John Kerrigan, Ronald Jackson, Peter Ladetto, Jack Harris, Paul Smith, George McLaughlin, and Ronald Fisher had been condemned to death. A moratorium failed passage in July, but Volpe managed to win acceptance of the measure. *Boston Traveler*, August 8, 1967.

31. *Commonwealth v. Tracy*, 349 Mass. 87, 89–94 (1965).

32. Ibid. at 95, 102. A majority of the court rejected Tracy's argument that the incriminating statements he made when he was interrogated by a police officer while he lay wounded at the hospital violated his constitutional right to remain silent and to an attorney as stated by the Supreme Court in *Escobedo v. Illinois*, 378 U.S. 478 (1964).

33. *Boston Herald*, September 24, 1966. Between 1950 and 1960 Boston lost about one hundred thousand whites and gained twenty-five thousand blacks, and in early 1965 the Boston branch of the NAACP filed suit in federal court against the Boston School Committee, alleging it denied black children equal protection. Alan Lupo, *Liberty's Chosen Home* (Boston, 1978), 143–51.

34. *Boston Globe*, November 28, 1966. See also *Beverly Times*, December 2, 1966.

35. "Boston College Faculty Petition for Charles E. Tracy," Ehrmann Papers. Foley, Hoag, and Eliot was founded by Henry I. Foley, a member of the Boston College Law School faculty from 1929 to 1939. Todd F. Simon, *Boston College Law School after Fifty Years: An Informal History* (Boston, 1980), 13.

36. *Boston Globe*, December 8, 1966.

37. *Boston Herald*, August 8, 1967. Cushing's statement appeared originally in *The Mentor: A Penal Publication*, March 1967, and was reprinted by the MCADP

along with an interview, Ehrmann Papers. MCADP had long opposed a popular referendum on the question of capital punishment; see, for example, *Worcester Telegram*, October 24, 1957; and Ehrmann to Attorney General Edward McCormack, March 18, 1959, Ehrmann Papers.

38. Charles W. Bartlett, "The President's Page," *Boston Bar Journal*, February 1967, 3–4. After her "retirement" Ehrmann remained active until 1988 in the Friends of Prisoners and the Norfolk Lifer's Group. Sara Ehrmann died March 17, 1993, at the age of ninety-seven. *Boston Globe*, March 20, 1993. The MCADP's office, at 14 Pearl Street, Brookline, was demolished as part of an urban renewal project in 1968. David Skerry, a Boston College Law School student, worked with Ehrmann in the summer of 1967 to sort through her vast anti-capital punishment collection. She initially thought her collection might be housed at Boston College Law School, but that plan fell through. The collection went to Northeastern University Law School, but after several years the collection was moved to Northeastern University's main library. See David Skerry to Ehrmann, September 17, 1967, Ehrmann Papers.

39. Following passage of the mercy bill in 1951 Ehrmann predicted that "lawyers themselves will come to demand abolition of capital punishment." Ehrmann to Charles Sprague, June 19, 1951, Ehrmann Papers. According to a letter sent to all MCADP members in June 1971, Tribe and Silber testified before the Judiciary Committee in 1970 and 1971. In the same letter the new president of MCADP also reported that John Flackett, a professor at Boston College Law School, and Frank Heffron, formerly with the NAACP Legal Defense Fund, had met with Governor Sargent to work out ways to extend the respites due to expire for four men on death row. For a list of Bedau's publications on the death penalty, see Hugo Adam Bedau, ed., *The Death Penalty in America: Current Controversies* (New York, 1997), 474–75.

40. *Elections Statistics: The Commonwealth of Massachusetts* (Boston, 1968), 400–406; *Boston Globe*, July 25, 1965. Sargent's 1970 campaign statement, *Boston Globe*, December 10, 1973.

41. *Boston Globe*, February 16, March 1, 8, 1972.

42. *Boston Herald Traveler*, May 24, 1972. At Walpole State Prison, Bond killed himself when a bomb he was making exploded.

43. *Boston Globe*, September 20, 1993; *Commonwealth v. Gilday*, 367 Mass. 474, 477 (1975). Saxe's first trial ended in a hung jury. She later pleaded guilty to manslaughter and received a twelve-to-fourteen-year sentence. She was paroled in 1982. *New York Times*, October 7, 1993. For Power, see *Boston Globe*, September 15, 1993.

44. Valeri's testimony, *Boston Globe*, February 24, 1972. The *Boston Record-American*, June 30, 1972, reported the number of men in Massachusetts under sentence of death. By joint resolution in 1971 the Massachusetts legislature abolished Walpole Prison's "death row" and allowed prisoners under sentence of death to

mix with other felons. *General Laws of Massachusetts* (Boston, 1972), chap. 279, sec. 44, amended by *Acts and Resolves, 1971* (Boston, 1972), chap. 1055.

45. *Furman v. Georgia*, 408 U.S. at 239–40; *Boston Record-American*, June 30, 1972.

46. *Furman v. Georgia*, 408 U.S. at 320, 299–300, 305, 358–59; *Trop v. Dulles*, 356 U.S. at 101. See generally, Stuart Banner, *The Death Penalty: An American History* (Cambridge, Mass., 2002), chap. 9.

47. *Furman v. Georgia*, 408 U.S. at 250–51, 256.

48. Ibid. at 309–10 (Justice Stewart), 311 (Justice White).

49. Ibid. at 310, 400.

50. *New York Times*, July 1, 1972; Robert M. Bohm, "American Death Penalty Opinion, 1936–1986," in *The Death Penalty in America: Current Research*, ed. Bohm (Cincinnati, Ohio, 1991); *Boston Globe*, June 30, 1972.

51. *Furman v. Georgia*, 408 U.S. at 239–40; *Stewart v. Massachusetts*, 408 U.S. 845 (1972); *Commonwealth v. Gilday*, 367 Mass. at 485; *Commonwealth v. A Juvenile* [Alphonso Pickney], 364 Mass. 103 (1973); *Commonwealth v. O'Neal*, 369 Mass. 242 (1975) (hereafter *O'Neal II*). Courts in Delaware and North Carolina struck down their state's mercy laws. *State v. Dickerson*, 298 A.2d 761 (Del. 1972); *State v. Waddell*, 282 N.C. 431 S.E.2d 19 (1973).

52. Lee Epstein and Joseph F. Kobylka, *The Supreme Court and Legal Change: Abortion and the Death Penalty* (Chapel Hill, N.C., 1992), 84–89.

53. *Commonwealth v. LeBlanc*, 364 Mass. 1, 14 (1973).

54. *Commonwealth v. A Juvenile*, 364 Mass. at 109, 106. The mandatory death penalty for felony rape-murder, *General Laws*, chap. 265, sec. 2 (1970). The applicable juvenile statute, *General Laws*, chap. 119, sec. 61. *Commonwealth v. A Juvenile*, 364 Mass., "Supplemental Brief for the Defendant," 5, quoting *Furman v. Georgia*, 408 U.S. at 309–10, and "Supplemental Brief," 6–8, Supreme Judicial Court [SJC] Records and Briefs, Judicial Archives, Massachusetts States Archives, Boston. See also Stephen E. Weyl, "The Supreme Judicial Court and the Death Penalty: The Effects of Judicial Choice on Legislative Options," *Boston University Law Review* 54 (1974): 158. Weyl argues that the SJC applied an expansive discretion per se reading of Furman; that is, the SJC "assumed that any capital statute discretionary on its face was unconstitutional" (164, 170).

55. *Commonwealth v. A Juvenile*, 364 Mass. at 108–9. See also Hugo A. Bedau, "Felony Murder Rape and the Mandatory Death Penalty: A Study in Discretionary Justice," *Suffolk University Law Review* 10 (1976): 493. Bedau's pioneering article was intended to provide empirical data to buttress the abolitionists' claim that a mandatory death penalty law was no less arbitrary and unconstitutional than those statutes struck down in *Furman*.

56. *Journal of the Massachuestts. House of Representatives* 7231 (August 7, 1973); *Boston Globe*, March 6, August 9, 1973. Before the 1951 debate over the mercy law, Sara Ehrmann had provided data that manifested jury discretion. Her study showed that of first-degree murder indictments and convictions from 1925 to 1941 in six Massachusetts counties, there were only three convictions for first-degree murder on 129 indictments. Ehrmann, "The Death Penalty and the Administration of Justice," in Bedau, *Death Penalty in America*, 415. "Request for Opinions from Supreme Judicial Court on Proposed House Bill No. 7231." Brief for Attorney General, 12 (1973), SJC Records and Briefs. Hugo Bedau, "Furman's Wake in the Land of the Bean and Cod," *Prison Journal* 53 (1973): 9, reports that at the hearing there was a good deal of vague talk about the supposed deterrent effect of the death penalty.

57. "Request for an Advisory Opinion," Brief for Attorney General, 12, 14–16 (1973), SJC Records and Briefs; *Trop v. Dulles*, 356 U.S. at 101; *Furman v. Georgia*, 408 U.S. at 286–87.

58. The vote, *Boston Globe*, October 2, 1973; the murders, *Boston Globe*, October 3, 5, 1973; House vote, *Boston Globe*, November 26, 1973.

59. John Schroeder was murdered on November 30, 1973, three years and thirty-seven days after his brother Walter was murdered. Terrell Walker was charged and convicted for John Schroeder's murder. *Boston Globe*, November 30, 1973. Silber's comments, *Boston Globe*, December 4, 1973; the police chiefs' letter was reported the same day. The governor's meeting with the six hundred police, *Boston Globe*, December 6, 1973.

60. *Boston Globe*, December 9, 10, 1973. Sargent's constitutional objections were reportedly based on Attorney General Quinn's belief that any death penalty statute violates Article 26 of the Massachusetts Declaration of Rights.

61. *Boston Globe*, December 15, 1973, March 6, 12, 26, 28, April 2, 1974.

62. Ibid., April 4, 1982. Dukakis's veto, *New York Times*, April 30, 1975; and *Boston Globe*, April 30, 1975. Senate president Kevin Harrington (D-Salem) cast the deciding vote against overriding Dukakis's veto. *Boston Globe*, May 2, 1975. During the 1988 presidential campaign, George H. W. Bush was critical of Dukakis's veto of death penalty legislation.

63. *O'Neal I* at 442; *Boston Globe*, June 9, August 9, 1973.

64. *Massachusetts Law Quarterly* 61 (Spring 1976); *Boston Globe*, October 7, 1994. G. Joseph Tauro, "Memorial," 421 Mass. 1603 (1995) provides details of Tauro's life and career.

65. *Lombardo v. D.F. Frangioso and Co.*, 339 Mass. 529, 536 (1971); *United Factory Outlet v. Jay's Stores, Inc.*, 361 Mass. 35, 52 (1972); *Commonwealth v. Cain*, 361 Mass. 224 (1972); *Commonwealth v. Mutina*, 366 Mass. 811 (1975).

66. *People v. Anderson*, 6 Cal. 3rd 628 (1972). Oregon and Louisiana courts also found death penalty statutes unconstitutional. *State v. Quinn*, 290 Or. 383 (1981); *Louisiana v. David*, 468 So. 2nd 1126 (1984). See also Hugo Adam Bedau, *Death Is Different: Studies in the Morality, Law, and Politics of Capital Punishment* (Boston, 1987), 185-94.

67. Justice William Brennan is credited with spurring the move to state constitutionalism; see his dissent in *Michigan v. Mosely*, 423 U.S. 96, 120 (1975). Herbert P. Wilkins, "Judicial Treatment of the Massachusetts Declaration of Rights in Relation to Cognate Provisions of the United States Constitution," *Suffolk University Law Review* 14 (1980): 887, 890-91. Chief Justice Hennessey's comment encouraging lawyers to make greater use of the Massachusetts Declaration of Rights, *Boston Globe*, August 3, 1986. Justice Paul Liacos, *Commonwealth v. Harris*, 371 Mass. 462, 471-72 (1976), quoting *Brown v. Mississippi*, 297 U.S. 278, 287 (1936).

68. *O'Neal I* at 443, 444.

69. Ibid. at 446, 447, 447 n. 5, 449-50.

70. Ibid, at 451, 453. Twenty-one states ban "cruel and unusual punishment," twenty-one prohibit "cruel or unusual punishment," and six forbid only "cruel punishment."

71. *O'Neal II*, "Commonwealth's Supplemental Brief, 6, 8, 10, 35; Ehrlich, "The Deterrent Effect of Capital Punishment: A Question of Life and Death," *American Economic Review* 65 (1975): 414. The commonwealth's brief stated as an absolute Ehrlich's argument that one execution "may" save lives (10).

72. *O'Neal II*, "Defendant's Supplemental Brief," 2, 12, 20, 28.

73. *O'Neal II* at 245n1, 246 n. 3, 244. The *Boston Globe*, December 22, 1975, noted the SJC's decision was "marked by unprecedented concurring and dissenting opinions by all seven judges."

74. *O'Neal II* at 252-53, 254, 255, 258, 261. In his opinion Tauro cited empirical studies by Hugo Bedau, president of the American League to Abolish Capital Punishment, and Sara Ehrmann, past president of the Massachusetts Council Against the Death Penalty (ibid. at 247 n. 5, 250, 257, 259, 260, 261, 256 n. 14).

75. Ibid. at 263-64, 274, 276, 276 n. 1.

76. Ibid. at 264-65, 267, 273. Reardon argued the SJC should wait until the Supreme Court made a decision in *Fowler v. North Carolina*, 422 U.S. 1039 (1975), a case originally involving the constitutionality of a mandatory death penalty statute. Justice Douglas's illness and subsequent resignation delayed oral argument on the case. By September 1975 when the Court was ready to hear *Fowler*, North Carolina had changed its statute to one permitting a jury's consideration of aggravating and mitigating circumstances in the penalty phase.

77. *Boston Globe*, December 23, 26, 1975; Harold Stanley and Richard G. Niemi, *Vital Statistics in American Politics* (Washington, D.C., 1992), 30.

78. *Gregg v. Georgia*, 328 U.S. 153 (1976). By the *Gregg* decision there were more than five hundred people under sentence of death; the names of those executed from July 1, 1976, to May 1986, Amnesty International, *United States of America: The Death Penalty* (London, 1987), 192–95. *Opinion of the Justices to the House of Representatives*, Mass. 364 N.E.2d 184, 186 (1977). The opinion was signed by five of the SJC's seven justices.

79. King-Dukakis primary battle, *Boston Globe*, May 21, 1978, August 31, September 1, 19, 20, 1978.

80. *Acts and Resolves, 1979* (Boston, 1980), chap. 488; *Boston Globe*, August 15, 1979.

81. *Acts and Resolves, 1979* (Boston, 1980), chap. 488. The law went into effect ninety days after August 15, 1979. *Boston Globe*, November 17, 1979. Police arrested Watson and Clay but were unable to locate the third suspect. Clay was sixteen years old at the time of the murder, and therefore his case followed a different legal path than Watson's. *Commonwealth v. Watson*, 388 Mass. 536, 539 (1983). Boyajian was the seventy-eighth person murdered in Boston to date in 1979. For Flanagan's request for a declaratory judgment, see *District Attorney v. Watson*, 381 Mass. 648.

82. *Boston Globe*, December 22, 1975, praised Hennessey's SJC for extending "personal liberties, in some areas, beyond the guarantees of the United States Constitution." Robert J. Brink, "A Lawyer's Lawyer and a Judge's Judge," *Massachusetts Law Review*, Fall 1989, 132. Dargo's interview, *New England Law Review* 24 (1990): iii–iv.

83. *District Attorney v. Watson*, 381 Mass. at 661, 662.

84. Ibid. at 662, 670.

85. Ibid. at 672, 673–74.

86. *Boston Globe*, May 8, 1999; *District Attorney v. Watson*, 381 Mass. at 676, 685. Justice Quirico dissented, arguing that the legislature had the power to enact any reasonable law including punishing a murderer by death. *Commonwealth v. Watson*, 381 Mass. at 701. State Senator Mel King said he believed the "soul of the state" was "more humane than punitive." *Boston Globe*, October 29, 1980.

87. *Boston Globe*, January 13, 1982, April 4, 1982.

88. Ibid., September 5, 10, 1982.

89. Ibid., September 15, 16, October 19, November 3, 1982.

90. Ibid., November 11, 12, December 8, 12, 14; 23, 1982.

91. *General Laws*, chap. 265, sec. 2; *General Laws*, chap. 279, secs. 4, 57–71, as amended by St. 1982, chap. 554, secs. 3–8.

92. *Boston Globe*, February 27, 28, 1983, February 2, 1984; *Commonwealth v. Colon-Cruz*, 393 Mass. 150. The defendant was convicted of murder in the first degree and sentenced to life imprisonment. *Commonwealth v. Colon-Cruz*, 408 Mass. 533 (1990).

93. *General Laws*, chap. 265, sec. 2; *General Laws*, chap. 279, secs. 4, 57–71, as amended by St. 1982.

94. *Boston Globe*, March 18, 1976; *Commonwealth v. Colon-Cruz*, 393 Mass. at 157, 158, 158 n. 10, 163. In *Commonwealth v. Colon-Cruz*, 393 Mass. at 173, Chief Justice Hennessey cited *U.S. v. Jackson*, 390 U.S. 570, 581 (1968), in which the Court had found unconstitutional a similar statute. Of the three dissenters, Wilkins, Joseph R. Nolan, and Neil L. Lynch, the latter two were King appointees.

EPILOGUE

1. *Commonwealth v. Colon-Cruz*, 393 Mass. 150 (1984). Six years later Colon-Cruz argued that the Miranda warning read to him after the murder of state trooper George Hanna was defective because the police officer who translated the warning into Spanish was biased. The court denied the motion, *Commonwealth v. Colon-Cruz*, 408 Mass. 533 (1990). Dukakis reiterated his opposition to the death penalty during the campaign, *Boston Globe*, July 31, 1983, April 19, 1992. John Silber reversed his life-long opposition to capital punishment during the campaign and also spoke about rationing health care.

2. Ibid., January 10, 1993, July 1, June 26, 1994, May 24, 1995.

3. Ibid., May 24, August 30, 1995.

4. Ibid., July 29, September 18, 1997.

5. Ibid., October 22, 1997.

6. Ibid., October 26, 1997.

7. Ibid., October 26, 29, 1997; *Boston Herald*, October 28, 1997.

8. Helen Prejean, *Dead Man Walking: An Eyewitness Account of the Death Penalty in the United States* (New York, 1994). *Boston Pilot*, October 27, 1997.

9. *Boston Globe*, October 29, 1997.

10. Ibid., November 7, 1997. Slattery also said his vote had been influenced by the Louise Woodward trial. She was a British au pair convicted a year earlier of second-degree murder in the death of an infant. Slattery thought the case showed the fragility of the jury process.

11. *Boston Globe*, November 7, 8, 9, 1997. Slattery and Cellucci were reelected in 1998.

12. Ibid., November 8, 13, December 11, 16, 1998, March 29, 1999, June 14, 2001.

13. Ibid., November 20, 2002. The *Globe* reported that the biggest change occurred in the Senate: in 1997 the Senate voted 23 to 15 in favor of a death penalty bill, but a 2002 poll showed a proposed death penalty bill losing by a 21-to-19 margin. The *Berkshire Eagle*, August 22, 2002, labeled Romney's call for re-instating the death penalty "a cheap appeal to bloodlust."

14. Press Release, Commonwealth of Massachusetts, September 23, 2003; *Boston Globe*, September 24, 2003.

15. Press Release, Commonwealth of Massachusetts, September 23, 2003.

16. *Report of the Governor's Council on Capital Punishment* (Commonwealth of Massachusetts, 2004), 3–4; *New York Times*, May 3, 2004.

17. *Boston Globe*, May 3, 5, 2004; *New York Times*, May 3, 2004.

18. *Boston Herald*, July 15, 2005; *Boston Globe*, May 16, 2005.

INDEX